CANADIAN HISTORY: A READER'S GUIDE
VOLUME 2: CONFEDERATION TO THE PRESENT

EDITED BY DOUG OWRAM

Canadian History:
A Reader's Guide
Volume 2: Confederation
to the Present

UNIVERSITY OF TORONTO PRESS
Toronto Buffalo London

© University of Toronto Press Incorporated 1994
Toronto Buffalo London
Printed in Canada

ISBN 0-8020-2801-2 (cloth)
ISBN 0-8020-7676-9 (paper)

Canadian Cataloguing in Publication Data

Main entry under title:

Canadian history : a reader's guide

Includes index.
Contents: v. 1. Beginnings to Confederation /
edited by M. Brook Taylor – v. 2. Confederation
to the present / edited by Doug Owram.
ISBN 0-8020-5016-6 (v. 1: bound)
ISBN 0-8020-6826-X (v. 1 : pbk.)
ISBN 0-8020-2801-2 (v. 2 : bound)
ISBN 0-8020-7676-9 (v. 2 : pbk.)

1. Canada – History – To 1763 (New France) –
Bibliography. 2. Canada – History – 1763–
Bibliography.* I. Taylor, M. Brook (Martin Brook),
1951– . II. Owram, Douglas, 1947– .

Z1382.C35 1994   016.971   C94-930029-2

Contents

PREFACE / xi
ABBREVIATIONS / xvii

National Politics and Government   *John English* / 3
The Canadian Centenary Series / 5
Modern Constitutional and Federal Issues / 9
The Age of Macdonald / 11
The Age of Laurier / 20
From the Great War to the Great Depression / 27
The 1930s: Depression and Dissent / 32
The War / 36
The Postwar Era / 40
The Tenth Decade: Diefenbaker and Pearson / 42
The Trudeau Years / 46

Foreign Relations and Defence Policy   *Robert Bothwell* / 51
Bibliographies / 51
Official Sources / 52
Periodicals / 53
General Histories / 54
Early History: 1867–1914 / 55
World War I and After: 1914–1939 / 60
War and Cold War: 1939–1990 / 68

Working-Class History   *Craig Heron* / 86
Historiography and General Texts / 87

Family and Household / 89
Neighbourhood and Community / 94
Wage-Earners' Struggles / 98
1850–1890 / 102
1890–1925 / 105
1925–1950 / 109
1950–1975 / 111
Post-1975 / 113
Industry and Union Studies / 113
Workers and Politics / 118
Biographies / 121

Business and Economic History   *Ben Forster* / 123
Reference Materials and General Texts / 124
Collections of Readings and Historiography / 129
Banking, Money, and Finance / 131
Transportation and Communications / 133
Primary Production / 136
Industrial Development and Manufacturing / 141
Distribution and Retailing / 144
Business Structure, Management, and Labour / 145
Elites / 147
Business–Government Relations / 149
Multinationals and Foreign Ownership / 153

Intellectual, Cultural, and Scientific History   *Doug Owram* / 157
General / 158
Confederation and the Victorian Age / 159
Science and Medicine / 160
Religion, the Social Gospel, and Secularization / 161
Writing on the Regions / 165
Politics / 169
Education / 172
The University World / 173
Media / 176
Music and Art / 177

Native History   *J.R. Miller* / 179
General and Reference Works / 179

Indian Policy Studies / 182
Regional Studies / 183
Treaty-making / 191
Northwest Rebellion / 192
The Métis / 192
The Policy of the Bible and the Plough / 195
Land Questions / 198

Women's History   *Wendy Mitchinson* / 202
General / 204
The Woman's Movement / 206
Unpaid Work / 211
Wage Labour / 214
White-Collar Work / 215
Unions and the State / 218
Education and Law / 219
The Private Lives of Women / 221
Religion / 224
Race and Ethnicity / 225

Urban History   *Paul Voisey* / 228
Bibliographies, Guides, and Journals / 229
General Works and Collections / 230
Urban Biography / 231
Approaches to Inter-Urban and Hinterland Relations / 233
Economic Development and Urban Growth / 234
Built Environment / 237
Social Structure and Social Life / 239
Municipal Government and Politics / 242

Atlantic Provinces   *T.W. Acheson*   246
Periodicals, Bibliographies, and General Studies / 247
The Consolidation of Confederation / 249
New Brunswick Schools / 250
The Staples Economy / 250
The National Policy and Economic Development to 1918 / 252
From Maritime Rights to DREE / 253
Politics in the Maritimes / 255
Newfoundland / 256
Religion / 257

Education / 258
Labour / 259
Women / 261
The Acadians / 262
Ethnic and Racial Minorities / 264
Social Movements and Social Problems / 264
Urban History / 265
Migration / 266
Culture / 266

Quebec   *Andrée Lévesque*   / 268
Bibliographies and General Works / 268
Political History / 270
Economic History / 276
Social History / 279
Labour and Working-Class History / 280
Women and the Family / 283
Ethnicity / 286
Urban History / 287
Regional History / 288
French outside Canada / 289
Cultural and Intellectual History / 289
The Media, Art, and Literature / 292

Ontario   *David Mills*   / 296
Bibliographical Works / 300
The People / 301
Demography / 302
Immigrant Groups and Ethnicity / 305
Women's History and Gender Studies / 308
Regional and Local Studies and Urban History / 311
The Economy and Class Formation / 316
Social and Cultural History / 324
Politics / 333

The West and the North   *John Herd Thompson*   / 341
Atlases, Bibliographies, and Scholarly Journals / 341
General Histories and Collections of Articles / 344
Extending Canadian Control West and North / 346
Economic Change / 353

'Limited Identities': Ethnicity / 361
'Limited Identities': Class / 363
'Limited Identities': Gender / 365
Political History / 367
Intellectual and Cultural History / 372

CONTRIBUTORS / 375
AUTHOR INDEX / 377
SUBJECT INDEX / 407

Preface

CANADIAN HISTORIOGRAPHY

Understanding the nature of Canadian history involves two related tasks. The first is to master some of the facts and conclusions that make up the history. The second is to comprehend, in at least a basic fashion, the structures and interpretations that shape historical writing. This is known formally as historiography or, in more informal terms, the history of historical writing. The chapters that follow will give significant detail on both the historical and historiographic aspects of the various areas of Canadian history. This brief section attempts to act as bibliographic primer to Canadian history and historiography.

The place to start for any understanding of Canadian historiography is Carl Berger, *The Writing of Canadian History: Aspects of English-Canadian Historical Writing since 1900* (2nd ed., T: UTP 1986). It intelligently and lucidly traces both the giant figures and the main trends of Canadian historical writing, and develops the major schools of thought and issues of interpretation. M. Brook Taylor, *Promoters, Patriots, and Partisans: Historiography in Nineteenth-Century English Canada* (T: UTP 1989) covers the period between 1867 and 1900, as well as pre-Confederation history. The one gaping hole in both of these studies is any coverage of francophone historians. For these, see Serge Gagnon, *Quebec and Its Historians, 1840 to 1920* (M: Harvest House 1982), and his *Quebec and Its Historians: The Twentieth Century* (M: Harvest House 1988). Ramsay Cook, *The Maple Leaf Forever: Essays on Canadian Nationalism* (2nd ed., T: M&S 1977) has excellent historiographical articles on both French and English writing. A useful additional source for understanding Canadian historiography is a recent work edited by John Schultz, *Writing about Canada: A Handbook for*

Modern Canadian History (T: PH 1990). It provides a collection of essays discussing the major fields of Canadian historical writing. Also helpful is Carl Berger, *Contemporary Approaches to Canadian History* (T: CPP 1987). Terry Crowley, *Clio's Craft: A Primer of Historical Methods* (T: CPP 1988) contains discussion on various methodologies rather than historiography as such. Historiographic assessments, retrospectives, and commentaries are also common to the major journals, such as the *Journal of Canadian Studies*, *Acadiensis*, and, less often, the *Canadian Historical Review*. These are usually on subfields rather than on the state of historical writing as a whole, and many examples are given in the chapters that follow.

There are also a few articles about Canadian history that are especially important in that they helped define the direction of the field over the years. In chronological order, such a list includes W.A. Mackintosh, 'Economic Factors in Canadian History,' *CHR* 1923; and W.L. Morton, 'Clio in Canada,' first published in 1946 and reprinted in A.B. McKillop, ed., *Contexts of Canada's Past: Selected Essays of W.L. Morton* (T: MAC 1980). The same year Frank H. Underhill gave a Canadian Historical Association presidential address which challenged many existing tendencies in Canadian historical writing. See his 'Some Reflections on the Liberal Tradition,' in his *In Search of Canadian Liberalism* (T: MAC 1960). Two articles by J.M.S. Careless are also crucial: 'Frontierism, Metropolitanism, and Canadian History,' *CHR* 1954, and 'Limited Identities' in Canada, *CHR* 1969.

The 'limited identities' thesis has had a tremendous impact upon Canadian historical writing. Practically every subfield contained in this volume has been shaped by the notion that Canadian history must be viewed in its parts rather than as a single entity. However some doubts have arisen as to the overall impact of such fragmentation upon the discipline as a whole. For a modification of his own views, see J.M.S. Careless, '"Limited Identities": Ten Years Later,' *Manitoba History* 1980, and most recently Michael Bliss, 'Privatizing the Mind: The Sundering of Canadian History, The Sundering of Canada,' *JCS* 1991–2. It is striking, however, that historiographic articles now have their major impact on particular subdisciplines and not on the field as a whole. Many such articles are important, but are best listed in the individual chapters.

General history texts are another special area, distinct from any particular subdiscipline. Forty or fifty years ago, the general textbook was something most major historians aspired to write. Then, for a period in the 1960s and 1970s, the writing of textbooks fell out of favour owing in part no doubt to the reorganization of the discipline that was occurring. Instructors were often forced to turn to books originally written decades before.

Fortunately, recent years have seen a revival of textbook writing, and a wealth of choice now faces both student and instructor. These books are ably discussed by John English in the first part of his essay in this volume.

One other source should be mentioned. Document collections were once a staple of Canadian historical work, but in the past couple of decades they have fallen from favour. A recent publication, however, does an excellent job of providing those interested with a run of the basic documents in Canadian history from Confederation to the present. See Dave de Brou and Bill Waiser, eds., *Documenting Canada: A History of Modern Canada in Documents* (S: Fifth House 1992).

THE GUIDE AND HOW TO USE IT

This is the third version of the *Guide to Canadian History*. It is also the first new edition in over a decade and is a complete rearrangement and rewrite of the earlier guides. Different authors and different subject headings reflect the fact that the field has evolved considerably over the past decade.

Three themes have shaped this new edition. First, as with the others, it is designed to be selective rather than definitive. This is both an issue of cost and of usefulness. The intention here is to introduce those interested in a topic to the key works. Some of the best historians in their respective fields have been chosen to write the chapters, not only for their knowledge but for their judgment. The books and articles included in the following pages are thought to be the best available on any given topic. In addition, authors will frequently make comments on the strengths or weaknesses of a book. Ideally, therefore, this guide will allow a researcher quick and easy access to the essential material in any subject area.

Second, we wanted this work to be affordable to those who would use it. A bibliography is helpful only if it is available, and to have produced a very expensive library work known only to a few would have defeated the purpose. The desire to be affordable, however, meant limitations on length. Choices had to be made, not only about the works cited but also the very chapters to be included. In the last guide the emphasis was on regions, which fit the historiographic interests of the time. It seemed to me that in the last decade at least two fields of history had developed sufficient scholarship and prominence to warrant their own chapters – women's history and Native history. This required that other topics be cut back and the simplest way for me (if not for John Thompson) was to merge the Prairies, British Columbia, and the North into one section on the West. Some may see this as just another example of the presumption that the

West is the Prairies, but a reading of Thompson's article will indicate, I think, that neither the North nor BC has been slighted. Two other fields were seriously considered. The first, social history, was rejected because it has become too big to be meaningful. Much of it has now been subsumed under fields like women's history, working-class history, and so on. Indeed, most fields – including intellectual history and political history – have been tremendously influenced by social history. It is hard to envisage a chapter on the area that would not have repeated most of the contents of the guide as a whole. The other field that was carefully considered, but eventually gave way to space demands, was ethnic history. This is unfortunate, but several of the regional chapters look specifically at ethnic history. Other smaller subdisciplines – legal history, scientific history, and so on – suffer the same fate. None receives separate chapters, but all are dealt with under subheadings. As one assessor of the *Guide* aptly noted, these emerging fields may very well be the ones that will displace some of the current ones by the time the next version of this book is written!

This *Guide* is intended to stand alone. Initially, there was some thought of making this an 'update' of earlier editions. That would be cumbersome for the student and impracticable for the authors of the pieces. These bibliographies depend on the author's sense of the structure of the field as a whole and, in developing that structure, old as well as new works must be considered. At the same time the selective approach means that older works which have not withstood the test of time naturally drop away. The emphasis in these chapters is, overall, on the most recent scholarship.

The *Guide* makes emphatic use of the principle of creative redundancy. Books often fit into several categories and can be used by researchers approaching an issue from any of several perspectives. If the work was to appear only in its 'most likely' place, a researcher could very easily miss it. Thus books appear wherever the individual authors think they should, and this often means more than one reference to a work. To take one specific example: A. Ross McCormack, *Reformers, Rebels, and Revolutionaries: The Western Canadian Radical Movement, 1899–1919* (T: UTP 1977), a history of Western radical thought, appears in the chapters on the West, on intellectual history, and on working-class history. The repetition was employed successfully in earlier versions and is, we think, one of the points that makes these guides readily usable. The user, however, should also employ redundancy in searching for material. Topics can be approached in different ways; for example, a student looking at female suffrage should consult not only the chapter on women's history but also that on the West and on politics and government.

The limitations on the size of the *Guide* also mean that authors have emphasized more readily available published works. Theses have been given relatively little attention, appearing only where no reasonable published alternative exists. Still, for anyone interested in detailed research in Canadian history, theses can provide a wealth of information and analysis. To see what is available up to the early 1980s, consult Donald M. Tupling, *Canada: A Dissertation Bibliography* and the *Supplement* (Ann Arbor: University Microfilms International 1980, 1983).

Finally, as editor I am painfully aware of the alternate ways of organizing a guide such at this. Other editors, no doubt, would have arranged things differently. No selection can please everybody, but I am confident of one thing. Given the organizational choices made at the outset, the individual writers have more than fulfilled their tasks. Their work has led to an impressive, up-to-date, and coherent survey of the works in their fields. I thank them all.

Doug Owram
University of Alberta

Abbreviations

The following abbreviations have been used in the citations within the chapters.

PLACE OF PUBLICATION

B	Brandon
C	Calgary
E	Edmonton
F	Fredericton
H	Halifax
K	Kingston
L	London, England
M	Montreal
NY	New York
O	Ottawa
Q	Quebec City
R	Regina
S	Saskatoon
T	Toronto
V	Vancouver
Vi	Victoria
W	Winnipeg
Wa	Waterloo

PUBLISHERS

ANQ	Assemblée Nationale du Québec
AP	Acadiensis Press

B	Les Editions du Boréal
BANQ	Bibliothèque de l'Assemblée Nationale du Québec
BE	Boréal Express
BNQ	Bibliothèque Nationale du Québec
BUT	Butterworths
CC	Copp Clark
CCLH	Canadian Committee on Labour History
CCP	Copp Clark Pitman
CHA	Canadian Historical Association
CI	Clarke Irwin
CIIA	Canadian Institute of International Affairs
CIUS	Canadian Institute of Ukrainian Studies
CPRC	Canadian Plains Research Center
CS	Champlain Society
HBJ	Harcourt Brace Jovanovich
HMH	Editions Hurtubise HMH
HRW	Holt, Rinehart & Winston
HUP	Harvard University Press
IQRC	Institut québécois de recherche sur la culture
IRP	Institut de recherche publique
ISER	Institute for Social and Economic Research, Memorial University of Newfoundland
ISSS	Institut Supérieur des sciences sociales
JL	James Lorimer
KP	King's Printer
M&S	McClelland and Stewart
MAC	Macmillan
MH	McGraw-Hill
MHR	McGraw-Hill Ryerson
MHSO	Multicultural History Society of Ontario
MQUP	McGill-Queen's University Press
MUN	Memorial University of Newfoundland
OUP	Oxford University Press
P	Préambule
PH	Prentice-Hall
PUL	Les Presses de l'Université Laval
PUM	Les Presses de l'Université de Montréal
PUQ	Les Presses de l'Université du Québec
Q/A	Editions Québec/Amérique
QP	Queen's Printer

RCHTQ	Le Regroupement des chercheurs en histoire des travailleurs et travailleuses du Québec
RP	Ryerson Press
RSC	Royal Society of Canada
UAP	University of Alberta Press
UBCP	University of British Columbia Press
UCP	University of Calgary Press
UMP	University of Manitoba Press
UOP	University of Ottawa Press
UTP	University of Toronto Press
WLUP	Wilfrid Laurier University Press
WPPB	Western Producer Prairie Books

JOURNALS

BCHQ	*British Columbia Historical Quarterly*
BCS	*BC Studies*
CES	*Canadian Ethnic Studies*
CHA *AR*	Canadian Historical Association *Annual Report*
CHA *HP*	Canadian Historical Association *Historical Papers*
CHR	*Canadian Historical Review*
CJE	*Canadian Journal of Economics*
CJEPS	*Canadian Journal of Economics and Political Science*
CJPS	*Canadian Journal of Political Science*
CJPST	*Canadian Journal of Political and Social Theory*
CJS	*Canadian Journal of Sociology*
CRSA	*Canadian Review of Sociology and Anthropology*
HS/SH	*Histoire sociale/Social History*
IJCS	*International Journal of Canadian Studies*
JCHA	*Journal of the Canadian Historical Association*
JCS	*Journal of Canadian Studies*
OH	*Ontario History*
QQ	*Queen's Quarterly*
RHAF	*Revue d'histoire l'Amérique française*
Ri/IR	*Relations industrielles/Industrial Relations*
RS	*Recherches Sociographiques*
TRSC	*Transactions of the Royal Society of Canada*
UHR	*Urban History Review*

CANADIAN HISTORY: A READER'S GUIDE
VOLUME 2: CONFEDERATION TO THE PRESENT

JOHN ENGLISH

National Politics and Government

National history is a category that fits remarkably little Canadian history written by the generation of Canadian historians working in the 1970s, 1980s, and 1990s. The 'nation' has not been a popular conceptual framework for historians in Canada and elsewhere because nations are pre-eminently political, and political history has not been fashionable recently. Moreover, Canada seems less a 'nation' than it did in the 1950s and early 1960s. Ian McKay, in a thoughtful essay (*Labour/Le travail* 1991) that examines how Marxist historians have tended 'to marginalize questions of belonging' which do not arise from class, suggests that Canadian historians face greater problems because the future may be not only post-modern but also post-Canadian. The great national histories of Canada, Donald Creighton's *Dominion of the North: A History of Canada* (T: MAC 1944), W.L. Morton's *The Kingdom of Canada: A General History from Earliest Times* (T: M&S 1963), A.R.M. Lower's *Colony to Nation: A History of Canada* (T: Longmans 1946), and J.M.S. Careless's *Canada: A Story of Challenge* (Cambridge: Cambridge UP 1953) were grounded in the optimism and English-Canadian nationalism of their time, neither of which survived the 1960s. There have been histories of Canada written in the past twenty years, but they are normally collaborative efforts that are chronologically limited and without overarching interpretation.

Kenneth Osborne of the University of Manitoba, who has studied what high school students are taught about history, has found that courses are taught around topics, themes, or issues, and that the earlier dominance of political and constitutional history and the chronological approach identified with political themes has ended, and has been replaced by an emphasis on social and cultural themes. Both social historians and, more recently, cultural historians have been critical of the traditional national historian's focus on the state. For social historians, the focus on political institutions obscured questions of economic power and class and tended to treat the dominant elites in analytical isolation. Cultural historians criticized their theoretical sloppiness and unwillingness to consider the meaning of language. There are, however, some indications of a reinvigorated interest in the state and its importance. A leading social historian, Michael Bliss, has claimed that historians' avoidance of political themes and questions of Canadian identity has paralleled and, perhaps, reflected the national disunity and political uncertainty of Canada since 1970. Gerald Friesen, who is critical of such complaints, nevertheless does believe that for historians and their students and readers 'What's been lost is a sense of nation – a sense of collective past and present' (*Globe and Mail*, Feb. 1992).

Canadian historians, then, reflect not only an international trend in the turn towards social history but also particular Canadian circumstances. The American bicentennial, for example, brought a flood of interpretive works on American national history. Ambitious new interpretations of American history appeared, such as David Hackett Fischer's remarkable *America: A Cultural History*, vol. 1, *Albion's Seed* (NY: OUP 1989), which proposes an interpretation of the development of contemporary American culture based upon the emigration of the British to America in the seventeenth and eighteenth centuries. It is the type of book that no professional historian wrote about Canada in the 1970s and 1980s. Popular historians are not so reluctant; June Callwood's *Portrait of Canada* (Garden City: Doubleday 1981) sees Canada through contemporary civil libertarian eyes, and Glen Frankfurter's *Baneful Domination: The Idea of Canada in the Atlantic World, 1581–1971* (Don Mills: Longmans 1971) spied upon Canadian history through a nationalist lens. Such books have had a poor reception from professional historians. Popular response has also been muted. Pierre Berton and Peter C. Newman have been by far the best-selling historians of the last generation. Berton wrote two major works of political history in the post-Centennial glow, *The National Dream: The Great Railway, 1871–1881* and *The Last Spike: The Great Railway, 1881–1885* (T: M&S 1970, 1971), but more recent work on the opening of the West, the Dionne quintuplets, and the Depression is much less political in orientation. Newman's history of the Hudson's Bay Company, which has had harsher treatment from professional historians than it merits, is a form of 'national history'; but in the post-Confederation period, it is, quite naturally, a business history.

A few professional historians have written national histories during the 1980s, although nearly all were directed towards the textbook market. Kenneth McNaught's brief but venerable *Pelican History of Canada*

(Harmondsworth: Penguin Books 1975), which is the Canadian book most likely to be found in foreign bookshops, was brought up to date. Desmond Morton has written two surveys, *A Short History of Canada* (E: Hurtig 1983) and *A Military History of Canada* (E: Hurtig 1990). Both books are written in Morton's lively and sometimes opinionated style and are impressive in their condensation of a wide range of scholarship. Craig Brown was joined by Morton and five others in the writing of *The Illustrated History of Canada* (T: Lester & Orpen Dennys 1987). Although some popular historians, notably Pierre Berton, took their revenge on academic reviewers when *The Illustrated History* appeared, the book was a remarkable achievement, reflecting the latest scholarship and Brown's outstanding editorial skills, and incorporating splendid illustrations and photographs, and (*pace* Berton) telling a lively story. A French edition of the book, produced under the expert supervision of Paul-André Linteau and called *Histoire générale du Canada* (M: BE 1990), is of similar high quality.

Douglas Francis, Richard Jones, and Donald Smith have written a text-book called *Destinies: Canadian History since Confederation* (2nd ed., T: HRW 1992) which not only covers the post-Confederation period well but in-dicates to students what the major historiographical debates are. Each chapter is followed by a good bibliography. There are even some footnotes which also offer bibliographical guidance. The second edition is better than the first, and *Destinies* is the counterpart of *Origins: Canadian History to Confederation*, which covers the pre-Confederation period. J.L. Finlay and D.N. Sprague, *The Structure of Canadian History* (3rd ed., Scarborough: PH 1989) is used in many courses and is somewhat more likely to enter into controversies than is *Destinies*. Its bibliographies are briefer and there are no footnotes.

Other collaborative efforts have a narrower time span. J.L. Granatstein, David Bercuson, Blair Neatby, Craig Brown, and Irving Abella produced two editions of *Twentieth-Century Canada* (T: MHR 1983). They added T.W. Acheson and the first twenty-three years of Confederation and called it *Nation: Canada since Confederation* for the third edition. Although *Nation* incorporates regional and social history, its core remains national politics. The various editions naturally reflect the interests of the authors, and there is, accordingly, a generous serving of both working-class and immigration history.

THE CANADIAN CENTENARY SERIES

The Canadian Centenary Series is a multi-authored history of Canada which now provides the best overview of the first century of Confederation. The quality of the individual volumes varies, but, taken together, they represent a tribute to the accomplishment of Canadian historians since 1960. Nearly all volumes incorporate archival research, most make extensive use of the numerous graduate theses written during the 1960s and 1970s, and all can be used in classrooms. Bibliographies would have been helpful but, alas, they are mostly absent. There are, however, copious footnotes which the enterprising student may scan to get a sense of the best literature on the period or subject. W.L. Morton, *The Critical Years: The Union of British North America, 1857–1873* (T: M&S 1964) begins the coverage of post-Confederation history. The book is not Morton's best, particularly the sections dealing with post-Confederation Canada. The West, as one would expect, is covered well, Ottawa less effectively. Morton's volume is followed by Peter B. Waite, *Canada 1874–1896: Arduous Destiny* (T: M&S 1971). Waite writes clearly and tells a good story. Although social and economic historians might find the book deficient in their areas, the political history is based upon a good knowledge of primary sources and secondary works. Nevertheless, Waite's later and excellent biography of Sir John Thompson offers a much better view of Ottawa than does *Arduous Destiny*.

R.C. Brown and Ramsay Cook, *Canada 1896–1921: A Nation Transformed* (T: M&S 1974) is not only a readable and remarkable survey that maintains its freshness but also a major landmark in Canadian historiography. Brown and Cook, who had supervised or taught many of the best young historians of the 1960s and early 1970s, wrote a brilliant synthesis that drew upon a rich lode of theses and incorporated their own archival work. It grounded the political events of the time in the social and economic changes that occurred in the first two decades of the century. The chapters on wartime politics remain the best short survey of the subject. John Herd Thompson with the assistance of Allen Seager, *Canada 1922–1939: Decades of Discord* (T: M&S 1985), tried to follow the Brown-Cook model with some success, although political history is not the book's strongest area. Both social historians, Thompson and Seager are strongest on what they know best and tend to rely on secondary works for other areas.

Donald Creighton's *Canada 1939–1957: The Forked Road* (T: M&S 1976) is not based on primary research, but this deficiency in evidence did not affect the vociferousness of the argument. Much criticized, *The Forked Road* is often vitriolic, especially when discussing Mackenzie King and the Liberals, and it often has the air of personal reminiscence. It presents a strong critique of the liberal view of Canada and of the growth of Canadian internationalism and dualism. As such, it bears reading, as does Creighton's highly personal *Canada's First Century, 1867–1967* (T: MAC 1976). For those who believe that Canada has followed the wrong path since 1945 the book provides ammunition.

The final volume, chronologically, of the Centenary Series is J.L. Granatstein, *Canada 1957–1967: The Years of Uncertainty and Innovation* (T: M&S 1986). In marked contrast to the Creighton volume, *Canada 1957–1967* is based on extensive archival research. Like Creighton, Granatstein does not shrink from expressing strong opinions, nor is he sententious. He tends to let documents speaks for themselves and then crisply states his own conclusion. The 1957 to 1967 period, the so-called tenth decade, was marked by controversies and Granatstein directly confronts several of them: Diefenbaker's government, defence reunification, medicare, nationalism, the Quebec crisis, and cultural politics. As this list suggests, the focus is on Ottawa, with journeys to other significant political capitals. Granatstein argues that the period is so complex that he was forced to be selective; there is little on social trends, for example. Nevertheless, what Granatstein explores he does so with skill and care. It is a fine volume, the best on the period.

Robert Bothwell, Ian Drummond, and John English also reflect their interests in *Canada 1900–1945* (rev. ed., T: UTP 1990) and *Canada since 1945: Power, Politics, and Provincialism* (2nd ed., T: UTP 1989). As the subtitle of the latter volume suggests, there is a consistent theme in these volumes, one that has brought some criticism from readers who contend that 'limited identities' are not properly represented.

For a much different point of view about Canada's historical development, one might look at R.T. Naylor's *Canada in the European Age, 1453–1919* (V: New Star 1987), which is traditional in its historical approach but not in its perceptions. Naylor is an economist, and economists and political scientists have been more willing than most historians to embrace political history topics. The increasing tendency of political scientists to write broad accounts of Canadian historical development either from a case-study approach or as grounding for theoretical generalization is discussed in John English, 'The Second-Time Around: Political Scientists Writing History,' *CHR* 1986. One of the best-selling academic works of the late seventies and the eighties was Leo Panitch, ed., *The Canadian State: Political Economy and Political Power* (T: UTP 1977). This collection of essays brought together diverse work by the so-called new political economists who traced their lineage in Canada not only to Marx, Habermas, and Milliband, but also to Harold A. Innis and Clare Pentland. Although many of the essays in the book dealt with contemporary questions, several were explicitly historical and most adventurously so. Reginald Whitaker, for example, wrote a long essay on images of the state in Canada, of the type so rarely written by historians. The same ambitious overviews are to be found in other work of the political economists, such as Jorge Niosi's *La bourgeoisie canadienne: La formation et le développement d'une classe dominante* (M: BE 1980).

Political scientists have also been more active than historians in studying the post-1950 period, especially in regard to such topics as political parties, voting behaviour, and the Constitution and its changes. They have rarely wandered into pre–World War II terrain, but even there some important works have been published. Most of this scholarship is marked by a predisposition to place the subject within a theoretical framework, a tendency that has aroused the ire of many historians. The best of it, however, blends the theory with solid archival research. Scholarship of both types written by non-historians will be identified wherever possible in the following sections of this article. There are some general works, however, that bear mention here because they are important sources of information on the entire span of Canadian post-Confederation history.

Janine Brodie and Jane Jenson have written a history of Canadian voting behaviour since Confederation: *Crisis, Challenge and Change: Party and Class in Canada* (Agincourt: Methuen 1980). Although historians may question some of the bold judgments and feel uncomfortable with contemporary models of party and class, the book does offer a perspective on Canadian elections that is absent from most historical writing in its use of polling data and quantitative techniques to study elections. An older book that reflected the approach of an earlier generation of political scientists, J. Murray Beck's *Pendulum of Power: Canada's Federal Elections* (T: PH 1968) remains useful because the essays about the elections are so intelligently written. D. Owen Carrigan's *Canadian Party Platforms: 1867–1968* (T: CC 1968) is a valuable primary source, but in recent times party platforms have mattered much less. Recognizing the 'two solitudes' between historians and political scientists, political scientist R. Kenneth Carty and historian W. Peter Ward organized joint sessions at the Canadian Historical Association and Canadian Political Science Association annual meetings which combined historians and political scientists. The result was *National Politics and Community in Canada* (V: UBCP 1986). The book begins with a lament that 'the part and not the whole has come to dominate thinking about our society and its most important institutions.' This tendency was more marked among historians than political scientists.

As disciplinary borders have become higher there has been less collaboration, and history has become somewhat incidental in the presentation of a theoretical argument. There are notable exceptions which will be identified below: these exceptions are nearly always so-called 'case studies' of particular incidents or periods. Most are in the area of diplomatic history/international relations. Two broader surveys, both of which are excellent, are James Eayrs's *The Art of the Possible: Government and Foreign Policy in Canada* (T: UTP 1961) and Kim Richard Nossal's *The Politics of Canadian Foreign Policy* (Scarborough: PH 1984). The latter survey reflects more recent interpretations and covers the period since Eayrs's. Other general works by political scientists that can be used profitably by historians include David Shugarman and Reg Whitaker, eds., *Federalism and Political Community: Essays in Honour of Donald Smiley* (Peterborough: Broadview 1989), a *Festschrift* to Smiley. Smiley's own *The Canadian Political Nationality* (T: Methuen 1967) and his later *Canada in Question: Federalism in the Seventies* (T: MHR 1972) are of interest to historians, not only because Smiley uses historical arguments but also because he had great influence on political scientists and federal-provincial bureaucrats. Smiley saw Canadian federalism as a system in which resurgent provincial interests had to be accommodated, and he posited an intrastate federalist model to understand the changes that were occurring in the post-1960 period in 'The Structural Problem of Canadian Federalism,' *Canadian Public Administration* 1971.

MODERN CONSTITUTIONAL AND FEDERAL ISSUES

Historians, on the whole, have resisted Smiley's approach and have largely abandoned writing about the subjects of the Constitution and federalism, though they have been so predominant in Canadian life in the post-1960 period. Unlike the Royal Commission on Dominion-Provincial Relations of the late 1930s and even the Royal Commission on Bilingualism and Biculturalism of the 1960s, the mid-1980s Royal Commission on the Economic Union and Development Prospects for Canada offered almost no contracts for historians (J.L. Granatstein wrote a study of free trade) but many for political scientists, whose writing about the Constitution and federalism had come to predominate. Smiley, for example, collaborated with Ronald L. Watts on *Intrastate Federalism in Canada* (T: UTP 1985).

Watts is a Queen's political scientist who has played a central role as a prime ministerial adviser in Canada. He and his colleagues at Queen's took up Smiley's notion of intrastate federalism and developed it into a program of constitutional revision. The best-known work of this genre is probably Richard Simeon's *Federal-Provincial Diplomacy: The Making of Recent Policy in Canada* (T: UTP 1972), which points to the emergence of 'diplomacy' within Canada's borders. The many special studies for the Royal Commission on the Economic Union and Development Prospects derive largely from this work by political scientists, which has had little parallel among historians. When the Meech Lake Accord was debated, the political scientist Allan Cairns of the University of British Columbia noted how few political scientists were to be found among its opponents, whereas historians such as Granatstein, Michael Bliss, Robert Bothwell, Michael Behiels, and David Bercuson were among its most vocal opponents. Ramsay Cook, another opponent, had initially confronted Smiley's approach to Canadian federalism [see *The Maple Leaf Forever: Essays on Nationalism and Politics in Canada* (T: MAC 1971)], but in the 1980s, although troubled by the rise of executive federalism, as 'co-operative federalism' came to be called, Cook expressed his doubts in presentations to committees and shorter essays such as 'Alice in Meechland or the Concept of Quebec as a Distinct Society,' in *QQ* 1987. Two works by historians, nevertheless, are important even though both are principally contributions to public debate rather than historical analyses. Michael Behiels edited the exhaustive *The Meech Lake Primer: Conflicting Views of the 1987 Constitutional Accord* (O: UOP 1989), and David J. Bercuson joined with political scientist Barry Cooper to write the most strongly argued denunciation of recent constitutional history: *Deconfederation: Canada without Quebec* (T: Key Porter 1991). When one compares *Deconfederation* with the work of the so-called Queen's school, one becomes aware of a fundamental difference in the understanding of 'facts.' The early Thomas Kuhn would have pointed to the existence of separate paradigms which created a situation where debate was impossible. Nevertheless, a few political scientists besides the renegade Cooper continued to pay attention to historians and their views: interestingly, they tended to be the few who had doubts about Meech Lake, its antecedents and its heirs, and they tended to fall outside the Ottawa-Toronto-Kingston axis. This group included Allan Cairns of Vancouver, Al Johnson (a former public servant in Saskatchewan), and Roger Gibbins of Calgary, but they themselves sensed their isolation (see Cairns, 'Political Science, Ethnicity and the Canadian Constitution,' in Shugarman and Whitaker, eds., *Federalism and Political Community*).

Whatever their point of view, political scientists have dominated the writing of post-1945 political history. Historians have paid more attention to the earlier period, although even there recent contributions are relatively few.

THE AGE OF MACDONALD

The approach of the centennial of Confederation created an efflorescence of books about Confederation, but not even the constitutional quarrels of the 1970s and 1980s have maintained interest in what the fathers of Confederation said and did. The standard accounts remain Morton, *The Critical Years*, and Peter Waite, *The Life and Times of Confederation 1864–1867: Politics, Newspapers, and the Union of British North America* (T: UTP 1962). The Maritimes have been the focus of much attention as to the causes and results of Confederation. Philip Buckner, with characteristic provocativeness, called for a reassessment of the Maritimes and Confederation, a challenge that was taken up by Peter Waite and William Baker, 'CHR Dialogue: The Maritimes and Confederation: A Reassessment,' *CHR* March 1990. Buckner's challenge originally appeared in Ged Martin, ed., *The Causes of Canadian Confederation* (Fredericton: Acadiensis Press 1990), which includes a fine article by Martin, 'The Case against Canadian Confederation, 1864–1867.' Gordon T. Stewart has written an interesting and assertive book, *The Origins of Canadian Politics: A Comparative Approach* (V: UBCP 1986), that tries to place Canadian politics into a broader Anglo-American context. His controversial conclusion that, from the 1840s, when modern Canadian party formation began, 'only the party leader/prime minister and perhaps one or two lieutenants ... take long term national interests into account' reflects his judgment that the Canadian party system served the nation well in the days of Macdonald and Laurier but has been inadequate for most of the twentieth century. Stewart stresses the importance of patronage in the nineteenth-century party system, a theme that is also stressed in Brian Beaven, 'Partisanship, Patronage, and the Press in Ontario, 1880–1914,' *CHR* 1983, and much earlier in the writings of Frank Underhill and Goldwin Smith. Underhill's influential arguments can be examined in 'The Development of National Parties in Canada,' in his *In Search of Canadian Liberalism* (T: MAC 1960) and in a series of radio lectures, *The Image of Confederation* (T: Canadian Broadcasting Corporation 1964). Paul Rutherford also gives many details on the link between parties and newspapers in his major work on the Victorian press: *A Victorian Authority: The Daily Press in Late Nineteenth-Century Canada* (T: UTP 1982).

For Donald Creighton, however, patronage was a subject that was thoroughly obscured by broader and grander deeds associated with building a new nation. His biography of Macdonald, *John A. Macdonald*, vol. 2, *The Old Chieftain* (T: MAC 1955) keeps a clear focus on the House of Commons and on Macdonald's dominance of Canadian political life for the first twenty-five years of Confederation. In this biography, Creighton describes the character of Confederation as he had sketched out its circumstances in *British North America at Confederation* (O: King's Printer, 1939). Criticism of Creighton's views may be found in Ralph Heintzman, 'The Spirit of Confederation: Professor Creighton, Biculturalism, and the Use of History,' *CHR* 1971, and, less directly, in Ramsay Cook, *Canada and the French Canadian Question* (T: MAC 1966). Although Creighton did not himself reply to these criticisms of his view of the 'spirit' of Confederation, David Hall did in 'The Spirit of Confederation: Ralph Heintzman, Professor Creighton, and the Bicultural Compact Theory,' *JCS* 1974. A later work that avoids much of the detail of these controversies but maintains a favourable view of Macdonald and his achievement is found in Donald Swainson, *Sir John A. Macdonald: The Man and the Politician* (2nd ed., K: Quarry Press 1989). The same applies to Peter Waite's sprightly *Macdonald: His Life and World* (Scarborough: MHR 1975). For those who want to encounter Macdonald directly, the best sources remain his secretary Joseph Pope's *Memoirs of the Right Honourable Sir John Alexander Macdonald, First Prime Minister of the Dominion of Canada*, 2 vols. (O: J. Durie 1894) and *Correspondence of Sir John Macdonald: Selections from the Correspondence of Sir John Alexander Macdonald* (T: OUP 1921).

Other fathers of Confederation have also attracted biographers. Brian Young, *George-Etienne Cartier: Montreal Bourgeois* (M and K: MQUP 1981) is an important work that places Cartier within the context of mid-nineteenth-century Quebec political economy. Alistair Sweeney, *George-Etienne Cartier: A Biography* (T: M&S 1976) is more traditional and biographical in its approach. Hector Langevin is the subject of Andrée Désilets, *Hector-Louis Langevin: Un père de la confédération canadienne, 1826–1906* (Q: PUL 1969). George Brown is fortunate to have had one of Canada's finest historians choose him as a subject. J.M.S. Careless's *Brown of the Globe*, vol. 2, *Statesman of Confederation* (T: MAC 1963) is one of the best Canadian historical biographies. It is a major contribution not only to the history of Confederation but also to the history of journalism and business in Ontario. Despite his importance, Alexander Tilloch Galt has received little attention since O.D. Skelton, *The Life and Times of Sir Alexander Tilloch Galt* (T: OUP 1920). The standard source on Charles Tupper is also dated: E.M. Saunders, *The Life and Letters of the Rt. Hon. Sir Charles Tupper, bart.*

K.C.M.G., 2 vols. (NY: Cassell 1916). The most fortunate of Macdonald's colleagues is Sir John Thompson, about whom Peter Waite has written a splendid study: *The Man from Halifax: Sir John Thompson, Prime Minister* (T: UTP 1985), which completely supersedes J. Castell Hopkins, *Life and Work of Sir John Thompson, Prime Minister of Canada* (T: Bradley Garretson 1895). His fellow Nova Scotian, Joseph Howe, initially an opponent of Confederation, is the subject of J. Murray Beck, *Joseph Howe*, vol. 2, *The Briton Becomes Canadian, 1848–1873* (M and K: MQUP 1983). Another important Maritimer, Timothy Warren Anglin, is the subject of a well-researched and valuable biography by William Baker: *Timothy Warren Anglin, 1822–96: Irish Catholic Canadian* (T: UTP 1977).

The creation of a national political party system was the product of various forces in different regions of the country. These were recognized in the creation of the first cabinet, the subject of 'The Cabinet of 1867,' in Frederick W. Gibson, eds., *Cabinet Formation and Bicultural Relations: Seven Case Studies*, vol. 6, *Studies of the Royal Commission on Bilingualism and Biculturalism* (O: QP 1970). Gibson's book should be consulted for cabinet-making in later governments as well. On the broader question of provincial interests and the nature of Confederation, the same Royal Commission sponsored Ramsay Cook's excellent brief study, *Provincial Autonomy, Minority Rights, and the Compact Theory, 1867–1921* (O: QP 1969). There has been considerable interest in opposition or adaptation of local interests to the demands of a new nation. This subject is covered in Beck's biography of Howe, and also Kenneth Pryke, *Nova Scotia and Confederation, 1864–1874* (T: UTP 1979), and Colin Howell, 'Nova Scotia's Protest Tradition and the Search for a Meaningful Federalism,' in D.J. Bercuson, ed., *Canada and the Burden of Unity* (T: Gage 1980), a book that has many essays which touch upon regional discontent with Confederation. D.A. Muise draws upon his thesis on party development in Nova Scotia in 'Parties and Constituencies: Federal Elections in Nova Scotia 1867–1896, CHA *AR* 1971. On Prince Edward Island, see David Weale and Harry Baglole, *The Island and Confederation: The End of an Era* (Summerside: Williams and Crue 1973), and Francis Bolger, *Prince Edward Island and Confederation, 1863–1873* (Charlottetown: St Dunstan's UP 1964). On Newfoundland's decision not to join, see James Hiller, 'Confederation Defeated: The Newfoundland Election of 1869,' in Hiller and Peter Neary, eds., *Newfoundland in the Nineteenth and Twentieth Centuries: Essays in Interpretation* (T: UTP 1980). For New Brunswick, the distinguished political scientist Hugh G. Thornburn's *Politics in New Brunswick* (T: UTP 1961) is essential, although dated. Two other works that should be consulted are Ernest R. Forbes, *Aspects of Maritime Regionalism, 1867–1927* (O: CHA 1983), and George Rawlyk, ed., *The Atlantic Provinces and the Problems of Confederation* (St John's: Breakwater 1980).

The province of Quebec and Confederation is, of course, the focus of some general works, including those by Creighton and Cook discussed above. A.I. Silver takes a broad and long view of the subject in *The French-Canadian Idea of Confederation, 1864–1900* (T: UTP 1982). Two texts also have valuable sections on Quebec's entry into Confederation: Paul-André Linteau, René Durocher, and Jean-Claude Robert, *Histoire du Québec contemporain*, vol. 1, *De la confédération à la Crise, 1867–1929* (M: BE 1979). There is also an English edition, *Quebec: A History, 1867–1929* (T: JL 1982). Susan Mann Trofimenkoff's *The Dream of Nation: A Social and Intellectual History of Quebec* (T: MAC 1982) is notable for its attempt to place the entry of French Canada into Confederation in the context of separate spheres, a concept which she sees as significant in the history of women and the church in nineteenth-century Quebec. The image of Confederation as a marriage, a mixed and bad one, is developed in Lionel Groulx, *La Confédération canadienne: ses origines* (M: Le Devoir 1918), which is polemical and dated but still extremely influential. More balanced are Jean-Charles Bonenfant, *La naissance de la Confédération* (M: Lemeac 1969); Walter Ullman, 'The Quebec Bishops and Confederation,' *CHR* 1963; and Paul G. Cornell, *The Alignment of Political Groups in Canada, 1841–1867* (T: UTP 1962). This last book reminds us that political groups took form in the United Canadas where Quebec politicians formed and broke alliances with Upper Canadians.

Upper Canada, of course, is popularly seen as identical with the movement towards Canadian Confederation. In fact, in the nineteenth century, Ontario was a vigorous exponent of provincial rights and was often uneasy with the nature of the new union. The major work on this subject is Christopher Armstrong's valuable *The Politics of Federalism: Ontario's Relations with the Federal Government, 1867–1942* (T: UTP 1981). Armstrong has also written about the early years in Donald Swainson, ed., *Oliver Mowat's Ontario* (T: MAC 1972), which is a valuable collection of articles about Ontario's first decades. Ontario's rather peculiar first premier, John Sandfield Macdonald, is the subject of a short biography by Bruce W. Hodgins, *John Sandfield Macdonald, 1812–1872* (T: UTP 1971). Most of the book is about the pre-Confederation period: only two chapters cover the post-Confederation period. Margaret Evans, who has written many articles on the far more significant Ontario premier, Oliver Mowat, has brought together this work in a biography, *Sir Oliver Mowat* (T: UTP 1992). Mowat succeeded Edward Blake as premier after Blake decided to opt for Ottawa rather than Toronto in 1872. Joseph Schull has written a two-volume biography of Blake which used the research of Frank Underhill, whose long fascination with Blake never resulted in a sustained treatment of that most complex figure. *Edward Blake: The Man of the Other Way, 1833–1881* and *Edward Blake: Leader and Exile, 1881–1912* (T: MAC 1975, 1976) do not succeed in capturing the elusive lawyer-intellectual-politician but they are the best studies we have.

Blake chose Ottawa in part because of his vision of what the new nation and, in particular, the Canadian West should be. The West and the early years of Confederation have attracted much scholarly attention because it seemed in the late 1860s and early 1870s that the fate and character of the new nation would be determined by how the West became part of it. This theme is very much present in Silver's *The French-Canadian Idea of Confederation* and in Doug Owram's fascinating study of what the West meant to its promoters, *Promise of Eden: The Canadian Expansionist Movement and the Idea of the West* (T: UTP 1980). The challenge to 'Canadian' aims in the West came primarily from two sources: the Americans to the South and the Métis in Manitoba. On the former, Alvin C. Gluek, *Minnesota and the Manifest Destiny of the Canadian Northwest: A Study in Canadian-American Relations* (T: UTP 1965) is useful. There is extensive literature on the resistance in Manitoba. W.L. Morton's introduction to *Alexander Begg's Red River Journal and Other Papers Relative to the Red River Resistance of 1869–1870* and the journal itself (T: CS 1956) are important as is the extensive discussion of Manitoba and Confederation in his *Manitoba: A History* (T: UTP 1957). The resistance is also described in Frits Pannekoek, *A Snug Little Flock: The Social Origins of the Riel Resistance of 1869–1970* (W: Watson and Dwyer 1991), as is the Canadian response to it in George F.G. Stanley, *Toil and Trouble: Military Expeditions to Red River* (T: Dundurn 1989). Two other works by Stanley deal with Western Canada and Confederation: *The Birth of Western Canada: A History of the Riel Rebellions* (3rd ed., T: UTP 1992), and *Louis Riel* (Scarborough: MHR 1972). Macdonald received much criticism for his western policies both from contemporaries and historians. He is defended by Donald Creighton in 'John A. Macdonald, Confederation, and the Canadian West,' in his *Towards the Discovery of Canada: Selected Essays* (T: MAC 1972). British Columbia and Confederation are dealt with in a useful collection of essays edited by W. George Shelton, *British Columbia and Confederation* (Vi: University of Victoria 1967). The relevant chapters in Margaret Ormsby's *British Columbia: A History* (T: MAC 1958) are also worthwhile.

The West which Macdonald believed so fundamental to his conception of the new nation caused him the most trouble in his first government: both the Riel resistance and the Pacific Scandal which led to his defeat arose from his efforts to build a railway westward. His defeat established the Canadian political maxim that oppositions do not win elections but governments lose them. The Liberal government under Alexander Mackenzie which succeeded the Macdonald Conservatives was an all-too-loose collection of Macdonald's foes that further proved the point about governments losing elections. Nevertheless, Canadian liberalism was congealing as a doctrine, one that was much influenced by the strength of British and American liberalism. The international context is described in Robert Kelley, *The Transatlantic Persuasion: The Liberal-Democratic Mind in the Age of Gladstone* (NY: Knopf 1969). The liberal tradition is also analysed in William Christian and Colin Campbell, *Political Parties and Ideologies in Canada: Liberals, Conservatives, Socialists, Nationalists* (2nd ed., T: MHR 1983). Frank Underhill was an earlier student of the subject. His numerous articles include 'Edward Blake and Canadian Liberal Nationalism,' in Ralph Flenley, ed., *Essays in Canadian History Presented to George M. Wrong* (T: MAC 1939), and 'Political Ideas of Upper Canadian Reformers, 1867–1878,' in his *In Search of Canadian Liberalism* (T: MAC 1960), a collection of Underhill's essays which illustrates well his not entirely successful search to define what Canadian liberalism was and should be.

Alexander Mackenzie was not the type who paid much attention to such lofty notions, a fact made clear in Dale C. Thomson, *Alexander Mackenzie: Clear Grit* (T: MAC 1960). Mackenzie receives somewhat harsher treatment in Berton's *The National Dream*. During Mackenzie's period, labour became a political factor. This is discussed in Bernard Ostry's two articles 'Conservatives, Liberals, and Labour in the 1870s,' *CHR* 1960, and 'Conservatives, Liberals, and Labour in the 1880s,' *CJEPS* 1961. These articles have been superseded by two books which, in their authors' view, are certainly not political or 'national' histories but which nevertheless discuss labour politics in the 1870s and 1880s in some detail: Gregory S. Kealey, *Toronto Workers Respond to Industrial Capitalism, 1867–1892* (2nd ed., T: UTP 1991), and Bryan D. Palmer, *A Culture in Conflict: Skilled Workers and Industrial Capitalism in Hamilton, Ontario 1860–1914* (M and K: MQUP 1979).

Mackenzie Liberalism depended on Quebec *rouge* support. During the 1870s the *rouge* tradition was transformed into Quebec liberalism. This transformation is discussed in Jean-Paul Bernard, *Les Rouges: libéralisme, nationalisme et anticléricalisme au milieu du XIXe siècle* (M: PUQ 1971). Wilfrid Laurier is, of course, central not only to this transformation but also to later Canadian political history, and the historiography of Laurier will be discussed below. Laurier's and the *rouges'* difficulties with the Church and, in particular, the ultramontanes are important in understanding national politics. An interpretation which incorporates class and sociological analysis is Nadia Fahmy-Eid, *Le clergé et le pouvoir politique au Québec: une analyse de l'idéologie ultramontaine au milieu du XIXe siècle* (M: HMH 1978). Good summaries of the question are available in Linteau et al., chapters 13–15 and, particularly Trofimenkoff, chapter 8. In fact, the Liberals survived the challenge; the Conservatives had persistent difficulties after 1873 as is explained in Andrée Desilets, 'La succession de Cartier, 1873–1891,' CHA *HP* 1968 and in her biography of Hector Langevin, *Hector-Louis Langevin: Un Père de la Confédération Canadienne (1826–1906)* (Q: PUL 1969), and in Blair Neatby and J.T. Saywell, 'Chapleau and the Conservative Party in Quebec,' *CHR* 1956.

Despite such difficulties, Macdonald returned to power in 1878, and his return is normally credited to his adoption of the National Policy. That policy of national development involving tariffs, immigration, and western expansion through the building of the CPR has attracted the attention it merits from historians, economists, and others. Critics of the National Policy point to the high cost economy it created, the dependence of the private sector on the state, and the branch-plant economy that it spawned. Best known of these critiques are John H. Dales, *The Protective Tariff in Canada's Development: Eight Essays on Trade and Tariff When Factors Move, with Special Reference to Canadian Protectionism, 1870–1955* (T: UTP 1966); Michael Bliss, *Northern Enterprise: Five Centuries of Canadian Business* (T: M&S 1987), especially chapter 9, and his admirably succinct statement of the argument, 'Canadianizing American Business: The Roots of the Branch,' in Ian Lumsen, ed., *Close the 49th Parallel etc.: The Americanization of Canada* (T: UTP 1972); the much earlier Edward Porritt, *Sixty Years of Protection in Canada, 1846–1907: Where Industry Leans on the Politician* (L: MAC 1908); and Goldwin Smith, *Canada and the Canadian Question* (1891, T: UTP 1971). The last two are worth reading to see how contemporary critics associated the policy with the rise of political corruption in Canada, a theme later taken up by Frank Underhill. The controversy about the National Policy is examined in a special issue of the *Journal of Canadian Studies*, 'The National Policy, 1879–1979,' Spring 1978. A well-researched account which tends to avoid the historical gusts which swirl around the national policy is Ben Forster, *A Conjunction of Interests: Business, Politics, and Tariffs, 1825–1879* (T: UTP 1986). The view of the National Policy as a necessary component of the nationalizing processes of the first decades of Confederation is found in R. Craig Brown, *Canada's National Policy, 1883–1900: A Study in Canadian-American Relations* (Princeton: Princeton UP 1964) and, of course, Donald Creighton, *Macdonald*. Pierre Berton, *The National Dream* and *The Last Spike*, put forward a similar argument traced along the path of the building of the CPR. For a critique of Berton's assumptions about nationalism and the CPR, see A.A. den Otter, 'Nationalism and the Pacific Scandal,' *CHR* 1986; and Robert A.J. Macdonald, 'Victoria, Vancouver, and the Economic Development of British Columbia, 1886–1914,' in Alan Artibise, ed., *Town and City: Aspects of Western Canadian Urban Development* (R: CPRC 1981). Macdonald argues that the CPR had much less effect than its business and historical promoters believed. Harold A. Innis, *A History of the Canadian Pacific Railway* (1923, T: UTP 1971) is now of interest only to those interested in Innis, not the railway. Of continuing importance, however, is W. Kaye Lamb, *A History of the Canadian Pacific Railway* (T: MAC 1977), which draws upon CPR papers as well as Lamb's unrivalled knowledge of the papers in the Public Archives of Canada, renamed the National Archives after he stepped down as archivist.

The CPR, as every Canadian schoolchild knows, brought the troops to put down Riel. The Riel controversy is one with deep resonance in late twentieth-century Canadian political life. There is now more published work on Riel than on Macdonald or, for that matter, any other Canadian political figure. A major Canadian government-funded project brought forth George F.G. Stanley et al., eds., *The Collected Writings of Louis Riel*, 5 vols. (E: UAP 1985). A sample of Riel can be found in Thomas Flanagan, ed., *The Diaries of Louis Riel* (E: Hurtig 1986). The division on Riel was set out in George Stanley, *Louis Riel: Patriot or Rebel?* (2nd ed., O: CHA 1970). Stanley's own biography of Riel portrayed him as an unfortunate if misguided victim of careless Ottawa expansionism. He directly confronted the view set out in Creighton's *Macdonald*, which tended to portray Riel as a dangerous lunatic who threatened all that Confederation represented. Thomas Flanagan in two books, a psychobiography of Riel, *Louis 'David' Riel: Prophet of the New World* (T: UTP 1979) and *Riel and the Rebellion: 1885 Reconsidered* (S: WPPB 1983) argued that Riel was a self-interested, deluded leader who ignored chances to avoid conflict and who created many of the Metis' troubles. Flanagan was bitterly attacked by Metis groups who supported Manitoba historian D.N. Sprague in the writing of *Canada and the Metis, 1869–1885* (Wa: WLUP 1988). Sprague blames Macdonald and the federal government for the problems and even suggests a conspiracy to force Riel to rebel in order that he and his people could be crushed in 1885. An excellent account of the rebellion itself is Bob Beal and Rod Macleod, *Prairie Fire: The 1885 North-West Rebellion* (E: Hurtig 1984). The best way to begin sorting out this historiographical muddle is with J.R. Miller's moderation and wisdom found in 'From Riel to the Metis,' *CHR* 1988.

Miller knows not only how the Riel resistance affected the Canadian West but also how it influenced the development of Quebec nationalism. He traced one controversial issue in *Equal Rights: The Jesuit Estates' Act Controversy* (M and K: MQUP 1979), which looked at the antagonism that grew out of Ontario suspicions of special privilege for French Canada and its church. Silver's *The French-Canadian Idea of Confederation* and Cook's *Provincial Autonomy, Minority Rights, and the Compact Theory* should be consulted on this subject as well. Robert Rumilly gives a traditional nationalist view in *Honoré Mercier et son temps*, 2 vols. (M: Fides 1975). Roberto Perin has written widely on the subject of the Vatican and its role in Quebec politics. His work is best examined in *Rome and Canada: The Vatican and Canadian Affairs in the Late Victorian Age* (T: UTP 1990). The swirl around the church and politics crystallized in the Manitoba school dispute of the 1890s. The best place to begin is Lovell Clark's collection *The Manitoba School Question: Majority Rule or Minority Rights?* (T: CC 1968). Paul Crunican has written the standard account in *Priests and Politicians: Manitoba Schools and the Election of 1896* (T: UTP 1974), although a different interpretation that tends to minimize the impact of the issue is found in Kenneth McLaughlin's unpublished University of Toronto PhD thesis (1975), 'Race, Religion, and Politics: The Election of 1896 in Canada.' John T. Saywell, ed., *The Canadian Journal of Lady Aberdeen, 1893–1898* (T: CS 1960) remains invaluable, not least because of Saywell's excellent introduction.

The questions of 'race and religion' outlived Macdonald, but the profound differences between the Liberals and Conservatives over the national policy did not. The 1891 election was Macdonald's last, and it was fought on the issue of Canada's economic relationship with the United States. The Liberals' flirtation with closer economic and political ties with the United States, expressed in extreme form by Goldwin Smith, pushed Macdonald into a protectionist stance where tariffs were linked directly with national survival. Smith's argument in *Canada and the Canadian Question* (cited above) should be read. The complexities for the Liberals are described in Roger Graham, 'Sir Richard Cartwright, Wilfrid Laurier, and the Liberal Party Trade Policy, 1887,' *CHR* 1952; Ian Grant, 'Erastus Wiman: A Continentalist Replies to Canadian Imperialism,' *CHR* 1972; and

Frank Underhill, 'Edward Blake, the Liberal Party, and Unrestricted Reciprocity,' CHA *AR* 1939.

The 1891 victory of Macdonald was decisive even though it was very close in terms of the popular vote. After 1891 Laurier was determined to smother the differences between the two major parties on the issue of loyalty and its economic component, the national policy. In Quebec he also sought to manage the contentious issues of church and state. He was assisted by deep divisions in the Conservative Party after Macdonald and by the difficulties the party had in finding a successor to Macdonald. The best account of these difficulties is now found in Peter Waite's biography of John Thompson, *The Man from Halifax*. Saywell's introduction to Lady Aberdeen's journal is still useful as is McLauglin's thesis mentioned above.

THE AGE OF LAURIER

Laurier was a major figure in Canadian political life from his entry into Parliament in 1874. Prime minister for fifteen years, architect of the Liberal dominance in the province of Quebec, the first French Canadian to be prime minister, Laurier has attracted surprisingly little serious interest from professional historians in the last two decades. Public attention has concentrated upon Laurier's relationship with Emilie Lavergne and whether it was physically consummated. Sandra Gwyn's colourful *The Private Capital: Ambition and Love in the Age of Macdonald and Laurier* (T: M&S 1984) has many pages on the subject. Gwyn's book is splendid on the social life of the capital and has many wise things to say about Canada's politics and politicians. Her Laurier, however, it too much a *tabula rasa* upon which Emilie leaves her mark. Heather Robertson in *More Than a Rose: Prime Ministers, Wives, and Other Women* (T: Seal 1991) does not accept such notions and discusses Laurier's wife as well, but she does not seem to grasp the complex character of Laurier because of the narrowness of the sources used. The same might be said of nearly all works on Laurier. Although several are worthy efforts, certainly none is definitive. Réal Bélanger, however, has written a good popular biography based upon excellent knowledge of the relevant primary materials: *Wilfrid Laurier: quand la politique devient passion* (Q: PUL 1986). Richard Clippingdale's *Laurier: His Life and World* (T: MHR 1979) is also an intelligent popular biography. Two older studies are very important not simply because of their discussions of Laurier but also because the authors were major figures in Canadian political and intellectual life. John Willison's *Sir Wilfrid Laurier and the Liberal Party: A Political History*, 2 vols.

(T: G.N. Morang 1903) was written just before Willison became disillusioned with Laurier. It tries to argue that Laurier was essential to Canadian unity and was responsible for the increasing optimism in Canada. The argument is not so bad as Willison later thought it was. O.D. Skelton never became disillusioned with Laurier. Indeed, he seems to have conveniently lost evidence that Laurier opposed Confederation and to have cut out Laurier's signatures from his letters to preserve them as personal icons. Skelton's *Life and Letters of Sir Wilfrid Laurier*, 2 vols. (T: OUP 1922) is the official biography of Laurier based upon apparently full access to the Laurier papers and extensive interviews with Laurier. It is relentlessly partial to Laurier and, in many places, it distorts the record. Nevertheless, it is obviously the product of a first-class mind. In casual asides, Skelton makes profound remarks about Canadian political history. Long before Carl Berger argued that Canadian imperialists were essentially nationalists, Skelton, the imperialists' foe, had noticed this. And he does know Laurier: the sense of a personal encounter and of what Laurier thought of events and politicians is abundantly clear. A valuable corrective to Skelton's Laurier is J.W. Dafoe's *Laurier: A Study in Canadian Politics* (T: M&S 1922), which was originally published as an extended review of Skelton. Dafoe, who also knew Laurier well, sees traces in him of Machiavelli as well as the Sir Galahad depicted by Skelton. Joseph Schull, *Laurier: The First Canadian* (T: MAC 1965) follows the Skelton interpretation, but the original is to be preferred. Another contemporary source which reflects its author's admiration for Laurier is the French sociologist André Siegfried's *The Race Question in Canada* (E. Nash 1906). Certainly the finest study of Canadian politics by a non-Canadian, Siegfried's insightful work argues that Canada's political leaders worked together to quell the angry spirits that lurked in the constituencies. Later scholars called this the Canadian process of elite accommodation but Siegfried described it first – without jargon. Another outside observer (although it was controversial to call a Briton a foreigner in those times) was Lord Minto, the governor general in Laurier's early years. His writings have been collected and offer fascinating views on Canadian life and politics at the turn of the century: Paul Stevens and John Saywell, eds., *Lord Minto's Canadian Papers: A Selection of the Public and Private Papers of the Fourth Earl of Minto, 1898–1904*, 2 vols. (T: CS 1981, 1989).

Lord Minto pushed the government toward closer links with the Empire, and in Laurier's first years this imperial question was his major one. The phenomenon of Canadian imperialism is discussed in Carl Berger's highly influential *The Sense of Power: Studies in the Ideas of Canadian Imperialism*,

1867–1914 (T: UTP 1970). Berger emphasizes the nationalism of Canadian imperialism and places it in the broader context of late-nineteenth-century racism, militarism, and nationalism. The details of Canadian policy-making in this area are ably presented in C.P. Stacey, *Canada and the Age of Conflict: A History of Canadian External Policies*, vol. 1, *1867–1921* (T: UTP 1981). The major crisis Laurier faced was the Boer War, to which he eventually agreed to send Canadian volunteers. The event is covered well in Stacey. Norman Penlington, *Canada and Imperialism, 1896–1899* (T: UTP 1965) emphasizes the importance of Canadian-American relations in the decision to send Canadians to South Africa. Other works worth consulting on this subject include Robert J.D. Page, ed., *Imperialism and Canada, 1895–1903* (T: HRW 1972) and 'Canada and the Imperial Idea in the Boer War,' *JCS* 1970; Carman Miller, *The Canadian Career of the Fourth Earl of Minto: The Education of a Viceroy* (Wa: WLUP 1980); Carl Berger, ed., *Imperial Relations in the Age of Laurier* (T: UTP 1969); H.B. Neatby, 'Laurier and Imperialism,' CHA *AR* 1955, and Richard Preston, *Canada and 'Imperial Defense': A Study of the Origins of the British Commonwealth's Defense Organization, 1867–1919* (Durham: Duke UP 1967).

The Boer War caused a profound rift in the Quebec branch of the Liberal Party and may have been the proximate cause of the rise of nationalist sentiment in Quebec. This movement coalesced originally around Liberal MP Henri Bourassa's challenge to Laurier. The relevant documents are found in Joseph Levitt, ed., *Henri Bourassa on Imperialism and Biculturalism, 1900–1918* (T: CC 1970). Other sources include James Corcoran, 'Henri Bourassa et la guerre sud-africaine,' *RHAF* 1964, 1965; and Casey Murrow, *Henri Bourassa and French Canadian Nationalism* (M: Harvest House 1968). Bourassa's challenge to Laurier, which included a critique of his broader political philosophy, is the subject of Joseph Levitt, *Henri Bourassa and the Golden Calf: The Social Program of the Nationalists of Quebec, 1900–1914* (2nd ed., O: UOP 1972). Robert Rumilly, *Henri Bourassa: la vie publique d'un grand Canadien* (M: Chantecler 1953) is dated but benefits from Rumilly's personal background as a Quebec nationalist. More remains to be said about Bourassa.

Laurier was a brilliant political leader whose skill in creating a Quebec base for his party while balancing other interests is described in H. Blair Neatby's *Laurier and a Liberal Quebec: A Study in Political Management* (T: M&S 1973). His colleagues, however, were not always so happy with his style and, sometimes, the substance of his politics. One who had many difficulties and who left the cabinet was the very able minister of the interior in Laurier's first governments, Sir Clifford Sifton. D.J. Hall has written an excellent two-volume biography of this secretive and difficult figure: *Clifford Sifton: The Young Napoleon, 1861–1900* and *Clifford Sifton: A Lonely Eminence, 1901–1929* (V: UBCP 1981, 1985). J.W. Dafoe's *Sir Clifford Sifton in Relation to His Times* (1931; Freeport, NY: Books for Libraries Press 1971) remains important because the author knew the subject and his times intimately. Laurier's other ministers have not fared so well. His finance minister, W.S. Fielding, is the subject of a thin biography by C.B. Fergusson, *Mr. Minister of Finance: Rt. Hon. W.S. Fielding*, 2 vols. (Windsor: Lancelot 1970, 1971). Richard Cartwright wrote his own autobiography *Reminiscences* (T: William Briggs 1912), which is one of the best of the early period. Mackenzie King, of course is covered in many works, but four concentrate on the earlier period: H.B. Ferns and Bernard Ostry, *The Age of Mackenzie King* (2nd ed., T: JL 1976); Fred A. McGregor, *The Fall and Rise of Mackenzie King, 1911–1919* (T: MAC 1962); R. MacGregor Dawson, *William Lyon Mackenzie King: A Political Biography*, vol. 1, *1874–1923* (T: UTP 1958); and Paul Craven, *'An Impartial Umpire': Industrial Relations and the Canadian State, 1900-1911* (T: UTP 1980). The first is highly critical of King and has not stood up well. The second is by King's secretary and is anodyne. The third is the official biography. It is traditional and based upon a good knowledge of the King papers, but is disappointing in the narrowness of its approach. The last is an important study of King's work in the department of labour that places King's approach to labour questions in a broader context. The minister of militia, Frederick Borden, was also a reformer, and these reforms are discussed in Carman Miller, 'Sir Frederick William Borden and Military Reform, 1896–1911,' *CHR* 1969.

Three of the major issues facing Laurier in the first five years of the new century were the demand for a new national railway, the Alaska Boundary Dispute, and the school problem in the Canadian West. These are covered ably in the Hall biography of Sifton, for the minister of the interior was at the centre of these issues until he resigned from the Laurier government in 1905. The complex railway issue, one where so many bad decisions were made, is analysed in T.D. Regehr, *The Canadian Northern Railway: Pioneer Road of the Northern Prairies, 1895–1918* (T: MAC 1976). The Canadian Northern's success in securing government funds was due to the skills of Sir William Mackenzie, whose career is discussed in R.B. Fleming, *The Railway King of Canada: Sir William Mackenzie, 1849–1923* (V: UBCP 1991). George R. Stevens, *Canadian National Railways*, 2 vols. (T: CI 1960) is dated but remains a readable account. The Alaska boundary dispute is covered very well in Stacey, *Canada and the Age of Conflict*, vol. 1. Two other books, the first emphasizing the American point of view and the second a good collection of the relevant primary sources and secondary works, are Norman Penlington, *The Alaska Boundary Dispute: A Critical Reappraisal* (T: MHR 1972), and John Munro, ed., *The Alaska Boundary Dispute* (T: CC 1970). The dispute over schools in the new provinces of Alberta and Saskatchewan is studied in Manoly Lupul, *The Roman Catholic Church and the North-West School Question: A Study in Church-State Relations in Western Canada, 1875–1905* (T: UTP 1974). David Hall's biography of Sifton is also essential on this question in that he argues that Sifton was basically in favour of a 'melting pot' with the public school as the pot. The literature is reviewed in J. William Brennan, 'The "Autonomy Question" and the Creation of Alberta and Saskatchewan, 1905,' in Howard Palmer and Donald Smith, eds., *The New Provinces: Alberta and Saskatchewan, 1905–1980* (V: Tantalus 1980).

Most western Canadians favoured the 'melting pot' but the over-whelming immigration to the West in that period swamped those 'Canadianizing' institutions which Sifton and others favoured. The formation of immigration policy is discussed in Hall's biography, and the imperial 'dreams' in London and elsewhere are ably presented in R.G. Moyles and Doug Owram, *Imperial Dreams and Colonial Realities: British Views of Canada, 1880–1914* (T: UTP 1988). Other works dealing with particular aspects are Donald Avery, *'Dangerous Foreigners': European Immigrant Workers and Labour Radicalism in Canada, 1896–1932* (T: M&S 1979); Patricia Roy, *A White Man's Province: British Columbia Politicians and Chinese and Japanese Immigrants, 1858–1914* (V: UBCP 1989); and Hugh Johnston, *The Voyage of the Komogata Maru: The Sikh Challenge to Canada's Colour Bar* (Delhi: OUP 1970). Pierre Berton, *The Promised Land: Settling the West, 1896–1914* (T: M&S 1984) is highly anecdotal, lively, and should not be ignored by students.

After 1905 the Laurier government seemed to lose its energy. In Ontario the party lost considerable strength. The problem of leadership is described in Paul Stevens, 'Laurier, Aylesworth, and the Decline of the Liberal Party in Ontario,' CHA *AR* 1968. Michael Bliss's outstanding biography of Sir Joseph Flavelle, *A Canadian Millionaire: The Life and Business Times of Sir Joseph Flavelle, bart., 1858–1939* (2nd ed., T: UTP 1992) is excellent in tracing Flavelle's growing suspicion of Laurier's 'sunny ways.' Robert Cuff wrote two articles that support Stevens's argument that in Ontario the Liberals had weakened greatly before the reciprocity issue administered the final blow: 'The Conservative Party Machine and the Election of

1911 in Ontario,' *OH* 1965; and 'The Toronto Eighteen and the Election of 1911,' *OH* 1965. The literature on the reciprocity question itself is disappointing. Lewis E. Ellis, *Reciprocity, 1911: A Study in Canadian-American Relations* (1939, 2nd ed., NY: Greenwood Press 1968) is dated. Paul Stevens, ed., *The 1911 General Election: A Study in Canadian Politics* (T: CC 1970) is a collection of readings. William Baker, 'A Case Study of Anti-Americanism in English-Speaking Canada,' *CHR* 1970, uses newspapers to study anti-Americanism in the Tory campaign; again, the focus is mainly on Ontario. The major issue in Quebec was the naval crisis. Robert Rumilly's *Henri Bourassa* is a strong defence of Bourassa and his alliance with the Tories to defeat Monk. John English wrote about the Nationalist-Tory matchmaker Frederick Monk in Carty and Ward, eds., *National Politics and Community*. The best understanding of the nationalists' motives and their difficulties is found in a valuable but relatively unknown biography by Réal Bélanger on Albert Sévigny: *L'impossible défi: Albert Sévigny et les conservateurs fédéraux* (Q: PUL 1983). Based upon extensive newspaper research, as manuscript material is scarce, this biography presents clearly the dilemmas the Quebec nationalists faced in Ottawa in the heyday of British-Canadian nationalism.

The best account of the election is in R.C. Brown's excellent biography of the victor, Conservative leader Robert Borden. *Robert Laird Borden: A Biography*, vol. 1, *1854–1914* (T: MAC 1975) rescues Borden from the stuffiness of his own memoirs: Henry Borden, ed., *Robert Laird Borden: His Memoirs*, 2 vols. (T: MAC 1938). The memoirs are wooden and reveal little of Borden himself. Brown is sympathetic to Borden, but in his account of the 1911 election and in his description of the war years, he criticizes Borden's failure to understand Quebec. Nevertheless, Brown clearly establishes that Borden was a highly intelligent and committed leader who led Canada through one of its most difficult periods. The Conservative party under Borden is the subject of John English, *The Decline of Politics: The Conservatives and the Party System, 1901–1920* (2nd ed., T: UTP 1993). This book argues that the pre-war party system that had been an integrative force broke down under the pressures of the enormous transformation of Canadian society in the first two decades of this century.

The major agent of transformation in Canada, as in the Western world more generally, was World War I. The best description of the broad impact of war on Canadian society, politics, and economics remains the relevant chapters of Brown and Cook, *Canada 1896–1921*. The impact on Quebec and on nationalist politics is summarized well by Susan Mann Trofimenkoff in her book *The Dream of Nation:* 'Nationalists in Quebec have never forgotten the First World War and Liberal politicians have been a close second in reminding voters of its political ravages. For many nationalists the war years turned French Canada into Quebec. For many Liberals the blunders of federal Conservatives during the same years provided electoral ammunition for generations to come.' Trofimenkoff's chapter 13, which begins with these statements, is essential reading on Quebec and the war. So is Elizabeth Armstrong, *The Crisis of Quebec, 1914–1918* (1937, T: M&S 1974). Armstrong, an American state department official, used newspapers to write this study of Quebec's reaction to the war, which also, to some extent, reflects her conversations with Canadians in the 1930s who still recalled 'the clash.'

The clash, of course, was mainly over conscription, but other factors played a major part, notably the Ontario bilingual schools issue, which is described in Marilyn Barber, 'The Ontario Bilingual Schools Issue: Sources of Conflict,' *CHR* 1966, and Margaret Prang, 'Clerics, Politicians, and the Bilingual Schools Issue in Ontario, 1910–1917,' *CHR* 1960. *N.W. Rowell: Ontario Nationalist* (T: UTP 1975), Prang's detailed and important biography of Newton Rowell, the Ontario Liberal leader who joined with Borden in supporting conscription, is also important in understanding an Ontario nationalist's response to French Canada and the war. For the origins of the school question in the Mowat period, Chad Gaffield, *Language, Schooling, and Cultural Conflict: The Origins of the French-Language Controversy in Ontario* (M and K: MQUP 1987) supersedes Robert Choquette, *Language and Religion: A History of English-French Conflict in Ontario* (O: UOP 1975), although the latter does contain some important material on the attitude of the clergy.

Conscription itself is discussed in J.L. Granatstein and J.M. Hitsman, *Broken Promises: A History of Conscription in Canada* (T: OUP 1977), a study which is sternly critical of Borden for making the decision to implement conscription and for the manner in which he carried it out. For a different point of view, see the article by A.M. Willms, 'Conscription 1917: A Brief for the Defence,' in a useful collection edited by Carl Berger, *Conscription 1917* (T: UTP 1969). Craig Brown does not defend the Union government's manipulation of the franchise, but he does argue cogently that the pressures of British-Canadian nationalism left Borden with no choice and that his leadership was, on the whole, responsible in these circumstances. Matt Bray has also illustrated the increasing strength of 'patriotic sentiment' in 'Fighting as an Ally: The English Canadian Patriotic Response to the Great War,' *CHR* 1980. Granatstein, in fact, seems to have moderated the harsh view expressed in *Broken Promises* in his more recent collaboration with Desmond Morton, *Marching to Armageddon: Canadians and the Great War 1914–1919* (T: Lester & Orpen Dennys 1989), a well-illustrated summary of the war and its impact on Canada. Another general work is Daniel G. Dancocks, *Spearhead to Victory: Canada and the Great War* (E: Hurtig 1987).

Canada's war effort is eloquently described in John Swettenham, *To Seize the Victory: The Canadian Corps in World War One* (T: RP 1965). Some individuals merit individual biographies. The controversial minister of militia Sam Hughes is the subject of Ronald Haycock, *Sam Hughes: The Public Career of a Controversial Canadian, 1885–1916* (Wa: WLUP 1986). Although Haycock tries to be fair to Hughes, a reader must conclude that at a dangerous time Hughes was not the right man; indeed, at moments, he seemed mad. Arthur Currie was an odd man, but a fine general. A.M.J. Hyatt has written a biography, which focuses on the latter: *General Sir Arthur Currie: A Military Biography* (T: UTP 1987). The veterans' path after the war is followed in an excellent scholarly study by Desmond Morton and Glenn T. Wright, *Winning the Second Battle: Canadian Veterans and the Return to Civilian Life, 1915–1930* (T: UTP 1987).

On the organization of the war, see the excellent sections in Brown and Cook, *Canada 1896–1921*, and Robert Cuff, 'Organizing for War: Canada and the United States During World War I,' CHA *AR* 1969. The war and farmers are discussed in an outstanding article by William Young, 'Conscription, Rural Depopulation, and the Farmers of Ontario, 1917–1919,' *CHR* 1972; and in John Herd Thompson, *The Harvests of War: The Prairie West, 1914–1919* (T: M&S 1978). The peace movement receives detailed attention in Thomas Socknat, *Witness against War: Pacifism in Canada, 1900–1945* (T: UTP 1987). Catherine Cleverdon's *The Woman Suffrage Movement in Canada: The Start of Liberation, 1900–1920* (T: UTP 1974) should be supplemented by the relevant sections in Alison Prentice et al., *Canadian Women: A History* (T: HBJ 1988). Finally, J. Castell Hopkins, *The Canadian Annual Review of Public Affairs 1917* (T: Canadian Annual Review 1918) gives the reader the intense flavours of that extraordinary year in undiluted form.

FROM THE GREAT WAR TO THE GREAT DEPRESSION

Social unrest, political disunity, and bitter animosities followed the war's end. The end of Union government is described in Craig Brown, *Robert Laird Borden*, vol. 2, *1914–1937*; and John English, *The Decline of Politics*. The West, which had supported Union government so strongly in 1917, defected quickly. Two older works remain essential in understanding the political expression of Western discontent: Ramsay Cook, *The Politics of John W. Dafoe and the Free Press* (T: UTP 1963); and W.L. Morton, *The Progressive Party in Canada* (T: UTP 1950). Gerald Friesen, *The Canadian Prairies: A History* (T: UTP 1984), chapter 14, should be consulted as well. On the radicalism of Western labour, which was expressed most vociferously in the streets of Winnipeg in 1919, the major work is David Bercuson, *Confrontation at Winnipeg: Labour, Industrial Relations, and the General Strike* (rev. ed., M and K: MQUP 1990). Other works that deal more generally with the subject include Bercuson's study of the One Big Union: *Fools and Wise Men: The Rise and Fall of the One Big Union* (Scarborough: MHR 1978); A. Ross McCormack, *Reformers, Rebels, and Revolutionaries: The Western Canadian Radical Movement, 1899–1919* (T: UTP 1977); and Gerald Friesen, '"Yours in Revolt": The Socialist Party of Canada and the Western Labour Movement,' *Labour* 1976. Martin Robin, *Radical Politics and Canadian Labour, 1880–1930* (K: Queen's University Industrial Relations Centre, 1968) is dated.

The Progressives seemed to represent the future to many journalists in 1919, and the Liberal Party seemed yet another casualty of the war. It was not, even though Laurier's successor was quickly dismissed as unworthy by many Canadian journalists in 1919. In fact, Mackenzie King stitched together a new coalition which eventually became the political party that dominated national politics until the mid-1980s. Although a later generation of journalists has tended to make King a risible figure, prone to talk to spirits and consort with prostitutes, historians have become increasingly generous to Canada's most venerable cabinet minister and prime minister. J.L. Granatstein has written the best short biography of King: *Mackenzie King: His Life and World* (Scarborough: MHR 1977). The first volume of the official biography by R. MacGregor Dawson was followed by two thoughtful and well-written volumes by Blair Neatby: *The Lonely Heights*, vol. 2, *1924–1932* and *The Prism of Unity*, vol. 3, *1933–1939* (T: UTP 1970, 1975). C.P. Stacey's muckraking *A Very Double Life: The Private World of Mackenzie King* (T: MAC 1976) concentrates upon King's peccadillos but does contain material on his political career. It contrasts strangely with Stacey's fine account of King's policies in *The Age of Conflict*, vol. 2, and his thoughtful and elegant *Mackenzie King and the Atlantic Triangle* (T: MAC 1977). Stacey, it seems, did not like King, but admits, most grudgingly, that King's political skills were probably the finest Canada has ever seen. Joy Esberey, *Knight of the Holy Spirit: A Study of W.L. Mackenzie King* (T: UTP 1980) is a psychobiography of King that confuses more than it illuminates. The distinguished Freudian scholar Paul Roazen has discovered important new material relating to King that is essential for any such psychobiography. We await the fruits of his labours. Additional material on King can be found in John English and John O. Stubbs, eds., *Mackenzie King: Widening the Debate* (T: MAC 1977), and in the debate between Reg Whitaker and Paul Craven in *Labour* (1977, 1979): 'The Liberal Corporatist Ideas of Mackenzie King,' and 'King and Context: A Reply to Whitaker.' Finally, one can take King straight by consulting his voluminous diaries, which are available on microfiche (T: UTP 1980). For those wanting a weaker dose, J.W. Pickersgill and Donald Forster, eds., *The Mackenzie King Record*, vols. 1–4 (T: UTP 1960–1970) are adequate although they cover only the post-1939 period and ignore the personal peculiarities of Mackenzie King.

The 1920s were a decade that most historians ignored for reasons that W.L. Morton enumerated in an essay on the decade in J.M.S. Careless and R.Craig Brown, eds., *The Canadians: 1867–1967* (T: MAC 1967). He described and, perhaps, recalled it as an age of Babbittry and mediocrity in Canada; one has the impression that Morton thought that Mackenzie King fitted it well. In the last fifteen years, however, historians in North America, beginning first in the United States and then in Canada, began to sketch a portrait of a more complex and innovative decade. The conventional picture of the women's movement 'losing its nerve' is supplanted by a more complicated definition of politics and gender in Veronica Strong-Boag, *The New Day Recalled: Lives of Girls and Women in English Canada, 1919–1939* (T: CCP 1988). There is much material on the first decade in which women could vote in national elections in Linda Kealey and Joan Sangster, eds., *Beyond the Vote: Canadian Women and Politics* (T: UTP 1989). Sangster has also written *Dreams of Equality: Women on the Canadian Left, 1920–1950* (T: M&S 1989). T.A. Crowley has written a sympathetic and sensitive biography of Agnes Macphail, the first woman MP, *Agnes Macphail and the Politics of Equality* (T: JL 1990), and Valerie Knowles has focused upon the first woman senator in *First Person: A Biography of Cairine Wilson, Canada's First Woman Senator* (T: Dundurn 1988).

Many of the fresh political ideas came from the West despite the decline of the Progressive movement at the federal level. David Laycock in *Populism and Democratic Thought in the Canadian Prairies, 1910–1945* (T: UTP 1990) discusses the Progressive tradition and its lasting impact on Western politics. The Maritimes Rights movement also established some of the major themes of Maritime political response in the twentieth century. The leading scholar of the movement is E.R. Forbes, whose sympathetic view is expressed in *The Maritime Rights Movement: A Study in Canadian Regionalism, 1919–1927* (M and K: MQUP 1979). The Communist Party of Canada gained life in the 1920s, although its influence was not felt until the following decades. Ivan Avakumovic is not a sympathetic historian in *The Communist Party in Canada: A History* (T: M&S 1975); Norman Penner, whose family was involved in the party in Manitoba, is: the author of *The Canadian Left: A Critical Analysis* (Scarborough: PH 1977). The most balanced study remains William Rodney, *Soldiers of the International: A History of the Communist Party of Canada, 1919–1929* (T: UTP 1968). The moderate left took form in the aftermath of the 1919 strikes in Calgary and Winnipeg. J.S. Woodsworth and the so-called Ginger Group in the House of Commons were the seed that sprouted later Canadian social democracy. Woodsworth is the subject of much study, but the best works are Kenneth McNaught's highly sympathetic *A Prophet in Politics: A Biography of J.S. Woodsworth* (T: UTP 1959), and Allen Mills, *Fool for Christ: The Political Thought of J.S. Woodsworth* (T: UTP 1991), which casts a sterner eye on Woodsworth and his motives.

On the national level, the 1920s were notable for the growth of the modern bureaucratic state. This growth became possible with the reforms in the civil service that followed the election of the coalition Union government in 1917. The role of the civil service commission is traced in J.E. Hodgetts et al., *The Biography of an Institution: The Civil Service Commission of Canada, 1908–1967* (M and K: MQUP 1972). Hodgetts's *The Canadian Public Service: A Physiology of Government, 1876–1970* (T: UTP 1973) tends to generalize and is of less value to students. On specific departments, there are some valuable studies, notably Doug Owram, *Building for Canadians: A History of the Department of Public Works, 1840–1960* (O: Public Works 1979), and John Hilliker, *Canada's Department of External Affairs*, vol. 1, *The Early Years, 1909–1946* (M and K: MQUP 1990). The history of Canada's trade activities by O. Mary Hill, *Canada's Salesman to the World: The Department of Trade and Commerce, 1892–1939* (M and K: MQUP 1977), is less satisfactory. The growth of a professional public service, which is so much associated with O.D. Skelton, who came to Ottawa from Queen's University in the 1920s, is the subject of two important books: J.L. Granatstein, *The Ottawa Men: The Civil Service Mandarins, 1935–1957* (T: OUP 1982), and Douglas Owram, *The Government Generation: Canadian Intellectuals and the State, 1900–1945* (T: UTP 1986). As Granatstein's title indicates, the emergence of the so-called Ottawa mandarinate did not occur until the mid-1930s, but the 1920s were a critical transitional period. In this respect, Owram's chapter on 'The

Social Sciences and the Service State' is essential reading and a model blend of intellectual and political history. He reveals how in the 1920s there was a transformation in the perception of what a state's functions were and the place of social scientists in defining the role. With the end of traditional forms of patronage, a professional public service could emerge which was complemented by the secularization of the civil service. University training mattered and professional skills were valued. It led, in time, to a revolution in government.

Mackenzie King's own background in political economy seemed ʰo fit this new age in the view of many intellectuals, although his apparent willingness to tolerate 'old-style politics' such as were seen in the Beauharnois Scandal did much to alienate them. See T.D. Regehr, *The Beauharnois Scandal: A Story of Canadian Entrepreneurship and Politics* (T: UTP 1990). Nevertheless, King found that he captured the spirit of the young and those who were discouraged with the past through a Canadian nationalism which was increasingly expressed in Canada's relationship with Great Britain during the 1920s. C.P. Stacey, *Canada and the Age of Conflict*, vol. 2, *1921–1940, The Mackenzie King Era* (T: UTP 1981) is excellent on the 1920s, in part because Stacey himself came of age politically in that period. His ambivalence towards King and nationalism is not shared in the Dawson and Neatby volumes of the official biography. Hostility is found in Roger Graham, *Arthur Meighen: A Biography*, vol. 2, *And Fortune Fled* (T: CI 1963), which admiringly traces Meighen's futile attempts to puncture King's pomposity. He did so rhetorically but not politically. Their decisive contest was the election of 1926 in which the major issue was the so-called King-Byng affair. This constitutional controversy is analysed from different points of view in Neatby's biography of King and Graham's biography of Meighen. Graham also edited a book which presents documents and arguments reflecting both sides of the controversy: *The King-Byng Affair, 1926: A Question of Responsible Government* (T: CC 1967).

The question of 'responsible government' refers, of course, to Canada's relationship with Great Britain. The evolution of this relationship in the 1920s is admirably traced by Philip Wigley, *Canada and the Transition to Commonwealth: British-Canadian Relations, 1917–1926* (Cambridge: Cambridge UP 1977), and by Norman Hillmer, 'A British High Commissioner for Canada, 1927–1928,' *Journal of Imperial and Commonwealth History* 1973; 'The Canadian Diplomatic Tradition,' in Andrew Cooper, ed., *Canadian Culture: International Dimensions* (T: CIIA 1985); and his brilliant exegesis of the attitudes and policies of O.D. Skelton, 'The Anglo-Canadian Neurosis: The Case of O.D. Skelton,' in Peter Lyon, ed., *Britain and Canada: Survey of a Changing Relationship* (L: Frank Cass 1976). Many of the best academic minds of the 1920s and 1930s focused upon the 'constitutional question' and the associated topic of Canadian nationality. Their work gathers dust today as the Anglo-Canadian neurosis has passed like yesterday's dream. To get the sense of the debate, students should consult the *Canadian Historical Review*, *Canadian Journal of Economics and Political Science*, and *Canadian Forum* for the 1920s and 1930s.

THE 1930s: DEPRESSION AND DISSENT

The Depression brought home to Canadians how much of their basic livelihood depended upon events far beyond their borders. Few of them noticed the collapse of Kreditanstalt in central Europe, and even the collapse of Wall Street in October 1929 did not seem initially portentous beyond Bay and St James streets. By the election of 1930, however, they realized their lives were fundamentally altered and they turned to R.B. Bennett and the Conservatives. Later, they tried other nostrums for their economic ailments ranging from Social Credit, populism, socialism, and communism to fascism, but they tested these on the provincial levels. At the federal level, R.B. Bennett and Mackenzie King, the former a great capitalist, the latter a cautious and traditional Liberal, dominated the 1930s.

Bennett had been one of the least-known Canadian prime ministers, but two recent works add much to our knowledge: James H. Gray, *R.B. Bennett: The Calgary Years* (T: UTP 1991), and Larry Glassford, *Reaction and Reform: The Politics of the Conservative Party under R.B. Bennett, 1927–1938* (T: UTP 1992). Gray is openly sympathetic to Bennett, seeing him as a remarkably generous person who was, perhaps, not equipped for those harsh times. Bennett's eccentricity as well as his generosity are evident in Michael Bliss and Linda Grayson, eds., *The Wretched of Canada: Letters to R.B. Bennett, 1930–1935* (T: UTP 1971). Peter Waite, Gray's collaborator, is working on a successor volume that will do much to illuminate Bennett's political career. An excellent short study by Waite is *The Loner: Three Sketches of the Personal Life and Ideas of R.B. Bennett: 1870–1947* (T: UTP 1992). Glassford has written a fine party history based upon detailed archival research. Two older books, Ernest Watkins, *R.B. Bennett: A Biography* (T: Kingswood House 1963), and Lord Beaverbrook, *Friends: Sixty Years of Intimate Personal Relations with Richard Bedford Bennett* (L: Heineman 1959) have been superseded, although the latter remains a curiosity item. There is excellent material, much of it drawn from unpublished theses, on Bennett and external policy in Robert Bothwell and Norman Hillmer, eds., *The In-Between Time: Canadian External Policy in the 1930s* (T: CC 1975). Two other selections of documents are very useful for the domestic arena: Michiel Horn, *The Dirty Thirties: Canadians in the Great Depression* (T: CC 1972), and Richard Wilbur, *The Bennett New Deal: Fraud or Portent?* (T: CC 1968). The attitude of business to Bennett's New Deal is analysed in Alvin Finkel, *Business and Social Reform in the Thirties* (T: JL 1979), which is most unsympathetic to business.

Wilbur has also written a short biography of Bennett's difficult colleague H.H. Stevens, who left the cabinet to form the Reconstruction Party: *H.H. Stevens, 1878–1973* (T: UTP 1977). Bennett dominated his government, and his other colleagues who remained have received deserved short shrift from the historians. This is not true of the provincial leaders of the time, many of whom played a major part in certain scenes on the national stage. The ablest premier of the age was Nova Scotia's Angus L. Macdonald, the subject of an admiring but not very able biography by John Hawkins, *The Life and Times of Angus L.* (Windsor: Lancelot 1969). The two Quebec premiers of the 1930s, Louis-Alexandre Taschereau and Maurice Duplessis, were strongly contrasting figures, as is made clear in two well-researched but very different studies of the two leaders: Bernard Vigod, *Quebec before Duplessis: The Political Career of Louis-Alexandre Taschereau* (M and K: MQUP 1986), and Conrad Black, *Duplessis* (T: M&S 1977). Both are based upon extensive archival research. Black's study is deliberately revisionist and often argumentative. It is a valuable antidote to writings from the national perspective, which are nearly always hostile towards Duplessis. It should be read, however, in conjunction with the relevant sections of Trofimenkoff, *The Dream of Nation*, and Paul-André Linteau et al., *Quebec since 1930* (T: JL 1989). A very critical treatment of Duplessis is found in Herbert Quinn, *The Union Nationale: A Study in Quebec Nationalism* (T: UTP 1963). Fernand Dumont et al., *Idéologies au Canada français, 1930–1939* (Q: PUL 1978), and René Durocher, 'Taschereau, Hepburn, et les relations Québec-Ontario,' *RHAF* 1970, are also useful.

Hepburn is the subject of a splendidly researched and lively biography which shows the warts but also manages to convey Hepburn's annoyance with Ottawa and his genuine populist appeal: John T. Saywell, *'Just call me Mitch': The Life of Mitchell F. Hepburn* (T: UTP 1991). The much less flamboyant Manitoba premier John Bracken has also been fortunate in his biographer John Kendle in *John Bracken: A Political Biography* (T: UTP

1979). Jimmy Gardiner dominated Saskatchewan politics, first as premier between 1925 and 1935 and then as the principal Prairie representative in Mackenzie King's cabinet. Two of Canada's finest political scientists, Norman Ward and David Smith, collaborated on *Jimmy Gardiner: Relentless Liberal* (T: UTP 1990). Less satisfactory is David Elliot and Iris Miller, *Bible Bill: A Biography of William Aberhart* (E: Reidmore 1987), which should be supplemented by Alvin Finkel's revisionist *The Social Credit Phenomenon in Alberta* (T: UTP 1989). Finkel's study does not entirely supersede C.B. Macpherson, *Democracy in Alberta: Social Credit and the Party System* (T: UTP 1953, 1962), or John A. Irving, *The Social Credit Movement in Alberta* (T: UTP 1959). Finkel, like Macpherson and Irving, uses Social Credit in Alberta as a means of explaining broader characteristics of twentieth-century representative democracy, particularly its economic and psychological roots. Finally, Duff Pattullo of British Columbia, a Liberal much attracted to Franklin Roosevelt's New Deal and much annoyed by the policies of Canada's federal Liberals, is the subject of a sympathetic and well-researched biography by Robin Fisher, *Duff Pattullo of British Columbia* (T: UTP 1991). Fisher, like several other biographers of the Depression-era premiers, shows how the provincial leaders looked to Ottawa in their desperation to find a solution to the economic crisis. They also found that antagonism towards Ottawa created affection among their voters. The result was an angry decade of confrontation.

Blair Neatby has written an excellent short study of the decade: *The Politics of Chaos: Canada in the 1930s* (T: MAC 1972). There is much detail on the economic difficulties of the period in Bothwell et al., *Canada 1900–1945*, and on the social changes in Thompson and Seager, *Canada 1922–1939*. Pierre Berton, *The Great Depression, 1929–1939* (T: M&S 1990) has a wealth of anecdotes but does not capture the complex political and social changes of the 1930s. It is determinedly hostile to the politicians and thoroughly populist in its attitude. Those who consult the abundant literature on economic thought, international trade, and the Canadian economy in the 1930s will derive a different impression. A.E. Safarian, *The Canadian Economy in the Great Depression* (T: UTP 1959) remains essential. Michael Bliss in *Northern Enterprise*, chapter 14, counters Finkel, Berton, and others in analysing business during the Depression. On economic thought, Owram, *The Government Generation*, is excellent in tracing the intellectual sea change that occurred as the events of the 1930s overwhelmed traditional attitudes. One who inspired these changes was the brilliant economist–public servant Robert B. Bryce, who did much to educate North Americans in the new economic approaches suggested by

Keynes. With full access to government sources, Bryce has written *Maturing in Hard Times: Canada's Department of Finance through the Great Depression* and (M and K: MQUP 1986). In the reinvigoration of the Canadian financial system, the Bank of Canada played a central role, as can be seen in the biography of its founding governor by Douglas Fullerton, *Graham Towers and His Times* (T: M&S 1986). International negotiations are discussed in the important study by Ian M. Drummond and Norman Hillmer, *Negotiating Freer Trade: The United Kingdom, the United States, Canada, and the Trade Agreements of 1938* (Wa: WLUP 1989). The problems of national security policy in the interwar years are traced in James Eayrs, *In Defence of Canada*, vol. 1, *From the Great War to the Great Depression*, and vol. 2, *Appeasement and Rearmament* (T: UTP 1964, 1965). King's answer to the perplexities of mid-1930s political economy was to set up a royal commission. Although it responded too late to affect policy in the 1930s, the Rowell-Sirois report should be consulted by all who want to understand political economy in the 1930s. An abbreviated version is available: Donald Smiley, ed., *The Rowell-Sirois Report: An Abridgement of Book One of the Rowell-Sirois Report on Dominion-Provincial Relations* (T: MAC 1963). David Fransen's unpublished doctoral thesis 'Unscrewing the Unscrutable: The Rowell-Sirois Commission, The Ottawa Bureaucracy, and Public Finance Reform, 1935–1941' (University of Toronto 1985) is essential for those who want to understand the commission, its origins, and its work.

There are numerous more specialized works that touch upon important areas of national politics in the 1930s. Irving Abella and Harold Troper are harshly critical of Canadian immigration policies and, at least implicitly, of Canadians in *None Is Too Many: Canada and the Jews of Europe, 1933–1938* (T: Lester & Orpen Dennys 1982). Deportation of undesirables is described in Barbara Roberts, *Whence They Came: Deportation from Canada, 1900–1935* (O: UOP 1988). The suspicion of the 'foreign' marked the 1930s. French-Canadian anti-Semitism is made clear in Pierre Anctil, *Le rendez-vous manqué: les Juifs de Montréal face au Québec de l'entre-deux-guerres* (Q: IQRC 1988). That the rest of Canada was not much better is apparent in Lita-Rose Betcherman, *The Swastika and the Maple Leaf: Fascist Movements in Canada in the Thirties* (T: Fitzhenry and Whiteside 1975). Canadian prejudice, however, did not have the hard edge of its Central European counterparts. Jonathan Wagner has examined the appeal of Nazism in Canada in *Brothers beyond the Sea: National Socialism in Canada* (Wa: WLUP 1982) and has found that its main appeal lay outside the mainstream. Communists often suffered because of anti-Semitism, as is made clear in Andrée Lévesque, *Virage à gauche interdit: les communistes, les socialistes et leurs ennemis au Québec, 1929–1939* (M: BE 1984).

One lasting response to the Depression was the Canadian socialist movement which took the form of the Co-operative Commonwealth Federation. It and its successor, the New Democratic Party, have had much support among academics and, not surprisingly, have attracted much academic attention. Among the major works are the biographies of its first leader, J.S. Woodsworth, by McNaught and Mills mentioned above; Walter D. Young, *The Anatomy of a Party: The National CCF, 1932–61* (T: UTP 1969); and Michiel Horn, *League for Social Reconstruction: Intellectual Origins of the Democratic Left in Canada, 1930–1942* (T: UTP 1980), a fine study of the intellectuals who combined to give eastern and intellectual ballast to a Prairie political movement. S.M. Lipset, *Agrarian Socialism: The Co-operative Commonwealth Federation in Saskatchewan, a Study in Political Economy* should be read in its later edition (NY: Doubleday 1968), which includes some articles which amplify or disagree with Lipset's characterization of Saskatchewan agrarian protest as socialism. The role of one intellectual who played a major part in the CCF's early years is most ably discussed in R. Douglas Francis, *Frank Underhill: Intellectual Provocateur* (T: UTP 1986). Sandra Djwa, *The Politics of the Imagination: A Life of F.R. Scott* (T: M&S 1987) is weak on Scott's politics, and Scott's contemporary writings are much to be preferred. The leftist intellectuals associated with the CCF can be directly encountered in their *Social Planning for Canada*. It should be read in the later edition in which they reflect on their socialism of the 1930s (T: UTP 1975).

THE WAR

The insufficient demand that made the Depression so severe and protracted ended with the coming of war and the stoking of the Canadian economy by the need for war production. Many of the Depression's major actors survived the 1930s, most importantly Mackenzie King. The official biography comes to an end in 1939, but J.L. Granatstein, *Canada's War: The Politics of the Mackenzie King Government, 1939–1945* (2nd ed., T: UTP 1990) is an excellent supplement to the earlier volumes, along with Pickersgill and Forster, *The Mackenzie King Record*, vols. 1–4. Brian Nolan, *King's War: Mackenzie King and the Politics of War, 1939–1945* (T: Random House 1988) should be ignored. There are, however, two good popular histories by historians which concentrate on the military effort but do not ignore other aspects: W.A.B. Douglas and Brereton

Greenhous, *Out of the Shadows: Canada in the Second World War* (T: OUP 1977), and J.L. Granatstein and Desmond Morton, *A Nation Forged in Fire: Canadians and the Second World War, 1939–1945* (T: Lester & Orpen Dennys 1989). The finest work on World War II that combines diplomatic, military, and political history is C.P. Stacey's magisterial *Arms, Men, and Governments: The War Policies of Canada, 1939–1945* (O: QP 1970). Sidney Aster edited several papers that cover particular aspect of the war experience: *The Second World War as a National Experience* (O: Canadian Committee for the History of the Second World War 1981). The experience of Canadian ethnic groups is the subject of a rather uneven book produced by the same organization: Norman Hillmer et al., eds., *On Guard for Thee: War, Ethnicity, and the Canadian State, 1939–1945* (O: Canadian Committee for the History of the Second World War 1988).

Reg Whitaker, *The Government Party: Organizing and Financing the Liberal Party of Canada, 1930–1958* (T: UTP 1977) is probably the finest history of a national party that exists. It is especially good on the turn to 'modern' means of influencing voters in the 1940s. Based on extensive research in the Liberal Party papers and the King collection, it does much to explain Liberal pre-eminence from 1935 to 1957. J.L. Granatstein also offers an explanation – Tory incompetence – in *The Politics of Survival: The Conservative Party of Canada, 1939–1945* (T: UTP 1967). Whitaker has described how one political party was repressed in the early year in 'Official Repression of Communism during World War II,' *Labour* 1986. The role of labour in Canadian politics is explained in Irving Martin Abella, *Nationalism, Communism, and Canadian Labour: The CIO, the Communist Party and the Canadian Congress of Labour, 1935–1956* (T: UTP 1973).

King's wartime cabinet is usually considered one of Canada's finest, and there are several studies that describe the role of individuals. C.D. Howe, the 'minister of everything,' is the subject of Robert Bothwell and William Kilbourn, *C.D. Howe: A Biography* (T: M&S 1979), an important work that reveals how much Howe was involved in the Liberal Party as well as in the overall direction of the Canadian war effort. In *Jimmy Gardiner* Ward and Smith describe how a party loyalist handled the problem of conscription, which he opposed. Ward also edited the excellent and delightful memoirs of Charles G. 'Chubby' Power, *A Party Politician: The Memoirs of Chubby Power* (T: MAC 1966). Louis St Laurent is the subject of Dale Thomson, *Louis St Laurent: Canadian* (T: MAC 1967), which is disappointing, although Thomson, St Laurent's secretary, knew his subject and his papers well. J.W. Pickersgill, *My Years with Louis St Laurent: A Political Memoir* (T: UTP 1975) is good on the reaction of

Ottawa to St Laurent and on St Laurent's initial clumsiness in office. It concentrates, however, on the later period when St Laurent was prime minister. General McNaughton, whom King tried to recruit for federal politics but who could not survive the electoral test, is the subject of a long biography by John Swettenham: *McNaughton*, 3 vols. (T: RP 1968, 1969, 1969). Angus L. Macdonald is the subject of John Hawkins's inadequate biography, *The Life and Time of Angus L.* (cited above). Many of the finest ministers, Ilsley, Ralston, Abbott, Lapointe, and Rogers await their biographers; David Bercuson's biography of Claxton will appear soon (T: UTP 1994). Some of King's advisers, however, have received deserved attention. J.L. Granatstein, *A Man of Influence: Norman A. Robertson and Canadian Statecraft, 1929–1968* (O: Deneau 1981) is that prolific historian's finest work. Meticulously researched, clearly written, and carefully crafted, it places Robertson within the larger context of Canadian statecraft. *A Man of Influence* is particularly good on Robertson's 'finest hour,' World War II, when he became King's most trusted adviser. Robertson had replaced Skelton, who had recruited him and several other highly intelligent and articulate young men to External Affairs. Being articulate, they left records. Among the finest of the over fifty books written by public servants of the war years are Hugh Keenleyside, *Memoirs of Hugh L. Keenleyside*, 2 vols. (T: M&S 1981); Escott Reid, *Radical Mandarin: The Memoirs of Escott Reid* (T: UTP 1989); Lester Pearson, *Mike: The Memoirs of the Right Honourable Lester B. Pearson*, 3 vols. (T: UTP 1971, 1973, 1975); John W. Holmes, *The Shaping of Peace: Canada and the Search for World Order, 1943–1957*, 2 vols. (T: UTP 1979, 1982); and Vincent Massey, *What's Past Is Prologue: The Memoirs of The Right Honourable Vincent Massey* (T: MAC 1963). In a separate category is the best autobiography by a Canadian federal politician. Paul Martin, who entered Parliament in 1935, King's cabinet in 1945, and served under three subsequent prime ministers, was assisted by the very able professional historian William Young in writing *A Very Political Life*, 2 vols. (O: Deneau 1983, 1985), which is based on extensive research in manuscript materials as well as Martin's own memory.

Young himself wrote the best study of wartime propaganda in his unpublished 1978 University of British Columbia thesis, 'Making the Truth Graphic: The Canadian Government's Home Front Information Structure and Programme during World War II.' A sample of his excellent work may be glimpsed in 'Academics and Social Scientists versus the Press: The Policies of the Bureau of Public Information and the Wartime Information Board, 1939–1945' CHA *HA* 1978. The role of women in wartime is analysed in Ruth Roach Pierson, *'They're Still Women After All':*

The Second World War and Canadian Womanhood (T: M&S 1986). E.R. Forbes argues that the Maritimes were treated badly by C.D. Howe and Ottawa in 'The Maritimes and the Industrialization of Canada during the Second World War,' *Acadiensis* 1986. Robert Young casts serious doubt upon Forbes's interpretation of events in his '"And the People Will Sink into Despair": Reconstruction in New Brunswick, 1942–1952' *CHR* 1988. The coming of the social welfare state is the subject of considerable attention. The *Journal of Canadian Studies* (1986) devoted an entire issue to Leonard Marsh, whose Canadian counterpart of the Beveridge report is regarded as a landmark in Canadian social policy. An earlier special issue in 1979 dealt with other aspects of the growth of the social service state in Canada. There is also relevant material in Allan Moscovitch and Jim Albert, eds., *The 'Benevolent' State: The Growth of Welfare in Canada* (T: Garamond 1987). Malcolm G. Taylor, *Health Insurance and Canadian Public Policy: The Seven Decisions that Created the Canadian Health Insurance System* (M and K: MQUP 1978), and in Granatstein, *Canada's War*.

The major political issue of wartime was conscription. The best study is the relevant section of Granatstein and Hitsman, *Broken Promises*. R. MacGregor Dawson, *The Conscription Crisis of 1944* (T: UTP 1961) has been superseded by Granatstein and Hitsman, and by Stacey, *Arms, Men, and Governments*. The problem, of course, was the serious difference of opinion between French and English Canada. The views of a strong opponent of conscription are presented in André Laurendeau, *La crise de la conscription 1942* (M: Editions du Jour 1962), and in Philip Stratford, ed., *André Laurendeau: Witness for Quebec* (T: MAC 1973). Several of the above works, notably *The Mackenzie King Record*, contain much material on conscription.

The other major historical controversy is the treatment of Japanese Canadians. Popular historians have been very harsh on the King government's policies; see Ken Adachi, *The Enemy That Never Was: A History of the Japanese Canadians* (T: M&S 1976); Barry Broadfoot, *Years of Sorrow, Years of Shame: The Story of the Japanese Canadians in World War Two* (T: Doubleday 1977); and Ann Gomer Sunahara, *The Politics of Racism: The Uprooting of Japanese Canadians during the Second World War* (T: JL 1981). J.L. Granatstein first questioned whether racism was the primary motivation of policy makers in *The Man of Influence*. He was followed with a major study in collaboration with Patricia Roy and two Japanese historians, Masako Iino and Hiroko Takamura, *Mutual Hostages: Canadians and Japanese during the Second World War* (T: UTP 1990). They wrote the book 'with the intention of examining the events of the war years as dispassion-

ately as possible and trying to explain them in the context of their times.'
They criticized earlier works as inadequately researched and as being too
ready to point fingers and to sketch the matter in black and white. If they
hoped to quell passions, they have not, as an angry review by Reginald
Whitaker (*CHR* 1991) proves.

THE POSTWAR ERA

Mackenzie King liked to point out in his diary that only he and Stalin
among wartime leaders survived 1945. He remained as Canadian prime
minister until 1948, but his influence waned in this period. He gave up
the critical External Affairs portfolio to Louis St Laurent in 1946, and
two years later St Laurent became prime minister. The major historical
controversies surrounding this period involve Canada's international relationships, in particular its political and economic links to the United
States. In *The Forked Road* Donald Creighton argues that an arrogant and
Americanized Liberal government took the wrong fork in the road in the
1940s and followed a path that led to the loss of Canadian independence.
Granatstein in *Canada's War* and, more directly, in *How Britain's Weakness Forced Canada into the Arms of the United States* (T: UTP 1989) rejects
Creighton's analysis and is fatalistic about Canada's choices. In two earlier works, however, Granatstein and his co-author Robert Cuff had been
critical of the lack of independence in Canadian policy in the 1940s,
especially after the Cold War began: *Ties That Bind: Canadian-American
Relations in Wartime from the Great War to the Cold War* (Toronto: Hakkert
1977) and *American Dollars-Canadian Prosperity: Canadian-American Economic Relations, 1945–1950* (T: Samuel Stevens 1978). Other works that
take a middle view include Granatstein's *A Man of Influence*; Holmes, *The
Shaping of Peace*; James Eayrs, *In Defence of Canada*, vol. 3, *Peacemaking
and Deterrence*, and vol. 4, *Growing Up Allied* (T: UTP 1972, 1980); and
John English, *Shadow of Heaven: The Biography of Lester Pearson* (T: Lester
& Orpen Dennys 1989). A.F.W. Plumptre, *Three Decades of Decision: Canada
and the World Monetary System, 1944–1975* (T: M&S 1977) is critical of
the 'revisionism' of Granatstein and Cuff. Other works are discussed in
the foreign and defence sections of this book.

   Creighton is correct in pointing to the continuity of wartime Liberalism
dominance, and the result is the continuing importance of several works
listed above. *The Forked Road* covers events until 1957, and Whitaker, *The
Government Party*, probes the decline of the party in the 1950s as St Laurent

paid less attention to party matters and concentrated on 'the administration of things.' Many of the things are described in Bothwell and Kilbourn, *C.D. Howe*. Kilbourn wrote the best study of one Howe project that was economically successful but politically disastrous: *Pipeline: Trans Canada and the Great Debate, A History of Business and Politics* (T: CI 1970). Ward and Smith point out how the West was ignored in *Jimmy Gardiner*, a theme developed at much greater length and with great sophistication in Smith's *The Regional Decline of a National Party: Liberals on the Prairies* (T: UTP 1981). The first edition of Bothwell, *Canada since 1945*, has detail of economics and politics in the St Laurent era. Black and Quinn on Duplessis also have much material on the postwar Duplessis governments and their relationships with Ottawa. They must be supplemented by Michael Behiels's important *Prelude to Quebec's Quiet Revolution: Liberalism versus Neo-Nationalism, 1945–1960* (M and K: MQUP 1985). William D. Coleman, *The Independence Movement in Quebec, 1945–1980* (T: UTP 1984) is disappointing in its coverage of the pre-1960 period. Some general background, including some valuable statistical information, is presented in Kenneth McRoberts, *Quebec: Social Change and Political Crisis* (T: M&S 1988).

The unravelling of the Liberal government came quickly after 1954. Earlier strengths such as its international policies and its economic policies became weaknesses. Philip Resnick, *The Land of Cain: Class and Nationalism in English Canada, 1945–1975* (V: New Star 1977) shows how concern about foreign investment suddenly appeared. The government learned how strong emotions about American investment were during the pipeline debate, which is discussed in Kilbourn, *Pipeline*, and in J.W. Pickersgill, *My Years with Louis St Laurent*, in which the opposition attitude is strongly criticized. Walter Gordon, a prominent Liberal who was appointed to head a Royal Commission on Canada's Economic Prospects, certainly was doubtful about the government's behaviour and its policies: see Walter L. Gordon, *A Political Memoir* (T: M&S 1977). A wonderful and remarkably insightful memoir by a Tory backroom operator offers an opposition view of what happened to the Liberals: Dalton Camp, *Gentlemen, Players, and Politicians* (O: Deneau 1979). The best analysis of what happened in the election of 1957 remains a pioneering study of Canadian political behaviour by one of Canada's most eminent political scientists, John Meisel, in *The Canadian General Election of 1957* (T: UTP 1962). The best contemporary source that captures the optimism of mid-1950s middle-class Canada is the distinguished journalist Bruce Hutchison's *Canada: Tomorrow's Giant* (Don Mills: Longman 1957). The world he sketches now seems very far away.

THE TENTH DECADE: DIEFENBAKER AND PEARSON

The period from 1957 to 1967 has been treated as a unit by most historians and by one of the finest historical television series in Canada: 'The Tenth Decade.' In that CBC documentary Diefenbaker, Pearson, and their colleagues recall their times. It is a model of visual history which all students of the period should consult. The Granatstein volume in the Centenary Series is excellent, particularly in its balanced account of the two dominant political personalities, Pearson and Diefenbaker. Peter C. Newman's two books on the tenth decade transformed Canadian political journalism. *Renegade in Power: The Diefenbaker Years* (T: M&S 1963) is a harsh portrait of John Diefenbaker as an indecisive outsider who never fitted the office of prime minister. In *The Distemper of Our Times: Canadian Politics in Transition, 1963–1968* (T: M&S 1968), Newman turns a bright spotlight on the Pearson years and exposes many wrinkles and flaws. Based upon a 'leak' from a senior Pearson cabinet minister, his account of the cabinet's workings is remarkably accurate. Both accounts convey the 'distemper' of 1960s politics exceptionally well.

Liberals and Conservatives fumed when Newman published his books and accused him of exaggerating the bitterness of the times, but later work has proved that he captured the mood and the times very well. The extent of the animosities can be glimpsed in four useful works. Peter Stursberg, a well-known reporter, was commissioned by the Public (now National) Archives of Canada to interview the major political figures of the Diefenbaker-Pearson era. The Archives connection, the lack of attention to secondary figures on the part of the media, and the passions that the sixties stirred combined to produce remarkably frank interviews. Several of the principals claimed that they never knew that Stursberg intended to publish large portions of the interviews. Nothing like it had ever been done before, and it is likely that politicians of a later age, much more distrustful of journalists and of public scrutiny, would never agree to such interviews in the first place. Two of the books deal with the Diefenbaker years and reveal clearly how profound the suspicion was in the Diefenbaker governments and how that suspicion vitiated all attempts to govern successfully: *Diefenbaker: Leadership Gained, 1956–1962* and *Diefenbaker: Leadership Lost, 1962–1967* (T: UTP 1975, 1976). Pearson's colleagues are not much kinder to him, but his governments, although chaotic, seem to have had a sense of accomplishment: *Lester Pearson and the Dream of Unity* (T: Doubleday 1978) and *Lester Pearson and the American Dilemma* (T: Doubleday 1980).

Another primary source for the post-1960 period is the *Canadian Annual Review* (T: UTP 1960–), which has excellent articles on the Constitution, Quebec, foreign policy, and national politics. The 'Parliament and Politics' articles by John T. Saywell are masterly syntheses that stand up very well. Some other contemporary works seem too close to the events: see Robert Coates, *The Night of the Knives* (Fredericton: Brunswick Press 1969); James Johnston, *The Party's Over* (T: Longman's 1971); and Thomas Van Dusen, *The Chief* (T: MH 1968). In a separate category is Donald Fleming's very long and unfortunate memoir, *So Very Near: The Political Memoirs of the Hon. Donald M. Fleming* 2 vols. (T: M&S 1985), which is laced with strong doses of both bitterness and smugness. More balanced in tone are biographies of three Diefenbaker ministers, George Pearkes, George Nowlan, and Alvin Hamilton: Reginald Roy, *For Most Conspicuous Bravery: A Biography of Major-General George R. Pearkes* (V: UBCP 1977); Margaret Conrad, *George Nowlan: Maritime Conservative in National Politics* (T: UTP 1986); and Patrick Kyba, *Alvin: A Biography of the Hon. Alvin Hamilton, P.C.* (CR: CPRC 1989).

Denis Smith is currently preparing a biography of Diefenbaker. Diefenbaker's own memoirs, *One Canada: The Memoirs of the Rt. Hon. John G. Diefenbaker*, 3 vols. (T: MAC 1975–7) begin well but end in a morass of anecdote and recrimination. There are, however, three excellent works that deal with different aspects of his career. Basil Robinson was Diefenbaker's personal assistant in the foreign policy area. He is also a splendid writer with a wonderful eye for detail. His *Diefenbaker's World: A Populist in Foreign Affairs* (T: UTP 1989) is sympathetic to Diefenbaker personally but is very critical of his obsessive jealousies that ultimately destroyed him and his government. Jealousy poisoned Canadian-American relations during this period as Diefenbaker's resentment towards John Kennedy swelled in the early 1960s. Kennedy responded with contempt. Knowlton Nash, who knew both leaders well, describes their poor relationship in his excellent *Kennedy and Diefenbaker: Fear and Loathing across the Undefended Border* (T: M&S 1990). Garrett Wilson and Kevin Wilson are Saskatchewan Liberals but their study of Diefenbaker's early years is remarkably sympathetic. *Diefenbaker for the Defence* (T: JL 1988) portrays Diefenbaker as the quintessential outsider, even in Prince Albert. Obviously highly intelligent and endowed with remarkable oratorical skills. Diefenbaker found modern people and modern Canada difficult. Heather Robertson in *More Than a Rose* indicates that his personal life was also deeply troubled.

Diefenbaker's opponents have taken pride in how they broke his government so quickly. There are two very different accounts of the recovery of the Liberal Party after the great defeat of 1958. J.W. Pickersgill keeps his focus on the House of Commons and the work of the parliamentarians in exposing the government's weaknesses in *The Road Back: By a Liberal in Opposition* (T: UTP 1986). A strong contrast to Pickersgill's interpretation is offered in Tom Kent, *A Public Purpose: An Experience of Liberal Opposition and Canadian Government* (M and K: MQUP 1988), which argues that the rebuilding was largely due to the efforts of Walter Gordon and the rethinking of policy that took place before, at, and after the famous Kingston Conference. The second volume of Pearson's memoirs falls somewhere in between these two interpretations as does the good account of the Liberal resurgence in Granatstein's *Canada 1957–1967*. One should also consult Joseph Wearing, *The L-Shaped Party: The Liberal Party of Canada, 1958–1980* (T: MHR 1981), and John Meisel, ed. *Papers on the 1962 Election* (T: UTP 1964). A good contemporary account of how Diefenbaker conservatism collapsed is Peter Regenstreif's influential *The Diefenbaker Interlude: Parties and Voting in Canada, an Interpretation* (T: Longmans 1965). The notion of Diefenbaker's government as an 'interlude' appears also in George Perlin, *The Tory Syndrome: Leadership Politics in the Progressive Conservative Party* (M and K: MQUP 1980). The decline of the Liberals in the 1980s and the election of two Conservative majority governments suggest that the 'interlude' can be overstated.

That Diefenbaker's fall was not entirely the product of forces within Canada is now widely accepted. Nash in *Kennedy and Diefenbaker* is most sympathetic to Kennedy but admits that the American president did everything he could, and that he would have liked to have done more, to get rid of the obnoxious Canadian prime minister. Earlier evidence for this argument is found in Jocelyn Ghent, 'Canada, the United States and the Cuban Missile Crisis,' *Pacific Historical Review* 1979, and 'Did He Fall or Was He Pushed? The Kennedy Administration and the Collapse of the Diefenbaker Government,' *International History Review* 1979. The classic statement of the conspiracy thesis is found in George Grant's polemical but influential *Lament for a Nation: The Defeat of Canadian Nationalism* (T: M&S 1965). Grant is not convincing in his attempt to make Diefenbaker the embodiment of history but his dislike of the Liberals and his former friend Lester Pearson pervades this tract.

Pearson was too bland and too willing to compromise with the Americans in Grant's later view. Others shared the view, but few members of the American government did. An angry attack on Pearson and Canada is made by former American secretary of state Dean Acheson in Livingston

Merchant, ed., *Neighbors Taken For Granted: Canada and the United States* (NY: Praeger 1966). If Pearson seemed too bland for many tastes, his prime ministerial period was not. Biographical material and a discussion of his prime ministerial period can be found in John English, *The Worldly Years: The Life of Lester Pearson*, vol. 2, *1949–1972* (T: Knopf 1992); Robert Bothwell, *Lester Pearson: His Life and World* (T: MHR 1978), and Bruce Thordarson, *Lester Pearson: Diplomat and Politician* (T: OUP 1974). Several of his colleagues' memoirs reflect the period's complex flavour, notably Walter Gordon, *Memoirs*; Paul Martin, *A Very Public Life*, vol. 2; Paul Hellyer, *Damn the Torpedoes: My Fight to Unify Canada's Armed Forces* (T: M&S 1990); Judy LaMarsh, *Memoirs of a Bird in a Gilded Cage* (T: M&S 1969); and Gérard Pelletier, *Years of Choice: 1960–1968* (T: Methuen 1987). LaMarsh and Gordon are very critical of Pearson as is Kent in *A Public Purpose*. Other essential works on the Pearson government are Denis Smith, *Gentle Patriot: A Political Biography of Walter Gordon* (E: Hurtig 1973); Keith Davey, *The Rainmaker: A Passion for Politics* (T: Stoddart 1986); and two excellent works by the the political journalist Richard J. Gwyn, *The Shape of Scandal: A Study of a Government in Crisis* (T: CI 1965) and *Smallwood: The Unlikely Revolutionary* (T: M&S 1968). *The Shape of Scandal* describes the numerous scandals that affected the Pearson government in the mid-1960s, while *Smallwood* brilliantly illuminates politics in Newfoundland, both federally and provincially, for 'Joey' dominated both levels.

One of the paradoxes of the Pearson years was that Canada's most eminent diplomat presided over the postwar government that had to face the greatest domestic crisis, the challenge from Quebec. Pearson's difficult relationship with his Ottawa colleague, Jean Lesage, is described in Dale Thomson, *Jean Lesage and the Quiet Revolution* (T: MAC 1984). Thomson has also written the definitive account of Charles de Gaulle's intervention in Canadian politics: *Vive le Québec libre* (T: Deneau 1988). The political memoirs of Quebec's leading civil servant, Claude Morin, who negotiated so shrewdly with Ottawa, must be consulted: *L'art de l'impossible: la diplomatie québécoise depuis 1960* (M: BE 1987). Edward McWhinney, a constitutional adviser to several governments throughout the period, surveys the question in *Quebec and the Constitution, 1960–1978* (T: UTP 1979). *The Preliminary Report* (O: Information Canada 1965) of the Royal Commission on Bilingualism and Biculturalism is an important contemporary document. In retrospect, some provincial politicians in Quebec and elsewhere have claimed that the problems arose from the federal government's general unwillingness to share taxes fairly. These claims may be judged in

R.M. Burns, *The Acceptable Mean: The Tax Rental Agreements 1941–1962* (T: Canada Tax Foundation 1980). Another case of federal-provincial controversy arose over the Columbia River, a topic that is ably analysed in Neil Swainson, *Conflict over the Columbia: The Canadian Background to an Historic Treaty* (M and K: MQUP 1979). The emergence of regional development policies which became central to federal-provincial relations and to federal government redistributive policies is discussed in M. Janine Brodie, *The Political Economy of Canadian Regionalism* (T: HBJ 1990), and James Bickerton, *Nova Scotia, Ottawa, and the Politics of Regional Development* (T: UTP 1990). Tom Kent, in *The Public Purpose*, describes the evolution of this policy in which he played a very large part. Many times regional development policy involved subsidies of industries. The weaknesses of such a strategy is argued in Philip Mathias, *Forced Growth: Five Studies of Government Involvement in the Development of Canada* (T: J. Lewis & Samuel 1971).

THE TRUDEAU YEARS

In regional development policies, foreign policy, and language policy, historians now tend to see the Trudeau years as a continuation of the Pearson years despite Trudeau's self-professed distinctiveness. There can be no doubt, however, that Trudeau was, as an individual, very different from any previous Canadian prime minister. There are several biographical works, the most notable of which is Stephen Clarkson and Christina McCall, *Trudeau and Our Times* (T: M&S 1990). This volume is the first of a two-volume work on Trudeau. The authors claim, correctly, that their study is not strictly a biography. Certainly it is not chronologically organized as biographies traditionally are. It is as eclectic as its subject and, like him, has flashes of brilliant insights, and is sometimes hard to follow. More traditional and more critical is Richard Gwyn, *The Northern Magus: Pierre Trudeau and Canadians* (T: M&S 1980). More admiring is George Radwanski, *Trudeau* (T: MAC 1978). Both are obviously dated since they fail to consider Trudeau's last government, but they do reflect two different points of view and are useful for students. Radwanski had privileged access to Trudeau and his colleagues, and his interviews are fascinating. Michel Vastel, *Trudeau le Québécois* (M: Editions de l'homme 1989) is determined to prove that Trudeau is not what the title suggests. It does present some interesting material on his early years.

Trudeau can be sampled directly in *Federalism and the French Canadians* (T: MAC 1968). This collection of his pre-parliamentary writings reveals a mind determined to be different. The articles often surprise students who are puzzled that a leader identified with Canadian nationalism is so critical of nationalism. Although attempts have been made to claim consistency, the fact is that he simply changed his mind and adjusted to political circumstances. More of Trudeau is found in *Conversations with Canadians* (T: UTP 1972), although this is best regarded as campaign material. His former principal secretary, Tom Axworthy, joined with Trudeau to edit *Towards a Just Society: The Trudeau Years* (Markham: Viking 1990). Trudeau's own contribution, the book's final chapter, is outstanding and makes one thirst for the memoirs of this most eloquent and elegant public person. Some of the other contributions are largely puffery. Nevertheless, the book is essential reading for students of Trudeau and the Trudeau era. Finally, his sharp criticism of the Supreme Court's approaches are found in *Fatal Tilt: Speaking Out about Sovereignty* (T: Harper Collins 1991).

The first major study of an aspect of Trudeau's governments that has had access to manuscript materials is the justly praised and brilliantly titled *Pirouette: Pierre Trudeau and Canadian Foreign Policy* (T: UTP 1990) by J.L. Granatstein and Robert Bothwell. It supersedes several earlier works, although Peter Dobell, *Canada in World Affairs, 1971–1973* (T: CIIA 1985) is useful for the readjustment of Canadian policies in the aftermath of the foreign policy review. On energy policy, the standard account is now Bruce Doern and Glen Toner, *The Politics of Energy: The Development and Implementation of the NEP* (T: Methuen 1985), but this should be read with Marc Lalonde's defence of those policies in *Towards a Just Society*. Garth Stevenson, *The Politics of Canada's Airlines from Diefenbaker to Mulroney* (T: UTP 1987) and Sandford F. Borins's study of the controversy over 'French in the air,' *The Language of the Skies: The Bilingual Air Traffic Control Conflict in Canada* (M and K: MQUP 1983), are also important.

The Constitution and its reform are, of course, central to Trudeau's leadership. There are numerous studies of the subject including some of the works listed above which contain important sections dealing with the topic. Among the others are Richard Simeon, ed., *Must Canada Fail?* (M and K: MQUP 1977); R.B. Byers and Robert Reford, eds., *Canada Challenged: The Viability of Confederation* (T: CIIA 1979); Garth Stevenson, *Unfulfilled Union: Canadian Federalism and National Unity* (3rd ed., T: Gage 1989); and several studies on the referendum, patriation, and the Charter of Rights and Freedom: Robert Sheppard and Michael Valpy, *The National Deal: The Fight for a Canadian Constitution* (T: Fleet 1982); Keith

Banting and Richard Simeon, eds., *And No One Cheered: Federalism, Democracy, and the Constitution Act* (T: Methuen 1983); Alan Cairns and Cynthia Williams,' eds., *Constitutionalism, Citizenship, and Society in Canada* (T: UTP 1985); David Milne, *Tug of War: Ottawa and the Provinces under Trudeau and Mulroney* (T: JL 1986); Roy Romanow, John Whyte, and Howard Leeson, *Canada ... Notwithstanding: The Making of the Constitution, 1976–1982* (T: Carswell/Methuen 1984); and Peter Brimelow, *The Patriot Game: National Dreams and Political Realities* (T: Key Porter 1986), which is critical of all politicians and academics in Canada who play the 'national unity' game.

Several of Trudeau's colleagues and associates have written memoirs which present different perspectives on Trudeau. Jean Chrétien, *Straight from the Heart* (T: Key Porter 1985) is the best-selling political memoir in Canadian history. Chrétien's charm and a few interesting nuggets make the book worthwhile for students. Davey, *The Rainmaker*, is more important for Trudeau than for Pearson. Patrick Gossage, *Close to the Charisma: My Years between the Press and Pierre Elliott Trudeau* (T: M&S 1986) is a well-written and often amusing reminiscence. Donald J. Johnston, *Up the Hill* (M: Optimum 1986) offers a view from English Montreal of what the Liberals accomplished. Johnston was Trudeau's lawyer and knew him well personally. He is often frank about his client/leader. Kent, *A Public Purpose*, is harsh towards Trudeau, accusing his government of lacking innovation. Roy MacLaren, *Honourable Mentions: The Uncommon Diary of an MP* (T: Deneau 1986) is well-written and perceptive. Eugene Whelan, with Rick Archbold, *Whelan: The Man in the Green Stetson* (T: CI 1986) is laudatory towards Trudeau but very harsh towards his successor, John Turner. The best memoir is Don Jamieson, *The Political Memoirs of Don Jamieson*, vol. 1, *No Place for Fools*, and vol. 2, *A World unto Itself*, ed. C. McGrath (St John's: Breakwater Press 1989, 1991).

The brief Conservative government under Joe Clark attracted the attention of one of Canada's finest political journalists. Jeffrey Simpson's *Discipline of Power: The Conservative Interlude and the Liberal Restoration* (T: MAC 1980) argues convincingly that the Tories were not prepared for power. Ron Graham treats Clark harshly in *One-Eyed Kings: Promise and Illusion in Canadian Politics* (T: Collins 1986), although Clark has much company in his misery, for Graham seems to admire few politicians beyond Trudeau and Chrétien. John Turner is a target for Graham as well as for Greg Weston in his controversial and poorly researched *Reign of Error: The Inside Story of John Turner's Troubled Leadership* (T: MHR 1986). A fairer book on Turner is Jack Cahill, *John Turner* (T: M&S 1984). The

1984 campaign which Turner lost is the subject of Norman Snider, *The Changing of the Guard: How the Liberals Fell from Grace and the Tories Rose to Power* (T: Lester & Orpen Dennys 1985). The NDP leader throughout this period is the subject of an adoring biography by Judy Steed, *Ed Broadbent: The Pursuit of Power* (Markham: Viking 1988).

Brian Mulroney's road to power is traced in great detail by John Sawatsky in *Mulroney: The Politics of Ambition* (T: Macfarlane, Walter & Ross 1991), a troubling but fascinating book. It lacks footnotes and bibliography. It depends on interviews, many of them carried out by undergraduate journalism students who were just learning their trade. It does not identify interviewees yet takes their comments at face value. In the absence of evidence, anecdotes suffice. Because these are not the standards of evidence or research that must be expected from undergraduate history students, *Mulroney* is a book that instructors should suggest their students treat with great caution. Sawatsky ends with Mulroney winning the 1984 election. His early years in office are the subject of David Bercuson, J.L. Granatstein, and William Young, *Sacred Trust?: Brian Mulroney and the Conservative Party in Power* (T: Doubleday 1986), which draws upon numerous 'inside' sources to sketch a portrait of the new government's agenda. They predicted that Mulroney would be a one term prime minister. He was not, largely because of free trade and because Quebec rallied behind him in 1988 as in 1984.

There are many accounts of the election of 1988 but the best so far is Graham Fraser, *Playing for Keeps: Making of the Prime Minister, 1988* (T: M&S 1989). The 1988 election confirmed the profound changes that the Canadian party system had undergone in the previous twenty years as leadership came to be a decisive factor and traditional party attachment counted less. These changes were followed in a series of studies on elections in Canada: John Meisel, ed., *Working Papers on Canadian Politics* (M and K: MQUP 1975); Howard Penniman, ed., *Canada at the Polls: The General Election of 1974* (Washington: American Enterprise Institute 1975); Howard Penniman, ed., *Canada at the Polls, 1979 and 1980: A Study of the General Elections* (Washington: American Enterprise Institute 1981); Alan Frizell et al., *The Canadian General Election of 1984: Politicians, Parties, Press, and Polls* (O: CUP 1985). A valuable book on the subject of leadership is Patrick Martin, Allan Gregg, and George Perlin, *Contenders: The Tory Quest for Power* (Scarborough: PH 1983).

The best study of the Meech Lake Accord, which represented Mulroney's attempt to conciliate nationalist forces in Quebec, is Andrew Cohen, *A Deal Undone: The Making and Breaking of the Meech Lake Accord*

(V: Douglas and McIntyre 1990). A good collection that tries to present 'both sides' of the question even though its editor was strongly anti-Meech is Michael Behiels, ed., *The Meech Lake Primer: Conflicting Views of the 1987 Constitutional Accord* (O: UOP 1989). Obviously the constitutional turmoil of the 1980s and early 1990s has yet to find its historian and its resolution. Future analyses of patriation, Meech Lake, and the so-called Canada Round will necessarily depend upon the outcome, which is far from clear at this point.

Like Meech Lake, free trade required a 'leap of faith' to use the term many of its proponents and opponents preferred. It is, of course, too early to assess whether the faith was justified. The proponents can find arguments for their case in Richard Lipsey, *Trade-Offs on Free Trade: The Canada-US Free Trade Agreement* (T: Carswell 1988); the opponents can find support in Mel Hurtig's polemical *The Betrayal of Canada* (T: Stoddart 1991). Both works are period pieces, the one the product of a late twentieth-century neo-classical economist, the other the outburst of a frustrated nationalist. They are, perhaps, the late twentieth-century replicas of Goldwin Smith, on the one hand, and Colonel George Denison, on the other.

The future of Canadian national history partly depends on the future of Canada. Many of the works mentioned above will become like the musty volumes on the evolution of dominion status that seldom move from library shelves. Other books, however, may become classics in explaining how Canada dissolved or was renewed. For the student of national history, the road is not forked: it is overgrown with thickets and covered with dense fog. It may lift soon, and the reader's path will become clearer. But it must be admitted that Canadian national history of the past twenty-five years has been written mostly by political scientists and journalists. Here is a fundamental difference between the recent and more distant past. Canadian national history depends partly on the nation's future and partly on the future of the writing of national history of Canada by professional historians. Their voices are now conspicuously muted in the current national debate.

ROBERT BOTHWELL

Foreign Relations and Defence Policy

In an earlier edition of this book, this chapter began with the words, 'The scholarly literature on foreign and defence policy in Canada is still not large.' Decades of effort by political scientists, economists, and historians have undermined this observation. The study of Canadian external relations is now formidable in bulk, even if it is unevenly distributed and some of it, alas, so academic as to be almost incomprehensible.

This bibliography is necessarily selective as to quantity and quality, especially as we approach the present. It is always difficult deciding between the illustrative and pertinent, and the merely ephemeral; equally, it is difficult to select between the efforts of hundreds of political scientists and economists in the field, and those of the still relatively few historical specialists.

BIBLIOGRAPHIES

The basic bibliographies in this field have been published by the Canadian Institute of International Affairs. They are: Donald M. Page, comp., *A Bibliography of Works on Canadian Foreign Relations, 1945–1970* (T: CIIA 1973); Page, comp., *A Bibliography ... 1971–1975* (T:CIIA 1977), Jane R. Barrett and Jane Beaumont, comps., *A Bibliography ... 1976–1980* (T: CIIA 1982); and Barrett, Beaumont, and Lee-Anne Broadhead, comps., *A Bibliography ... 1981–1985* (T: CIIA 1987). These volumes supersede *A Reading Guide to Canada in World Affairs, 1945–71* (T: CIIA 1972), compiled by Laurence Motiuk and Madeleine Grant. On defence policy, Larry R. Stewart, ed., *Canadian Defence Policy: Selected Speeches and Documents, 1964–1981* (K: Centre for International Relations, Queen's University 1982) contains useful bibliographies. Motiuk has also published an annual

Strategic Studies Reading Guide (O: 1984-9). Current bibliographies appear in the *Canadian Historical Review*'s regular feature, 'Recent Publications Relating to Canada.'

Grace F. Heggie, ed., *Canadian Political Parties, 1867-1968: An Historical Bibliography* (T: MAC 1977) identifies valuable materials, as does Gregory Mahler, *Contemporary Canadian Politics: An Annotated Bibliography, 1970-1987* (NY: Greenwood Press 1988), which has sections on 'high' and 'low' foreign relations. André Donneur and Stephane Roussel have produced *Politique étrangère canadienne: bibliographie, 1985-1989* (M: Département de science politique, Université du Québec à Montréal 1990). Theses on Canadian subjects, including foreign relations, are indexed in Donald M. Tupling, *Canada: A Dissertation Bibliography* (Ann Arbor: University Microfilms International 1980), with a supplement published in 1983. On the military side, there is a mimeographed bibliography by Rand Flem-Ath on *Canadian Security and Intelligence* (Vi: University of Victoria 1985). Owen A. Cooke's *The Canadian Military Experience, 1867-1967: A Bibliography/Bibliographie de la vie militaire au Canada, 1867-1967* (O: Department of National Defence 1979) is a good guide to books, but omits articles.

OFFICIAL SOURCES

The basic documentary series on Canadian foreign policy is the Department of External Affairs's *Documents on Canadian External Relations* (DCER [O: QP]), published sporadically since 1967. In 1994 the series covered the years 1909-47, 1952, and 1953. The quality of the volumes varies markedly (they are better after 1939), and throughout there is an over-emphasis on the 'plumbing' of External Affairs – the exchange of missions and the like – as opposed to high policy. Nevertheless, the volumes are an invaluable aid to the study of the subject.

The Canadian document series should be supplemented by its American cousin, *The Foreign Relations of the United States* [FRUS Washington: US Government Printing Office]. This multi-volume enterprise published by the US State Department often contains information and analysis on Canadian reactions to international events, although naturally through an American filter. Because this series is largely complete for the 1950s and is well advanced into the 1960s, it often serves as a unique source for such topics as Canadian policy on Vietnam, or Canadian-American differences over the Castro regime in Cuba. British, French, and Italian official series exist, especially for the inter-war period, but are not as comprehensive, or, except for real specialists, as useful for Canadian diplomatic endeavours.

There is the Department of External Affairs's long-running series, *Statements and Speeches*, indexed in the CIIA's bibliographies. This collection of offprints of speeches and other official pronouncements may be found in most large libraries. The department also produces an annual report, useful for statistics. Of interest are the *Debates* of the House of Commons, and the proceedings of its various committees, especially the Standing Committee on External Affairs and Defence. The reports of various committees of the Canadian Senate are interesting: an example is the standing Senate Committee on Foreign Affairs, whose publications, such as *Canada-United States Relations*, 2 vols. (O: QP 1975), often contain both valuable information and insights into the conduct and limitations of Canadian foreign policy.

The most important official statements on external affairs have been collected in three paperback volumes: R.A. MacKay, *Canadian Foreign Policy, 1945–1954: Selected Speeches and Documents* (T: M&S 1970), Arthur Blanchette, *Canadian Foreign Policy, 1955–1965: Selected Speeches and Documents* (T: M&S 1977), and Blanchette, *Canadian Foreign Policy, 1966–1976: Selected Speeches and Documents* (T: Gage 1980). Larry Stewart's *Canadian Defence Policy*, already mentioned, does the same for defence policy. Most, but not all, meetings between Canadian prime ministers and American presidents are treated in a collection of official documents edited by Roger Frank Swanson, *Canadian American Summit Diplomacy, 1923–1973: Selected Speeches and Documents* (T: M&S 1975).

PERIODICALS

There is no single periodical devoted to Canadian international relations, although there are several on international affairs in general. The CIIA's *International Journal* followed the subject fairly closely until the late 1960s, when it switched to a thematic approach, which considerably reduced its usefulness to historians and other students of Canadian foreign policy. It was and is supplemented by the CIIA's *Behind the Headlines* series, which features single issues of importance to Canada. The *International History Review* publishes occasional articles in the area, as does the *Canadian Historical Review*. *Canadian Public Policy*, *Policy Options*, *Etudes Internationales* (from the Centre québécois des relations internationales), and *Bout de papier* (the organ of the Professional Association of Foreign Service Officers) also publish in the field. *International Canada*, published since 1989, carries on the external affairs chronology that formerly appeared in *International Perspectives*. Students should also consult *Diplomatic History*, an American publication, which occasionally carries material relevant to the history of Canadian foreign policy. The publications of the C.D. Howe Research Institute and the Fraser Institute are frequently useful. On defence, there is the *Canadian Defence Quarterly*; although its coverage is sometimes spotty, it has made a serious effort to engage professional historians for articles on aspects of Canadian military history.

From 1900 to 1937 the *Canadian Annual Review* was published out of Toronto by J. Castell Hopkins. Revived in 1960 by J.T. Saywell, it became the more narrowly focused *Canadian Annual Review of Politics and Public Affairs* (T: UTP 1961–) in 1971. It remains the most reliable, continuous chronology of Canadian external affairs – at least, at time of printing, for the period to 1987. For the period 1938 to 1959, however, researchers should check the chronologies in the official *Canada Year Book*, which also contains copious statistics on important subjects such as trade. Researchers should also consult, for the period 1937–84, the series *Canada in World Affairs*, now defunct, and for 1984 to date, *Canada among Nations*.

GENERAL HISTORIES

There are only two general histories of Canadian foreign policy. The first, by the bureaucrat and scholar G.P. de T. Glazebrook, *A History of Canadian External Relations*, 2 vols. (rev. ed., T: M&S 1966), is seriously dated and of interest primarily to historiographers. The second, *Canada and the Age of Conflict: A History of Canadian External Policies*, vol. 1, *1867–1921* and vol. 2, *1921–1948* (1977, T: UTP 1981, 1984), by C.P. Stacey, covers the subject up to 1948. Based on primary sources and extensive scholarship, Stacey's work is the first port of call for students of pre-1950 Canadian foreign policy. It takes a mildly positive attitude towards its material, favourable alike to Sir Robert Borden and Mackenzie King.

There are a number of useful general histories of Canadian defence policies. G.F.G. Stanley, *Canada's Soldiers: The Military History of an Unmilitary People* (3rd ed., T: MAC 1974) covers the field in a lively and sometimes opinionated way; Desmond Morton, *A Military History of Canada* (3rd ed., T: M&S 1992) is also useful as an introduction to Canadian military history. Donald J. Goodspeed, *The Armed Forces of Canada, 1867–1967: A Century of Achievement* (O: QP 1967) is a fine and elegant summary, complete with well-chosen illustrations and maps.

The volumes of the Canadian Centenary Series all contain sections on external relations. Peter B. Waite, *Canada, 1874–96: Arduous Destiny* (T: M&S 1971) and, especially, Robert Craig Brown and Ramsay Cook, *Canada, 1896–1921: A Nation Transformed* (T: M&S 1974) are handy guides to their periods, as is J.L. Granatstein, *Canada, 1957–67: The Years of Uncertainty and Innovation* (T: M&S 1986).

EARLY HISTORY: 1867–1914

As a colony of Great Britain, Canada had no constitutional role in foreign relations, which remained the preserve of the imperial government in London. Nevertheless, there were continual cross-border relations with the United States in a wide variety of areas, not to mention commercial relations with the United States and other countries. There the Canadian government was a quasi-independent actor, since it, and it alone, controlled the raising of government revenue, including tariffs. And finally, the Canadian government enjoyed a large measure of autonomy over immigration and citizenship, which certainly involved foreign relations on a significant scale.

Students of Canadian foreign relations in this period must therefore consult analyses of British colonial and foreign policies. There are a number of general surveys: Bernard Porter, *The Lion's Share: A Short History of British Imperialism, 1850–1970* (L: Longmans 1975) is a useful, but brief, introduction. James Morris, *Pax Britannica*, 3 vols. (L: Faber and Faber 1968) is better at evoking the imperial atmosphere than it is as a general history. Nicholas Mansergh, *The Commonwealth Experience*, vol. 1, *The Durham Report to the Anglo-Irish Treaty* and vol.2, *From British to Multi-Racial Commonwealth* (2nd ed., T: UTP 1983), sums up a lifetime of scholarship in the area. Judicious and well-informed, Mansergh is not adventurous. Max Beloff, *Imperial Sunset*, vol.1, *Britain's Liberal Empire, 1897–1921* (2nd ed., Basingstoke: MAC 1987) successfully sites Canada in the ideological and political struggles of early twentieth-century Britain. Beloff makes better use of Canadian publications than most other British imperial historians, although Canadian students may still find his approach curiously remote. More typical is Correlli Barnett, who takes a consistently censorious attitude to Canada's foreign and defence policy, sometimes based on exotic interpretations that Canadian scholars find unfounded; nevertheless, researchers in imperial history should consult his *The Collapse of British Power* (L: Eyre Methuen 1972) for a stimulating, if frequently uninformed, appraisal of Britain and its empire. A.P. Thornton, *The Imperial Idea and Its Enemies: A Study in British Power* (2nd ed., L: MAC

1985) remains the classic analysis and interpretation of the ideological underpinnings of the British Empire; it is paralleled for Canada by Carl Berger, *The Sense of Power: Studies in the Ideas of Canadian Imperialism, 1867-1914* (T: UTP 1970), a penetrating study of the ideas of certain Canadian imperialists at the turn of the century. Berger has also edited a useful collection of articles on the subject, *Imperialism and Nationalism, 1884-1914: A Conflict in Canadian Thought* (T: CC 1969).

There are also many more specific studies. Foremost among these is Kenneth Bourne, *Britain and the Balance of Power in North America, 1815-1908* (Berkeley: University of California Press 1967), which for some purposes updates and supersedes C.P. Stacey, *Canada and the British Army: A Study in the Practice of Responsible Government, 1846-1871* (1936, rev. ed., T: UTP 1963). J. Mackay Hitsman, *Safeguarding Canada, 1763-1871* (T: UTP 1968) contains a masterful summary of the growing strategic burden Canada posed to the empire in its final chapters.

Brian Jenkins, *Britain and the War for the Union*, 2 vols. (M and K: MQUP 1974, 1980) is essential for the foreign policy context of Canadian confederation in the 1860s. His *Fenians and Anglo-American Relations during Reconstruction* (Ithaca: Cornell UP 1969) is also worthwhile, although more peripheral. Richard A. Preston, *Canada and 'Imperial Defense': A Study in the Origins of the British Commonwealth's Defense Organization, 1867-1919* (T: UTP 1967) covers a vast subject; unfortunately its organization and tedious prose make finishing the book something of an ordeal. Desmond Morton, *Ministers and Generals: Politics and the Canadian Militia, 1868-1904* (T: UTP 1970) is a mine of valuable insights into the sometimes troubled relations between British professional officers and their colonial subordinates.

The institutional side of Anglo-Canadian relations is adequately covered in David M.L. Farr, *The Colonial Office and Canada, 1867-1887* (T: UTP 1955). The governors general of the period have been captured in three Champlain Society publications: C.W. de Kiewiet and Frank Underhill, eds., *The Dufferin-Carnarvon Correspondence, 1874-1878* (T: CS 1955), J.T. Saywell, ed., *The Canadian Journal of Lady Aberdeen, 1893-1898* (T: CS 1960), and Saywell and Paul Stevens, eds., *Lord Minto's Canadian Papers: A Selection of the Public and Private Papers of the Fourth Earl of Minto, 1898-1904*, 2 vols. (T: CS 1981, 1983). The Aberdeen and Minto introductions are especially valuable. There is also a useful biography of Lord Minto: Carman Miller, *The Canadian Career of the Fourth Earl of Minto: The Education of a Viceroy* (Wa: WLUP 1980). Lord Lansdowne, governor general in the 1880s, was memorialized by Lord Newton in a biography; but *Lord*

Lansdowne: A Biography (L: MAC 1929) is better on context than on Canada.

The emergence of common imperial institutions is imaginatively and authoritatively covered in John Kendle, *The Colonial and Imperial Conferences, 1887–1911: A Study in Imperial Organization* (L: Longmans 1967). Kendle's work is more than the dry title implies: the conferences were very wide-ranging, as is Kendle's approach. His subsequent book, *The Round Table Movement and Imperial Union* (T: UTP 1975), should be read in conjunction with Robert Bothwell, *Loring Christie and the Failure of Bureaucratic Imperialism* (NY: Garland 1988); together, these two books chronicle the rise and fall of the attempt to found a new British Empire on rational, bureaucratic principles.

Tariffs and trade were often a contentious issue between colonial Canada, protectionist and fascinated by the lure of the neighbouring American market, and the imperial government, free-trading in principle and, usually, in practice. There are two widely differing surveys of the Canadian tariff. John H. Young, *Canadian Commercial Policy* (O: QP 1957) originated as a special study for the Royal Commission on Canada's Economic Prospects (The Gordon Commission). The Commission prefaced Young's study with a disclaimer; the book survived its warning and is the best short history and explanation of the Canadian tariff. O.J. McDiarmid, *Commercial Policy in the Canadian Economy* (Cambridge: HUP 1946) is longer, much more detailed, and duller – although still very reliable. Douglas R. Annett, *British Preference in Canadian Commercial Policy* (T: RP 1948) relies on official sources and secondary studies, but it is still the best study of the pre-1932 Canadian love affair with British preference.

The question of trade relationships with the United States is sketched in J.L. Granatstein, 'Free Trade between Canada and the United States: The Issue That Will Not Go Away,' in Denis Stairs and Gilbert R. Winham, eds., *The Politics of Canada's Economic Relationship with the United States* (T: UTP 1985), a special study for the Royal Commission on the Economic Union. Some of the same material is covered in three, now dated, studies: L.B. Shippee, *Canadian-American Relations, 1849–1874* (2nd ed., NY: Russell and Russell 1970), C.C. Tansill, *Canadian-American Relations, 1875–1911*(2nd ed., Gloucester, Mass: P. Smith 1964), and L.E. Ellis, *Reciprocity 1911: A Study in Canadian-American Relations* (NY: Greenwood Press 1968).

The related question of the political and economic integration of North America was once a favourite theme of American historians, and it still attracts considerable attention. Albert Weinberg, *Manifest Destiny: A Study of Nationalist Expansion in American History* (2nd ed., Chicago: Quadrangle Books 1963) is the classic study. It has been supplemented by, among others, Frederick Merk, *Manifest Destiny and Mission in American History: A Reinterpretation* (NY: Knopf 1963). Most recently, Reginald C. Stuart has surveyed the field in his *United States Expansionism and British North America, 1775–1871* (Chapel Hill: University of North Carolina Press 1988). Stuart argues that the strong cultural connections between Canada and the United States during the nineteenth century were a foundation for continuing American political interest in Canada.

Cross-border population movements receive attention in Marcus Lee Hansen, *The Mingling of the Canadian and American Peoples* (New Haven: Yale UP 1940), a part of the Carnegie series *The Relations of Canada and the United States*. To be preferred are Alvin C. Gluek jr., *Minnesota and the Manifest Destiny of the Canadian Northwest: A Study in Canadian-American Relations* (T: UTP 1965), and R.C. Brown, *Canada's National Policy, 1883–1900: A Study in Canadian-American Relations* (Princeton: Princeton UP 1964). Worth noting is D.F. Warner, *The Idea of Continental Union: Agitation for the Annexation of Canada to the United States, 1849-1893* (Lexington: University of Kentucky Press 1960), which is intelligent although frequently unreliable. From the Canadian side, two historians, R.C. Brown and S.F. Wise, have sketched out Canadian attitudes towards the United States in their *Canada Views the United States: Nineteenth Century Political Attitudes* (T: MAC 1967). Especially interesting is a concluding commentary by the American historian David Potter, in which Canadian opinions are considered as a 'reflex of Canadian values.'

Biographies of individuals involved in national politics are also of considerable service. Canadian prime ministers also of necessity handled imperial relations, and the distinction between internal and external affairs was, in colonial days, inevitably blurred. Sir John A. Macdonald's efforts are covered in Donald Creighton's very favourable *John A. Macdonald*, vol. 2, *The Old Chieftain* (T: MAC 1955). The unsuccessful mission to Washington of Macdonald's rival, George Brown, receives ironic treatment in J.M.S. Careless, *Brown of the Globe*, vol. 2, *Statesman of Confederation, 1860–1880* (T: MAC 1963). Laurier's efforts are still best covered, from a biographical point of view, in O.D. Skelton, *Life and Letters of Sir Wilfrid Laurier*, 2 vols. (T: OUP 1921), although Skelton is far from impartial towards his subject. His Prairie lieutenant, Clifford Sifton, who was involved in the Alaska Boundary dispute as well as serving as minister responsible for immigration, is treated in D.J. Hall, *Clifford Sifton*, 2 vols. (V: UBCP 1981, 1985). Hall's work catches the spirit of English-Canadian nationalism of the period and is essential for any issue in which Sifton was involved. R.C. Brown's *Robert Laird Borden: A Biography*, 2 vols. (T: MAC 1975, 1980) is fair-minded and extremely judicious in treating Borden's contacts with the British and the Americans before and during World War I. He supersedes Henry Borden, ed., *Robert Laird Borden: His Memoirs*, 2 vols., (T: MAC 1938). Harold A. Wilson, *The Imperial Policy of Sir Robert Borden* (Gainesville: University of Florida Press 1966) takes a somewhat eccentric view of Borden and his policies; students should approach Wilson's analysis with caution.

The three main external relations issues to affect Canadian politics before 1914 were the Boer War, the Alaska Boundary dispute, and the Naval Question. All are are dealt with in the biographies of the political leaders of the day, especially Laurier, Bourassa, and Sifton. Henri Bourassa is the subject of a lengthy biography by the prolific political publicist Robert Rumilly (M: 1953); his views on the Boer War and the Naval Question are amply chronicled there, and in Bourassa's own writings. On the conduct of the war itself, see Desmond Morton's biography of General W.D. Otter, *The Canadian General, Sir William Otter* (T: Hakkert 1974). The Alaska Boundary dispute receives differing treatments in John A. Munro, ed., *The Alaska Boundary Dispute* (T: CC 1970), and in Norman Penlington, *The Alaska Boundary Dispute: A Critical Appraisal* (T: MHR 1972). The overall context of the dispute is presented in a rather old-fashioned approach by Bradford Perkins, *The Great Rapprochement: England and the United States, 1895–1914* (NY: Antheneum 1968). The Naval Question also had a strong Quebec component; nevertheless, the best point of departure is naval: Arthur Marder, *From the Dreadnought to Scapa Flow: The Royal Navy in the Fisher Era, 1904-1914*, vol. 1, *The Road to War, 1904–1914* (L: OUP 1961). Gilbert Norman Tucker, *The Naval Service of Canada: Its Official History*, 2 vols. (O: KP 1952) is obviously much more detailed on the subject, but manages nevertheless to be less informative. James A. Boutilier, ed., *The RCN in Retrospect, 1910–1968* (V: UBCP 1982) avoids the general subject but fills in some of the periphery. Michael L. Hadley and Roger Sarty, *Tin-Pots and Pirate Ships: Canadian Naval Forces and German Sea-Raiders, 1880–1918* (M and K: MQUP 1991) is the best Canadian authority on the subject. The politics of the issue, and especially Sir Robert Borden's fateful pact with Bourassa's *nationalistes*, are intelligently analysed in John English, *The Decline of Politics: The Conservatives and the Party System* (2nd ed., T: UTP 1993).

The RCN was not the only government creation in the period. The Department of Trade and Commerce, founded in 1892, is memorialized in a scattered and anecdotal history, O. Mary Hill, *Canada's Salesman to the World: The Department of Trade and Commerce, 1892–1939* (M and K: MQUP 1977). Throughout this period, Trade and Commerce was a marginal ministry, and Hill does nothing to alter this impression. The Department of External Affairs, founded in 1909, has received a much more professional history in John Hilliker, *Canada's Department of External Affairs*, vol. 1, *The Early Years, 1909–1946* (M and K: MQUP 1990). No future historian of Canadian diplomacy can ignore this careful and detailed discussion of the diplomatic bureaucracy. Its first undersecretary or deputy minister, Sir Joseph Pope, left behind a diary, assembled by his son, Maurice Pope, into *Public Servant: The Memoirs of Sir Joseph Pope* (T: OUP 1960), which has some utility. Hilliker's volume largely supersedes Gordon Skilling, *Canadian Representation Abroad: From Agency to Embassy* (T: RP 1945). Nancy Gelber, ed., *Canada in London: An Unofficial Glimpse of Canada's Sixteen High Commissioners, 1880-1980* (L: Canada House 1980) adds some information on the personalities holding the London post. The biographies of Sir A.T. Galt, *The Life and Times of Sir Alexander Tilloch Galt*, by O.D. Skelton (T: OUP 1920); Sir Charles Tupper, *The Life and Letters of the Rt. Hon. Sir Charles Tupper* by E.M.Saunders; 2 vols. (NY: Frederick A. Stokes 1916), and Lord Strathcona, *The Life and Times of Lord Strathcona* (L: E. Nash 1914), by W.T.R. Preston, high commissioners all, provide additional data on the nature of Canada's external representation.

WORLD WAR I AND AFTER: 1914–1939

World War I naturally called forth a plethora of military history, too numerous for a complete list here. The easiest summary is Goodspeed, *The Armed Forces of Canada*, mentioned earlier. The standard source on the Canadian army, beautifully mapped, is G.W.L. Nicholson, *The Canadian Expeditionary Force, 1914–1919: Official History of the Canadian Army in the First World War* (O: QP 1962). More opinionated, more interesting, and still reliable, is John Swettenham, *To Seize the Victory: The Canadian Corps in World War One* (T: RP 1965). It strongly defends Sir Arthur Currie, commanding general of the Canadian Corps, a favourite whipping boy in other popular accounts of the war. Swettenham also wrote the biography of General A.G.L. McNaughton, *McNaughton*, 3 vols. (T: RP 1968–9); the first volume, covering the period to 1939, is by far the best. Canada's war effort in the air is covered in S.F. Wise, *Canadian Airmen and the First World War* (T: UTP 1980), vol. 1 of the official history of the Royal Canadian Air Force. Since there was no Canadian air force as such, the story is sometimes difficult to follow, but the compilation of individual efforts is very well done, a testament to years of careful work by the historical staff at the Department of National Defence. Tucker, *The Naval Service of Canada* (cited above) is dull but competent on the war effort at sea; Hadley and Sarty, *Tin-Pots and Pirate Ships*, already mentioned, is to be preferred.

Conscription, which convulsed Canadian politics between 1914 and 1918, and after, is dealt with in the National Politics section of this essay, but the handiest survey is J.L. Granatstein and J.M. Hitsman, *Broken Promises: A History of Conscription in Canada* (T: OUP 1977). The military side – the actual numbers drafted into the army, and why conscription became an inevitability – may be found in R.C. Brown and Donald Loveridge, 'Unrequited Faith: Recruiting and the CEF, 1914–1918,' *Revue internationale d'histoire militaire* 1982.

Canada's massive war effort required considerable administrative and political coordination, which was sought through the establishment of an overseas ministry in London; its existence is chronicled in Desmond Morton, *A Peculiar Kind of Politics: Canada's Overseas Ministry in the First World War* (T: UTP 1982). Most histories and biographies dealing with the war are very critical of Canada's defence minister, Sir Sam Hughes; much less critical is Ronald G. Haycock, *Sam Hughes: The Public Career of a Controversial Canadian, 1885–1916* (Wa: WLUP 1986).

Brown's *Borden*, vol. 2, is the standard and very reliable account of Sir Robert Borden during the war and after. Brown also summarized the complex issues of wartime Anglo-Canadian relations in a skilful essay. 'Sir Robert Borden, the Great War, and Anglo-Canadian Relations.' This piece, originally written for a *festschrift* for Donald Creighton – J.S. Moir, ed., *Character and Circumstance: Essays in Honour of Donald Grant Creighton* (T: MAC 1970) – is conveniently included in J.L. Granatstein, ed., *Towards a New World: Readings in the History of Canadian Foreign Policy* (T: CCP 1992). Borden's minister of trade and commerce, Sir George Foster, who attended a number of imperial conferences as well as the Paris Peace Conference, kept a diary which was the basis for W. Stewart Wallace's *The Memoirs of the Rt. Hon. Sir George Foster* (T: MAC 1933). N.W. Rowell, a Liberal Unionist who joined the government in 1917, was often consulted on external affairs; his influence is described in Margaret Prang, 'N.W. Rowell and Canada's External Policy, 1917–1921,' CHA *AR* 1960. Borden's principal assistant for external affairs, Loring Christie, is the subject of Robert Bothwell's already mentioned biography, which also deals with

Canadian relations with both the empire and the United States between 1913 and 1922. Canadian-American relations are covered in R.D. Cuff and J.L. Granatstein, *Canadian-American Relations in Wartime: From the Great War to the Cold War* (T: Hakkert 1975); they concentrate on the economic relationships, which included a 'war mission' in Washington. War production, which in Canada depended heavily on British and American orders, is dealt with in Michael Bliss's biography of Canada's munitions czar, Sir Joseph Flavelle: *A Canadian Millionaire: The Life and Business Times of Sir Joseph Flavelle, Bart., 1858–1939* (2nd ed., T: UTP 1992). A subsequent article by Bliss, 'War Business as Usual: Canadian Munitions Production, 1914–1918,' in N.F. Dreisziger, *Mobilization for Total War: The Canadian, American, and British Experience, 1914–1918, 1939–1945* (Wa: WLUP 1981), is a useful summary of Canada's war production record.

The deployment of Canadian troops in Russia in 1918–9 as part of a wider effort to restore the eastern front and combat bolshevism is best described in John Swettenham, *Allied Intervention in Russia, 1918–1919: And the Part Played by Canada* (T: RP 1967). On the broader subject of Canadian-Soviet relations, there is an unimaginative although sometimes usable discussion in Aloysius Balawyder, *Canadian-Soviet Relations between the World Wars* (T: UTP 1972). The impoverished state of communist history is revealed in Tim Buck, *Canada and the Russian Revolution: The Impact of the World's First Socialist Revolution on Labour and Politics in Canada* (T: Progress Books 1967).

The most comprehensive account of the Anglo-Canadian relations during and after the war is Philip G. Wigley, *Canada and the Transition to Commonwealth: British-Canadian Relations, 1917–1926* (Cambridge: CUP 1977). Some of the same material – Anglo-Canadian-American relations – is handled in Roger Graham, *Arthur Meighen*, vol. 2, *And Fortune Fled* (T: CI 1963), and in Michael G. Fry, *Illusions of Security: North Atlantic Diplomacy, 1918–1922* (T: UTP 1972). G.P. de T. Glazebrook also wrote, many years ago, a very fair account of *Canada at the Paris Peace Conference* (T: OUP 1942), based on then secret materials; it is still reliable. Seth P. Tillman, *Anglo-American Relations at the Paris Peace Conference of 1919* (Princeton: Princeton UP 1961) was written before secret British materials became available; nevertheless, it places the issues at the conference in a wider context. Volume 2 of the *DCER* is a handy guide, as, for the very serious student, are the twenty-one volumes by the American David Hunter Miller, *My Diary at the Conference of Paris* (NY: np 1924). Also useful, particularly for the controversial termination of the Anglo-Japanese alliance in 1921, is Ian H. Nish, *Alliance in Decline: A Study in Anglo-Japanese Relations, 1908–1923* (L: Athlone Press 1972). Imperial relations are also the subject of a collection of essays, *The First British Commonwealth: Essays in Honour of Nicholas Mansergh*, edited by Norman Hillmer and Philip Wigley (L: Frank Cass 1980); the Canadian Expeditionary Force and the 1926 Imperial Conference are among the topics included.

Foreign policy in the postwar period was largely the policy of the Liberals and MacKenzie King. There are a number of older biographies, of which Bruce Hutchison, *The Incredible Canadian: A Candid Portrait of Mackenzie King, his work, his times, and his nation* (T: Longmans 1953) is still worth consulting; it was based on reporters' notes from the period. C.P. Stacey, who was both fascinated and repelled by King, wrote a great deal on this subject. His essay 'Laurier, King, and External Affairs,' published in John Moir, ed., *Character and Circumstance*, and republished in Granatstein, *Towards a New World*, is characteristically incisive; it should be read in conjunction with his later *Canada in the Age of Conflict*, vol. 2. Stacey's brief *Mackenzie King and the Atlantic Triangle* (T: MAC 1976) is a splendid summary of King's often complicated relations with Great Britain and the United States. Finally, his extended essay on King's private life and character, *A Very Double Life: The Private World of Mackenzie King* (T: MAC 1976), repays reading, even if most Canadian historians are highly sceptical of some of its conclusions.

The official life of King, *William Lyon Mackenzie King: A Political Biography*, vol. 1, *1874–1923* (T: UTP 1958), by R. MacGregor Dawson, suffers by comparison with Stacey. Well-researched but tortuous, Dawson's book is all but forgotten. The succeeding volumes in the official life, vol. 2, *The Lonely Heights, 1924–1932*, and vol. 3, *The Prism of Unity, 1932–1939*, by H. Blair Neatby (T: UTP 1963, 1976), are much better than Dawson's and serve as an interesting contrast to Stacey. King almost monopolized foreign relations at the political level; the only significant minister with influence on the subject, Ernest Lapointe, left few papers and little to tempt a biographer. C.G. Power, King's political organizer in Quebec, explained in his fascinating memoir, *A Party Politician: The Memoirs of Chubby Power*, edited by Norman Ward (T: MAC 1966), how the threat of conscription could be used as a brake on Canadian foreign policy in the interwar years. More significant than anyone else in King's cabinet was O.D. Skelton, undersecretary from 1924 to 1941. Skelton wrote many biographies, and has received none, as yet, in return. The best essay on Skelton's ideology is Norman Hillmer, 'The Anglo-Canadian Neurosis: The Case of O.D. Skelton,' in Peter Lyon, ed., *Britain and Canada: Survey of a Changing Relationship* (L: Frank Cass 1976). Skelton's role in External Affairs is treated at length in Hilliker, *Canada's Department of External Affairs*, especially chapters 4 and 5. Doug Owram, *The Government Generation: Canadian Intellectuals and the State, 1900–1945* (T: UTP 1986) also deals with the context of the formation of a professional foreign service.

Two surveys of the field should be mentioned for the interwar period. John Herd Thompson with Allen Seager, *1922–1939; Canada Decades of Discord* (T: M&S 1985), a volume in the Canadian Centenary series, is stronger on domestic events than on foreign policy. Max Beloff, *Imperial Sunset*, vol. 2, *Dream of Commonwealth, 1921–1942* (L: Methuen 1969) continues his history of the British empire. Less reliable on facts, although analytically perceptive, is R.F. Holland, *Britain and the Commonwealth Alliance*, 1918–1939 (L: MAC 1981). Canadian readers may have difficulty recognizing certain Canadian events and attitudes.

Anglo-Canadian relations in the later 1920s are analysed in Norman Hillmer, 'The Foreign Office, the Dominions, and the Diplomatic Unity of the Empire, 1925–1929,' in David Dilks, ed., *Retreat from Power: Studies in Britain's Foreign Policy of the Twentieth Century*, vol. 1, *1906–1939* (L: MAC 1981). The question of diplomatic representation abroad, first broached in the 1910s (see Robert Bothwell, 'Canadian Representation at Washington: A Study in Colonial Responsibility,' *CHR* 1972), was consummated in 1926 with the appointment of Vincent Massey as minister in Washington. On Massey's extensive diplomatic career, which lasted until 1946, readers should consult Massey himself, assisted by a ghost writer, *What's Past is Prologue: Memoirs* (T: MAC 1963), and the two volumes of Claude Bissell's study, *The Young Vincent Massey* and *The Imperial Canadian: Vincent Massey in Office* (T: UTP 1981, 1986). The latter two, although gracefully written, are far stronger on Massey's career as a patron of the arts and the Liberal party than they are on his diplomatic activities. Massey's subordinate in Washington and at a later posting in London, Lester B. Pearson, wrote of his experiences as a Canadian diplomat in his memoir *Mike: The Memoirs of the Right Honourable Lester B. Pearson*, vol. 1 (T: UTP 1972). The book is charmingly written and displays its author's talents to good effect, but it has its omissions, especially on appeasement. To be preferred is John English, *Shadow of Heaven: The Life of Lester Pearson*, vol. 1, *1897–1948* (T: Lester & Orpen Dennys 1989), a thorough and objective analysis of Pearson's career as a professional diplomat. A second volume on Pearson's later career as a politician was produced in 1992: *The Worldly Years: The Life of Lester Pearson*, vol. 2, *1949–1972* (Toronto: Knopf 1992). Charles Ritchie, another, more junior, foreign service officer, compressed his diaries and memoirs into an elegant and evocative book, *The Siren Years: A Canadian Diplomat Abroad, 1937–1945* (T: MAC 1974). Hugh Keenleyside, *Memoirs of Hugh L. Keenleyside*, vol. 1, *Hammer the Golden Day* (T: M&S 1981) is less well written, less perceptive, but more thorough. Escott Reid, *Radical Mandarin: The Memoirs of Escott Reid* (T: UTP 1989), viewed in the 1930s both from the standpoint of an interested private commentator, seeing affairs from the left, and, later, as a diplomat. Paul Martin, a young MP in the 1930s, has written on King and foreign policy as viewed from the backbenches in his memoir, *A Very Public Life*, vol. 1, *Far from Home* (O: Deneau 1983). Norman Robertson, one of Canada's ablest diplomats, has been memorialized in a comprehensive biography by J.L. Granatstein, *A Man of Influence: Norman A. Robertson and Canadian Statescraft, 1929–68* (O: Deneau 1981).

Mackenzie King was never fond of generals, and in peacetime defence questions were usually confided to second-rate ministers. James Eayrs, *In Defence of Canada*, vol. 1, *From the Great War to the Great Depression* (T: UTP 1964) touches some of the high points, including the Canadian general staff's war plans exercises – or fantasies. Stephen J. Harris, *Canadian Brass: The Making of a Professional Army, 1860–1939* (T: UTP 1988), deals with what might be called the inner life of the army, although he does not answer all the questions that might arise about the formation of Canada's officer corps. Students of defence history should also consult a collection of readings, Marc Milner, ed., *Canadian Military History: Selected Readings* (T: CCP 1993).

The long border with the United States had already called forth an international investigatory and regulatory body, the International Joint Commission. It and other Canadian-American governmental creatures are described in William R. Willoughby, *The Joint Organizations of Canada and the United States* (T: UTP 1979). Relations between Canadian prime ministers and American presidents are chronicled in a journalistic survey, Lawrence Martin, *The Presidents and the Prime Ministers: Washington and Ottawa Face to Face: The Myth of Bilateral Bliss, 1867–1982* (T: Doubleday 1982).

Economic relations were thoroughly covered in W.K. Hancock, *Survey of British Commonwealth Affairs*, vol. 2, *Problems of Economic Policy, 1918–1939* parts 1 and 2 (L: OUP 1964). These books are still useful for context, and for intellectual and political atmosphere. On economic policy, strictly defined, they have been superseded by more recent books: Ian M. Drummond, *British Economic Policy and the Empire, 1919–1939* (L: Allen and Unwin 1972), which contains a valuable documentary appendix, and his more detailed *Imperial Economic Policy, 1917–1939: Studies in Expansion and Protection* (L: Allen and Unwin 1974). Both deal at length with the Ottawa conference of 1932, and the system of imperial preference. Drummond and Norman Hillmer have also written conclusively about the Anglo-American-Canadian trade negotiations of 1936-8 in their *Negotiating Freer Trade: The United Kingdom, the United States, Canada, and the Trade Agreements of 1938* (Wa: WLUP 1989). Trade of a different kind is discussed in Allan S. Everest, *Rum across the Border: The Prohibition Era in Northern New York* (Syracuse UP 1978), a popular history of a once flourishing Canadian export industry. Canadian-American economic relations are described and analysed in Herbert Marshall, Frank A. Southard, and Kenneth W. Taylor, *Canadian-American Industry: A Study in International Investment* (1936, T: M&S 1976). A later account worth consulting is Peter Kresl, 'Before the Deluge: Canadians on Foreign Ownership, 1920–1955,' *American Review of Canadian Studies* 1976. H.F. Angus, *Canada and Her Great Neighbour: Sociological Surveys of Opinion's and Attitudes in Canada Concerning the United States* (T: RP 1938) is essential for any student of public opinion in the 1930s. On that point, see also the article by Robert Bothwell and John English, 'The View from Inside Out: Canadian diplomats and their Public,' *International Journal* 1983–4. The deputy minister of trade and commerce, Leolyn Dana Wilgress, left a record in *Memoirs* (T: RP 1967), but it has little value except as anecdotage.

An interesting and somewhat controversial redefinition of American policy towards Canada may be found in Gordon Stewart, 'A Special Contiguous Country Economic Regime,' *Diplomatic History* 1982, republished in Norman Hillmer, ed., *Partners Nevertheless: Canadian-American Relations in the Twentieth Century* (T: CCP 1989). A different approach is taken in Robert Bothwell and John Kirton, 'A Sweet Little Country: American Attitudes towards Canada, 1925–1963,' also in *Partners Nevertheless*, originally published in *QQ* 1983. A rather more limited version is Peter Kasurak, 'American Foreign Policy Officials and Canada, 1927–1941: A Look through Bureaucratic Glasses,' *International Journal* 1977.

In 1919 the Canadian government rather reluctantly joined the League of Nations, an organization that purported to safeguard collective security. Canada's adventures in the League are described in Richard Veatch, *Canada and the League of Nations* (T: UTP 1975), and in Donald Page's PhD thesis, University of Toronto 1972, 'Canadians and the League of Nations before the Manchurian Crisis,' a discussion of Canadian public opinion and pressure groups during the 1920s. Donald C. Story's PhD thesis, 'Canada's Covenant: Canada, the League of Nations, and Collective Security,' University of Toronto 1976, is very informative. Canada's permanent representative at the League, Walter Riddell, left behind a memoir, *World Security by Conference* (T: RP 1947); it is dated and in some respects inaccurate. Also flawed is Mack Eastman, *Canada at Geneva: An Historical Survey and Its Lessons* (T: RP 1946), which is nevertheless informed by its author's strong commitment to its subject. Better is Gwendolen Carter, *The British Commonwealth and International Security: The Role of the Dominions, 1919–1939* (T: RP 1947), still worth consulting because of its thoroughness. On the Ethiopian crisis, Robert Bothwell and John English have written 'Dirty Work at the Crossroads,' CHA *AR* for 1972, republished in Bothwell and Norman Hillmer, eds., *The In-Between Time: Canadian External Policy in the 1930s* (T: CC 1975). This book is a collection of contemporary comments, some from unpublished documents, and later commentaries by scholars. Charles Woodsworth, son of J.S., wrote a thoughtful analysis of *Canada and the Orient: A Study in International Relations* (T: MAC 1941), just in time for World War II.

The Spanish civil war was a highly divisive issue in Canadian politics. Victor Hoar, *The Mackenzie-Papineau Battalion: Canadian Participation in the Spanish Civil War* (T: CC 1969) deals with those Canadians who went to fight in Spain.

Appeasement is the subject of a number of studies. Ritchie Ovendale, *'Appeasement' and the English-speaking World: Britain the United States, the Dominions, and the Policy of 'Appeasement' 1937–1939* (Cardiff: University of Wales Press 1975) is well founded, although a trifle dated where Canada is concerned. J.L. Granatstein and Robert Bothwell have also published an analysis of Mackenzie King's foreign policy in the late 1930s, 'A Self-Evident National Duty,' in the *Journal of Imperial and Commonwealth History* 1975, republished in Granatstein, ed., *Canadian Foreign Policy*. On the 1937 imperial conference, see Norman Hillmer, 'The Pursuit of Peace: Mackenzie King and the 1937 Imperial Conference,' in John English and John O. Stubbs, eds., *Mackenzie King: Widening the Debate* (T: MAC 1977). An older, harsher, but still interesting view of the diplomacy of the 1930s is contained in James Eayrs, *In Defence of Canada*, vol. 2, *Appeasement and Rearmament* (T: UTP 1965). Of passing interest, because of its inaccuracy, is the brief description of Canadian foreign policy in Donald Cameron Watt, *How War Came: The Immediate Origins of the Second World War, 1938–1939* (NY: Pantheon 1989). Finally, no list of imperial histories would be complete without again citing the bizarre analysis of Correlli Barnett, *The Collapse of British Power* in which he makes the case that the dominions, and especially Canada (and within Canada, Mackenzie King), subverted imperial strength.

The 1930s also saw a multiplication of Canadian commentaries on foreign affairs. Two of them are especially noteworthy: R.A. MacKay and E.B. Rogers, *Canada Looks Abroad* (T: OUP 1938), which has valuable commentary on public opinion, and F.H. Soward et al., *Canada in World Affairs: The Pre-War Years* (T: OUP 1941). The latter is the first volume in a series published for many years by the Canadian Institute of International Affairs, and covering, ultimately, the period down to 1984. Originally intended to provide readers with up-to-date commentaries on the very recent past in two- or three-year bites, the series gradually fell behind and was finally wound up with a belated summary volume on Pierre Trudeau's foreign policy. All the volumes are worth checking, although inevitably some (the war years, 1946–9, 1955–65, 1971–3) are better than others.

WAR AND COLD WAR: 1939–1990

The basic documents for the war and postwar period continue to be the *Documents on Canadian External Relations*, volumes 7 to 13, covering 1939 to 1947, and 18 and 19, covering 1952 and 1953. A number of general histories cover the period. Robert Bothwell, Ian Drummond, and John English, *Canada 1900–1945* (T: UTP 1987) and *Canada since 1945: Power, Politics, and Provincialism* (2nd ed., T: UTP 1989) deal with political, economic, and social trends, including foreign economic and political relations. Donald Creighton, *The Forked Road: Canada, 1939–1957* (T: M&S 1976), in the Canadian Centenary Series, is interesting for its anti-Liberal bias, but should be carefully checked against other sources. Creighton's own sources are almost entirely secondary.

For the view from the top, the Mackenzie King diaries have been compressed into *The Mackenzie King Record*, edited by J.W. Pickersgill and D.F. Forster, 4 vols. (T: UTP 1960, 1968, 1970). The last three volumes in particular, covering 1944 to 1948, are comprehensive and extremely useful. The unexpurgated main diary (not including the so-called dream diary) may be viewed on microfiche; see *The Mackenzie King Diaries, 1932–1949* (T: UTP 1980).

During the war, Canada was a minor diplomatic player, its efforts confined to housekeeping on the political front. Militarily and economically, however, Canada had large interests at play. Financially, Canada was able to render considerable assistance to the British; the events are well described in the official British history, R.S. Sayers, *Financial Policy, 1939–1945* (L: HM Stationery Office 1956). Canada's war production minister (and his dealings with the Americans and the British clients of Canadian factories) is treated in Robert Bothwell and William Kilbourn,

C.D. Howe: A Biography (T: M&S 1979). A summary may also be found in Robert Bothwell, 'Who's Paying for Anything These Days? War Production in Canada, 1939–1945,' in Dreisziger, ed., *Mobilization for Total War* (cited above). A contemporary discussion, still usable, is A.F.W. Plumptre, 'Organizing the Canadian Economy for War,' in J.F. Parkinson, ed., *Canadian War Economics* (T: UTP 1941). R. Warren James, *Wartime Economic Cooperation* (T: RP 1949) is best on the systems and processes of wartime economic and production priorities between Canada and the United States.

Canadian relations with Japan during the war are discussed in Patricia Roy, J.L. Granatstein, Masako Iino, and Hiroko Takamura, *Mutual Hostages: Canadians and Japanese during the Second World War* (T: UTP 1990), a fruitful example of international collaboration. Its close competitor is John A. Schultz, ed., *Canada and Japan in the Twentieth Century* (T: OUP 1991).

As the end of the war approached, the Canadian government was concerned about shoring up its traditional trading relationship with Great Britain, while providing for a future that would be dominated by American economic power. The most accessible description of Anglo-Canadian engagements in this period is L.S. Pressnell, *External Economic Policy since the War*, vol. 1, *The Postwar Financial Settlement* (L: HM Stationery Office 1986); Pressnell includes Lend-Lease, Bretton Woods, and the American and Canadian loans of 1945–6. A more strictly Canadian perspective is presented in Robert Bothwell and John English, 'Canadian Trade Policy in the Age of American Dominance and British Decline, 1943–47,' *Canadian Review of American Studies* 1977. Wheat was also a factor in Anglo-Canadian relations through most of the twentieth century; on the Anglo-Canadian wheat trade, and in particular on the Anglo-Canadian wheat agreement of 1946, see Charles F. Wilson's massive (and massively dull) *A Century of Canadian Grain: Government Policy to 1951* (S: WPPB 1978). The recollections of a participant are to be found in Douglas LePan, *Bright Glass of Memory: A Set of Four Memoirs* (T: MHR 1979), 'Introduction to Economics.'

The single best volume on the higher politics and diplomacy of Canada's war effort is still C.P. Stacey's superb *Arms, Men, and Governments: The War Policies of Canada, 1939–1945* (O: QP 1970). Covering everything from manpower problems to atomic energy, Stacey is an indispensable source for any serious student of Canada in World War II. J.L. Granatstein, *Canada's War: The Politics of the Mackenzie King Government, 1939–1945* (2nd ed., T: UTP 1990) is the best description of politics in wartime, but it is also very useful for such subjects as Canadian-American relations. The military side of the war is dealt with in Stacey's official histories of the Canadian army, *Six Years of War: The Army in Canada, Britain, and the Pacific*, and *The Victory Campaign: The Operations in North-West Europe, 1944–1945* (O :QP 1955, 1960), and in G.W.L. Nicholson's *The Canadians in Italy, 1943–1945* (O: QP 1956). Much of the generalship of the Canadian army is explained in J.L. Granatstein's *The Generals* (T: Stoddart 1993). The second volume of the RCAF official history, W.A.B. Douglas, *The Creation of a National Air Force* (T: UTP 1986), treats the air force between the wars, the air force in Canada during the war, and the air force's role in the Battle of the Atlantic. The third volume, Brereton Greenhous et al., *The Crucible of War, 1939–45*, will be published early in 1994. Murray Peden, *A Thousand Shall Fall* (Stittsville: Canada's Wings 1979) is a vivid and moving memoir of a bomber pilot. The navy, science, and anti-submarine warfare are covered in two books, Marc Milner, *North Atlantic Run: The Royal Canadian Navy and the Battle for the Convoys* (T: UTP 1985), and David Zimmerman, *The Great Naval Battle of Ottawa* (T: UTP 1989). Boutilier, *The RCN in Retrospect* has a number of essays on the RCN during the war. There are passing references to the Canadian military in Chester Wilmot, *The Struggle for Europe* (L: Collins 1952), and John Keegan, *Six Armies in Normandy: From D-Day to the Liberation of Paris, June 6th–August 25th, 1944* (NY: Viking 1982). Nigel Hamilton, *Monty*, vol. 2, *Master of the Battlefield, 1942–1944*, and vol. 3, *The Field Marshal, 1944–76* (L: Hamilton 1983, 1986), affords interesting sidelights on Canadian generalship during the war, although from a rather one-sided point of view; it should be read in conjunction with Granatstein's *The Generals*. Canadian-American military questions are considered in Stanley W. Dziuban, *Military Relations between the United States and Canada, 1939–1945* (Washington: Department of the Army 1959). Dziuban uses only US records for his work; on larger questions, therefore, Stacey is to be preferred.

Diplomatic relations with the United States are covered in Nancy Harvison Hooker, ed., *The Moffat Papers: Selections from the Diplomatic Journals of Jay Pierrepont Moffat, 1919–1943* (Cambridge: HUP 1956). The St Pierre and Miquelon episode is the subject of a number of books, including Douglas G. Anglin, *The St Pierre and Miquelon Affaire of 1941: A Study in Diplomacy in the North Atlantic Quadrangle* (T: UTP 1966), and William A. Christian, *Divided Island: Faction and Unity on Saint Pierre* (Cambridge: HUP 1969).

Atomic energy is the focus of two books by Robert Bothwell, *Eldorado:*

Canada's National Uranium Company (T: UTP 1984) and *Nucleus: The History of Atomic Energy of Canada Limited* (T: UTP 1988). They deal with among other things, Canada's supply of uranium to its allies' atomic weapons projects, and Canada's role as a designer and producer of nuclear reactors. The two should be read in conjunction with Margaret Gowing's excellent *Britain and Atomic Energy, 1939–1945* (L: MAC 1964) and her subsequent *Independence and Deterrence: Britain and Atomic Energy, 1945–1952*, 2 vols. (L: MAC 1974). The comparable American books, Richard G. Hewlett and Oscar E. Anderson, *A History of the US Atomic Energy Commission*, vol. 1, *The New World, 1939–1946* (University Park: Pennsylvania State UP 1962), and vol. 2, *Atomic Shield, 1947–1952*, (Springfield, Va.: National Technical Information Service 1972), and Hewlett and Jack M. Holl, *Atoms for Peace and War, 1953–1961: Eisenhower and the Atomic Energy Commission* (Berkeley: University of California Press 1989), are not in the same league, although occasional snippets may be gleaned. Spencer R. Weart, *Scientists in Power* (Cambridge: HUP 1979), covering the adventures of French refugee scientists in the Anglo-Canadian atomic project, is, however, very useful.

A particular episode in Canadian foreign affairs, relations with Newfoundland, is captured in David MacKenzie, *Inside the Atlantic Triangle: Canada and the Entrance of Newfoundland into Confederation, 1939–1949* (T: UTP 1986), and Peter Neary, *Newfoundland in the North Atlantic World, 1929–1949* (M and K: MQUP 1988). There is also a three-volume collection of relevant documents, vol. 1, *Defence, Civil Aviation, and Economic Affairs, 1935–1949* (O: Department of External Affairs 1974) and vol. 2, in two parts, *Confederation, 1940–1949* (O: Department of External Affairs 1984).

The memoirs and biographies of Pearson, Keenleyside, Robertson, Ritchie, and Reid, already mentioned, continue through the war. Also of interest are the perceptive memoirs of General Maurice Pope, *Soldiers and Politicians: The Memoirs of Lt.-Gen. Maurice A. Pope* (T: UTP 1962). Pope worked in Mackenzie King's office, and later served in Washington and Berlin. H.S. Ferns, *Reading from Left to Right: One Man's Political History* (T: UTP 1983) is the memoir of a Canadian Communist in the 1930s, who moved into the Department of External Affairs during the war – and out of the party. Another Communist from the 1930s, Herbert Norman, also joined External Affairs; unlike Ferns, his Communist past later became the subject of bitter controversy which ended in tragedy. Norman is featured in two contrasting biographies, one unsympathetic by James Barros, *No Sense of Evil: Espionage, The Case of Herbert Norman* (T: Deneau

1986), one markedly more supportive by Roger W. Bowen, *Innocence Is Not Enough: The Life and Death of Herbert Norman* (V: Douglas & McIntyre 1988). Both books treat the question of loyalty and security, and give some attention to the implications of Communist allegiance. From a different angle, so does Robert Bothwell and J.L. Granatstein, eds., *The Gouzenko Transcripts: The Evidence Presented to the Kellock–Taschereau Royal Commission of 1946* (O: Deneau 1982), an edition of the Royal Commission inquiry into the Gouzenko spy scandal.

The Cold War and its origins have not provoked the same magnitude of historical controversy in Canada as in the United States. The orthodox version of the Cold War, Canadian style, is contained in the relevant volumes of *Canada in World Affairs*, appearing soon after the events described. To a much greater extent than in the United States, the actual protagonists, literate intellectuals all, set the terms of the debate and for a very long time were its only serious participants. The Mackenzie King *Diary*; Pearson, *Mike*, vols. 1 and 2; Reid, *Radical Mandarin*; Keenleyside, *Memoirs*, vol. 2, *On the Bridge of Time* (T: M&S 1982); and, especially, Escott Reid's very interesting (although oddly organized) *Time of Fear and Hope: The Making of the North Atlantic Treaty, 1947–1949* (T: M&S 1977), a history of the origins of NATO, are testimony to that fact. Reid's book is invaluable on the subject, but its assertions are often a matter of opinion – strong opinion; it should be read in conjunction with Sir Nicholas Henderson's contemporary account (published long after), *The Birth of NATO* (L: Weidenfeld & Nicolson 1982). A very useful essay is Mary Halloran, 'Canada and the Origins of the Post-War Commitment,' in Margaret O. MacMillan and David S. Sorenson, eds., *Canada and NATO: Uneasy Past, Uncertain Future* (Wa: WLUP 1990).

A Reporter Reports (T: RP 1954), by Canadian journalist I. Norman Smith, records impressions of Mackenzie King unwillingly confronting the Russians in Paris in 1946. A contrasting contemporary view is Leslie Roberts, *Home from the Cold Wars* (T: S.J. Saunders 1948). Merrily Weisbord, *The Strangest Dream: Canadian Communists, the Spy Trials, and the Cold War* (T: Lester & Orpen Dennys 1983) is a retrospective 'view from the inside' of the Communist party, based on interviews with survivors of the 1930s and 1940s.

Public opinion generally supported the government in its approach to foreign policy during the Cold War. Don Munton has written a somewhat frustrating but nevertheless informative article on the interrelationship of press and public: 'Public opinion and the Media in Canada from the Cold War to Detente to New Cold War,' *International Journal* 1983–4.

The most comprehensive account of Canada's diplomacy in the 1940s and 1950s is John W. Holmes, *The Shaping of Peace: Canada and the Search for World Order, 1943–1957*, 2 vols. (T: UTP 1979, 1982). Holmes, who participated as a Canadian diplomat in the events described, interpreted Canadian policy for a later generation, drawing on archival sources. His study is charmingly written and often persuasive, but it suffers from inadequate footnotes and at times an unexpected opacity in its analysis. Holmes's most valuable contribution is to site the Cold War in the context of a broader Canadian foreign policy, one dealing with the United Nations, the Commonwealth, and the United States. Denis Smith, *Diplomacy of Fear: Canada and the Cold War, 1941–1948* (T: UTP 1988) is something of a disappointment. It is strongest as a presentation, through extensive quotation, of the views of Canadian politicians and diplomats; it is weakest in its representation of the United States, to which the Canadians were reacting. Lawrence Aronsen and Martin Kitchen, *The Origins of the Cold War in Comparative Perspective: American, British, and Canadian Relations with the Soviet Union, 1941–1948* (NY: St Martins's 1988) has merit but is rather thin, on the Canadian side at least. D.F. Harrington, 'As Others Saw Us: A Canadian View of US Policy towards the Soviet Union, 1947,' *Diplomatic History* 1983, is of some interest. Reg Whitaker, 'Fighting the Cold War on the Home Front, America, Britain, Australia, and Canada,' *The Socialist Register* 1984, treats the domestic side of the Cold War in comparative perspective, and from a left-wing point of view. A close-up view of the Cold War on the diplomatic front may be found in Escott Reid's diary of his early adventures at the United Nations, *On Duty: A Canadian at the Making of the United Nations, 1945–1946* (T: M&S 1983).

James Eayrs published two volumes on the postwar era in his *In Defence of Canada* series; vol. 3, *Peacemaking and Deterrence* (T: UTP 1972), does little to clarify the crucial questions of budgeting, although it has some perceptive character sketches. His fourth volume, *Growing Up Allied* (T: UTP 1980), is much better; it makes good use of the extremely useful unpublished memoirs of Canada's defence minister, Brooke Claxton.

Many pre-war attitudes changed with the experience of the war, and the achievement of prosperity after 1945. Immigration (treated elsewhere in this *Guide*) was one. Refugees, the involuntary movement of populations displaced by catastrophes of various kinds, were always a lively issue. Of use is Gerald E. Dirks, *Canada's Refugee Policy: Indifference or Opportunism?* (M and K: MQUP 1977), updated by Dirks in *Behind the Headlines* 1988.

Canadians greeted the end of the war with economic apprehension, captured in J. Douglas Gibson, ed., *Canada's Economy in a Changing World*

(T: MAC 1948). Economic diplomacy in the postwar period is considered in a number of specialized studies. A.F.W. Plumptre, *Three Decades of Decision: Canada and the World Monetary System, 1944–75* (T: M&S 1977) is rather thin on day-to-day history, but there is nothing else. R.D. Cuff and J.L. Granatstein, *American Dollars, Canadian Prosperity: Canadian-American Economic Relations, 1945–1950* (T: Samuel Stevens 1978) is extremely useful on the abortive Canadian-American negotiations for a customs union in 1947–8 and on Canada's role in the Marshall Plan. It should be read in conjunction with Robert Bothwell and John English, 'Canadian Trade Policy in the Age of American Dominance and British Decline, 1943–47,' *Canadian Review of American Studies* 1984, republished in Granatstein, ed., *Canadian Foreign Policy*. B.W. Muirhead, *The Development of Postwar Canadian Trade Policy: The Failure of the Anglo-European Option* (M and K: MQUP 1992) is an interesting discussion of the development of the details of trade policy, and is an effective refutation of Donald Creighton's fantasies about the postwar Liberals; nevertheless, Muirhead does not spend as much time as he might on the overall shaping of policy.

The Korean War stimulated an official military history, H.F. Wood, *Strange Battleground: The Operations in Korea and Their Effects on the Defence Policy of Canada* (O: QP 1966); it is cautious and respectful of Canada's allies in the conflict. Denis Stairs, *The Diplomacy of Constraint, the Korean War, and the United States* (T: UTP 1974) is a superb treatment of Canadian attitudes and policies during the war, but it is perhaps less well informed about American policy – in this case rather like the Canadian government of the day. The extensive release of American papers since the publication of Stairs in any case makes cross-referencing mandatory. For a more recent view, taking into account American sources, see Robert Prince, 'The Limits of Constraint: Canadian-American Relations and the Korean War, 1950–51,' in *JCS* 1993. Of collateral interest, especially on the question of the Commonwealth and Korea, see the excellent New Zealand official history, *New Zealand and the Korean War*, vol. 1, *Politics and Diplomacy* (Auckland: OUP 1992). The subject is summarized, along with the rest of postwar Canadian-American relations, in Robert Bothwell, *Canada and the United States: The Politics of Partnership* (T: UTP 1992).

Canadian-American relations in the 1950s are the subject of a number of specialized studies. Air defence is the subject of Joseph T. Jockel, *No Boundaries Upstairs: Canada, the United States, and the Origins of North American Air Defence, 1945–1958* (V: UBCP 1987), which makes use of Canadian and American records and is probably the definitive work on air defence. Robert W. Reford, *Canada and Three Crises* (T: CIIA 1968) deals with the Quemoy and Matsu crisis of 1955, as well as the Suez and Cuba crises. The Canadian ambassador in Washington, the very discreet Arnold Heeney, wrote a memoir on his deathbed, *The Things That Are Caesar's: Memoirs of a Canadian Public Servant* (T: UTP 1972); it is inaccurate in spots but nevertheless contains much information – although not as much as it might. An intelligent American perspective, closely reflecting the US embassy in Ottawa, is Joseph Barber, *Good Fences Make Good Neighbors: Why the United States Provokes Canadians* (T: M&S 1958). The controversy over the TransCanada Pipeline, which focused anti-American sentiment in 1956, is discussed in William Kilbourn, *Pipeline: TransCanada and the Great Debate, A History of Business and Politics* (T: CI 1970), and in Bothwell and Kilbourn, *C.D. Howe*.

Not only business was involved in Canadian-American controversy. Canadian labour was closely connected to American trade unionism. On that subject there is a general study by Irving Martin Abella, *Nationalism, Communism, and Canadian Labour: The CIO, the Communist Party, and the Canadian Congress of Labour, 1935–1956* (T: UTP 1973), and a more detailed and very perceptive case study, William Kaplan, *Everything That Floats: Pat Sullivan, Hal Banks, and the Seamen's Unions of Canada* (T: UTP 1987), which covers the violent history of the Seafarers' International Union. Labour's first cousin, the CCF party, is discussed in Greg Donaghy, 'Solidarity Forever: The Cooperative Commonwealth Federation and Its Search for an International Role, 1939–1949,' *IJCS* 1992.

Canadian-Israeli relations are treated in two books by David J. Bercuson: *Canada and the Birth of Israel: A Study in Canadian Foreign Policy* (T: UTP 1985), which considers the diplomatic side of events, and *The Secret Army* (T: Lester & Orpen Dennys 1983), on private Canadian efforts on behalf of the fledgling Jewish state. Canadian contacts with Israel were, however, limited until the Suez crisis of 1956. Reford, *Canada and Three Crises*, already mentioned, deals with that subject among others. So does Terence Robertson, *Crisis: The Inside Story of the Suez Conspiracy* (T: M&S 1964), an early account based on then-secret Canadian documents. The views of Canada's prime minister on British behaviour are accurately reflected in Dale C. Thomson's rather pedestrian biography, *Louis St. Laurent: Canadian* (T: MAC 1967). Much water has passed under the bridge since then. With most British and American documents declassified, as well as Canadian ones, it is possible to consult a much more sophisticated and comprehensive collection of essays on the subject: *Suez 1956: The Crisis and Its Consequences* (NY: OUP 1989), edited by William Roger Louis and Roger

Owen. The relevant volume of the official *Foreign Relations of the United States*, vol. 16 of the 1955–1957 series (Washington: US Government Printing Office 1990) should be consulted for the day-to-day development of the crisis. For a somewhat different perspective, see Escott Reid, *Hungary and Suez, 1956: A View from New Delhi* (Oakville: Mosaic 1986); Reid was then high commissioner in New Delhi, and faced with the problem of achieving some kind of community of interest with the Indian government.

The larger question of relations between Canada and the Third World, especially India, is treated in Reid's book, *Envoy to Nehru* (T: Oxford 1981); for a contrasting view from Nehru's defence minister, see Michael Brecher, *India and World Politics: Krishna Menon's View of the World* (L: Oxford 1968). India, a Commonwealth partner, was also conceived of as an outlet for Canadian technology; see Robert Bothwell, *Nucleus*. China, on the other hand, was regarded as a strategic threat at worst, and as an undesirable complication at best. On Canadian-Chinese relations, see Chester Ronning's somewhat uncritical account, *A Memoir of China in Revolution: From the Boxer Rebellion to the People's Republic* (NY: Pantheon 1974). Much of Ronning's book was based on the diary he kept while serving in the Canadian embassy in Nanking. South America has frequently been neglected by Canadian historians. An exception is J.C.M. Ogelsby, whose *Gringos from the Far North: Essays in the History of Canadian-Latin American Relations, 1866–1968* (T: MAC 1976) contains some useful essays. Duncan McDowall, *The Light: Brazilian Traction, Light, and Power Co., Ltd., 1899–1945* (T: UTP 1988) is a fascinating study of Brazilian Traction, a Canadian-owned utility company in Brazil. The book does, however, suffer from frequent repetition.

The Soviet Union absorbed a considerable amount of Canada's diplomatic talent during this period. Dean Beeby and William Kaplan, eds., *Moscow Despatches: Inside Cold War Russia* (T: JL 1987) presents the dispatches of Canada's mid-1950s ambassador, John Watkins. A more tough-minded account, stretching from the 1940s to the 1980s, is Robert A.D. Ford, *Our Man in Moscow: A Diplomat's Reflections on the Soviet Union* (T: UTP 1989); these are the memoirs of Canada's very able ambassador in Moscow in the 1960s and 1970s.

The Diefenbaker interval in Canadian foreign policy is best captured in H. Basil Robinson, *Diefenbaker's World: A Populist in Foreign Affairs* (T: UTP 1989); although some contemporary observers have some disagreement with its nuances; also useful is Knowlton Nash, *Kennedy and Diefenbaker: Fear and Loathing across the Undefended Border* (T: M&S 1990).

Two earlier collections of interviews by Peter Stursberg, *Diefenbaker: Leadership Gained, 1956–1962* (T: UTP 1975) and *Diefenbaker: Leadership Lost, 1962–1967* (T: UTP 1976) cast considerable light on 'the Chief's' performance in foreign and defence policy. Defence policy is the subject of Jon B. McLin, *Canada's Changing Defense Policy, 1957–1963: The Problems of a Middle Power in Alliance* (Baltimore: Johns Hopkins UP 1967), which has stood the test of time for its information and analysis. J.L. Granatstein, *Canada 1957–1967: The Years of Uncertainty and Innovation* (T: M&S 1986), and 'When Push Comes to Shove: Canada and the United States,' in Thomas G. Paterson, ed., *Kennedy's Quest for Victory: American Foreign Policy, 1961–1963* (NY: OUP 1989), are reliable and authoritative. Researchers should also consult Jocelyn Ghent, 'Did He Fall or Was He Pushed?' *International History Review* 1979. Diefenbaker's own memoirs, *One Canada: Memoirs of the Right Honourable John G. Diefenbaker*, 3 vols. (T: MAC 1975–7), are simply dreadful, and of slight use to students of foreign policy. Similarly dreadful, but more candid and useful, are the memoirs of the minister of finance, Donald Fleming, *So Very Near: The Political Memoirs of the Hon. Donald M. Fleming*, 2 vols. (T: M&S 1985). The biography of Diefenbaker's minister of defence, *For Most Conspicuous Bravery: A Biography of Major-General George R. Pearkes, VC* (V: UBCP 1977), by Reginald Roy, is also rather unsatisfactory. A related defence subject, the Defence Production Sharing Agreement, is reported in John Kirton, 'The Consequences of Integration: The Case of the Defence Production Sharing Agreements,' in W. Andrew Axline et. al., eds., *Continental Community? Independence and Integration in North America* (T: M&S 1974).

One issue of the Diefenbaker period did not go away: the limitations of the Canadian government's power in foreign affairs. These limitations were revealed in the episode of the Columbia River Treaty, described in Neil A. Swainson, *Conflict over the Columbia: The Canadian Background to an Historic Treaty* (M and K: MQUP 1979). Another, the St Lawrence Seaway, was more or less resolved: see William R. Willoughby, *The St Lawrence Waterway: A Study in Politics and Diplomacy* (Madison: University of Wisconsin Press 1961). Diefenbaker's troubles with the Commonwealth are discussed in J.D.B. Miller, *Survey of Commonwealth Affairs: Problems of Expansion and Attrition, 1953–1969* (L: Oxford 1974); they are also mentioned in Alistair Horne, *Harold Macmillan*, vol. 2, *1957–1986* (NY: Viking 1989).

Lester Pearson's foreign policy is covered, up to a point, in Pearson's memoir, *Mike*, vol. 3 (T: UTP 1975); it is expanded – and reflected –

upon in John English's second volume of his biography of Lester Pearson, *The Worldly Years*. Peter Stursberg collected, but did not sufficiently edit, the opinions of Pearson's contemporaries in his *Lester Pearson and the American Dilemma* (T: Doubleday 1980). Paul Martin, Pearson's minister of external affairs, penned a useful memoir, *A Very Public Life*, vol. 2, *So Many Worlds* (T: Deneau 1985); it is, however, excessively defensive in tone, especially over Vietnam.

The unhappy story of Canadian diplomacy and Vietnam is contained in Douglas A. Ross, *In the Interests of Peace: Canada and Vietnam, 1954–1973* (T: UTP 1984); while Ross's book is both thorough and fair, it is best on events down to the early 1960s, after which it rather runs out of steam. John English, 'Speaking Out on Vietnam, 1965' in Don Munton and John Kirton, *Canadian Foreign Policy: Selected Cases* (Scarborough: PH 1992), is a valuable supplement. Victor Levant, *Quiet Complicity: Canadian Involvement in the Vietnam War* (T: Between the Lines 1986) takes a radically different stand from Ross; its assertions are frequently questionable, while its statistics should be compared with those in the *Canada Year Book*. Charles Taylor, *Snow Job: Canada, the United States, and Vietnam, 1954 to 1973* (T: Anansi 1975) is interesting both as a contemporary point of view and for its rhetorical fervour. The overview by David van Praagh, 'Canada and Southeast Asia,' in Peyton V. Lyon and Tareq Y. Ismael, eds., *Canada and the Third World* (T: MAC 1976), is the shortest and most judicious discussion. The volume by James Eayrs, *In Defence of Canada*, vol. 5, *Indochina: Roots of Complicity* (T: UTP 1983), is a somewhat incomplete study which is better on roots than on complicity.

Canadian-American relations did not benefit from Vietnam, or from a simultaneous rise in Canadian nationalistic feeling. A group of prominent Canadians and Americans produced a book edited by Livingston T. Merchant, a former American ambassador, entitled *Neighbors Taken for Granted: Canada and the United States* (T: Burns and McEachern 1966). Its most interesting contribution is by Dean Acheson, 'Canada: Stern Daughter of the Voice of God'; it should be remembered that Acheson's parents were Canadian. Charles Ritchie, ambassador in Washington, called his memoir of the period *Storm Signals: More Undiplomatic Diaries, 1962–1971* (T: MAC 1983). Peter C. Newman, the chief journalistic chronicler of the decade, wrote *The Distemper of Our Times: Canadian Politics in Transition, 1963–1968* (T: M&S 1968), which, among other things, dealt with the tribulations of Walter Gordon as minister of finance. Dave Godfrey and Mel Watkins, eds., *Gordon to Watkins to You, Documentary: The Battle for Control of our Economy* (T: New Press 1970) explained the apostolic succession in Canadian economic nationalism during the decade. Another contemporary nationalist book, with a self-explanatory title, is Ian Lumsden, ed., *Close the 49th Parallel Etc.: The Americanization of Canada* (T: UTP 1970). For a calm and reflective overview, readers should also consult a very fine essay by John Holmes, one of his last, 'Merchant-Heeney Revisited: A Sentimental Overview,' in Laure McKinsey and Kim Richard Nossal, eds., *America's Alliances and Canadian-American Relations* (T: Summerhill 1988).

The American investment question may be perused in A.E. Safarian, *Foreign Ownership of Canadian Industry* (2nd ed., T: UTP 1973); a contrasting view is Kari Levitt, *Silent Surrender: The Multinational Corporation in Canada* (T: MAC 1970). Walter L. Gordon, *A Political Memoir* (T: M&S 1977), gives his side of the case.

One of the most vivid controversies in Pearson's period was the unification of the armed forces; on that subject, and the Pearson government more generally, see the memoirs of his defence minister, Paul Hellyer, *Damn the Torpedoes: My Fight to Unify Canada's Armed Forces* (T: M&S 1990).

The Commonwealth was finally equipped with a permanent secretariat in Pearson's time; on that subject, and on Canada's relations with the Commonwealth in the 1960s and 1970s, see Arnold Smith, with Clyde Sanger, *Stitches in Time: The Commonwealth in World Politics* (Don Mills General 1981). It is a very informative account, especially on Biafra, Bangladesh, and South Africa. Sanger also wrote a study of Canadian foreign aid, as did Keith Spicer, *A Samaritan State? External Aid in Canada's Foreign Policy* (T: UTP 1966). Later experiences with foreign aid (and sometimes the lack of it) were documented in a valuable series of monographs from the North-South Institute. Particularly good examples are Roger Young, *Canadian Development Assistance to Tanzania: An Independent Study* (O: North-South Institute 1983); Roger B. Ehrhardt, *Canadian Development Assistance to Bangladesh: An Independent Study* (O: North-South Institute 1983); and Glenn P. Jenkins, *Costs and Consequences of the New Protectionism: The Case of Canada's Clothing Sector* (2nd ed., O: North-South Institute 1985).

South Africa became an increasingly sore point in relations between the Canadian government and its foreign public policy. Clarence G. Redekop, 'Commerce over Conscience: The Trudeau Government and South Africa, 1968–84,' originally published in *JCS* 1984–5, and republished in J.L. Granatstein, ed., *Towards a New World*, is valuable for following the twists and turns of policy.

Much has been written on the Trudeau period. Trudeau's overall record in foreign policy, including defence, the Third Option, and aid and trade, is considered in J.L. Granatstein and Robert Bothwell, *Pirouette: Pierre Trudeau and Canadian Foreign Policy* (T: UTP 1990). The best biography of Trudeau to date is Richard Gwyn, *The Northern Magus: Pierre Trudeau and Canadians* (T: M&S 1980). B.W. Powe,'The Quiet Civil War of Pierre Trudeau,' in his *The Solitary Outlaw* (T: Lester & Orpen Dennys 1987), is perceptive and informative, as is George Radwanski, *Trudeau* (T: MAC 1978). Incomplete, as yet, is Stephen Clarkson and Christina McCall, *Trudeau and Our Times* (T: M&S 1990); much is expected of its second volume, due to appear in 1994. One of Trudeau's foreign ministers, Don Jamieson, left two volumes of his diary, *The Political Memoirs of Don Jamieson*, edited by Camelita McGrath: *No Place for Fools* and *A World unto Itself* (St John's: Breakwater 1989, 1991). Jamieson's posthumous memoir confirms his reputation for intelligence and perception, but his descriptions of events ought to be checked against those of his colleagues. Trudeau's principal secretary, Tom Axworthy, has written a trifling analysis of his master's foreign policy. '"To stand not so high perhaps but always alone": The Foreign Policy of Pierre Elliott Trudeau,' in Axworthy and Trudeau, eds., *Towards a Just Society: The Trudeau Years* (Markham: Viking 1990). Paul Martin, high commissioner in London during the 1970s, published excerpts from his diaries, *Paul Martin: The London Diaries, 1975–1979* (O: UOP 1988), edited by William R. Young. They contain interesting reflections on Canadian relations with Europe as well as Great Britain. The overseas effects of the Quebec crisis of the time are also discussed. Two early studies, Bruce Thordarson, *Trudeau and Foreign Policy: A Study in Decision-Making* (T: OUP 1972), and Peter C. Dobell, *Canada's Search for New Roles: Foreign Policy in the Trudeau Era* (T: OUP 1972), catch the flavour of the period and add interesting details. At the time of writing, Trudeau's own memoirs were anticipated but had not yet appeared.

The Law of the Sea and the extension of Canada's maritime boundaries were a considerable challenge to Canada's capacity in international law. On the negotiations over the Law of the Sea, see Clyde Sanger, *Ordering the Oceans: The Making of the Law of the Sea* (T: UTP 1987), and Barbara Johnson and Mark W. Zacher, eds., *Canadian Foreign Policy and the Law of the Sea* (V: UBCP 1977). On maritime boundaries, one handy source is Edward Collins, 'The East Coast Maritime Boundary of Canada and the United States,' in Robert Lecker, ed., *Borderlands: Essays in Canadian-American Relations* (T: ECW Press 1991).

Defence policy is not usually regarded as the Trudeau government's strong suit. It did however issue an important White Paper, *Defence in the 70s* (O: Information Canada 1971). At the time, some commentators praised the government's emphasis on arms control and *détente*: an example is Colin S. Gray, *Canadian Defence Priorities: A Question of Relevance* (T: CI 1972). A different point of view is set down in Nils Orvik, *Canadian Defence Policy: Priorities and Directions* (Kingston: Centre for International Relations, Queen's University 1980), which argues that Trudeau's emphasis on northern defence was misplaced, if not utterly wrong-headed. Two books by Larry R. Stewart, *Canada's European Force, 1971–1980: A Defence Policy in Transition*, and *Canadian Defence Policy: Selected Speeches and Documents, 1964–1981*, both from Queen's University (K: Centre for International Relations 1980, 1982), are very handy in outlining the sometimes unfeasible commitments and doctrines of the period.

Much of the Trudeau period was spent in studying process. The Department of External Affairs commissioned studies, reviews, and consultations galore, while political scientists earnestly polled, quantified, and computerized the results. Some of the atmosphere, along with some useful information derived from polls in Canada and abroad, may be found in Peyton V. Lyon and Brian W. Tomlin, *Canada as an International Actor* (T: MAC 1979). Not to be forgotten is the department's own emission, *Foreign Policy for Canadians*, 6 vols. (O: Information Canada 1970), and what eventually supplemented or supplanted it, Mitchell Sharp, 'Canada-US Relations: Options for the Future,' *International Perspectives* 1972. The latter is probably the key statement of the Trudeau government's aspirations in foreign affairs, and it remains a monument to hopes indefinitely deferred. Sharp's own memoir, *Which Reminds Me ... A Memoir* (T: UTP 1993), is especially illuminating for its overviews of Canadian government, including the processes of foreign relations from the 1940s to the 1980s.

Sharp's 1972 paper dealt with the interface of politics and economics. In the latter category, energy policy was increasingly prominent. Of great interest is Marc Lalonde, former minister of energy, 'Riding the Storm: Energy Policy, 1968–1984,' in Axworthy, *Towards a Just Society*. Students of energy policy, and the minerals trade generally, should consult Carl E. Beigie and Alfred O. Hero, Jr., eds., *Natural Resources in US-Canadian Relations*, 2 vols. (Boulder: Westview Press 1980). Richard H.K. Vietor, *Energy Policy in America since 1945: A Study of Business Government Relations* (Cambridge: CUP 1984) contains much valuable information. Those interested in the global context should consult Ethan B. Kapstein, *The Insecure Alliance: Energy Crises and Western Politics since 1944* (NY: OUP 1990).

David Leyton-Brown, 'Canadianizing Oil and Gas: The National Energy Program, 1980–83,' deals with Trudeau's most controversial domestic policy; it is an excerpt from Leyton-Brown, *Weathering the Storm: Canadian-US Relations, 1980–83* (T: Canadian-American Committee 1985). See also Edward Wonder, 'The US Government Response to the Canadian National Energy Program,' *Canadian Public Policy* 1982. Much of Canada's energy policy centred on the Arctic and on Native rights; in this area there is a first-class study available: Robert Page, *Northern Development: The Canadian Dilemma* (T: M&S 1986).

The other great issue of Canadian politics during the 1960s, 1970s, and 1980s was 'What does Quebec want?' The question had an external dimension, because among other things the government of Quebec preached that it had a constitutional role in external affairs even inside the Canadian federal state. Separatists, naturally, sought foreign approbation for their efforts, and sometimes they got it. The best study of the 1960s is Dale C. Thomson, *Vive le Québec libre* (T: Deneau 1988). More partisan, and from a separatist standpoint, is Claude Morin's informative *L'Art de l'impossible: la diplomatie québécoise depuis 1960* (M: BE 1987); also of considerable interest is Morin's *Mes Premiers Ministres: Lesage, Johnson, Bertrand, Bourassa, et Lévesque* (M: BE 1991), which contains a number of documents from the period. It is unclear how much of Morin's testimony is undermined by his double role in the 1970s as a high Quebec functionary and an informant of the RCMP. Pierre O'Neill and Jacques Benjamin, *Les mandarins du pouvoir: l'exercice du pouvoir au Québec de Jean Lesage à René Lévesque* (M: Q/A 1978) illuminates the Quebec higher civil service in the period. There is a fascinating, but on some points uncorroborated, biography, *Daniel Johnson*, vol. 2, *1964–1968: la difficile recherche de l'égalité*, by Pierre Godin (M: Editions de l'homme 1980).

On the French side, there is a considerable literature. Jean Lacouture, *De Gaulle*, 3 vols. in French, 2 vols. in English, (English edition, NY: Norton 1990–1992), describes the general's 1967 intervention in Canada in considerable detail. Pierre-Louis Mallen, *Vivre le Québec Libre* (M: Presses de la Cité 1978), by the very committed Radio-France correspondent in Canada, draws on and publishes some confidential information. The French consul general in Quebec City, Pierre de Menthon, wrote a brief memoir, interesting for the light it sheds on de Gaulle's attention to detail, as well as on the French government's failure to provide economic underpinnings for its political bravado: *Je témoigne: Québec 1967, Chili 1973* (Paris: Cerf 1978). In the aftermath, Jean-Marc Léger, an enthusiast for la francophonie, wrote a memoir on the subject, *La francophonie: grand dessein, grande ambiguité* (LaSalle: HMH 1987). Also of interest is a more general survey, Sylvie and Pierre Guillaume, *Paris-Québec-Ottawa: un ménage à trois* (Paris: Editions Entente 1987).

Much of the war between Canada and Quebec was fought in Africa, where the two governments competed for support from bemused French-speaking, aid-receiving governments. On that subject, see John P. Schlegel, *The Deceptive Ash: Bilingualism and Canadian Policy in Africa, 1957–1971* (Lanham: UP of America 1978). Also useful, although hard to find, is Jean Baulin, *Conseiller du President Diori* (Eurofor 1986). Some of the American dimension of the Canada-Quebec conundrum is described in Jean-François Lisée's very well-researched *In the Eye of the Eagle* (T: HarperCollins 1990). American-Quebec relations receive more general consideration in Alfred Hero and Louis Balthazar, *Contemporary Quebec and the United States, 1960–1985* (Lanham: UP of America 1988). A more recent publication, edited by R. Kent Weaver, entitled *The Collapse of Canada?* (Washington: Brookings Institution 1992), is interesting as an attempt to explain to Americans why they should be concerned by the continuing Canada-Quebec crisis. Quebec's premier from 1970 to 1976, and 1985 to 1994, Robert Bourassa, has so far been the subject of one major biography, *Bourassa* (T: MAC 1992) by the ultra-nationalist Quebec journalist, Michel Vastel; unfortunately it says little about Bourassa's obsession with northern hydroelectric power, which linked Quebec's hopes so closely with US energy demand.

Canadian-American relations did not cease while Trudeau dealt with Quebec. Energy policy has already been mentioned, for which readers should also consult Stephen Clarkson's well-documented study, *Canada and the Reagan Challenge: Crisis and Adjustment, 1981–1985*, which should be used in its second edition (2nd ed., T: JL 1985). On energy, see G. Bruce Doern and Glen Toner, *The Politics of Energy: The Development and Implementation of the NEP* (T: Methuen 1985). More generally, there is Richard Gwyn's thoughtful *The 49th Paradox: Canada in North America* (T: M&S 1985), or the special studies for the Royal Commission on the Economic Union, edited by John Whalley and Roderick Hill, *Canada-United States Free Trade* (T: UTP 1985), and Stairs and Winham, *The Politics of Canada's Economic Relationship with the United States* (cited above). From an American (and political science) perspective, there is Annette Baker Fox, Alfred O. Hero , Jr. , and Joseph S. Nye, eds., *Canada and the United States: Transnational and Transgovernmental Relations* (NY: Columbia UP 1976). John W. Holmes, the dean of Canadian foreign relations analysts, penned a thoughtful essay, *Life with Uncle: The Canadian-American Relationship*

(T: UTP 1981). Charles F. Doran, an American political scientist, has written a good contemporary study, *Forgotten Partnership: US-Canada Relations Today* (Baltimore: John Hopkins UP 1984).

Canadian relations with Europe had their ups and downs in the 1970s and 1980s. Of particular value is Robert Spencer, ed., *Conference on Security and Cooperation in Europe* (T: Centre for International Studies, University of Toronto 1984). Human rights, a particular focus for the Conference on Security and Cooperation in Europe, but of more general application in Canadian foreign policy, are discussed in Robert O. Matthews and Cranford Pratt, eds., *Human Rights in Canadian Foreign Policy* (M and K: MQUP 1988). Interesting for its line of thought is Tom Keating and Larry Pratt, *Canada, NATO, and the Bomb: The Western Alliance in Crisis* (E: Hurtig 1988), which argues NATO's utility as a counterweight to the United States. Canadian relations with China, and especially the recognition question, have been studied in Paul M. Evans and B. Michael Frolic, eds., *Reluctant Adversaries: Canada and the People's Republic of China, 1949–1970* (T: UTP 1991).

The Mulroney government's foreign relations are sometimes treated in more general books on the subject of the government. Its main foreign policy achievement, the Free Trade Agreement (FTA) with the United States, is already the subject of a vast literature. The best book to date is G. Bruce Doern and Brian W. Tomlin, *Faith and Fear: The Free Trade Story* (Don Mills: Stoddart 1991). Peter Morici, *A New Special Relationship: Free Trade and US-Canada Economic Relations in the 1990s* (O: Centre for Trade Policy and Law 1991) gives, despite its title, a historical account of the evolution of free trade, plus an analysis of the agreement and an essentially optimistic view of its prospects. There is also an excellent article by Michael Hart, one of the negotiators, 'Negotiating Free-Trade, 1985–1988', in Munton and Kirton, eds., *Canadian Foreign Policy*. Lawrence Martin, *Pledge of Allegiance: The Americanization of Canada in the Mulroney Years* (T: M&S 1993) contains some marvellous anecdotage; nevertheless, its analysis is weak and its logic flawed.

The vexed question of acid rain is the subject of Don Munton and Geoffrey Castle, 'Reducing Acid Rain, 1980s,' in Munton and Kirton, *Canadian Foreign Policy*. See also John E. Carroll, *Environmental Diplomacy: An Examination and a Prospective of Canadian-US Transboundary Environmental Relations* (Ann Arbor: University of Michigan Press 1983). The Persian Gulf War of 1991 is treated in John Kirton, 'Liberating Kuwait: Canada and the Persian Gulf War, 1990–91,' in Munton and Kirton, eds., *Canadian Foreign Policy*, and in Jocelyn Coulon, *La dernière croisade: la guerre du Golfe et le role caché du Canada* (M: Meridien 1992). Defence policy in general is covered in B.B. Hunt and R.G. Haycock, *Canada's Defence* (T: CCP 1993). Unfortunately, much of the existing literature predates the complete collapse of the Soviet system and is therefore somewhat dated. Lewis MacKenzie, *Peacekeeper: The Road to Sarajevo* (V: Douglas & McIntyre 1993) is an interesting and well-written discussion of the peacekeeping general's professional career culminating in a lengthy discussion in diary form of his time in the Balkans. The ultimate story of Canada's encounter with the world under Mulroney still awaits historical analysis. Finally, there is a summary overview, with essays covering most aspects of Canadian external relations from the 1940s to the 1990s, in John English and Norman Hillmer, eds., *Making a Difference? Canada's Foreign Policy in a Changing World Order* (T: Lester 1992).

As we approach the end of the century a few trends in this field deserve to be highlighted. First, there continues to be a relative paucity of material in French. Second, the gap between political science and history, though not unbridged, remains wide. Third, a certain interest in Canadian foreign policy has begun to be manifested abroad as a result of government encouragement of 'Canadian Studies.' The result may be a further proliferation of literature in the field.

CRAIG HERON

Working-Class History

Workers were once described as being on the margins of Canadian history. Now they spill all over the pages. A flood of books, articles, and theses over the past twenty years has brought their particular history into the full light of historical reflection, and into the mainstream of Canadian historical writing. Most history departments in Canadian universities now offer courses on Canadian labour history. Academic conferences invariably offer sessions on working-class history that attract large audiences and stimulate lively discussion. And the main academic mouthpiece for the field, *Labour/Le Travail*, published by the Canadian Committee on Labour History, continues to produce some of the most interesting, sophisticated work in Canadian social history. Quebec labour historians also maintain their own vigorous organization, Le Regroupement des chercheurs en histoire des travailleurs et travailleuses du Québec, which puts out its own *Bulletin*.

The historical investigation of Canadian workers actually includes far more than the work of these specialized practitioners. In many ways, almost the whole project of the new social history was centrally concerned with the working class, often from the perspective of middle- and upper-class activists who were anxious about workers' health, housing, child-rearing practices, schooling, leisure patterns, and morality in general. In other disciplines, the expanding field of political economy also brought to light many more areas of working-class life, especially workers' interaction with the Canadian state.

The massive output of new literature on Canadian working-class history is staggering, and the following discussion of useful readings in the field cannot do more than suggest the more important books and some of the most perceptive articles. For a fuller bibliography, consult G. Douglas

Vaisey et al., comps., *The Labour Companion: A Bibliography of Canadian Labour History Based on Materials Printed from 1950 to 1975* (H: CCLH 1980); Peter Weinrich, comp., *Social Protest from the Left in Canada, 1870–1970* (T:UTP 1982); and the annual bibliographies in *Labour/Le Travail*.

HISTORIOGRAPHY AND GENERAL TEXTS

Aside from the debates within French-Canadian history, no branch of Canadian historical writing has sparked as much heated controversy as working-class history. The salient critiques include Bryan D. Palmer, 'Working-Class Canada: Recent Historical Writing,' *QQ* 1979/80 and his 'Listening to History Rather Than Historians: Reflections on Working-Class History,' *Studies in Political Economy* 1986; Gregory S. Kealey, 'Labour and Working-Class History: Prospects in the 1980s,' *Labour* 1981; David J. Bercuson, 'Through the Looking Glass of Culture: An Essay on the New Labour History and Working-Class Culture in Recent Canadian Historical Writing,' *Labour* 1981; Kenneth McNaught, 'E.P. Thompson vs. Harold Logan: Writing about Labour and the Left in the 1970s,' *CHR* 1981; Desmond Morton, 'E.P. Thompson dans les arpents de neiges: les historiens canadiens anglais et la classe ouvrière,' *RHAF* 1983; Ian McKay, 'Historians, Anthropology, and the Concept of Culture,' *Labour* 1981/82; James Conley, '"More Theory, Less Fact?" Social Reproduction and Class Conflict in a Sociological Approach to Working-Class History,' in Gregory S. Kealey, ed., *Class, Gender, and Region: Essays in Canadian Historical Sociology* (St John's: CCLH 1988); Bettina Bradbury, 'Women's History and Working-Class History,' *Labour* 1987; Bruno Ramirez, 'Ethnic Studies and Working-Class History,' *Labour* 1987; and Fernand Ouellet, 'The Social Question, 1880–1930: Historiographical and Critical Perspectives,' in Ouellet, *Economy, Class, and Nation in Quebec: Interpretive Essays*, ed. Jacques A. Barbier (T: CCP 1991). For a survey of the main lines of the debates, see Gregory S. Kealey, 'Writing about Labour,' in John Schultz, ed., *Writing about Canada: A Handbook for Modern Canadian History* (Scarborough: PH 1990). Useful reflections on the state of the field can also be found in James Naylor, 'Working-Class History in English Canada in the 1980s: An Assessment,' *Acadiensis* 1989; and Joanne Burgess, 'Exploring the Limited Identities of Canadian Labour: Recent Trends in English-Canada and in Quebec,' *IJCS* 1990.

For many years, there was no single book that attempted to synthesize a wide range of the themes in working-class history. An interesting effort with limited circulation was H. Clare Pentland, *A Study of the Changing Social, Economic, and Political Background of the Canadian System of Industrial Relations* (O: QP 1968). Two collections of primary documents that appeared in the 1970s suggested the kind of material that should be included. They still remain quite useful: Michael S. Cross, ed., *The Workingman in the Nineteenth Century* (T: OUP 1974); and Irving Abella and David Millar, eds., *The Canadian Worker in the Twentieth Century* (T: OUP 1978). The first two general histories to emerge reflected the two polar positions in the developing historiographical debate. In *Working People: An Illustrated History of the Canadian Labour Movement* (3rd ed., T: Summerhill Press 1990), Desmond Morton and Terry Copp tell the social-democratic version of the story, with plenty of swipes at the 'reds' along the way. It is well illustrated and often informative. But its treatment of the nineteenth century is woefully brief, and its rambling, weakly structured narrative style can be confusing. Bryan D. Palmer offered a more theoretically informed, wide-ranging, and controversial survey in *Working-Class Experience: The Rise and Reconstitution of Canadian Labour, 1800–1980* (T: BUT 1983), which was substantially revised and reissued as *Working-Class Experience: Rethinking the History of Canadian Labour, 1800–1991* (2nd ed., T: M&S 1992), a subtle statement on historical materialism. This new edition reflects Palmer's engagement with the new research and intense debates of the 1980s, and, while still dense for the uninitiated reader, is a useful overview of the field. Syntheses need not be national, and two publications taking a single city as their focus attempt to cut wide swaths through the local workers' history by linking old photographs and text: Craig Heron et al., *All That Our Hands Have Done: A Pictorial History of the Hamilton Workers* (Oakville: Mosaic Press 1981); and most sensitive to all the new concerns, the Working Lives Collective, *Working Lives: Vancouver, 1886–1986* (V: New Star 1985).

There are also several collections of essays that span a wide range of issues: see, in particular, Gregory S. Kealey and Peter Warrian, eds., *Essays in Canadian Working-Class History* (T: M&S 1976); Bryan D. Palmer, ed., *The Character of Class Struggle: Essays in Canadian Working-Class History, 1850–1985* (T: M&S 1986); Kealey, ed., *Class, Gender, and Region* (cited above); David J. Bercuson, ed., *Canadian Labour History: Selected Readings* (T: CCP 1987); and W.J.C. Cherwinski and G.S. Kealey, ed., *Lectures in Canadian Labour and Working-Class History* (St John's and T: CCLH/New Hogtown Press 1985). Regional collections include Rennie Warburton and David Coburn, eds., *Workers, Capital, and the State in British Columbia: Selected Papers* (V: UBCP 1988); Harley Dickinson and

Robert Russell, ed., *The Politics of Work in the West: Historical and Contemporary Perspectives* (S: Department of Sociology, University of Saskatchewan 1985); and Michael Earle, ed., *Workers and the State in Twentieth Century Nova Scotia* (F: AP 1989). Some international comparisons are drawn in Deian R. Hopkin and Gregory S. Kealey, eds., *Class, Community, and the Labour Movement: Wales and Canada, 1850–1930* (Aberystwyth and St John's: Llafur and CCLH 1989); and in Gregory S. Kealey and Greg Patmore, eds., *Canadian and Australian Labour History: Towards a Comparative Perspective* (Sydney and St John's: Australian Society for the Study of Labour History/CCLH 1990).

FAMILY AND HOUSEHOLD

The best studies of working-class families and households recognize not only the importance of family economies as the central survival strategy of working people, but also the gendered inequalities that exist within them. Several good examples can be found in Joy Parr, ed., *Childhood and Family in Canadian History* (T: M&S 1982); and in Bettina Bradbury, ed., *Canadian Family History: Selected Readings* (T: CCP 1992). Bradbury has also produced by far the most sensitive treatment of nineteenth-century working-class family households in *Working Families: Age, Gender, and Daily Survival in Industrializing Montreal* (T: M&S 1993). The household responsibilities of children in Ontario's working-class family economies are discussed in John Bullen, 'Hidden Workers: Child Labour and the Family Economy in Late Nineteenth-Century Urban Ontario,' *Labour* 1986. The continuing role of children in the family economy is noted in Chad Gaffield, 'Children, Schooling, and Family Reproduction in Nineteenth-Century Ontario,' *CHR* 1991; Jane Synge, 'The Transition from School to Work: Growing Up Working Class in Early 20th Century Hamilton, Ontario,' in K. Ishwaran, ed., *Childhood and Adolescence in Canada* (T: MHR 1979); Rebecca Coulter, 'The Working Young of Edmonton, 1921–1931,' in Parr, ed., *Childhood and Family*: and Neil Sutherland, '"We Always Had Things To Do": The Paid and Unpaid Work of Anglophone Children between the 1920s and the 1960s,' *Labour* 1990. Anthony B. Chan explores the households of single male wage-earners in 'Chinese Bachelor Workers in Nineteenth-Century Canada,' *Ethnic and Racial Studies* 1982, while the dynamics of Italian boarding-houses are examined in Robert F. Harney's two articles, 'Boarding and Belonging: Thoughts on Sojourner Institutions,' *UHR* 1979; and 'Men without Women: Italian Migrants in Canada, 1885–1930,' *Canadian Ethnic Studies* 1979. Meg Luxton brilliantly elucidates the domestic labour of twentieth-century working-class house-wives in *More Than a Labour of Love: Three Generations of Women's Work in the Home* (T: Women's Press 1980). See also the collection of essays she co-edited with Harriet Rosenberg and Sedef Arat-Koc, *Through the Kitchen Window: The Politics of Home and Family* (2nd ed., T: Garamond Press 1990), and Susan Prentice's study of the politics of child care, 'Workers, Mothers, Reds: Toronto's Postwar Daycare Fight,' *Studies in Political Economy* 1989. Franca Iacovetta draws a vivid portrait of the links between household and paid work in *'Such Hardworking People': Italian Immigrants in Postwar Toronto* (M and K: MQUP 1992). Mark Rosenfeld probes the same relationship within families headed by railway workers in 'It Was a Hard Life: Class and Gender in Work and Family Rhythms of a Railway Town, 1920s–1950,' CHA *AR* 1988. Kathryn Harvey raises the issue of potential conflict within these families in 'To Love, Honour, and Obey: Wife Battering in Working-Class Montreal, 1869–79,' *UHR* 1990, while Suzanne Morton probes the rituals surrounding family formation in 'The June Bride as the Working-Class Bride: Getting Married in a Working-Class Neighbourhood in the 1920s,' in Bradbury, ed., *Canadian Family History*.

Several other books and articles open the doors to working-class households of the past. Michael B. Katz has made full use of nineteenth-century manuscript censuses to construct a detailed, if bloodless, portrait of class and community in one Ontario city in two consecutive studies: first, *The People of Hamilton, Canada West: Family and Class in a Mid-Nineteenth-Century City* (Cambridge: HUP 1975); and, then, with Michael J. Doucet and Mark J. Stern, *The Social Organization of Early Industrial Capitalism* (Cambridge: HUP 1982). These books reveal a good deal about the rigidities of the Canadian class structure and family strategies for coping, but stop well short of a full appreciation of life in working-class households. Gordon Darroch and Michael Ornstein offer a wider comparative perspective in 'Family and Household in Nineteenth-Century Canada: Regional Patterns and Regional Economies,' *Journals of Family History* 1984. Gregory S. Kealey presents a quick overview of the living standards of late-Victorian Toronto workers in *Hogtown: Working-Class Toronto at the Turn of the Century* (2nd ed., T: New Hogtown Press 1975), while Jean de Bonville does the same for Montreal workers in *Jean-Baptiste Gagnepetit: les travailleurs montréalais à la fin du XIXe siècle* (M: Editions de l'Aurore 1975). David Gagan and Rosemary Gagan attempt a more statistical analysis in 'Working-Class Standards of Living in Late-Victorian Urban Ontario: A Review of the Miscellaneous Evidence on the Quality of Material Life,' *JCHA* 1990. For detailed local studies, see Gordon Darroch, 'Early Industrialization and Inequality in Toronto, 1861–1905,' *Labour* 1983; and Gilles Lauzon, *Habitat ouvrier et révolution industrielle: le cas du village Saint-Augustin (municipalité de St.-Henri)* (M: RCHTQ 1989). Judith Fingard provides a glimpse of those living on the margins in an Atlantic seaport in *The Dark Side of Life in Victorian Halifax* (Potters Lake: Pottersfield Press 1989).

The grim working-class living standards of the early twentieth-century boom years are explored in depth, although without a clear elucidation of the working of family economies, in Terry Copp, *The Anatomy of Poverty: The Condition of the Working Class in Montreal, 1897–1929* (T: M&S 1974); Michael J. Piva, *The Condition of the Working Class in Toronto, 1900–1921* (O: UOP 1979) and his 'Urban Working Class Incomes and Real Incomes in 1921: A Comparative Analysis,' *HS/SH* 1983; and Eleanor A. Bartlett, 'Real Wages and the Standard of Living in Vancouver, 1901–1929,' *BCS* 1981. Ian M. Drummond offers a less convincing perspective on living standards with more emphasis on prosperity than poverty in *Progress without Planning: The Economic History of Ontario from Confederation to the Second World War* (T: UTP 1987). Post-World War II poverty has been subjected to studies far too numerous to cite here; for a sampling, see Ian Adams et al., *The Real Poverty Report* (E: Hurtig 1971); S.D. Clark, *The New Urban Poor* (T: MHR 1978); and David P. Ross, *The Working Poor: Wage Earners and the Failure of Income Security Policies* (T: JL 1981).

Working-class housing is discussed in Joann Latremouille, *Pride of Home: The Working Class Housing Tradition in Nova Scotia, 1749–1949* (Hantsport: Lancelot Press 1986); R. Harris, G. Levine, and B.S. Osborne, 'Housing Tenure and Social Classes in Kingston, 1881–1901,' *Journal of Historical Geography* 1981; Richard Harris, 'Working-Class Home Ownership and Housing Affordability across Canada in 1931,' *HS/SH* 1986; Deryck W. Holdsworth's two articles, 'House and Home in Vancouver: Images of West-Coast Urbanism, 1886–1929,' in Gilbert A. Stelter and Alan F.J. Artibise, eds., *The Canadian City: Essays in Urban and Social History* (2nd ed., T: Carleton UP 1984) and 'Cottages and Castles for Vancouver Home-Seekers,' *BCS* 1986; and Michael J. Doucet and John Weaver, *Housing the North American City* (M and K: MQUP 1991). Several studies consider the social engineering behind certain housing schemes for working-class families; see, for example, Eileen Golz, 'A Corporate View of Housing and Community in a Company Town: Copper Cliff, 1886 to 1920,' *OH* 1990; Shirley Spragge, 'A Confluence of Interests: Housing Reform in Toronto, 1900–1920,' in Alan F. J. Artibise and Gilbert A. Stelter, eds.,

The Usable Urban Past: Planning and Politics in the Modern Canadian City (T: MAC 1979); and Albert Rose, *Regent Park: A Study in Slum Clearance* (T: UTP 1958). The limited state role in providing housing for workers is considered in Albert Rose, *Canadian Housing Policies (1935–1980)* (T: BUT 1980); John Bacher, *Keeping to the Marketplace: The Evolution of Canadian Housing Policy* (M and K: MQUP 1993); and John R. Miron et al., eds., *House, Home, and Community: Progress in Housing Canadians, 1945– 1986* (M and K: MQUP 1993).

Many working-class families had to turn in desperation to charities for help. Judith Fingard surveys the charitable resources available to pre-industrial workers in 'The Poor in Winter: Seasonality and Society in Pre-industrial Canada,' in Michael S. Cross and Gregory S. Kealey, eds., *Readings in Canadian Social History*, vol. 2, *Pre-Industrial Canada, 1760–1849* (T: M&S 1982). The situation in Lower Canada gets a fuller treatment in Jean-Marie Fecteau, *Un nouvel ordre des choses: la pauvreté, le crime, l'Etat au Québec, de la fin du XVIIIe siècle à 1840* (M: VLB 1989). For the later nineteenth century, three articles are helpful: Stephen Speisman, 'Munificent Parsons and Municipal Parsimony: Voluntary vs. Public Poor Relief in Nineteenth Century Toronto,' *OH* 1973; Joey Noble, '"Class-ifying the Poor": Toronto Charities, 1850–1880,' *Studies in Political Economy* 1979; and James M. Pitsula, 'The Treatment of Tramps in Late Nineteenth Century Toronto,' CHA *AR* 1980. So far the only book-length studies of these voluntary institutions are Richard B. Splane's plodding history of institutional development, *Social Welfare in Ontario, 1791–1893: A Study of Public Welfare Administration* (T: UTP 1965), and Huguette Lapointe-Roy's *Charité bien ordonnée: le premier réseau de lutte contre la pauvreté a Montrèal au 19e siécle* (M: BE 1987). For discussions of early twentieth-century charity and relief work, see Diane L. Matters, 'Public Welfare Vancouver Style, 1910–1920,' *JCS* 1977; Wendy Johnston, 'Keeping Children in School: The Response of the Montreal Roman Catholic School Commission to the Depression of the 1930s,' CHA *HP* 1985; Anne MacLennan, 'Charity and Change: Montreal English Protestant Charity Faces the Crisis of Depression,' *UHR* 1987; Jim Overton, 'Public Relief and Social Unrest in Newfoundland in the 1930s: An Evaluation of the Ideas of Piven and Cloward,' *Canadian Journal of Sociology* 1988; H.M. Cassidy, *Unemployment and Relief in Ontario, 1929–1932: A Survey and Report* (T: Dent 1932); and Leonard C. Marsh, *Canadians In and Out of Work: A Survey of Economic Classes and Their Relations to the Labour Market* (T: OUP 1940). Christina Simmons probes the operations of one charitable organization with notable sensitivity in '"Helping the Poorer Sisters":

The Women of the Jost Mission, Halifax, 1905–1945,' *Atlantis* 1984. The middle-class 'rescue' of children from these families is discussed in Patricia T. Rooke and R.L. Schnell, *Discarding the Asylum: From Child Rescue to the Welfare State in English Canada (1800–1950)* (Lanham: UP of American 1983); Joy Parr, *Labouring Children: British Immigrant Apprentices to Canada, 1869–1924* (2nd ed., T: UTP 1994); Andrew Jones and Leonard Rutman, *In the Children's Aid: J.J. Kelso and Child Welfare in Ontario* (T: UTP 1981); and Neil Sutherland, *Children in English-Canadian Society: Framing the Twentieth-Century Consensus* (T: UTP 1976). On the growth of the social work profession in these institutions, see James Pitsula, 'The Emergence of Social Work in Toronto,' *JCS* 1979; James Struthers, 'A Profession in Crisis: Charlotte Whitton and Canadian Social Work in the 1930s,' *CHR* 1981; Patricia T. Rooke and R.L. Schnell, *No Bleeding Heart: Charlotte Whitton, A Feminist on the Right* (V: UBCP 1987); and Franca Iacovetta, 'Making "New Canadians": Social Workers, Women, and the Reshaping of Immigrant Families,' in Iacovetta and Mariana Valverde, eds., *Gender Conflicts: New Essays in Women's History* (T: UTP 1992).

State intervention to guarantee some measure of social security came only in the mid-twentieth century. Veronica Strong-Boag looks at one of the first, parsimonious initiatives in 'Wages for Housework: Mother's Allowances and the Beginnings of Social Security in Canada,' *JCS* 1979, while Desmond Morton explores another early program in 'Resisting the Pension Evil: Bureaucracy, Democracy, and Canada's Board of Pension Commissioners, 1916–33,' *CHR* 1987. The arrival of a more elaborate 'welfare state' is covered in Dennis Guest, *The Emergence of Social Security in Canada* (2nd ed., V: UBCP 1985); in the essays collected in Allan Moscovitch and Jim Albert, eds., *The 'Benevolent' State: The Growth of Welfare in Canada* (T: Garamond Press 1987); and in James Struthers, 'How Much Is Enough? Creating a Social Minimum in Ontario, 1930–44,' *CHR* 1991. Stimulating discussion of one of the most important measures for workers – unemployment insurance – can be found in James Struthers, *No Fault of Their Own: Unemployment and the Canadian Welfare State, 1914–1941* (T: UTP 1983); Leslie A. Pal, *State, Class, and Bureaucracy: Canadian Unemployment Insurance and Public Policy* (M and K: MQUP 1988); and Ruth Roach Pierson, 'Gender and Unemployment Insurance Debates in Canada, 1934–1940,' *Labour* 1990. For the impact of another crucial social-security program, see Dominique Jean, 'Family Allowances and Family Autonomy: Quebec Families Encounter the Welfare States, 1945–1955,' in Bradbury, ed., *Canadian Family History*. The changes in the Canadian welfare state that followed World War II can be traced in the chapters of Allan Moscovitch and Glenn Drover, eds., *Inequality: Essays on the Political Economy of Social Welfare* (T: UTP 1981), and Jacqueline S. Ismael, ed., *The Canadian Welfare State: Evolution and Transition* (E: UAP 1987). The essays in James Dickinson and Bob Russell, eds., *Family Economy, and State: Essays on the Social Reproduction Process under Capitalism* (T: Garamond Press 1986), also provide many useful insights, as does Jane Ursel, *Private Lives, Public Policy: One Hundred Years of State Intervention in the Family* (T: Women's Press 1992). Allan Moscovitch has assembled an excellent bibliographic tool, *The Welfare State in Canada: A Selected Bibliography, 1840 to 1978* (Wa: UW Press 1983).

NEIGHBOURHOOD AND COMMUNITY

The essence of community life in Canadian working-class neighbourhoods has escaped most writers other than novelists such as Hugh Garner or Gabrielle Roy. Rex A. Lucas presents a drier sociological anatomy in *Minetown, Milltown, Railtown: Life in Canadian Communities of Single Industry* (T: UTP 1971). Rolf Knight provides some warmer, more revealing vignettes in *Along the No. 20 Line: Reminiscences of the Vancouver Waterfront* (V: New Star 1980). Donna McCririck and Graeme Wynn sketch the emergence of early working-class suburbs in 'Building "Self-Respect and Hopefulness": The Development of Blue-Collar Suburbs in Early Vancouver,' in Wynn, ed., *People, Places, Patterns, Processes: Geographical Perspectives on the Canadian Past* (T: CCP 1990). One local study that looks at working-class community building is Errol Black and Tom Black, 'The Making of the East End Community Club,' *Labour* 1983. W.E. Mann describes a postwar inner-city neighbourhood in 'The Social System of a Slum: The Lower Ward, Toronto,' in S.D. Clark, ed., *Urbanism and the Changing Canadian Community* (T: UTP 1961). A rare snapshot of Toronto's Anglo-Saxon working-class householders at the end of the 1960s appears in James Lorimer and Myfanwy Phillips, *Working People: Life in a Downtown City Neighbourhood* (T: James Lewis and Samuel 1971). Photographic collections on working-class life can often capture the special qualities of local working-class communities; see especially the Working Lives Collective, *Working Lives*; Heron et al., *All That Our Hands Have Done*; Leslie Shedden, *Mining Photographs and Other Pictures, 1948–1968: A Selection from the Negative Archives of Sheddon Studio, Glace Bay, Cape Breton*, edited by Benjamin H.D. Buchlock and Robert Wilkie (H: Press of the Nova Scotia College of Art and Design/University College of Cape Breton Press 1983); and Alan Noon, *East of Adelaide: Photographs of Com-*

mercial, Industrial, and Working-Class Urban Ontario, 1905–1930 (London: London Regional Art and Historical Museums 1989).

Some of the best discussions of community building in working-class neighbourhoods can be found in the new writing on ethnicity. David Frank provides an exemplary study of the weaving of ethnic and working-class history in 'Tradition and Culture in the Cape Breton Mining Community in the Early Twentieth Century,' in Kenneth Donovan, ed., *Cape Breton at 200: Historical Essays in Honour of the Island's Bicentennial, 1785–1985* (Sydney: University College of Cape Breton Press 1985). Ross McCormack reminds us of the ethnic ties of English newcomers in 'Cloth Caps and Jobs: The Ethnicity of English Immigrants in Canada, 1900–1914,' in Jorgen Dahlie and Tissa Fernando, eds., *Ethnicity, Power, and Politics in Canada* (T: Methuen 1981). Robert F. Harney has drawn together a useful collection of ethnic neighbourhood portraits in *Gathering Place: Peoples and Neighbourhoods of Toronto, 1834–1945* (T: MHSO 1985). See also Bruno Ramirez and Michael Del Balso, *The Italians of Montreal: From Sojourning to Settlement, 1900–1921* (M: Editions du Courant 1980). Women's roles in these communities are discussed by the various contributors to Jean Burnet, ed., *Looking into My Sister's Eyes: An Exploration in Women's History* (T: MHSO 1986), and in Varpu Lindström-Best, *Defiant Sisters: A Social History of Finnish Immigrant Women in Canada* (T: MHSO 1988).

The popular culture in which Canadian workers participated was rich and varied. Donald G. Wetherell and Irene Kmet touch on many facets of it in *Useful Pleasures: The Shaping of Leisure in Alberta, 1896–1945* (R: CPRC 1990), although without always making clear the class boundaries of leisure activities that are described more insightfully in Robert A.J. McDonald, '"Holy Retreat" or "Practical Breathing Spot"?: Class Perceptions of Vancouver's Stanley Park, 1910–1913,' *CHR* 1984. See also Yvan Lamonde, Lucia Ferretti, and Daniel Leblanc, *La culture ouvrière à Montrèal (1880–1920): bilan historiographique* (Q: IQRC 1982). Respectable pursuits have only slowly been studied more closely. On the continuing working-class interest in education, see Jean Barman, '"Knowledge is Essential for Universal Progress but Fatal to Class Privilege": Working People and the Schools in Vancouver during the 1920s,' *Labour* 1988; Bill Maciejko, 'Public Schools and the Workers' Struggle: Winnipeg, 1914–1921,' in Nancy M. Sheehan et al., eds., *Schools in the West: Essays in Canadian Educational History* (C: Detselig 1986); George L. Cook with Marjorie Robinson, '"The Fight of My Life": Alfred Fitzpatrick and Frontier College's Extramural Degree for Working People,' *HS/SH* 1990;

Michael R. Welton, ed., *Knowledge for the People; The Struggle for Adult Learning in English-Speaking Canada, 1828–1973* (T: OISE Press 1987); and Hayden Roberts, *Culture and Adult Education: A Study of Alberta and Quebec* (E: UAP 1982). The literary side of working-class communities is explored in F.W. Watt, 'The Literature of Protest,' in C.F. Klinck, ed., *Literary History of Canada: Canadian Literature in English*, vol. 1 (2nd ed., T: UTP 1976); Ron Verzuh, *Radical Rag: The Pioneer Labour Press in Canada* (O: Steel Rail Press 1988); Dawn Fraser, *Echoes from Labor's Wars: Industrial Cape Breton in the 1920s: Narrative Verse* (T: New Hogtown Press 1976); N. Brian Davis, ed., *The Poetry of the Canadian People, 1720–1920: Two Hundred Years of Hard Work* (T: NC Press 1976), and *The Poetry of the Canadian People, 1900–1950* (T: NC Press 1978); Richard Wright, ed., *Eight Men Speak and Other Plays from the Canadian Workers' Theatre* (T: New Hogtown Press 1976); Toby Gordon Ryan, *Stage Left: Canadian Workers' Theatre, 1929–1940* (T: Simon and Pierre 1985); and Tom Wayman, *Inside Job: Essays on the New Work Writing* (Madiera Park: Harbour Publishing 1983). Studies of the place of religion in working-class communities are scarce; five studies that open up the question in fascinating ways are Lynne Marks's two articles, 'The "Hallelujah Lasses": Working-Class Women in the Salvation Army, 1882–1892,' in Iacovetta and Valverde, eds., *Gender Conflicts*, and 'The Knights of Labor and the Salvation Army: Religion and Working-Class Culture in Ontario, 1882–1890,' *Labour* 1991; Gerard Bouchard, 'Les prêtres, les capitalistes et les ouvriers à Chicoutimi, 1896–1930,' *Le mouvement social* 1980; Benoît Lacroix and Jean Simard, eds., *Religion populaire, religion des clercs?* (Q: IQRC 1984); and Lucia Ferretti, *Entre Voisins: La société paroissiale en milieu urbain: Saint-Pierre-Apotre de Montréal, 1848–1930* (M: BE 1992).

'Rougher' working-class pastimes also deserve more careful attention. The role of alcohol in workers' social lives has unfortunately escaped the kind of thorough study it deserves, but insights can be drawn from Peter DeLottinville, 'Joe Beef of Montreal: Working-Class Culture and the Tavern, 1869–1889,' *Labour* 1981/82, James H. Gray, *Booze: The Impact of Whisky on the Prairie West* (T: MAC 1972); James H. Morrison and James Moreira, eds., *Tempered by Rum: Rum in the History of the Maritime Provinces* (Porters Lake: Pottersfield Press 1988) and Cheryl Krasmich Warsh, ed., *Drink in Canada: Historical Essays* (M and K: MQUP 1993). Male activities tend to predominate in studies of working-class sports; see S.F. Wise, 'Sport and Class Values in Old Ontario and Quebec,' in W.H. Heick and Roger Graham, eds., *His Own Man: Essays in Honour of Arthur Reginald Marsden Lower* (M and K: MQUP 1974); Colin D. Howell, 'Baseball,

Class, and Community in the Maritime Provinces, 1870–1910,' *HS/SH* 1989; Alan Metcalfe's numerous publications, especially 'Leisure, Sport, and Working-Class Culture: Some Insights from Montreal and the North-East Coalfield of England,' in Hart Cantelon and Robert Hollands, eds., *Leisure, Sport, and Working-Class Cultures: Theory and History* (T: Garamond Press 1988); 'Organized Sport and Social Stratification in Montreal: 1840–1901,' in Richard S. Gruneau and John G. Albinson, eds., *Canadian Sport: Sociological Perspectives* (Don Mills: Addison-Wesley 1976); and Alan Metcalfe, *Canada Learns to Play: The Emergence of Organized Sport, 1807–1914* (T: M&S 1987). The music in workers' lives has been studied in Edith Fowke, 'Labor and Industrial Protest Songs in Canada,' *Journal of American Folklore* 1969; David Frank, 'The Industrial Folk Song in Cape Breton,' *Canadian Folklore Canadien* 1986; and John Gilmore, *Swinging in Paradise: The Story of Jazz in Montreal* (M: Véhicule 1988). Thomas W. Dunk has drawn a finely textured portrait of the informal social life of modern male workers in *It's a Working Man's Town: Male Working-Class Culture in Northwestern Ontario* (M and K: MQUP 1991).

Moral regulation of much of this working-class popular culture has a long history. Bryan D. Palmer suggests the possibilities of a self-regulated morality in 'plebian' communities in 'Discordant Music: Charivaris and Whitecapping in Nineteenth-Century North America,' *Labour* 1978. Most writing, however, has focused on outside intervention. Curbing the consumption of alcohol was one such concern discussed in E.R. Forbes, 'Prohibition and the Social Gospel in Nova Scotia,' *Acadiensis* 1971, and in Gerald A. Hallowell, *Prohibition in Ontario, 1919–1923* (O: Ontario Historical Society 1972). The equally determined sabbatarian campaigns are treated in Christopher Armstrong and H.V. Nelles, *The Revenge of the Methodist Bicycle Company: Sunday Streetcars and Municipal Reform in Toronto, 1888–1897* (T: Peter Martin Associates 1977); Barbara Schrodt, 'Sabbatarianism and Sport in Canadian Society,' *Journal of Sport History* 1977; and Gene Howard Homel, 'Sliders and Backsliders: Toronto's Sunday Tobogganing Controversy of 1912,' *UHR* 1981. Carolyn Strange presents a fascinating analysis of the moral scrutiny of leisure and courtship patterns of 'working girls' in 'From Modern Babylon to a City upon a Hill: The Toronto Social Survey Commission of 1915 and the Search for Sexual Order in the City,' in Roger Hall et al., eds., *Patterns of the Past: Interpreting Ontario's History* (T: Dundurn 1988); see also Andrée Lévesque, 'Eteindre le "Red Light": les réformateurs et la prostitution à Montréal, 1865–1925,' *UHR* 1989; John P.S. McLaren, 'Chasing the Social Evil: Moral Fervour and the Evolution of Canada's Prostitution Laws, 1867–

1917,' *Canadian Journal of Law and Society* 1986; James H. Gray, *Red Lights on the Prairies* (T: MAC 1971); and S.W. Horrall, 'The (Royal) North-West Mounted Police and Prostitution on the Canadian Prairies,' *Prairie Forum* 1985. Malcolm Dean surveys the censorship of movies, a popular form of working-class entertainment, in *Censored! Only in Canada: The History of Film Censorship – the Scandal off the Screen* (T: Virgo Press 1981). For the role and attitudes of the police and police courts that had to implement much of the moral legislation aimed at working-class behaviour, see Paul Craven, 'Law and Ideology: The Toronto Police Court, 1850–80,' in David H. Flaherty, ed., *Essays in the History of Canadian Law*, vol. 2, (T: UTP 1983); John Weaver, 'Social Control, Martial Conformity, and Community Entanglement: The Varied Beats of the Hamilton Police, 1895–1920,' *UHR* 1990; Gene Howard Homel, 'Denison's Law: Criminal Justice and the Police Court in Toronto, 1877–1921,' *OH* 1982; and Dorothy E. Chunn, *From Punishment to Doing Good: Family Courts and Socialized Justice in Ontario, 1880–1940* (T: UTP 1992).

WAGE-EARNERS' STRUGGLES

By far the largest volume of writing on the Canadian working class has explored the world of wage labour and the struggles of organized wage-earners. The first general overviews of organized wage-earners' history were the political economist Harold A. Innis's edited collection, *Labor in Canadian-American Relations* (T: RP 1937), the labour economist H.A. Logan's *Trade Unions in Canada: Their Development and Functioning* (T: MAC 1948), and the political activist Charles Lipton's *The Trade Union Movement of Canada, 1827–1959* (4th ed., T: NC Press 1978). Two short pamphlets cover some of the same terrain: Eugene A. Forsey, *The Canadian Labour Movement, 1812–1902* (O: CHA 1974), and Irving M. Abella, *The Canadian Labour Movement, 1902–60* (O: CHA 1975). A brief overview that attempts to integrate these workers' movements into a wider social history is Craig Heron, *The Canadian Labour Movement: A Short History* (T: JL 1989). In the 1960s, Eugene Forsey set out to document the whole nineteenth-century Canadian labour movement and produced a massive compilation of scarcely digested detail, which was eventually published in abridged form as *Trade Unions in Canada, 1812–1902* (T: UTP 1982). It remains a useful, if dense, reference source. Gloria Montero put together a more anecdotal version of the twentieth-century story based on oral interviews with key labour leaders in *We Stood Together: First-Hand Accounts of Dramatic Events in Canada's Labour Past* (T: JL 1979). For a lively summary of mid-twentieth-century developments, see Wayne Roberts and John Bullen, 'A Heritage of Hope and Struggle: Workers, Unions, and Politics in Canada, 1930–1982,' in Michael S. Cross and Gregory S. Kealey, eds., *Readings in Canadian Social History*, vol. 5, *Modern Canada, 1930–1980s* (T: M&S 1984). Stuart Marshall Jamieson wrote an extremely useful study of strikes over the course of the twentieth century for the federal Task Force on Labour Relations, *Times of Trouble: Labour Unrest and Industrial Conflict in Canada, 1900–66* (O: Task Force on Labour Relations 1968). Two articles from *Labour* (1987) offer a more statistically rigorous picture of wage-earners' militancy: Bryan D. Palmer, 'Labour Protest and Organization in Nineteenth-Century Canada', and Douglas Cruikshank and Gregory S. Kealey, 'Canadian Strike Statistics, 1891–1950.' Jacques Rouillard presents an interesting interprovincial comparison in 'Le militantisme des travailleurs au Québec et en Ontario, niveau de sydicalisation et mouvement de gréve (1900–1980),' *RHAF* 1983.

Almost every province has its own general history of wage-earners' struggles and workers' movements, usually brimming with fascinating photographs. Moving from east to west, a reader may usefully consult Bill Gillespie, *A Class Act: An Illustrated History of the Labour Movement in Newfoundland and Labrador* (St John's: Newfoundland and Labrador Federation of Labour 1986); Gregory S. Kealey, *The History and Structure of the Newfoundland Labour Movement* (St John's: Royal Commission on Employment and Unemployment, Newfoundland and Labrador 1986); Paul MacEwan, *Miners and Steelworkers: Labour in Cape Breton* (T: Hakkert 1976); Doug Smith, *Let Us Rise!: A History of the Manitoba Labour Movement* (V: New Star 1985); Warren Caragata, *Alberta Labour: A Heritage Untold* (T: JL 1979); and Paul Phillips, *No Power Greater: A Century of Labour in British Columbia* (V: British Columbia Federation of Labour 1967). Quebec's particular development is evident in a reading of Confederation des syndicats nationaux and Centrale de l'enseignement du Québec, *The History of the Labour Movement in Quebec* (M: Black Rose 1987); Jacques Rouillard, *Histoire du syndicalisme au Québec: des origines à nos jours* (M: BE 1989) and his *Histoire de la CSN, 1921–1981* (M: BE 1981); and two collections of essays edited by Fernand Harvey, *Aspects historiques du mouvement ouvrier au Québec* (M: BE 1973), and *Le mouvement ouvrier au Québec: aspects historiques* (M: BE 1980).

Numerous studies in recent years have explored the complex and difficult experience of women wage-earners and their relationship to the male-controlled workers' movements. Many groups of female workers in Quebec are discussed in Nadia Fahmy-Eid and Michèline Dumont, eds.,

Maîtresses de maison, maîtresses d'école: femmes, famille, et éducation dans l'histoire du Québec (M: BE 1983); Marie Lavigne and Yolande Pinard, *Travailleuses et féministes: les femmes dans la société québécoise* (M: BE 1983); and Francoise Barry, *Le travail de la femme au Québec: l'évolution de 1940 à 1970* (M: PUQ 1977). Helpful general discussions of the history of women in unions can be found in Nadia Fahmy-Eid and Lucie Piché, *Si le travail m'était conté autrement: les femmes dans la Confédération des syndicats nationaux depuis 1920* (M: CSN 1987); Sylvie Murray, *A la jonction du mouvement ouvrier et du mouvement des femmes: la ligue auxiliaire de l'Association internationale des machinistes, Canada, 1903-1980* (M: RCHTQ 1990); and Linda Briskin and Lynda Yantz, eds., *Union Sisters: Women in the Labour Movement* (T: Women's Press 1983). By far the most compelling and stimulating study of gender and wage-earning is Joy Parr, *The Gender of Breadwinners: Women, Men, and Change in Two Industrial Towns, 1880–1950* (T: UTP 1990).

Primary Producers

Canadian working-class historians have generally been preoccupied with urban workers and have been slow to investigate the relationship between older forms of production and wage labour. Arthur J. Ray is one of the few to carry the story of Native peoples in the capitalist labour market into the post-Confederation period in his *The Canadian Fur Trade in the Industrial Age* (T: UTP 1990), as do Rolf Knight in *Indians at Work: An Informal History of Native Labour in British Columbia, 1858–1930* (V: New Star 1978); Alicja Muszynski in 'Race and Gender: Structural Determinants in the Formation of British Columbia's Salmon Cannery Labour Force,' in Kealey, ed., *Class, Gender, and Religion*; and John Lutz in 'After the Fur Trade: The Aboriginal Labouring Class of British Columbia, 1849–1890,' *CHAJ* 1992.

The complex connections between agriculture and wage labour are addressed in Allan Greer, 'Fur-Trade Labour and Lower Canadian Agrarian Structures,' CHA *HP* 1981; Marjorie Griffin Cohen, *Women's Work, Markets, and Economic Development in Nineteenth-Century Ontario* (T: UTP 1988); Rusty Bittermann, 'The Hierarchy of the Soil: Land and Labour in a 19th Century Cape Breton Community,' *Acadiensis* 1988; Beatrice Craig, 'Agriculture and the Lumberman's Frontier in the Upper St John Valley, 1800–1870,' *Journal of Forest History* 1988; René Hardy and Normand Séguin, *Forêt et société en Mauricie: la formation de la région de Trois-Rivières, 1830–1930* (M: BE 1984); L.D. McCann, '"Living a Double

Life": Town and Country in the Industrialization of the Maritimes,' in Douglas Day et al., eds., *Geographical Perspectives on the Maritime Provinces* (H: St Mary's University 1988); Bruno Ramirez, *On the Move: French-Canadian and Italian Migrants in the North Atlantic Economy, 1860–1914* (T: M&S 1991); Alan A. Brookes and Catherine A. Wilson, '"Working Away" from the Farm: The Young Women of North Huron, 1910–30,' *OH* 1985; and Everett C. Hughes, *French Canada in Transition* (4th ed., Chicago: University of Chicago Press 1963). The literature on waged labour on farms includes Joy Parr, 'Hired Men: Ontario Agricultural Wage Labour in Historical Perspective,' *Labour* 1985; John Herd Thompson, 'Bringing in the Sheaves: The Harvest Excursionists, 1890–1929,' *CHR* 1978; W.J.C. Chernwinski, 'In Search of Jake Trumper: The Farm Hand and the Prairie Farm Family'; and Cecilia Danysk, '"Showing These Slaves Their Class Position": Barriers to Organizing Prairie Farm Workers,' both in David C. Jones and Ian MacPherson, eds., *Building beyond the Homestead: Rural History on the Prairies* (C: UCP 1985).

The primary producers of the fishing industry have enjoyed considerable attention recently. The early years get careful scrutiny in Rosemary E. Ommer, ed., *Merchant Credit and Labour Strategies in Historical Perspective* (F: AP 1990). The growing 'semi-proletarianization' of these people is addressed in Alicja Muszynski, 'Class Formation and Class Consciousness: The Making of Shoreworkers in the BC Fishing Industry,' *Studies in Political Economy* 1986; and 'The Organization of Women and Ethnic Minorities in a Resource Industry: A Case Study of the Unionization of Shoreworkers in the BC Fishing Industry, 1937–1949,' *JCS* 1984; L. Gene Barrett, 'Underdevelopment and Social Movements in the Nova Scotia Fishing Industry to 1938,' in R.J. Brym and R. James Sacouman, eds., *Underdevelopment and Social Movements in Atlantic Canada* (T: New Hogtown Press 1979); and Barbara Neis, 'Competitive Merchants and Class Struggle in Newfoundland,' *Studies in Political Economy* 1981. The long series of producers' organizations in the industry are described in Ian D.H. McDonald, *'To Each His Own': William Coaker and the Fishermen's Protective Union in Newfoundland Politics, 1908–1925* (St John's: ISER 1987); Wallace Clement, *The Struggle to Organize: Resistance in Canada's Fishery* (T: M&S 1986); Gordon Inglis, *More Than Just a Union: The Story of the NFFAWU* (St John's: Jesperson Press 1985); Silver Donald Cameron, *The Education of Everett Richardson: The Nova Scotia Fishermen's Strike, 1970–71* (T: M&S 1977); David Macdonald, *Power begins at the Cod End: The Newfoundland Trawlermen's Strike, 1974–75* (St John's: ISER 1980); and Patricia Marchak et al., eds., *Uncommon Property: The Fishing and Fish-*

Processing Industries in British Columbia (V: Methuen 1987). Gender dimensions in fishing are examined in Hilda Murray, *More Than 50%: Woman's Life in a Newfoundland Outport, 1900–1950* (St John's: Breakwater Books 1979); Martha MacDonald and M. Patricia Connelly, 'Class and Gender in Fishing Communities in Nova Scotia,' *Studies in Political Economy* 1989; and Marilyn Porter, '"She Was the Skipper of the Shore-Crew": Notes on the History of the Sexual Division of Labour in Newfoundland,' *Labour* 1985.

1850–1890

For a fascinating introduction to nineteenth-century wage earning (and many other features of working-class life), readers should consult Gregory S. Kealey's abridged version of testimony presented to the Royal Commission on the Relations of Labour and Capital in the late 1880s, *Canada Investigates Industrialism: The Royal Commission on the Relations of Labor and Capital, 1889 (Abridged)* (T: UTP 1973). Fernand Harvey analyses the Quebec evidence in *Révolution industrielle et travailleurs: une enquête sur les rapports entre le capital et le travail au Québec à la fin du 19e siècle* (M: BE 1978). Various studies have brought to light the working lives of particular groups of wage-earners. Sailors have been treated to thorough analysis in Judith Fingard, *Jack in Port: Sailortowns of Eastern Canada* (T: UTP 1982) and Eric W. Sager, *Seafaring Labour: The Merchant Marine of Atlantic Canada, 1820–1914* (M and K: MQUP 1989), while most of the essays in Rosemary E. Ommer and Gerald Panting, eds., *Working Men Who Got Wet* (St John's: Maritime History Group 1980) are densely statistical and much less informative.

Aside from Marjorie Cohen's *Women's Work, Markets, and Economic Development*, the only book-length study of women's waged work in nineteenth-century Canada is Claudette Lacelle, *Urban Domestic Servants in 19th Century Canada* (O: Environment Canada 1987); but see also Bettina Bradbury, 'Women and Wage Labour in a Period of Transition: Montreal, 1861–1881,' *HS/SH* 1984; Susan Trofimenkoff, 'One Hundred and Two Muffled Voices: Canada's Industrial Women in the 1880s,' *Atlantis* 1978; Muszynski, 'Race and Gender'; Michèle Martin, 'Feminization of the Labour Process in the Communications Industry: The Case of the Telephone Operators, 1876–1904,' *Labour* 1988; and several of the essays in Janice Acton et al., eds., *Women at Work: Ontario, 1850–1930* (T: Women's Press 1974). The use of child labour in this period is discussed in Bettina Bradbury, *Working Families*; John Bullen, 'Hidden Workers'; Fernand Harvey, 'Children of the Industrial Revolution in Quebec,' in R. Douglas Francis and Donald B. Smith, eds., *Readings in Canadian History*, vol. 2, *Post-Confederation* (3rd ed., T: HRW 1990); Robert MacIntosh's three articles, 'The Boys in Nova Scotia Coal Mines, 1873–1923,' *Acadiensis* 1987, 'Canada's Boy Miners,' *The Beaver* 1987–8, and '"Grotesque Faces and Figures": Child Labourers and Coal Mining Technology in Victorian Nova Scotia,' *Scientia Canadensis* 1988; Joy Parr, *Labouring Children*; and Lorna Hurl, 'Restricting Child Factory Labour in Late Nineteenth-Century Ontario,' *Labour* 1988.

Mining was one of the important new industries of the industrial age. A largely anecdotal tale of British Columbia's coal miners in this period can be found in Eric Newsome, *The Coal Coast: The History of Coal Mining in BC – 1835–1900* (Vi: Orca Books 1989); for more substantial assessments, see John Douglas Belshaw, 'Mining Techniques and Social Division on Vancouver Island, 1848–1900,' *British Journal of Canadian Studies* 1986, and Jeremy Mouat, 'The Politics of Coal: A Study of the Wellington Miners' Strike of 1890–91,' *BCS* 1988. Elinor Barr opens up the little-known world of the nineteenth-century northern Ontario miner in *Silver Islet: Striking It Rich in Lake Superior* (T: Natural Heritage/Natural History Inc. 1988). Nova Scotia's miners are analysed with more rigour in Del Muise, 'The Making of an Industrial Community: Cape Breton Coal Towns, 1867–1900,' in Don Macgillivray and Brian Tennyson, eds., *Cape Breton Historical Essays* (Sydney: University College of Cape Breton Press 1980); and in Ian McKay's three articles, 'The Crisis of Dependent Development: Class Conflict in the Nova Scotia Coalfields, 1872–1876,' in Kealey, ed., *Class, Gender, and Region*; '"By Wisdom, Wile or War": The Provincial Workmen's Association and the Struggle for Working-Class Independence in Nova Scotia, 1879–97,' *Labour* 1986; and 'The Realm of Uncertainty: The Experience of Work in the Cumberland Coal Mines, 1873–1927,' *Acadiensis* 1986.

Urban industrial workers have stood at the centre of much of the writing on this period. The work experience of Quebec wage-earners in the nineteenth century is chronicled in Noel Bélanger et al., *Les travailleurs québécois, 1851–1896* (2nd ed., M: PUQ 1975); Joanne Burgess, 'L'industrie de la chaussure à Montréal, 1840–1870: le passage de l'artisanat à la fabrique,' *RHAF* 1977; Jacques Ferland's two articles, 'Les Chevaliers de Saint-Crépin du Québec, 1869–71: une étude en trois tableaux,' *CHR*

1991, and 'Syndicalism "parcellaire" et syndicalisme "collectif": une interpretation socio-technique des conflits ouvriers dans deux industries québécoises, 1880–1914,' *Labour* 1987; and Bettina Bradbury, *Working Families*. Peter DeLottinville opens up the lives of New Brunswick cotton-mill workers in 'Trouble in the Hives of Industry: The Cotton Industry Comes to Milltown, New Brunswick, 1879–1892,' *CHAR* 1980. The two most influential community studies of this period cover skilled male workers in southern Ontario's leading factory centres: Bryan D. Palmer, *A Culture in Conflict: Skilled Workers and Industrial Capitalism in Hamilton, Ontario, 1860–1914* (M and K: MQUP 1979); and Gregory S. Kealey, *Toronto Workers Respond to Industrial Capitalism, 1867–1892* (2nd ed., T: UTP 1991). But, for different perspectives, see also Peter Bischoff, 'La formation des traditions de solidarité ouvrière chez les mouleurs montréalais: la longue marche vers le syndicalisme, 1859–1881,' *Labour* 1988; and Ian McKay's two essays, 'Capital and Labour in the Halifax Baking and Confectionery Industry during the Last Half of the Nineteenth Century,' *Labour* 1978, and 'Class Struggle and Mercantile Capitalism: Craftsmen and Labourers on the Halifax Waterfront, 1850–1900,' in Palmer, ed., *The Character of Class Struggle*. The pattern of strikes in Quebec in the nineteenth century is outlined in Jean Hamelin et al., *Répertoire des grèves dans la province de Québec au XIXe siècle* (M: Presses de l'Ecole des hautes études commerciales 1970).

Some work has concentrated more specifically on the growth of the first institutions of the labour movement, notably Stephen Langdon, 'The Emergence of the Canadian Working-Class Movement, 1845–75,' *JCS* 1973; and John Battye, 'The Nine-Hour Pioneers: The Genesis of the Canadian Labour Movement,' *Labour* 1979. Bernard Ostry penned two early studies of the relations between these unions and the state, which have largely been surpassed by subsequent research: 'Conservatives, Liberals, and Labour in the 1870s,' *CHR* 1960; and 'Conservatives, Liberals, and Labour in the 1880s,' *CJEPS* 1961. Kealey and Palmer have also produced a compelling study of the late-nineteenth-century labour movement in *Dreaming of What Might Be: The Knights of Labour in Ontario, 1880–1900* (2nd ed., T: New Hogtown Press 1987), which overshadows the older, less sophisticated work by Douglas R. Kennedy, *The Knights of Labor in Canada* (London: University of Western Ontario 1956). A briefer parallel study of the Knights in Quebec is available in Fernand Harvey, 'Les Chevaliers du Travail, les Etats-Unis, et la société québécoise, 1882–1902,' in Harvey, *Aspects historiques*. For the English-Canadian labour journalism of this period, see Ron Verzuh, *Radical Rag*.

1890–1925

The early twentieth century has attracted more attention than any other single period in Canadian working-class history, although much of the new scholarship remains in article and thesis form. The new managerial practices of the age have been brought to light in several studies, notably Craig Heron, *Working in Steel: The Early Years in Canada, 1883-1935* (T: M&S 1988); Graham S. Lowe, *Women in the Administrative Revolution: The Feminization of Clerical Work* (T: UTP 1987); and Richard Rajala, 'Managerial Crisis: The Emergence and Role of the West Coast Logging Engineer, 1900–1930,' *Canadian Papers in Business History* (Vi: Public History Group 1989).

One of the first studies of male workers in the period was Edmund Bradwin, *The Bunkhouse Man: A Study of Work and Play in the Camps of Canada, 1903-1914* (1928, T: UTP 1972). Since then, a great deal more scholarly energy has been directed to Western Canadian workers. Indeed a whole historiographical current has emerged to assert the case for 'Western exceptionalism' within Canadian working-class history; see David J. Bercuson, 'Labour Radicalism and the Western Industrial Frontier,' *CHR* 1977; Ross McCormack, 'The Western Working-Class Experience,' in Cherwinski and Kealey, *Lectures in Canadian Labour and Working-Class History*; and H. Clare Pentland, 'The Western Canadian Labour Movement, 1897–1919,' *Canadian Journal of Political and Social Theory* 1979. For a careful reconsideration of this historiographical current, see Jeremy Mouat, 'The Genesis of Western Exceptionalism: British Columbia's Hard-Rock Miners, 1895–1903,' *CHR* 1990. McCormack surveys the radical labour movements that emerged in that region in *Reformers, Rebels, and Revolutionaires: The Western Canadian Radical Movement, 1899–1919* (T: UTP 1977), while Carlos A. Schwantes places them in a cross-border comparison in *Radical Heritage: Labor, Socialism, and Reform in Washington and British Columbia, 1885–1917* (V: Douglas & McIntyre 1979). A more in-depth treatment of one strand of that radicalism can be found in Mark Leier, *Where the Fraser River Flows: The Industrial Workers of the World in British Columbia* (V: New Star 1990). Robert A.J. McDonald assesses the particularities of the West-Coast metropolis in 'Working-Class Vancouver, 1886–1914: Urbanism and Class in British Columbia,' in Patricia E. Roy, ed., *A History of British Columbia: Selected Readings* (T: CCP 1989), while John Norris analyses one crucial strike of the period in 'The Vancouver Island Coal Miners' Strike, 1912–1914,' *BCS* 1980. The Prairie experience gets careful examination in Glen Makahonuk, 'Class Conflict in a

Prairie City: The Saskatoon Working-Class Response to Prairie Capitalism, 1906–19, *Labour* 1987.

A much different picture of central-Canadian labour and its links with
American unions emerges in Robert H. Babcock, *Gompers in Canada: A
Study in American Continentalism before the First World War* (T: UTP 1974).
Craig Heron and Bryan D. Palmer offer a more nuanced reading of
workplace dynamics and workers' responses in that region in 'Through
the Prism of the Strike: Industrial Conflict in Southern Ontario, 1901–
1914,' *CHR* 1977; in a similar vein, see also Craig Heron, 'The Crisis of
the Craftsman: Hamilton Metal Workers in the Early Twentieth Century,'
Labour 1981; and Wayne Roberts's two stimulating analyses of Toronto
craft workers, 'Artisans, Aristocrats, and Handymen: Politics and Unionism among Toronto Skilled Building Trades Workers, 1896–1914,' *Labour*
1976, and 'The Last Artisans: Toronto Printers, 1896–1914,' in Kealey and
Warrian, *Essays in Canadian Working Class History*. Jacques Rouillard discusses the distinctive history of Quebec workers in these years in *Les
travailleurs du coton au Québec, 1900–1915* (M: PUQ 1974) and *Les syndicats
nationaux au Québec de 1900 à 1930* (Q: PUL 1979). See also James
Thwaites, 'La grève au Québec: une analyse quantitative exploratoire
portant sur la période 1896–1915,' *Labour* 1984. The struggles of the
workers in Atlantic Canada are rigorously analysed in Ian McKay's
sweeping article, 'Strikes in the Maritimes, 1901–1914,' *Acadiensis* 1983:
Robert Babcock's two studies of New Brunswick workers, 'The Saint
John Street Railwaymen's Strike and Riot, 1914,' *Acadiensis* 1982, and 'Saint
John Longshoremen during the Rise of Canada's Winter Port, 1895–
1922,' *Labour* 1990; Melvin Baker et al., *Workingmen's St. John's: Aspects of
Social History in the Early 1900s* (St John's: Harry Cuff Publications 1982);
and Jessie Chisholm, 'Organizing on the Waterfront: The St. John's
Longshoremen's Protective Union (LPSU), 1890–1914,' *Labour* 1990. J.H.
Tuck explores the early union experience of railway workers in 'Canadian
Railways and Unions in the Running Trades, 1865–1914,' *Ri/IR* 1981; 'The
United Brotherhood of Railway Employees in Western Canada, 1898–
1905,' *Labour* 1983; and 'Union Authority, Corporate Obstinacy, and the
Grand Trunk Strike of 1910,' CHA *HP* 1976. Bill Doherty discusses the
first stirrings of organization among federal civil servants in *Slaves of
the Lamp: A History of the Federal Civil Service Organizations, 1865–1924*
(Vi: Orca Books 1991).

Women wage-earners in this period are treated in Wayne Roberts's
path-breaking pamphlet, *Honest Womanhood: Feminism, Femininity, and Class
Consciousness among Toronto Working Women, 1893–1914* (T: New Hogtown

Press 1976); see also contributions to Acton et al., eds., *Women at Work: Ontario 1850–1930*; Jennifer Stoddart, 'Ouvrières et travailleuses montréalaises, 1900–1940,' in Marie Lavigne and Yolande Pinard, *Travailleuses et féministes* (M: BE 1983); Mercedes Steedman, 'Skill and Gender in the Canadian Clothing Industry, 1890–1940,' in Heron and Storey, *On the Job*; Gillian Cresse, 'The Politics of Dependence: Women, Work, and Unemployment in the Vancouver Labour Market before World War II,' *Canadian Journal of Sociology* 1988. *Labour* has published several useful articles on wage-earning women: three in 1989, Michele Dagenais, 'Itineraires professionels masculins et féminins en milieu bancaire: le cas de la Banque d'Hochelega, 1900–1929'; Margaret McCallum, 'Separate Spheres: The Organization of Work in a Confectionery Factory: Ganong Bros., St Stephen, N.B.'; and Jacques Ferland's challenging interpretation of structural constraints in the labour process, '"In Search of Unbound Promethia": A Comparative View of Women's Activism in Two Quebec Industries, 1869–1908'; and in 1991, Shirley Tillotson, '"We May All Soon Be 'First Class Men'": Gender and Skill in Canada's Early Twentieth Century Urban Telegraph Industry.' Their difficulties in overcoming the sexism of male trade unionists in this period are documented in Joan Sangster, 'The 1907 Bell Telephone Strike: Organizing Women Workers,' *Labour* 1978; Marie Campbell, 'Sexism in British Columbia Trade Unions, 1900–1920,' in Barbara K. Latham and Cathy Kess, eds., *In Her Own Right: Selected Essays on Women's History in BC* (Vi: Camosun College 1980); Mary Horodyski, 'Women and the Winnipeg General Strike of 1919,' *Manitoba History* 1986; Linda Kealey, 'No Special Protection – No Sympathy': Women's Activism in the Canadian Labour Revolt of 1919,' in Hopkin and Kealey, *Class, Community, and the Labour Movement*; and Ruth A. Frager's two penetrating studies of union culture, 'No Proper Deal: Women Workers and the Canadian Labour Movement, 1870–1940,' in Briskin and Yanz, *Union Sisters*; and *Sweatshop Strife: Class, Ethnicity, and Gender in the Jewish Labour Movement of Toronto, 1900–1939* (T: UTP 1992).

The difficult cross-currents of race and ethnicity have also been examined in Robert Harney, 'Montreal's King of Italian Labour: A Case Study of Padronism,' *Labour* 1979; Jean Morrison, 'Ethnicity and Violence: The Lakehead Freight Handlers before World War I,' in Kealey and Warrian, *Essays in Canadian Working Class History*; Stanley Scott, 'A Profusion of Issues: Immigrant Labour, the World War, and the Cominco Strike of 1917,' *Labour* 1977; Donald Avery, *'Dangerous Foreigners': European Immigrant Workers and Labour Radicalism in Canada, 1896–1932* (T: M&S 1979); Allen Seager, 'Class, Ethnicity, and Politics in the Alberta Coalfields,

1905–1945,' in Dirk Hoerder, ed., 'Struggle a Hard Battle': Essays on Working-Class Immigrants (DeKalb, Northern Illinois UP 1986); W. Peter Ward, 'Class and Race in the Social Structure of British Columbia,' BCS 1980; Jin Tan, 'Chinese Labour and the Reconstituted Social Order of British Columbia,' Canadian Ethnic Studies 1987; Gillian Creeses's excellent articles, 'Organizing against Racism in the Workplace: Chinese Workers in Vancouver before the Second World War,' Canadian Ethnic Studies 1987; 'Class, Ethnicity, and Conflict: The Case of Chinese and Japanese Immigrants, 1880–1923,' in Warburton and Coburn, eds., Workers, Capital, and the State; and 'Exclusion of Solidarity? Vancouver Workers Confront the "Oriental Problem,"' BCS 1988; and Agnes Calliste, 'Sleeping Car Porters in Canada: An Ethnically Submerged Split Labour Market,' Canadian Ethnic Studies 1987.

There has been a great outpouring of research and writing on the working-class revolt at the end of World War I. D.C. Masters first explored the most famous incident of the period in The Winnipeg General Strike (T: UTP 1950). David Jay Bercuson presents a fuller treatment that situates the strike in the history of the city's industrial relations in Confrontation at Winnipeg: Labour, Industrial Relations, and the General Strike (2nd ed., M and K: MQUP 1990). In this book, and in Fools and Wise Men: The Rise and Fall of the One Big Union (T: MHR 1878), Bercuson also attacks the left-wing leadership of the Western Canadian labour movement for deflecting the revolt along fruitless radical paths. By contrast, Norman Penner emphasizes the radical politics of the Winnipeg strike, and the period in general, in his introduction to Winnipeg 1919: The Strikers' Own History of the Winnipeg General Strike (T: James Lewis and Samuel 1973). Gregory Kealey broadens this argument to the whole country in his challenging article, '1919: The Canadian Labour Revolt,' Labour 1984. He also contests the claim by McCormick, Bercuson, and others that this was a purely Western revolt. Many other historians now make the same argument, most notably David Frank, 'Class Conflict in the Coal Industry: Cape Breton, 1922,' in Kealey and Warrian, Essays in Canadian Working Class History; Nolan Reilly, 'The General Strike in Amherst, Nova Scotia, 1919,' Acadiensis 1980; Suzanne Morton, 'Labourism and Economic Action: The Halifax Shipyards Strike of 1920,' Labour 1988; and James Naylor, The New Democracy: Challenging the Social Order in Industrial Ontario, 1914–25 (T: UTP 1991). Larry Peterson sets much of this activity in a wider context in 'The One Big Union in International Perspective: Revolutionary Industrial Unionism, 1900–1925,' Labour 1981.

1925–1950

This period of wage-earners' history fell into two distinct phases: the agonizing failures of the 1920s and 1930s and the breakthroughs of the 1940s. Some of the managerial adjustments inaugurated during the post–World War I revolt are surveyed in Margaret McCallum, 'Corporate Welfarism in Canada, 1919–1939,' *CHR* 1990; for more sensitive local studies, see the following articles published in *Labour*: Bruce Scott, '"A Place in the Sun": The Industrial Council at Massey-Harris, 1919–1929,' 1976; Robert Storey, 'Unionization versus Corporate Welfare: The "Dofasco Way,"' 1983; and José Igartua, 'La mobilité professionnelle des travailleurs de l'aluminium à Arvida, 1925–1940,' 1987. Women's wage-earning experience during these years is covered in Veronica Strong-Boag, 'The Girl of the New Day: Canadian Working Women in the 1920s,' *Labour* 1979; Marie Lavigne and Jennifer Stoddart, 'Les travailleuses montréalaises entre les deux guerres,' *Labour* 1977; Gail Cuthbert Brandt's three valuable articles, 'Weaving It Together: Life Cycle and the Industrial Experience of Female Cotton Workers Workers in Quebec, 1910–1950,' *Labour* 1981, 'The Transformation of Women's Work in the Quebec Cotton Industry, 1920–1950,' in Palmer, *The Character of Class Struggle*, and '"Pigeon-Holed and Forgotten": The Work of the Subcommittee on the Post-War Problems of Women, 1943' *HS/SH* 1982; Joy Parr, *Gender of Breadwinners*; Ruth Roach Pierson's pioneering articles, 'Women's Emancipation and the Recruitment of Women into the Canadian Labour Force in World War II,' CHA *AR* 1976, and, with Marjorie Cohen, 'Educating Women for Work: Government Training Programs for Women before, during, and after World War II,' in Cross and Kealey, *Readings in Canadian Social History*, vol. 5; and Nancy Forestell, 'The Necessity of Sacrifice for the Nation at War: Women's Labour Force Participation, 1939–1946,' *HS/SH* 1989.

Organizing the unemployed has been a major theme in the writing on the 1930s. Two excellent pamphlets document the struggles of families on relief: Patricia V. Schulz, *The East York Workers' Association: A Response to the Great Depression* (T: New Hogtown Press 1975), and Carmela Patrias, *Relief Strike: Immigrant Workers and the Great Depression in Cowland, Ontario 1930–1935* (T: New Hogtown Press 1990). Sean Cadigan looks at another local struggle in Newfoundland in 'Battle Harbour in Transition: Merchants, Fishermen, and the State in the Struggle for Relief in a Labrador Community during the 1930s,' *Labour* 1990; while Gordon Hak considers activity on the West Coast in 'The Communists and the Unemployed in the Prince George District, 1930–1935,' *BCS* 1985–6. Irene Howard resurrects women's particular role in this kind of agitation in 'The Mothers' Council of Vancouver: Holding the Fort for the Unemployed,' *BCS* 1986. For the story of the battles of single unemployed men, see Victor Howard, *'We Were the Salt of the Earth!': A Narrative of the On-to-Ottawa Trek and the Regina Riot* (R: CPRC 1985) and Lorne Brown, *When Freedom Was Lost: The Unemployed, the Agitator, and the State* (M: Black Rose 1987).

Several books are now available on the efforts of wage-earners to organize on the job in this period. Don Taylor and Bradley Dow produced a brief, disappointing synthesis of much of this history: *The Rise of Industrial Unionism in Canada – A History of the CIO* (K: Industrial Relations Centre, Queen's University 1988). Irving Martin Abella offers a more useful examination of the major political battles within the new industrial unions of this period in *Nationalism, Communism, and Canadian Labour: The CIO, the Communist Party, and the Canadian Congress of Labour, 1935–1956* (T: UTP 1973). Unfortunately there is no comparable study of the developments within craft-union organizations, especially the Trades and Labor Congress of Canada. Numerous writers have spotlighted organizing efforts in specific industries and localities. Abella's collection of essays reveals some moments of major industrial conflict: *On Strike: Six Key Labour Struggles in Canada, 1919–1949* (T: James Lewis and Samuel 1974). Allen Seager has produced fascinating studies of coal miners' struggles in 'Class, Ethnicity, and Politics' and 'Minto, New Brunswick: A Study in Class Relations between the Wars,' *Labour* 1980. Michael Earle tells the story of East-Coast miners in 'The Coalminers and Their "Red" Union: The Amalgamated Mine Workers at Nova Scotia, 1932–1936,' *Labour* 1988, while Robert Robson discusses the Prairies' hardrock miners in 'Strike in a Single Enterprise Community: Flin Flon, Manitoba – 1934,' *Labour* 1981/2. For another local study, see Richard C. McCanless, 'Vancouver's "Red Menace" of 1935: The Waterfront Situation,' *BCS* 1974. Myrtle Woodward Bergren brought to light the BC loggers' story in *Tough Timber: The Loggers of BC – Their Story* (2nd ed., V: Elgin 1979) but a fuller account is available in Jerry Lembcke and William M. Tattam, *One Union in Wood: A Political History of the International Woodworkers of America* (Madeira Park: Harbour Publishing 1984). Evelyn Dumas describes the difficult labour battles in Quebec in *The Bitter Thirties in Quebec* (M: Black Rose 1975). Terry Copp sketches the particular Montreal experience in 'The Rise of Industrial Unions in Montreal, 1935–1945,' *Ri/IR* 1982.

Ontario factory workers' unionizing efforts get some attention in John Manley, 'Communists and Autoworkers: The Struggle for Industrial Unionism in the Canadian Automobile Industry, 1925–36, *Labour* 1986; Duart Snow, 'The Holmes Foundry Strike of March 1937,' *OH* 1977; Terry Copp, ed., *Industrial Unionism in Kitchener, 1937–47* (Elora: Cumnock Press 1976); and Robert H. Storey, 'The Struggle to Organize Stelco and Dofasco,' *Ri/IR* 1987. Laurel Sefton MacDowell provides thorough accounts of pivotal wartime strikes in *'Remember Kirkland Lake':* *The Gold Miners' Strike of 1941–42* (T: UTP 1983), and 'The 1943 Steel Strike against Wartime Wage Controls,' *Labour* 1982. Two memorable confrontations from the later 1940s are dissected in Pierre Elliott Trudeau, ed., *The Asbestos Strike* (1965, T: James Lewis and Samuel 1974); and Eileen Sufrin, *The Eaton Drive: The Campaign to Organize Canada's Largest Department Store, 1948–1952* (T: Fitzhenry and Whiteside 1982). The impact of the Cold War on the labour movement in the late 1940s gets its fullest treatment in Abella's books and in the publications on the radical Canadian Seamen's Union and its gangster-led successor, the Seafarers' International Union, especially Jim Green's sympathetic portrait of the Communist-led union, *Against the Tide: The Story of the Canadian Seamen's Union* (T: Progress Books 1986) and William Kaplan's more anti-Communist treatment, *Everything That Floats: Pat Sullivan, Hal Banks, and the Seamen's Unions of Canada* (T: UTP 1987). See also Mike Solski and John Smaller, *Mine Mill: The History of the International Union of Mine, Mill, and Smelter Workers in Canada since 1895* (O: Steel Rail Press 1985); and Terry Copp, *The IUE in Canada: A History* (Elora: Cumnock Press 1980).

1950–1975

By the early 1950s, the much enlarged labour movement had won a solid place for itself in many industries and most regions. Useful studies of unions that were consolidated in this postwar period include: Bill Freeman, *1005: Political Life in a Union Local* (T: JL 1982); Jean Gérin-Lajoie, *Les métallos, 1936–1981* (M: BE 1982); and Wayne Roberts, *Cracking the Canadian Formula: The Making of the Energy and Chemical Workers Union* (T: Between the Lines 1990). Guy Belanger presents a useful reminder that not all unions enjoyed such acceptance and stability in 'La grève de Murdochville (1957),' *Labour* 1981/2. Outside the largely ahistorical work of industrial relations writers, relatively little has been published on the years of quiet institutional consolidation in the 1950s and early 1960s. David Kwavnick presents a dry discussion of labour lobbying in *Organized*

Labour and Pressure Politics: The Canadian Labour Congress, 1956–1968 (M and K: MQUP 1972). The essays in Richard Miller and Fraser Isbester, eds., *Canadian Labour in Transition* (T: PH 1971) suggest some of the new developments, although without much analytical profundity.

The new directions in unions, especially the radicalization and sensitivity to American control, are outlined in Robert Laxer, *Canada's Unions* (T: JL 1976); Bank Book Collective, *An Account to Settle: The Story of the United Bank Workers (SORWUC)* (V: Press Gang 1979); and David Kettler et al., 'Unionization and Labour Regimes in Canada and the United States: Considerations for Comparative Research,' *Labour* 1990. The rise of public-sector unionism in the 1960s deserves more attention than it has so far received. Bruce McLean presents an official history in *'A Union amongst Government Employees': A History of the British Columbia Government Employees Union, 1919–1979* (Burnaby: BC Government Employees' Union 1979). The Nova Scotia counterpart gets more detached treatment in Anthony Thomson's two articles, 'The Nova Scotia Civil Service Association, 1956–1967,' *Acadiensis* 1983, and 'From Civil Servants to Government Employees: N.S.G.E.A., 1967–1973,' in Earle, *Workers and the State*. The major new federal union is discussed in Maurice Lemelin, *The Public Service Alliance of Canada: A Look at a Union in the Public Sector* (Los Angeles: Institute of Industrial Relations, University of California 1978). The new female activism in Canadian unionism in this period is discussed in Heather Jon Maroney, 'Feminism at Work,' in Palmer, *The Character of Class Struggle*, and Julie White, *Mail and Female: Women and the Canadian Union of Postal Workers* (T: Thompson Educational Publishing 1990).

Several writers have been particularly interested in the wave of militancy that lasted from the mid-1960s to the mid-1970s. John H.G. Crispo and H.W. Arthurs gave the early orthodox interpretation in 'Industrial Unrest in Canada: A Diagnosis of Recent Experience,' *Ri/IR* 1968. G.F. MacDowell considers one particularly bitter incident in *The Brandon Packers' Strike: A Tragedy of Errors* (T: M&S 1971). Walter Johnson brings together lively studies of different settings in *The Trade Unions and the State*, and *Working in Canada* (M: Black Rose 1978, 1975). C.H.J. Gilson, ed., does the same for Nova Scotia in *Strikes: Industrial Relations in Nova Scotia, 1957–1987* (Hantsport: Lancelot 1987). Robert Lacroix assesses the whole wave of militancy in *Les grèves au Canada: causes et conséquences* (M: PUM 1987).

The dramatic explosions of Quebec labour can be traced in Emile Boudreau and Leo Roback, *L'histoire de la FTQ: des tout débuts jusqu'en 1965* (M: FTQ 1988); H. Tremblay, *Le syndicalisme québécois: idéologies de la CSN et de la FTQ, 1940–1970* (M: PUM 1972); Jean-François Cardin,

La crise d'Octobre 1970 et le mouvement syndical québécois (M: RCHTQ 1988); Daniel Drache, ed., *Quebec: Only the Beginning: The Manifestoes of the Common Front* (T: New Press 1972); André Beaucage, *Syndicats, salaires, et conjuncture économique: l'expérience des fronts communs du secteur public québécois de 1971 à 1983* (Sillery: PUQ 1989); and Carla Lipsig-Mumme, 'Quebec Unions and the State: Conflict and Dependence,' *Studies in Political Economy* 1980.

POST-1975

Around 1975 Canadian workers and their unions began to face new pressures from their employers and the state. Some of their responses are discussed in Bryan D. Palmer, *Solidarity: The Rise and Fall of an Opposition in British Columbia* (V: New Star 1987); Jerry White, *Hospital Strike: Women, Unions, and Public Sector Conflict* (T: Thompson Educational Publishing 1990); Robert Argue et al., eds., *Working People and Hard Times: Canadian Perspectives* (T: Garamond Press 1987); Jacob Finkelman and Shirley B. Goldenberg, eds., *Collective Bargaining in the Public Service: The Federal Experience in Canada* (M: Institute for Research on Public Policy 1983); Mark Thompson and Gene Swimmer, eds., *Conflict or Compromise: The Future of Public Sector Industrial Relations* (M: Institute for Research on Public Policy 1984); Gregg M. Olsen, ed., *Industrial Change and Labour Adjustment in Sweden and Canada* (T: Garamond Press 1988); Miriam Smith, 'The Canadian Labour Congress: From Continentalism to Economic Nationalism,' *Studies in Political Economy* 1992; and several of the essays in Daniel Drache and Meric S. Gertler, eds., *The New Era of Global Competition: State Policy and Market Power* (M and K: MQUP 1991). For the perspective of the discipline of industrial relations on the emerging industrial relations 'system' in Canada, see John C. Anderson, Morley Gunderson, and Allen Ponak, eds., *Union-Management Relations in Canada* (2nd ed., Don Mills, Addison-Wesley 1989). These developments are surveyed regularly in Pradeep Kumar et al., *The Industrial Relations Scene in Canada* (K: Industrial Relations Centre, Queen's University annual).

INDUSTRY AND UNION STUDIES

Numerous books have appeared that cover the history of workers in one union or one industry over many decades. One of the best in situating union developments within a larger social and economic context is Ian McKay, *The Craft Transformed: An Essay on the Carpenters of Halifax, 1885-*

1985 (H: Holdfast Press 1985). Much narrower in focus is Sally F. Zerker, *The Rise and Fall of the Toronto Typographical Union, 1832–1972: A Case Study of Foreign Domination* (T: UTP 1982). Elaine Bernard provides a rich analysis of telephone company workers over the course of the twentieth century in *The Long Distance Feeling: A History of the Telecommunications Workers Union* (V: New Star 1982). William E. Greening wrote two early but still somewhat useful union histories: *Paper Makers in Canada: A History of the Paper Makers Union in Canada* (Cornwall: International Brotherhood of Paper Makers 1952) and, with M.M. Maclean, *It Was Never Easy, 1908–1958: A History of the Canadian Brotherhood of Railway, Transport, and General Workers* (O: Mutual Press 1961). Lynne Bowen has made extensive use of oral history to rediscover the story of Vancouver Island coal miners since the turn of the century in two books, *Boss Whistle: The Coal Miners of Vancouver Island Remember* and *Three Dollar Dreams* (Lantzville: Oolichan Books 1982, 1987). Jean Bourassa tackles the Quebec miner in *Le travailleur minier, la culture, et le savoir ouvrier: quatres analyses de cas* (Q: IQRC 1982), while Gail Weir brings a group of East Coast miners to light in *The Miners of Wabana: The Story of the Iron Ore Miners of Bell Island* (St John's: Breakwater Books 1989). Donald MacKay surveys the colourful history of Canadian loggers in *The Lumberjacks* (T: MHR 1978). The workers in Quebec's forest industries are extensively covered in Gilbert Vanasse, *Histoire de la Fédération des travailleurs du papier et de la forêt*, tome 1, *1907–1958* (M: Editions Saint Martin 1986), and those in the aluminum industry in Luc Coté, *Les enjeux du travail à l'Alcan, 1901-1951* (Hull: Editions Asticou 1990). ILWU Local 500 Pensioners put together *'Man along the Shore': The Story of the Vancouver Waterfront as Told by Longshoremen Themselves, 1860s–1975* (V: ILWU Local 500 Pensioners 1975).

Salaried professionals still await more attention, but teachers have come into fuller light in Marta Danylewycz, Beth Light, and Alison Prentice, 'The Evolution of the Sexual Division of Labour in Teaching: A Nineteenth-Century Ontario and Quebec Case Study,' *HS/SH* 1983; Susan Gelman, 'The "Feminization" of the High Schools? Women Secondary School Teachers in Toronto, 1871–1930,' *Historical Studies in Education* 1990; Cecilia Reynolds, 'Hegemony and Hierarchy: Becoming a Teacher in Toronto, 1930–1980,' *Historical Studies in Education* 1990; Norman H. Fergusson, *The Story of the Nova Scotia Teachers' Union: From the Formation of the Old Union in 1895 to the 1980s* (Armdale: Nova Scotia Teachers' Union 1990); Alison Prentice and Marjorie R. Theobald, eds., *Women Who Taught: Perspectives on the History of Women and Teaching* (T: UTP 1991);

and Rennie Warburton, 'The Class Relations of Public School Teachers in British Columbia,' *Canadian Review of Sociology and Anthropology* 1986.

Several writers have undertaken these industry studies with more sensitivity to the labour processes involved and workers' experience with them. The books by Heron and Lowe on steelworkers and clerical workers are important examples, as is Sager, *Seafaring Labour*. Ian Radforth analyses logging with exemplary rigour and clarity in *Bushworkers and Bosses: Logging in Northern Ontario, 1900–1980* (T: UTP 1987); see also Patricia Marchak, *Green Gold: The Forest Industry in British Columbia* (V:UBCP 1983); Jean-Pierre Charland, *Les pâtes et papiers au Québec, 1880–1980: technologies, travail, et travailleurs* (Q: IQRC 1990); and Wallace Clement, *Hardock Mining: Industrial Relations and Technological Change at INCO* (T: M&S 1981). The particular labour-process experience of women is creatively analysed in Charlene Gannage, *Double Day, Double Bind: Women Garment Workers* (T: Women's Press 1986), and Michèle Martin, *'Hello Central?': Gender, Technology, and Culture in the Formation of Telephone Systems* (M and K: MQUP 1991). Heather Menzies explores the impact of automation in *Women and the Chip: Case Studies of the Effects of Informatics on Employment in Canada* (M: Institute for Research on Public Policy 1981) and in *Computers on the Job: Surviving Canada's Microcomputer Revolution* (T: JL 1982). Craig Heron and Robert Storey have collected several shorter studies of the evolving labour process in *On the Job*. Occupational health and safety has been a growing concern within this literature; for a wide-ranging survey of the issues past and present, see Charles E. Reasons et al., *Assault on the Worker: Occupational Health and Safety in Canada* (T: BUT 1981).

State Responses

Wage-earners regularly bumped up against the might of the state in their struggles. For the courts' early hostility to workers' organizations, see Paul Craven, 'The Law of Master and Servant in Mid-Nineteenth-Century Ontario,' in David H. Flaherty, ed., *Essays in the History of Canadian Law*, vol. 1 (T: UTP 1981) and his 'Workers' Conspiracies in Toronto, 1854–72, *Labour* 1984; and Eric Tucker, '"That Indefinite Area of Toleration": Criminal Conspiracy and Trade Unions in Ontario, 1837–77,' *Labour* 1991. Military repression of workers' movements has been documented in Desmond Morton, 'Aid to the Civil Power: The Canadian Militia in Support of Social Order, 1867–1914,' in Michiel Horn and Ronald Sabourin, eds., *Studies in Canadian Social History* (T: M&S 1974); Don

Macgillivray, 'Military Aid to the Civil Power: The Cape Breton Experience in the 1920s,' in Macgillivray and Tennyson, eds., *Cape Breton Historical Essays* (cited above); and J.J.B. Pariseau, *Disorders, Strikes, and Disasters: Military Aid to the Civil Power in Canada, 1867–1933* (O: Directorate of History, National Defence Headquarters 1973). The policing function of the RCMP, including covert surveillance and regression of radicalism, is studied in William M. Baker, 'The Miners and the Mounties: The Royal North West Mounted Police and the 1906 Lethbridge Strike,' *Labour* 1991; S.W. Horrall, 'The Royal Northwest Mounted Police and Labour Unrest in Western Canada, 1919,' *CHR* 1980; Barbara Roberts, 'Shovelling Out the "Mutinous": Political Deportation from Canada before 1936,' *Labour* 1986; J. Petryshyn, 'R.B. Bennett and the Communists: 1930–1935,' *JCS* 1974; Gregory S. Kealey and Reginald Whitaker, eds., *RCMP Security Bulletins: The War Series, 1939–1941* and *The Early Years, 1919–29* (St John's: CCLH 1989, 1991). The state's heavy-handedness continued into the Cold War era; see Whitaker, 'Official Repression of Communism during World War II,' *Labour* 1986, and Alvin Finkel, 'The Cold War, Alberta, and the Social Credit Regime,' *Labour* 1988. Since 1975, federal and provincial governments once again have been using a heavier hand to curb labour militancy; see Allan M. Maslove and Gene Swimmer, *Wage Controls in Canada, 1975–78: A Study in Public Decision Making* (M: Institute for Research on Public Policy 1980), Leo Panitch and Donald Swartz, *The Assault on Trade Union Freedoms: From Consent to Coercion Revisited* (rev. ed., T: Garamond Press 1988), and Larry Haiven et al., eds., *Regulating Labour: The State, Neo-Conservatism, and Industrial Relations* (T: Garamond 1991). Stuart Jamieson offers an insightful overview in 'Some Reflections on Violence and the Law in Industrial Relations,' in D.J. Bercuson and L.A. Knafla, eds., *Law and Society in Historical Perspective* (C: University of Calgary 1979).

The state has also been interested in promoting industrial peace through a mediating role, as revealed in several studies, especially Paul Craven's brilliant monograph, *'An Impartial Umpire': Industrial Relations and the Canadian State, 1900–1911* (T: UTP 1980); H.A. Logan's now dated, *State Intervention and Assistance in Collective Bargaining: The Canadian Experience, 1943–1956* (T: UTP 1956); Laurel Sefton McDowell, 'The Formation of the Canadian Industrial Relations System during World War II,' *Labour* 1978; Jeremy Webber, 'Compelling Compromise: Canada Chooses Conciliation over Arbitration, 1900–1907,' *Labour* 1991, and his 'The Malaise of Compulsory Conciliation: Strike Prevention during World War II,' in Palmer, ed., *The Character of Class Struggle*; Judy Fudge,

'Voluntarism, Compulsion, and the Transformation of Canadian Labour Law during World War II,' in Kealey and Patmore, *Canadian and Australian Labour History*; John A. Willes, *The Ontario Labour Court, 1943–1944* (Kingston: Industrial Relations Centre, Queen's University 1979); and Christopher Huxley, 'The State, Collective Bargaining, and the Shape of Strikes in Canada,' *Canadian Journal of Sociology* 1979. For the ineffectual attempts to promote a corporatist option, see Roy Adams, 'The Federal Government and Tripartism,' *Ri/IR* 1982, and Donald M. Wells, *Empty Promises: Quality of Working Life Programs and the Labour Movement* (NY: Monthly Review Press 1987). Bob Russell's attempt to integrate the whole twentieth-century experience with state intervention into workplace relations is theoretically interesting but methodologically flawed; see *Back to Work?: Labour, State, and Industrial Relations in Canada* (Scarborough: Nelson 1990).

At moments of labour militancy and middle-class outrage, the Canadian state has also enacted measures to guarantee certain labour standards. Several studies have documented the limited impact of these measures; see, in particular, Eric Tucker's lucid analysis of the first factory acts, *Administering Danger in the Workplace: The Law and Politics of Occupational Health and Safety Regulation in Ontario, 1850–1914* (T: UTP 1990), his more general discussion, 'The Determination of Occupational Health and Safety Standards in Ontario, 1860–1982: From the Market to Politics to ... ?' *McGill Law Journal* 1984, and Michael Piva's less rigorous 'The Workmen's Compensation Movement in Ontario,' *OH* 1975. Minimum-wage legislation is analysed in Margaret McCallum, 'Keeping Women in Their Proper Place: The Minimum Wage in Canada, 1910–25,' *Labour* 1988, and in Bob Russell, 'A Fair or a Minimum Wage? Women Workers, the State, and the Origins of Wage Regulation in Western Canada,' *Labour* 1991. Mark Cox assesses Ontario's industrial standards legislation of the 1930s in 'The Limits of Reform: Industrial Regulation and Management Rights in Ontario,' *CHR* 1987. Shirley Tillotson takes a refreshing look at the introduction of equal-pay legislation in 'Human Rights Law as Prism: Women's Organizations, Unions, and Ontario's Female Employees Fair Remuneration Act of 1951,' *CHR* 1991. The federal and provincial governments have also attempted some rationalization of the labour market; see Struthers, *No Fault of Their Own*, and Udo Sautter's two articles, 'The Origins of the Unemployment Service of Canada, 1900–1920,' *Labour* 1980, and 'Measuring Unemployment in Canada: Federal Efforts before World War II, *HS/SH* 1982.

Many of these dimensions of state labour policy, particularly as it affected men, are dealt with in Esdras Minville, *Syndicalisme, legislation ouvrière, et régime social au Québec avant 1940* (M: Fides 1986); Warburton and Coburn, *Workers, Capital, and the State*; and Earle, *Workers and the State*, which includes Craig Heron's overview essay, 'Male Wage-Earners and the Canadian State.'

WORKERS AND POLITICS

Scholars and writers of many political stripes have had a longstanding interest in the political organizations that workers have created or joined in coalition with other groups. All too often these studies have never moved beyond the internal life of the parties, their ideologies, and leaders, and lack much social, economic, or even political context. On the early years, readers may consult the first heavily detailed synthesis of this activity, Martin Robin, *Radical Politics and Canadian Labour, 1880–1930* (Kingston: Industrial Relations Centre, Queen's University 1968), but should beware of factual errors. A more reliable source is Ross McCormack's lively *Reformers, Rebels, and Revolutionaries*; see also Allen Seager, 'Socialists and Workers: The Western Canadian Coal Miners, 1900–21,' *Labour* 1985. East Coast radicalism is documented in David Frank and Nolan Reilly, 'The Emergence of the Socialist Movement in the Maritimes, 1899–1916,' in Brym and Sacouman, eds., *Underdevelopment and Social Movements in Atlantic Canada* (cited above), and in Frank's fascinating articles, 'Company Town/Labour Town: Local Government in the Cape Breton Coal Towns, 1917–1926,' *HS/SH* 1981, and 'Working-Class Politics: The Election of J.B. McLachlan, 1916–1935,' in Kenneth Donovan, ed., *The Island: New Perspectives on Cape Breton's History, 1713–1990* (F: AP 1990). Toronto's early socialist culture is explored in Gene Howard Homel, '"Fading Beams of the Nineteenth Century": Radicalism and Early Socialism in Canada's 1890s,' *Labour* 1980. Craig Heron has sketched the main contours of working-class reformism across the country in the early twentieth century in 'Labourism and the Canadian Working Class,' *Labour* 1984. Groups of radical immigrants from non-Anglo-Celtic backgrounds made an important contribution to the early Canadian socialist movement; on this subject, see Avery, *'Dangerous Foreigners.'* For contrasting views of Ukrainian workers' radicalism, see Peter Krawchuk, *The Ukrainian Socialist Movement in Canada (1907–1918)* (T: Progress Books 1979); John Kolasky, *The Shattered Illusion: The History of Ukrainian Pro-Communist Organizations in Canada* (T: Peter Martin Associates 1979); and Orest T. Martynowych, 'The Ukrainian Socialist Movement in

Canada, 1900–1918,' *Journal of Ukrainian Graduate Studies* 1978. The Finnish workers' radicalism is evident in Edward W. Laine, 'Finnish Canadian Radicalism and Canadian Politics: The First Forty Years, 1900–1940,' in Dahlie and Fernando, *Ethnicity, Power, and Politics*, and Lindström-Best, *Defiant Sisters*. On Jewish radicals, see Irving Abella, 'Portrait of a Jewish Revolutionary: The Recollections of Joshua Gershman,' *Labour* 1977; Roz Uisikin, 'The Winnipeg Jewish Community: Its Radical Elements, 1905–1918,' Historical and Scientific Society of Manitoba, *Transactions* 1976–77; and Frager, *Sweatshop Strife*.

The left-wing workers' movements split into Communist and social-democratic streams in the 1920s. The literature on the Communists has generally been obscured by Cold War loyalties. The Communist Party of Canada has produced its own version of the story, *Canada's Party of Socialism: History of the Communist Party of Canada, 1921–1976* (T: Progress Books 1982). The anti-Communist works include William Rodney, *Soldiers of the International: A History of the Communist Party of Canada, 1919–1929* (T: UTP 1968), and Ivan Avakumovic, *The Communist Party in Canada: A History* (T: M&S 1975). For studies that maintain a critical distance but never lose some sympathy for their subjects, see Ian Angus, *Canadian Bolsheviks: The Early Years of the Communist Party of Canada* (M: Vanguard 1981), and Lita-Rose Betcherman, *The Little Band: The Clashes between the Communists and the Political and Legal Establishment in Canada, 1928–1932* (O: Deneau 1982). Several studies of Communism in Quebec have been published: Marcel Fournier, *Communisme et anti-communisme au Québec, 1920–1950* (M: Edition Albert Saint-Martin 1979); Robert Comeau and Bernard Dionne, *Communists in Quebec, 1936–1956: The Communist Party of Canada/Labour Progressive Party* (M: Presses de l'Unite 1982), and their *Le droit de se taire: histoire des communistes au Québec, de la Première Guerre mondiale à la Révolution tranquille* (Outrement: VLB 1989); and Andrée Lévesque, *Virage à gauche interdit: les communists, les socialistes, et leurs ennemis au Québec, 1929–1939* (M: BE 1984). The party's leadership in mobilizing workers on international issues is addressed in Victor Hoar, *The Mackenzie-Papineau Battalion: Canadian Participation in the Spanish Civil War* (T: CC 1969), and William Beeching, *Canadian Volunteers: Spain, 1936–1939* (R: CPRC 1989). William Repka and Kathleen M. Repka discuss the wartime internment of Communists in *Dangerous Patriots: Canada's Unknown Prisoners of War* (V: New Star 1982). Norman Penner has undertaken the most sweeping reinterpretation of the party's history yet, first in *The Canadian Left: A Critical Analysis* (Scarborough: PH 1977), and then in *Canadian Communism: The Stalin Years and Beyond* (T: Methuen

120   Craig Heron

1988). Merrily Weisbord uses oral history to tackle the years in which this stream in Canadian politics was essentially snuffed out in *The Strangest Dream: Canadian Communists, the Spy Trials, and the Cold War* (T: Lester & Orpen Dennys 1983).

The social democrats, who generally trace their roots to the founding of the Co-operative Commonwealth Federation in 1933, have had more favourable treatment on the whole. Neither this organization nor its successor, the New Democratic Party, was ever a purely working-class organization, but workers and their representatives were active at all levels of the party. Ivan Avakumovic offers a sketchy overview of these organizations' histories in *Socialism in Canada: A Study of the CCF-NDP in Federal and Provincial Politics* (T: M&S 1978). Two general treatments of the early years are Walter D. Young, *The Anatomy of a Party: The National CCF, 1932–61* (T: UTP 1969), and Gad Horowitz, *Canadian Labour in Politics* (T: UTP 1968). More detailed studies can be found in J. William Brennan, ed., *'Building the Co-operative Commonwealth': Essays on the Democratic Socialist Tradition in Canada* (R: CPRC 1984); Allen Mills, *Fool for Christ: The Political Thought of J.S. Woodsworth* (T: UTP 1991); Gerald L. Caplan, *The Dilemma of Canadian Socialism: The CCF in Ontario* (T: M&S 1973); J. Terence Morley, *Secular Socialists: The CCF/NDP in Ontario, A Biography* (M and K: MQUP 1984); and Nelson Wiseman, *Social Democracy in Manitoba: A History of the CCF/NDP* (W: UMP 1983). The fortunes of the NDP are covered in Desmond Morton's regularly updated brief study, currently entitled *The New Democrats, 1961–1986: The Politics of Change* (3rd ed., T: CCP 1986). Keith Archer concentrates on the complex relationship between unions and the party in *Political Choices and Electoral Consequences: A Study of Organized Labour and the New Democratic Party* (M and K: MQUP 1990).

The women in these left-wing organizations are brought out of their long obscurity in the historical record in Linda Kealey, 'Canadian Socialism and the Woman Question, 1900–1914,' *Labour* 1984; Janice Newton, 'The Alchemy of Politicization: Socialist Women and the Early Canadian Left,' in Iacovetta and Valverde, eds., *Gender Conflicts*; Lindström-Best, *Defiant Sisters*; Joan Sangster, *Dreams of Equality: Women on the Canadian Left, 1920–1950* (T: M&S 1989); Terry Crowley, *Agnes Macphail and the Politics of Equality* (T: JL 1990); and Linda Kealey and Joan Sangster, eds., *Beyond the Vote: Canadian Women and Politics* (T: UTP 1989).

Little has yet been written about the workers who supported other parties. Janine Brodie and Jane Jensen present an overview in *Crisis, Challenge, and Change: Party and Class in Canada Revisited* (rev. ed.,

O: Carleton UP 1988). Michael Piva looks at working-class toryism in 'Workers and Tories: The Collapse of the Conservative Party in Urban Ontario, 1908–1919,' *UHR* 1977. Quebec's working-class voters are discussed in Tremblay, *Le syndicalisme québécois*, Edwidge Munn, 'L'action politique partisane de la FTQ (1957–76),' *Labour* 1983, and Maurice Pinard, 'Working-Class Politics: An Interpretation of the Quebec Case,' *Canadian Review of Sociology and Anthropology* 1970.

BIOGRAPHIES

Biographies and autobiographies of working people are often the most accessible avenue to the study of working-class history. Many have appeared in the past decade, usually dealing with working-class activists in unions or radical politics. They may be personally written memoirs, texts ghost-written by sympathetic writers (usually journalists), pieces of oral history shaped by the extensive questioning of historians, or simply biographies in which the subject played no part in the writing. There are several books on the working-class participants in left-wing politics. The social democrats include Leo Heaps, *The Rebel in the House: The Life and Times of A.A. Heaps, MP* (L: Niccolo 1970); Anthony Mardiros, *William Irvine: The Life of a Prairie Radical* (T: JL 1979); and Dorothy G. Steeves, *The Compassionate Rebel: Ernest E. Winch and the Growth of Socialism in Western Canada* (2nd ed., V: J.J. Douglas 1977). Radical socialists and Communists have attracted more attention; see, especially, Claude Lariviere, *Albert Saint-Martin, militant d'avant-garde, 1865–1947* (Laval: Editions Albert Saint-Martin 1979); Susan Mayse, *Ginger: The Life and Death of Albert Goodwin* (Madeira Park: Harbour Publishing 1990); Rolf Knight and Maya Koizumi, *A Man of Our Times: The Life-History of a Japanese-Canadian Fisherman* (V: New Star 1976); Tim Buck, *Yours in the Struggle: Reminiscences of Tim Buck*, edited by William Beeching and Phyllis Clarke (T: NC Press 1977); Catharine Vance, *Not by Gods But by People: The Story of Bella Hall Gauld* (T: Progress Books 1968); Louise Watson, *She Was Never Afraid: The Biography of Annie Buller* (T: Progress Books 1976); Jean Evans Sheils and Ben Swankey, *'Work and Wages': Semi-Documentary Account of the Life and Times of Arthur H. (Slim) Evans* (V: Trade Union Research Bureau 1977); Peter Hunter, *Which Side Are You On Boys: Canadian Life on the Left* (T: Lugus Productions 1988); Tom McEwen, *The Forge Glows Red: From Blacksmith to Revolutionary* (T: Progress Books 1974); George MacEachern, *George MacEachern, An Autobiography: The Story of a Cape Breton Radical*, edited by David Frank and

Donald MacGillivray (Sydney: University College of Cape Breton Press 1987); Milan Bosnich, *One Man's War: Reflections of a Rough Diamond* (T: Lugus Productions 1988); Gérard Fortin and Boyce Richardson, *Life of the Party* (M: Véhicule 1984); Rick Salutin, *Kent Rowley, the Organizer: A Canadian Union Life* (T: JL 1980); Bruce Magnuson, *The Untold Story of Ontario's Bushworkers: A Political Memoir* (Toronto Progress Books 1990); Howard White, *A Hard Man to Beat: The Story of Bill White, Labour Leader, Historian, Shipyard Worker, Raconteur: An Oral History* (V: Pulp Press 1983); and Jack Scott, *A Communist Life: Jack Scott and the Canadian Workers' Movement, 1927–1985*, edited by Bryan D. Palmer (St John's: CCLH 1988).

Biographies can also shed light on life inside unions. See Alfred Charpentier, *Cinquante ans d'action ouvrier: les mémoires d'Alfred Charpentier* (Q: PUL 1971); Bob Miner, *Miner's Life: Bob Miner and Union Organizing in Timmins, Kirkland Lake, and Sudbury*, edited by Wayne Roberts (Hamilton: McMaster University Labour Studies Programme 1979); Alf Ready, *Organizing Westinghouse: Alf Ready's Story*, edited by Wayne Roberts (Hamilton: McMaster University Labour Studies Programme 1979); Cyril W. Strong, *My Life as a Newfoundland Union Organizer: The Memoirs of Cyril W. Strong, 1912–1987*, edited by Greg Kealey (St John's: CCLH 1987); Max Swerdlow, *Brother Max: Labour Organizer and Educator* (St John's: CCLH 1990); Peter Edwards, *Waterfront Warlord: The Life and Violent Times of Hal C. Banks* (T: Key Porter 1987); Joe Davidson and John Deverell, *Joe Davidson* (T: JL 1978); Jack Munro and Jane O'Hara, *Union Jack: Labour Leader Jack Munro* (V: Douglas & McIntyre 1988); and Bob White, *Hard Bargains: My Life on the Line* (T: M&S 1987). A rank-and-filer's story is available in W.J. Chafe, *I've Been Working on the Railroad: Memoirs of a Railwayman, 1911–1962* (St John's: CCLH 1987).

Finally, the only book-length autobiography of a working-class woman is Phyllis Knight's *A Very Ordinary Life, as Told to Rolph Knight* (V: New Star 1974), a fascinating chronicle of an extraordinary person.

As this partial listing of books and articles indicates, Canadian workers continue to fascinate and inspire large numbers of writers and scholars. Exploring the many facets of workers' lives, however, has become a far more complex process. Having established the legitimacy of using class as a category of historical analysis, historians are becoming more aware of the need to integrate gender and ethnicity/race as crucial factors in shaping the Canadian working-class experience. The field thus continues to evolve dynamically in innovative directions.

BEN FORSTER

Business and Economic History

Business and economic history are separate, although related, as is evident in the way these fields developed. Business history is a recent area of specialization in Canada. There was an initial impulse at organizing a self-conscious subdiscipline in the late 1960s and early 1970s; this submerged, to reappear more effectively and strongly in 1984 and beyond. Business history before the 1970s was primarily an offshoot of economic history, or consisted of journalistic biographies of businessmen and companies, most of them commissioned.

The traditions of professional economic history are much more deeply rooted. In Canada, this kind of history had its ancestry in a late-nineteenth and early-twentieth century fiscal, institutional, and economic policy tradition, typified by Adam Shortt and Oscar D. Skelton [see Shortt and Arthur G. Doughty, eds., *Canada and Its Provinces; A History of the Canadian People and Their Institutions* (T: Publishers' Association of Canada 1914–17), especially vols. 9 and 10]. That was partly displaced in the 1920s and 1930s by the staples thesis as developed by Harold A. Innis, whose various books, most especially for our purposes, *The Cod Fisheries: The History of an International Economy* (1940, T: UTP 1954), have overshadowed William A. Mackintosh's contribution, 'Economic Factors in Canadian History,' *CHR* 1923 (and examine his *The Economic Background of Dominion-Provincial Relations: Appendix III of the Royal Commission Report on Dominion-Provincial Relations*, [1964, T and O: MAC 1979] John H. Dales, ed.). Only more recently has the explanatory power of the staples thesis been questioned in terms of its determinism and its limited scope of inquiry. The thesis only awkwardly or partially explained Canada's industrialization and urbanization. Its explanatory power sharply declined when one closely examined individual firms, as Douglas McCalla demonstrated in

The Upper Canada Trade, 1834–1872: A Study of the Buchanans' Business (T: UTP 1979). Neither could it effectively encompass new social and intellectual history approaches, exemplified by Michael Bliss's first work, *A Living Profit: Studies in the Social History of Canadian Business, 1883–1911* (T: M&S 1974).

These new approaches to business taken by historians writing in the 1970s and beyond were heavily influenced by trends in historical writing in the United States and Great Britain. However, the institutionalist, organizational synthesis which has ruled business history in the United States in the last few decades (see Louis Galambos, 'Technology, Political Economy, and Professionalization: Central Themes of the Organizational Synthesis,' *Business History Review* 1983) is only currently being grappled with in Canada. Perhaps this is partly because Canadian economic and business history already had a powerful institutional bias in its pervasive concerns with business-government relations. As well, in Canada the companies displaying the strategic and structural elements favoured by the leading business historian in the organizational synthesis, Alfred Chandler, were often foreign subsidiaries or in the public sector.

But where had economic history gone in the mean time? The powerful tradition of historical analysis in economics affirmed through H.A. Innis (and of which he was highly conscious – see the historiographical/bibliographical essay, 'The Teaching of Economic History in Canada,' in *Essays in Canadian Economic History*, Mary Quayle Innis, ed. (T: UTP 1956)) – reeled under the impact of the new economics and its stress on theory and on resolving specific problems. The chief function of the staples thesis, in the hands of some of its devotees, was to interpret underdevelopment on a regional or national basis. In this fashion the thesis was enveloped in one of the overriding concerns of the day. Other economists, in escaping the confines of the staple thesis, also escaped history and political economy. The strained mating of theory, problem-oriented modelling, and the analysis of historical continuities in William L. Marr and Donald G. Paterson, *Canada: An Economic History* (T: MAC 1980), indicates some of the difficulties which have resulted. But that strained union also shows how reluctant many economists were to give up the explanatory power of history.

REFERENCE MATERIALS AND GENERAL TEXTS

The range of bibliographical sources for economic and business history is relatively limited. Trevor J. O. Dick's once-thorough review, *Economic*

History of Canada: A Guide to Information Sources (Detroit: Gale 1978), should be consulted on the economic side. While there are national bibliographies of business history for the United States and Great Britain, nothing like this exists for Canada. The citations and comments provided by Michael Bliss in his *Northern Enterprise: Five Centuries of Canadian Business* (T: M&S 1987) are an important resource in this regard. Jerry Mulcahy's *Business and History at Western: A Guide to Selected Resources* (London: UWO Library System 1992) is a wide-ranging citation guide to books on American and British, as well as Canadian, topics. Paul Craven, Anne Forrest, and Tom Traves, comp., *Canadian Company Histories: A Checklist* (2nd ed., Downsview: York University 1978) is now well out-of-date, but remains useful. A source for short short histories of the largest Canadian corporations is Thomas Derdak and John Simley, eds., *International Directory of Company Histories* (Chicago: St James Press 1988–91).

If one wishes to do research beyond secondary sources on Canadian business, there are few useful guides. The *Canadian Business Periodicals Index* (T: Information Access 1975–1980) followed by the *Canadian Business Index* (T: Micromedia 1980–) gives access to material on the recent past. *Canadian Business and Current Affairs* (T: Micromedia 1987–) is a computer file on CD-ROM; *America: History and Life* (Santa Barbara: ABC-CLIO, ongoing) contains a vast amount of Canadian information, and is available on CD-ROM, or through the DIALOG database, to which many university libraries subscribe. A wonderful boon to business historians is the recently available Gordon R. Adshead, comp., *Index to the Financial Post* (T: Micromedia 1990). For those with hostile intent, Manuel Gordon's *Researching Canadian Corporations* (T: New Hogtown Press 1977) is inadequate, but is nonetheless serviceable for anyone seeking some guidance to contemporary sources.

Full of compressed information about twentieth century Canadian business and economic institutions and practices is David Crane, *A Dictionary of Canadian Economics*, (E: Hurtig 1980). Strictly on the business side is the idiosyncratic, entertaining, and instructive T. Kelly Dickinson, *Elementary Finance and Glossary of Financial Terms* (W: National Press 1930), although it is not available everywhere.

Canadian economic history has been well served by a variety of general texts. Those produced by an older generation of scholars are dominated by the staples approach: W.T. Easterbrook and Hugh G.J. Aitken, *Canadian Economic History*, (1956, T: UTP 1988) is strong on the nineteenth century, but sharply flawed by its staples emphasis in dealing with the twentieth; the schematic, staple-oriented, W.T. Easterbrook, *North American Patterns of Growth and Development: The Continental Context*, Ian Parker, ed. (T: UTP 1990); and of course Mary Quayle Innis, *An Economic History of Canada* (2nd ed., T: RP 1954) are key examples.

A second generation of texts has partly transcended the staples obsession. Marr and Paterson's book, mentioned above, offers a great deal to the patient reader. The iconoclastic, uneven treatment of Richard Pomfret, *The Economic Development of Canada* (Agincourt: Methuen 1981) is a good introduction to some major disputes in Canadian economic history. The recent K.H. Norrie and Doug Owram, *A History of the Canadian Economy* (T: HBJ 1991), in great contrast to Pomfret, provides a smooth continuous analytical narrative.

None of these texts can offer much as business histories. There is only one general text in Canadian business history: Michael Bliss's comprehensive, entertainingly astringent *Northern Enterprise*. Bliss eschews grand theory; Peter Baskerville and Graham Taylor's *A Concise* [though not short] *History of Canadian Business* (T: OUP 1994) is an analysis somewhat more in keeping with the model of American organizational business history.

While not business or economic history texts, there are a number of general studies, the content of which includes a great deal that is useful. Various volumes of McClelland and Stewart's Centenary Series contain much economic material. Particularly notable here are R. Craig Brown and Ramsay Cook, *Canada 1896–1921: A Nation Transformed* (T: M&S 1974) and, though its ideological perspective is strikingly different, John H. Thompson and Allen Seager, *Canada 1922–1939: Decades of Discord* (T: M&S 1985). In Robert Bothwell, Ian Drummond, and John English, *Canada since 1945: Power, Politics, and Provincialism* (rev. ed., T: UTP 1989) and *Canada, 1900–1945* (T: UTP 1987), some modest attention is given to business cycle ups and downs amid considerable analysis of economic and policy history.

There are also provincial and regional surveys which must be mentioned. Robert Armstrong, *Structure and Change: An Economic History of Quebec* (T: Gage 1984) is a useful place to start for that province. Jean Hamelin and Yves Roby, *Histoire économique de Québec, 1851–1896* (M: Fides 1971) is a classic; a more obviously opinionated work with high business and economics content is Brian Young and John A. Dickinson, *A Short History of Quebec: A Socio-economic Perspective* (T: CCP 1988). One can continue to gain a great deal from the work of Albert Faucher and M. Lamontagne, 'History of Industrial Development,' in Marcel Rioux and Yves Martin, eds., *French-Canadian Society*, vol. 1 (T: M&S 1964). Intensely systematic in approach, as is typical of much modern French-Canadian historiography, Paul-André Linteau, René Durocher, and Jean-Claude Robert, *Histoire du Québec contemporain, De la confederation à la crise, 1867–1929*, and with F. Ricard, tome II, *Le Québec depuis 1930* (2nd ed., M: BE 1989, and available in English translation) have very extensive materials on economic history, and should be consulted by any student of modern Canada.

Rich in detail, and unrepentant in its economic liberalism, is Ian Drummond, *Progress without Planning: The Economic History of Ontario from Confederation to the Second World War* (T: UTP 1987), although it emphasizes sectoral analysis and eschews any interest in business cycles. Even the title reveals how important is the notion of progress in stimulating the writing of modern economic history. For an interesting exchange on the book's approaches, see *CHR* 1988. Kenneth J. Rea's *The Prosperous Years: The Economic History of Ontario, 1939–1975* (T: UTP 1985) provides a careful economic survey. These two books are rounded out by Douglas McCalla's *Planting the Province: The Economic History of Upper Canada, 1784–1870* (T: UTP 1993), which can provide deep background for the student of post-Confederation Ontarian studies. McCalla has continued the assault on the Innisian staple-export bias of Canadian economic history. That assault, in muted, unassuming fashion, is found as early as James M. Gilmour's *Spatial Evolution of Manufacturing: Southern Ontario, 1851–1891* (T: UTP 1972).

Stanley A. Saunders, *The Economic History of the Maritime Provinces*, T.W. Acheson, ed., (Fredericton: Acadiensis Press 1984) was originally a study for the Royal Commission on Dominion-Provincial Relations, and is where all students of regional underdevelopment in the Maritimes should begin. The student then might go to the journal *Acadiensis*, lush with business and economic history, much of it at least implicitly on the issue of development and its absence. T.W. Acheson's 'The National Policy and the Industrialization of the Maritimes, 1880–1910,' *Acadiensis* 1972, is now being transcended but remains a combative piece. A recent, further, assessment using different methodology is Kris Inwood, 'Maritime Industrialization from 1870 to 1910: A Review of the Evidence and Its Interpretation,' *Acadiensis* 1991. This has been reprinted along with other articles from *Acadiensis* and some five others previously unpublished in Kris Inwood, ed., *Farm, Factory and Fortune: New Studies in the Economic History of the Maritime Provinces* (Fredericton: Acadiensis Press 1993). One might particularly note Neil C. Quigley, Ian M. Drummond, and Lewis T. Evans, 'Regional Transfers of Funds through the Canadian Banking System and Maritime Economic Development, 1895–1935,' which, although technical, will make it difficult for scholars to continue blaming the banks for the economic troubles of the region.

On the West, one good place to start is Gerald Friesen, *The Canadian Prairies: A History* (T: UTP 1984), as it has a fair bit about settlement, the National Policy, and urban business development. A great deal of the literature on agricultural development deals with the Canadian West (see below). One may disagree with the counter-factual assumptions of John H. Thompson, *The Harvests of War: The Prairie West, 1914–1918* (T: M&S 1978), but the book does contain considerable material on the industrial development of the West in wartime. Alan F.J. Artibise, *Winnipeg: A Social History of Urban Growth, 1874–1914* (M and K: MQUP 1975) contains valuable material on a city dominated by a 'growth ethic.' One can extend this quasi-geographical focus by consulting Peter J. Smith, ed., *The Prairie Provinces* (T: UTP 1972) as it not only has chapters dealing with the physical characteristics of the Prairies, but also on economic development, population, and urban life.

Morris Zaslow examined the moving frontier of northern staples development in two thorough, splendidly detailed narratives: *The Opening of the Canadian North, 1870–1914* (T: M&S 1971), and *The Northward Expansion of Canada, 1914–1967* (T:M&S 1988). K. J. Rea has written a study of economic development in the Yukon and Northwest, *The Political Economy of the Canadian North: An Interpretation of the Course of Development in the Northern Territories of Canada to the Early 1960s* (T: UTP 1968).

While most economic historians are content to deal with structural change rather than the more slippery impact of the business cycle, the business cycle has received substantial attention. Thus, O.J. Firestone focused on the growth of the economy in the late nineteenth century, rather than its considerable ups and downs, in his *Canada's Economic Development, 1867–1953: With Special Reference to Changes in the Country's National Product and National Wealth* (L: Bowes & Bowes 1958), also available in earlier mimeographed versions. This data has been revised and refined in M.C. Urquhart, 'New Estimates of Gross National Product, Canada, 1870–1926: Some Implications for Canadian development,' in Stanley L. Engerman and Robert E. Gallman, eds., *Long-term Factors in American Economic Growth* (Chicago: Chicago UP 1986), and in Morris Altman's 'A Revision of Canadian Economic Growth: 1870–1910,' *CJE* 1987, which makes the case for major discontinuities. Urquhart has now expanded and summed up his work in *Gross National Product, 1870–1926: Derivation of Estimates* (M and K: MQUP 1993). Two articles by Keith

A.J. Hay, 'Money and Cycles in Post-Confederation Canada,' *Journal of Political Economy* 1966, and 'Early Twentieth-Century Business Cycle in Canada,' *CJEPS* 1967, were ground-breaking in their tracing of cycles. An early study of the international flow of money and the process of economic growth which has retained an impressive reputation in Jacob Viner, *Canada's Balance of International Indebtedness, 1900–1913: An Inductive Study in the Theory of International Trade* (1924; 2nd ed., T: M&S 1975 with an introduction by H.C. Eastman). Georg Rich, *The Cross of Gold: Money and the Canadian Business Cycle, 1867–1913* (O: Carleton UP 1988), makes considerable effort to examine the relationship of money availability to the business cycle, and criticizes the conclusions of Hay and Viner. Viner and Rich will be viewed by many students as overly complex and difficult.

There was one major downturn that has received detailed attention: the Depression of the 1930s. A.E. Safarian provided a close analysis of major elements and developments in *The Canadian Economy in the Great Depression* (T: M&S 1970). On this decade one should also consult Edward Marcus, *Canada and the International Business Cycle, 1927–1939* (NY: Bookman 1954). An interesting recent attempt to couple structural change and cyclical developments is Kris Inwood and Thomasis Stengos, 'Discontinuities in Canadian Economic Growth, 1870–1985,' *Explorations in Entrepreneurial History* 1991.

COLLECTIONS OF READINGS AND HISTORIOGRAPHY

Two recent and thoughtful overviews of business history are Michael Bliss, 'Canadian Business History at the Crossroads,' *Business Quarterly* 1992, and Graham Taylor, 'Writing about Business,' in John Schultz, ed., *Writing about Canada: A Handbook for Modern Canadian History* (Scarborough: PH 1990). Some trends in economic history are discussed in articles by Robin Neill and Hugh G.J. Aitken in *JCS* 1977. Certainly Ian M. Drummond, 'Writing about Economics,' in Schultz, ed., *Writing about Canada* provides key insights on current trends.

Discussions of developments in business and economic history are to be found to be in virtually all of the edited collections of articles. One of the earliest collections of articles is David S. MacMillan, ed., *Canadian Business History: Selected Studies, 1497–1971* (T: M&S 1972), in which Fred A. Armstrong has a bibliographic essay. Tom Traves, ed., *Essays in Canadian History* (T: M&S 1984), with its fine introduction, consists of reprints and is aimed at classroom use. Douglas McCalla's two useful books of readings, *The Development of Canadian Capitalism: Essays in Business History* (T: CCP 1990), to which he provides a discerning introduction, and *Perspectives on Canadian Economic History* (T: CCP 1987), use different sets of reprinted articles. Three business history conferences have produced publications of original papers: *JCS* 1985, and Peter A. Baskerville, ed., *Canadian Papers in Business History*, vol. 1 (Vi: Public History Group 1989) and *Canadian Papers in Business History*, vol. 2 (Vi: Public History Group 1993). W.T. Easterbrook and M.H. Watkins, eds., *Approaches to Canadian Economic History: A Selection of Essays* (T: M&S 1967) remains a notable collection with a staples emphasis. It contains a bibliographical essay, now dated. Craufurd D.W. Goodwin went into considerable effort to outline a cohesive *Canadian Economic Thought: The Political Economy of a Developing Nation, 1814–1914* (L: UP 1961); the odds were not on his side. Thirty years of scholarly work permitted Robin Neill to provide a picture integrated in part through his own vigorous opinions in *A History of Canadian Economic Thought* (L: Routledge 1991). Both of these books can function as substantial bibliographies, although that is not their first purpose, and there are some gaps.

Useful articles on Canadian business and economic history are found in virtually the full range of Canadian historical and economics journals, although of late the *Canadian Journal of Economics* has not carried many; the defunct *Canadian Journal of Economics and Political Science* (1935–1967) had a fair number. Non-Canadian journals in which material relevant to Canada occasionally appears include *Journal of Economic History*, the British *Business History*, and especially Harvard's *Business History Review*. The last published a special issue on Canada (1973), which later appeared as *Enterprise and National Development: Essays in Canadian Business and Economic History* (T: Hakkert 1973), Glenn Porter and Robert D. Cuff, eds.

The *Dictionary of Canadian Biography* (T: UTP various dates) now has several volumes which include numerous entries on businessmen active after Confederation through to 1900, and more will be forthcoming. Its very thorough nominal, geographic, and topical index will be reissued to cover recent volumes, I trust. *On the Job: Confronting the Labour Process in Canada* (M and K: MQUP 1986), Craig Heron and Robert Storey eds., provides insights from the perspective of labour history on transportation and communications, mining, clothing manufacture, office work, lumbering, and steel manufacturing. The book is indicative of the broadening of labour history to include the history of whole enterprises, a signal development to which business historians should pay serious attention. The three volumes of *The Historical Atlas of Canada* (T: UTP 1987, 1990,

1993) contain masses of economic information that deserve repeated examination. *The Canadian Encyclopedia* (E: Hurtig 1985) has rich offerings in business and economic history, M.C. Urquhart and Kenneth A.H. Buckley, *Historical Statistics of Canada* (2nd ed., O: Statistics Canada 1983) is an absolute goldmine for the statistically inclined, as are the two volumes of Clifford A. Curtis, Kenneth W. Taylor, and Humfrey Michell, *Statistical Contributions to Canadian Economic History* (T: MAC 1931).

BANKING, MONEY, AND FINANCE

A specialized documentary collection is Edward P. Neufeld, ed., *Money and Banking in Canada: Historical Documents and Commentary* (T: M&S 1964). One should see Shortt, *Canada and Its Provinces*, vol. 10. Irving Brecher, *Monetary and Fiscal Thought and Policy in Canada, 1919–1939* (T: UTP 1957) is on the intellectual debate and public thought concerning subjects such as inflation and central banking. A look at the place of the credit card in Canadian society is Sandra Martin and Ann Finlayson, *Card Tricks* (T: Penguin 1993); the banks do not come off well. Arthur F.W. Plumptre, *Three Decades of Decision: Canada and the World Monetary System, 1944–75* (T: M&S 1977) is an accessible discussion of the international management of the monetary system. The high temple of Canadian financial institutions, the Bank of Canada, has not received much published historical analysis. E.P. Neufeld's technical *Bank of Canada Operations and Policy* (T: UTP 1958) is one good place to look.

The most important book on financial institutions is E.P. Neufeld's descriptive economic history, *The Financial System of Canada, Its Growth and Development* (T: MAC 1972), which provides much material on individual firms. One should also see H.H. Binhammer, *Money, Banking and the Canadian Financial System* (5th ed., Scarborough: Nelson 1988). A virtual history of Canadian banking in dense narrative form is to found in Victor Ross and Arthur St. L. Trigge, *A History of the Canadian Bank of Commerce, with an   account of the other banks which now form part of its organization* (T: OUP 1920–1934). Merrill Denison, *Canada's First Bank: A History of the Bank of Montreal* (NY: Dodd, Mead 1966–67) is a substantial account by one of Canada's journalist-historians. Duncan McDowall's *Quick to the Frontier: Canada's Royal Bank* (T: M & S 1993) is a fine narrative analysis by a leading business historian. Ronald Rudin's *Banking en français: The French Banks of Quebec, 1835–1925* (T: UTP 1985) provides intriguing insights not only into banking but into historiography of French-Canadian economic life. Rubin extends his social history of financial institutions in Quebec with his question, *In Whose Interest?: Quebec's Caisses Populaires, 1990–1945* (M and K: MQUP 1990). The Bank of Nova Scotia has come in for criticism on its regional functions in J.D. Frost, 'The "Nationalization" of the Bank of Nova Scotia, 1880–1910,' *Acadiensis* 1982; N.C. Quigley has shown that bank as a dynamic, profit-seeking institution in its international operations: 'The Bank of Nova Scotia in the Caribbean, 1889–1940,' *Business History Review* 1989. An enjoyable read, although focused on the personalities of CEOs, is Rod McQueen, *The Money-Spinners: An Intimate Portrait of the Men who Run Canada's Banks* (Don Mills: MAC 1983).

If the banks deserve more historical attention, then certainly insurance, trust, and brokerage firms do. Ian Drummond's 'Canadian Life Assurance Companies and the Capital Market, 1890–1914,' *CJEPS* 1962, is one of the few analytical perspectives available. Joseph Schull's slim *Century of the Sun: The First Hundred Years of Sun Life Assurance Company of Canada* (T: MAC 1971) manages to obscure much that has been vital about a controversial financial institution – and it is one of the best of the lot on life insurance. On fire, marine, and general insurance we have very little indeed, although Christopher L. Hives's celebratory *The Underwriters: The History of the Insurers' Advisory Organization and Its Predecessors ... (1883–1983)* (T: Phelps Publishing 1985) is a solid starting point.

Work on stock exchanges and brokers is thin. Doug Fetherling, *Gold Diggers of 1929: Canada and the Great Stock Market Crash* (T: MAC 1979), while inconsistent, gives a racy and informative account of some aspects of the crash, focusing on Toronto; David Cruise and Alison Griffiths, *Fleecing the Lamb: The Inside Story of the Vancouver Stock Exchange* (T: Douglas & McIntyre 1987) leads readers to hide money under mattresses; *The Traders: Inside Canada's Stock Markets* (T: Collins 1984) is Alexander Ross's attempt to persuade us to haul the money out. The early history of the Toronto and Montreal stock exchanges are given balanced and sophisticated treatment in two articles: J.F. Whiteside, 'The Toronto Stock Exchange and the Development of the Share Market to 1985,' *JCS* 1985, and R.C. Michie, 'The Canadian Securities Market, 1850–1914,' *Business History Review* 1988, which provides international comparisons. The reader who wonders how stocks and bonds got sold might look at Christopher Armstrong's article, 'Making a Market: Selling Securities in Atlantic Canada before World War I,' *CJE* 1980. Gregory Marchildon soon will be producing interesting work on Max Aitken (in the meantime, see his 'Promotion, Finance, and Mergers in Canadian Manufacturing Industry, 1885–1918,' PhD thesis, LSE 1990).

Trust companies have fared better. David Mackenzie has written a short, direct, and insightful history of Guaranty Trust, *A Commitment to Quality: Guaranty Trust Company of Canada, 1926–86* (T: Guaranty Trust Company of Canada 1986). Canada Trust has now a full narrative history by Philip Smith, *The Trust-Builders: The Remarkable Rise of Canada Trust* (T: MAC 1989). Terence Corcoran and Laura Reid, *Public Money, Private Greed: The Greymac, Seaway, and Crown Trusts Affairs* (T: Collins 1984), have shown us how trust companies could be abused as vehicles for aggrandizement. With a similar thrust, Patricia Best and Ann Shortell have taken a broader look at trust companies in the fine *A Matter of Trust: Power and Privilege in Canada's Trust Companies* (Markham: Viking 1985).

TRANSPORTATION AND COMMUNICATIONS

The place to start on transportation remains George P. de T. Glazebrook, *A History of Transportation in Canada* (2nd ed., T: M&S 1964). Arthur W. Currie, *Canadian Transportation Economics* (T: UTP 1967) varies in quality; however it not only deals with railways, but tries to encompass highways, trucking, automobiles, and shipping.

The history of shipping and shipbuilding has received increased attention from the work of the Maritime History Project at Memorial University. A brief introduction is Eric W. Sager and Lewis R. Fischer, *Shipping and Shipbuilding in Atlantic Canada, 1820–1914* (O: CHA 1986). Several books of essays emerged from the project: among them are Lewis R. Fischer and Eric W. Sager, eds., *The Enterprising Canadians: Entrepreneurs and Economic Development in Eastern Canada, 1820–1914* (St John's: Memorial University 1979) and their *Merchant Shipping and Economic Development in Atlantic Canada* (St John's: Maritime History Group, Memorial University 1982); and David Alexander and Rosemary Ommer, eds., *Volumes Not Values: Canadian Sailing Ships and World Trades* (St John's: Maritime History Group, Memorial University 1979). How the shipping business worked up to World War I can be grasped through Eric W. Sager's *Seafaring Labour: The Merchant Marine of Atlantic Canada, 1820–1914* (M and K: MQUP 1989) and, with Gerald E. Panting, his *Maritime Capital: The Shipping Industry in Atlantic Canada, 1820–1914* (M and K: MQUP 1990). Transatlantic shipping with a Canadian element is to be found in Francis E. Hyde's impressive *Cunard and the North Atlantic, 1840–1973: A History of Shipping and Financial Management* (L: MAC 1975). Canals are primarily an early nineteenth-century phenomenon in Canada with the St Lawrence Seaway being the great exception. On that, one should consult a good, short introduction: Jennifer Sussman, *The St Lawrence Seaway: History and Analysis of a Joint Water Highway* (M: C.D. Howe Research Institute 1978). Shipping on the Great Lakes has generated considerable literature, as the 72 pages of *Canadian Great Lakes Shipping: An Annotated Bibliography*, complied by Susan S. Patterson (T: Centre for Urban and Community Studies 1976), clearly shows.

Canadian history has a romantic involvement with railways, and they have been deemed vital instruments of national development. Consequently we have broad surveys and highly specific studies in considerable number. Robert F. Legget, *Railways of Canada* (V: Douglas & McIntyre 1980) is a very readable general survey. The CPR has been done over several times, most completely by W. Kaye Lamb in *History of the Canadian Pacific Railway* (T: MAC 1977), but also in H.A. Innis's turgidly written *A History of the Canadian Pacific Railway* (2nd ed., T: UTP 1970), the second edition of which has a thought-provoking counter-factual introduction by Peter George. George questions the necessity for haste in construction and the need for massive government support for the CPR, premises otherwise not questioned except by late-nineteenth-century Liberals. A thoroughly accessible history of the building of the Canadian Pacific Railway which unquestioningly accepts the nationalist premises George does not are Pierre Berton's two volumes, *The National Dream: The Great Railway, 1871–1881* (T: M&S 1970) and *The Last Spike: The Great Railway, 1881–1885* (T: M&S 1971). Very considerable detail on the constituent parts of the Canadian National Railway system is given by George R. Stevens, in his two volumes on *Canadian National Railways* vol. 1: *Sixty Years of Trial and Error, 1836–1896*; vol. 2: *Towards the Inevitable, 1896–1922* (T: CI 1960, 1962). A fascinating story of western entrepreneurship in making the railway which lay at the heart of the CNR is to be found in T.D. Regehr, *The Canadian Northern Railway: Pioneer Road of the Northern Prairies, 1895–1918* (T: MAC 1976). A broader narrative regional study in which business enterprises plays only a part is John A. Eagle, *The Canadian Pacific Railway and the Development of Western Canada, 1896–1914* (M and K: MQUP 1989). Albert Tucker, *Steam into Wilderness: Ontario Northern Railway, 1902–1962* (T: Fitzhenry & Whiteside 1978) provides an extensive political and economic context for Ontario Northland Railway to 1960. A. A. den Otter, *Civilizing the West: The Galts and the Development of Western Canada* (E: UAP 1982), examines the involvement of a family in regional railway and coal-mining development. The title of William J. Wilgus, *The Railway Interrelations of the United States and Canada* (1937, NY: Russell & Russell 1970) is self-explanatory, and corrects the notion that railways were simply a bulwark against continental integration.

But road, rather than rail, has increasingly dominated continental transportation in the last half century, and we really don't know that much about it. Donald F. Davis is systematically exploring the function of some elements of automobile transport: 'Dependent Motorization: Canada and the Automobile to the 1930s.' *JCS* 1986. S. Davies, '"Reckless Walking Must Be Discouraged": The Automobile Revolution and the Shaping of Modern Urban Canada to 1930,' *UHR* 1989, provides an interesting spin. Material on the history of the automobile in Canada is remarkably limited. James Dykes, *Canada's Automotive Industry* (T: MH 1970) is a slim volume in more ways than one, and needs to be supplemented by Canada, Royal Commission on the Automobile Industry, *Report* (O: QP 1961). A satisfying slice of the automobile history pie, covering the bicycle and public transport in addition to the car, is the industrious Geoffrey W. Taylor's *The Automobile Saga of British Columbia, 1864–1914* (Victoria: Morriss Publishing 1984). The omnipresent trucking industry has not received its fair attention, although some beginnings have been made in the well-organized reminiscences of Andy A. Craig, *Trucking: British Columbia's Trucking History* (Saaninchton: Hancock House 1977). An anonymous work, *The Golden Years of Trucking: Commemorating Fifty Years of Service by the Ontario Trucking Association, 1926–1976* (Rexdale: Ontario Trucking Association 1977) offers a thorough chapter by R. Jerry on trucking technology in Canada. It is striking that the intellectual contexts of the history of road transportation are so distant from the national concerns that drove writing about railways and canals.

Some notion of the history and role in the 1960s of the humble yet vital people-mover, the bus, can be garnered from Derek Scrafton and Susan van Steenburgh, *The Inter-City Motor Coach Industry in Canada: A Report on the operations of the Bus and Coach Industry in Canada* (O: Ministry of Transport, Transportation Policy, and Research Branch 1970). Donald F. Davis has an interest in public transport too: 'Competition's Moment: The Jitney-bus and Corporate Capitalism in the Canadian City, 1914–29,' *UHR* 1989. It is a great caution to see how evanescent systems of public transport can be. Not only Davis touches on history almost lost: John F. Due, *The Intercity Electric Railway Industry in Canada* (T: UTP 1966) re-creates an industry of a century ago.

Philip Smith, *It Seems Like Only Yesterday: Air Canada, The First 50 Years* (T: M&S 1986) mixes insiders' anecdotes aimed at employees with insightful narrative analysis of the development of Air Canada. That story cannot escape the issue of government policy and involvement, as David Mackenzie's *Canada and International Civil Aviation, 1932–1948* (T: UTP 1989) elaborates.

For a general, broad, history of the media in Canada, see Paul Rutherford's *The Making of the Canadian Media* (T: MHR 1978). If you want to know how newspapers worked a hundred years ago, you can consult his *A Victorian Authority: The Daily Press in Late Nineteenth-Century Canada* (T: UTP 1982). Ross Harkness, *J.E. Atkinson of the Star* (T: UTP 1963) has scattered information on the business of running a newspaper. A good biography with large business-history content is Michael Nolan, *Walter J. Blackburn: A Man for All Media* (T: MAC 1989). Paul Rutherford has treated the history of television as a social phenomenon in *When Television Was Young: Primetime Canada, 1952–1967* (T: UTP 1990). The politics behind broadcasting policy are discussed in Frank W. Peers, *The Politics of Canadian Broadcasting, 1920–1951* (T: UTP 1969) and *The Public Eye: Television and the Politics Canadian Broadcasting, 1952–1968* (T: UTP 1979). The impression Peers provides of a necessarily public broadcasting system is questioned by Michael Nolan, 'An Infant Industry: Canadian Private Radio, 1919–36,' *CHR* 1989. On book publishing, see two background studies for the Ontario Royal Commission on Book Publishing, H. Pearson Gundy's *The Development of Trade Book Publishing in Canada* (T: QP 1972), and D. McGill, *The Marketing of Trade Books in Canada* (T: QP 1972).

Telecommunications has a useful popular history in Edmon B. Ogle, *Long Distance Please: The Story of the TransCanada Telephone System* (T. Collins 1979), but serious company histories are lacking. One place to go is Graham Taylor, 'Charles F. Sise, Bell Canada, and the Americans: A Study of Managerial Autonomy, 1880–1905,' CHA *HP* 1982, which functions as a useful case critique on generalizations about American multinationals in Canada, as well as analysing managerial functions. The telephone, now ubiquitous, was not always so, as is indicated in R.M. Pike's brief history and case study of the Kingston area, *Adopting the Telephone: The Social Diffusion and Use of the Telephone in Urban Central Canada, 1876–1914* (K: Queen's University 1987).

PRIMARY PRODUCTION

Even the oldest staple industries, fishing and the fur trade, have received substantial treatments recently. There was much room for such works: on the fur trade, the early Harold A. Innis, *The Fur Trade in Canada: An*

Introduction to Canadian Economic History (3rd ed., T: UTP 1970) has only one short chapter on the post-Confederation era. Now, however, one can go to Arthur J. Ray, *The Canadian Fur Trade in the Industrial Age* (T: UTP 1990), which discusses the Hudson's Bay Company's marketing, company organization, and relations with natives in the last hundred years. Peter C. Newman's third volume on the company, *Merchant Princes* (T: Viking 1991), offers the author's usual vigorous mix of the sprawling and anecdotal.

As the fishing industry off Newfoundland has staggered in ecological torment, historians, ironically, gave it increasing attention, puzzling as to why three centuries of exploitation had not led to a reasonably healthy regional economy: underdevelopment is the theme. *The Cod Fisheries* (cited above) was H.A. Innis's seminal contribution to this literature, long before the cod were in trouble. More recently, see the creative work of David Alexander: *Atlantic Canada and Confederation: Essays in Canadian Political Economy* (T: UTP 1983). Rosemary Ommer has continued with the very aptly titled 'What's Wrong with Canadian Fish,' *JCS* 1985, which has an insightful comparative element. The concern with development and its absence apparent in Ommer's work is extended in a discussion of 'Merchant Credit and the Informal Economy: Newfoundland, 1919–1929,' CHA *HP* 1989. Peter R. Sinclair has gathered together essays dealing with the role and development of the Newfoundland fisheries: *A Question of Survival: The Fisheries and Newfoundland Society* (St John's: Institute for Social and Economic Research 1988) and *State Intervention and the Newfoundland Fisheries: Essays on Fisheries Policy and Social Structure* (London: Gower Publishing 1987). The only notable company history of the fisheries is that by Stephen Kimber, *Net Profits: The Story of National Sea* (H: Nimbus Publishing 1989), which gives a good sense of the processes of commercial fishing, but with blindness to the depletion of the resource. Shannon Ryan, *Fish Out of Water: The Newfoundland Saltfish Trade, 1814–1914* (St John's: Breakwater 1986) finds the troubles of Newfoundland rooted in a decline in export markets beginning late in the nineteenth century.

A.B. McCullough's minor gem, *The Commercial Fishery of the Canadian Great Lakes* (O: Environment Canada 1989), extends this basic staple inland. For the west coast, one might well begin with William A. Carrothers's old but viable short study, *The British Columbia Fisheries* (T: UTP 1941). Dianne Newell, ed., provides a substantial introduction to *The Development of the Pacific Salmon-Canning Industry: A Grown Man's Game* (M and K: MQUP 1989), which covers the papers of the packer Henry Doyle,

Patricia Marchak, Neil Guppy, and John McMullan, eds., *Uncommon Property: The Fishing and Fish-Processing Industries in British Columbia* (T: Methuen 1987) offers a series of essays on the west coast fisheries and fish packers with good contemporary historical content.

Lumber

In *Bushworkers and Bosses: Logging in Northern Ontario, 1900–1980* (T: UTP 1987), Ian Radforth assesses changes in the character of work as a management response to rising labour costs. A.R.M. Lower's *The Northern American Assault on the Canadian Forest: A History of the Lumber Trade Between Canada and the Untied States* (T: RP 1938) entrenched notions of the industry's wastefulness even after the decline of the trade in square timber. Do not ignore the shorter studies on the Maritimes by Stanley A. Saunders and on British Columbia by William A. Carrothers, packaged with Lower. The problem of linkages between this industry and secondary manufacturing is scrutinized in J. Lutz, 'Losing Steam: The Boiler and Engine Industry as an Index of British Columbia's Deindustrialization, 1880–1915,' CHA *HP* 1988. Geoffrey W. Taylor, *Timber: History of the Forest Industry in BC* (V: J.J. Douglas 1975) is a brief overview. There are two substantial commissioned company histories. Ernest G. Perrault, *Wood and Water: The Story of Seaboard Lumber and Shipping* (V: Douglas & McIntyre 1985) shows how independent lumber millers could compete with an *Empire of Wood: The Macmillan Bloedel Story* (V: Douglas & McIntyre 1982), by Donald McKay. His *The Lumberjacks* (T: MHR 1978) gives superb insights into the field operations of lumbering in the late nineteenth and twentieth centuries.

Mining

Readers will not go wrong to consult the well-aged H.A Innis, *Settlement and the Mining Frontier* (T: MAC 1936). The prolific Philip Smith's *Harvest from the Rock: A History of Mining in Ontario* (T: MAC 1986) provides a survey history of Ontario Mining; Donat M. LeBourdais, *Metals and Men: The Story of Canadian Mining* (T: M&S 1957) was not thereby replaced. LeBourdais's *Sudbury Basin: The Story of Nickel* (T: RP 1953) combined with Oscar W. Main, *The Canadian Nickel Industry, 1885–1939: A Study in Market Control and Public Policy* (T: UTP 1955), and Wallace Clement, who describes Inco surface and mining operations in Sudbury in *Hardrock Mining: Industrial Relations and Technological Changes at*

Inco (T: M&S 1981), can give the reader a grasp of the development, structure, and technology of this industry. A fine company study of a public-sector mining corporation – although only loosely controlled by government – is Robert Bothwell's *Eldorado: Canada's National Uranium Company* (T: UTP 1984). The range of Eugene Forsey's concerns encompassed coal in Nova Scotia. See his *Economic and Social Aspects of the Nova Scotia Coal Industry* (T: MAC 1926), which is still a good source of information. David Frank has undertaken explorations of the coal industry from a labour perspective which are illuminating; see 'The Cape Breton Coal Industry and the Rise and Fall of the British Empire Steel Corporation,' *Acadiensis* 1977. While John N. McDougall's brief, compelling *Fuels and the National Policy* (T: BUT 1982) is devoted not to the processes of private enterprises, but to the development of national economic policy concerning coal, gas, and oil, his work is vital to understanding the context in which these industries operated.

Oil and Gas

Journalist-historians have made signal contributions to the history of the oil industry. Some of the key literature really deals with government-business relations (separately discussed later), but because of economic and technical elements cannot be excluded here. On the first ten years of the post-war industry in Alberta, consult Eric J. Hansen, *Dynamic Decade: The Evolution and Effects of the Oil Industry in Alberta* (T: M&S 1958), which also discusses petrochemicals. Half of John Richards and Larry Pratt, *Prairie Capitalism: Power and Influence in the New West* (T: M&S 1979) discusses Alberta oil (the other half is Saskatchewan potash) and shows how oil, because it required regulation, became a vehicle for provincial economic planning. Barry G. Ferguson, *Athabasca Oil Sands: Northern Resource Exploration, 1875–1951* (E: Alberta Culture and Canadian Plains Research Centre 1985) contributes much insight into the technicalities of oil sands exploitation and production; his book should be teamed with G. Taylor, 'Sun Oil Company and Great Canadian Oil Sands Ltd.: The Financing and Management of a Pioneer Enterprise, 1962–1974,' in *JCS* 1985. The immense uncertainties, the potential for failure, the intense excitement of success in oil exploration is all effectively explored in Philip Smith's *The Treasure-Seekers: The Men who Built Home Oil* (T: MAC 1978). Earle Gray describes the struggle to make deals, sell and move products, and the ever-present hand of government in *Wildcatters: The Story of Pacific Petroleums and Westcoast Transmission* (T: M&S 1982).

William Kilbourn has much to say about business-government relations and the growing intensity of Canadian economic nationalism in the 1950s in his *Pipeline: TransCanada and the Great Debate, A History of Business and Politics* (T: CI 1970). In his examination of the Dome oil exploration debacle *Other People's Money: The Banks, the Government and Dome* (Don Mills: Collins 1983), Peter Foster captures the mix of entrepreneurial dynamism and governmental stimulus which marked one era in the oil patch. David H. Breen's massive study of the oil industry in Alberta, *Alberta's Petroleum Industry and the Conservation Board* (E: UAP 1993) is now available.

Hydroelectricity

John H. Dales, *Hydroelectricity and Industrial Development: Quebec, 1889–1940* (Cambridge: HUP 1957) develops a persuasive argument about late industrialization in Quebec in his industry study. *The Beauharnois Scandal: A Story of Canadian Entrepreneurship and Politics* (T: UTP 1990), by T.D. Regehr, examines the political and business scandal with detailed care. The development of an integrated, province-wide energy supply system in Saskatchewan is covered in Clinton O. White, *Power for a Province: A History of Saskatchewan Power* (Regina: CPRC 1976). Keith R. Fleming, in *Power at Cost: Ontario Hydro and Rural Electrification, 1911–1958* (M and K: 1992) has extended the work on Ontario hydro begun by H.V. Nelles (see below) in ways far beyond the business demand for electricity. Merrill Denison, *The People's Power: The Story of Ontario Hydro* (T: M&S 1960) remains a reasonably effective treatment of this organization prior to nuclear power. The development of a single major hydroelectrical resource is explored in a massive work by Philip Smith: *Brinco: The Story of Churchill Falls* (T: M&S 1975).

Agriculture

Concerns about the role of government are pervasive. Vernon C. Fowke, *The National Policy and the Wheat Economy* (T: UTP 1957) and his *Canadian Agricultural Policy: The Historical Pattern* (T: UTP 1946) loom large. Along with Fowke's work, George E. Britnell, editor's preface by H.A. Innis, *The Wheat Economy* (T: UTP 1939) is permeated by concerns with the staples thesis. Charles F. Wilson's *A Century of Canadian Grain: Government Policy to 1951* (S: WPPB 1978) talks policy and marketing for over a thousand pages. The western focus of this literature is complemented by David Breen, *The Canadian Prairie West and the Ranching Frontier, 1874–1924* (T: UTP 1983), which details the economics of cattle-raising and conflict between ranches and farmers, and by Paul Voisey's *Vulcan: The Making of a Prairie Community* (T: UTP 1988), which furnishes an examination of the capitalist farmer. Fundamental information for understanding the patterns of settlement in Canada is found in Chester Martin, *Dominion Lands Policy* (2nd ed., T: M&S 1973). There is a sizeable journal literature on the rate and timing of western rural settlement: one might start into this by consulting Kenneth Norrie, 'The Rate of Settlement of the Canadian Prairies, 1870–1911,' *Journal of Economic History* 1975. A rip-roaring controversy among economic historians concerning the role of prairie wheat – and implicitly, the validity of the staples thesis – is partly summarized in Gordon W. Bertram, 'The Relevance of the Wheat Boom in Canadian Economic Growth,' *CJE* 1973.

A central Canadian emphasis could be found by consulting Robert L. Jones, *History of Agriculture in Ontario, 1613–1880* (1946, T: UTP 1977). John McCallum, *Unequal Beginnings: Agricultural and Economic Development in Quebec and Ontario until 1870* (T: UTP 1980) is a brilliant exposition of the notion of staple product linkages to the process of industrialization. The volumes of *Canadian Papers in Rural History* provide a diversity of studies in the economics of agriculture. The latter half of Marjorie Cohen's *Women's Work, Markets, and Economic Development in Nineteenth-Century Ontario* (T: UTP 1988) furnishes material on the role of women in the dairying industry and in Ontario's industrialization. Ian MacPherson has been a one-person industry in exploring the origins and development of farmers' cooperative business organizations. See, to begin with, his *Each for All: A History of the Co-operative Movement in English Canada 1900–1945* (T: MAC 1979). A survey of recent rural history by C.A. Wilson with strong reference to the Maritimes is in *Acadiensis* 1991, where R. McKinnon's 'Farming the Rock: The Evolution of Commercial Agriculture around St John's, Newfoundland to 1945' can also be found. A series of effective essays on agriculture in Quebec is Normand Séguin, ed., *Agriculture et colonisation au Québec: aspect historiques* (M: BE 1980).

INDUSTRIAL DEVELOPMENT AND MANUFACTURING

Development requires technology. John J. Brown's compendiun of Canadian inventions, *Ideas in Exile: A History of Canadian Invention* (T: M&S 1967) reflects nationalist concerns about presumed slow Canadian economic development; Bruce Sinclair, Norman R. Ball, and James O.

Petersen edited a collection of primary source readings in *Let Us Be Honest and Modest: Technology and Society in Canadian History* (T: OUP 1974). On the works of professional engineers, see Norman R. Ball, *'Mind, Heart, and Vision': Professional Engineering in Canada, 1887 to 1987* (O: National Museum of Science and Technology 1988). Really a book about the professionalization of engineering in Canada, but important to an understanding of the role of engineers in turn-of-the century advances is J. Rodney Millard, *The Master Spirit of the Age: Canadian Engineers and the Politics of Professionalism, 1887–1922* (T: UTP 1988). Norman Ball and John Vardalas have produced a business history with technical and engineering focus in *Ferranti-Packard: Pioneers in Canadian Electrical Manufacturing* (M and K: MQUP 1993). One volume with very useful material on technological transfer is Christopher Armstrong and H.V. Nelles, *Monopoly's Moment: The Organization and Regulation of Canadian Utilities, 1830–1930* (2nd ed., T: UTP 1988). On pulp and paper, see the superbly thorough Jean-Pierre Charland, *Les pâtes et papiers au Québec, 1880–1980: technologies, travail et travailleurs* (Québec: IQRC 1990), which describes technology and labour processes in major plants and is supplemented by excellent illustrations. In a careful case study, Jacques Ferland explores the character of technological dependence: '"Not for sale" – American Technology and Canadian Shoe Factories: the United Shoe Machinery Company of Canada, 1899–1912,' *The American Review of Canadian Studies* 1988. *Material History Review* 1992 has a number of articles on technology in Canada, including Larry McNally's on nails in Montreal.

One Canadian industry which has received substantial attention is the iron and steel industry. Kris Inwood's careful, exhaustive *Decline and Rise of Charcoal Iron, The Case of Canada: The Canadian Charcoal Iron Industry, 1870–1914* (NY: Garland 1986) traces in detail one dominant early form of iron production. But the industry as it emerged in the early twentieth century needs to be seen through William Kilbourn, *The Elements Combined: A History of the Steel Company of Canada* (T: CI 1960), and Duncan McDowall, *Steel at the Sault: Francis H. Clergue, Sir James Dunn, and the Algoma Steel Corporation, 1901–1956* (T: UTP 1984) McDowall, while stressing the function of personality and government involvement in Algoma's growth, shows that the organizational systems beloved by A.D. Chandler were not well-established at Algoma during Dunn's reign. The development of the steel industry can be observed in Craig Heron, *Working in Steel: The Early Years in Canada, 1883–1935* (T: M&S 1988), in which Heron, a labour historian, traces the considerable weaknesses of the early-twentieth century industry. K. Inwood has carefully traced the weakness of the Nova Scotian iron and steel industry to the resource base, rather than to managerial iniquities, in 'Local control, resources, and the Nova Scotia Steel and Coal Company,' CHA *HP* 1986. W.J.A. Donald, *The Canadian Iron and Steel Industry: A Study in the Economic History of a Protected Industry* (Boston: Houghton Mifflin 1915), old and useful, emphasizes the tariff – another source of weakness. How did an industry so riddled with defects survive?

The locational aspects of strategic planning for a major automotive firm are analysed in Gerald T. Bloomfield's *Locational Processes at Work: The Ford Car Assembly Plant at St. Thomas, Ontario* (Guelph: Dept. of Geography, University of Guelph 1990). W.G. Philips, *The Agricultural Implement Industry in Canada: A Study of Competition* (T: UTP 1956) is the right place to start, though gnomic in its exploration. Merrill Denison's journalistic study of the Masseys, *Harvest Triumphant: The Story of Massey-Harris* (T: M&S 1948) has weathered well as a discussion of agricultural equipment manufacturing, and must be used with E.P. Neufeld and P. Cook, cited below.

Food Processing

In biographical form, Michael Bliss, *A Canadian Millionaire: The Life and Business Times of Sir Joseph Flavelle, Bart., 1858–1939* (T: UTP 1992), gives the reader an understanding not just of food processing, but banking, finance, and the organization of an economy for war in the late nineteenth and early twentieth centuries. The breweries have received a fair bit of attention: Merrill Denison, *The Barley and the Stream: The Molson Story, a Footnote to Canadian History* (T: M&S 1955) does a good job, and certainly was not replaced by Shirley E. Woods, Jr, *The Molson Saga, 1763–1983* (T: Doubleday 1983). To understand how the industry achieved its modern form in Canada, one must consult Richard Rohmer, *E.P. Taylor: The Biography of Edward Plunket Taylor* (T: M&S 1978). An even more alcoholic food has been explored, again in biographical form, in Peter C. Newman, *Bronfman Dynasty: The Rothschilds of The New World* (T: M&S 1978). The latter should be read only with Michael Marrus's *Mr. Sam: The Biography of Samuel Bronfman* (T: MAC 1991) in hand. Several background studies (especially those on the Molson Companies, Argus Corporation, Rothmans of Pall Mall, and Carling O'Keefe Limited), for Canada, Royal Commission on Corporate Concentration, provide some insight into the world of Canadian holding companies and conglomerates with strong interests in food processing.

Textiles and Furniture

A superior general survey of the primary textile industry primarily before 1940 is A.B. McCullough, *The Primary Textile Industry in Canada: History and Heritage* (O: Environment Canada 1992). Some elements of the woollen manufacturing industry in the nineteenth century have received substantial attention. *The Development of the Woollen Industry in Lanark, Renfrew and Carleton Counties* (n.p.: North Lanark Historical Society 1978), and Richard Reid, 'The Rosamond Woolen Company of Almonte: Industrial Development in a Rural Setting,' *Ontario History* 1983, are excellent starting points.

Barbara Austin's 'Life cycles and the Strategy of a Canadian Company – Dominion Textile: 1873–1983,' (PhD thesis, Concordia University 1985) has a Chandlerian emphasis on strategy, structure, and management, using some most instructive techniques. Caroline Pestieau, *The Quebec Textile Industry in Canada* (M: C.D. Howe Research Institute 1978), and Rianne Mahon, *The Politics of Industrial Restructuring: Canadian Textiles* (T: UTP 1984) both assess the contemporary industry in the context of international competition and domestic government support.

A fine book which offers much insight into the roles of women and men in textile and furniture manufacturing is Joy Parr, *The Gender of Breadwinners: Women, Men, and Change in Two Industrial Towns, 1880–1950* (T: UTP 1990), which downplays technological change. Ben Forster, 'Finding the Right Size: Markets and Competition in the Mid- and Late-Nineteenth-Century Ontario,' in Roger Hall, William Westfall, and Laurel S. MacDowell, eds., *Patterns of the Past: Interpreting Ontario's History* (T: Dundurn 1988) leans the other way in examining an era of intensifying competition from the examples of woollens and furniture manufacture. Ruth Cathcart, *Jacques & Hay: 19th Century Toronto Furniture Makers* (Erin: Boston Mills Press 1986) provides much detail on one major nineteenth-century furniture manufacturer.

DISTRIBUTION AND RETAILING

We certainly don't know a great deal about wholesale distribution in this country. Douglas McCalla has given us a good picture of a large-scale wholesaler just at the time of Confederation in *The Upper Canada Trade* (cited above). Albert D. Cohen styles himself as one of *The Entrepreneurs: The Story of Gendis Inc.* (T: M&S 1985), openly reporting on the Cohen-dominated firm's distributing deals and close relationships with Sony.

The self-serving *Net Worth: The Memories of C.E. Pickering* (T: Yorkminster Pub. 1973), based on interviews by Dean Walker, is remarkably frank in its portrayal of a driven salesman who through simple hard work accumulated a fortune in the distribution and manufacturing of cleaning products.

Eaton's has received repeated treatments: Joy L. Santink's recent *Timothy Eaton and the Rise of His Department Store* (T: UTP 1990) is the best of these and emphasizes Eaton's organization and retailing. Another family-dominated retailing concern is discussed by Douglas E. Harker, *The Woodwards: The Story of a Distinguished British Columbia Family, 1850–1975* (V: Mitchell Press 1976), which stresses family more than firm. David Monad's emphasis on organizational and marketing characteristics is refreshingly unusual in 'Bay Days: The Managerial Revolution and the Hudson's Bay Company Department Stores, 1912–1939,' in CHA *HP* 1986. The operations of a clothing manufacturer *cum* retailer are described by Alan Wilson in one of the earliest Canadian biographies explicitly written as business history, *John Northway: A Blue Serge Canadian* (T: Burns and MacEachern 1965). *Freewheeling: The Feuds, Broods, and Outrageous Fortunes of the Billes Family and Canada's Favorite Company* (T: HarperCollins 1989), by Ian Brown, is a highly coloured examination of the history of Canadian Tire, and provides much insight into the firm's operational characteristics and into the special difficulties faced by family-dominated firms. Keith Walden, 'Speaking Modern: Language, Culture, and Hegemony in Grocery Window Displays, 1887–1920,' *CHR* 1989, is an interesting, although strained, effort to plumb the full meaning of commercial window displays.

BUSINESS STRUCTURE, MANAGEMENT, AND LABOUR

As elements of the organizational analysis of American cases, there has been much emphasis on managerial structures, the techniques of management, and consequently on some elements of labour relations. Such literature is not at all rich in Canadian historiography. Efforts are now under way to focus attention on issues of management, and certainly the volume of essays which were the product of the business history conference in Victoria in 1988, Baskerville, ed., *Canadian Papers in Business History* (cited above – see those of Radforth on furniture manufacturing, R. Rajala on technology and management in BC lumbering, and G. Taylor on Vickers Canada) indicates that a transition in focus is taking place. One early article which attempted to direct attention to the managerial issue was that of Peter Baskerville, 'Professional vs. Proprietor: Power Distribution in the Railroad World of Upper Canada/Ontario, 1850 to 1881,' CHA *HP* 1978 – not surprisingly as railways were one of the great breeding grounds for professional management in the United States and Britain.

Case studies remain in limited availability for Canadian firms. Mark C. Baetz and Paul W. Beamish, *Strategic Management: Canadian Cases* (Homewood: Irwin 1987), which functions as a general text on strategic management, offers some 36 brief case studies of Canadian firms as diverse as Redpath, Magna International, Canadian Tire, and the Toronto Sun. A good entry into the history of systematic and scientific management, although the empirical base is narrow, is by Graham S. Lowe, *Women in the Administrative Revolution: The Feminization of Clerical Work* (T: UTP 1987). The vast American literature on welfare work – the paternalistic mode of large corporations – finds no replication in Canada, but entrance to this important area is provided by Margaret McCallum, 'Corporate Welfarism in Canada, 1919–39,' *CHR* 1990. Edward B. Mellett, *From Stopwatch to Strategy: A History of the First Twenty-five years of the Canadian Association of Management Consultants* (T: Canadian Association of Management Consultants 1988) provides a brief, popular history of a group devoted to the technical improvement of management.

A wide array of formal and informal institutions and organizations give business and economic life expression. While the history of business education has not fared well, there has been some groundwork laid in Max Von Zur-Muehlen, *Business Education and Faculty at Canadian Universities* (O: Information Canada 1971). Chartered accountancy in its educational and institutional aspects has been given an evocative and thorough treatment in Philip Creighton, *A Sum of Yesterdays: Being a History of the First One Hundred Years of the Institute of Chartered Accountants of Ontario* (T: The Institute 1984). Why Clarkson Gordon alone deserves two company histories, when so many other accountancy firms go begging is not easy to understand; see Arthur J. Little, *The Story of the Firm, 1864–1964: Clarkson, Gordon & Co.* (T: Clarkson Gordon 1964), and David MacKenzie, *The Clarkson Gordon Story: In Celebration of 125 Years* (T: Clarkson Gordon 1989). Frederick Elkin, *Rebels and Colleagues: Advertising and Social Change in French Canada* (M and K: MQUP 1973) looks at the role of advertising in Quebec's Quiet Revolution; almost as an incidental benefit, we learn about agencies and the technology of advertising. Carol Wilton did a great deal to stimulate interest in an undeveloped area when she brought business and legal historians together to begin a dialogue in

Beyond the Law: Lawyers and Business in Canada, 1830 to 1930 (T: Osgoode Society 1990).

The approach fostered by Alfred D. Chandler is cogenial to large corporations. Yet much of the business world has been made up of small joint-stock firms, and of firms that are family-held. Such firms have faced functional and structural problems not always open to Chandlerian analysis: what of succession problems in family firms, for example? An effort to deal with some of these matters outside the framework of biography and family history is apparent in articles by Margaret McCallum, 'Law and the Problems of Succession at Ganong Bros.,' and Henry C. Klassen, 'Family business and inheritance in Alberta and Montana,' and Barbara Austin, 'Structural Adaptation in a Family Firm: Hamilton Cotton/ Hamilton Group 1832–1991,' in P. Baskerville, ed., *Canadian Papers in Business History*, vol. 2 (cited above). Many family firm histories (see I. Brown, *Freewheeling* cited above, for example) as well as biographies such as M. Nolan, *A Man for All Media* (cited above) touch on the special problems of family-dominated firms.

ELITES

Biography, indeed, has been one of the favoured modes of treating Canadian business life. Peter Foster's careful *The Master Builders: How the Reichmanns Reached for an Empire* (T: Key Porter 1986) does not deal with the spectacular fall of the Reichmanns' Olympia and York (Owe and Why? or Oh, why?), but Foster provides carefully laid clues as to some of that empire's flaws. In his recently published *Towers of Debt: The Rise and Fall of the Reichmanns* (T: Key Porter 1993) he has extended his exploration into Reichmanns' downfall. Much criticized for its congratulatory tone, Rohmer's *E.P. Taylor* (cited above) nonetheless lets us see key elements in the formation of a holding-company conglomerate. The astonishing dominance of the Irving family in New Brunswick can be explored in Russell Hunt and Robert Campbell, *K.C. Irving: The Art of the Industrialist* (T: M&S 1973) and especially in John DeMont, *Citizens Irving: K.C. Irving and His Legacy: The Story of Canada's Wealthiest Family* (T: Doubleday 1991). The family is Canada's no longer: K.C.'s will saw to that. The McCains, the other power in New Brunswick, have not yet had their innings in the books, although others in the Maritimes have: *Frank Sobey: The Man and the Empire* (T: MAC 1985), by Harry Bruce, is a relatively full tale. Conrad Black's own strained mixture of bluster and honesty, *A Life in Progress* (T: Key Porter 1993), partly replaces P.C.

Newman's *The Establishment Man: A Portrait of Power* (T: M & S 1982). Susan Goldenberg, *The Thomson Empire* (T: Methuen 1984) is less about newspapers than family wealth, acquisition, and the making of a conglomerate. Roger Lacasse, *Joseph-Armand Bombardier: An Inventor's Dream Come True* (M: Libre Expression 1988) gives the reader a clear perception of how entrepreneurship, invention, and family ties could be the basis of an international transportation conglomerate; it also appears to be a success story in terms of government involvement.

Wealth and power are closely related, and it has been suggested more than once that people of wealth and power form broad social networks which control and direct Canadian life. Indeed, academics stressing class and elites often come to question the public-good emphasis of some nationalist interpretations of Canadian economic and business history. An early muckraking examination of the monied elite is Gustavus Myers, *A History of Canadian Wealth*, vol. 1 (1914, 2nd ed., T: J. Lewis and Samuel, 1972, with an introduction by Stanley Ryerson). R. Tom Naylor, *The History of Canadian Business, 1867–1914* (T: JL 1975) combines muckraking schismatic marxism with an effort to blame the nineteenth-century mercantile elite of Canada for a presumed failure of Canada to industrialize. John A. Porter, *The Vertical Mosaic: An Analysis of Social Class and Power in Canada* (T: UTP 1965) laid out the basis for the study of contemporary elites in Canada. Wallace Clement elaborated on Porter from a marxist perspective: see his *The Canadian Corporate Elite: An Analysis of Economic Power* (T: M&S 1975) and *Continental Corporate Power: Economic Elite Linkages between Canada and the United States* (T: M&S 1977). See also William K. Carroll, *Corporate Power and Canadian Capitalism* (V: UBCP 1986). An iconoclastic, brief, and unsubtle elite-analysis of the contemporary business world is Jorge Niosi, *The Economy of Canada: A Study of Ownership and Control* (2nd ed., M: Black Rose 1982). Peter C. Newman has combined the scholarly notion of elites – rather too loosely, most academics think – with the widespread public fascination with people of money in his two volumes on *The Canadian Establishment* (T: M&S 1975, 1981) and his earlier *Flame of Power: Intimate Profiles of Canada's Greatest Businessmen* (T: M&S 1965).

A stress on entrepreneurialism weaves into this biographical and elite-oriented material, although the entrepreneurial emphasis very frequently rejects the notion of close business-government relations. An exception to this is Matthew Fraser, *Quebec Inc.: French-Canadian Entrepreneurs and the New Business Elite* (T: Key Porter 1987), which ties together entrepreneurship, elites, and government support of business, although some of his cases have become tarnished. Other writers simply appeal to the reading public's interest in the successful and rich. 'How they made it – and how you can too,' trumpets the front cover of Allen Gould, *The New Entrepreneurs: 80 Canadian Success Stories* (2nd. ed., T: Bantam 1987). Fortunately the book is somewhat more than recipes for success. Paul Grescoe and David Cruise, *The Money Rustlers: Self-Made Millionaires of the New West* (Markham: Viking 1985); Alexander Ross, *The Risk Takers* (T: MacLean-Hunter 1975) enters the same racy vein.

BUSINESS–GOVERNMENT RELATIONS

Virtually all Canadian business history touches on the issue of business-government relations. A number of general surveys on business-government relations are worth examination: William D. Coleman, *Business and Politics: A Study of Collective Action* (M and K: MQUP 1988), while contemporary in bias, had useful historical content. W.T. Stanbury, *Business-Government Relations in Canada: Gripping with Leviathan* (T: Methuen 1986) should be consulted as well. The most compelling explanation for the close relationship remains in two essays by Hugh G.J. Aitken: 'Defensive Expansionism: The State and Economic Growth in Canada,' in Aitken, ed., *The State and Economic Growth* (NY: Social Science Research Council 1959) and 'Government and Business in Canada: An Interpretation,' *Business History Review* 1964.

Aitken's explanation is permeated with geographic and economic determinism. It is rich in nationalist implications, and consequently fosters the nationalist/continentalist dichotomy which has deep roots in debates over economic policy. The historical basis of the dichotomy in political life is traced by R. Craig Brown, *Canada's National Policy, 1883–1900: A Study in Canadian-American Relations* (Princeton: Princeton UP 1964) and in his article in Peter Russell, ed., *Nationalism in Canada* (T: MH 1966). Edward Porritt's early, passionate *Sixty Years of Protection in Canada, 1846–1907, Where Industry Leans on the Politician* (L: MAC 1908) gives away its perspective in the title. John H. Dales, in *The Protective Tariff in Canadian Development: Eight Essays on Trade and Tariffs when Factors Move with Special Reference to Canadian Protectionism, 1870–1955* (T: UTP 1966), and in his article in Russell, ed., *Nationalism in Canada*, explicitly rejects the continentalist label which his economic liberalism apparently acquired. Some implicit effort to escape the compelling force of Aitkin's thinking is to be found in a whole series of articles on one or another national policy in *JCS* 1979. Indeed, interest-group analyses may enrich, soften, or rebuff parts of Aitken's perspective. Ben Forster's discussion of the National Policy of tariffs, *A Conjunction of Interests: Business, Politics, and Tariffs, 1825–1879* (T: UTP 1986), emphasizes a pluralist interest-group approach sceptical about protectionist nationalism. More synthetic in tone on tariff policy is Orville J. McDiarmid, *Commercial Policy in the Canadian Economy* (Cambridge: HUP 1946), which covers a longer time span.

Tariffs lead into the issues of trade relations. A. broader historical examination in *Canada-United States Economic Relations* (O: QP 1957), by Irving Brecher and S.S. Reisman (now of FTA fame), has useful material on business cycles and on foreign investment as well. The making of the Free Trade Agreement with the United States stimulated a renewed bout of explorations of trade relations: a useful book of readings on the controversy the FTA generated is Duncan Cameron, ed., *The Free Trade Papers* (T: JL 1986).

The issue of commercial relations with the United States has had much previous economic analysis (and see above, on tariffs). An overview is Randall White, *Fur Trade to Free Trade: Putting the Canada-US Trade Agreement in Historical Perspective* (2nd ed., T: Dundurn 1989). Set within the broader context of Canadian-American relations, commercial relations are examined with care by Lester B. Shippee, *Canadian-American Relations, 1849–1874* (1939, NY: Russell and Russell 1970), and Charles Tansill, *Canadian-American Relations, 1875–1911* (1943, Glouster: P. Smith 1964), for the nineteenth and early twentieth centuries. Lewis E. Ellis, *Reciprocity 1911: A Study in Canadian-American Relations* (1939, NY: Greenwood 1968) examines in detail the negotiations and politics of the proposed 1911 trade agreement. The drift toward more protectionist policies in the 1930s is examined in Richard N. Kottman, *Reciprocity and the North Atlantic Triangle, 1932–1938* (Ithaca: Cornell UP 1968), and the closer relations stimulated by World War II are skilfully assessed by Robert Cuff and J.L. Granatstein in *American Dollars/Canadian Prosperity: Canadian-American Economic Relations, 1945–50* (T: Samuel Stevens 1978).

There are numerous departments of government concerned with economic matters. Two histories of such institutions can prove valuable from various perspectives: Robert B. Bryce drew heavily on his own experience in *Maturing in Hard Times: Canada's Department of Finance through the Great Depression* (T: Institute of Public Administration 1986), although the book is based on documentary sources; and O. Mary Hill, *Canada's Salesman to the World: The Department of Trade and Commerce, 1892–1939* (M and K: MQUP 1977) details efforts to foster international trade.

The curious beginnings of Canadian competition policy are traced in

M. Bliss, 'Another Anti-Trust Tradition: Canadian Anti-Combines Policy, 1889–1910,' *Business History Review* 1973. A careful analytical study of the goals of competition policy derived from the stated motives of its architects, the provisions of legislation, and from the case law, is Paul K. Gorecki and W.T. Stanbury, *The Objectives of Canadian Competition Policy, 1888–1983* (M: Institute for Research on Public Policy 1984). Lloyd G. Reynolds, *The Control of Competition in Canada* (Cambridge: HUP 1940) continues to be a worthy source.

The regulatory process, of which competition policy is one element, is an area of exploration where disparate themes in business-government relations sometimes fuse together. The continued strong interest in the history of regulation and government intervention in business is apparent in a number of articles in P. Baskerville, ed., *Canadian Papers in Business History*, vol. 2 (cited above). G. Bruce Doern, ed., *The Regulatory Process in Canada* (T: MAC 1978) provides contemporary views from political science. Undoubtedly the greatest contributors to the discussion of regulation from a historical perspective have been H.V. Nelles and Christopher Armstrong. H.V. Nelles, *The Politics of Development: Forests, Mines, and Hydro-Electric Power in Ontario, 1849–1941* (T: MAC 1974) is a huge, discursive, and insightful book on Ontario policy formation on mining, hydro, and lumbering. *The Revenge of the Methodist Bicycle Company: Sunday Streetcars and Municipal Reform in Toronto, 1888–1897* (T: Peter Martin Associates 1977) is Armstrong and Nelles's obscurely titled, amusingly written discussion of relations between utility operators, the public, and Toronto City Hall in the late nineteenth century. That work evolved into their study of disaggregated regulatory evolution in the Canadian utilities sector, *Monopoly's Moment*.

An early, and relatively unsophisticated, exponent of the 'capture' theory of regulation (that regulatory agencies are the creatures of the industries regulated) is Alvin Finkel, *Business and Social Reform in the Thirties* (T: JL 1979). Tom Traves traces a more tortured trail of the development of regulation under business impetus in newsprint, autos, and steel in *The State and Enterprise: Canadian Manufacturers and the Federal Government, 1917–1931* (T: UTP 1979). Ken Cruikshank's treatment of one of the earliest national regulatory agencies, the Board of Railway Commissioners, *Close Ties: Railways, Government, and the Board of Railway Commissioners, 1851–1933* (M and K: MQUP 1991), rejects capture and develops the intriguing notion of regulatory pluralism based on interest-group politics.

Wars, not economy and geography, are the exogenous shocks which created the scope and the character of modern business-government relations, it has been suggested. While not business history, Doug Owram, *The Government Generation: Canadian Intellectuals and the State, 1900–1945* (T: UTP 1986) expresses this in a moderate way. Owram does trace the roots of government interventionism to social changes early this century. J.L. Granatstein, *The Ottawa Men: The Civil Service Mandarins, 1935–1957* (T: OUP 1982) pivots much more on the war, and opens the way to understanding government involvement in the economy in the last fifty years. The extent of government interventionism during World War I is usefully described in J.A. Corry, 'The Growth of Government Activities in Canada 1914–1921,' CHA *AR* 1940. The role of women, vital in wartime manufacturing but deemed less so in the aftermath, is analysed in Ruth R. Pierson, *'They're Still Women After All': The Second World War and Canadian Womanhood* (T: M&S 1986). M. Bliss provides a more detailed account of intervention in World War manufacturing in his biography of Joseph Flavelle (cited above) and in a brief article in N.F. Dreisziger, ed., *Mobilization of Total War: The Canadian, American, and British Experience, 1914–1918, 1939–1945* (Wa: WLUP 1981), where Robert Bothwell also provides his perspectives on the financing of World War Two. Despite their lengthy discussion of government interventionism in the economy during that war and after [*C.D. Howe: A Biography* (T: M&S 1979)], Bothwell and William Kilbourn vehemently denied Michael Bliss's assertion that Howe set in place modern business dependence on government. Bothwell has gone over the topic from other perspectives: see his narrative discussions in *Eldorado* (cited above) and *Nucleus: The History of Atomic Energy of Canada Limited* (T: UTP 1988).

It is currently high fashion to reject all overt government involvement in business activity, just as growing government involvement was almost uncritically accepted as a public good for thirty years or more after World War II. When Peter Mathias had his *Forced Growth: Five Studies of Government Involvement in the Development of Canada* (T: J. Lewis and Samuel 1971) published in 1971 his was a lonely voice denouncing the interference of the state. Rather later, Peter Foster continued with great verve and skill the attack begun by Mathias; in his assault on the National Energy Policy in *The Sorcerer's Apprentices: Canada's Super-Bureaucrats and the Energy Mess* (T: Collins 1982) meddling bureaucrats get the short end of the stick. M. Trebilcock's *The Political Economy of Business Bailouts* (T: Ontario Economic Council 1985) is a scholarly examination of the way governments can throw good money after bad. One racy tale of an individual company is H.A. Fredericks and Allan Chambers, *Bricklin* (Fredericton: Brunswick Press 1977). Richard D. French, *How Ottawa*

Decides: Planning and Industrial Policy-Making 1968–1980 (T: JL 1980) shows us an Ottawa in an orgy of bureaucratic strategic planning, although French remains hopeful for the future of such centralization activity. A comparative examination of government involvement by Sanford F. Borins with Lee Brown, *Investments in Failure: Five Government Corporations that cost the Canadian Taxpayer Billions* (T: Methuen 1986), is cautious in its conclusions, finding common flaws in the cases examined, but finding that creative and effective involvement is possible. Certainly the excesses of the 1960s and 1970s provided much grist for the mill of laissez-faire critics. Yet involvement of the state in economic life has been one of the touchstones of the Canadian experience, and in practice no business person, no student – no academic! – can claim the biblical honour of casting the first stone.

MULTINATIONALS AND FOREIGN OWNERSHIP

Government intervention was for a long time deemed to be a major method of reducing foreign ownership in Canadian business, and for overcoming underdevelopment, the deemed consequence of foreign ownership. The staples thesis generated controversial ideas about the nature of Canadian economic and business development in these regards, rooted in the notion of a 'staples trap,' the end result of which is supposed to be a stunted or dependent industrial sector. Melville Watkins articulated the notion in *JCS* 1977. One should read his much more optimistic elaboration of staples as an engine of development, 'A staple theory of economic growth,' in Easterbrook and Watkins, eds., *Approaches to Canadian Economic History* (cited above). The most substantial historical treatment is to be found in Naylor, *The History of Canadian Business* (cited earlier). A number of Canadian economic nationalists adopted the 'staple trap' thesis in part or in whole: Kari Levitt, *Silent Surrender: The Multinational Corporation in Canada* (T: MAC 1970) is so fuelled. The great popularity of theses perspectives in the 1960s and 1970s has waned. One set of arguments surrounding the dangers of foreign investment which does not derive from the theoretical conceptions outlined above is the report put together by Liberal cabinet minister Herb Gray, which is handily presented in The Canadian Forum, eds., *A Citizen's Guide to the Gray Report* (Don Mills: PaperJacks 1971).

To balance this nationalist literature, one might start with Herbert Marshall, Frank Southard, and Kenneth W. Taylor, *Canadian-American Industry: A Study in International Investment* (1936, T: M&S 1976) and then continue with the unpassionate A.E. Safarian, *Foreign Ownership of Canadian Industry* (2nd. ed., T: UTP 1973). Balanced, although incomplete and dated, perspectives are to be found in Hugh G.J. Aitken [and others], *The American Economic Impact on Canada* (Durham: Duke UP 1959). A. Dow, 'Finance and Foreign Control in Canadian Base Metal Mining, 1918–55,' *Economic History Review* 1984, shows Canadian money and entrepreneurship utilizing some American finance to exploit mineral resources.

The considerable historical role of British investment in Canada is underplayed in this context. Donald G. Paterson, *British Direct Investment in Canada, 1890–1914: Estimates and Determinants* (T: UTP 1976), indicates the extent of British portfolio investment in early twentieth century Canada; how the money actually got here can be seen through G.P. Marchildon, '"Hands across the Water": Canadian Industrial Financiers in the City of London, 1905–20,' *Business History* 1992.

Despite the body of work on foreign investments, close examinations of the operational and financial aspects of foreign multinationals in Canada remain largely lacking. There are some materials in Canada in Mira Wilkins and Frank E. Hill, *American Business Abroad: Ford on Six Continents* (Detroit: Wayne State 1964), and there is excellent substance on Newfoundland pulp and paper in the well-known British business historian William J. Reader's *Bowater: A History* (Cambridge: Cambridge UP 1981). Decisions concerning major multinational operations in Canada were not necessarily filtered through sophisticated managerial structures, Jose E. Igartua argues in '"Corporate" Strategy and Locational Decision-Making: The Duke-Price-Alcoa Merger, 1925,' *JCS* 1985. J. Laureyssens, 'Growth of the Multidivisional Corporation: The Genstar Case,' *Business History Review* 1982, shows a strong Chandlerian influence in an examination of a Belgian-based multinational in Canada. Several articles by Graham Taylor indicate his interest in the area: 'A Merchant of Death in the Peaceable Kingdom: Canadian Vickers, 1911–27,' in Baskerville, ed., *Canadian Papers in Business History*, vol. 1 (cited above), on Sun Oil (see above) and in the journal next cited. The special July 1992 issue of *Business History* is devoted to multinationals in Canada and to international finance, so the subject is receiving increasing emphasis.

Curiously enough, historians have paid attention to Canadian entrepreneurs and companies functioning abroad. The domestic and state-side business operations of Canada's best-known nineteenth-century photographer are explored, with ample illustration, in Roger Hall, W.D. Dodds, and S. Triggs, *The World of William Notman* (T: M&S 1993). Christopher Armstrong and H.V. Nelles, *Southern Exposure: Canadian Promoters in Latin America and the Caribbean, 1896–1930* (T: UTP 1988) deals with Canadian entrepreneurs in utilities in the Caribbean and South America; Duncan McDowall gives the company now called Brascan a thorough examination in *The Light: Brazilian Traction, Light, and Power Company Limited, 1899–1945* (T: UTP 1988). E.P. Neufeld, *A Global Corporation: A History of the International Development of Massey-Ferguson Limited* (T: UTP 1969) was path-breaking in its emphasis on organizational matters, but perhaps did not probe deeply into the flaws generated by the corporation's climb to international stature; Peter Cook, *Massey at the Brink: The Story of Canada's Greatest Multinational and its Struggle to Survive* (T: Collins 1981) is a required corrective. Robert Campeau's success as a developer is praised in Michael Babad and Catherine Mulroney, *Campeau: The Building of an Empire* (T: Doubleday 1989), which traces his rise and apogee; John Rothchild, *Going for Broke: How Robert Campeau Bankrupted the Retail Industry, Jolted the Junk Bond Market, and Brought the Booming Eighties to a Crashing Halt* (T: Simon and Schuster 1991) stresses his personality flaws rather than errors in management and structure for the disaster in retailing which resulted.

The stress on international competitiveness is pervasive in the Macdonald Commission Report, more formally known as Canada, Royal Commission on the Economic Union and Development Prospects for Canada, *Report* (O: Supply and Services Canada 1985). The report laid the groundwork for the current Free Trade Agreement with the United States. To balance its conclusions one might look at Daniel Drache and Duncan Cameron, eds., *The Other Macdonald Report: The Consensus on Canada's Future that the Macdonald Commission Left Out* (T: JL 1985), which derives conclusions of an economic nationalist character from a significant group of submissions to the Commission.

One of the few books that examine Canadian multinationals on a comparative basis is Alan M. Rugman and John McIlveen, *Megafirms: Strategies for Canada's Multinationals* (T: Methuen 1985), and it reaches some clear and useful conclusions. Jorge Niosi, *Canadian Multinationals* (T: Garamond Press 1985) has a fundamentally different perspective. The analysis made by Michael Porter in his *Canada at the Crossroads: The Reality of a New Competitive Environment* (O: Business Council on National Issues 1991) uses a sophisticated and complex, but rigidly formulistic, model which probably does not suit the Canadian case. Both the Rugman and the Porter studies emphasize international competition.

Canadian business history had the fortune or misfortune of emerging in, and contributing to, an era of fragmentation in historical studies. Unlike economic history, in business history a common approach, a dominant interpretation, or generally accepted techniques of analysis have never been apparent. Intellectual and social histories of business life, studies which emphasize regions, approaches which can really be viewed as labour or gender history, and other forms of assessment have evolved. An interest in business-government relations has provided a highly important theme. The most powerful American methods have become increasingly fashionable – although they are still not in widespread use – but techniques which involve accounting and financial appraisal are virtually unknown. It may be, too, that comparative and industry-wide excurses such as have marked some recent work in the United States may reaffirm links to economic history when adapted to Canada.

Most historians, economic and otherwise, would agree that the decline from dominance of the staples thesis has been beneficial. But even though substantial fragmentation has taken place in economic history, there are extremely powerful methodological commonalities in that discipline, and at least some schools based on different assumptions. The problem-driven, theory-dominated approaches which have saturated the subdiscipline are at a considerable remove from methods and techniques common in other historical subdisciplines. Economic historians can face difficulties in making their work accessible while maintaining professional sophistication; however, some economic history of the last decade has merged theoretical considerations with effective analytical description. Pervasive concerns with development and underdevelopment continue to provide the impetus for the discipline's undertakings.

DOUG OWRAM

Intellectual, Cultural, and Scientific History

Although the roots of Canadian intellectual and cultural history can be traced back to the early twentieth century, it is only since the 1960s that the field has been sufficiently developed to be distinguished as a separate area of study. As with other subfields the line between it and other areas is often blurred. Traditionally intellectual history has been described as having two subfields. One, termed the history of ideas, has an affinity with philosophy and is interested in tracing the lineage and origins of ideas. A discussion of the major Canadian thinkers on the question of Darwinian thought, for example, would fall into this category. On the other side intellectual history is employed to discover not so much the lineage of ideas as their impact upon a society. The natural affinity for this field is with social history. Both fields are crucial to the overall structure of intellectual history. Cultural history is a loosely employed term. Sometimes it relates to the concept of anthropological culture, which is to say, any trait or value which shapes the society. Other times it is used more specifically to refer to the study of the arts and arts institutions – painting, music, and so on. Most recently the term cultural history has become loosely associated with such notions as postmodernism, deconstructionism, and semiotics. These theories, drawn from linguistics and literary criticism's search for status, have had only a modest influence on Canadian historical writing to date, especially in English Canada.

What follows is at best a selective listing of those themes and works which have most dominated Canadian intellectual and cultural history. For the most part cultural history has been defined as the history of arts institutions, thus avoiding the rather too amorphous problems of defining anthropological culture. Still, the definition must be pragmatic for there are certain themes which straddle social and cultural history and which, for lack of a better place, appear below.

GENERAL

There is no overview of Canadian intellectual history to parallel works that exist in political and economic history. Maria Tippett, *Making Culture: English-Canadian Institutions and the Arts before the Massey Commission* (T: UTP 1990) is a study of the evolution of cultural institutions rather than ideas or movements. It is complemented by her article 'The Writing of English-Canadian Cultural History, 1970–85,' *CHR* 1986. A.B. McKillop's collected essays, *Contours of Canadian Thought* (T: UTP 1987) provides a series of essays by one of Canada's more reflective intellectual historians. It is a good work but was never designed as a synthesis. There has been considerable attention paid to the history of historical writing however. The standard work here is Carl Berger, *The Writing of Canadian History: Aspects of English-Canadian Historical Writing since 1900*, (2nd ed., T: UTP 1986). In Quebec, there is Serge Gagnon, *Quebec and Its Historians, 1840 to 1920* (M: Harvest House 1982) and his *Quebec and Its Historians: The Twentieth Century* (M: Harvest House 1985). Also helpful is Yvan Lamonde, *L'histoire des idées au Québec, 1760–1960: bibliographie des études* (M: BNQ 1989), a bibliography of important works in the field.

In addition, several people have sought to define intellectual history and to trace its evolution in Canada. A.B. McKillop's essays, 'Nationalism, Identity, and Canadian Intellectual History,' and 'So Little on the Mind,' in his above-mentioned *Contours of Canadian Thought* provide useful introduction to the nature of the field as does Clarence Karr, 'What Is Canadian Intellectual History?' *Dalhousie Review* 1975, and J.M. Bumsted, 'Canadian Intellectual History and the Buzzing Factuality,' *Acadiensis* 1977. To the extent that the purpose of these articles is to discuss the existing state of intellectual history, however, they must be seen as historical documents reflecting the state of the field after about a decade or so of existence. More recent writings include Doug Owram, 'Writing about Ideas,' in John Schultz, ed., *Writing about Canada: A Handbook for Modern Canadian History* (Scarborough: PH 1990), and Clarence Karr, 'What Happened to Canadian Intellectual History?' *Acadiensis* 1989. The Influence and role of postmodernism is studied from a critical left-wing perspective in Bryan Palmer, *Descent into Discourse: The Reification of Language and the Writing of Social History* (Philadelphia: Temple UP 1990). This work, although written by a Canadian historian, is not specifically about Canada.

CONFEDERATION AND THE VICTORIAN AGE

Writing on Canadian intellectual history has not been spread evenly but has focused instead on a few key areas. For example, the decades surrounding Confederation have attracted much attention as Canadian historians sought to understand key forces in the formation of our elusive national character. The process began perhaps with P.B. Waite's now dated but still useful *The Life and Times of Confederation: Politics, Newspapers, and the Union of British North America, 1864–1867* (T: UTP 1962), but it was really Carl Berger's *The Sense of Power: Studies in the Ideas of Canadian Imperialism, 1867–1914* (T: UTP 1970) and its assessment of the post-Confederation outlook on imperialism that set the standard. A.I. Silver, *The French-Canadian Idea of Confederation, 1864–1900* (T: UTP 1982) re-examined the French-Canadian attitude towards Confederation and in doing so undermined many old shibboleths about the nature of Confederation. Doug Owram, *Promise of Eden: The Canadian Expansionist Movement and the Idea of the West, 1856–1900* (2nd ed., T: UTP 1992) looked at the relationship between Confederation and expansion westward. Also worth mentioning is the work written by one of Canada's leading intellectuals, Goldwin Smith. His *Canada and the Canadian Question* (1891, T: UTP 1971) provides a pessimistic analysis of Canada that concludes its natural destiny lies as a part of the United States. It has long been the classic statement of pessimism about Canada's future. When set beside another contemporary classic, George M. Grant's *Ocean to Ocean: Sandford Fleming's Expedition through Canada in 1872* (1872, E: Hurtig 1967) one gets a good sense of the opposing sides of Victorian Canadian nationalism.

The Confederation era was also a part of the Victorian period and issues of Confederation have broadened into wide considerations of the values and concerns of that age. Peter Waite, 'Sir Oliver Mowat's Canada: Reflections on an Un-Victorian Society,' helped define the era in Donald Swainson, *Oliver Mowat's Ontario* (T: MAC 1972). Carl Berger identified one of the most enduring national myths in his 'True North Strong and Free: The Myth of the North in Canadian History,' in P. Russell, ed., *Nationalism in Canada* (T: MH 1966). It has since been reprinted several times, most recently in J.L. Granatstein et al., *Twentieth-Century Canada: A Reader* (T: MHR 1986). More recently Allan Smith, 'The Myth of the Self-made Man in English Canada, 1850–1914,' *CHR* 1978, and J.R. Miller, 'Anti-Catholic Thought in Victorian Canada,' *CHR* 1985, set out other important aspects of Victorian Canada. W. Peter Ward, *Courtship, Love, and Marriage in Nineteenth-Century English Canada*

(M and K: MQUP 1990) looks at an important side of Victorian life in a highly readable book. On a related subject see James Snell, 'The White Life for Two: The Defence of Marriage and Sexual Morality in Canada, 1890–1914,' *HS/SH* 1983. All are important to understanding the values of the latter half of the nineteenth century. Carol Lee Bacchi, *Liberation Deferred? The Ideas of the English-Canadian Suffragists, 1877–1918* (T: UTP 1983) looks at one of the most important reform periods of turn-of-the-century society. Mariana Valverde, *The Age of Light, Soap, and Water: Moral Reform in English Canada, 1885–1925* (T: M&S 1991) is a work that hovers between social and intellectual history. It is also a useful overview of the whole issue of middle-class reformism in the late Victorian-Edwardian era.

The culture of business is less fully described, but in two works Michael Bliss does much to capture a sense of the Victorian business community. In *A Living Profit: Studies in the Social History of Canadian Business, 1883–1911* (T: M&S 1974) he looks broadly at business attitudes in the late nineteenth century. In his *A Canadian Millionaire: The Life and Times of Sir Joseph Flavelle, Bart, 1858–1939* (2nd ed., T: UTP 1992) he captures the ideology of one of Canada's most prominent turn-of-the-century businessmen. Both books complement Allan Smith's 'Myth of the Self-made Man,' mentioned above. Stephen Leacock, *Arcadian Adventures with the Idle Rich* (1914, T: M&S 1959) provides a humorous contemporary view of the pre–World War I business class.

SCIENCE AND MEDICINE

Other areas of considerable passion for the Victorians were science and medicine. Both areas are receiving an increasing amount of coverage and several excellent books have appeared, particularly on the decades between Confederation and the World War I.

The relationship between nationalism and science is explored in Suzanne Zeller, *Inventing Canada: Early Victorian Science and the Idea of a Transcontinental Nation* (T: UTP 1987). Works by J. Rodney Millard, *The Master Spirit of the Age: Canadian Engineers and the Politics of Professionalism* (T: UTP 1988), and Morris Zaslow, *Reading the Rocks: The Story of the Geological Survey of Canada, 1842–1972* (T: MAC 1975), although not strictly intellectual history, both describe the rise of professional organizations in nineteenth-century Canada and tell a great deal about the tendency to professionalization in the post-Confederation decades. They are complemented by W.A. Waiser, *The Field Naturalist: John Macoun, the*

Geological Survey, and Natural Science (T: UTP 1989), which looks at the rise of an important part of Canada's intellectual establishment, the scientific community.

Until relatively recently medical history was written as hagiography. Physicians or family members of physicians tended to write the accounts and to see medicine as a study of the triumph of great men over adversity. The past decade or so has seen a new sophistication develop in the field, and there is now a considerable body of good medical history. One of the first of the new approach, and still a standard collection, is S.E.D. Shortt, ed., *Medicine in Canadian Society: Historical Perspectives* (M and K: MQUP 1981). C.G. Roland, ed., *Health, Disease, and Medicine: Essays in Canadian History* (T: CI 1984) is a collection and therefore uneven, but there are several individual pieces that are very useful to those interested in Canadian medical history. The most recent collection is Wendy Mitchinson and Janice Dickin McGinnis, eds., *Essays in Canadian Medical History* (T: M&S 1988). For Quebec see Jacques Bernier, *La Médecine au Québec: Naissance et évolution d'une profession* (Q: PUL 1989). Wendy Mitchinson, *The Nature of Their Bodies: Women and Their Doctors in Victorian Canada* (T: UTP 1991) combines medical and social history in an excellent study which shows how prejudice, custom, and science combined to affect the medical profession's understanding of women. Michael Bliss, *Plague: A Story of Smallpox in Montreal* (T: HarperCollins 1991) uses a medical event, the smallpox plague of 1885, as a vehicle to investigate the attitudes and fears prevalent in the era. S.E.D. Shortt, *Victorian Lunacy: Richard M. Bucke and the Practice of Late-Nineteenth-Century Psychiatry* (Cambridge: Cambridge UP 1986) looks at one of Canada's more influential psychiatric figures. Jefferson Lewis, *Something Hidden: A Biography of Wilder Penfield* (T: Doubleday 1981) provides one of the better biographies of a Canadian medical figure. In the area of specific diseases there is the strong study by Geoffrey Bilson, *A Darkened House: Cholera in Nineteenth-Century Canada* (T: UTP 1980). Michael Bliss's *The Discovery of Insulin* (T: M&S 1982) brilliantly shows the combination of luck, foolishness, and skill which led to one of Canada's most famous medical discoveries. This is complemented by his biography of Frederick Banting, *Banting: A Biography* (2nd ed., UTP 1992).

RELIGION, THE SOCIAL GOSPEL, AND SECULARIZATION

The emphasis on the Victorian era flows almost seamlessly into the interest on religion. Perhaps this is because so much of the discussion about religion in Canada over the last twenty years has focused on the late Victorian and Edwardian eras, when religion underwent a spiritual crisis and a diminution in role in Canada. The last few years, however, have seen a revival in religious history which concentrates on religion its own sake and not just on the nature of its passing.

Over the decades there have been a great many works on religion. Only a small percentage of them are worth mentioning. On the history of Catholicism the best work has been done in French. Pierre Savard, *Aspects du catholicisme Canadien-français au XIXe siècle* (M: Fides 1980), and Jean Hamelin and Nicole Gagnon, *Histoire du catholicisme québécois*, 3 vols., (M: BE 1984–1991) provide good overviews. Serge Gagnon, *Plaisir d'Amour et Crainte de Dieu: Sexualité et confession au Bas-Canada* (Q: PUL 1990) looks at the important role the church played in one area of personal morality. There have been numerous books and articles on Protestantism over the decades but until recently much of this was amateur history or mere chronology. Religious history is undergoing a revival, however, and over the last few years much useful work has begun to appear. John Webster Grant, *The Church in the Canadian Era: The First Century of Confederation* (T: MHR 1972) provides a readable overview which, although general, has many insights into the course of religion in modern Canada. George Rawlyk, ed., *The Canadian Protestant Experience, 1760– 1990* (Burlington: Welch 1991) is a collection of essays by various authors. Arranged in chronological order, it provides much useful material on the general trends of Protestant religion. The most recent collection is Mark G. McGowan and David B. Marshall, *Prophets, Priests, and Prodigals: Readings in Canadian Religious History, 1680 to Present* (T: MHR 1992). This is a collection of articles that previously appeared elsewhere, some of which are crucial to our understanding of Canadian religious history. Also worth looking at is the book by Reginald W. Bibby, *Fragmented Gods: The Poverty and Potential of Religion in Canada* (T: Irwin 1987). It is sociological and somewhat journalistic but has useful information on post-1945 religious history.

There are also several books that look at religion within various parts of the country. W.H. Brooks, 'Methodism in the Canadian West in the Nineteenth Century,' PhD thesis, University of Manitoba, 1972, is useful. John Webster Grant, *A Profusion of Spires: Religion in Nineteenth-Century Ontario* (T: UTP 1988) looks at Ontario religion. William Westfall, *Two Worlds: The Protestant Culture of Nineteenth-Century Ontario* (M and K: MQUP 1989) sees Protestant religion as a binding force in shaping the Ontario sense of community. Michael Gauvreau, *The Evangelical Century:*

College and Creed in English Canada from the Great Revival to the Great Depression (M and K: MQUP 1991) looks at aspects of the interrelated educational and religious experience of the period. It fills an important gap in our understanding of the transition from the age of denomination-alism to the modern secular era. Also crucial is David B. Marshall's recent work, *Secularizing the Faith: Canadian Protestant Clergy and the Crisis of Belief, 1850–1940* (T: UTP 1992). Marguerite Van Die examines a sig-nificant individual in *An Evangelical Mind: Nathanael Burwash and the Methodist Tradition in Canada, 1839–1918* (M and K: MQUP 1989).

All the major Protestant denominations have had histories written about them and some are even good. John S. Moir, *Enduring Witness: A History of the Presbyterian Church in Canada* (T: Bryant Presbyterian Church in Canada 1975); Philip Carrington, *The Anglican Church in Canada: A History* (T: Collins 1963); and M. James Penton, *Apocalypse Delayed: The Story of Jehovah's Witnesses* (T: UTP 1985) are all worth looking at. Canada's largest Protestant church, the United Church, has received an especially large amount of attention, not only because of its size but because of the controversy surrounding church union. See John Webster Grant, *The Canadian Experience of Church Union* (L: Lutterworth 1967), and N. Keith Clifford, *The Resistance to Church Union in Canada, 1904–1939* (V: UBCP 1985).

If there has been a single dominating issue in intellectual and cultural history it has been the process of secularization that occurred in the early twentieth century. The debate brings together religious thought, social activism, and a discussion of the fate of the shift from the religious world of the nineteenth century to the secular one of the twentieth. Richard Allen really began the debate twenty years ago with his important, if overly detailed, *The Social Passion: Religion and Social Reform in Canada, 1914–28* (T: UTP 1971). His argument that the 'social gospel' was both an important force for reform and a signal of a successful transition by the church to a new era reinvigorated the study of religious ideas in Canada. Historians soon discovered and reprinted many of the classic expositions of the social gospel written by its proponents. Among the most enduring of these are J.S. Woodsworth, *My Neighbor: A Study of City Conditions, A Plea for Social Service*, with an introduction by Richard Allen (1911, T: UTP 1972), and Salem Bland, *The New Christianity, or the Reli-gion of the New Age*, also with an introduction by Richard Allen (1920, T: UTP 1973).

Allen's assertion of the importance of the social gospel occasioned much discussion and re-examination among historians of the process of adaptation and secularization. S.E.D. Shortt, *Six Intellectuals and Their Convictions in an Age of Transition* (T: UTP 1976) shifted the emphasis to the philosophical aspect of the debate. A.B. McKillop, *A Disciplined Intelligence: Critical Inquiry and Canadian Thought in the Victorian Era* (M and K: MQUP 1979) continued that debate and has provided one of the most important of works on religion, philosophy, and social values yet written in Canada, although it is not for the philosophically faint-hearted. Easier to read are Ramsay Cook, *The Regenerators: Social Criticism in Late Victorian English Canada* (T: UTP 1985), and Carl Berger, *Science, God, and Nature in Victorian Canada* (T: UTP 1983). Both extend the implications of the McKillop/Shortt discussion and significantly challenge the assumptions of Allen. Michael Gauvreau, 'The Taming of History: Reflections on the Canadian Methodist Encounter with Biblical Criticism, 1830–1900,' *CHR* 1984, helps explain the thinking of one of the most important of the nineteenth-century Protestant churches. David Marshall's already mentioned *Secularizing the Faith* looks at the religious issues surrounding the movement to a more secular society. George Rawlyk, *Champions of the Truth: Fundamentalism, Modernism, and the Maritime Baptists* (M and K: MQUP 1990) looks at a somewhat more fundamentalist denomination and its response to the social gospel on a regional basis. Jerold K. Zeman, *Baptists in Canada: Search for Identity amidst Diversity* (Burlington: Welch 1980) also contains a couple of articles on the issue of modernism. Especially noteworthy are John S. Moir, 'The Canadian Baptists and the Social Gospel Movement, 1897–1914,' and Clark Pinnock, 'The Modernist Impulse at McMaster University, 1887–1927.' Thomas P. Socknat, *Witness against War: Pacifism in Canada, 1900–1945* (T: UTP 1987) turns away from the problem of secularization to the ongoing sense of moral and religious conviction. Discussed below and also important for an understanding of the role of religion are the political biographies of people like Eugene Forsey, F.R. Scott, and William Lyon Mackenzie King.

One of the potentially most important areas for study involves women and religion. At the moment there are vast gaps yet to be filled but there are also promising signs as important new studies appear. Ruth Compton Brouwer, *New Women for God: Canadian Presbyterian Women and India Missions, 1876–1914* (T: UTP 1990) looks at the recruitment of women for overseas missionary work and at the women who were involved in the movement. Marta Danylewycz, *Taking the Veil: An Alternative to Marriage, Motherhood, and Spinsterhood in Quebec, 1840–1920* (T: M&S 1987) looks at the importance of religious orders. Neither work was conceived primarily as intellectual history but both add considerably to our understanding of the ideas of the time.

WRITING ON THE REGIONS

The emphasis on regional historical writing over the last ten to fifteen years means that considerable writing on Canadian intellectual history has also come forth from a regional perspective. In Atlantic Canada there is some excellent work although there is not yet sufficient material written to give us an adequate understanding of the rich intellectual and cultural traditions of the region. On the historiography of the region see E.R. Forbes, 'In Search of a Maritime Post-Confederation Historiography,' in his *Challenging the Regional Stereotype: Essays on the 20th Century Maritimes* (F: AP 1989). Intellectual history has received much less attention than, for example, the economic history of the region. There are notable exceptions in the area of religion, however (see above). Standard works on other aspects of Atlantic Canada's rich intellectual heritage include Patrick O'Flaherty, *The Rock Observed: Studies in the Literature of Newfoundland* (T: UTP 1979). Important for the mainland literary tradition is Janice Kulyk Keefer, *Under Eastern Eyes: A Critical Reading of Maritime Fiction* (T: UTP 1987). Naomi Griffiths, 'Longfellow's Evangeline: The Birth and Acceptance of a Legend,' in P.A. Buckner and David Frank, eds., *Atlantic Canada after Confederation: The Acadiensis Reader*, vol. 2, (F: AP 1985), traces the evolution of an important regional myth. So too does Ian McKay, 'Tartanism Triumphant: The Construction and Uses of Scottishness in Nova Scotia,' *Acadiensis* 1981. An important social movement is discussed in E.R. Forbes, 'Prohibition and the Social Gospel in Nova Scotia,' *Acadiensis* 1971.

Quebec intellectual history is perhaps more closely tied to politics than its counterpart in English Canada. As a result, overviews of intellectual history tend to focus on the question of ideology. Denis Monière, *Ideologies in Quebec: The Historical Development* (T: UTP 1981) provides the best overview available in English, although it is not completely satisfying. In the French language the choices broaden. J.P. Bernard, *Les idéologies québécoises au 19e siècle* (M: BE 1973), Fernand Dumont, Jean Hamelin, and Jean-Paul Montminy, *Les Idéologies au Canada français, 1850–1900* (Q: PUL 1971) and *Idéologies au Canada français, 1900–1929* (Q: PUL 1973) are all useful. English-Canadian historians have also written some excellent material on Quebec. Ramsay Cook, *Canada, Quebec, and the Uses of Nationalism* (T: M&S 1986) is a collection of Cook's articles over the years, most of them on Quebec. It should not lead readers to ignore the older but still useful work by Cook, *The Maple Leaf Forever: Essays on Nationalism and Politics in Canada* (2nd ed., T: M&S 1977), which should be read for his comments on 'la survivance.'

Important for an understanding of nineteenth-century Quebec thought is Jean-Paul Bernard, *Les Rouges: liberalisme, nationalisme et anticlericalisme au milieu du XIXe siècle* (M: PUQ 1971). The intellectual climate of the early twentieth century is captured in a number of works. Michael Behiels, 'L'ACJC and the Quest for a Moral Regeneration, 1903–1914' *JCS* 1978, leads nicely into Susan Trofimenkoff, *Action Française: French-Canadian nationalism in the twenties* (T: UTP 1975). Some of the leading intellectuals and their varied approaches to the national issue are dealt with in Pierre Savard, *Jules-Paul Tardivel: la France et les Etats-Unis, 1851–1905* (Q: PUL 1967), and Joseph Levitt, 'Henri Bourassa on Imperialism and Biculturalism, 1900–1918,' in R. Douglas Francis and Donald B. Smith, *Readings in Canadian History: Post Confederation* (3rd ed., T: HRW 1990). Abbé Groulx has received a fair bit of attention; see P.M. Senese, 'Catholique d'abord!: Catholicisim and Nationalism in the Thought of Lionel Groulx,' *CHR* 1979, and two works by Susan Mann Trofimenkoff: *Abbé Groulx: Variations on a Nationalist Theme* (T: CC 1973) and 'The Urban Tocsin: Lionel Groulx and French Canadian Nationalism,' in Bruce Hodgins and Robert Page, eds., *Canadian History since Confederation: Essays and Interpretations* (T: Irwin-Dorsey 1972).

Recent Quebec history has focused on the transformation of the state and of ideas in the years before and after the Quiet Revolution. For the rise of the Quiet Revolution see Michael D. Behiels, *Prelude to Quebec's Quiet Revolution: Liberalism versus Neo-Nationalism, 1945–1960* (M and K: MQUP 1985). On the intellectual climate of the 1960s see two works which reprint one of the foremost exponents of the values of the Quiet Revolution, André Laurendeau. One is an edited collection of Laurendeau's writings: Philip Stratford, ed., *André Laurendeau: Witness for Quebec*, (T: MAC 1973); the other is *The Diary of André Laurendeau, Written during the Royal Commission on Bilingualism and Biculturalism, 1964–1967* (T: JL 1991). The classic exposition of federalist thinking from the years around the Quiet Revolution comes in Pierre E. Trudeau, *Federalism and the French Canadians* (T: MAC 1968). The already mentioned Cook, *Canada, Quebec, and the Uses of Nationalism* contains several useful articles on the origins and development of the ideas of the Quiet Revolution.

There are exceptions to the political emphasis of Quebec intellectual history. Yvan Lamonde and Esthier Trepanier, eds., *L'avènement de la modernité culturelle au Québec* (Q: IQRC 1986), and Roger Levasseur, *Loisir et culture au Québec* (M: BE 1982), looks at the culture in the broad anthropological sense of popular inclinations and attitudes. There is also a considerable literature on religion which has been listed above under that subheading.

In the West there has been a great deal of attention paid to intellectual history, and a rich literature seeking to comprehend the Prairie identity has been the result. The tendency toward radical, even utopian, ideals was discussed long ago in W.L. Morton's still germane 'Bias of Prairie Politics,' and his observations on the West eremain valuable. The easiest way to get a sense of Morton's assessment is through A.B. McKillop, ed., *Contexts of Canada's Past: Selected Essays of W.L. Morton* (T: MAC 1980), which contains 'Bias of Prairie Politics' and other useful articles. Also useful for some insight into the nature of Western Canada is J.E. Rea, 'The Roots of Prairie Society,' in David Gagan, ed., *Prairie Perspectives* (T: HRW 1970).

Western politics has been a fascinating blend of the weird, the influential, and the transitory. In particular the CCF and Social Credit have come in for more than their share of study. All the specifics, however, should be set against themes like Morton's 'Bias of Prairie Politics' mentioned above. The radical tradition in the West has been examined in A. Ross McCormack, *Reformers, Rebels, and Revolutionaries: The Western Canadian Radical Movement, 1899–1919* (T: UTP 1977), and Walter Young, *Democracy and Discontent: Progressivism, Socialism, and Social Credit in the Canadian West* (T: RP 1969). More recently these studies have been supplemented by David Laycock, *Populism and Democratic Thought in the Canadian Prairies, 1910 to 1945* (T: UTP 1990). Social Credit has fascinated historians for a long time and the existence of those studies of Social Credit undertaken by largely eastern Canadian academics after World War II are in themselves a historiographic phenomenon. C.B. Macpherson, *Democracy in Alberta: Social Credit and the Party System* (2nd ed., T: UTP 1962) provides one of the more interesting interpretations, although later works have brought many of his conclusions into question. More recently Alvin Finkel, *The Social Credit Phenomenon in Alberta* (T: UTP 1989) probes the radical roots of Social Credit. David Elliot and Iris Miller, *Bible Bill: A Biography of William Aberhart* (E: Reidmore Books 1987) looks at Aberhart's theology. The CCF has not had an intellectual history, which is perhaps a bit surprising. Still their origins and leadership have been probed in a number of pieces. Allen, *The Social Passion*, looks at one of the most potent forces for reform influencing many of the leaders of the CCF. Allen Mills, *Fool for Christ: The Political Thought of J.S. Woodsworth* (T: UTP 1991) provides a much-needed and excellent account of the thought of the founder of the party. Subsequent leaders have not been as well-studied; see, however, Lewis H. Thomas, ed., *The Making of a Socialist: The Recollections of T.C. Douglas* (E: UAP 1982).

As the titles by Allen and Mills indicate, religious utopianism has played a large part in Prairie life. Perhaps the first serious academic study on religion in the West was William E. Mann, *Sect, Cult, and Church in Alberta* (T:UTP 1955). It is now dated and many of the conclusions have been called into question. Nonetheless, it identified an important intellectual force in western history. A more recent study is A.W. Rasporich 'Utopian Ideals and Community Settlements in Western Canada,' in R. Douglas Francis and Howard Palmer, eds., *The Prairie West: Historical readings* (2nd ed., E: Pica Press 1992). Benjamin Smillie, ed., *Visions of the New Jerusalem: Religious Settlement on the Prairie* (E: NeWest Press 1983) is a collection of disparate articles on religious communities. The collection is uneven but several pieces are worth reading. E.K. Francis, *In Search of Utopia: The Mennonites in Manitoba* (Altona: D.W. Friesen 1955) and George Woodcock and Ivan Avakumovic,*The Doukhobors* (T: M&S 1977) and two older but reliable studies of specific religious communities in the West.

Utopianism showed up in movements as well as in religion. Western labour is infused with a radical utopian tradition that does not exist elsewhere in Canada. Worth looking at in this regard is David J. Bercuson, *Fools and Wise Men: The Rise and Fall of the One Big Union* (T: MHR 1978) and McCormack's already mentioned *Reformers, Rebels and Revolutionaries*. Louis Riel continues to attract considerable attention although perhaps less than a couple of decades ago. The most recent collection of his myth is Ramon Hathorn and Patrick Holland, *Images of Louis Riel in Canadian Culture* (Lewiston: Edwin Mellen 1992). Doug Owram, 'The Myth of Louis Riel,' *CHR* 1982, assesses the interpretations of Riel over the past century. For the historian of ideas, Thomas Flanagan, *Louis 'David' Riel: Prophet of the New World* (T: UTP 1979) puts Riel in the context of religious belief. Another western myth is assessed in Keith Walden, *Visions of Order: The Canadian Mounties as Symbol and Myth* (T: BUT 1982).

The Prairie West has produced a rich literature. Two of the best attempts to come to grips with it are Dick Harrison, *Unnamed Country: The Struggle for a Canadian Prairie Fiction* (E: UAP 1977). More recently Robert Thacker, *The Great Prairie Fact and Literary Imagination* (Albuquerque: University of New Mexico Press 1989) undertakes a cross-border analysis. It doesn't replace the earlier works but does add new perspectives to them. Although not really a literary assessment, Ronald Rees, *New and Naked Land: Making the Prairies Home* (S: WPPB 1988) adds much to our understanding of the western identity.

For some reason intellectual and cultural historians have not paid as much attention to British Columbia. Aside from the important works on Emily Carr (see Art) there is little writing on BC intellectual history as such. There are some notable exceptions however. Hugh Brody, *Maps and Dreams: Indians and the British Columbia Frontier* (V: Douglas & McIntyre 1981) is a fascinating study of varying perceptions of geographical and cultural reality. Attitude studies – part intellectual, part social, and part political history – have been important. All have, in various ways, tried to probe the complex sense of racial, ethnic, and class identities which have shaped British Columbia's history. The first of these was W. Peter Ward's excellent work, *White Canada Forever: Popular Attitudes and Public Policy towards Orientals in British Columbia* (M and K: MQUP 1978). It was followed by Patricia Roy, *A White Man's Province: British Columbia Politicians and Chinese and Japanese Immigrants, 1858–1914* (V: UBCP 1989). Patrick A. Dunae has investigated another aspect of ethnicity, British Columbia's particular sense of Britishness, in his *Gentlemen Emigrants; From the British Public Schools to the Canadian Frontier* (V: Douglas and McIntyre 1981). Jean Barman, *Growing Up British in British Columbia: Boys in Private School, 1900–1950* (V: UBCP 1984) follows the same theme. Both books are useful but it is surprising that more has not been done on the Britishness of BC culture.

POLITICS

Political thought and political debate were the first areas of study in Canadian intellectual history and they remain lively; partly a branch of political history, partly of intellectual history, and partly of biography. Long gone are the old assumptions that Canadian political leaders were dull pragmatists without an ideology. Debate on political issues has remained central to this nation's tradition.

There is no overarching historical assessment or synthesis of Canadian political thought. G.P. de T. Glazebrook, *A History of Canadian Political Thought* (T: UTP 1966) does not really fulfil the purpose. Gad Horowitz, *Canadian Labour in Politics* (T: UTP 1968) brought Hartzian notions to the assessment of Canadian political thought as did Kenneth McRae's article on New France in Louis Hartz, *The Founding of New Societies: Studies in the History of the United States, Latin America, South Africa, Canada, and Australia* (NY: Harcourt Brace 1964). The Hartzian notions were always more popular in pre-Confederation history and, at any rate, historians use them much less than they did than a couple of decades ago, although the paradigm continues to have influence on both history and political science. See H.D. Forbes, 'Hartz-Horowitz at Twenty: Nationalism, Toryism, and Socialism in Canada and the United States,' *CJPS* 1987. No new single paradigm has replaced the Hartzian notions that were so once so popular. For a general overview of Canadian political thought see H.D. Forbes, ed., *Canadian Political thought* (T: OUP 1985). It provides a useful collection of primary writings from before Confederation to the 1960s. The *Journal of Canadian Studies* 1991 also devoted a special issue to political thought in Canada.

One of the first cross-over points between politics and intellectual history was in the everlasting attempt of Canadians to define themselves and their nationality. Old but important works on this topic include W.L. Morton, *The Canadian Identity* (T: UTP 1961); Frank H. Underhill, *In Search of Canadian Liberalism* (T: MAC 1960); and George P. Grant, *Lament for a Nation: The Defeat of Canadian Nationalism* (T: M&S 1965). Donald Creighton, *Canada's First Century* (T: MAC 1970) is ostensibly a historical text but is in reality a bitter diatribe against modernism and liberalism by a strong and embittered conservative. A more detailed and less satisfying format for Creightonian diatribe is also found in his *The Forked Road: Canada 1939–1957* (T: M&S 1976). Charles Taylor, *Radical Tories: The Conservative Tradition in Canada* (T: Anansi 1982) also looks at the conservative tradition but is overall a disappointingly shallow work. Looking at the issue of Canadian nationalism from a liberal-bicultural viewpoint is Cook, *The Maple Leaf Forever*. The classic federalist position of the Quebec Quiet Revolution is Pierre Trudeau, *Federalism and the French Canadians*. A left-of-centre analysis is given in the various essays in Leo Panitch, ed., *The Canadian State: Political Economy and Political Power* (T: UTP 1977). Especially relevant to intellectual history is the article in this collection by Reg Whitaker, 'Images of the State in Canada.' One of the striking things about Canadian national thought in recent years has been its anti-national character. History, political science, and economics have all emphasized the regional or fractious aspects of Canadian nationalism. In history the new trend began with J.M.S. Careless, '"Limited Identities" in Canada,' *CHR* 1969. See also J.M.S. Careless, '"Limited Identities": Ten Years Later,' *Manitoba History* 1980.

Political historians in Canada now accept the fact that ideologies affected Canadian politicians and political parties. John English, *The Decline of Politics: The Conservatives and the Party System* (2nd ed., T: UTP 1992) is ostensibly about shifts in party structures and organization but draws as well upon changing outlooks and values of politicians. Reg Whitaker, 'The Liberal-Corporatist Ideas of MacKenzie King,' and 'Reason, Passion, and Interest: Pierre Trudeau's Eternal Triangle,' both in Reg Whitaker, *A Sovereign Idea: Essays on Canada as a Democratic Community* (M and K: MQUP 1992), puts a great deal of emphasis on ideology. Norman Penner, *The Canadian Left: A Critical Analysis* (Scarborourgh: PH 1977) is interested in party ideology and development on the left. Also important for thought on the left is the massive work by the League for Social Reconstruction, *Social Planning for Canada* (1935, T: UTP 1975).

The emphasis on ideas that developed in the 1970s has continued. Mackenzie King has been particularly important in this regard, and there have been several attempts to understand his complex and unusual mind. Perhaps the best success is achieved in Paul Craven, *An Impartial Umpire: Industrial Relations and the Canadian State, 1900–1911* (T: UTP 1980). Like English's book this contains a great deal more intellectual history than the title implies. Joy E. Esberey, *Knight of the Holy Spirit: A Study of William Lyon Mackenzie King* (T: UTP 1980) is one of the relatively rare attempts to bring psychological analysis to the understanding of history. It has not been that influential. Thomas Flanagan, 'Problems of Psychobiography,' *QQ* 1982, sums up some of the reservations about the field. Anyone trying to understand King should not overlook the man's own view as expressed in William Lyon Mackenzie King, *Industry and Humanity: A Study in the Principles Underlying Industrial Reconstruction* (1919, T: UTP 1973).

With the precedent set by the studies of King, political biographies increasingly allow for the importance of ideas in shaping political lives. John English, *Shadow of Heaven: The Life of Lester Pearson*, vol. 1, *1897–1948* (T: Lester & Orpen Dennys 1989) and vol. 2, *The Worldly Years, 1949–1976* (T: Knopf Canada 1992) integrates ideas and politics well. J.S. Woodsworth has always been seen as understandable only through an analysis of his ideas. Most recently Allen Mills, *Fool for Christ*, undertakes a full-blown intellectual biography of this influential leader.

Intellectual biographies have been most popular, however, in those works on academics who were active in political issues. Doug Owram, *The Government Generation: Canadian Intellectuals and the State, 1900–1945* (T: UTP 1986) emphasizes those academics and other intellectuals who formed connections in the civil service and government. Michiel Horn, *The League for Social Reconstruction: Intellectual Origins of the Democratic Left in Canada, 1930–1942* (T: UTP 1980) focuses on the influential 'think-tank' that developed in the Depression. Paul Litt, *The Muses, the Masses, and the Massey Commission* (T: UTP 1992) looks at the premier event in cultural politics, the 1949 Royal Commission on National Development in the Arts, Letters, and Sciences. The original report of the commission is also worth looking at. Several of these people have also received individual treatment or left memoirs. Sandra Djwa, *The Politics of the Imagination: A Life of F.R. Scott* (T: M&S 1987) is the literary-oriented biography of that formative constitutional lawyer, political activist, and poet. The life of F.H. Underhill is written in R. Douglas Francis, *Frank H. Underhill: Intellectual Provocateur* (T: UTP 1986). There is no published biography of Eugene Forsey, but two works between them do a good job of filling the gap. The first are Forsey's own memoirs, *A Life on the Fringe: The Memoirs of Eugene Forsey* (T: OUP 1990). The second is Frank Milligan, 'Eugene A. Forsey: An Intellectual Biography,' PhD thesis, University of Alberta, 1987. Memoirs are also very popular with this highly literate group. Amongst the best, if somewhat longish, are Hugh Keenleyside. *Memoirs of Hugh L. Keenleyside*, vol. 1, *Hammer the Golden Day* and vol. 2, *On the Bridge of Time* (T: M&S 1981, 1982), and Escott Reid, *Radical Mandarin: The Memoirs of Escott Reid* (T: UTP 1989).

EDUCATION

The history of education is a field unto itself, often taught in faculties of education rather than in departments of history. It is vast and specialized. For the general purposes of the historian, however, a few key works stand out as a means of gaining at least a rudimentary acquaintance with the evolution of education in Canada. Amongst the best are Susan E. Houston and Alison Prentice, *Schooling and Scholars in Nineteenth-Century Ontario* (T: UTP 1988), and Alison Prentice, *The School Promoters: Education and Social Class in Mid-Nineteenth-Century Upper Canada* (T: M&S 1977). Although primarily a pre-Confederation study the latter book does cover the period up to 1880s and tells much about the roots of modern public education. Also important is Robert M. Stamp, *The Schools of Ontario, 1876–1976* (T: UTP 1982). R.D. Gidney and W.P.J. Millar look at an important issue in *Inventing Secondary Education: The Rise of the High School in Nineteenth-Century Ontario* (M and K: MQUP 1990). See as well the edited collection by J.D. Wilson et al., *Canadian Education: A History* (T: PH 1970). An older work by F. Henry Johnson, *A History of Public Education in British Columbia* (V: UBC 1964) is still useful. For Quebec, Roger Magnuson, *A Brief History of Quebec Education: From New France to the Parti Québécois* (M: Harvest House 1980) has the advantage of being in English but is very brief indeed. It does, however, give at least a quick sketch of Quebec education. There are also several works by Louis Phillipe

Audet including his *Histoire du Conseil de l'Instruction publique de la province du Québec, 1856–1964* (M: Léméac 1964) and with Armand Gauthier, *Le Systéme Scolaire du Québec: organisation et fonctionnement* (M: Beauchemin 1967). The best study of the pre–Quiet Revolution system is Claude Garneau's study of the crucial classic colleges, *Les colleges classique au Canada français* (M: Fides 1978).

THE UNIVERSITY WORLD

Until the last couple of decades histories of universities tended to be fairly superficial chronicles of the major 'highlights' of an institution. This changed considerably and several universities now boast excellent studies. Two volumes also seem to be the rule. Some of the better histories, from east to west, included Malcolm MacLeod, *A Bridge Built Halfway: A History of Memorial University College, 1925–1950* (M and K: MQUP 1990); John G. Reid, *Mount Allison University: A History, to 1963* (T: UTP 1984); Robert Gagnon, *Histoire de l'Ecole Polytechnique de Montreal* (M: BE 1991); Stanley B. Frost, *McGill University: For the Advancement of Learning*, vol. 1, *1805–1895* and vol. 2, *1895–1971* (M and K: MQUP 1980). There is also Stanley B. Frost, *The Man in the Ivory Tower: F. Cyril James of McGill* (M and K: MQUP 1991), which looks at McGill's wartime president. Hilda Neatby, *To Strive, to Seek, to Find and Not to Yield: Queen's University*, vol. 1, *1841–1917* and Frederick W. Gibson, *To Serve and yet be Free: Queen's University*, vol. 2, *1917–1961* (M and K: MQUP 1978, 1983); Charles M. Johnston, *McMaster University*, vol. 1, *The Toronto Years* and vol. 2, *The Early Years in Hamilton, 1930–1957* (T: UTP 1976, 1981). Surprisingly, there is no study of the University of Toronto as yet, but the gap is partly filled by studies of colleges and by studies of individual administrators. James G. Greenlee, *Sir Robert Falconer: A Biographer* (T: UTP 1988) provides a look at one of the more important presidents of that institution. Claude Bissell, *Halfway Up Parnassus: A Personal Account of the University of Toronto, 1932–1971* (T: UTP 1974) provides personal memoirs of another. Douglas Richardson, '*A Not Unsightly Building': University College and Its History* (Oakville: Mosaic Press 1990) looks at one of the university's more important colleges. A different but useful perspective on the university is given in Robert H. Blackburn, *Evolution of the Heart: A History of the University of Toronto Library up to 1981* (T: UT Library 1989). A comprehensive study of the rise of the university in Ontario is A.B. McKillop's *Matters of Mind: The University in Ontario, 1791–1951* (T: UTP 1994).

Until recently western universities were little studied. There are still notable gaps but several works have appeared which do much to improve the situation. W.L. Morton, *One University: A History of the University of Manitoba* (T: UTP 1957) is one of the first serious university studies. For a long time it stood as a model but is now dated. There is also Michael Hayden, *Seeking a Balance: The University of Saskatchewan, 1907–1982* (V: UBCP 1983). Walter Johns, *A History of the University of Alberta, 1908–1969* (E: UAP 1981) is less analytical. West of the Rockies the full histories of the British Columbia universities are just now being written. Worth looking at for UBC, however, is the study of one of UBC's more significant and controversial presidents, Peter B. Waite, *Lord of Point Grey: Larry MacKenzie of UBC* (V: UBCP 1987).

There are dozens of specific studies of the development of departments and areas of study in Canadian higher education. They vary greatly depending on the author and the purpose. The best is Marlene Shore, *The Science of Social Redemption: McGill, the Chicago School, and the Origins of Social Research in Canada* (T: UTP 1987). Also good are Ian Drummond, *Political Economy at the University of Toronto: A History of the Department, 1888–1982* (T: UT Faculty of Arts and Science 1983); Robert Bothwell, *Laying the Foundation: A Century of History at the University of Toronto* (T: UT History Department 1991); and Barry Ferguson, *Remaking Liberalism: The Intellectual Legacy of Adam Shortt, O.D. Skelton and W.A. Mackintosh 1890–1925* (M and K: MQUP 1993). The growth of different fields can also be looked at through studies of individuals. This is done for sociology in Harry H. Hiller, *Society and Change: S.D. Clark and the Development of Canadian Sociology* (T: UTP 1982). Leslie Armour and Elizabeth Trott, *The Faces of Reason: An Essay on Philosophy and Culture in English Canada, 1850–1950* (Wa: WLUP 1981) follows individuals rather than institutions in its assessment of the evolution of philosophy in Canadian thought. Also useful is Michael Gauvreau, 'Philosophy, Psychology, and History: George Sidney Brett and the Quest for a Social Science at the University of Toronto, 1910–1940,' CHA *HP* 1988. The sciences are not as well documented, but see Yves Gingras, *Physics and the Rise of Scientific Research in Canada* (M and K: MQUP 1991).

There have also been various studies which look at non-institutional aspects of higher education. The first of these was the encyclopedia-like survey by Robin S. Harris, *A History of Higher Education in Canada, 1663–1960* (T: UTP 1976). It gives many useful facts but provides neither compelling analysis nor interesting reading. Worth looking at is Paul Axelrod and John G. Reid, eds., *Youth, University, and Canadian Society:*

Essays in the Social History of Higher Education (M and K: MQUP 1989), a series of essays by various experts on aspects of students and university life from the late nineteenth century on. The perspective of one exceptional nineteenth-century woman student is provided in Elizabeth Smith, *A Woman with a Purpose: The Diaries of Elizabeth Smith, 1872–1884*, edited and with an introduction by Veronica Strong-Boag (T: UTP 1980). The role of women is also looked at in John G. Reid, 'The Education of Women at Mount Allison, 1854–1914,' *Acadiensis* 1983. The best single study of student life is Paul Axelrod, *Making a Middle Class: Student Life in English Canada during the Thirties* (M and K: MQUP 1990). The great explosion of universities in post-World War II period is coming under increased scrutiny. For a view from the administrative and governmental perspectives see H.B. Neatby, 'Visions and revisions: The View from the President's Offices of the Ontario Universities since the second World War,' CHA *HP* 1988; Paul Axelrod, *Scholars and Dollars: Politics, Economics, and the Universities of Ontario, 1945–1980* (T: UTP 1982). Also important is Patricia Jasen, 'Ways of Knowing: An Intellectual History of the Liberal Arts Curriculum in English-Canadian Universities,' PhD thesis, University of Manitoba, 1987. The student perspective on the rapid changes that were taking place is less well-documented as yet. Cyril Levitt, *Children of Privilege: Student Revolt in the Sixties* (T: UTP 1984) looks at the elite of the radical left. Myrna Kostash, *Long Way from Home: The Story of the Sixties Generation in Canada* (T: JL 1980) provides a more personal account of the decade. It might be pushing the definition to call David Sharpe's *Rochdale, The Runaway College* (T: Anansi 1987) a history of an educational institution, but it does illuminate much about the sixties.

The attention paid to individual intellectuals within the university milieu is endless. Particularly singled out are the international 'stars' of the intellectual tradition in Canada – Harold Innis, Marshall McLuhan, and Northrop Frye. Many of these are mentioned under topics such as social reform and only a few of the most important works can be mentioned here. Harold Innis remains a major figure in Canadian scholarship. Donald Creighton's hagiographic *Harold Adams Innis: Portrait of a Scholar* (T: UTP 1957) is now badly dated as analysis but remains a useful summary of Innis's life. More recent works, however, have added considerable depth to our understanding of Innis. Aside from Berger's assessment in *The Writing of Canadian History* there is William Christian, ed., *The Idea File of Harold Adams Innis* (T: UTP 1980) for the truly dedicated Innis scholar. Mel Watkins, 'The Innis Tradition in Canadian Political Economy,' *Canadian Journal of Political and Social Thought* 1982, tries to claim Innis for the left-nationalist. Innis was neither a nationalist in the modern sense nor a leftist in any sense but the claim is interesting for what it says about the cult of Innis. More useful is a special issue on Innis in *The Journal of Canadian Studies* 1977. More esoteric for the historian is Robin Neill, *A Theory of Value: The Canadian Economics of H.A. Innis* (T: UTP 1972). This is a work more for economists than historians.

Marshall McLuhan, once the guru of Canadian pop-think, has fallen from favour lately. This in no way diminishes the fascinating story of both his thought and the reasons why he became such a cult star. An enjoyable and revealing biography is Philip Marchand, *Marshall McLuhan: The Medium and the Messenger* (Mississauga: Random House 1989). For a list of McLuhan's writings see *The Writings of Marshall McLuhan: Listed In Chronological Order from 1934 to 1975* (Fort Lauderdale: Wake-Brook House 1975). McLuhan's intellectual dependence on Innis is traced in Graeme Patterson, *History and Communications: Harold Innis, Marshall McLuhan, the Interpretation of History* (T: UTP 1990). Northrop Frye is perhaps the most studied of all three figures, is also one of the most prolific; see Robert Denham, *Northrop Frye: An Annotated Bibliography of Primary and Secondary Sources* (T: UTP 1987).

Another major figure on the Canadian intellectual landscape has been philosopher George P. Grant. Grant because well known in the 1960s for his nationalism and for his critique of technology, both of which struck a chord in that tumultuous decade. See George P. Grant, *Lament for a Nation*, and *Technology and Empire: Perspectives on North America* (T: Anansi 1969). For a discussion of Grant's philosophy see Joan E. O'Donovan, *George Grant and the Twilight of Justice* (T: UTP 1984). Most recent is William Christian, *George Grant: A Biography* (T: UTP 1993).

MEDIA

Although much work remains to be done on the media there are now several useful works on the history of radio, television, and newspapers in Canada. Paul Rutherford, *The Making of the Canadian Media* (T: MHR 1978) provides a quick overview of media as a whole. The senior medium, newspapers, are dealt with in Paul Rutherford, *A Victorian Authority: The Daily Press in Late Nineteenth-Century Canada* (T: UTP 1982). In French Canada the most detailed work is Jean de Bonville, *La Presse Québécoise de 1884 à 1914: Genèse d'un média de masse* (Q: PUL 1988). See also Yvan Lamonde, *Imprime au Quebec: aspects historioques* (18e–20e siècles) (Q: IQRC

1983). On radio and television see Frank W. Peers, *The Politics of Canadian Broadcasting, 1920–1951* (T: UTP 1969) and his *The Public Eye: Television and the Politics of Canadian Broadcasting, 1952–1968* (T: UTP 1979). The most ambitious attempt to look at television as culture rather than institution is Paul Rutherford, *When Television Was Young: Primetime Canada, 1952–1967* (T: UTP 1990). This vast 637-page book looks at early programs and programming as a means of illustrating both the nature of the industry and the age. One of the most recent contributions to the field is Mary Vipond, *Listening In: The First Decade of Canadian Broadcasting, 1922–1932* (M and K: MQUP 1992).

Much less has been written about film in Canada. Peter Morris, *Embattled Shadows: A History of Canadian Cinema, 1895–1939* (M and K: MQUP 1978) is the most general but is limited by the fact it ends before World War II. The National Film Board has been the centre of Canadian film activity through much of the period, and Gary Evans, *In the National Interest: A Chronicle of the National Film Board of Canada* (T: UTP 1991) is the closest thing to a national study for the post-war years. Also important in understanding a key national institution is Gary Evans, *John Grierson and the National Film Board: The Politics of Wartime Propaganda* (T: UTP 1984). As well *The Journal of Canadian Studies* had a special issue on film in Canada in 1981.

MUSIC AND ART

The coverage of the cultural and theatre world is mixed. Aside from Maria Tippett's article mentioned in the introduction to this chapter, there are specific studies of various institutions. The Canada Council is discussed in J.L. Granatstein, 'Culture and Scholarship: The First Ten Years of the Canada Council,' *CHR* 1984. The history of music is surveyed in Helmut Kallmann, *A History of Music in Canada, 1534–1914* (2nd ed., T: UTP 1987). Helmut Kallmann, et al., *The Encyclopedia of Music in Canada* (2nd ed., T: UTP 1992) is a tremendously useful reference source.

In contrast to this thin historiography, the world of art in Canada is well covered. J. Russell Harper, *Painting in Canada: A History* (2nd ed., T: UTP 1977) provides the standard overview. Dennis Reid, *Our Own Country Canada: Being an Account of the National Aspirations of the Principal Landscape Artists in Montreal and Toronto* (O: National Gallery 1979) adds to this with a more detailed look at the nineteenth century. Much of the best work has been done on the major art figures who have dominated Canadian painting. Krieghoff is written up in J. Russell Harper, *Krieghoff*

(T: UTP 1979). Peter Mellen, *The Group of Seven* (T: M&S 1970) provides an excellent overview of that all-important group and its impact. See as well Douglas Cole, 'An Inquiry into the Success of the Group of Seven,' *JCS* 1978. Ramsay Cook, 'Landscape Painting and National Sentiment in Canada,' in his *Maple Leaf Forever*, does an excellent job of tying the Group of Seven to the general intellectual and nationalist climate of the age. For the West Coast there are two important studies of Emily Carr. Maria Tippett, *Emily Carr: A Biography* (T: OUP 1979) concentrates on the life of the painter while Doris Shadbolt, *Emily Carr* (T: Douglas & McIntyre 1990) is a useful supplement, especially on the art itself. On the Prairies, see Ronald Rees, *Land of Earth and Sky: Landscape Painting of Western Canada* (S: WPPB 1984). Ramsay Cook, 'William Kurelek: A Prairie Boy's Vision' in Ramsay Cook, *Canada, Quebec, and the Uses of Nationalism* provides a perceptive look at the eccentric Prairie artist. Some insight is provided into a contemporary painter in William Metson and Cheryl Lean, eds., *Alex Colville: Diary of a War Artist* (H: Nimbus 1981). Maria Tippett, *By a Lady: Celebrating Three Centuries of Art by Canadian Women* (T: Viking 1992) looks at the varied contributions of women artists.

Writing about intellectual and cultural history in Canada has developed considerably in the last quarter century but compared to the wealth of material available in, say, the United States, the coverage in Canada still looks relatively uneven. Insightful works in certain areas have inspired debate, discussions, and replies, yielding a rich bibliography. Typical of this is the discussion of religion and secularization mentioned above. Yet other areas remain virtually untouched. This uneven coverage is also reflected in the virtual absence of any overarching interpretation of Canadian thought. Perhaps the nation is just too small and too culturally dependent upon the United States and Great Britain. Perhaps the historiographic tendency toward 'limited identities' has also made such an interpretation too daunting to historians. In spite of this, however, the field has yielded much about the nature of Canadians – their thoughts and their cultural enthusiasms or obsessions.

J.R. MILLER

Native History

The fields of Native history and of the history of Native/non-Native relations have grown dramatically in recent years. In fact, when an earlier edition of this *Guide* was published a decade ago, it was not considered essential to include a section of works on these themes. However, if it was possible to overlook Native subjects in 1982, it is not now. The involvement of Indian, Inuit, and Métis in constitutional confrontations, as well as more spectacular conflicts at such places as Akwesasne and Kanesatake, has catapulted Native peoples into the consciousness of the general public. And the explosion of historical writing since 1982 on the history of the First Nations and their relations with European newcomers to Canada, an eruption partly attributable to the greater concern of the general public about Aboriginal issues, makes examination of Native historiography as feasible academically as it is compelling politically.

GENERAL AND REFERENCE WORKS

As for most topics in Canadian history, fruitful use can be made of the *Dictionary of Canadian Biography*, thirteen vols. to date (T: UTP 1966–) for brief biographies of the most prominent actors. A comprehensive bibliography of the topic is not available, but a useful starting point is the bibliography of writings on the Canadian government's policy towards Indians and Inuit that was prepared for the Newberry Library Center for the History of the American Indian Bibliographical Series by Robert J. Surtees: *Canadian Indian Policy: A Critical Bibliography* (Bloomington: Indiana UP for the Newberry Library 1982). For a few topics, such as education, specialized bibliographies including I.R. Brooks, comp., *Native Education in Canada and the United States: A Bibliography* (C: UCP 1976), are available.

Most scholarly Canadian historical journals carry articles on Native peoples from time to time. A few periodicals, such as the *Canadian Journal of Native Studies* (Brandon University) and the *Native Studies Review* (University of Saskatchewan), both of which appear erratically, are devoted exclusively to materials on the First Peoples. Specialized regional journals, such as Quebec's *Recherches amérindiennes*, naturally focus on the Aboriginal peoples of their respective parts of the country. The number of Australian, New Zealand, and American journals that sometimes treat Canadian Native history is far too great to list here, but mention should be made of two US publications: *Ethnohistory* and the *American Indian Culture and Research Journal*.

General works fall into three categories: ethnographic surveys of the Native peoples, overviews of their relationship with non-Natives, and collections of previously published material known as 'readers.' Generations of students interested in the history of the original inhabitants have cut their scholarly teeth on the work of an anthropologist, born in New Zealand, who carried out his research at the other end of the earth. Diamond Jenness first published *The Indians of Canada* in 1932, but it has gone through many editions and is still in print (7th ed., T: UTP 1977). Jenness's study was in part an ethnographic survey of the indigenous peoples group by group and culture area by culture area, but it also contained a few chapters that examined the impact Europeans have had since contact. Jenness's *Indians of Canada* has been supplanted by Alan D. McMillan's *Native Peoples and Cultures of Canada: An Anthropological Overview* (V: Douglas & McIntyre 1988) as the principal ethnographic survey. Older works of this nature that continue to be of some use to students of history are Selwyn Dewdney and Franklin Arbuckle, *They Shared to Survive: The Native Peoples of Canada* (T: MAC 1975); Alice B. Kehoe, *North American Indians: A Comprehensive Account* (Englewood Cliffs: PH 1981); and R. Bruce Morrison and C. Roderick Wilson, eds., *The Native Peoples: The Canadian Experience* (T: M&S 1986).

Diamond Jenness was also one of the first scholars to present information on the Inuit (Eskimo) in an accessible form. The Inuit were a responsibility that neither level of senior government wanted, but the Supreme Court in 1939 ruled that they were 'Indians' for purposes of the Indian Act. The history of these bureaucratically unwanted people is found principally in narrow examinations of particular aspects of Arctic life. Although oceans of ink have been spilled in celebrating the exploits of European explorers, which were usually made possible by Inuit knowledge and labour, a general account of these peoples since Confederation does not exist. (Now it is possible to find out what they thought of at least one explorer by examining David C. Woodman, *Unravelling the Franklin Mystery: Inuit Testimony* [M and K: MQUP 1991]). Jenness's *People of the Twilight* (NY: MAC 1928) and *Eskimo Administration*, 5 vols. (M: Arctic Institute of North America 1962–8) are sensible places to begin, as is the popular work of Farley Mowat, *People of the Deer* (Boston: Little Brown 1951). Also helpful are some of the articles in Victor F. Valentine and Frank G. Vallee, eds., *Eskimo of the Canadian Arctic* (T: M&S 1968). The perceptive observations in Hugh Brody's *The People's Land: Eskimos and Whites in the Eastern Arctic* (Harmondsworth: Penguin 1975) should not be missed.

Studies of the history of relations between Natives and immigrants are only slightly more numerous than studies of the Inuit. The first useful summary of the relationship of Natives and newcomers since the sixteenth century was E. Palmer Patterson III, *The Canadian Indian: A History since 1500* (Don Mills: Collier-Macmillan 1972), which placed the Canadian experience of cultural contact within a comparative framework of similar British colonial experiences. Although welcome as a pioneering work, Patterson's study was uneven in quality. In general, it was strongest on the peoples of the Northwest Coast, as Patterson had done specialized research on aspects of their history. A different approach to surveying the relationship between the First Nations and the immigrant peoples was taken in J.R. Miller, *Skyscrapers Hide the Heavens: A History of Indian-White Relations in Canada* (2nd ed., T: UTP 1991). Often building on other scholars' more specialized studies, Miller sought to trace the relationship through five centuries, placing its various stages in different parts of the country within a single interpretive framework. Some critics considered his application of that framework rather forced in places. Others have pointed out that the supposedly comprehensive survey is lamentably lacking in coverage of the Atlantic region after the middle of the eighteenth century and of the far north at any time. The greatest strength of *Skyscrapers* is its analysis of the evolving relationship from the end of the era of military alliance in the early nineteenth century to the emergence of powerful Native political organizations in the later twentieth century.

A different approach was taken by Olive P. Dickason in *Canada's First Nations: A History of Founding Peoples from Earliest Times* (T: M&S 1992). Particularly in its early chapters, Dickason's treatment examines one specific cultural group after another. For the period after the War of 1812, a combination of thematic, cultural, and geographical approaches is used, sometimes with a resulting loss of focus. All the same, *Canada's First Na-*

tions contains a wealth of information on the post-Confederation era, and many of its endnotes provide helpful leads to further reading. Against the richness of factual detail must be set a tendency to shift focus and the absence of an interpretative framework. On balance, Dickason's study is essential reading for any student of Native history.

The rapidly expanding literature on Native peoples and their relations with newcomers that made surveys such as Miller's and Dickason's possible also facilitated the appearance of three useful collections of articles. Ian A.L. Getty and Antoine S. Lussier, eds., *As Long as the Sun Shines and Water Flows: A Reader in Canadian Native Studies* (V: Nakoda Institute and UBCP 1979) made available a group of articles on the period since 1763, the year of the Royal Proclamation. Two University of Northern British Columbia historians, Kenneth S. Coates and Robin Fisher, sought to train the scholarly searchlight more directly on the Native people themselves in their collection *Out of the Background: Readings on Canadian Native History* (T: CCP 1988). J.R. Miller, ed., *Sweet Promises: A Reader on Indian-White Relations in Canada* (T: UTP 1991) briefly considered missionary and fur-trade activities in New France before following the relationship in a pattern that tracked the organization of his general survey.

Although both the quality and quantity of the general and reference works available to students are much improved over what existed in 1982, major gaps remain. There is no bibliography of historical aspects of the Native peoples and their interactions with non-Natives, and no truly comprehensive survey of the history of the relationship.

INDIAN POLICY STUDIES

The new Dominion's attempt to acquire and integrate vast territories necessarily forced the federal government to pay attention to Native peoples, especially to the Indians of the Prairies and of British Columbia. Pre-Confederation policies of a number of colonial jurisdictions had to be searched for a national policy towards Indians, and a coherent approach had to be developed if Canada was effectively to occupy and develop both the territories it possessed and those it coveted in 1867. Regrettably, there is no single analysis of post-Confederation Indian policy, as there is none for colonial times. A brief outline of policy is found in a pioneering article by John L. Tobias, 'Protection, Civilization, Assimilation: An Outline History of Canada's Indian Policy,' *The Western Canadian Journal of Anthropology* 1976. One measure of this piece's value is the fact that it was included in both the Getty/Lussier and Miller anthologies (cited above).

A number of longer studies of policy, some general and others more specialized, are also available. Although the Indian Act, which first attempted to consolidate legislation on Indians in 1876, was not the sum total of Indian policy, it was a major component. The Treaties and Historical Research Centre (THRC) of Indian and Northern Affairs Canada has produced a highly useful overview in *The Historical Development of the Indian Act* (2nd ed., O: THRC 1978), edited by John Leslie and Ron Maguire. Its examination of the emergence and revision of the Act over the decades is far more than a descriptive account, often explaining the origins of specific amendments and providing analyses of the impact of particular clauses of the statute. A work that provides a helpful introduction to general Indian policy from the late nineteenth century until the Depression is E. Brian Titley's study of the most important of the deputy ministers of Indian Affairs, Duncan Campbell Scott. *A Narrow Vision: Duncan Campbell Scott and the Administration of Indian Affairs in Canada* (V: UBCP 1986) is perceptive, both in regard to policy in general and a number of specific topics such as education and political control as well. THRC also commissioned John Leonard Taylor's *Canadian Indian Policy during the Inter-War Years, 1918–1939* (O: THRC 1984), which is a useful introduction to government policy in the 1920s and 1930s. J. Rick Ponting and Roger Gibbins explain the context of Indian Affairs policy in *Out of Irrelevance: A Socio-Political Introduction to Indian Affairs in Canada* (T: BUT 1980), and Sally M. Weaver explains the controversy over the 1969 White Paper clearly in *Making Canadian Indian Policy: The Hidden Agenda, 1968–1970* (T: UTP 1981). More specialized studies of government Indian policy are found below under specific headings.

REGIONAL STUDIES

Given the importance of acquiring and integrating the West, it is not surprising that the strongest areas in historical writing on Native peoples after Confederation are the Prairies and British Columbia. As is the case for most Prairie topics, the indispensable starting point for the historical inquirer is Gerald Friesen's *The Canadian Prairies: A History* (T: UTP 1984). Separate chapters deal in turn with the Métis and the Plains Indians during the critical change that occurred before and after Confederation, although a number of other chapters contain useful information on the Native peoples of the Prairies as well. Friesen was one of the first historians to write Native peoples into a general history of a region as central characters, rather than as bit players or the Aboriginal equivalent of a Greek chorus. As for most regions of Canada, coverage of the nineteenth-century experience of Native peoples in the Prairies is stronger than the twentieth.

Other aspects of the Indian experience in the West can be examined in a series of monographs of high quality. P. Doug Elias, *The Dakota of the Canadian Northwest: Lessons for Survival* (W: UMP 1988) not only surveys the experience of these refugees from the American military, but also provides valuable insights into how one Native group adjusted economically to the flood of European settlers that threatened to engulf them. The variety of ways in which the Dakota learned their 'lessons for survival' serves as a salutary warning against over-generalization about 'the Native experience' in a single region, let alone Canada as a whole. Rather less scholarly, but still useful, is an account by a Catholic missionary to the Dakota. *The Dakota Sioux in Canada* (W: DLM Publications 1991) by Oblate Gontran Laviolette makes up in enthusiasm what it lacks in scholarly apparatus.

Other Prairie groups have not been as well served by historians as the Dakota. Only the final chapter of John S. Milloy's excellent *The Plains Cree: Trade, Diplomacy, and War, 1790 to 1870* (W: UMP 1988) has anything to do with the post-Confederation period, but it remains indispensable. Most of the other writing on the Cree is ethnographic in nature, the standard work being David G. Mandelbaum's *The Plains Cree: An Ethnographic, Historical, and Comparative Study* (2nd ed., R: CPRC 1979). Special mention should be made of one of the most influential articles ever published in Native history, because its focus was the Cree's resistance to the assertion of Canadian authority in the 1870s and 1880s. John L. Tobias's 'Canada's Subjugation of the Plains Cree, 1879–1885,' *CHR* 1983, revolutionized historians' understanding of the post-treaty experience and laid to rest forever any lingering delusions about the beneficence of Canadian government policy towards the western Indians. Tobias's article, which he has followed up with related studies of article length, has been reprinted in both Coates and Fishers *Out of the Background* and Miller's *Sweet Promises*. Useful both as a regional treatment and a policy study is Hana Samek, *The Blackfoot Confederacy 1880–1920: A Comparative Study of Canadian and US Indian Policy* (Albuquerque: University of New Mexico Press 1987); its international approach points in the direction that at least some western Canadian Native history studies will undoubtedly take in the future.

Hugh Dempsey's work on the Indians of Alberta deserves to be singled out for consideration in its own right and on its own merit. Dempsey, closely connected with both the Glenbow Museum in Calgary and the Blood Nation of southern Alberta, has played a crucial role in the creation and popularization of Native history, both as editor of *Alberta History* and as author of a series of studies of prominent individuals. Unconstrained by the narrow-mindedness about sources that has been one of the limiting influences on academic history, Dempsey made extensive use of the oral history of Blood Indians and has conducted meticulous research in published records of government and other agencies. The result has been an impressive collection of books that document large parts of Alberta Indian history, especially that of the Blood Indians. *Charcoal's World* (S: WPP 1978) examines the process of change through the life of an individual who came into conflict with the law. *Crowfoot: Chief of the Blackfeet* (E: Hurtig 1972) and *Big Bear: The End of Freedom* (V: Douglas & McIntyre 1984) similarly capture the passing of the traditional Plains economy and culture through examinations of the lives of prominent representatives of the Blackfoot and Cree peoples respectively. Dempsey's biographies of two less-known Blood leaders are also important for historians: *Red Crow: Warrior Chief* (S: WPPB 1980) and *The Gentle Persuader: A Biography of James Gladstone, Indian Senator* (S: WPPB 1986). *Gentle Persuader* is significant for several reasons: Gladstone was a mixed-blood man who managed to obtain status as a registered Indian; he was the first Indian appointed to the Senate; and he was Dempsey's father-in-law.

Biography was the chosen form for examining the lives of a number of other important Prairie Indians. Prolific popular historian Grant MacEwan devoted his pen both to the spectacular, in *Sitting Bull: The Years in Canada* (E: Hurtig 1973), and to the less flamboyant but for Canadians historically more significant, *Tatanga Mani: Walking Buffalo of the Stonies* (E: Hurtig 1969). Journalist Norma Sluman began a task that some professionally trained historian should complete in her impressionistic study of a Cree chief in *Poundmaker* (T: RP 1967), and she collaborated with the subject's natural daughter on an important biography of a little-known Cree organizer and leader in *John Tootoosis* (2nd ed., W: Pemmican 1984). Also important is the history and the personal statement about the Stoney by one of their leaders, John Snow, in *These Mountains Are Our Sacred Places: The Story of the Stoney People* (T: Samuel Stevens 1977). In a class by itself for both its depth of research and its subject is Donald B. Smith, *From the Land of Shadows: The Making of Grey Owl* (S: WPPB 1990). Grey Owl – Englishman Archie Belaney – was not an Indian at all, but an early 'wannabe,' someone who emulated the Indians' ways. While masquerading as a Native he broadcast a message of respect for both the North American environment and the first dwellers in it throughout North America and western Europe.

The strangest thing about Grey Owl was that he spent his Canadian career in northern Ontario and Saskatchewan's Prince Albert National Park, rather than the homeland of most of post-Confederation Canada's notoriously flaky characters – British Columbia. Perhaps the richness and diversity of the First Peoples of the Northwest Coast, interior, and northern forests of BC were too overwhelming even for a masterful con artist like him. Certainly the numbers, heterogeneity, and fascinating social structures of the Indian peoples of the Pacific province account in large part for the profusion and excellence of the historical literature that is available about them.

As with the Prairies, BC is well served by a regional history that reflects recent trends in historical scholarship by paying much more attention to Native peoples than earlier works did. Jean Barman, *The West beyond the West: A History of British Columbia* (T: UTP 1991), while perhaps not as successful as Friesen's *Canadian Prairies* in peopling the canvas with Indians, still gives their experience both sympathy and prominence. Barman, like all other students of BC's Native peoples, is greatly in the debt of Wilson Duff, *The Indian History of British Columbia*, vol. 1, *The Impact of the White Man* (2nd ed., Vi: Royal British Columbia Museum 1969). Unfortunately, Duff's premature death prevented the appearance of volume 2, but one of his students, Robin Fisher, carried on the tradition in an excellent survey of Native/non-Native relations to the 1880s, *Contact and Conflict: Indian-European Relations in British Columbia, 1774–1890* (2nd ed., V: UBCP 1992). Fisher applied insights from both his native New Zealand and anthropology to produce a gripping account of the relationship from the cooperation of the fur trade to dispossession in the age of missionaries, settlers, and government administrators. The second edition contains a useful bibliographical preface but is otherwise unaltered. One major aspect of Fisher's account, the land question that has bedevilled British Columbia since the 1870s, was carried through to the late twentieth century in Paul Tennant, *Aboriginal Peoples and Politics: The Indian Land Question in British Columbia, 1849–1989* (V: UBCP 1990). Tennant's concern for tracing the emergence of Indian political organizations makes his monograph a vehicle for following the story that Fisher began so well through ten more decades.

The literature, historical and otherwise, on the large number of Indian groups in BC is simply massive. A useful, although now dated, starting point is a work by a man who later produced a similar survey of the conditions in which Canada's Indians found themselves in the 1960s: H.B. Hawthorn, et al., *The Indians of British Columbia* (T: UTP 1960). For the enormous anthropological and ethnographic literature, it is advisable to consult Fisher's sources or a specialized bibliography. A few biographies are available to provide readers with insights into both traditional ways and the process of culture change among the Kwakiutl: James Spradley, *Guests Never Leave Hungry: The Autobiography of James Sewid*, a Kwakiutl Indian (New Haven: Yale UP 1969); Clellan S. Ford, *Smoke from Their Fires: The Life of a Kwakiutl Chief* [Charles Nowell] (New Haven: Yale UP 1941); and Harry Assu with Joy Inglis, *Assu of Cape Mudge: Recollections of a Coastal Indian Chief* (V: UBCP 1989). These studies go far beyond personal reminiscences, throwing light on how the Indian peoples lived and how they responded to Europeans in the late nineteenth and twentieth centuries. Nowell, the source of *Smoke from Their Fires*, had a fascinating career as an assistant and supplier to museum parties that ransacked the Northwest Coast for Indian artifacts. This story is told well in a revealing study by Douglas Cole, *Captured Heritage: The Scramble for Northwest Coast Artifacts* (V: Douglas & McIntyre 1985). Less glamorous forms of employment for BC Indians are considered in Rolf Knight, *Indians at Work: An Informal History of Native Indian Labour in British Columbia, 1858–1930* (V: New Star Press 1978); like Elias on the Dakota, this is one of the few examinations of how Indians fitted themselves into the economy that the newcomers established.

Other regions have not been as well served as the Prairies and British Columbia by students of the Native peoples. The North, long the focus of those who celebrated the explorers to the region, has of late yielded some excellent studies that focus on the people whose lands were explored by these Europeans and whose resources often were exploited by the same people. The necessary starting point is the work of Morris Zaslow: *The Opening of the Canadian North, 1870–1914* (T: M&S 1971) and *The Northward Expansion of Canada, 1914–1967* (T: M&S 1988). The fur trade is another useful path of entry. Most important are two works by Arthur J. Ray: *Indians in the Fur Trade: Their Role as Hunters, Trappers, and Middlemen in the Lands Southwest of Hudson Bay, 1600–1870* (T: UTP 1974) and *The Canadian Fur Trade in the Industrial Age* (T: UTP 1990). Hugh Brody was a participant-observer of the Beaver Indians and his *Maps and Dreams: Indians and the British Columbia Frontier* (V: Douglas & McIntyre 1981), although actually about a region of northeast British Columbia, describes a way of life and an economy that is truly 'northern.'

Beyond the land of the Beaver Indians are those of the Tagish, Tutchone, Gwitch'in, and other groups. Their interaction with southerners since the onset of fur trading has been told compellingly in Kenneth S. Coates, *Best Left as Indians: Native-White Relations in the Yukon Territory, 1840–1973*, (M and K: MQUP 1991). To a degree that is unusual among historians, Coates employed the techniques of anthropologists, ethnohistorians, and educational historians to explain a pattern of Aboriginal permanence and southern transiency that has left most Indians in the Yukon as economically marginalized as those in the south. Also worth examining on the fur trade is Peter J. Usher, *Fur Trade Posts of the Northwest Territories, 1870–1970* (O: Indian and Northern Affairs 1971).

The general story of Native peoples and their relations with immigrants in the Northwest Territories is somewhat more difficult to piece together, inasmuch as there is not yet a companion volume to *Best Left as Indians*. Keith J. Crowe, *A History of the Original Peoples of Northern Canada* (rev. ed., M and K: MQUP 1991) is a fairly basic approach. For the most part, students have to rely on more narrowly focused studies, such as Richard Slobodin, *Métis of the Mackenzie District* (O: St. Paul's University 1966), R. Fumoleau, *As Long as This Land Shall Last: A History of Treaty 8 and Treaty 11, 1870–1939* (T: M&S nd), and several articles by Kerry Abel: 'Prophets, Priests, and Preachers: Dene Shamans and Christian Missions in the Nineteenth Century,' CHA *AR* 1986; 'Of Two Minds: Dene Response to the Mackenzie Missions, 1858–1902,' in K.S. Coates and W.R. Morrison, eds., *Interpreting Canada's North: Selected Readings* (T: CCP 1989); and '"Matters are growing worse": Government and the Mackenzie Missions, 1870–1921,' in K.S. Coates and W.R. Morrison, eds., *For Purposes of Dominion: Essays in Honour of Morris Zaslow* (North York: Captus Press 1989). There is also Abel's longer study, *Drum Songs: Glimpse of Dene History* (M and K: MQUP 1993). For recent political and constitutional developments, students should consult R. Quinn Duffy, *The Road to Nunavut: The Progress of the Eastern Arctic Inuit since the Second World War* (M and K: MQUP 1988), and Peter Jull, 'Building Nunavut,' *Northern Review* 1988.

The early contact period in the Arctic is best approached via studies of whaling and the European whalers' relations with the Inuit. W.G. Ross, *Whaling and Eskimos: Hudson Bay, 1860–1915* (O: National Museum of Man [now Canadian Museum of Civilization] 1975) is an excellent overview, while Philip Goldring's 'Inuit Economic Responses to Euro-American Contacts: Southeast Baffin Island, 1824–1940,' CHA *AR* 1986, concentrated more on the Inuit side of the relationship. Dorothy Harley

Eber's *When the Whalers Were Up North: Inuit Memories from the Eastern Arctic* (M and K: MQUP 1989) also pursued the subject from the Inuit point of view. The latter work was also noteworthy for its reliance on Inuit oral tradition, the type of source upon which historians of Native peoples in all regions increasingly are relying. Another work that pays close attention to Native peoples' outlooks and interests in the matter of harvesting animal resources in the North is George Wenzel, *Animal Rights, Human Rights: Ecology, Economy, and Ideology in the Canadian Arctic* (T: UTP 1991).

The northerly regions of the central provinces are much better covered than the more southerly portions. Several studies of the fur trade, for example, bring their story down to at least part of the post-Confederation era. Charles A. Bishop, *The Northern Ojibwa and the Fur Trade: An Historical and Ecological Study* (T: HRW 1974), and Daniel Francis and Toby Morantz, *Partners in Furs: A History of the Fur Trade in Eastern James Bay, 1600–1870* (M and K: MQUP 1985), are both first-rate. A fascinating introduction to northwestern Ontario and parts of Manitoba is Chief Thomas Fiddler and James R. Stevens, *Killing the Shamen* (Moonbeam: Penumbra Press 1985). Blending oral history of the Indians and records of the Europeans, this volume follows the involvement of increasingly perplexed Indian peoples with the white strangers and their justice system. The cause of the confusion was the Euro-Canadians' insistence on prosecuting for murder individuals who carried out the band's will to destroy a woman who was possessed by a bad spirit. A more recent consideration of the incompatibility of Euro-Canadian and Aboriginal legal systems is Rupert Ross, *Dancing with a Ghost: Exploring Indian Reality* (Markham: Octopus 1992), which also focuses on northwestern Ontario. Further south the Ojibwa have been chronicled sympathetically by Peter S. Schmalz, *The Ojibwa of Southern Ontario* (T: UTP 1991), of which the last two substantive chapters deal with the post-Confederation era.

Unfortunately, no one has done the same job for other Indians residing in Ontario. Particularly regrettable is the absence of reliable studies of the Iroquois Loyalists who located near Brantford and Belleville. Bruce W. Hodgins and Jamie Benedickson have studied the Algonkian people who call themselves the Teme-augama Anishnabai (people of the deep water) in *The Temagami Experience: Recreation, Resources, and Aboriginal Rights in the Northern Ontario Wilderness* (T: UTP 1989), whose subtitle gives some indication of the range and complexity of this excellent regional study. The dreadful impact of a different form of 'development' on northwestern Ontario Indians is Anastasia M. Shkilnyk, *A Poison Stronger Than Love: The*

Destruction of an Ojibwa Community (New Haven: Yale UP 1985), a truly horrifying account of the cumulative effects of economic dislocation and social disintegration. A model analysis of a government-inspired economic disaster in the same region is Paul Driben and Robert S. Trudeau, *When Freedom Is Lost: The Dark Side of the Relationship between Government and the Fort Hope Band* (T: UTP 1983).

Daniel Francis's *A History of the Native Peoples of Quebec, 1760–1867* (O: Indian and Northern Affairs 1983), sponsored by THRC, unfortunately has not been followed by a second volume to carry on the story. However, another monograph from the same agency, by Larry Villeneuve (revised and updated by Daniel Francis), *The Historical Background of Indian Reserves and Settlements in the Province of Quebec* (O: Indian and Northern Affairs 1984) can be read with profit. The 1990 crisis at Oka inspired a special issue on 'Les Mohawks' in *Recherches amérindiennes au Québec* (1991) that has many useful articles. There is as yet no reliable history of the Indians at Kanesatake, but Sylvia Du Vernet, *An Indian Odyssey: Tribulation, Trials, and Triumphs of the Gibson Band of the Mohawk Tribe of the Iroquois Confederacy*, (np: Muskoka Publications 1986), chronicles the experience of some who were persuaded to move from Oka to a reserve in the Muskoka district of Ontario in the early 1880s. Of the plethora of books on Oka, the only worthwhile one is Geoffrey York and Loreen Pindera, *People of the Pines: Warriors and the Legacy of Oka* (T: Little, Brown 1991). York and Pindera, both journalists who covered the story in 1990, provide a good journalistic account of the crisis itself, but one lacking much historical depth. For the most part, other Indian groups in Quebec must be studied in the ethnographic, rather than the historical, literature for the period after Confederation.

The Indians of Atlantic Canada, like those of Quebec, had their heyday long before 1867, at least judging by the historical literature about them. In contrast to the wealth of titles on Beothuk, Micmac, Abenaki, Maliseet, Penobscot, and Passamaquoddy down to the eighteenth century, little is available about their experiences in the late nineteenth century and beyond. H.F. McGee, *The Native Peoples of Atlantic Canada: A History of Indian-European Relations* (O: Carleton UP 1983) has only a few post-Confederation pieces, none of them historical in orientation. A great deal of material unfortunately remains only in article form or in unpublished dissertations. An uneven account that is nonetheless worth reading is Olga McKenna, *Micmac by Choice: Elsie Sark – An Island Legend* (H: Formac 1990), a rare portrait of a Caucasian woman (and an Englishwoman at that!) who married into and lived alongside a Micmac band on Prince

Edward Island. Also of interest is an anthropological study of settlers' social construction of group identity in relation to Native peoples: Evelyn Plaice, *The Native Game: Settler Perceptions of Indian/Settler Relations in Central Labrador* (St John's: ISER 1990). Also worth attention are several books on Micmac culture and legend by Halifax ethnographer Ruth Holmes Whitehead that take the non-Native reader literally into a different world. Worth sampling, too, are the insights of Micmac poet Rita Joe, whose *Poems of Rita Joe* (H: Abanaki Press 1978) are a source of distilled history.

TREATY-MAKING

Treaty-making, although not new in 1867, still provided novelty for the young Dominion, not to mention dozens of titles for anyone interested in Native history. The logical starting point for the numbered treaties is a primary source, first published in 1880 and most recently republished in 1991. Alexander Morris, treaty commissioner for the negotiations of a number of the treaties, set out an account of the background, his version of the proceedings, and the text of the Prairie treaties in *The Treaties of Canada with the Indians of Manitoba and the North-West Territories*, (1880, S: Fifth House 1991). Good accounts of Treaty 8 and Treaty 11 can be found in Fumoleau, *As Long*, and Treaty 9 is the subject of a chapter of Titley's *Narrow Vision* (cited above). The best historical overview of treaty-making in the 1870s is Friesen, *Canadian Prairies* (cited above), and an extremely important reinterpretation of the Indians' role is John L. Taylor, 'Canada's North-West Indian Policy in the 1870s: Traditional Premises and Necessary Innovations,' in D.A. Muise, ed., *Approaches to Native History in Canada* (O: Museum of Man 1977). Taylor's article is anthologized in Miller, *Sweet Promises* (cited above). Also not to be missed is Jean Friesen's sensitive interpretation of treaty-making: 'Magnificent Gifts: The Treaties of Canada with the Indians of the Northwest, 1869–1876,' *TRSC* 1986. Still useful is the first section of George F.G. Stanley, *The Birth of Western Canada: A History of the Riel Rebellions* (2nd ed., T: UTP 1960). A Reprints in Canadian History (RICH) edition of Stanley's *Birth*, containing an introduction by Thomas Flanagan, was issued by UTP in 1992.

As important as the actual treaty-making was the aftermath, to appreciate which it is vital to understand the differing viewpoints of Indians and government about the treaties. Important for the Indian side are three articles by John L. Tobias: 'Indian Reserves in Western Canada: Indian Homelands or Devices for Assimilation,' Muise, ed., *Approaches* (cited above); 'The Origins of the Treaty Rights Movement in Saskatchewan,' in F. Laurie Barron and J.B. Waldram, eds., *1885 and After: Native Society in Transition* (R: CPRC 1986); and 'Canada's Subjugation of the Plains Cree' (cited above). Also valuable are the essays on Treaty 7 and Treaty 8 in R. Price, ed., *The Spirit of the Alberta Indian Treaties* (2nd ed., E: Pica Pica Press 1987). The Ottawa view of the treaties is most easily captured in Stanley, *Birth* (cited above).

NORTHWEST REBELLION

Historians have long followed Stanley in portraying the 1885 rebellion in the Saskatchewan country as a clash between two ways of life, a confrontation exacerbated by the aftermath of treaty-making in the 1870s. More recently, however, a different interpretation has become predominant. This version, in which the Indians are not much involved in the rising, owes a great deal to the work of John L. Tobias (cited above) and of A. Blair Stonechild, 'The Indian View of the 1885 Uprising,' in Barron and Waldram, eds., *1885 and After* (cited above). Essentially, any scholar who has looked at 1885 through the eyes of the Indians has found that the insurrection was almost exclusively a Métis event. Examples include W.B. Fraser, 'Big Bear, Indian Patriot,' *Alberta Historical Review* 1966; R.S. Allen, 'Big Bear,' *Saskatchewan History* 1972; and the work of Hugh Dempsey on southern Alberta Indians (cited above). Worthy of particular note is Dempsey's 'The Fearsome Fire Wagons,' in Dempsey, ed., *The CPR West: The Iron Road and the Making of a Nation* (V: Douglas & McIntyre 1984), which advances reasons for the quiescence of some southern plains Indians. Métis nationalist historians resist this recent reinterpretation of 1885, preferring still to see the resistance as Stanley did, a united Native front against the encroaching Euro-Canadian agricultural frontier.

THE METIS

In part because of Louis Riel, the mixed-blood communities generically labelled the Métis have attracted enormous, if sometimes myopic, attention. In fact, there are many Métis communities across the country, even though those of Red River and the Saskatchewan have enjoyed most of the scholarly attention. Furthermore, the Métis are divisible into at least two main ethnic sub-groupings: the anglophone mixed-blood peoples sometimes in the West called 'the country born,' and the francophone group or Métis proper. Here the term will be used generically. For these fascinating people the historical road to Red River, Batoche, and beyond is a lengthy one, with many curves – and perhaps even a couple of dead ends.

The grand ethnographic-historical survey of the Métis, now available in a graceful English translations thanks to George Woodcock, is Marcel Giraud's *The Métis in the Canadian West*, 2 vols, (1945 [French], Lincoln: University of Nebraska Press 1986 [English]). Much less ambitious, but still useful as an introduction, is D.B. Sealey and A.S. Lussier, *The Métis: Canada's Forgotten People* (W: Pemmican 1975). These general accounts should be supplemented by two innovative fur-trade studies that effectively explain the economic and biological reasons for the emergence of the mixed-blood community. Sylvia Van Kirk, *'Many Tender Ties': Women in Fur Trade Society, 1670–1870* (W: Watson & Dyer 1979) and Jennifer S.H. Brown, *Strangers in Blood: Fur Trade Company Families in Indian Country* (V: UBCP 1980), take different paths to the same destination: a reinterpretation of the western fur trade that puts Native women at the centre of the picture and thereby greatly enriches our understanding both of the commerce and of the unique social collectivities that were produced by it. Also instructive are a number of essays in Jacqueline Peterson and Jennifer S.H. Brown, eds., *The New People: Being and Becoming Métis in North America* (W: UMP 1985). Helpful on more modern aspects of the mixed-blood experience (especially legal matters) is Donald J. Purich, *The Métis* (T: Lorimer 1988). Much of this literature has been surveyed and evaluated in J.R. Miller, 'From Riel to the Métis,' *CHR* 1988.

The entanglement of the western Métis with the Canadian state after 1867 has been responsible for the destruction of a small forest. Articles and books on Riel and the resistance pour forth steadily from the presses. D.N. Sprague, *Canada and the Métis, 1869–1885* (Wa: WLUP 1988) argued convincingly that the Dominion, after the Red River Resistance of 1869–70, mistreated the Métis community of Manitoba, contrary to its statutory obligations. Historians persuaded by Sprague's depiction of government mishandling of Métis land in the 1870s in Manitoba drew back at the author's rather more strained contention that there was a government conspiracy to foment the Northwest Rebellion in 1885 by ignoring and/or riding roughshod over the Métis in the South Saskatchewan River valley. In part, Sprague was responding to portrayals of Canadian Native policy in the West as benevolent and foresighted; in part, he was reacting to the other main protagonist (see below) in what has become a major historiographical debate about the Métis and their fate.

Thomas Flanagan, a political scientist rather than a historian, entered the fray over the Métis with a study of Riel, his political thought, and his leadership: *Louis 'David' Riel: Prophet of the New World* (T: UTP 1979). This was a Riel the likes of which had been unknown to readers of earlier biographies, such as G.F.G. Stanley's *Louis Riel* (T: MHR 1963). Stanley's Riel had been a heroic defender of his people against Canadian intolerance and government blundering. Flanagan's Riel was a religious zealot, a prophet-king with a divine mission to refashion the Canadian West into a homeland for the Indians, the Métis, and the dispossessed of Europe. If Flanagan tried to reveal Riel's peculiar vision, a historical sociologist, Gilles Martel, sought to explain that the Métis were susceptible to Riel's message because they were in the throes of social and economic dislocation. Martel provided this analysis in *Le messianisme de Louis Riel* (Wa: WLUP 1984), which was more persuasive on the message and the state of the audience than it was in establishing a cause-and-effect linkage between the two. Flanagan took his analysis one step further in *Riel and the Rebellion: 1885 Reconsidered* (S: WPPB 1983), in which he countermanded Stanley's *Birth* (cited above) and provoked Sprague by holding the Métis leader almost solely responsible for the rebellion of 1885.

Amidst this donnish scrapping, a few scholars tried to analyse the 1885 troubles in less pugnacious terms. George Woodcock wrote a sensitive biography, *Gabriel Dumont: The Métis Chief and His Lost World* (E: Hurtig 1975), that, not surprisingly given Woodcock's own political philosophy, painted the Métis as anarchists and Dumont as the closest thing that anarchist communes got to leadership. Bob Beal and Rod Macleod, *Prairie Fire: The 1885 North-West Rebellion* (E: Hurtig 1984), settled for telling the complicated story of the rebellion and its suppression clearly and intelligently. Doug Owram, 'The Myth of Louis Riel,' *CHR* 1982, delineated the role that Riel has played in popular culture and political thought in the decades since his execution in 1885.

The debate that Sprague and Flanagan began over the (mis)treatment of the Métis has moved backward chronologically, as other scholars joined in the debate over what had happened in Red River and Manitoba after the assertion of Canadian rule. Frits Pannekoek had begun his research into the society of Red River well before the larger historiographical war began, and his *A Snug Little Flock: The Social Origins of the Riel Resistance* (W: Watson & Dwyer 1991) contended that sectarian and racial tensions had underlain the unrest at Red River in the 1860s, and that Riel had not led a united mixed-blood community in the resistance to Canada in 1869–70. Economic historian Irene Spry countered this view in articles, most notably 'The Métis and Mixed-Bloods of Rupert's Land before 1870,' in Peterson and Brown, *New Peoples* (cited above). Increasingly the debate has centred on economic questions, such as the adaptability of the Manitoba Métis to change, and their (in)ability to capitalize upon the promise of 1.4 million acres in the Manitoba Act of 1870. Sprague's *Canada and the Métis*, of course, addresses these issues head-on. Thomas Flanagan argued a contrary view – that the Métis were not mistreated by government – in *Métis Lands in Manitoba* (C: UCP 1991). This debate, increasingly focused on samples of Métis who did or did not get the land coming to them, has tended to wander into a methodological bog.

Deliverance might come in the form of detailed community studies, which, by eschewing the grand historiographical questions, often provide more useful insights. Trudy Nicks has done such work on the Métis of Grande Cache, Alberta (in Peterson and Brown, *New Peoples*), and Diane Payment has produced several valuable studies of Batoche that correct a number of generalizations about the Métis and the impact of Canadian authority. Her most recent work is '*The Free Peoples – Otipemisiwak*': *Batoche, Saskatchewan, 1870–1930*, (O: Supply and Services 1990). For Red River, illuminating work on local communities has been produced by Gerhard Ens: 'Kinship, Ethnicity, Class, and the Red River Métis: The Parishes of Saint-François and St. Andrews,' PhD thesis, University of Alberta 1989 (forthcoming as a monograph from UTP, 1994 or 1995) and 'Dispossession or Adaptation: Migration and Persistence of the Red River Métis, 1835–1890,' CHA *AR* 1988; and by Nicole St-Onge: 'Race, Class, and Marginality: A Métis Settlement in the Manitoba Interlake, 1850–1914,' PhD thesis, University of Manitoba 1990, and 'Race, Class, and Marginality in an Interlake Settlement, 1850–1950,' in James Silver and Jeremy Hull, eds., *The Political Economy of Manitoba* (R: CPRC 1990). By concentrating carefully on one corner of the big canvas, these authors throw light on all of it. Whatever the result of the Sprague-Flanagan debate, there should be little doubt that the Métis, Riel, and the troubles in the Canadian West in the generation after Confederation will continue to attract the attention of historians for some time yet.

THE POLICY OF THE BIBLE AND THE PLOUGH

Following the making of the Western treaties in the 1870s, and with more urgency after the Northwest Rebellion, Ottawa turned its hand to controlling, and assimilating the Indians of the country and to making them self-sufficient. The policies that were developed in pursuit of these ends, known collectively as 'the policy of the Bible and the plough,' included efforts to control Indians politically, to limit their movements, to suppress traditional cultural practices, to assimilate and equip them to earn a living in Euro-Canadian fashion in residential schools, and to instruct those who lived in appropriate regions in horticulture. Anthropologist Noel Dyck examines this complex of policies under the heading 'coercive tutelage' and relates it to earlier forms of Native-newcomer relations in *What is the Indian 'Problem'?: Tutelage and Resistance in Canadian Indian Administration* (St John's: ISER 1991). Dyck's examination is the logical starting point for this broad theme of political control, economic adaptation, and cultural suppression.

Little analysis of government interference with Indians' political structures and movements since Confederation is available. Titley's *A Narrow Vision* (cited above) has an excellent chapter on efforts to force Mohawk on the Six Nations reserve in Ontario to abandon their customary system of having clan mothers select chiefs from certain hereditary lines. There is also some information on a similar struggle at Kanesatake/Oka in York and Pindera, *People of the Pines* (cited above). The fascinating efforts to thwart Prairie Indian diplomats by limiting Indians' freedom of movement extra-legally by a pass system has been dealt with briefly by Tobias in 'Subjugation' (cited above) and more systematically by F. Laurie Barron in 'The Indian Pass System in the Canadian West, 1882–1935,' *Prairie Forum* 1988. Much remains to be discovered about both the pass system and Ottawa's imperialistic effort at political interference.

More is known about the government's attempts to suppress traditional practices such as the Potlatch on the West Coast and the Sun or Thirst Dance on the Prairies. F.E. LaViolette, *Indian Cultures and the Protestant Ethic in British Columbia* (T: UTP 1961) has been supplanted by a much more sophisticated study, Douglas Cole and Ira Chaikin, *An Iron Hand upon the People: The Law against the Potlatch on the Northwest Coast* (V: Douglas & McIntyre 1990). However, LaViolette's account has some interesting detail that is still useful, and *Iron Hand* has been criticized by some Indians as having less than a complete grasp of the nature and purpose of the Potlatch ceremonial. A legal perspective that contains interesting insights about the ambiguity and limitations of government power in such situations is Tina Loo, 'Dan Cranmer's Potlatch: Law as Coercion, Symbol, and Rhetoric in British Columbia, 1884–1951,' *CHR* 1992. J.R. Miller has also tried to point out that Indians had means to resist the coercion of the pass system, cultural suppression, and residential schools in 'Owen Glendower, Hotspur, and Canadian Indian Policy,' *Ethnohistory* 1990.

Unfortunately, material on Prairie dances and government efforts to suppress them is not yet bountiful. A beginning can be made in Titley's *Narrow Vision* and Dempsey's *Red Crow* (cited above). Katherine Pettipas's paper 'The Prairie Dance Law and Indian Resistance' (CHA 1990) is unpublished, but her longer study, *Severing the Ties That Bind: Government Repression of Indigenous Religious Ceremonies on the Prairies*, is soon to be published by University of Manitoba Press.

The residential school fiasco is better documented, although no comprehensive account is available of it either. John Webster Grant, *Moon of Wintertime: Missionaries and the Indians of Canada in Encounter since 1534* (T: UTP 1984), has reliable material on the missionary background to these institutions, as it does for cultural suppression in general. J. Barman, Y. Hébert, and D. McCaskill, eds., *Indian Education in Canada*, 2 vols. (V: Nakoda Institute and UBCP 1986–7), has a number of good essays, particularly in the first volume. Jacqueline [Kennedy] Gresko, 'White "Rites" and Indian "Rites": Indian Education and Native Responses in the West, 1870–1910,' in A.W. Rasporich, ed., *Western Canada Past and Present* (C: M&S 1975), is unusual in its attention to Indian resistance as well as missionary coercion. Brian Titley, 'Indian Industrial Schools in Western Canada,' in Nancy M. Sheehan and J. Donald Wilson, eds., *Schools in the West: Essays on Canadian Educational History* (C: Detselig 1986), surveys the ambitious schools that attempted for a brief time after 1883 to teach trades to Indian children. A detailed study of the missionary side of the residential school effort that yields surprising results about the impact that attempts at cultural replacement had on the oppressor is David A. Nock's analysis of E.F. Wilson, *A Victorian Missionary and Canadian Indian Policy* (Wa: WLUP 1988). There is also useful material on residential schools in Coates, *Best Left*, and Miller, 'Owen Glendower' (cited above). Finally, more specialized studies are well worth consulting: Jean Usher, *Duncan of Metlakatla* (O: Museum of Man 1974), and David Mulhall, *The Will to Power: The Missionary Career of Father Morice* (V: UBCP 1986).

Studies of the 'plough' portion of the policy of the Bible and the plough have been dominated by the fine work of Sarah Carter. Prior to the appearance of her publications, Noel Dyck provided a useful beginning in 'An Opportunity Lost: The Initiative of the Reserve Agricultural Programme in the Prairie West,' in Barron and Waldram, eds., *1885 and After* (cited above). However, Carter's well-executed case study, *Lost Harvests: Prairie Indian Reserve Farmers and Government Policy* (M and K: MQUP 1990), showed clearly that Indian Affairs did not so much direct attempts to assist Western Indians into agriculture after the disappearance of the buffalo as sabotage the Indians' efforts to make the transition their own way. *Lost Harvests* is an impressive, if depressing, account. Carter pursued the theme of a malignant federal government in 'Demonstrating Success: The File Hills Farm Colony,' *Prairie Forum* 1991, an analysis that is relevant to the history of the residential schools as well as Indian agriculture. Economist Helen Buckley adopted Carter's analysis of late nineteenth-century agricultural policy and extended it through the twentieth century in *From Wooden Ploughs to Welfare: Why Indian Policy Failed in the Prairie Provinces* (M and K: MQUP 1992). Buckley showed convincingly that Ottawa learned nothing from its early disasters in agricultural development. Whether or not her conclusion that the solution to these problems lies in Aboriginal self-government is sound remains to be seen.

LAND QUESTIONS

The 'land question,' which the federal government prefers to term 'land claims,' is as much the product of the overwhelming of a traditional Indian economy and society as were efforts to suppress cultural traditions and to remake children in residential schools. In the absence, yet again, of a reliable general account, the best starting point is a publication of THRC. Richard C. Daniel, *A History of Native Claims Processes in Canada, 1867–1979* (O: Indian and Northern Affairs 1980) is invaluable, although the successive crises in this area in the 1980s have left it somewhat out of date. A more recent collection that takes a provincial and regional approach to this complex topic is K.S. Coates, ed., *Aboriginal Land Claims in Canada: A Regional Perspective* (Mississauga: CCP 1992). To pursue the story in detail, one should begin where the protests over loss of lands did, in British Columbia. Robert E. Cail, *Land, Man, and Law: The Disposal of Crown Lands in British Columbia, 1871–1913* (V: UBCP 1974) has been superseded by Tennant, *Aboriginal Peoples and Politics* (cited above), but is still of some value. Donald J. Purich, *Our Land: Native Rights in Canada* (T: JL 1986) is particularly helpful in untangling the legal and constitutional complexities of both the land question and Aboriginal self-government. Land issues have stimulated the appearance of some fascinating statements by the Indians themselves. Joanne Drake-Terry, *The Same as Yesterday: The Lillooet Chronicle the Theft of Their Lands and Resources* (np: Lillooet Tribal Council 1989), and Gisday Wa and Delgam Uukw, *The Spirit in the Land: The Opening Statement of the Gitksan and Wet-suwet'en Hereditary Chiefs in the Supreme Court of British Columbia, May 11, 1987* (Gabriola: Gitksan and Wet'suwet'en Hereditary Chiefs 1989) contain a great deal of history.

Access to Native lands and to the resources and energies to be found there has since 1945 led to both some mighty struggles and some enlightening historical literature. Robert Page, *Northern Development: The Canadian Dilemma* (T: M&S 1986) provides a broad overview of the issues. Thomas R. Berger's inquiry into the viability of a pipeline up the Mackenzie Valley produced *Northern Frontier/Northern Homeland: The Report of the Mackenzie Valley Pipeline Inquiry*, 2 vols. (O: Supply and Services 1977), as well as a shorter treatment by Martin O'Malley, *The Past and Future Land: An Account of the Berger Inquiry into the Mackenzie Valley Pipeline* (T: Peter Martin Associates 1976). The political response of the inhabitants is displayed in Mel Watkins, ed., *Dene Nation: The Colony Within* (T: UTP 1977). The assault by the Quebec government under Robert Bourassa on the homeland of the Cree for the purpose of generating hydroelectricity for export produced a journalistic indictment by Boyce Richardson, *Strangers Devour the Land* (2nd ed., V: Douglas & McIntyre 1991), and a more scholarly analysis by Richard F. Salisbury, *A Homeland for the Cree: Regional Development in James Bay, 1971–1981* (M and K: MQUP 1986). Parallel developments in Manitoba and Saskatchewan have been carefully examined and assessed in James B. Waldram, *As Long as the Rivers Run: Hydroelectric Development and Native Communities in Western Canada* (W: UMP 1988).

Journalist John Goddard exposed the chicanery to which one Native group had been subjected by oil companies and the Alberta government in *The Last Stand of the Lubicon Cree* (V: Douglas & McIntyre 1991). A new wrinkle to these disputes over access to Native lands containing resources was added in the 1980s in Labrador. There the issue between the Innu and Canadian government was the air space above Indian lands, which Ottawa wanted to use for fighter aircraft training flights that disturbed the game animals on whom the Innu depended. The events of this sorry chapter have been summarized to date by a Newfoundland-based CBC journalist, Marie Wadden, in *Nitassinan: The Innu Struggle to Reclaim Their Homeland* (V: Douglas & McIntyre 1992). Many of these late twentieth-century confrontations over resource lands have been addressed in a volume aimed at the quincentennial of Christopher Columbus's arrival in the Caribbean: Thomas R. Berger, *A Long and Terrible Shadow: White Values, Native Rights in the Americas, 1492–1992* (V: Douglas & McIntyre 1991).

Through the 1980s and 1990s, battles over territory have regularly spilled over onto legal and constitutional turf, especially during the constitutional sturm und drang precipitated by the efforts of the Trudeau and Mulroney governments to reinvent the country. Indeed, legal scholars have long worked in the area of Native rights. Peter A. Cumming and Neil H. Mickenberg, eds., *Native Rights in Canada* (2nd ed., T: Indian-Eskimo Association 1972) was the first scholarly exploration. A more recent consideration is available in Purich, *Our Land* (cited above). Collections of cases relevant to the evolution of Native law and of Native legal rights are Derek G. Smith, ed., *Canadian Indians and the Law: Selected Documents, 1663–1972* (T: M&S 1975), and B.W. Morse, ed., *Aboriginal Peoples and the Law: Indian, Metis, and Inuit Rights in Canada* (O: Carleton UP 1985). The latter title is much more complete, although its organization makes it a repetitious nightmare for historians to use. As yet no comprehensive accounts of the constitutional heroics have appeared. However, students can make a productive beginning with an anthropologist, Michael Asch, *Home and Native Land: Aboriginal Rights and the Canadian Constitution* (T: Methuen 1984), and with two journalists, Robert Sheppard and Michael Valpy, *The National Deal: The Fight for a Canadian Constitution* (T: Fleet Books 1984). Obviously neither of these dealt with the 1987–90 battle over the Meech Lake Accord or the agonies that followed in 1991–2.

Finally, students of Native history might want to consider some of the surveys of the conditions in which Native peoples lived. The definitive study for its time was the government-sponsored H.B. Hawthorne et al., *A Survey of the Contemporary Indians of Canada*, 2 vols, (O: Indian Affairs 1966–7). A powerful Indian writer, Harold Cardinal, was inspired by the White Paper and the political tumult of the 1970s to produce two moving portraits – *The Unjust Society: The Tragedy of Canada's Indians* (E: Hurtig 1969), and *The Rebirth of Canada's Indians* (E: Hurtig 1977) – whose cover illustrations speak volumes. One of the country's best journalistic commentators on Native affairs, Geoffrey York, demonstrated that things had not improved much in the 1970s and 1980s in his *The Dispossessed: Life and Death in Native Canada* (T: Lester & Orpen Dennys 1989). York's conclusion was underlined by another journalistic study produced by Larry Krotz, *Indian Country: Inside Another Canada* (T: M&S 1990). Unfortunately, there is every reason to expect that a decade from now there will be a longer list of such works on the sorry results of the history of the Native peoples in Canada.

During the past quarter-century the scholarly attention devoted to Native history has grown dramatically. Although many specific topics remain untreated and comprehensive works are lacking for a number of important areas, considerable progress has been achieved in making academic analysis of many themes available. Increasingly researchers have moved beyond merely depicting the Native communities as victims of Euro-Canadians and their government in the decades since Confederation. A growing proportion of studies produced in the 1980s and 1990s emphasized that Native groups were active and assertive in their resistance, although there is at yet no scholarly consensus on the degree of activity or the Aboriginal communities' success is resisting coercive assimilation. Rather less slowly researchers have begun to broaden the range of research materials that they employ, putting aside the near-total dependence on government records that used to typify work in this area, and gradually incorporating more Native sources, many of them oral. Unfortunately, at the same time there has been a tendency to neglect the denominational religious archives that are now fuller and more accessible than they have ever been. The final development in the recent historiography that should be noted is the beginnings of a 'Native history' produced by Native scholars. The recent publication by Georges E. Sioui, a Wendat (Huron), of *For an Amerindian Autohistory: An Essay on the Foundations of a Social Ethic*, Sheila Fischman, trans., (M and K: MQUP 1992; French ed. Q: PUL 1991) is a hopeful sign in that regard. Sioui's reinterpretation of the relationship between Natives and newcomers concentrates on the seventeenth century, but it holds clues to post-Confederation patterns as well. All students of recent Native history should hope that Sioui or some other Aboriginal scholar will carry on the story chronologically.

WENDY MITCHINSON

Women's History

Women's history is one of most exciting and vibrant areas of current historical research and has posed major challenges to the discipline of history. It has broadened the topics of historical research to include the family, the body, life cycles, sexuality, and unpaid work. Women's history has also expanded the definition of historical source material, as much of it has incorporated the methodology of both material and oral history. Most significantly, as suggested by Sylvia Van Kirk in 'What Has the Feminist Perspective Done for Canadian History?' in Ursula Franklin et al., *Knowledge Reconsidered: A Feminist Overview* (O: Canadian Research Institute for the Advancement of Women 1984), it has challenged historians to rethink the way they have examined the past. Van Kirk argues that it is simply impossible to integrate the history of women into a structure that focused on political and economic events to measure the passage of time rather than the lives of Canadians themselves. Historians of women have also introduced the concept of gender as a central variable of historical analysis, that is, that female and male roles are socially constructed rather than biologically determined.

The problems associated with trying to write the history of more than half the population, and the fact that most historians of women are feminists and thus influenced by the theoretical shifts within the feminist movement, have made historians examine how they approach the history of women. This led Ruth Roach Pierson and Alison Prentice in 'Feminism and the Writing and Teaching of History,' *Atlantis* 1982, to discuss how their own feminist ideology intersected with their research and teaching. Concerns about terminology and concepts as applied to women were raised in Joy Parr's 'Nature and Hierarchy: Reflections in Writing in the History of Women and Children,' *Atlantis* 1985, and in a beautifully crafted essay '"Sundays Always Make Me Think of Home": Time and Place in Canadian Women's History,' in Barbara K. Latham and Roberta J. Pazdro, eds., *Not Just Pin Money: Selected Essays on the History of Women's Work in British Columbia* (Vi: Camosun College 1984), Margaret Conrad describes the way in which women measure the passage of time through births, deaths, anniversaries, and through the changes in their own bodies. Recently, Ruth Roach Pierson has stimulated our thinking about women's history in 'Experience, Difference, Dominance, and Voice in the Writing of Canadian Women's History,' in Karen Offen, Ruth Roach Pierson, and Jane Rendall, eds., *Writing Women's History: International Perspectives* (Bloomington: Indiana UP 1991), and in 'Colonization and Canadian Women's History,' *Journal of Women's History* 1992.

Reflecting the vitality of the field of women's history are periodic historiographical examinations, most of which are useful bibliographic sources as well. Ruth Pierson and Beth Light wrote an excellent overview of trends in the field in 'Women in the Teaching and Writing of Canadian History,' *The History and Social Science Teacher* 1982. In that same year the *CHR* published Elaine Leslau Silverman's 'Writing Canadian Women's History, 1970–82: An Historiographical Analysis.' This was followed by Margaret Conrad's 'The Re-Birth of Canada's Past: A Decade of Women's History,' *Acadiensis* 1983, and most recently by Gail Cuthbert Brandt's insightful 'Postmodern Patchwork: Some Recent Trends in the Writing of Women's History in Canada,' *CHR* 1991, which begins the examination of the historiography where Silverman's article in the same journal ended, 1982. To help researchers keep up with the flow of new work there are several standard bibliographic sources. The *CHR* has a separate section on women's history in the bibliographic section published in each issue, and *Resources for Feminist Research* keeps track of recent publications on women, and also does periodic reviews of specialized topics. The standard bibliography is Beth Light and Veronica Strong-Boag, comps., *True Daughters of the North: Canadian Women's History, An Annotated Bibliography* (T: OISE Press 1980), which in its detail has not been surpassed. Of less value but more up-to-date is Carol Mazur and Sheila Pepper, eds., *Women in Canada: A Bibliography, 1965–1982* (3rd ed., T: OISE Press 1984), which is an interdisciplinary compilation of sources. Most recent is Diana Pedersen, *Changing Women, Changing History: A Bibliography of the History of Women in Canada* (T: Green Dragon Press 1992).

Although there is no specific journal devoted to the history of Canadian women there are several which regularly publish articles on the topic. Among journals devoted to women, *Atlantis* and *Canadian Woman Studies* are the most likely to contain historical articles. Of more limited use is the *Canadian Journal of Women and the Law*. The *Canadian Feminist Periodical Index, 1972–1985* has indexed the major women's periodicals and will make finding journal articles easier for the time period it covers. History journals which favour women's history are *Histoire Sociale/Social History*, *Labour/Le Travail*, and *Revue d'histoire de l'Amérique française*. One trend that does seem to be emerging is for various journals to devote theme issues to the history of women, for example, the December 1991 issue of the *Canadian Historical Review* and *Canadian Bulletin of Medical History* 1991.

GENERAL

General historical studies of women in Canada are not numerous. Early efforts of a restricted nature were written but the publication of two works has superseded them. With *Quebec Women: A History* (T: Women's Press 1987) by the Clio Collective, first published in French in 1982 and with a new French edition in 1992, women's history came of age. It revealed the depth of research in the field and challenged the periodization usually followed by historians of Quebec in that more than half the book focused on the twentieth century. While at times the authors tended to see women as victims, this reflected the historiography of the early 1980s when the book was written. Less pessimistic in approach and the only general survey of women in Canada is Alison Prentice et al., *Canadian Women: A History* (T: HBJ 1988). For anyone wanting a place to start learning about women's history, this is it. Like other historians of women, the authors have pointed out that traditional periodization does not hold. Certainly 1867 and Confederation were essentially meaningless for most women (and most men) living at the time. More significant were the 1850s and the beginning of industrial development with its impact on the family and women's work experience. Equally important was World War I, not because it was a war, but because during it women finally received the vote and achieved one of their long-worked-for reforms – prohibition. While not covering the same breadth of time as the above, Veronica Strong-Boag's *The New Day Recalled: Lives of Girls and Women in English Canada, 1919–1939* (T: CCP 1988) is an intensive study of two decades. Using the life-cycle approach, she has written a stimulating examination of the various levels of women's lives in the interwar period, encompassing most of the topics discussed below. More specialized is Ruth Roach Pierson's masterful *'They're Still Women After All': The Second World War and Canadian Womanhood* (T: M&S 1986), which explores the world of women working in the military and their involvement in non-military employment and in volunteer fields.

Collections of essays on the history of women have been vital in the advancement of the field and four in particular stand out. Two are edited by Susan Mann Trofimenkoff and Alison Prentice, *The Neglected Majority: Essays in Canadian Women's History*, 2 vols, (T: M&S 1977, 1985). These, along with Veronica Strong-Boag and Anita Clair Fellman, eds., *Rethinking Canada: The Promise of Women's History* (2nd ed., T: CC 1991), and Franca Iacovetta and Mariana Valverde, eds., *Gender Conflicts: New Essays in Women's History* (T: UTP 1992), are designed for use in women's history courses, so the essays contained within them cover a wide time frame and range of topics. All four volumes are excellent sources. Collections of research essays also have been published with a specific regional focus. Among them are Marie Lavigne and Yolande Pinard, eds., *Les femmes dans la société québécoise: aspects historiques* (M: BE 1977); Barbara Latham and Cathy Kess, eds., *In Her Own Right: Selected Essays on Women's History in British Columbia* (Vi: Camosun College 1980); Gillian Cresse and Veronica Strong-Boag, eds., *British Columbia Reconsidered: Essays on Women* (V: Press Gang 1992); and Mary Kinnear, ed., *First Days, Fighting Days: Women in Manitoba History* (R: CPRC 1987), all of which contain a wide selection of excellent essays, as does *Looking into My Sister's Eyes: An Exploration in Women's History* (T: MHSO 1986), edited by Jean Burnet. This last volume has been particularly welcome in that it has done much to focus historians' attention on the lives of minority women.

One popular approach to women's history has been compilations of documents written by women in the past, allowing them to speak for themselves. One of the first of these was Ramsay Cook and Wendy Mitchinson, eds., *The Proper Sphere: Women's Place in Canadian Society* (T: OUP 1976), which largely focuses on the perceptions women and men alike about the role women were to play in Canadian society in the late nineteenth century and early decades of the twentieth. Since it was published, the life-cycle perspective has become the organizational focus in such collections, as revealed in three volumes from Toronto's New Hogtown Press – Beth Light and Alison Prentice, eds., *Pioneer and Gentlewomen of British North America, 1713–1867* (1980); Beth Light and Joy Parr, eds. *Canadian Women on the Move, 1867–1920* (1983), and Beth Light and Ruth Roach Pierson, eds., *No Easy Road: Women in Canada, 1920s to 1960s* (1990). Each volume traces the experience of women through girlhood, education, work, courtship, marriage, childbearing, and

widowhood. The documents chosen are insightful, as are the introductory essays in each. Allowing the women themselves to be heard has also
been the desire of Denise Lemieux and Lucie Mercier in their *Les femmes
au tournant du siècle, 1880–1940: âges de la vie, maternité et quotidien* (Q:
IQRC 1989), which uses autobiographical accounts organized around the
life cycle. Perhaps one of the most sensitive examples of this approach is
the collection edited by Margaret Conrad, Toni Laidlaw, and Donna
Smyth, *No Place Like Home: Diaries and Letters of Nova Scotia Women,
1771–1938* (H: Formac 1988). Of published diaries none can surpass the
three volumes pertaining to the life of Lucy Maud Montgomery. In *The
Selected Journals of L.M. Montgomery*, vol. 1, *1889–1910*, vol. 2, *1910–
1921*, and vol. 3, *1921–1929* (T: OUP 1985, 1987, 1992), Mary Rubio
and Elizabeth Waterston have made public the inner life of one of Canada's
most famous authors. In her journals Montgomery reveals her fears,
dreams, and joys, and details the frustrations of living the life of a woman.

The first women's history written was biographical. For an introduction to the biographies of over five hundred women covering the period
from New France to 1970, Jean Bannerman's *Leading Ladies: Canada,
1639–1967* (Belleville: Mika Publishing 1977) is a good place to begin.
Less encompassing but more detailed is *The Clear Spirit: Twenty Canadian
Women and Their Times* (T: UTP 1966), edited by Mary Quayle Innis,
which has chapter biographies on women who made their mark in the
arts, politics, reform, and the church. *Wilderness Women: Canada's Forgotten History* (T: Peter Martin Associates 1973) by Jean Johnston focuses on
women who experienced life away from settled areas. Relevant for the
period after the mid-nineteenth century are the studies of Amelia Douglas, Charlotte Bompas, and Martha Louise Black. All of the above depict
women as heroines.

THE WOMEN'S MOVEMENT

One area of interest for historians of women has been the ideology of
woman's proper place in Canadian society. Many of the documentary
sources mentioned above address this issue as they juxtaposed the images
with the reality of women's lives. Susan Mann Trofimenkoff's work has
been more analytical. In two articles, one on Henri Bourassa in *The
Neglected Majority*, vol. 1, and 'Les femmes dans l'oeuvre de Groulx,'
RHAF 1978, she examines the thinking of two of Quebec's leading opinion makers, both of whom believed strongly in women maintaining their
traditional role in the home as a way to protect the well-being of French

culture. Similarly focused on ideology is Mona-Josée Gagnon's *Les femmes vues par le Québec des hommes: 30 ans d'histoire des idéologies, 1940–1970* (M: Editions du jour 1974). For English Canada, three articles stand out. Two examine the popular press: Susannah Wilson, 'The Changing Image of Women in Canadian Mass Circulating Magazines, 1930–1970,' *Atlantis* 1977, and Susan M. Bland, 'Henrietta the Homemaker and "Rosie The Riveter": Images of Women in Advertising in *Maclean's Magazine*, 1930–1950,' *Atlantis* 1983. Yvonne Mathews-Klein turns her attention to the National Film Board in 'How They Saw Us: Images of Women in National Film Board Films of the 1940s and 1950s,' *Atlantis* 1979. Ideology provides the context in which women had to act and helps explain why they made the decisions they did.

In the early years of writing women's history, many researchers were intrigued by how women gained the vote. Catherine Cleverdon's *The Woman Suffrage Movement in Canada: The Start of Liberation* (2nd ed., T: UTP 1974) is an excellent survey with particular emphasis on the struggles in each province. More critical of the suffragists themselves is Carol Lee Bacchi, *Liberation Deferred? The Ideas of the English-Canadian Suffragists, 1877–1918* (T: UTP 1983). Unlike Cleverdon's book, Bacchi focuses largely on central Canada and ignores regional variations, although she does emphasize the discontent of farm and labour women with the suffrage efforts as run from Toronto. An excellent critique of Bacchi's book, and one that explores the complexities of the movement, is Ernest Forbes, 'A Review of Carol Lee Bacchi's *Liberation Deferred? The Ideas of the English-Canadian Suffragists, 1877–1918,'* *Atlantis* 1985. In keeping with the desire to study individual women, several works on the more prominent suffragists have appeared. Nellie L. McClung has had several of her books reprinted, including *In Times Like These* (1915, T: UTP 1972), a series of essays which reveal the wit of McClung and her ideas on women and men in society. Particularly compelling is the second volume of her autobiography *Clearing in the West: My Own Story* (1935, T: Thomas Allen 1976), which describes her writing career and her reform activities. Another reprint of note is Elsie MacGill's biography of her mother, activist and suffragist Helen MacGill: *My Mother the Judge: A Biography of Judge Helen Gregory MacGill* (T: Peter Martin Associates 1981). Both this book and *In Times Like These* have excellent introductory essays written by Naomi Black and Veronica Strong-Boag respectively.

In examining the suffrage movement, it became evident to scholars that many women's involvement in it originally stemmed not from any desire to have the vote but rather from what they thought they could achieve with the vote. Women at the turn of the century were engaged in all sorts of charitable, philanthropic, and reform activities which they had determined would better society and the vote became a means to an end. This can be seen in Veronica Strong-Boag's pioneering study *The Parliament of Women: The National Council of Women of Canada, 1893–1929* (O: National Museum of Man 1976), in which she explores the many activities of this major women's organization. This was echoed in the various articles appearing in Linda Kealey, ed., *A Not Unreasonable Claim: Women and Reform in Canada, 1880s–1920s* (T: Women's Press 1979), many of which probe what some historians refer to as the 'maternal feminist' approach of the women reformers. The involvement of women in organizations which they created and ran has been the focus of numerous studies. For example, the YWCA has received attention as an organization which was one of the first to recognize women's experience in the work force and the new demands this placed on them. Its beginnings were traced by Wendy Mitchinson in 'The YWCA and Reform in the Nineteenth Century,' *HS/SH* 1979, and Diana Pedersen in '"Building Today for the Womanhood of Tomorrow": Businessmen, Boosters, and the YWCA, 1890–1930,' *UHR* 1987, continued the study of this group through the early twentieth century. A fascinating dissection of women's reform efforts can be found in Mariana Valverde, *The Age of Light, Soap, and Water: Moral Reform in English Canada, 1885–1925* (T: M&S 1991).

Not everyone who examined the woman's movement saw it the same way. Wayne Roberts was not sympathetic to the middle-class ideology of many of the women's organizations. He criticized their class bias and tried to reveal an alternative perspective in *Honest Womanhood: Feminism, Femininity, and Class Consciousness among Toronto Working Women, 1893–1914* (T: New Hogtown Press 1976). Certainly the diversity of the reformers and the inadequacy of trying to generalize about them is evident when studies of individual women are examined. Terry Crowley's article on Adelaide Hoodless, 'Madonnas before Magdalenes: Adelaide Hoodless and the Making of the Canadian Gibson Girl,' *CHR* 1986, focuses on what he sees as the conservatism of Hoodless. More sympathetic is Cheryl MacDonald's biography of Hoodless, *Adelaide Hoodless: Domestic Crusader* (T: Dundurn 1986). Ruth Brouwer has written a sensitive exploration of one woman's intellectual complexity in 'Moral Nationalism in Victorian Canada: The Case of Agnes Machar,' *JCS* 1985, and Ramsay Cook has done likewise for the pacifist Frances Marion Beynon in 'Frances Marion Beynon and the Crisis of Christian Reformism,' in Carl Berger and Ramsay Cook, eds., *The West and the Nation: Essays in Honour of W.L. Morton*

(T: M&S 1976). The difficulty of classifying feminism is probed in Ernest Forbes's excellent article 'Battles in Another War: Edith Archibald and the Halifax Feminist Movement,' in his *Challenging the Regional Stereotype: Essays on the 20th Century Maritimes* (F: AP 1989).

No historical overview of the Quebec suffrage movement exists that is as extensive as Cleverdon's study of the Canadian movement as a whole. One general account written by a political scientist is Chantal Maillet, *Les Québécoises et la conquête du pouvoir politique: Enquête sur l'émergencce d'une élite feminine au Québec* (M: Éditions Saint-Martin 1990). Because Quebec women did not receive the vote until 1940, a discussion of their efforts to gain the franchise focuses on the interwar period. Jennifer Stoddart has written a detailed analysis of the Dorion Commission in 'The Dorion Commission, 1926–1931: Quebec's Legal Elites Look at Women's Rights,' in David H. Flaherty, ed., *Essays in the History of Canadian Law*, vol. 1 (T: UTP 1981). She traces the ideology of the members of the commission and the largely unsuccessful requests by various Quebec women's groups to have women granted more autonomy. Thérèse F. Casgrain's autobiography, *A Woman in a Man's World* (T: M&S 1972), is entertaining and details the life of this major player in the efforts to achieve the vote for women in Quebec. An attempt to explain the reason Quebec women received the vote so late can be found in Sylvie d'Augerot-Arend, 'Why So Late? Cultural and Institutional Factors in the Granting of Quebec and French Women's Political Rights,' *JCS* 1991. While Augerot-Arend argues that one reason for the delay was that the church in Quebec did the work which lay women in Protestant Canada were doing, it would be untrue to suggest that women's organizations in Quebec were non-existent or even removed from the women-centred issues of English Canada. Hélène Pelletier-Baillargeon, in her fascinating study of a family of reform women, *Marie-Gérin Lajoie: De mère en fille, la cause des femmes* (M: BE 1985), reveals the deep commitment of these women to social betterment throughout the decades of the twentieth century. Additional studies also indicate the activism of Quebec women (see below for work on religious women and farm women in Quebec).

While many Quebec women were working hard in their organizations throughout the interwar period, English-Canadian women also continued their struggle, although their interests were no longer as unified as they had been. Many became involved in the peace movement, as seen in Deborah Gorham's and Veronica Strong-Boag's articles in Ruth Roach Pierson, ed., *Women and Peace: Theoretical, Historical, and Practical Perspectives* (L: Croom Helm 1987), and in articles by Thomas Socknat, Randi

Warne, and Barbara Roberts in Janice Williamson and Deborah Gorham, eds., *Up and Doing: Canadian Women and Peace* (T: Women's Press 1989). Studies of individual women whose lives were outside the normative experience of women also suggest that the interwar period was an active one. The reprint of Alice A. Chown's autobiography, *The Stairway* (1921, T: UTP 1988), with its excellent introduction by Diana Chown, reveals a woman searching for a life unrestricted by social constraints. Perhaps the most sophisticated biography of a woman during this period is that by Patricia T. Rooke and R.L. Schnell, *No Bleeding Heart: Charlotte Whitton, A Feminist on the Right* (V: UBCP 1987). It is a sensitive portrayal of the woman who dominated the development of social welfare in Canada and who went on to become the infamous mayor of Ottawa. Not always likeable but difficult to ignore, Whitton was a woman who lived in a woman's world but worked in a man's. Equally welcome are Mary Kinnear's *Margaret McWilliams: An Interwar Feminist* (M and K: MQUP 1991) and Irene Howard's *The Struggle for Social Justice in British Columbia: Helena Gutteridge, the Unknown Reformer* (V: UBCP 1992).

Even after the success of receiving the vote, women's political involvement has remained of interest. However, historians of women have redefined what is meant by political. Linda Kealey and Joan Sangster have edited a valuable collection of articles, *Beyond the Vote: Canadian Women and Politics* (T: UTP 1989), in which the various contributors examine women in mainstream parties, minority parties, lobbying groups, and community associations in order to probe the meaning of 'political.' Perhaps because the major parties were unwelcoming to women, most of the political studies to date have focused on women in minority parties. Joan Sangster has written a commanding study in *Dreams of Equality: Women on the Canadian Left, 1920–1950* (T: M&S 1989). Agnes MacPhail, the first woman to be elected a member of Parliament and a prime mover in the CCF, has been the subject of several studies, the most recent and analytical being Terry Crowley's *Agnes MacPhail and the Politics of Equality* (T: JL 1990). More mainstream in terms of party affiliation is Valerie Knowles's *First Person: A Biography of Cairine Wilson, Canada's First Woman Senator* (T: Dundurn 1988). Once past World War II, the historical material on women in politics is thin, but Judy LaMarsh's wonderful autobiography *Memoirs of a Bird in a Gilded Cage* (T: M&S 1969), which details her experience in the cabinet of Lester B. Pearson, is worth the read.

Little historical research has been done on the modern feminist movement. Cerise Morris, 'Determination and Thoroughness': The Movement for a Royal Commission on the Status of Women in Canada,' *Atlantis* 1980, traces efforts made to get the commission going. The chair of the commission, Florence Bird, has written her autobiography, which provides a certain amount of detail on the hearings in *Anne Francis: An Autobiography* (T: CI 1974). In *Feminist Organizing for Change: The Contemporary Women's Movement in Canada* (T: OUP 1988), Nancy Adamson, Linda Briskin, and Margaret McPhail have made a start at delineating the complexities of modern feminism. Two recent studies have continued the analysis of the modern period: Constance Backhouse and David H. Flaherty, eds., *Challenging Times: The Women's Movement in Canada and the United States* (M and K: MQUP 1992); and Jill Vickers, Pauline Rankin and Christine Appelle, *Politics As If Women Mattered: A Political Analysis of the National Action Committee on the Status of Women* (T: UTP 1993).

UNPAID WORK

Women and work has been a major area of research in women's history and many of its themes have been reviewed in Bettina Bradbury, 'Women's History and Working-Class History,' *Labour* 1987. In women's history, however, the definition of work has been expanded to include both wage and non-wage endeavours. The importance of the latter is seen in two bibliographies: *Farm Women on the Prairie Frontier: A Sourcebook for Canada and the United States* (Metuchen: The Scarecrow Press 1983), compiled by Carol Fairbanks and Sara Brooks; and Kathryn McPherson, *A 'Round the Clock Job': A Selected Bibliography on Women's Work at Home in Canada* (O: Canadian Research Institute for the Advancement of Women 1983). While recent research has made the value of non-wage work explicit, early historiography accepted that notion implicitly. This is particularly evident in the accounts of pioneer women which, more often than not, emphasize the tremendous physical efforts women made to build homes out of the wilderness. Such accounts abound. In *A Flannel Shirt and Liberty: British Emigrant Gentlewomen in the Canadian West, 1880–1914* (V: UBCP 1982), Susan Jackel has written a fine contextual introduction for the narratives of women who emigrated to the Canadian West. Less class-oriented is Elaine Leslau Silverman's *The Last Best West: Women on the Alberta Frontier, 1880–1930* (M: Eden Press 1984), a rich portrayal of the memories of early women settlers, which is arranged by Silverman according to life cycle. More eclectic is *A Harvest Yet to Reap: A History of Prairie Women* (T: Women's Press 1976), edited by Linda Rasmussen et al., which reprints journal extracts, newspaper articles, and photographs to provide the reader with a mélange of women's experiences in the Canadian West through the first four decades of this century. Individual accounts of pioneering vary in quality. One of the best is the reprint of Georgina Binnie-Clark's experience as a farmer in the West at the turn of the century in *Wheat and Woman* (1914, T: UTP 1979), edited by Susan Jackel. Others worth noting are W.L. Morton, ed., *'God's Galloping Girl': The Peace River Diaries of Monica Storrs, 1929–31* (V: UBCP 1979); Elizabeth B. Mitchell, *In Western Canada before the War: Impressions of Early Twentieth Century Prairie Communities* (S: WPPB 1981), edited by Susan Jackel; Monica Hopkins, *Letters from a Lady Rancher* (C: Formac 1983); and Margaret Ormsby, ed., *A Pioneer Gentlewoman in British Columbia: The Recollections of Susan Allison* (V: UBCP 1976). As is evident, most of the accounts focus on the West and on women living in rural farming and ranching areas.

Two books which explicitly emphasize the economic importance of the unpaid work women did are Sylvia Van Kirk, *'Many Tender Ties': Women in Fur-Trade Society, 1670–1870* (W: Watson & Dwyer 1980), and Marjorie Griffin Cohen, *Women's Work, Markets, and Economic Development in Nineteenth-Century Ontario* (T: UTP 1988). Both stress how you cannot fully understand the economic development of this country without comprehending the contributions that women made, in Van Kirk's case to the fur trade, and in Cohen's to agriculture. Of course by the late nineteenth century the fur trade was in decline, but the importance of farming was on the rise. For this reason, women's historians have been directing their attention to the work of farm women in a way that emphasizes the hard physical work they did and how little recognition they received for it. Mary Kinnear in '"Do you want your daughter to marry a farmer?": Women's Work on the Farm, 1922,' in Donald Akenson, ed., *Canadian Papers in Rural History*, vol. 4 (Gananoque: Langdale Press 1988), raises the issue facing so many farm women. What appeared to many to be monotonous lives is analysed in Marilyn Barber, 'Help for Farm Homes: The Campaign to End Housework Drudgery in Rural Saskatchewan in the 1920s,' *Scientia Canadensis* 1985, as well as in Georgina Taylor, '"Should I Drown Myself Now or Later?": The Isolation of Rural Women in Saskatchewan and Their Participation in the Homemakers' Clubs, the Farm Movement, and the Co-operative Commonwealth Federation, 1910–1967,' in K. Storrie, ed., *Women: Isolation and Bonding, the Ecology of Gender* (T: Methuen 1987). As in other parts of the country, Quebec women joined organizations to counter their isolation. Yolande Cohen's study *Femmes de parole: L'histoire des cercles de fermières du Québec, 1915–1990*

(M: Editions Le Jour 1990) reveals the activism of farm organizations. Naomi Black and Gail Cuthbert Brandt in '"Il en faut un peu": Farm Women and Feminism in Quebec and France since 1945,' *JCHA* 1990, explore the subtleties of farm women's identification with what has been essentially an urban women's movement.

What all this literature on farming reveals is the interconnectedness between the work that women did and their personal lives. This was true for non-farm women as well, whether they were paid or not. Elizabeth Goudie's autobiography, *Woman of Labrador* (T: Peter Martin Associates 1973), edited by David Zimmerly, depicts the experiences of a woman living a self-sufficient trapping life with her family. Studies of East Coast fishing communities reveal that women's work was integral to that economy. Hilda Chaulk Murray in *More Than 50%: Woman's Life in a Newfoundland Outport, 1900–1950* (St John's: Breakwater Books 1979) has, through oral history, followed the lives of women Canadians know little about. But it is not only women who live in rural or outpost areas whose lives weave public and private together. In *Working Families: Age, Gender, and Daily Survival in Industrializing Montreal* (T: M&S 1993), Bettina Bradbury has sensitively explored the work which working-class women in Montreal did within the home. Whether paid or unpaid it helped keep their families together. Especially relevant are 'The Family Economy and Work in an Industrializing City: Montreal in the 1870s,' *CHA* 1979; 'Pigs, Cows, and Boarders: Non-Wage Forms of Survival among Montreal Families, 1861–1891,' *Labour* 1984; and 'Surviving as a Widow in Nineteenth-Century Montreal,' *UHR* 1989. More contemporary studies by non-historians are quite useful, such as Meg Luxton, *More Than a Labour of Love: Three Generations of Women's Work in the Home* (T: Women's Educational Press 1980).

While the focus of attention has been on the work of adult women, we should not forget that girls contributed to the family economy as well. Joy Parr's landmark study, *Labouring Children: British Immigrant Apprentices to Canada, 1869–1923* (2nd ed., T: UTP 1994), explored the experiences of children sent to Canada. Many of the girls were put to work as domestics either on farms or in the city. John Bullen examines non-immigrant children in his fine study 'Hidden Workers: Child Labour and the Household Economy in Early Industrial Ontario,' *Labour* 1986. Neil Sutherland continues the exploration of children as part of the labour force in '"We always had things to do". The Paid and Unpaid Work of Anglophone Children between the 1920s and the 1960s,' *Labour* 1990 and '"I can't recall when I didn't help": The Working Lives of Pioneering Children in Twentieth-Century British Columbia,' *HS/SH* 1991, as does

Rebecca Coulter in 'Youth Unemployment in Canada, 1920–1950,' *Canadian History of Education Association Bulletin* 1988. Twentieth-century Quebec is the interest of Therese Hamel, 'Obligation scolaire et travail des enfants au Québec, 1900–1950,' *RHAF* 1984, and Dominique Jean in 'Le recul du travail des enfants au Quebec entre 1940 et 1960: une explication des conflits entre les familles pauvres et l'Etat providence,' *Labour* 1989. In the latter, Jean makes it evident that the needs of working-class families have not changed very much over time.

WAGE LABOUR

Despite the recognition of non-paid labour's importance, most of the literature on women and work has been on women's involvement in the paid labour force. The primary focus of this research is on the late nineteenth and early twentieth centuries because of the interest in how industrialization affected women – the general conclusion being that it segregated them. There is no specific monograph that summarizes women's paid work experience but there are several collections of essays that provide insight into the breadth of women's endeavours. A general one is Paula Bourne, ed., *Women's Paid and Unpaid Work: Historical and Contemporary Perspectives* (T: New Hogtown Press 1985), which contains essays on both types of work and their interconnection. Most collections, however, have a regional focus. One of the first to be published was Janice Acton et al., eds., *Women at Work: Ontario, 1850–1930* (T: Canadian Women's Educational Press 1974), which surveys women in specific occupations, including domestic service, nursing, education, and prostitution. One of the strengths of such collections is the breadth of the articles, which makes up for the lack of synthesis. Other works on specific provinces are Marie Lavigne and Yolande Pinard, eds., *Travailleuses et féministes: les femmes dans la société québécoise* (M: BE 1983); Francine Barry, *Le travail de la femme au Québec: l'evolution de 1940 à 1970* (Q: PUQ 1977); and Barbara Latham and Roberta Pazdro, eds., *Not Just Pin Money*. What many of the individual studies included in the above emphasize is that women workers did not all conform to the stereotype of being young and single. Many older women had to work to support themselves and their dependants and many married women entered the work force as an additional, but necessary, family wage earner.

Specific areas of employment have attracted attention. The obvious one is domestic service because it was the largest employer of women in the country until 1921. Claudette Lacelle in *Urban Domestic Servants in*

Nineteenth Century Canada (O: National Historic Parks and Sites 1987) studies the work of domestics in Quebec City, Montreal, Halifax, and Toronto, using census material to trace the changing nature of the work and those who engaged in it. Prostitution was often the only alternative if a domestic servant lost her job. Two excellent articles describe in a sympathetic way the lives of prostitutes: Andrée Lévesque, 'Le Bordel: Milieu de travail controlé,' *Labour* 1987, and Judy Bedford 'Prostitution in Calgary, 1905–1914,' *Alberta History* 1981. Unfortunately James H. Gray's *Red Lights on the Prairies* (T: MAC 1971) is rather anecdotal and lacking in serious analysis but as a source it is valuable. Industrial work for women also has received its share of attention. Questions raised by historians usually concern how industrialization affected women and their work. Bettina Bradbury looks at this for the early years in 'Women and Wage Labour in a Period of Transition: Montreal, 1861–1881,' *HS/SH* 1983, as do Elizabeth Bloomfield and G.T. Bloomfield in *Canadian Women in Workshops, Mills, and Factories: The Evidence of the 1871 Census Manuscripts* (Guelph: University of Guelph 1991). The textile industry in its various guises has been central to industrial work. In a series of articles Gail Cuthbert Brandt has revealingly explored women in the Quebec cotton industry, looking at the transformation of women's work in the industry in terms of the power they held. See particularly her article in Bryan D. Palmer, ed., *The Character of Class Struggle: Essays in Canadian Working-Class History, 1850–1985* (T: M&S 1986). Joy Parr's *The Gender of Bread-winners: Women, Men, and Change in Two Industrial Towns, 1880–1950* (T: UTP 1990) is a beautifully written and sophisticated analysis of women's work in the knitting industry in small-town Ontario. What distinguishes Parr's work is her examination of gender and the interplay between the world of work and home for men as well as for women.

WHITE-COLLAR WORK

Not all women who were in paid employment worked in domestic service or in factories. Particularly in the late nineteenth century opportunities in 'white-collar' work emerged. In an in-depth examination of a technology closely aligned with women, Michèle Martin, *'Hello Central?': Gender, Technology, and Culture in the Formation of Telephone Systems* (M and K: MQUP 1991) delineates the changing nature of this type of work for much of the twentieth century. Most white-collar work is associated with women in clerical jobs, and Graham S. Lowe in *Women in the Administrative Revolution: The Feminization of Clerical Work* (T: UTP 1987) has

written a perceptive account of this type of work. The struggle of women
to be recognized as professionals makes up another area of research in
women's history. Because there were no standardized formal require-
ments, writing was a field open to women. A critical study of one journalist is *Kit's Kingdom: The Journalism of Kathleen Blake Coleman* (O: Carleton
UP 1989), by Barbara M. Freeman. A good biography of E. Cora Hind,
who made her journalistic career in the Canadian West and in the uncommon field of reporting on the farm economy, is Carlotta Hacker's
E. Cora Hind (T: Fitzhenry & Whiteside 1979). Maria Tippett, *By a Lady:
Celebrating Three Centuries of Art by Canadian Women* (T: Viking 1992) is
the starting point for anyone interested in researching women artists.
Emily Carr in particular has been well served by several biographers:
Maria Tippett, *Emily Carr: A Biography* (T: OUP 1979); Paula Blanchard,
The Life of Emily Carr (V: Douglas & McIntyre 1987); and Doris Shadbolt's
excellent view of the woman and especially her art in *Emily Carr* (V:
Douglas & McIntyre 1990). Contralto Maureen Forrester has written a
heartwarming and personally revealing portrait of herself both as a woman
and as a performer in *Out of Character: A Memoir* (T: M&S 1986). In
addition to the arts, women were also entering the field of photography,
advertising, and the sciences. An excellent collection of essays on these
occupations including medicine is *Despite the Odds: Essays on Canadian
Women and Science* (M: Véhicule Press 1990), edited by Marianne Gosztonyi
Ainley. A recent biography, *Harriet Brooks: Pioneer Nuclear Scientist* (M and
K: MQUP 1992), by Marelene F. Rayner-Canham and Geoffrey W.
Rayner-Canham, details the significance of Brooks's life and also the
obstacles she had to overcome. The recent *No Place for a Lady: The Story
of Canadian Women Pilots, 1928–1992* (W: Portage & Main Press 1992),
by Shirley Render, is a delightful exploration of women engaged in a
non-traditional occupation.

Two women's professions dominate the literature. The first is teaching.
So extensive is the research in this field that readers are referred to Susan
Gelman and Alison Prentice, *The History of Gender and Teaching: A Selected
Bibliography of English-Language Published Sources* (T: Centre for Women's
Studies in Education 1990), which contains an excellent listing of Canadian
and non-Canadian material, and to *Historical Studies in Education*, which has
published many articles on women. A good place to begin the study of
women teachers is *Gender and Education in Ontario: An Historical Reader*
(T: Canadian Scholars Press 1991), edited by Ruby Heap and Alison
Prentice. It is a fine collection of articles, some of which have been
previously published, which examine women both as teachers and stu-

dents at the various levels of the Ontario school system from the 1870s to the mid-twentieth century. Susan E. Houston and Alison Prentice have written a commanding history of education in Ontario in *Schooling and Scholars in Nineteenth-Century Ontario* (T: UTP 1988), in which women as both teachers and students play a significant role. For Quebec, Nadia Fahmy-Eid and Micheline Dumont have edited an invaluable collection of essays, *Maîtresses de maison, maîtresses d'école: Femmes, famille et éducation dans l'histoire du Québec* (M: BE 1983), which examine the life of the school and the home, both centres of socialization and education over the last two centuries. Irene Poelzer's *Saskatchewan Women Teachers, 1905–1920: Their Contributions* (S: Lindenblatt and Hamonic 1990) is a small but helpful book on women in the schools of that province.

The second professional field that has been a focus is medicine. A good general place to begin the study of women doctors is Carlotta Hacker's *The Indomitable Lady Doctors* (T: CI 1974), which consists of biographical chapters on some of Canada's early women physicians. Veronica Strong-Boag in *A Women with a Purpose: The Diaries of Elizabeth Smith, 1872–1884* (T: UTP 1980) has edited the diaries of Smith written while she was a student at the medical school in Kingston. In them, Smith describes her own turmoil and that of others about her decision to study medicine. For more information on women doctors, readers should check various histories of medical faculties and histories of medicine in Canada. But being a physician was not the only way that women could participate in health care. Even before they became doctors they were midwives and nurses. Historians have been intrigued by the decline of midwifery in Canada and several studies probe the reasons for this. The most extensive is Hélène Laforce's *Histoire de la sage-femme dans la région de Québec* (Q: IQRC 1985). Midwifery, however, did not decline everywhere in Canada. The vitality of it in Newfoundland for the first half of the twentieth century is revealed in Cecilia Benoit's *Midwives in Passage: The Modernization of Maternity Care* (St John's: ISER 1991). Nursing was also an important area of medicine in which women dominated. No general history of nursing in Canada exists, but G.W.L. Nicholson's *Canada's Nursing Sisters* (T: Hakkert 1975) is a good study of nursing in the armed forces. Joyce Nesbitt has written a valuable provincial survey in *White Caps and Black Bands: Nursing in Newfoundland to 1934* (St John's: Jesperson Press 1978). Margaret M. Street's biography of Ethel Johns, *Watch-fires on the Mountains: The Life and Writings of Ethel Johns* (T: UTP 1973), gives Johns an opportunity to speak and at the same time allows Street to analyse this nurse who was so central to the professionalization of nursing in the early decades of the twentieth century. Public health nurses have received special attention, perhaps because they more than other nurses enjoyed a measure of autonomy in their work. Marion Royce has written a well-researched biography of Eunice Dyke in *Eunice Dyke, Health Care Pioneer: From Pioneer Public Health Care Nurse to Advocate for the Aged* (T: Dundurn 1983), which explores the relationship between Dyke and the public health officers she worked under, some of whom were supportive and others who tried to curb the independence of the nurses. Meryn Stuart in 'Ideology and Experience: Public Health Nursing and the Ontario Rural Child Welfare Project, 1920–25,' *Canadian Bulletin of Medical History* 1989, also explored the antagonism of physicians to nurses encroaching on what doctors saw as their territory. The many-faceted nature of women's involvement in health care is seen in Nadia Fahmy-Eid and Lucie Piché, 'Le savoir négocie: les stratégies des associations de technologie médicale, de physiothérapie et de diététique pour l'access à une meilleure formation professionnelle (1930–1970),' *RHAF* 1990.

UNIONS AND THE STATE

Before women's history came to the fore, it had been assumed by many that women had not participated in the union movement to any great extent, indeed that they were difficult to organize. As with many preconceived ideas, when examined, this proved to be incorrect, as illustrated in Jacques Ferland, '"In Search of Unbound Prometheia": A Comparative View of Women's Activism in Two Quebec Industries, 1869–1908,' *Labour* 1989, a study of the cotton and boot and shoe industries. Joan Sangster's incisive study, 'The 1907 Bell Telephone Strike: Organizing Women Workers,' in *Rethinking Canada*, revealed the independence of these women workers and their solidarity with one another. Nadia Fahmy-Eid and Lucie Piche have written a more general study of Quebec women who organized and their treatment by their male colleagues in *Si le travail m'était conté autrement: les Femmes dans la Confédération des syndicats nationaux depuis 1920* (M: CSN 1987). Even broader is Ruth A. Frager's 'No Proper Deal: Women Workers and the Canadian Labour Movement, 1870–1940,' in *Union Sisters* (see below), in which the ambivalence of male unionists to women who worked was made evident.

Unions were one way that working women protected themselves; looking to the state was another. However working women soon discovered that the state had its own concepts of the proper place for women and its own priorities. This is traced in Veronica Strong-Boag's significant study

'Working Women and the State: The Case of Canada, 1889–1945,' *Atlantis* 1981. How minimum wage legislation was a mixed blessing has been explored by Margaret MacCallum in 'Keeping Women in Their Place: The Minimum Wage in Canada, 1910–25,' *Labour* 1986, and Bob Russell, 'A Fair or a Minimum Wage? Women Workers, the State, and the Origins of Wage Regulation in Western Canada,' *Labour* 1991. More often than not when the state determined to assist workers, it thought in terms of male workers, as made evident in Diane Matters's 'Public Welfare, Vancouver Style, 1910–1920,' *JCS* 1979, in which it was clear that the state believed that unemployed men should be helped because they posed a threat to society, but that unemployed women did not and so could be ignored. When attempts were made to help women workers they were usually directed towards a traditional role, as described by Ruth Pierson in 'Home Aide: A Solution to Women's Unemployment after the Second World War,' *Atlantis* 1977. In '"Pigeon-Holed and Forgotten": The Work of the Subcommittee on the Post-War Problems of Women, 1943,' *HS/SH* 1982, Gail Cuthbert Brandt examines the government's efforts to plan for a better future and to have a policy for working women included in that plan. Yet women were not a priority and the recommendations of its own agency were never considered by the government. Another postwar study is Shirley Tillotson's 'Human Rights Law as Prism: Women's Organizations, Unions, and Ontario's Female Employees Fair Remuneration Act, 1951,' *CHR* 1991. If, as these articles reveal, the state was not particularly supportive of working women, it did not seem to treat women who remained or who wanted to remain in the home any better. Veronica Strong-Boag elaborates on this with respect to mothers' allowances in *The New Day Recalled*. At least with mothers' allowances the government had to devise a program that took into account the existence of women. According to Margaret Hobbs and Ruth Roach Pierson in their exhaustive study '"A Kitchen That Wastes No Steps ...": Gender, Class, and the Home Improvement Plan, 1936–40,' *HS/SH* 1988, this was not always the case. The state's intervention in the family, whose care has traditionally been the work and responsibility of women, was considerable.

EDUCATION AND LAW

In both these fields the emphasis has been on the struggles of women to enter the educational system and to be treated equally under the law. For the education of young women, as with the field of women as teachers, readers should look to the myriad of articles in *Historical Studies in Educa-*

tion, as well as Susan Houston and Alison Prentice, *Schooling and Scholars in Nineteenth-Century Ontario*, and Ruby Heap and Alison Prentice, eds., *Gender and Education* (cited above). General histories of education usually include some examination of female students at various educational levels. Because education is a provincial responsibility, most of the literature is on individual provinces; the study of girls' education in Quebec is particularly well developed. An excellent survey is Micheline Dumont's *Girls' Schooling in Quebec, 1639–1960* (O: CHA 1990). Her edited book of essays with Nadia Fahmy-Eid, *Les couventines: l'éducation des filles au Québec dans les congrégations religieuses enseignantes, 1840–1960* (M: BE 1986), reveals the variety of educational possibilities and approaches within the church structure. The introduction of domestic science into the various school systems has intrigued historians, perhaps because it was so linked to the ideology of woman's place being the home. Any study of Adelaide Hoodless would have to address this issue (see under Reform).

The field of university education for women has a significant place in the literature. Since each institution is relatively autonomous, most research has focused on specific universities. Among individual studies, one of the best is *We Walked Very Warily: A History of Women at McGill* (M: Eden Press 1981), by Margaret Gillett. Lee Stewart, *'It's Up to You': Women at UBC in the Early Years* (V: UBCP 1990) does the same for UBC with special attention given to the development of domestic science and nursing, two fields in which UBC was at the forefront. University of Toronto has had its foibles about women exposed in Anne Rochon Ford's pithy *A Path Not Strewn with Roses: One Hundred Years of Women at the University of Toronto, 1884–1984* (T: University of Toronto 1985). Three excellent articles appear in Paul Axelrod and John G. Reid, eds., *Youth, University, and Canadian Society: Essays in the Social History of Higher Education* (M and K: MQUP 1989). In one, Diana Pedersen examines the interrelationship between the YWCA and college women; Nancy Kiefer and Ruth Roach Pierson provide a detailed analysis of women students at the University of Toronto during World War II; and Judith Fingard gives a description of Dalhousie co-eds between 1881 and 1927.

Our knowledge of the experience of women with the legal system is more limited than with education. The pioneering work of Constance Backhouse and her many articles on various aspects of nineteenth-century law and women have been brought together in *Petticoats and Prejudice: Women and Law in Nineteenth-Century Canada* (T: Women's Press 1991), in which she examines issues such as infanticide, birth control, prostitution, rape, divorce, and women's entry into the legal profession. *In the Shadow of the Law: Divorce in Canada, 1900–1939* (T: UTP 1991), by James G. Snell, is a wonderful study in which the author has been able, through the examination of divorce petitions, to delve into the marital lives of Canadians and discern not only what the law thought of marriage but also how Canadians, women and men, viewed it. Another aspect of women and the law is the study of women who legally transgress. Judith Fingard's excellent book *The Dark Side of Life in Victorian Halifax* (Porters Lake: Pottersfield Press 1989) is a study of the petty criminal class – where they lived, how they lived, and their contact with the law – through the lives of specific families and their members, including the women. More traditional in approach are Jane B. Price, '"Raised in Rockhead – Died in the Poor-house": Female Petty Crime in Halifax, 1864–1890,' in Philip Girard and Jim Phillips, eds., *Essays in the History of Canada Law*, vol. 3, Nova Scotia (T: UTP 1990), and Elizabeth Langdon's 'Female Crime in Calgary, 1914–1941,' in Louis A. Knafla, ed., *Law and Justice in a New Land: Essays in Western Canadian Legal History* (T: Carswell 1986). A detailed institutional study is 'The Criminal and Fallen of Their Sex: The Establishment of Canada's First Women's Prison, 1874–1901,' *Canadian Journal of Women and the Law* 1985, by Carolyn Strange.

THE PRIVATE LIVES OF WOMEN

Demography and family history have made significant contributions to women's history and, although the literature in these fields is vast, it is important to mention a few sources. The real value of family history has been to reveal the interplay between the private and public spheres, how class enters into family formation, and how gender, class, ethnicity, and so on determine age of marriage for both men and women, the size of the family and household, and the composition of the household. Michael B. Katz's *The People of Hamilton, Canada West: Family and Class in a Mid-Nineteenth-Century City* (Cambridge: HUP 1975) is a unique urban study of the lives of ordinary Canadians in the crucial period of early industrialization. David Gagan's *Hopeful Travellers: Families, Land, and Social Change in Mid-Victorian Peel County, Canada West* (T: UTP 1981) does the same for the rural countryside; Gagan examines the problems of family size in a period of declining economic prospects and the difficulties of inheritance for farm families and the repercussions of their solutions on daughters and wives. Douglas Campbell and David Neice in *Ties That Bind – Structure and Marriage in Nova Scotia* (Port Credit: Scribblers' Press 1979) have focused on the East Coast, but to date there is no study of the Canadian

West. More general in nature but valuable nonetheless are two collections of essays: Joy Parr, ed., *Childhood and Family in Canadian History* (T: M&S 1982), and Bettina Bradbury, ed., *Canadian Family History: Selected Readings* (T: CCP 1992). Demographic studies are significant for the actual data they provide on the patterns of lives. Ellen Gee, in a series of articles, has followed the marriage and fertility patterns of Canadians. Especially good are her 'Marriage in Nineteenth-Century Canada,' *Canadian Review of Sociology and Anthropology* 1982, and 'Female Marriage Patterns in Canada: Changes and Differentials,' *Journal of Comparative Family Studies* 1980. More encompassing are Jacques Henripin's ever useful *Trends and Factors of Fertility in Canada* (O: Statistics Canada 1972) and Hubert Charbonneau's *Vie et mort de nos ancetres: étude demographique* (M: PUM 1975).

Beneath the demographics, what was the relationship between the sexes? Peter Ward's *Courtship, Love, and Marriage in Nineteenth-Century English Canada* (M and K: MQUP 1990), while limited in focus, traces the changing nature of courtship, looking at where it takes place and who controls it. A delightful and personal insight into courtship practices in nineteenth-century Quebec comes from the diary of Henriette Dessaulles, *Hopes and Dreams: The Diary of Henriette Dessaulles, 1874–1881* (Willowdale: Hounslow Press 1986), translated by L. Hawke, which reveals Henriette's love for the boy next door and how she has to overcome the opposition of her stepmother before her path to marriage is clear. Marriage, however, could have its dark side. Wife abuse is not a new phenomenon, as is revealed in Terry Chapman's '"Til Death do us Part": Wife Beating in Alberta, 1905–1920,' *Alberta History* 1988, and Kathryn Harvey's 'To Love, Honour, and Obey: Wife-battering in Working-Class Montreal, 1869–79,' *UHR* 1990. A specific case where the wife fought back is described in Karen Dubinsky and Franca Iacovetta, 'Murder, Womanly Virtue, and Motherhood: The Case of Angelina Napolitano, 1911–1922,' *CHR* 1991. Karen Dubinsky has explored sexual violence against women in her groundbreaking work *Improper Advances: Rape and Heterosexual Conflict in Ontario 1880–1929* (Chicago: University of Chicago Press).

As historians delve further into the personal realm, they have had to come to terms with the issue of the body. Canadians in the past viewed women and men as belonging to separate spheres because of physical differences between them. Such perceptions led to different treatment. This was especially true in the history of women's sport, where, as Helen Lenskyj points out in *Out of Bounds: Women, Sport, and Sexuality* (T: Women's Press 1986), the kind of activities women engaged in reflected society's perception of what was proper for them more than it did their abilities. For further literature on sport, readers should consult the

Canadian Journal of the History of Sport. Within the last century and a half, doctors have increasingly had opinions on women's bodies. In *The Nature of Their Bodies: Women and Their Doctors in Victorian Canada* (T: UTP 1991) Wendy Mitchinson has brought together, in a new synthesis, her many articles on women and their treatment as patients. In this monograph she examines the physicality of women through a study of menstruation, menopause, sexuality, birth control, obstetrics, gynaecology, and nervous disorders. Andrée Lévesque, too, has addressed the interrelationship between doctors and women in 'Mères ou malades, les Québécoises de l'entre-deux-guerres vues par les médecins,' *RHAF* 1984, in which she illustrates the preconceived notions that physicians had of female frailty. Interest in the body has led to interest in sexuality. Michael Bliss's pioneering article '"Pure Books on Avoided Subjects": Pre-Freudian Sexual Ideas in Canada,' *CHA* 1970, introduced Canadians to the fact that our ancestors were perhaps not as repressive as we had thought. Since then there have been numerous studies focusing on female sexuality in particular. One of the best is Andrée Lévesque's detailed work on unwed mothers and prostitutes in *La Norme et les déviantes: des femmes au Québec pendant l'entre-deux-guerres* (M: Les Editions du remue-ménage 1989).

Childbearing is central to most women's lives, and birthing and its control by physicians is the partial focus of many of the articles in *Delivering Motherhood: Maternal Ideologies and Practices in the 19th and 20th Centuries* (L: Routledge 1990), edited by Katherine Arnup et al. Within several of the works, an underlying tone of criticism of the medical profession and its increasing control over childbirth is evident. Focusing not on the medical profession but on the health of mothers is W. Peter Ward and Patricia Ward, 'Infant Birth Weight and Nutrition in Industrializing Montreal,' *American Historical Review* 1984, which suggests that industrialization weakened the health of women so that their children's birth weight declined from what it had been. Suzanne Buckley, in a fine study of the Ottawa Civic Hospital, examines the issue of maternal mortality and how its causes were viewed by physicians in 'The Search for the Decline of Maternal Mortality: The Place of Hospital Records,' in Wendy Mitchinson and Janice Dickin McGinnis, eds., *Essays in the History of Canadian Medicine* (T: M&S 1988). The particular problems of rural and outpost mothers are explored in Cynthia Abeele, '"The Mother of the Land Must Suffer": Child and Maternal Welfare in Rural and Outpost Ontario, 1918–1940,' *OH* 1988.

The major source on birth control is Angus McLaren and Arlene Tigar McLaren, *The Bedroom and the State: The Changing Practices and Politics of Contraception and Abortion in Canada, 1880–1980* (T: M&S 1986), which traces the movement for the acceptance of birth control from the late nineteenth century to when it became legal in 1969. Other studies on this subject focus on local aspects, many of which the McLarens cover in their book. Of these studies notable is Dianne Dodd's 'The Canadian Birth Control Movement: Two Approaches to the Dissemination of Contraceptive Technology,' *Scientia Canadensis* 1985, in which it is clear that she and the McLarens differ on their assessment of the work of A.R. Kaufmann and the Parents Information Bureau. For many women, birth control was not effective and some resorted to infanticide. Such a choice was not easy to make and is difficult for historians to trace, but Mary Ellen Wright in 'Unnatural Mothers: Infanticide in Halifax, 1850–1875,' *Nova Scotia Historical Review* 1987, and Marie-Aimée Cliche 'L'infanticide dans la région de Québec (1660–1969),' *RHAF* 1990, have used sources in creative ways to delve into this subject.

RELIGION

Another aspect of the personal lives of women which straddles the boundaries between private and public is religion. The involvement of women within the church has been a function of their own beliefs and their desire to engage in activity which had some meaning for them and their society. Ruth Compton Brouwer, in a beautifully written study of Presbyterian missionaries, *New Women for God: Canadian Presbyterian Women and India Missions, 1876–1914* (T: UTP 1990), examines one group of these women and their lives in Canada as well as their work in the India missions. *A Sensitive Independence: Canadian Methodist Women Missionaries in Canada and the Orient, 1881–1925* (M and K: MQUP 1992), by Rosemary R. Gagan, equally appreciates the multidimensional aspect of such women. The organizations that supported most of these women have also been the subject of study. Wendy Mitchinson in 'Canadian Women and Church Missionary Societies in the Nineteenth Century: A Step towards Independence,' *Atlantis* 1977, argues that the work women did in these societies gave them the self-confidence to assert their power within the church. Several articles on missionary work can also be found in John S. Moir and C.T. McIntire, eds., *Canadian Protestant and Catholic Missions, 1820s–1960s: Historical Essays in Honour of John Webster Grant* (NY: Peter Lang 1988). As paid workers, women other than missionaries devoted themselves to the church. John Thomas, 'Servants of the Church: Canadian Methodist Deaconess Work, 1890–1926,' *CHR* 1984, examines what the twentieth century would see as religious social workers. The ordination of women has been a long struggle, and Mary Hallett in 'Nellie McClung and the Fight for the Ordination of Women in the United Church of Canada,' *Atlantis* 1979, has analysed this as an extension of McClung's other reform activities. Literature on women in the Catholic tradition also abounds. Readers are reminded to examine the literature on women and education and on women as teachers for references to teaching by nuns. One of the best accounts of the sisterhoods is Marta Danylewycz's study *Taking the Veil: An Alternative to Marriage, Motherhood, and Spinsterhood in Quebec, 1840–1920* (T: M&S 1987). In it she reveals the complexity of the orders and how they offered women both shelter and opportunity.

RACE AND ETHNICITY

Its seems appropriate to have a separate section on minority women because of the present-day interest in their experiences. While much of the early literature in women's history ignored such women, not all of it did and certainly recent studies have devoted more attention to them. This means that readers should consult the general studies and collections listed above. More work needs to be done on Native women and for those interested, Sylvia Van Kirk's *Toward a Feminist Perspective in Native History* (T: Centre for Women's Studies in Education 1987) is an excellent place to start as she builds on her work begun in *'Many Tender Ties.'* For Native women and education a good article in a valuable collection is Jean Barman's 'Separate and Unequal: Indian and White Girls at All Hallows School, 1884–1920; in Jean Barman et al., eds., *Indian Education in Canada* vol. 1, *The Legacy* (V: UBCP 1986). Contemporary but useful and powerful reading is Janet Silman's *Enough is Enough: Aboriginal Women Speak Out* (T: Women's Press 1987), a description of Native women's efforts to maintain their Indian status on the same grounds as men. A moving account is *Kohkominawak Otacimowiniwawa: Our Grandmothers' Lives, as Told in Their Own Words* (S: Fifth House 1992), edited by Freda Ahenakew and H.C. Wolpart.

The best place to begin a study of other minority women is *Looking into My Sister's Eyes* (cited above under General) and 'Women and Ethnicity,' a special issue of *Polyphony: The Bulletin of the Multicultural History Society of Ontario* 1986. Readers should also check *Canadian Ethnic Studies*. One woman's experience is given in *Confessions of an Immigrant's Daughter* (1939, T: UTP 1981), by Laura Goodman Salverson, introduced by K.P. Stich. In her account, Salverson recounts the pressures on her and her parents because of their Icelandic heritage while she was growing up on the Canadian Prairies in the early twentieth century. Another woman's experience is Rolf Knight's sensitive portrayal of his immigrant mother and her working life both inside and outside the home in Canada from 1928 until 1973 in *A Very Ordinary Life* (V: New Star 1974). Varpu Lindström-Best's study *Defiant Sisters: A Social History of Finnish Immigrant Women in Canada* (T: MHSO 1988) is a fine investigation of one group of immigrant women and how they adapted to their new country. *Feminists Despite Themselves: Women in Ukrainian Community Life, 1884–1939* (E: CIUS 1988), by Martha Bochachevsky-Choniak, chronicles the same for another group. Much broader in scope is Frances Swyripa, *Wedded to the Cause: Ukrainian-Canadian Women and Ethnic Identity, 1891–1991* (T: UTP 1993). The recent *Such Hardworking People: Italian Immigrants in Postwar Toronto* (M and K: MQUP 1992), by Franca Iacovetta, is a perceptive study which examines women and men in their separate experiences and also in those they shared. Subtly nuanced is Ruth A. Frager, *Sweatshop Strife: Class, Ethnicity, and Gender in the Jewish Labour Movement of Toronto, 1900–1939* (T: UTP 1992). A moving original document is Muriel Kitagawa's *This Is My Own: Letters to Wes and Other Writings on Japanese Canadians, 1941–1948* (V: Talon Books 1985), which reveals the anguish of one family's experience with the forced removal of Japanese-Canadians in BC during World War II.

Black women have a long history in Canada. Jim Bearden and Linda Butler have examined the career of one black woman in *Shadd: The Life and Times of Mary Shadd Cary* (T: NC Press 1977). Cary, a schoolteacher and publisher of *The Provincial Freeman* in Canada West, was involved with the fight for emancipation of blacks in the United States and the adjustment to freedom of those who escaped to Canada. Sylvia Hamilton's 'Our Mothers Grand and Great: Black Women in Nova Scotia,' *Canadian Woman Studies* 1982, is a celebratory article. One girl's experience of growing up black in Ontario is documented in Cheryl Foggo, *Pourin' Down Rain* (C: Detselig 1990). Another excellent source is the recent *No Burden to Carry: Narratives of Black Working Women in Ontario, 1920s–1950s* (T: Women's Press 1991), by Dionne Brand.

Despite the wealth of material that exists in women's history, it still has not been integrated with, for lack of a better term, traditional history. Any examination of survey texts in Canadian history will show a paucity of information on women. Two notable exceptions both focused on Quebec are Susan Mann Trofimenkoff's beautifully written *The Dream of*

Nation: A Social and Intellectual History of Quebec (T: MAC 1982), and Paul-André Linteau, Réne Durocher, and Jean-Claude Robert, *Quebec: A History, 1867–1929* (T: JL 1983). Nevertheless, advances have occurred. While women may not be fully integrated, it has become obligatory to at least acknowledge their existence. In addition, the concept of gender has begun to make an impact on the way historians approach all aspects of history.

PAUL VOISEY

Urban History

Urban history has long wrestled with the problem of how to define itself, which poses numerous problems for the compilation of a reading guide. Mounds of historical studies explore events, developments, and processes that occurred largely, or even exclusively, in cities. But although they illuminate urban history, the attention of their authors has been on some other major theme, and there has been no conscious attempt to link their topics to the specific physical and human environment that we know as urban. This tendency has increased in recent times. From its birth in the days of D.C. Masters and others who pioneered the study of urban history in Canada, the field appeared to enter a robust adolescence in the 1970s, when scholars wrote urban history with a greater sense of identity than ever before. In the 1980s, however, more of them joined the massive shift towards specialties in social history. Increasingly, gender, class, or ethnicity became the rallying cry for analysis – and place faded into the background. For the sake of brevity and to avoid needless overlap with other sections of this book, the following guide tries to stick to those studies that explicitly tie their themes to the urban scene. However, readers are well advised to consult other sections of this book for additional information.

What can be said about the current breadth and depth of urban historical knowledge in Canada? Geographically, its scope is quite unbalanced. More work, and in general better work, focuses on Montreal, Toronto, and Hamilton. Urban historians have also served the West reasonably well, but good post-Confederation studies of eastern Quebec and the Atlantic region are lacking. Chronologically, historians have studied the period from about 1880 to about 1920 far more than other periods. While it is not a concern of this volume, one of the most neglected eras has been the pre-Confederation period, in spite of some outstanding work. Serious neglect, however, also characterizes the decades after 1945. Social scientists have increasingly studied the postwar Canadian city, and while their work provides valuable snapshots at particular points in time, little of it analyses change over time. Historians have not rushed to remedy that deficiency. Only those social science works with a significant historical component have been included here, and the contributions of geography in that respect greatly outweigh those of other disciplines.

While a detailed assessment follows, a general point about the various approaches and themes that characterize the literature is in order here. Urban history is generally regarded as an interdisciplinary field, but closer inspection reveals that it is more often multidisciplinary. In other words, various disciplines have tackled urban history, but surprisingly few works actually blend different approaches into an integrated whole. One result is that while many diverse themes in urban history have been explored, there are few good studies that successfully tie them together.

As for a general comment on the quality of urban history in Canada, it would be a truism to say of it, like any field, that the quality is uneven. In the case of urban history, however, it is extremely uneven. The best work readily meets high international standards. Such an assessment, however, must include the better pre-Confederation studies, and to appreciate the potential of urban history, readers are advised to consider the superb studies by Michael B. Katz, *The People of Hamilton, Canada West: Family and Class in a Mid-Nineteenth-Century City* (Cambridge: HUP 1975); and T.W. Acheson, *Saint John: The Making of a Colonial Urban Community* (T: UTP 1985). By contrast, the broad bottom of the literary pyramid consists of pure junk, and in between almost every level of competence has been demonstrated. This range in itself poses special problems in compiling a reader's guide because, for certain topics, many good studies clamour for attention and some must be omitted. For other areas, however, it is necessary to cite a mediocre work for lack of anything better, or else to arbitrarily select a few middling examples from among a great many.

A final comment on the reading guide should be made: much urban history, and much of the best of it, has appeared in articles rather than books. Instead of piecing together important aspects of the topic by citing inordinately long lists of articles, the emphasis here is on books, although attention is given to collections of articles and special theme issues of journals.

BIBLIOGRAPHIES, GUIDES, AND JOURNALS

The field of urban history enjoys the luxury of an excellent general bibliography: Alan F.J. Artibise and Gilbert A. Stelter, *Canada's Urban Past: A*

Bibliography to 1980 and Guide to Canadian Urban Studies (V: UBCP 1981). With over seven thousand entries, it embraces many different sorts of material. They are organized chiefly by place rather than theme. Equally comprehensive annual updates are provided in the October issue of the *Urban History Review*. The field has also spawned many useful bibliographical, historiographical, and methodological essays – indeed, for many years, it looked as though Canadian urban history would be more talk than action. Such items rapidly became outdated, but start by reading Alan F.J. Artibise and Paul-André Linteau. *The Evolution of Urban Canada: An Analysis of Approaches and Interpretations* (W: Institute of Urban Studies/University of Winnipeg 1984), and Gilbert A. Stelter, 'A Sense of Time and Place: The Historians Approach to Canada's Urban Past,' in Carl Berger, ed., *Contemporary Approaches to Canadian History* (T: CCP 1987).

The field is also well served by its own specialized journal, the *Urban History Review*, which has steadily improved in quality from its inauspicious beginnings in 1972. It publishes an array of material including research articles, interpretive essays, methodological notes, illustrations, bibliographies, and archival and other primary source information, as well as news and commentary on conferences and other scholarly events. While these items focus almost wholly on Canada, the journal reviews both Canadian and non-Canadian books. Some Canadian material can also be found in the American *Journal of Urban History* (1974–) and the British *Urban History Yearbook* (1974–1991; renamed *Urban History* in 1992), which are both international in scope. *City Magazine* (1974–79, 1983–) sometimes publishes good history articles. Articles on Canadian urban history can also be found in a tremendous variety of other journals, both national and international, and in disciplines other than history. Fortunately, many of the best articles have been routinely assembled in edited collections and these are cited in the appropriate categories below.

GENERAL WORKS AND COLLECTIONS

Incredibly, there is no broad synthesis of Canadian urban history. The closest approximation of one is George A. Nader, *Cities of Canada*, vol. 1, *Theoretical, Historical, and Planning Perspectives*, and vol. 2, *Profiles of Fifteen Metropolitan Centres* (T: MAC 1975, 1976), which is intended to be an introduction to all aspects of Canadian urban studies. Unfortunately, the historical components are bland, badly organized, and deficient in important respects. Despite its title, Leroy O. Stone, *Urban Development in*

Canada: An Introduction to the Demographic Aspects (O: Dominion Bureau of Statistics 1967) is not a general text, but a statistical analysis of aspects of urbanization in the twentieth century. There are not even any comprehensive texts about the urban history of particular regions or provinces, although some regional studies noted below are available on particular themes.

By contrast, there are many good collections of readings on a broad spectrum of topics. See in particular three books edited by Gilbert A. Stelter and Alan F.J. Artibise: *The Canadian City: Essays in Urban and Social History* (2nd ed., O: Carleton UP 1984), *Power and Place: Canadian Urban Development in the North American Context* (V: UBCP 1986), and *Shaping the Urban Landscape: Aspects of the Canadian City-Building Process* (O: Carleton UP 1982). The latter book contains articles more wide-ranging than its title suggests. The most recent collection is Gilbert A. Stelter, ed., *Cities and Urbanization: Canadian Historical Perspectives* (T: CCP 1990). For the West, see A.R. McCormack and Ian Macpherson, eds., *Cities in the West: Papers of the Western Canada Urban History Conference* (O: National Museum of Man 1975), and Alan F.J. Artibise, ed., *Town and City: Aspects of Western Canadian Urban Development* (R: University of Regina 1981).

URBAN BIOGRAPHY

Comprehensive general histories of individual cities exist in abundance and there are few communities in Canada that do not boast some sort of local history. Many of these are antiquarian, consisting of little more than colourful anecdotes. For many places, however, including some sizeable cities, there is nothing better available. A common complaint about virtually all of them, however, is that they study their subjects in isolation, without sufficient comparisons or regard for broader developments. Nonetheless, good urban biographies are the only venue for studying the totality of the urban community, and they also provide much material for thematic studies. The best available histories of the most important regional centres are outlined below, moving from east to west.

Every major city east of Montreal now needs a good general history of the post-Confederation era. Exemplifying many of the problems of traditional local history is Paul O'Neill, *The Story of St John's, Newfoundland*, vol. 1, *The Oldest City*, and vol. 2, *A Seaport Legacy* (Erin: Press Porcépic 1975, 1976). Better, but still unsatisfactory, is Thomas Raddall, *Halifax, Warden of the North* (rev. ed., T: M&S 1971). The best introduction to

Charlottetown is a collection of essays: Douglas Baldwin and Thomas Spira, eds., *Gaslights, Epidemics, and Vagabond Cows: Charlottetown in the Victorian Era* (Charlottetown: Ragweed Press 1988). Saint John and Quebec desperately need good post-Confederation histories to match the outstanding volumes available for earlier periods, and nothing can be recommended. Although older histories of Montreal still offer some valuable insights, especially John I. Cooper, *Montreal: A Brief History* (M and K: MQUP 1969), they have now been surpassed by Paul-André Linteau, *Histoire de Montréal depuis la Confédération* (M: Boréal 1992).

Many cities west of Montreal have benefited from the *History of Canadian Cities* series published by James Lorimer and the National Museum of Man (now the Canadian Museum of Civilization). Although the texts are brief, each book is written by a well-known authority on his or her city, and each systematically pursues the same major themes. Each offers an abundance of statistical tables, maps, and especially photographs. For Ottawa, see John H. Taylor, *Ottawa: An Illustrated History* (T: JL 1986). Toronto gets two volumes: J.M.S. Careless, *Toronto to 1918: An Illustrated History* (T: JL 1983), and James Lemon, *Toronto since 1918: An Illustrated History* (T: JL 1985). These volumes supersede older histories of the city, but still worth noting is the brief study by Jacob Spelt and Donald P. Kerr, *Toronto* (Don Mills: Collier-Macmillan 1973). See also Victor L. Russell, ed., *Forging a Consensus: Historical Essays on Toronto* (T: UTP 1984). One of the best *History of Canadian Cities* volumes is John C. Weaver, *Hamilton: An Illustrated History* (T: JL 1982). M.J. Dear et al., eds., *Steel City: Hamilton and Region* (T: UTP 1987) is a useful supplement. Worthy books on other Ontario cities include Frederick H. Armstrong, *The Forest City: An Illustrated History of London, Canada* (T: Windsor Publications 1986), John English and Kenneth McLaughlin, *Kitchener: An Illustrated History* (Wa: WLUP 1983), and Gerald Tulchinsky, ed., *To Preserve and Defend: Essays on Kingston in the Nineteenth Century* (M and K: MQUP 1976).

Heading west, see Alan F.J. Artibise, *Winnipeg: An Illustrated History* (T: JL 1977). For a more intensive look at several major themes during Winnipeg's critical years of explosive growth, see Artibise, *Winnipeg: A Social History of Urban Growth, 1874–1914* (M and K: MQUP 1975). For Regina, see J. William Brennan, *Regina: An Illustrated History* (T: JL 1989). Moving north, see Don Kerr and Stan Hanson, *Saskatoon: The First Half-Century* (E: NeWest Press 1982). For a briefer work covering more recent developments, see William P. Delainey and William A.S. Sargeant, *Saskatoon, The Growth of a City*, part 1, *The Formative Years, 1882–1960* (S: Saskatoon Environmental Society 1974). Crossing into Alberta, see

Max Foran, *Calgary: An Illustrated History* (T: JL 1978). Also useful is Anthony W. Rasporich and Henry Klassen, eds., *Frontier Calgary: Town, City, and Region, 1875–1914* (C: M&S West 1975). Edmonton needs a better history, but see James G. MacGregor, *Edmonton: A History* (2nd ed., E: Hurtig 1975). For the Pacific Coast, see Patricia Roy, *Vancouver: An Illustrated History* (T: JL 1980). For a good comparative approach, read Norbert MacDonald, *Distant Neighbours: A Comparative History of Seattle and Vancouver* (Lincoln: University of Nebraska Press 1987). Victoria needs more help, but see Harry Gregson, *A History of Victoria, 1842–1970* (Vi: Victoria Observer Publishing 1970), or the much briefer study by Peter A. Baskerville, *Beyond the Island: An Illustrated History of Victoria* (Burlington: Windsor Publications 1986).

There are many book-length local histories of small urban centres, but no scholarly one that can be recommended as a model worthy of emulation. Many articles, however, effectively explore aspects of the history of small places. A sample is offered in L.D. McCann, ed., *People and Place: Studies of Small Town Life in the Maritimes* (F: AP 1987). Single-industry company towns have attracted much attention. For an introduction, see Gilbert A. Stelter and Alan F.J. Artibise, 'Canadian Resource Towns in Historical Perspective,' in *Shaping the Urban Landscape*, and several articles in Roy T. Bowles, ed., *Little Communities and Big Industries: Studies in the Social Impact of Canadian Resource Extraction* (T: BUT 1982). Sometimes a satisfactory quick sketch of a small centre (or even a large one) can be found in James H. Marsh, gen. ed., *The Canadian Encyclopedia*, 4 vols. (2nd ed., E: Hurtig 1988), which contains a large number of place-name entries.

APPROACHES TO INTER-URBAN AND HINTERLAND RELATIONS

In Canada, relationships between cities, towns, and countrysides have largely been studied within the context of metropolitanism. While it has a long historiographical tradition that stretches back to N.S.B. Gras and the Laurentian thesis, the seminal essay remains J.M.S. Careless, 'Frontierism, Metropolitanism, and Canadian History,' *CHR* 1954, in which Careless defines metropolitanism as a hierarchical structure whereby some cities came to dominate not only their own hinterlands, but other cities and their hinterlands. The application of Careless's approach can be seen in nearly all his writings, but his most recent views on the concept are provided in *Frontier and Metropolis: Regions, Cities, and Identities in Canada before 1914* (T: UTP 1989). L.D. McCann, 'The Myth of the Metropolis:

The Role of the City in Canadian Regionalism,' *UHR* 1981, argues that metropolitanism loses its explanatory power for the more recent past. The most vigorous assault on the approach, however, is provided by Donald F. Davis in 'The "Metropolitan Thesis" and the Writing of Canadian Urban History,' *UHR* 1985. Thus far, his criticism has had little impact. For a reply from Careless, see 'The View from Ontario: Further Thoughts on Metropolitanism in Canada,' in *Careless at Work: Selected Canadian Historical Studies* (T: Dundurn Press 1990). Meanwhile, Gilbert A. Stelter, 'A Regional Framework for Urban History,' *UHR* 1985, pleads for a metropolitan approach that considers urban relationships on various levels: international, national, regional, and local.

Canadian preoccupation with metropolitanism has led to the neglect of other approaches. Thus central-place theory, first expounded in Walter Christaller's classic *Central Places in Southern Germany* (1933, Englewood Cliffs: PH 1966) has never been prominent in Canadian urban writing, but it does share many essential features with metropolitanism. The 'systems' approach to understanding urban history has also been ignored. Pioneered most effectively by the American Allan R. Pred in, for example, *Urban Growth and the Circulation of Information: The United States System of Cities, 1790–1840* (Cambridge: HUP 1973), it eschews the notion of rivalry and hierarchy implicit in metropolitanism. By focusing on transportation and communication networks, it argues that large cities grow through integrated specialization in which change in one city necessarily sparks growth and change in others. While not particularly historical in approach, see James W. Simmons, *Canada as an Urban System: A Conceptual Framework* (T: Centre for Urban and Community Studies, University of Toronto 1974). For an example of historical writing influenced by this approach, see Peter G. Goheen, 'Communications and Urban Systems in Mid-Nineteenth Century Canada,' *UHR* 1986. A plea for integrating various approaches is found in F.A. Dahms, 'The Evolution of Settlement Systems: A Canadian Example, 1851–1970,' *Journal of Urban History* 1981, but the demonstration he offers is too brief and sweeping to be effective.

ECONOMIC DEVELOPMENT AND URBAN GROWTH

While virtually all the studies listed so far are concerned with the growth of cities, Canada has spawned a large and respectable literature that focuses specifically on this theme. Even so, there is no comprehensive national survey. For a brief, sweeping overview see J.M.S. Careless, *The Rise of Cities in Canada before 1914* (O: CHA 1978). For the period since 1914, the geography text most sensitive to the historical growth of cities in all regions is L.D. McCann, ed., *Heartland and Hinterland: A Geography of Canada* (Scarborough: PH 1982). In these and other studies, readers will detect a difference between the approach of geographers and historians. The former concentrate on various economic and locational factors to explain the rise of some cities relative to others, while the latter attach more importance to the actions of business elites to promote their cities through a variety of strategies commonly known as boosterism.

Both approaches can be found in the wealth of literature explaining the intensive urban-industrial development of southern Ontario. Among several books, the best regional study is still Jacob Spelt, *The Urban Development in South-Central Ontario* (T: M&S 1972), but see also James M. Gilmour, *Spatial Evolution of Manufacturing: Southern Ontario, 1851–1891* (T: UTP 1972), and W. Randy Smith, *Aspects of Growth in a Regional Urban System: Southern Ontario, 1851–1921* (T: Atkinson College, York University 1982). Of many pertinent articles, one of the most interesting and original is C.F.J. Whebell, 'Corridors: A Theory of Urban Systems,' *Annals, Association of American Geographers* 1969. A much greater focus on boosterism is provided in other articles, several of which appear in the journal *Ontario History*. See, for example, Elizabeth Bloomfield, 'Building the City on a Foundation of Factories: The "Industrial Policy" in Berlin, Ontario, 1870–1914,' *OH* 1983. Direct rivalries between cities to secure economic advantage is also an important theme. For a book-length case study, see David B. Knight, *A Capital for Canada: Conflict and Compromise in the Nineteenth Century* (Chicago: Department of Geography, University of Chicago 1977).

The literature on Western urban growth is rife with boosterism; see, for example, articles in the previously cited *Town and City*. Alan F.J. Artibise has written much on this theme, but see his *Prairie Urban Development, 1870–1930* (O: CHA 1981). Winnipeg's economic hegemony is discussed by almost every urban writer on the West, but the single full-length study is only moderately successful: Ruben Bellen, *Winnipeg First Century: An Economic History* (W: Queenston House 1978). A useful concept for explaining the sudden emergence of frontier metropolitan centres is provided by Andrew F. Burghardt, 'A Hypothesis about Gateway Cities,' *Annals, Association of American Geographers* 1969. One of the few studies to demonstrate how economic metropolitanism actually worked in practice is Donald Kerr, 'Wholesale Trade on the Canadian Plains in the Late Nineteenth Century: Winnipeg and Its Competition,' in Howard Palmer, ed., *The Settlement of the West* (C: Comprint Publishing 1977).

While students of Ontario and the West seek explanations for urban growth, those of the Atlantic region are more concerned with the lack of it. Many of their explanations are bound up in studies that examine economic problems in the region generally. The critical starting point for the urban historian is T.W. Acheson, 'The National Policy and the Industrialization of the Maritimes, 1880–1910,' *Acadiensis* 1972. Other articles with an urban focus can be found in Lewis R. Fischer and Eric W. Sager, eds., *The Enterprising Canadians: Entrepreneurs and Economic Development in Eastern Canada, 1820–1914* (St John's: Maritime History Group 1979), and in many issues of *Acadiensis*. The failure of urban elites to promote growth in spite of strenuous efforts is documented in Elizabeth W. McGahan, *The Port of Saint John*, vol. 1, *From Confederation to Nationalization, 1867–1927, A Study in the Process of Integration* (Saint John: National Harbours Board 1982). One of the best studies of the economic history of specialized production towns for any region in Canada is L.D. McCann, 'The Mercantile-Industrial Transition in the Metal Towns of Pictou County, 1857–1931,' *Acadiensis* 1981.

That French Canadians also participated in booster activity is documented in Ronald Rudin, 'Boosting the French-Canadian Town: Municipal Government and Urban Growth in Quebec,' *UHR* 1982. More detail is provided in the best monograph on urban economic development in the province: Paul-André Linteau, *The Promoters' City: Building the Industrial Town of Maisonneuve, 1883–1918* (1981; English ed., T: JL 1985). Linteau's previously cited *Histoire de Montréal* is also valuable on growth, but there is still room for a comprehensive study of Montreal's economic role as national metropolis to complement studies of its pre-Confederation rise to prominence. Like the Maritime historians, urban scholars in Quebec must also confront relative decline. Montreal's slip in stature relative to Toronto over the past half-century is an important development, but the only major work on the topic is disappointing: Benjamin Higgins, *The Rise – and Fall? of Montreal: A Case Study of Urban Growth, Regional Economic Expansion, and the National Development* (Moncton: Canadian Institute for Research on Regional Development 1986). Quebec City has had longer experience with relative decline and the best overview is Fernand Ouellet's neglected *Histoire de la Chambre de Commerce de Québec, 1809–1959* (Q: Centre de recherche de la faculté de commerce de l'Université Laval 1959). An important reason for the arrested development of other Quebec cities is suggested by Ronald Rudin, 'Montreal Banks and the Urban Development of Quebec, 1840–1910,' in the previously cited Stelter, *Shaping the Urban Landscape*.

BUILT ENVIRONMENT

The studies of urban growth and relationships cited above do not concern themselves with the physical changes that occur within cities. Such studies form a distinct genre that can be traced to the ecological approach of Chicago sociologists in the 1920s. The best work in this tradition strives to relate the layout and physical structure of the entire city to changes in its social structure, but few book-length studies in Canada attempt this feat. The one outstanding example is Peter G. Goheen, *Victorian Toronto, 1850–1900: Pattern and Process of Growth* (Chicago: Department of Geography, University of Chicago 1970), which charts the critical transition from a pre-industrial to an industrial setting. For an introduction to the many articles that focus on residential segregation during and after industrialization, see Richard Harris, 'Residential Segregation and Class Formation in Canadian Cities: A Critical Review,' *Canadian Geographer* 1984. Few studies assess the dramatic spatial changes after World War II in a historical fashion, but see P.J. Smith, 'Changing Forms and Patterns in the Cities,' in Smith, ed., *The Prairie Provinces* (T: UTP 1972).

Three books with almost identical titles provide sweeping histories of various aspects of the urban environment: Thomas Ritchie et al., *Canada Builds, 1867–1967* (T: UTP 1967) is chaotically organized, but contains a wealth of information about changing construction techniques and other aspects of the built urban environment. More concerned with the technology of utilities and other infrastructure is Norman R. Ball, ed., *Building Canada: A History of Public Works* (T: UTP 1988). There is a huge body of work on architectural history in Canada, but almost none of it links buildings to history in ways that historians find satisfying. The best survey in that regard is still Alan Gowans, *Building Canada: An Architectural History of Canadian Life* (T: OUP 1966). From the historian's perspective, the best architectural study of a single city is Jean-Claude Marsan, *Montreal in Evolution: Historical Analysis of the Development of Montreal's Architecture and Urban Environment* (1974; English ed., M and K: MQUP 1981). Although closer in spirit to old-fashioned muckraking than modern scholarship, James Lorimer's *The Developers* (T: JL 1978) is a useful overview of the role played by big developers in shaping the physical environment since World War II.

Houses are a particularly important part of the urban landscape, and again, an immense literature explores them from a variety of perspectives. Most of it is not historical, but anyone venturing into the subject should now begin with a mammoth study by Michael Doucet and John Weaver,

Housing the North American City (M and K: MQUP 1991). Although based on Hamilton, the book is well informed by work elsewhere, and offers a series of topical essays on the varied aspects of housing. For a social and demographic explanation of more recent development, see John R. Miron, *Housing in Postwar Canada: Demographic Change, Household Formation, and Housing Demand* (M and K: MQUP 1988). On the critical question of housing policy, also see the section below on municipal government and politics.

For the twentieth century, the rise of planning and zoning has also tied the study of the urban environment more closely to the subject of municipal government and politics. There is plenty of literature here, including a specialized journal, *Plan Canada* (1920–31, 1959–), which offers some historical articles. A comprehensive guide to early material is Ian Cooper and J. David Hulchanski, *Canadian Town Planning, 1900–1930: An Historical Bibliography*, 3 vols. (T: Centre for Urban and Community Studies, University of Toronto 1978), which, in addition to planning (vol. 1), also lists items on housing (vol. 2) and public health (vol. 3). A good introduction that pays attention to historical developments is Gerald Hodge, *Planning Canadian Communities: An Introduction to the Principles, Practice, and Participants* (T: Methuen 1986). Among many good articles, see in particular, Walter van Nus, 'The Fate of City Beautiful Thought in Canada, 1893–1930,' *CHAR* 1975. A biography that places Canada's most influential planner in his international context is Michael Simpson, *Thomas Adams and the Modern Planning Movement: Britain, Canada, and the United States, 1900–1940* (L and NY: Mansell 1985). Planners enjoyed more freedom to lay out new resource towns; for an introduction, see Oiva W. Saarienen, 'Single-Sector Communities in Northern Ontario: The Creation and Planning of Dependent Towns,' in Stelter and Artibise, *Power and Place* and a special issue of *Plan Canada* (1978).

One might have expected the physical impact of automobiles and trucks on Canadian cities to inspire historians, but this territory is virtually unexplored. For a cursory introduction, see a special issue of the *Urban History Review* (1989). Much of the American literature is useful, but because Canadian cities did not receive the same massive subsidies for freeway construction from their senior governments, important differences deserve attention.

Work on physically distinct neighbourhoods within cities is spotty. Waterfronts, transportation sites, office and warehouse districts, retail streets, industrial parks, shopping centres, skid rows, campus neighbourhoods, and other physical enclaves within the city have spawned few articles that treat their subjects historically. Nonetheless, preliminary examples of such work include Gunter Gad and Deryck W. Holdsworth, 'Building for City, Region, and Nation: Office Development in Toronto, 1834–1984,' in Russell, *Forging a Consensus*, and John E. Tunbridge, 'Clarence Street, Ottawa: Contemporary Change in an Inner City "Zone of Discard,"' *UHR* 1986. Urban parks have attracted more attention. There is a book-length study, but higher quality work can be sampled in Geoffrey Wall and John S. Marsh, eds., *Recreational Land Use: Perspectives on Its Evolution in Canada* (O: Carleton UP 1982). Also worthy is Robert A.J. McDonald, '"Holy Retreat" or "Practical Breathing Spot"?: Class Perceptions of Vancouver's Stanley Park, 1910–1913,' *CHR* 1984.

In spite of its hungry consumption of land in the modern city, even the residential suburb has attracted little historical attention. The best single reading is John C. Weaver, 'From Land Assembly to Social Maturity: The Suburban Life of Westdale (Hamilton), Ontario, 1911–1951,' *HS/SH* 1978, but for the more pervasive post-1945 suburb, see an introductory article by Paul-André Linteau, 'Canadian Suburbanization in a North American Context: Does the Border Make a Difference?' *Journal of Urban History* 1987. For a postwar case study, see John Sewell, 'Don Mills: E.P. Taylor and Canada's First Corporate Suburb,' in James Lorimer and Evelyn Ross, eds., *The Second City Book: Studies of Urban and Suburban Canada* (T: JL 1977).

SOCIAL STRUCTURE AND SOCIAL LIFE

Urban society is at once one of the most and least studied aspects of urban history. As an introduction noted, the bursting cornucopia of recent social history tells us much about developments that could only have occurred in an urban setting, but these studies usually fail to consider the city as an essential component of the analysis. This point must be kept in mind when considering the limited selection of readings suggested below. Much of the difficulty stems from the lack of historical studies that systematically compare urban and rural life. We do not know what is specifically urban about Canadian society, because we do not know what is non-urban. At critical points in time, cities owed much of their growth to the arrival of rural migrants, but urbanization as a social process in Canada is little understood. The very limited literature available, however, suggests rural-urban social differences may have been exaggerated by scholars in the past. Declining fertility rates, rapid geographical mobility, and increasingly rigid social structures, for examples, now seem common to both ways of life. See Chad Gaffield, 'Social Structure and the Urbanization Process: Perspectives on Nineteenth-Century Research,' in Stelter and Artibise, *The Canadian City* (2nd ed. only). My own study, Paul Voisey, *Vulcan: The Making of a Prairie Community* (T: UTP 1988) also suggests that a strong 'urban' ethos prevailed in at least some early twentieth-century rural and small town communities.

Unfortunately, urban sociologists no longer help historians solve these or other historical problems. Several textbooks on Canadian urban sociology exist, but the subdiscipline of historical sociology so skilfully pioneered by S.D. Clark and C.A. Dawson is virtually dead in English Canada, and barely alive in French Canada. Even the books by Katz on the social structure of pre-Confederation Hamilton failed to ignite much interest in comprehensive studies of urban social structure. Artibise, *Winnipeg: A Social History* (cited above) comes closest. Since 1972, the Social History of Montreal Project has also generated articles and research reports. For an assessment of the methodology and findings, read Paul-André Linteau and Jean-Claude Robert, 'Montréal au 19e siècle: bilan d'une recherche,' *UHR* 1985. For another city that has received particular attention, see Robert A.J. McDonald and Jean Barman, eds., *Vancouver Past: Essays in Social History* (V: UBCP 1986). Interestingly, some of the best accounts of social life can be found in articles on single-industry company towns. While not a work of history, a study historians should note is Rex A. Lucas, *Minetown, Milltown, Railtown: Life in Canadian Communities of Single Industry* (T: UTP 1971).

Particular urban social classes have received more attention. On the social characteristics of urban elites see, for example, Elizabeth Bloomfield, 'Community Leadership and Decision-Making: Entrepreneurial Elites in Two Ontario Towns [Berlin and Waterloo], 1870–1930,' in Stelter and Artibise, *Power and Place*; Paul Voisey, 'In Search of Wealth and Status: An Economic and Social Study of Entrepreneurs in Early Calgary,' in Rasporich and Klassen, *Frontier Calgary*; and Robert A.J. McDonald, 'Vancouver's "Four Hundred"; The Quest for Wealth and Status in Canada's Urban West, 1886–1914,' *JCS* 1990. Except in their capacity as urban reformers, the middle class is the most neglected group of all, but plenty of attention has been lavished on the working class and the poor. Thanks to reprints, two important books by contemporary reformers are widely available: J.S. Woodsworth's 1911 exposé, *My Neighbor: A Study of City Conditions, A Plea for Social Service* (1911, T: UTP 1972), and the 1897 survey by Herbert Brown Ames, *The City below the Hill: A Sociological Study of a Portion of the City of Montreal, Canada* (1897, T: UTP 1972).

Modern studies include Terry Copp, *The Anatomy of Poverty: The Condition of the Working Class in Montreal, 1897–1929* (T: M&S 1974), and Michael J. Piva, *The Condition of the Working Class in Toronto, 1900–1921* (O: UOP 1979). See also many articles in the journals *Labour/Le Travail* and *Histoire-sociale/Social History*. For an excellent study of the urban underclass, see Judith Fingard, *The Dark Side of Life in Victorian Halifax* (Porters Lake: Pottersfield Press 1989).

There are also many studies of ethnic groups in the city. For those most consciously urban in orientation, see Robert F. Harney and Harold Troper, *Immigrants: A Portrait of the Urban Experience, 1890–1930* (T: Van Nostrand Reinhold 1975); Robert F. Harney, ed., *Gathering Place: Peoples and Neighbourhoods of Toronto, 1834–1945* (T: MHSO 1985); Alan F.J. Artibise, 'Divided City: The Immigrant in Winnipeg Society, 1874–1921,' in Stelter and Artibise, *The Canadian City*, and special urban issues of *Canadian Ethnic Studies* (1977, 1980), *Urban History Review* (1978), and *Polyphony* (1984). One of the best works explaining the formation of a distinct ethnic neighbourhood is John Zucchi, *The Italian Immigrants of the St John's Ward [Toronto], 1875–1915: Patterns of Settlement and Neighbourhood Formation* (T: MHSO 1981). Because they are so physically conspicuous, more attention has been focused on Chinatowns: see David Chuenyan Lai, *Chinatowns: Towns within Cities in Canada* (V: UBCP 1988).

Several worthwhile studies probe particular aspects of urban social history. With some difficulty, Michael A. Goldberg and John Mercer, *The Myth of the North American City: Continentalism Challenged* (V: UBCP 1986), argue that Canadian cities are more livable than American ones because of deep-rooted value differences between the two nations. In a neglected essay, L.G. Thomas, 'The Rancher and the City: Calgary and Cattlemen, 1883–1914,' *TRSC* 1986, stands almost alone in exploring the social, rather than the economic, dimensions of city-hinterland relationships; it is also unique in documentating the cultural impact of the countryside on the city. His example has not inspired others. Except for boards of trade, there is also little on how particular voluntary organizations functioned as distinctly urban institutions, but the argument that all of them contributed to a sense of urban community is offered in Carl Betke, 'The Original City of Edmonton: A Derivative Prairie Urban Community,' in Artibise, *Town and City*. See also a special issue of *Urban History Review* (1983) for the role of sports in urban life. For the limited literature that specifically links women's history to urban history, see the annotated bibliography in Caroline Andrew and Beth Moor Milroy, eds., *Life Spaces: Gender, Household, Employment* (V: UBCP 1988), and a special issue of

Urban History Review (1989). See also Veronica Strong-Boag, 'Home Dreams: Women and the Suburban Experiment in Canada, 1945–60,' *CHR* 1991.

MUNICIPAL GOVERNMENT AND POLITICS

As with urban society, we know both a great deal and very little about the history of municipal government and politics. Urban reform movements have received an inordinate amount of attention, but the basic structures and processes that the reformers attacked are less understood. Of the many political scientists studying local government, few have attempted any long-range historical view. Historical introductions may be found in several textbooks, but the best and most comprehensive volume for the historian is Warren Magnusson and Andrew Sancton, eds., *City Politics in Canada* (T: UTP 1983). Its introductory overview is followed by historical surveys of politics in seven major cities, and the excellent notes and bibliographies direct the reader to more detailed studies. Another sweeping overview worth reading is John H. Taylor, 'Urban Autonomy in Canada: Its Evolution and Decline,' in Stelter and Artibise, *The Canadian City*. The best collection of historical articles is Alan F.J. Artibise and Gilbert A. Stelter, eds., *The Usable Urban Past: Planning and Politics in the Modern Canadian City* (T: MAC 1979). The peculiarities of local administration in single-industry resource towns, especially company-owned towns, have been explored in many articles. For an introduction see a special issue of the *Laurentian University Review* (1985).

Nearly every province has some sort of text on local government, but few are full-scale historical studies. The exceptions include J. Murray Beck, *The Evolution of Municipal Government in Nova Scotia, 1749–1973: A Study* (H: Royal Commission on Education, Public Services, and Provincial-Municipal Relations 1973); Hugh J. Whalen, *The Development of Local Government in New Brunswick* (F: QP 1963); and David G. Bettison et al., *Urban Affairs in Alberta* (E: UAP 1975). Since cities are legal children of the provinces, one might expect more historical studies of provincial-municipal relations rather than mere accounts of provincial policies and regulations, but this topic has been strangely ignored. Although federal-municipal relations are much less important, the topic has been examined for the period since 1935 in David G. Bettison, *The Politics of Canadian Urban Development* (E: UAP 1975).

Good biographies of municipal politicians are also rare. One of the best is Timothy J. Colton, *Big Daddy: Frederick G. Gardiner and the Building of Metropolitan Toronto* (T: UTP 1980), which can be read in conjunction with Albert Rose, *Governing Metropolitan Toronto: A Social and Political Analysis, 1953–1971* (Berkeley: University of California Press 1972). See also Brian McKenna and Susan Purcell, *Drapeau* (T: CI 1980), Desmond Morton, *Mayor Howland: The Citizens' Candidate* (T: Hakkert 1973), and for the period since 1935, Allan Levine, ed., *Your Worship: The Lives of Eight of Canada's Most Unforgettable Mayors* (T: JL 1989).

Urban reform has generated the most interest. Begin by reading Paul Rutherford, 'Tomorrow's Metropolis: The Urban Reform Movement in Canada, 1880-1920,' *CHAR* 1971, and Rutherford's collection of primary material in *Saving the Canadian City: The First Phase, 1880–1920* (T: UTP 1974). For more emphasis on the self-interest of the reformers, read two studies by John C. Weaver: *Shaping the Canadian City: Essays on Urban Politics and Policy, 1890–1920* (T: Institute of Public Administration in Canada 1977); and '"Tomorrow's Metropolis" Revisited: A Critical Assessment of Urban Reform in Canada, 1890–1920,' in Stelter and Artibise, *The Canadian City*. See also a special issue on reform in the *Urban History Review* (1976). More recent urban reform movements that first sprouted in the 1960s have not received historical treatment, but an introduction to them is provided in several articles and commentaries in the *International Journal of Urban and Regional Research* (1987, 1988).

Book-length studies of reform in particular cities are rare. Readers seeking a wealth of detail on three major cities might turn to Harold Kaplan's gargantuan *Reform, Planning, and City Politics: Montreal, Winnipeg, Toronto* (T: UTP 1982), but they will not appreciate the chaotic organization, the jargon, and the lack of documentation. Montreal has attracted special attention because it is the city presumed to have developed an American-style machine capable of thwarting reformers. See Annick Germain, *Les mouvements de réforme urbaine à Montréal au tournant du siècle: modes de développement, modes d'urbanisation, et transformations de la scène politique* (M: Centre d'information et d'aide à la recherche, Département de sociologie, Université de Montréal 1984). More satisfying, however, is Michel Gauvin, 'The Reformer and the Machine: Montreal Civic Politics from Raymond Préfrontaine to Médéric Martin,' *JCS* 1978.

Besides the political goals of eliminating corruption and restructuring municipal government, many urban reformers urged local councils to provide various utilities and services. On this topic, the physical and technical aspects have been dealt with under the 'Built Environment,' but utilities increasingly because political issues as more of them came under municipal ownership or regulation. There are many good articles, but readers should begin with the prize-winning book by Christopher

Armstrong and H.V. Nelles, *Monopoly's Moment: The Organization and Regulation of Canadian Utilities, 1830–1930* (2nd ed., T: UTP 1988), which introduces the complexities of the issue, explains local variations, and offers copious notes that indicate more specialized studies.

Specific utilities and services are the focus of much work. For introductory overviews on public transportation, sewers, streets, waterworks, electricity, and garbage collection see essays in the previously cited Ball, *Building Canada*. A useful reference guide to the introduction of many services in Ontario cities is provided in Elizabeth Bloomfield et al., *Urban Growth and Local Services: The Development of Ontario Municipalities to 1981* (Guelph: Department of Geography, University of Guelph, 1983). Streetcars are particular favourites in the literature, and mediocre books are available for many cities. There are many excellent articles, however. For a good comparative example, see Christopher Armstrong and H.V. Nelles, 'Suburban Street Railway Strategies in Montreal, Toronto, and Vancouver, 1896–1930,' in Stelter and Artibise, *Power and Place*. Alternative modes of public transportation, like buses and taxicabs, are virtually ignored in the literature.

Fire prevention and fire-fighting have ignited few historians, but there is one excellent article: John C. Weaver and Peter de Lottinville, 'The Conflagration and the City: Disaster and Progress in British North America during the Nineteenth Century,' *HS/SH* 1980. Crime and policing fare better; for several articles and an introduction and guide to further reading, see a special issue of the *Urban History Review* (1990). For a particularly good article that looks at policing from several perspectives, see Greg Marquis, '"A Machine of Oppression under the Guise of the Law": The Saint John Police Establishment, 1860–90,' *Acadiensis* 1986. The public-health movement inspired a host of related reforms including street cleaning, garbage collection, water and sewage improvements, and parks. There are many articles, but the most comprehensive study for any city is Heather MacDougall, *Activists and Advocates: Toronto's Health Department, 1883–1983* (T: Dundurn Press 1990).

Planning also became an important aspect of municipal government and reform; see the discussion under 'Built Environment.' Housing policy likewise affected urban development, but most often involved senior levels of government. In addition to the works cited earlier, see Andrew Eric Jones, *The Beginnings of Canadian Government Housing Policy, 1918–1924* (O: Centre for Social Welfare Studies, Carleton University 1978); Albert Rose, *Canadian Housing Policies, 1935–1980* (T: BUT 1980); and a special issue of the *Urban History Review* (1986).

As this survey indicates, many fine studies examine bits and pieces of Canadian urban history. There are also sweeping essays of quality that provide bold outlines and broad abstractions for its study. The most critical deficiency is the missing middle ground – studies that synthesize and link specialized works, while fleshing out or revising the more inter-pretive overviews. We need comprehensive period studies, broad surveys of regions, and thematic books that trace big topics over long spans of time. The paucity of such work undoubtedly reflects our lack of knowledge about many specific matters, but if Canadian urban history is to advance as a field, scholars must be more willing to explore the uncertain terrain that lies between research monograph and speculative generalization.

T.W. ACHESON

Atlantic Provinces

The past twenty-five years have witnessed a golden age of historical writing on the Maritime provinces and Newfoundland. Before 1965 historical studies of the region in the post-1867 period were few and often spotty in coverage. Most were the work of dedicated amateur historians writing for local and provincial historical societies. The remainder were unpublished and often inaccessible MA theses. The work of professional historians was overwhelmingly concerned with the careers of politicians and political administrations. In 1965 the existing literature could not sustain any attempt to write a synthetic history of the region in modern times.

All of this has changed. The growth of the historiography over the past generation – and especially since 1971 – has turned the unknown regional experience into the known. Many questions remain to be answered, and many of the answers which we now have remain to be modified, but we can finally provide some answers to most questions which historians consider to be important. Increasingly the historiography of the Atlantic provinces is coming to resemble that of New England in scope and sophistication of approach, although the depth is often uneven. The historiography of the pre-1930 period, for example, is much richer than that of the later era. Yet questions that deal with even the relatively recent past can usually find at least one study that charts what a few years ago was unknown territory, while the older themes now sometimes provide several stimulating explanations in answer to important questions. The range of themes has also widened. While the provincial governments and the relationships between the region and the Canadian state remain important, they have been supplemented by a growing literature on subjects as diverse as business and labour, women, religion and mentality, economic development, and social change. The literature reflects two tendencies: much of it is a conscious search for a 'regional' experience; much else seeks to address broader questions, with case studies drawn from the Atlantic provinces. Approaches and methodologies employed by historians have broadened greatly over the past three decades and now range from the more traditional interaction of character and circumstance to the search for broad patterns of meaning.

The question of whether or not the Atlantic provinces constitute a region remains a subject of debate. Even more controversial is the nature of regionalism. For some attempts to define the nature of the subject see J.M.S. Careless, 'Aspects of Metropolitanism in Atlantic Canada,' in Mason Wade, ed., *Regionalism in the Canadian Community, 1867–1967* (T: UTP 1969), and his 'Limited Identities,' *CHR* 1969; J. Murray Beck, 'The Maritimes: One Region or Three Provinces,' *TRSC* 1977; E.R. Forbes, *Aspects of Maritime Regionalism 1867–1927* (O: CHA 1983); and L.D. McCann, ed., *Heartland and Hinterland: A Geography of Canada* (2nd ed., T: PH 1987). See also George Rawlyk, 'Nova Scotia's Regional Protest, 1862–1967,' *QQ* 1962.

PERIODICALS, BIBLIOGRAPHIES, AND GENERAL STUDIES

The indispensable periodical for the history of the region is the journal *Acadiensis*. Published twice yearly since 1971, *Acadiensis* has been the vehicle through which most of the professional history of the region has been published. Other material related to the region can sometimes be found in the *Canadian Historical Review, Labour/Le Travail, Histoire sociale/ Social History*, Canadian Historical Association *Historical Papers, La Revue d'histoire de l'amérique française, The American Review of Canadian Studies*, and the *British Journal of Canadian Studies*. Interdisciplinary journals such as *La Revue de l'Université de Moncton, Newfoundland Studies*, and *The Journal of Canadian Studies* also sometimes contain useful articles. The region is home to a number of local and popular historical journals usually specializing in provincial or ethnic history. These include the venerable *New Brunswick Historical Society Collections* and *Collections of the Royal Nova Scotia Historical Society*, as well as *Les cahiers de la société historique acadienne*, the *Newfoundland Quarterly*, the *Island Magazine*, and the *Nova Scotia Historical Review*. Occasional pieces of historical interest are found in more general journals of opinion such as *The Dalhousie Review, New Maritimes, Queen's Quarterly*, and *The New England Quarterly*.

The most complete bibliography of work relating to the history of the Maritimes and Newfoundland since 1975 has been published in each issue of *Acadiensis*. A bibliography with a section on Atlantic Canada is also found in each issue of the *CHR*. For a bibliography of specialized bibliographies on the region see E.L. Swanick, 'Secondary Sources for Maritime Studies: A Bibliographical Guide,' in Philip A. Buckner, ed., *Teaching Maritime Studies* (F: AP 1986.

A major weakness of the regional historiography has been the lack of an overview through which a reader could gain easy access to the history of the region. With the recent publication of *The Atlantic Provinces in Confederation*, (T and F: UTP and AP 1993) edited by E.R. Forbes and D.A. Muise, this problem has been rectified. Prepared by thirteen leading historians of the region, this volume provides both a synthesis of the existing literature and an interpretative framework for the regional experience. It should be the starting point for any study of the region. There are no general provincial histories of New Brunswick and Nova Scotia since 1867. Newfoundland has been better served with Frederick W. Rowe, *A History of Newfoundland and Labrador* (T: MHR 1980). A brief topical look at the history of Prince Edward Island is found in Francis W.P. Bolger, ed., *Canada's Smallest Province: A History of PEI* (Charlottetown: PEI Heritage Foundation 1973). A similar survey of the Acadian people is found in Jean Daigle, ed., *Les Acadiens des Maritimes: études thématiques*, translated as *Acadians of the Maritimes: Thematic Studies* (Moncton: Centre d'études acadiennes 1980, 1982). A useful examination of the 1860s, 1880s, and 1920s is John G. Reid, *Six Crucial Decades: Times of Change in the History of the Maritimes* (H: Nimbus 1987). There are also several useful historiographical essays on the region, including E.R. Forbes, 'In Search of a Post-Confederation Maritime Historiography, 1900–1967,' *Acadiensis* 1978; Peter Neary, 'The Writing of Newfoundland History: An Introductory Survey,' in James Hiller and Peter Neary, eds., *Newfoundland in the Nineteenth and Twentieth Centuries: Essays in Interpretation* (T: UTP 1980); W. Godfrey, '"A New Golden Age": Recent Historical Writing on the Maritimes,' *QQ* 1984; John G. Reid, 'Toward the Elusive Synthesis: The Atlantic Provinces in Recent General Treatments of Canadian History,' *Acadiensis* 1987; P.A. Buckner, 'Limited Identities and Canadian Historical Scholarship: An Atlantic Provinces Perspective,' *JCS* 1988; I.R. Robertson, 'Historical Writing on Prince Edward Island since 1975,' *Acadiensis* 1988; J.M. Bumsted, '"The only island there is": The Writing of Prince Edward Island History,' in V. Smitheram et al., *The Garden Transformed: Prince Edward Island, 1945–1980* (Charlottetown: Ragweed Press 1982); and Judith Fingard, 'Ideas on the Periphery of Peripheral Ideas: The Intellectual and Cultural History of Atlantic Canada,' *JCS* 19?.

THE CONSOLIDATION OF CONFEDERATION

Long a concern of historians, the political pacification and integration of Nova Scotia in the years following Confederation is addressed in almost every study of the period, including Donald G. Creighton's *John A. Macdonald*, vol. 2, *The Old Chieftain* (T: MAC 1955), usually in terms of the personal relationships between Joseph Howe and his political enemies. The views on Howe are conveniently presented in George A. Rawlyk, ed., *Joseph Howe: Opportunist? Man of Vision? Frustrated Politician?* (T: CC 1967), and J.M. Beck, *Joseph Howe: Anti-confederate* (O: CHA 1965). The standard biography of Howe is J.M. Beck, *Joseph Howe*, vol. 2, *The Briton Becomes Canadian 1848–73* (M and K: MQUP 1983). More comprehensive and satisfying explanations of the issue are found in Kenneth G. Pryke, *Nova Scotia and Confederation, 1864–74* (T: UTP 1979), and his 'The Making of a Province: Nova Scotia and Confederation,' CHA 1968, as well as Brian D. Tennyson, 'Economic Nationalism and Confederation: A Case Study in Cape Breton, *Acadiensis* 1972, and in D.A. Muise, 'Parties and Constituencies: Federal Elections in Nova Scotia, 1867–1896,' CHA 1971. A useful study of later separatist efforts in Nova Scotia is Colin D. Howell, 'W.S. Fielding and the Repeal Elections of 1886 and 1887 in Nova Scotia,' *Acadiensis* 1979.

New Brunswick acquiesced more easily than Nova Scotia to Confederation and little has been written on the anti-confederates of that province. The best sources for the integration are A.G. Bailey, 'The Basis and Persistence of Opposition to Confederation in New Brunswick,' CHR 1942, and especially Carl Wallace, 'Albert Smith, Confederation, and Reaction in New Brunswick: 1852 to 1882,' CHR 1963. The story of Prince Edward Island's sudden entry into Confederation in 1873 is told in all general histories. The standard work is F.W.P. Bolger, *Prince Edward Island and Confederation, 1863–1873* (Charlottetown: St Dunstan's UP 1964). Another interpretation of the same event is David Weale and Harry Baglole, *The Island and Confederation: The End of an Era* (Summerside: Williams & Crue 1973).

Newfoundland's relationship with Canada in the late nineteenth century is documented in F.J. Newhook, 'Newfoundland's First Rejection of Confederation: The Election of 1869,' *Newfoundland Quarterly* 1961; J.K. Hiller, 'Confederation Defeated: The Newfoundland Election of 1869,' in J.K. Hiller and P. Neary, eds., *Newfoundland in the Nineteenth and Twentieth Centuries*; and Harvey Mitchell, 'Canada's Negotiations with Newfoundland, 1887–95,' CHR 1959.

NEW BRUNSWICK SCHOOLS

One of the earliest challenges to the viability of the new Canadian state was the decision of the New Brunswick government in 1871 to create a compulsory, non-sectarian public school system. The issue threatened to reignite the cultural antagonisms which had destroyed the first union of the Canadas. Perspectives on the issue are found in William M. Baker, *Timothy Warren Anglin, 1822–1896, Irish Catholic Canadian* (T: UTP 1977); Katherine F.C. MacNaughton, *The Development of the Theory and Practice of Education in New Brunswick, 1784–1900: A Study in Historical Background* (F: University of New Brunswick 1947); Peter Toner, 'New Brunswick Schools and the Rise of Provincial Rights,' in Bruce W. Hodgins et al., eds. *Federalism in Canada and Australia: The Early Years* (Wa: WLUP 1978); T.W. Acheson, 'George King,' *Dictionary of Canadian Biography (DBC)* XIII; Margaret Conrad, 'An Abiding Conviction of the Paramount Importance of Christian Education: Theodore Harding Rand and Education, 1860–1900,' in R.S. Wilson, ed., *An Abiding Conviction: Maritime Baptists and Their World* (Hansport: Lancelot Press 1988); and G.F.G. Stanley, 'The Caraquet Riots of 1875,' *Acadiensis* 1972. The schools issue was resolved by 1877, but cultural antagonisms remained close to the surface and could easily be used for political purposes. A fine case study is Michael Hatfield, 'H.H. Pitts and Race and Religion in New Brunswick,' *Acadiensis* 1975.

THE STAPLES ECONOMY

Some of the most significant regional scholarship of the past decade has been devoted to aspects of the traditional staples industries. An interesting social history of the sailor's life in port towns is Judith Fingard, *Jack in Port: Sailortowns of Eastern Canada* (T: UTP 1982). The best work on the shipping industry is contained in two fine volumes, Eric W. Sager with Gerald E. Panting, *Maritime Capital: The Shipping Industry in Atlantic Canada, 1820–1914* (M and K: MQUP 1990), and Sager, *Seafaring Labour: The Merchant Marine of Atlantic Canada, 1820–1914* (M and K: MQUP 1989). They are the fruition of the work done by the Atlantic Canada Shipping Project at Memorial University since the mid-1970s. They synthesize and largely supersede the work presented in the six volumes of conference proceedings published as part of the ongoing work of the project, although the specialized proceedings will repay consultation. They were all published by the Maritime History Group at Memorial and include Keith Matthews and G. Panting, eds., *Ships and Shipbuilding in the North Atlantic Region* (St John's: Maritime History Group 1978); Lewis R. Fischer and E.W. Sager, eds., *The Enterprising Canadians: Entrepreneurs and Economic Development in Eastern Canada, 1820–1914* (St John's: Maritime History Group 1979); David Alexander and Rosemary Ommer, eds., *Volumes Not Values: Canadian Sailing Ships and World Trade* (St John's: Maritime History Group 1979); R. Ommer and G. Panting, eds., *Working Men Who Got Wet* (St John's: Maritime History Group 1980); L.R. Fischer and E.W. Sager, eds., *Merchant Shipping and Economic Development in Atlantic Canada* (St John's: Maritime History Group 1982); L. Fischer and G. Panting, eds., *Change and Adaptation in Maritime History: The North Atlantic Fleets in the Nineteenth Century* (St John's: Maritime History Group 1985). See also D. Alexander and G. Panting, 'The Mercantile Fleet and Its Owners: Yarmouth, Nova Scotia, 1840–1889,' *Acadiensis* 1978; E.W. Sager and L.R. Fischer, 'Patterns of Investment in the Shipping Industries of Atlantic Canada, 1820–1900,' *Acadiensis* 1979; and their *Shipping and Shipbuilding in Atlantic Canada, 1820–1914* (O: CHA 1986).

The fishing industry has long been a concern of historians of the Atlantic provinces, particularly those working on Newfoundland. An interesting perspective on the significance of the fishery is provided in D. Alexander, 'Newfoundland's Traditional Economy and Development to 1934,' *Acadiensis* 1976. A good survey of the industry is Shannon Ryan, *Fish Out of Water: The Newfoundland Saltfish Trade, 1814–1914* (St John's: Breakwater Books 1986). The story is continued in D. Alexander, *The Decay of Trade: An Economic History of the Newfoundland Saltfish Trade, 1935–1965* (St John's: ISER 1977). An interesting case study is Rosemary Ommer, *From Outpost to Outport: A Structural Analysis of the Jersey-Gaspé Cod Fishery, 1767–1886* (M and K: MQUP 1991). An indication of the importance of the fishery in Nova Scotia in the Confederation era is found in R.S. Longley, 'Fisheries in Nova Scotia Politics, 1865–71,' *Collections of the Royal Nova Scotia Historical Society* 1942. More recent perspectives are reflected in L.G. Barrett, 'Capital and the State in Atlantic Canada: The Structural Context of Fishery Policy between 1939 and 1977,' in C. Lamson and A.J. Hanson, eds., *Atlantic Fisheries and Coastal Communities: Fisheries Decision-Making Case Studies* (H: Dalhousie University 1984).

Little scholarly work has been published on the important Maritime lumber industry between 1867 and 1914. The staples approach is presented in S.A. Saunders, 'Forest Industries in the Maritime Provinces,' in A.R.M.

Lower, ed., *The North American Assault on the Canadian Forest: A History of the Lumber Trade between Canada and the United States* (1938, NY: Greenwood 1968). A recent study is Raymond Léger, 'L'industrie du bois dans la péninsule acadienne, 1875–1900,' *La Revue d'histoire de la Société historique Nicolas Denys* 1988. See also Catherine Johnston, 'The Search for Industry in Newcastle, New Brunswick, 1899–1914,' *Acadiensis* 1983. The lumber industry and the pulp and paper industry are examined in L. Anders Sandberg, ed., *Trouble in the Woods: Forest Policy and Social Conflict in Nova Scotia and New Brunswick* (F: AP 1992). For the arrival of the pulp and paper industry in Newfoundland, see J.K. Hiller, 'The Origins of the Pulp and Paper Industry in Newfoundland,' *Acadiensis* 1982, and 'The Politics of Newsprint: The Newfoundland Pulp and Paper Industry, 1915–1931,' *Acadiensis* 1990.

THE NATIONAL POLICY AND ECONOMIC DEVELOPMENT TO 1918

Concern over the decline of maritime economic fortunes relative to those of the rest of Canada has led many historians to reassess the Maritime experience in the half century following Confederation. The result of their efforts produced a rich literature on the political economy of the region. The classic staples interpretation of the earlier period was offered in 1939 by S.A. Saunders in *The Economic History of the Maritime Provinces* (1939, F: AP 1984).

Most assessments of the impact of the National Policy on the region have been negative. These were challenged in T.W. Acheson, 'The National Policy and the Industrialization of the Maritimes, 1880–1910,' *Acadiensis* 1972. The theme of regional industrial development has become a central concern of historians. The process of development has been explored by L.D. McCann in three articles: 'Staples and New Industries in the Growth of Post-Confederation Halifax,' *Acadiensis* 1979; 'The Mercantile-Industrial Transition in the Metal Towns of Pictou County, 1857–1931,' *Acadiensis* 1981; and 'Metropolitanism and the Branch Businesses in the Maritimes,' *Acadiensis* 1983. A comparative study of Canadian and American regional development is found in Robert Babcock, 'Economic Development in Portland, Me., and St John, NB,' *American Review of Canadian Studies* 1979. The shift of capital from the traditional to the new enterprises is examined in G. Panting, 'Cradle of Enterprise: Yarmouth, Nova Scotia, 1840–1889,' in Fischer and Sager, eds., *The Enterprising Canadians*, and in P. Felt and L. Felt, 'Capital Accumulation and Industrial Development in New Brunswick,' in Fischer and Sager, eds.,

Merchant Shipping and Economic Development. Studies of the corporate development of the important Nova Scotia coal, iron, and steel industry are found in Don Macgillivray, 'Henry Melville Whitney Comes to Cape Breton,' *Acadiensis* 1979, and in David Frank, 'The Cape Breton Coal Industry and the Rise and fall of the British Empire Steel Corporation,' *Acadiensis* 1977. Two studies of industrial development in Halifax illustrate both the different ways in which development occurred and the approaches used by historians in writing business history: Ian McKay, 'Capital and Labour in the Halifax Baking and Confectionery Industry during the Last Half of the Nineteenth Century,' *Labour* 1978, and Christopher Armstrong and H.V. Nelles, 'Getting Your Way in Nova Scotia: Tweaking Halifax, 1909–1917,' *Acadiensis* 1976. The significance of the creation of an integrated banking system is explored in J. Frost, 'The "Nationalization" of the Bank of Nova Scotia,' *Acadiensis* 1982, and in Douglas O. Baldwin, 'The Growth and Decline of the Charlottetown Banks, 1854–1904,' *Acadiensis* 1986. The idea that the consolidation of much of the regional industry under central Canadian control in the 1890s presented a threat to the region is challenged by Kris Inwood in 'Local Control, Resources, and the Nova Scotia Steel and Coal Company,' CHA *AR* 1986.

The most useful studies of the other critical manifestation of the National Policy in the nineteenth-century Maritimes, the Intercolonial Railway, are G.R. Stevens, *The Canadian National Railways*, vol. 2, *Towards the Inevitable, 1896–1922* (T: CI 1962); Ken Cruikshank, 'The People's Railway: The Intercolonial Railway and the Canadian Public Enterprise Experience,' *Acadiensis* 1986, and his *Close Ties: Railways, Governments, and the Board of Railway Commissioners, 1851–1933* (M and K: MQUP 1991); and E.R. Forbes, 'Misguided Symmetry: The Destruction of Regional Transportation Policy for the Maritimes,' in David J. Bercuson, ed., *Canada and the Burden of Unity* (T: MAC 1977).

FROM MARITIME RIGHTS TO DREE

The interwar years were difficult ones in the Maritimes. An overview of some themes of the period is found in John Herd Thompson with Allen Seager, *Canada 1922–1939: Decades of Discord* (T: M&S 1985). The depression which wracked the Canadian economy between 1919 and 1923 devastated the manufacturing and processing industries of the Maritimes to the point that some scholars speak of the 'deindustrialization' of the region. The best study of the process and of the regional reaction to it is

E.R. Forbe's now classic *The Maritime Rights Movement, 1919–1927: A Study in Canadian Regionalism* (M and K: MQUP 1979). This should be supplemented by Forbes, 'Misguided Symmetry,' and his 'Origins of the Maritime Rights Movement,' *Acadiensis* 1975. Another explanation for the decline is provided in P.J. Wylie, 'When Markets Fail: Electrification and Maritime Industrial Decline in the 1920s,' *Acadiensis* 1987. T.W. Acheson's 'The Maritimes and "Empire Canada"' in *Canada and the Burden of Unity* is also useful as an overview of the post-1918 period. An interesting comparison of the product output of the Maritime and Newfoundland economies is found in D. Alexander, 'Economic Growth in the Atlantic Region, 1880 to 1940,' *Acadiensis* 1978.

Work on the political economy of the Maritimes after 1930 is scarce. The most important studies are two essays by E.R. Forbes, '"Cutting the Pie into Smaller Pieces": Matching Grants and Relief in the Maritime Provinces during the 1930s,' *Acadiensis* 1987, and 'Consolidating Disparity: The Maritimes and the Industrialization of Canada during the Second World War,' *Acadiensis* 1987. Another useful perspective on the region during the war and post-war period is R.A. Young, '"and the people will sink into despair": Reconstruction in New Brunswick, 1942–52,' *CHR* 1988. Provincial development policies are dealt with in R.A. Young, 'Planning for Power: The New Brunswick Electric Power Commission in the 1950s,' *Acadiensis* 1982, and his 'L'édification de l'état provinciale et le développement régionale au Nouveau-Brunswick,' *Egalité* 1984–5. One of the few scholarly studies of a regional leader operating as intermediary between the region and the federal government is Margaret Conrad's important book, *George Nowlan: Maritime Conservative in National Politics* (T: UTP 1986). She also examines the impact of federal policies on an important Nova Scotia industry in her article 'Apple Blossom Time in the Annapolis Valley, 1880–1957,' *Acadiensis* 1980. See also her 'The "Atlantic Revolution" of the 1950s,' in Berkeley Fleming, ed., *Beyond Anger and Longing: Community and Development in Atlantic Canada* (F: AP 1988).

Most postwar work on development has been written by economists, political scientists, and reporters. The most sustained analysis, beginning at Confederation but focused on the postwar period, is James P. Bickerton, *Nova Scotia, Ottawa, and the Politics of Regional Development* (T: UTP 1990). Other studies include popular biographies of the region's great business families, the most scholarly of which is John DeMont, *Citizens Irving: K.C. Irving and His Legacy, The Story of Canada's Wealthiest Family* (T: Doubleday 1991). See also John F. Graham, *Fiscal Adjustment and Economic Development: A Case Study of Nova Scotia* (T: UTP 1963); Roy E.

George, *A Leader and a Laggard: Manufacturing Industry in Nova Scotia, Quebec, and Ontario* (T: UTP 1970); and his *The Life and Times of Industrial Estates Limited* (H: Dalhousie University 1974); Philip Mathias, *Forced Growth: Five Studies of Government Involvement in the Development of Canada* (T: James Lewis & Samuel 1971); Anthony G.S. Careless, *Initiative and Response: The Adaptation of Canadian Federalism to Regional Economic Development* (M and K: MQUP 1977); and N.H. Lithwick, *Regional Economic Policy: The Canadian Experience* (T: MHR 1978).

POLITICS IN THE MARITIMES

For a region with so much politics there is little political history. Scholarly work on the general political history of the Maritimes is surprisingly sparse. The old political science surveys are Frank MacKinnon, *The Government of Prince Edward Island* (T: UTP 1951), Hugh G. Thorburn, *Politics in New Brunswick* (T: UTP 1961), and J. Murray Beck, *The Government of Nova Scotia* (T: UTP 1957). None of them now adequately reflects the literature on the political cultures of their respective provinces, but on many questions, Beck remains an important source. Moreover he has recently fleshed out his study in the two-volume *Politics of Nova Scotia*, vol. 1, *Nicholson–Fielding, 1710–1896* , and vol. 2, *Murray–Buchanan, 1896–1988* (Tantallon: Four East Publications 1985, 1988). There are few published histories of even the major administrations of the provinces. The best-documented administration is that of Fielding. Aspects of this government are examined in C.B. Fergusson's *Fielding: Mantle of Howe* (Windsor, NS: Lancelot Press 1970) and K.M. McLaughlin's 'W.S. Fielding and the Liberal Government in Nova Scotia, 1891–6,' *Acadiensis* 1974. There is a well-researched account of political corruption in New Brunswick during the Great War in A.T. Doyle, *Front Benches and Back Rooms: A Story of Corruption, Muckraking, Raw Partisanship, and Intrigue in New Brunswick* (T: Green Tree 1976). An examination of the political career of Louis Robichaud is found in Della M.M. Stanley, *Louis Robichaud: A Decade of Power* (H: Nimbus 1984). Brief biographies of the early premiers are found in the *DCB* notably those of I.R. Robertson on J.C. Pope (XI), T.W. Acheson on A.R. Wetmore (XII) and G.E. King (XIII), D.M. Young on J.J. Fraser (XII) and A.G. Blair (XIII), D.A. Sutherland on W. Annand (XI), and J.M. Beck on P.C. Hill (XII). The only systematic study of a provincial party is Wayne E. MacKinnon, *The Life of the Party: A History of the Liberal Party in Prince Edward Island* (Charlottetown: PEI Liberal Party 1973). A personal account of the provincial politics of the 1950s is found in Dalton Camp, *Gentlemen, Players, and Politics* (T: M&S 1974). A popular account of Nova Scotia politicians and the press is William March, *Red Line: The Chronicle-Herald and the Mail Star, 1875–1954* (H: Chebucto Agencies 1986).

The men who served as regional leaders in the federal cabinet have fared somewhat better than the provincial leaders, although there are some serious omissions. There is no satisfactory biography of Tupper and for Tilley see the doctoral thesis of Carl Wallace, 'Samuel Leonard Tilley: a political biography' (University of Alberta 1972). Thompson is well served in P.B. Waite's fine study, *The Man from Halifax: Sir John Thompson, Prime Minister* (T: UTP 1985). For Fielding there is C.B. Fergusson, *Fielding: Mr. Minister of Finance* (Windsor, NS: Lancelot Press 1971); for Foster see W. Stewart Wallace, *Memoirs of the Rt. Hon. Sir. George Foster* (T: MAC 1933); for Borden see R. Craig Brown's definitive biography, *Robert Laird Borden: A Biography*, 2 vols. (T: MAC 1975, 1980). Conrad's study of Nowlan remains the only scholarly study of a Maritime national leader in the post-1920 period.

NEWFOUNDLAND

Dominions are taken more seriously than provinces by historians, or at least that is the lesson that can be taken from the comparative richness of the twentieth-century political history of the Dominion. The standard work on Newfoundland politics is S.J.R. Noel, *Politics in Newfoundland* (T: UTP 1971). The indispensable study of the Commission period is Peter Neary's *Newfoundland in the North Atlantic World, 1929–1949* (M and K: MQUP 1988). Useful for the same period is St John Chadwick, *Newfoundland: Island into Province* (L: Cambridge UP 1967). An important examination of the movement to Confederation is David MacKenzie, *Inside the Atlantic Triangle: Canada and the Entrance of Newfoundland into Confederation, 1939–1949* (T: UTP 1986). Other studies of the movement include Peter Neary, 'Newfoundland's Union with Canada: Conspiracy or Choice?,' *Acadiensis* 1983, and J.H. Webb, 'Responsible Government and the Confederation Campaigns of 1948,' *Newfoundland Studies* 1989. On political leadership after Confederation see Peter Neary, 'Party Politicians in Newfoundland, 1947–71: Survey and Analysis,' *JCS* 1972. There are two popular but perceptive biographies of Joey Smallwood: Richard Gwyn's *Smallwood: The Unlikely Revolutionary* (rev. ed., T: M&S 1972), and Harold Horwood, *Joey: The Life and Political Times of Joey Smallwood*

(T: Stoddard 1989). For another significant difference between the Dominion and the provinces see also C.A. Sharpe, '"The Race of Honour": An Analysis of Enlistments and Casualties in the Armed Forces of Newfoundland, 1914–18,' *Newfoundland Studies* 1988. A useful examination of Canadian-Newfoundland pre-Confederation relations by Malcolm MacLeod is forthcoming in the CHA Historical booklet series.

The political economy of Newfoundland in the mid-twentieth century is dealt with in Peter Neary, ed., *The Political Economy of Newfoundland, 1929–1972* (T: CC 1973), and Ralph Matthews in *The Creation of Regional Dependency* (T: UTP 1983). For the late nineteenth-century experience see J.K. Hiller, 'The Railway and Local Politics in Newfoundland, 1870–1901,' in Hiller and Neary, eds., *Newfoundland in the Nineteenth and Twentieth Centuries*. Useful case studies of the development process are Neary, 'Traditional and Modern Elements in the Social and Economic History of Belle Ilse and Conception Bay,' CHA *AR* 1973; Melvin Baker, 'Rural Electrification in Newfoundland in the 1950s and the Origins of the Newfoundland Power Commission,' *Newfoundland Studies* 1990; W.G. Reeves, 'Alexander's Conundrum Reconsidered: The American Dimension in Newfoundland Resource Development, 1898–1910,' *Newfoundland Studies* 1989; Gerhard Bassler, '"Develop or Perish": Joseph R. Smallwood and Newfoundland's Quest for German Industry, 1949–1953,' *Acadiensis* 1986; and Philip Smith's popular account, *Brinco: The Story of Churchill Falls* (T: M&S 1975).

RELIGION

Given the significance of religion in the regional experience, the state of the historiography is disappointing. There are a number of mostly old, mostly filio-pietistic institutional surveys of individual denominations or parishes but there are few serious scholarly studies of religious manifestations within the region or of the interaction of religion and culture. The best of the denominational histories are George Levy, *The Baptists of the Maritime Provinces, 1753–1946* (Saint John: Barnes-Hopkins 1946), and A.A. Johnson, *History of the Roman Catholic Church in Eastern Nova Scotia*, vol. 2 (Antigonish: St Francis Xavier UP 1972).

Fortunately, the limited recent writing on the subject has been of high quality. Intriguing questions and approaches are suggested in E.R. Forbes, 'Prohibition and the Social Gospel in Nova Scotia,' *Acadiensis* 1971; in Gregory Baum, *Catholics and Canadian Socialism: Political Thought in the Thirties and Forties* (T: JL 1980); in R.N. Bérard, 'Moral Education in

Nova Scotia, 1880–1920,' *Acadiensis* 1984; in G.A. Rawlyk, 'Fundamental-ism, Modernism, and the Maritime Baptists in the 1920s and 1930s,' *Acadiensis* 1987, and his *Champions of the Truth: Fundamentalism, Modernism, and the Maritime Baptists* (M and K: MQUP 1990); in G.O. Rothney, 'The Denominational Basis of Representation in the Newfoundland Assembly, 1919–1962,' *CJEPS* 1962; and in the essays of Michael Gauvreau and T.W. Acheson in Charles H.H. Scobie and John Webster Grant, eds., *The Contribution of Methodism to Atlantic Canada* (M and K: MQUP 1992). See also Rawlyk, ed., *Canadian Baptists and Christian Higher Education* (M and K: MQUP 1988), and R.S. Wilson, ed., *An Abiding Conviction.*

EDUCATION

Scholarly publication on the history of the public school system of the region is disappointing. The standard survey for the country as a whole is J.D. Wilson, R.M. Stamp, and L.P. Audet, *Canadian Education: A History* (T: PH 1970), but the Maritimes largely disappear after the New Brunswick schools crisis. Still useful for the late nineteenth century is MacNaughton, *The Development of the Theory and Practice of Education in New Brunswick* (cited above). Newfoundland's unique education system is examined in F.W. Rowe, *The History of Education in Newfoundland* (T: RP 1952). There is a brief excursion into the development of Acadian education in A.J. Savoie, 'Education in Acadia from 1604 to 1970,' in Diagle, ed., *The Acadians of the Maritimes.* There has been little published on the significant twentieth-century structural and curricular changes or on the social changes which precipitated them; of it, the best work has been done on Newfoundland. See the essays in William A. McKim, ed., *The Vexed Question: Denominational Education in a Secular Age* (St John's: Breakwater 1988), and P. McCann, 'The Educational Policy of the Commission of Government,' *Newfoundland Studies* 1987. Two articles examine the origins of technical education in Nova Scotia: Donald MacLeod, 'Practicality Ascendant: The Origins and Establishment of Technical Education in Nova Scotia,' *Acadiensis* 1986, and Janet Guildford, 'Coping with De-industrialization: The Nova Scotia Department of Technical Education, 1907–1930,' *Acadiensis* 1987.

In contrast to the public school system, higher education has received considerable attention from historians. The most significant recent study of a Maritime university is John Reid's fine *Mount Allison University: A History*, vol. 1, *1843–1914*, and vol. 2, *1914–1963* (T: UTP 1984.) He has also examined the search for external funding by Maritime institutions in the interwar years in 'Health, Education, Economy: Philanthropic Foundations in the Atlantic Region in the 1920s and 1930s,' *Acadiensis* 1984. There are useful essays on university reform, Memorial students, and Acadia in the Great War by John G. Reid, Malcolm MacLeod, and Barry Moody in Paul Axelrod and Reid, eds., *Youth, University, and Canadian Society: Essays in the Social History of Higher Education* (M and K: MQUP 1989). An interesting insight into the impact of the university experience on the student body is offered in Axelrod, 'Moulding the Middle Class: Student Life at Dalhousie University in the 1930s,' *Acadiensis* 1985. Three innovative studies of medical practice examine the professionalization of medicine and medical education. See Colin Howell, 'Reform and the Monopolistic Impulse: The Professionalization of Medicine in the Maritimes,' *Acadiensis* 1981; Howell and Michael Smith, 'Orthodox Medicine and the Health Reform Movement in the Maritimes, 1850–1885,' *Acadiensis* 1989; and S.M. Penney, 'Marked for Slaughter: The Halifax Medical College and the Wrong Kind of Reform, 1868–1910,' *Acadiensis* 1989. See also two commissioned hospital histories: Howell, *A Century of Care: A History of the Victoria General Hospital in Halifax, 1887–1987* (H: Victoria General Hospital Foundation 1988), and P. O'Brien, *Out of Mind, Out of Sight: A History of the Waterford Hospital* (St John's: Breakwater 1989).

LABOUR

The growth of labour history in the Maritimes has paralleled and sometimes inspired the development of studies in the political economy of the region. Work in this area is also concerned with examining class relations and the emergence of a working-class culture. Much of the work in the field has focused on the coal-mining communities of eastern Nova Scotia. Eugene Forsey explored this territory in his *Economic and Social Aspects of the Nova Scotia Coal Industry* (T: MAC 1926), but the recent historiography begins with articles by Don Macgillivray, including 'Cape Breton in the 1920s: A Community Besieged,' in Brian Douglas Tennyson, ed., *Essays in Cape Breton History* (Windsor, NS: Lancelot 1973) and his study of federal intervention in local strikes, 'Military Aid to the Civil Power: The Cape Breton Experience in the 1920s,' *Acadiensis* 1974. Ian McKay has examined the coal miners' early unionism in '"By Wisdom, Wile or War": The Provincial Workmen's Association and the Struggle for Working-Class Independence in Nova Scotia, 1879–97,' *Labour* 1986. Two studies of the coal miners' struggle for control of the workplace are Ian McKay,

'The Realm of Uncertainty: The Experience of Work in the Cumberland Coal Mines, 1873–1924,' *Acadiensis* 1986, and David Frank, 'Contested Terrain: Workers' Control in the Cape Breton Coal Mines in the 1920s,' in Craig Heron and Robert Storey, eds., *On the Job: Confronting the Labour Process in Canada* (M and K: MQUP 1986). The problem child labour in the pits is examined in two articles by Robert McIntosh, 'Grotesque Faces and Figures: Child Labourers and Coal Mining Technology in Victorian Nova Scotia,' *Scientia canadiensis* 1988, and 'The Boys in the Nova Scotia Coal Mines, 1873 to 1923,' *Acadiensis* 1987. The coal-mining community is explored in David Frank, 'Tradition and Culture in the Cape Breton Mining Community in the Early Twentieth Century,' in Kenneth Donovan, ed., *Cape Breton at 200: Historical Essays in Honour of the Island's Bicentennial, 1785–1985* (Sydney: University College of Cape Breton Press 1985), 'Company Town/Labour Town: Local Government in the Cape Breton Coal Towns, 1917–1926,' *HS/SH* 1981, and in Michael Earle, 'The Coalminers and Their "Red" Union: The Amalgamated Mine Workers of Nova Scotia, 1932–1936,' *Labour* 1988. Allen Seager has written about the contrasting experience of the New Brunswick coal miners in 'Minto, New Brunswick: A Study in Class Relations between the Wars,' *Labour* 1980.

Beyond the coalfields there has also been a growing interest in the history of workers. Eugene Forsey's *Trade Unions in Canada, 1812–1902* (T: UTP 1982) is an encyclopedic work of reference for the nineteenth century. Important general patterns are found in Ian McKay, 'Strikes in the Maritimes, 1901–1914,' *Acadiensis* 1983, and in David Frank, 'The Struggle for Development: Workers in Atlantic Canada in the Twentieth Century,' in Gregory S. Kealey and W.J.C. Cherwinski, eds., *Lectures in Canadian Labour and Working-Class History* (St John's and T: CCLH and New Hogtown Press 1985). A fine local study is Peter Delottinville, 'Trouble in the Hives of Industry: The Cotton Industry Comes to Milltown, New Brunswick, 1879–1892,' CHA 1980. Important occupational groups are analysed in Robert Babcock. 'Saint John Longshoremen during the Rise of Canada's Winter Port, 1895–1922,' *Labour* 1990, and Craig Heron, 'The Great War and Nova Scotia's Steelworkers', *Acadiensis* 1987. Specific strikes are studied in detail in Babcock, 'The Saint John Street Railwaymen's Strike and Riot, 1914,' *Acadiensis* 1982; Nolan Reilly, 'The General Strike in Amherst, Nova Scotia, 1919,' *Acadiensis* 1980; and Suzanne Morton, 'Labourism and Economic Action: The Halifax Shipyards Strike of 1920,' *Labour* 1988. Two histories of individual unions are Ian McKay, *The Craft Transformed: An Essay on the Carpenters of Halifax, 1885–1985* (H: Holdfast Press 1985), and Sue Calhoun, *A*

Word to Say: The Story of the Maritime Fishermen's Union (H: Nimbus 1991).

Labour history in Newfoundland is well presented in Bill Gillespie, *A Class Act: An Illustrated History of the Labour Movement In Newfoundland and Labrador* (St John's: Newfoundland and Labrador Federation of Labour 1986). See the articles on Newfoundland labour in *Labour* 1990. Other articles in the same journal include B.C. Busch, 'The Newfoundland Sealers' Strike of 1902,' 1984, Nancy Forestell, 'Times Were Hard: The Pattern of Women's Paid Labour in St John's between the Two World Wars,' 1989, and Duff Sutherland, 'Newfoundland Loggers Respond to the Great Depression,' 1992. The history of the fishermen's unions can be followed in Ian D.H. McDonald, *'To Each His Own': William Coaker and the Fishermen's Protective Union in Newfoundland Politics, 1908–1925* (St John's: ISER 1987), and Gordon Inglis, *More Than Just a Union: The Story of the NFFAWU* (St John's: Jesperson 1985).

WOMEN

As a subject of serious scholarly examination, the history of women in the Atlantic Provinces since 1867 is not yet a decade old. Reference to the region is found in Catherine Cleverdon, *The Women Suffrage Movement in Canada: The Start of Liberation* (2nd ed., T: UTP 1974); Wendy Mitchinson presented her stimulating interpretation of the origins of the women's missionary societies in *Atlantis* 1977, and the early experience of Maritime women at university was explored in J.G. Reid, 'The Education of Women at Mount Allison, 1854–1914,' *Acadiensis* 1983. But the signal that Maritime women had a significant experience which could not be ignored was given with the publication of E.R. Forbes's 'The Ideas of Carol Lee Bacchi and the Suffragists of Halifax : A Review Essay on *Liberation Deferred? The Ideas of English-Canadian Suffragists, 1877–1918,*' *Atlantis* 1985. Work on the subject has expanded rapidly since that time. A recent examination of the historiography of Maritime women is found in G.G. Campbell, 'Canadian Women's History: A View From Atlantic Canada,' *Acadiensis* 1990. The literature has generally been concerned either with social issues and the legal status of women or with women in the workplace. On the former see the popular reference work by Elspeth Tulloch, *We, the undersigned: A Historical Overview of New Brunswick Women's Political and Legal Statues, 1784–1984* (Moncton: NB Status of Women 1985); C. Simmons, 'Helping the Poor Sisters: The Women of the Jost Mission, Halifax, 1905–19', *Acadiensis* 1984; J.D. Davison, *Alice of Grand Pré: Alice T. Shaw and Her Grand Pré Seminary, Female Education in*

Nova Scotia and New Brunswick (Wolfville: Acadia University 1981); Judith Fingard, 'College, Career, and Community: Dalhousie Co-eds, 1881–1921,' in Axelrod and Reid, eds., *Youth, University, and Canadian Society*; James G. Snell, 'Marital Cruelty: Women and the Nova Scotia Divorce Court, 1900–1930,' *Acadiensis* 1988; and the essays by K.S. Maynard and R. Viennot in Philip Girard and Jim Phillips, eds., *Essays in the History of Canadian Law*, vol. 3, *Nova Scotia* (T: UTP 1990). An interesting case study of working women in one Maritime plant is Margaret E. McCallum, 'Separate Spheres: The Organization of Work in a Confectionery Factory, Ganong Bros., St. Stephen, New Brunswick,' *Labour* 1989. An important examination of structural inequality is found in D.A. Muise, 'The Industrial Context of Inequality: Female Participation in Nova Scotia's Paid Labour Force, 1871–1921,' *Acadiensis* 1991. A similar study of Moncton is Gisette Lafleur, 'L'industrialization et le travail rémunéré des femmes,' in Daniel Hickey, ed., *Moncton, 1871–1929: changements socio-économiques dans une ville ferroviaire* (Moncton: Editions d'Acadie 1990). On the early feminist movement, see 'Battles in Another War: Edith Archibald and the Halifax Feminist Movement,' in E.R. Forbes, *Challenging the Regional Stereotype: Essays on the 20th Century Maritimes* (F: AP 1989). See also Michael Smith, 'Graceful Athletism or Robust Womanhood: The Sporting Culture of Women in Victorian Nova Scotia, 1870–1914,' *JCS* 1988. Three studies make effective use of diaries to explore the experience of Maritime women. See the introduction to Margaret Conrad et al., eds., *No Place Like Home: Diaries and Letters of Nova Scotia Women, 1771–1938* (H: Formac 1988); Conrad, *Recording Angels: The Private Chronicles of Women from the Maritime Provinces of Canada, 1750–1950* (O: Canadian Research Institute for the Advancement of Women 1982), and her '"Sundays always make me think of Home," Time and Place in Canadian Women's History,' in Veronica Strong-Boag and Anita Clair Fellman, eds., *Rethinking Canada: The Promise of Women's History* (2nd ed., T: CCP 1991).

THE ACADIANS

The Acadians are the largest and one of the oldest cultural minorities in the Maritimes. There is an extensive historical literature on them but it is overwhelmingly concentrated on the pre-1867 period. The community is served by three local historical journals which cover a wide range of subjects and should be consulted in connection with any topic relating to Acadian history. These are *Les cahiers de la société historique acadienne*, *La revue historique de la société historique Nicolas Denys*, and *La Société historique du Madawaska Revue.* In addition the *Revue d'université de Moncton* sometimes publishes pieces dealing with the history of the Acadians.

For general surveys of the Acadian experience since 1867 see Robert Rumilly's old but still useful *Histoire des Acadiens* (M: L'Académie canadienne-française 1935); Jean Diagle, ed., *Les Acadiens des Maritimes: Études Thématiques* (Moncton: Centre d'études acadiennes 1980, English translation cited above); J.C. Vernex, *Les Francophones du Nouveau-Brunswick*, 2 vols. (Lille: Atelier 1978); and Georges Arsenault, *Les Acadiens de l'Ile, 1720–1980* (Moncton: Editions d'acadie 1987). A survey of recent historical writing on the Acadians is found in J.P. Couturier, 'Tendances actuelle de l'historiographie acadienne (1970–1985),' CHA 1987. The late nineteenth century witnessed the development of a strong sense of corporate identity as a distinct people on the part of the Acadians. Aspects of this important movement are dealt with by Raymond Mailhot in 'Quelques éléments d'histoire économique de la prise de conscience acadienne, 1850–1891,' *Les cahiers de la société historique acadienne* 1976; Michel Roy, *L'Acadie, des origines à nos jours: essai de synthèse historique* (M: QA 1981); Phyllis Leblanc, 'Le rôle et l'impact du *Courrier des Provinces Maritimes* sur la population acadienne (1885–1903),' *Les Cahiers de la Société historique acadienne* 1978; Perry Biddiscombe, 'Le Tricolore et l'étoile: The Origin of the Canadian National Flag, 1867–1912,' *Acadiensis* 1990; and G.F.G. Stanley, 'The Flowering of the Acadian Renaissance' in David J. Bercuson and Phillip Buckner, eds., *Eastern and Western Perspectives* (T: UTP 1981).

On the struggle for the church see M.S. Spigelman, 'Race et religion: Les Acadiens et la hiérarchie catholique irlandaise du Nouveau-Brunswick,' *RHAF* 1975. On the important issue of education see Omer LeGresley, *L'Enseignement du français en Acadie, 1604–1926* (Mamers: Gabriel Enault 1925); H.D. Hody, 'The Development of Bilingual Schools of New Brunswick,' PhD thesis, University of Toronto 1964, and A.J. Savoie, *Un Siècle de Revendications Scholaire au Nouveau-Brunswick, 1871–1977* (M: A.J. Savoie 1979). On Acadian demographic and social development see Daniel Hickey, ed., *Moncton, 1871–1929*; Irene Landry, 'Saint Quentin et le retour à la terre: analyse socio-économique, 1910–1960,' *Revue de la société historique du Madawaska* 1987; and Nicole Lang, 'L'impact d'une industrie et les effects sociaux de l'arrivée de la Compagnie Fraser Limited à Edmunston, NB, 1900–1950,' *Revue de la société historique du Madawaska* 1987. A short biography of Pierre-Armand Landry is found in Della M.M. Stanley, *In the Service of Two Peoples: Pierre-Armand Landry* (F: Law Society of New Brunswick 1988).

ETHNIC AND RACIAL MINORITIES

The history of ethnic and racial minorities in the Atlantic Provinces since 1867, apart from the Acadians, has not been told. Most of the work dealing with these groups in the post-1867 era is the conclusion of studies centred in an earlier age. On the Scots see D. Campbell and Raymond MacLean, *Beyond the Atlantic Roar: A Study of the Nova Scotia Scots* (T: M&S 1974), and Charles W. Dunn, *Highland Settler: A Portrait of the Scottish Gael in Nova Scotia* (T: UTP 1953). On the Irish see A.A. MacKenzie, *The Irish in Cape Breton* (Antigonish: Formac 1979). There is virtually no work by historians on the Micmac or Maliseet experience of the past century; see, however, the epilogue to L.F.S. Upton, *Micmacs and Colonists: Indian-White Relations in the Maritimes, 1713–1867* (V: UBCP 1979). Black Maritimers fare somewhat better. See Robin W. Winks, *The Blacks in Canada: A History* (M and K: MQUP 1971), D.H.J. Clairmont, *Nova Scotian Blacks: An Historical and Structural Overview* (H: Dalhousie University 1970), and Clairmont's *Africville: The Life and Death of a Canadian Black Community* (rev. ed., T: Canadian Scholars Press 1987).

SOCIAL MOVEMENTS AND SOCIAL PROBLEMS

Historians have only recently begun to take an interest in social movements in the Atlantic provinces. The earliest social movement in the post-Confederation era was a nexus of temperance, social gospel, and feminism. The first significant work on the subject was E.R. Forbes, 'Prohibition and the Social Gospel in Nova Scotia' (cited above). Later studies of prohibition include J.P. Couturier, 'Prohiber ou contrôler? L'application de l'Acte de Témperance du Canada à Moncton, NB, 1881–1896,' *Acadiensis* 1988, and 'Splendeur et misère du sentiment prohibitioniste: étude des referendum sur le comté de Westmorland, NB, 1879–1899,' *Revue de l'Université de Moncton* 1987. The essays by C.M. Davis and Judith Fingard in J.H. Morrison and James Moreira, eds., *Tempered by Rum: Rum in the History of the Maritime Provinces* (Porters Lake: Pottersfield Press 1988), and E.R. Forbes's introduction to Clifford Rose, *Four Years with the Demon Rum, 1925–1929: The Autobiography and Diary of Temperance Inspector Clifford Rose* (F: AP 1980). In the woman's suffrage movement see Forbes, 'Battles in Another War.' An insight into the urban underclass is provided in Judith Fingard, *The Dark Side of Life in Victorian Halifax* (Porters Lake: Pottersfield Press 1989). Studies which link the earlier social gospel concerns with those for a cooperative social order include J.K. Chapman, 'Henry Harvey Stuart (1873–1952): New Brunswick Reformer,' *Acadiensis* 1976, and D. Frank and N. Reilly, 'The Emergence of the Socialist Movement in the Maritimes, 1899–1916,' in Robert J. Brym and R.J. Sacoumen, eds., *Underdevelopment and Social Movements in Atlantic Canada* (T: New Hogtown Press 1979), and George Boyle, *Father Tompkins of Nova Scotia* (T: RP 1953). On the cooperative movement see Gregory Baum, *Catholics and Canadian Socialism*, Jean Daigle, *Une Force qui nous appartient: La Fédération des caisses populaires acadiennes, 1936–1986* (Moncton: Editions d'acadie 1990); R.J. Sacouman, 'Underdevelopment and the Structural Origins of the Antigonish Movement Co-operatives and Eastern Nova Scotia,' *Acadiensis* 1977; Ian MacPherson, 'Patterns in the Maritime Co-operative Movement, 1900–1945,' *Acadiensis* 1975, and 'Appropriate Forms of Enterprise: The Prairies and Maritime Co-operative Movements, 1905–1955,' *Acadiensis* 1978, and his book *Each for All: A History of the Co-operative Movement in English Canada, 1900–1945* (T: MAC 1979); L.G. Barrett, 'Underdevelopment and Social Movements in the Nova Scotia Fishing Industry to 1938,' in Brym and Sacoumen, eds., *Underdevelopment and Social Movements in Atlantic Canada*. On the early development of the CCF see M. Earle and H. Gamberg, 'The United Mine Workers and the Coming of the CCF to Cape Breton,' *Acadiensis* 1989.

URBAN HISTORY

There has been a long tradition of community studies in the region. Almost all are antiquarian in nature but provide a perspective and a narrative of events that are often useful. The best known of the popular histories is Thomas Raddall, *Halifax: Warden of the North* (rev. ed., T: M&S 1971). A more recent study of St John's is Paul O'Neill, *The Story of St John's Newfoundland*, vol. 1, *The Oldest City* (Erin: Press Porcépic 1975). Recent scholarly studies have begun to provide insights into the structures and problems of the region's major urban centres. The nationalization of the port of Saint John, is examined by Elizabeth McGahan in *The Port Of Saint John*, vol.1, *From Confederation to Nationalization, 1867–1927, A Study in the Process of Integration* (Saint John: National Harbours Board 1982). Another insight into the social order of the city is provided by Greg Marquis in '"A Machine of Oppression under the Guise of the Law": The Saint John Police Establishment,' *Acadiensis* 1986. Aspects of the Halifax experience are found in Judith Fingard's *The Dark Side of Life*; in Henry Roper, 'The Halifax Board of Control: The Failure of Municipal Reform,

1906–1919,' *Acadiensis* 1985; in Suzanne Morton, 'The Halifax Relief Commission and Labour Relations during the Reconstruction of Halifax, 1917-1919,' *Acadiensis* 1989; and in the essays of Jim Phillips and B.J. Price in Girard and Phillips, eds., *Essays in the History of Canadian Law*, vol. 3. St John's is well served by a volume of essays by M. Baker, R. Cuff, and B. Gillespie *Workingman's St John's: Aspects of Social History in the 1900s* (St John's: Harry Cuff 1982). A similar collection serves the same purpose for Charlottetown; see Douglas Baldwin and Thomas Spira, eds., *Gaslights, Epidemics, and Vagabond Cows: Charlottetown in the Victoria Era* (Charlottetown: Ragweed Press 1988). On Moncton see the essays in Daniel Hickey, ed., *Moncton 1881–1929*. A brief overview of the early Nova Scotia experience is D.A. Muise, 'The Great Transformation: Changing the Urban Face of Nova Scotia, 1891–1921,' *Nova Scotia Historical Review* 1991.

MIGRATION

Given the centrality of migration to the regional experience there is a small, but growing literature on the subject. The most useful overview is Patricia Thornton, 'The Problem of Out-Migration from Atlantic Canada, 1871–1921,' *Acadiensis* 1985. See also A.A. Brookes, 'Out-Migration from the Maritime Provinces, 1860–1900: Some Preliminary Considerations,' *Acadiensis* 1976; and 'The Golden Age and the Exodus: The Case of Canning, Kings County,' *Acadiensis* 1981; T.W. Acheson, 'A Study in the Historical Demography of a Loyalist County,' *HS/SH* 1966; and Claire Quintal, *L'émigrant acadien vers les Etats-Unis: 1842–1950* (Q: Conseil du vie française en Amérique 1984). An interesting case study of intraregional migration is found in Ron Crawley, 'Off to Sydney: Newfoundlanders Emigrate to Industrial Cape Breton, 1890–1940,' *Acadiensis* 1988.

CULTURE

The cultural history of the region is also beginning to receive attention as a worthwhile area of study. The uses of the Loyalist legacy are discussed by Murray Barkley in 'The Loyalist Tradition in New Brunswick: The Growth and Evolution of a Myth,' in *Acadiensis* 1975. The image of the Acadians is considered in Naomi Griffiths, 'Longfellow's *Evangeline:* The Birth and Acceptance of a Legend,' *Acadiensis* 1982. Attitudes towards scientific discovery and the reconciliation of science and religion are found in Paul Bogaard, ed., *Profiles of Science and Society in the Maritimes prior to*

1914 (F: AP 1990). The literary history of the Maritimes is reviewed in Janice Kulyk Keefer, *Under Eastern Eyes: A Critical Reading of Maritime Fiction* (T: UTP 1987), and in Gwendolyn Davies, *Studies in Maritime Literary History, 1760–1930* (F: AP 1991). The role of the political cartoonist in the Maritime Rights movement is discussed by Margaret Conrad in 'The Political Cartoons of Donald McRitchie 1904–1937,' *Acadiensis* 1991. The romantic vision of regional culture is examined in two articles by Ian McKay, 'Among the Fisherfolk: J.F.B. Livesay and the Invention of Peggy's Cove,' *JCS* 1988, and 'Tartanism Triumphant: The Construction and Uses of Scottishness in Nova Scotia,' *Acadiensis* 1992. Two studies of the cultural meaning to be found in the built environment of the region are P. Ennals and D. Holdsworth, 'Vernacular Architecture and the Cultural Landscape of the Maritime Provinces – A Reconnaissance,' *Acadiensis* 1981, and Gerald Posius, *A Place to Stand: Community Order and Everyday Space in Calvert, Newfoundland* (M and K: MQUP 199).

The recent emergence of a small but significant body of historical writing relating to the general culture development of the Atlantic provinces is symbolic of the vitality of the regional historiography. The work of a generation of historians, reflected in this chapter, provides examples of virtually every genre, approach, and methodology found in the discipline. No Canadian historian in 1993 can speak of the Maritimes as a place where nothing happens and nothing changes.

ANDRÉE LÉVESQUE

Quebec

Each generation writes its own history. This is all the more true when the generations experience a war, or a quiet revolution, or important political or demographic changes. New subjects become worthy of historical enquiry; old ones call for a reinterpretation in the light of newly uncovered documents of contemporary concerns. In Quebec historiography, we have witnessed the shift from political history to broader social considerations and the study of social institutions and social groups; we have seen labour history moving from labour organization and political action to the experience of the working class. In this account of the essential canons, I have included all the significant recent books and a few articles but I have also retained most of the main titles found in previous editions of this volume. Students and researchers should still consult previous editions for references to the works I have had to discard, either because their interpretations have been superseded or, especially in the case of articles, because of ruthless choices I had to make to respect the suggested length of the chapter. This bibliography is limited to Quebec; with few exceptions, it does not deal with French Canada and francophones outside Quebec, as these citations will be found under the appropriate regional chapters.

BIBLIOGRAPHIES AND GENERAL WORKS

Quebec history has been the subject of a number of excellent bibliographies, some general and others very specialized. Any student of Quebec history has to start by consulting the latest comprehensive annotated bibliography, the *Guide d'histoire du Québec du Régime français à nos jours: bibliographie commentée* (M: Méridien 1991), edited by Jacques Rouillard with the collaboration of seventeen specialists, each presenting the state of the art in their particular field. Over a third of the book deals with the period since 1867. Here one finds historiographical essays assessing all the major, and some of the minor, books as well as a number of articles, covering the main fields of historical investigation.

More exhaustive but less analytical is Paul Aubin's multivolume and very thorough *Bibliographie de l'histoire du Québec et du Canada/Bibliography of the History of Quebec and Canada* (Q: IQRC 1981, 1985, 1987, 1991), which includes books, articles, and theses. The collection picks up where Claude Thibault left off, in 1946, in his *Bibliographica Canadiana* (T: Longmans 1973). There also exists a bibliography of bibliographies by H.-B. Boivin, *Bibliographie de bibliographies québécoises* (Q: BNQ 1979, 1981). Much Quebec historiography has focused on Montreal, and this is reflected in the excellent *Clés pour l'histoire de Montréal: bibliographie* (M: BE 1992), put together by Joanne Burgess, Louise Dechêne, Paul-André Linteau, and Jean-Claude Robert. All bibliographies suffer from the shortcomings inherent in this kind of work: by the time they are published, they are in need of updating. To keep up with the latest publications, one should go to the *Revue d'histoire de l'Amérique française*'s quarterly bibliographies, as well as those published by the *Canadian Historical Review* and *Labour/Le Travail*.

Historiographical reviews, such as Pierre Savard, 'Un quart de siècle d'historiographie québécoise, 1947–1972,' *RS* 1974, appear from time to time in most historical journals. Published in the 1980s, the following reflect their authors' preoccupations and specializations: Michael Behiels, 'Recent Contributions to the History of Twentieth-Century Quebec,' *CHR*, 1987; Fernand Ouellet, 'La modernisation de l'historiographie et l'émergence de l'histoire sociale,' *RS* 1985; Ronald Rudin, 'Recent Trends in Quebec Historiography,' *QQ*, 1985 and his 'Revisionism and the Search for a Normal Society: A Critique of Recent Quebec Historical Writing,' *CHR* 1992.

The basic survey of the history of the twentieth-century Quebec is Paul-André Linteau, René Durocher, and Jean-Claude Robert, *Quebec: A History*, vol. 1, *1867–1929* (T: JL 1983) and vol. 2, with François Ricard, *Quebec since 1930* (T: JL 1991). Organized by themes within each chronological period, this major synthesis is the result of the collective effort of specialists in political, social, urban, and cultural history. Brian Young and John A. Dickinson have produced a good but more general survey, from pre-contact Native society to Oka crisis in 1990, *A Short History of Québec: A Socio-Economic Perspective* (2nd. ed., Mississauga: CCP 1993). Those searching into the arcane details of provincial politics can probe

Robert Rumilly, *Histoire de la Province de Québec*, 35 vols. (M: various publishers 1940–69). Often referred to as a chronicle, this multivolume work would not meet the test of modern scholarship but remains useful for specific events, provided one goes on to other sources. Similarly, Mason Wade, *The French Canadians, 1760–1967* (rev. ed., T: MAC 1968), although a more rigorous piece of work, now possesses a mainly historiographical interest. Susan Mann Trofimenkoff, *The Dream of Nation: A Social and Intellectual History of Quebec* (T: MAC 1982), manages to weave the experience of women into the evolution of nationalism from New France to the 1980 referendum, and thus sheds new light on the growth of Quebec society and Quebec nationalism.

Finally, for statistical data, apart from government publications, researchers should consult Gérald Bernier and Robert Boily, *Le Québec en chiffres de 1850 à nos jours* (Q: Association canadienne-français pour l'avancement des sciences 1986).

POLITICAL HISTORY

There are a few up-to-date, specialized bibliographies of Quebec political history, although Robert Boily, *Québec, 1940–1969, Bibliographie: le système politique et son environnement* (M: PUM 1971) should be mentioned. There are also bibliographies collated by the Quebec National Assembly Library: Robert Comeau and Michel Lévesque, eds., *Le Parti Québécois: bibliographie rétrospective* (Q: BANQ 1991); Michel Lévesque and Robert Comeau, eds., *Le Parti Libéral du Québec: bibliographie rétrospective (1867–1990)* (Q; BANQ 1991); and Michel Lévesque, ed., *L'Union nationale: bibliographie* (Q: BANQ 1988).

Until 1970, Quebec history was mainly traditional political history, often framed in a conservative perspective, enumerating and dissecting the various nationalist currents, constitutional problems, and relations with Canada, as well as the interactions between religious and political elites. To this period belong both Robert Rumilly and Mason Wade (cited above). With the blooming of social and economic history, and the ideological concerns of the 70s, historians have turned away from political history, leaving much of the field to political scientists, sociologists, and journalists.

Among the exceptional historical monographs in this area, Marcel Hamelin, *Les premières années du parlementarisme québécois, 1867–1878* (Q: PUL 1974) contributes to the understanding of the immediate aftermath of Confederation. A.I. Silver, *The French-Canadian Idea of Confedera-*

tion 1864–1900 (T: UTP 1982) traces the evolution of the francophone attitude to Confederation from 1867 through the language and school crises in New Brunswick and Manitoba, the Riel affair, and the advent of the Laurier government.

Electoral politics, long referred to as Quebec's national sport, have generated both document collections and serious treatises. For raw data, one can consult Pierre Drouilly, *Atlas des élections au Québec, 1867–1985* (Q: BANQ 1989), and *Statistiques électorales fédérales du Québec, 1867–1985* (Q: VLB 1986). The question of parliamentary representation is broached by, among others, Louis Massicote and André Bernard, *Le scrutin au Québec: un miroir déformant* (M: HMH 1985). Vincent Lemieux's analysis of provincial elections since 1936 can be found in *Le quotient politique vrai: la vote provincial et fédéral au Québec* (Q: PUL 1973), to be supplemented by articles found in Lemieux, ed., *Personnel et partis politiques au Québec: aspects historiques* (M: BE 1982). In *Le Parti libéral du Québec: alliances rivalités, et neutralités* (Q: PUL 1993), Lemieux analyses more specifically the provincial Liberal Party since 1897, with a particular stress on the post-Duplessis period. For the uneasy position of the federal Conservative Party from the 1930s to the 1960s, and its valiant efforts to gain a foothold in Quebec, see Marc La Terreur, *Les Tribulations des conservateurs au Québec de Bennett à Diefenbaker* (Q: PUL 1973).

There is no lack of articles on recent elections. Of interest to historians are Vincent Lemieux et al., *Quatre élections provinciales au Québec: 1956–1966* (Q: PUL 1969), Jean Crête, ed., *Comportement électoral au Québec* (Chicoutimi: Gaëtan Morin 1984), and Rejéan Pelletier, *Partis politiques et société québécoise: de Duplessis à Bourassa, 1944–1970* (M: Q/A 1989). More specifically on electoral platforms, there is Jean-Louis Roy, *Les Programmes électoraux du Québec: un siècle de programmes politiques québécois*, 2 vols. (M: Leméac 1970, 1971). James Iain Gow, *Histoire de l'administration publique québécoise, 1867–1970* (M: PUM 1986) traces the development of government institutions as the state took an increasing role in Quebec society. Yves Vaillancourt's *L'évolution des politiques sociales au Québec, 1940–1960* (M: PUM 1988) looks at the implementation of the welfare state in the framework of class relations, and presents the interests and the social thinking of the workers, the middle class, and the capitalist bourgeoisie in the twenty years preceding the Quiet Revolution. Alain Pontaut, *Santé et sécurité: un bilan du régime québécois de santé et sécurité au travail, 1885–1985* (M: BE 1985) focuses on health and safety issues. Arthur Tremblay et al., *Le ministère de l'Education et le Conseil supérieur*, vol. 1, *antécédents et création, 1867–1964* (Q: PUL 1989), presents the evolution of Quebec public school system by one personally involved in the educational reforms of the 1960s.

For a long time, there were few biographies of Quebec politicians, and those that existed were mostly hagiographic. More recently, well-researched biographies, first of federal politicians then of provincial ones, have started filling this gap. Quebec's most famous Father of Confederation, George-Etienne Cartier, has inspired two biographies: one by Alastair Sweeney, (T: M&S 1976), and Brian Young's fine example of the new political history, *George-Etienne Cartier: Montreal Bourgeois*, (M and K: MQUP 1981). Cartier's successor as leader of the Conservative Party, Hector-Louis Langevin, is the subject of a solid biography by Andrée Désilets, *Hector-Louis Langevin: un père de la Confédération canadienne (1826–1906)* (Q: PUL 1969), which is also illuminating on church-state relations at the time of Confederation. For the same period, but on the provincial scene, Kenneth Munro, *The Political Career of Sir Adolphe Chapleau, Premier of Quebec, 1879–1882* (Lewiston: Edwin Mellen Press 1992) is the definitive biography of this nineteenth-century politician. The prime minister of 'Canada's Century,' Wilfrid Laurier, has inspired three biographies which reflect three generations of biographers: Joseph Schull, *Laurier: The First Canadian* (T: MAC 1965); H. Blair Neatby, *Laurier and a Liberal Quebec: A Study in Political Management* (T: M&S 1973): and Réal Bélanger, *Wilfrid Laurier: quand la politique devient passion* (Q: PUL CBC 1986).

The career of Henri Bourassa, journalist and politician active at the federal and provincial levels, has been sympathetically reported by Robert Rumilly, *Henri Bourassa: la vie d'un grand Canadien* (M: Chantecler 1953). Joseph Levitt, *Henri Bourassa and the Golden Calf: The Social Programme of the Nationalists of Quebec (1900–1914)* (2nd. ed., O: UOP 1972) explores the economic nationalism and the social ideas of Bourassa and five pre-1914 nationalists to refute the previously held belief that they opposed modern industrial development.

Bernard L. Vigod, *Quebec before Duplessis: The Political Career of Louis-Alexandre Taschereau* (M and K: MQUP 1986) paints a generous view of a premier long associated with corruption and longevity. In the 1920s, Taschereau was also responsible for important social legislation which, together with his opposition to nationalism, alarmed the clerical-nationalist elites of the time. Church-state relations under his premiership are the subject of Antonin Dupont, *Les relations entre l'Eglise et l'Etat sous Louis-Alexandre Taschereau, 1920–1936* (M: Guérin 1972). Paul Gouin, leader of the 1935 dissident liberal group, *L'Action libérale nationale*, has recently found a biographer in Philippe Ferland, *Paul Gouin* (M: Guérin 1991).

Maurice Duplessis's terms as premier, 1936–9 and 1944–59, have left a deep, and at times exaggerated, imprint on Quebec history, and it has taken a long time to produce scholarly assessments of those years. A bit dated and overly sympathetic is the published version of Conrad Black's MA thesis, *Duplessis* (T: M&S 1977). A good appraisal of his government, rather than only of the man himself, is Herbert F. Quinn, *The Union Nationale: Quebec Nationalism from Duplessis to Lévesque* (2nd ed., T: UTP 1979). Political scientist Gérard Boismenu's *Le Duplessisme: politiques économiques et rapport de force, 1944–1960* (M: PUM 1981) focuses on the premier's populism and his political representation of the Quebec bourgeoisie.

Both world wars resulted in painful rifts in Quebec politics and society, first on the question of participation, and more traumatically on that of conscription. On the Great War and Quebec opposition to conscription, the standard account remains Elizabeth H. Armstrong, *The Crisis of Quebec, 1914–1918* (1937, T: M&S 1974). André Laurendeau has left his personal assessment of the conscription crisis, *La Crise de la conscription, 1942* (M: Editions du Jour 1962). The conscription crises of both world wars are aptly and thoughtfully examined in J.L. Granatstein and J.M. Hitsman, *Broken Promises: A History of Conscription in Canada* (T: OUP 1977). Jean-Pierre Gagnon, *Le 22e bataillon (canadien-français), 1914–1919: étude socio-militaire* (Q: PUL 1986) is as much a social history as it is a military history of the largely francophone batallion.

The persecution of the Jehovah's Witnesses in Quebec belongs more to political history than to religious history. Journalist Michel Sarra-Bournet, *L'affaire Roncarelli: Duplessis contre les Témoins de Jéhovah* (Q: IQRC 1986) looks at the legal battle surrounding the restaurant owner who lost his licence for his beliefs until a provincial judgement was reversed by the Supreme Court of Canada.

There is no doubt that the Quiet Revolution marks a crucial turning point in the history of twentieth-century Quebec, but was it really such a break or did it not rather follow from the postwar unrest, or even from the transformations wrought by the war? Instead of a watershed, wasn't it more what Susan Mann Trofimenkoff, in *The Dream of Nation*, called a 'noisy evolution'? Claude Couture, *Le Mythe de la modernisation du Québec: des années 1930 à la Révolution tranquille* (M: Méridien 1991), supports this latter view by juxtaposing ideas expressed in Montreal and Quebec City's three major daily newspapers with government policies and pronouncements of the elites. The postwar years have now been called *la grande noirceur*, and emphasis on Maurice Duplessis's personal style and repressive policies has obscured the persistent opposition to the Union Nationale.

Léon Dion brings these elements to light in *Québec, 1945–1960*, vol. 1, *À la recherche du Québec*, and vol. 2, *Les intellectuels et le temps de Duplessis* (Q: PUL 1987, 1993). Michael Behiels, *Prelude to Quebec's Quiet Revolution: Liberalism versus Neo-nationalism, 1945–1960* (M and K: MQUP 1985) turns to federal-provincial relations in the postwar period as the roots of change. Articles on different aspects of that period are assembled in Michael Behiels, *Quebec since 1945: Selected Readings* (T: CCP 1987).

The Quiet Revolution never stops inspiring colloquia, conferences, collections of articles, and monographs. Kenneth McRoberts, *Quebec: Social Change and Political Crisis* (3rd ed., T: M&S 1988), is particularly concerned with modernization in the wake of the Quiet Revolution. Leader of the opposition in the 1950s and one of the most important reformers behind the 1960s Quiet Revolution, Georges-Emile Lapalme is the subject of a collection of papers published by Jean-François Léonard et al., eds., *Georges-Emile Lapalme* (Sillery: PUQ 1988). In *Jean Lesage and the Quiet Revolution* (T: MAC 1984), political scientist Dale Thomson has written a thorough biography of the premier closely identified with the reforms of the sixties. Yearly colloquia organized by the Université du Québec à Montréal on contemporary Quebec political leaders have yielded interesting, although at times uneven, collections of papers. Those prepared for the colloquium on Jean Lesage have been edited by Robert Comeau et al., in *Jean Lesage et l'éveil d'une nation: les débuts de la Révolution tranquille* (Sillery: PUQ 1989). The proceedings of another colloquium on Union Nationale Premier Daniel Johnson have been published in Robert Comeau, Michel Lévesque, and Yves Bélanger, eds., *Daniel Johnson: Rêve d'égalité et projet d'indépendance* (Sillery: PUQ 1991). Johnson also has been the subject of a biography by Pierre Godin, *Daniel Johnson*, 2 vols. (M: Editions de l'Homme 1980). A number of journalists have published impressions and interpretations of their ex-colleague Réne Lévesque. Jean Provencher, *René Lévesque: portrait d'un Québécois* (M: La Presse 1974), translated as *René Lévesque: Portrait of a Quebecois* (Markham: Paperjacks 1977), is quite dated but informative for the years before the election of Parti Québécois. Graham Fraser, *PQ: René Lévesque and the Parti Québécois in Power* (T: M&S 1984) is a very readable narrative of the post-1976 period.

Despite the dominance of bipartisan politics, third parties of the right and of the left have never been absent from the Québec scene. For CCF and Communist political action during the 1930s, see Andrée Lévesque's *Virage à gauche interdit: les communistes, les socialistes, et leurs ennemis au Québec, 1929–1939* (M: BE 1984). Paul-André Comeau, *Le Bloc Populaire, 1942–1948* (M: Q/A 1982) traces the meteoric career of this short-lived reformist party. Michael Behiels, 'The Bloc Populaire and the Origins of French-Canadian Neo-nationalism, 1942–48,' *CHR* 1982, describes the party's ideological slant and its social program. Resistance to modernization expressed in political protest forms the essence of the Social Credit Party. Michael B. Stein, *The Dynamics of Right-Wing Protest: A Political Analysis of Social Credit in Quebec* (T: UTP 1973) is a fundamental treatment of this form of populist politics in Quebec.

The nationalist ideology has generated political movements for Quebec independence whose development is surveyed in Jean-Claude Robert, *Du Canada français au Québec libre: histoire d'un mouvement indépendantiste* (Paris: Flammarion 1975). In *The Independence Movement in Quebec, 1945–1980* (T: UTP 1984), William D. Coleman looks at the economy and the social structure to find the roots of separatism. Ramsay Cook, *Canada and the French Canadian Question* (T: MAC 1966), also makes nationalism the unified theme of his essay. A severe critic of nationalism, he reaffirms his faith in Confederation on its one hundredth anniversary.

The trauma of the October 1970 crisis has given rise to a number of journalistic studies, but these should be supplemented by Louis Fournier, *FLQ: histoire d'un mouvement clandestin* (M: Q/A 1982), which deals with the Front de Libération du Québec, and by Jean-François Cardin, *Comprendre Octobre 1970: le FLQ, la crise et le syndicalisme* (M: Méridien 1990).

International affairs are of the federal domain but Quebec has long engaged in political and commercial relations with other countries. Pierre Savard, *Le Consulat général de France à Québec et à Montréal de 1859 à 1914* (Q: PUL 1970) approaches French-Quebec relations from the vantage point of the French missions in Quebec and Montreal between the eve of Confederation and the Great War. Since the 1960s, Quebec has stressed its privileged links with France. Dale C. Thomson, *De Gaulle et le Québec* (Saint-Laurent: Trécarré 1990), covers the years from World War II to the culmination of the French president's role as a catalyst in 1967 when his 'Vive le Québec libre' provoked a major diplomatic incident.

We are indebted to political scientists for insightful studies of Quebec relations with the United States. The rise of movements for independence in the 1960s, and more recently the debates over free trade with the United States, have inspired Alfred Olivier Hero, Jr, and Louis Balthazar, *Contemporary Québec and the United States, 1960–1985* (Lanham: UP of America 1988). Jean-François Lisée, *In the Eye of the Eagle* (T: HarperCollins 1990) concludes that the US, while preferring a united Canada, could adapt to an independent Quebec.

Until the 1960s, few political figures left their memoirs, but the generation active in the 1950s and 1960s is now revealing the inner workings of federal and provincial politics, and the relations between the two. Here are a few selections from the most fruitful first-hand writings: Gérard Pelletier, *Years of Impatience, 1950–1960* and *Years of Choice, 1960–1968* (T: Methuen 1984, 1987), and, awaiting translation, *L'aventure du pouvoir, 1968–1975* (M: Stanké 1992). A liberal journalist who has participated in many of the intellectual movements in Quebec since the 1930s, was chief editor of Quebec's largest daily, and who replaced André Laurendeau as chair of the Royal Commission on Bilingualism and Biculturalism, Jean-Louis Gagnon, in his memoirs *Les Apostasies*, 3 vols. (M: La Presse 1985, 1987), reflects on his long career in a lively, literate style and with courageous honesty not always found in personal literature. From a federalist champion of Quebec as a distinct society, a Liberal sitting in the Senate as a Conservative, we have *Regards* (M: Pierre Tisseyre 1966–1990), Solange Chaput-Rolland's multivolume memoir covering the years since the Quiet Revolution. Many more memoirs are being published each year, and can easily be found under their authors' names.

ECONOMIC HISTORY

Economist Gilles Paquet has lamented his colleagues' lack of interest in Quebec's economic history, and has taken stock of their different approaches in *La pensée économique au Québec français* (M: Association Canadienne-français pour l'avancement des sciences 1989) and in 'Le fruit dont l'ombre est la saveur – Réflexions aventureuses sur la pensée économique,' *RS* 1985.

Quebec's economic development, its 'backwardness' and its catching up, has inspired lively debates among historians and economists, yet there is no general economic history of Quebec since Confederation. For the early period, Jean Hamelin and Yves Roby, *Histoire économique du Québec, 1851–1896* (M: Fides 1971) is an excellent synthesis based on the state of the research at the time of publication. Robert Comeau, ed., *Economie québécoise* (Sillery: PUQ 1969) is a collection of essays from the 1960s, on a variety of topics, which cover a long period of time.

The main arguments explaining Quebec's economic development, as they stood some twenty years ago, were brought together in a collection of articles, *Le 'retard' du Québec et l'infériorité économique des Canadiens français* (M: BE 1971), edited by René Durocher and Paul-André Linteau. Maurice Séguin expounds on his thesis about the consequences of the

Conquest of 1763, but in this collection the traditional cultural explanations are superseded by those of Pierre Harvey and especially those of Albert Faucher and Maurice Lamontagne, who in 'L'histoire du développement industriel du Québec' put forth materialist causes such as the distribution of natural resources. This influential article was originally published some twenty years earlier in another important collection, edited by Jean-Charles Falardeau, *Essais sur le Québec contemporain/Essays on Contemporary Quebec* (Q: PUL 1953). An English translation of Faucher and Lamontagne's article is found in Marcel Rioux and Yves Martin, eds., *French Canadian Society* (T: M&S 1964). Their considerations have led to inquiries into French-Canadian representation in the business world, and the growth of the Quebec bourgeoisie. W.F. Ryan, *The Clergy and Economic Growth in Quebec, 1896–1914* (Q: PUL 1966), revises some clichés regarding the clergy's negative influence on industrialization, particularly in the primary sector.

Industrial development cannot be studied without reference to the international context, more specifically to foreign capital, first British, then American. Yves Roby, *Les Québécois et les investissements américains (1918–1929)* (Q: PUL 1976) analyses Quebec's cooperation with American capital to foster industrialization in the interwar period. Maurice Saint-Germain, *Une économie à libérer: le Québec analysé dans ses structures économiques* (M: PUM 1973), offers a socio-economic nationalist point of view of Quebec economic structures. For the pre–1940 period, Robert Armstrong, *Structure and Change: An Economic History of Quebec* (T: Gage 1984) gives an ambitious but partial analysis, focusing on a few key sectors of the economy. It remains a major attempt to grasp Quebec's economic structure and development although it somewhat neglects its North American context.

Staples, of great interest to political economists since the works of Harold A. Innis, have recently elicited the interest of historians. Marc Vallières, *Des mines et des hommes: histoire de l'industrie minérale québécoise des origines au début des années 1980* (Q: Publications du Québec 1989) is a government publication charting the development of a sector of growing importance, especially since World War II. Jean-Pierre Charland, *Les Pâtes et papiers au Québec 1880–1980: technologies, travail et travailleurs* (Q: IQRC 1990) offers a broad survey of Quebec's first industry. Pulp and paper and hydroelectricity developed symbiotically, and John H. Dales, *Hydroelectricity and Industrial Development: Quebec, 1898–1940* (Cambridge: HUP 1957) is still a reliable treatment of the early development of Quebec's main energy resource.

Acknowledging the importance of railway construction in the nineteenth century, Brian J. Young, *Promoters and Politicians: The North-Shore Railways in the History of Quebec, 1854–85* (T: UTP 1978) examines the close interconnection between business and politics. Although American capital plays an important role in Quebec's economic development, indigenous financial institutions have also aroused the interest of historians. Ronald Rudin, *Banking en français: The French Banks of Quebec, 1835–1925* (T: UTP 1985) documents nearly a century of francophone banking. In his revisionist interpretation of Quebec's banking institutions, Rudin uses the example of Lévis to produce *In Whose Interest? Quebec's Caisses Populaires, 1900–1945* (M and K: MQUP 1990). Adopting a class perspective, he concludes that the Caisses populaires were not so much a mass movement, as previously believed, as they were an instrument of the petite bourgeoisie. This view is at times at odds with previous histories of this cooperative institution, such as Yves Roby, *Alphonse Desjardins et les Caisses populaires, 1854–1920* (M: Fides 1964), and Pierre Poulin, *Histoire du Mouvement Desjardins*, vol. 1, *Desjardins et la naissance des Caisses populaires, 1900–1920* (M: Q/A 1990). For an inside view of the business world as seen by a French Canadian, see Joseph-Edmond McComber, *Mémoires d'un bourgeois de Montréal (1874–1949)* (M: HMH 1980). Yves Bélanger and Pierre Fournier, *L'entreprise québécoise: développement historique et dynamique contemporaine* (M: HMH 1987), a study of entrepreneurs and their businesses, is particularly useful for the last twenty years.

Regional studies, often fostered by the Institut québécois de recherche sur la culture, are filling some gaps in specific economic sectors in certain regions. Agriculture, Quebec's vocation according to generations of politicians and clergymen, has consequently long been neglected by historians eager to document Quebec's industrial contribution. This is now being remedied by monographs such as Normand Séguin, *La conquête du sol au 19e siècle* (M: BE 1977), and a collection he edited, *Agriculture et colonisation au Québec: aspects historiques* (M: BE 1980), which examine the close interrelationship between agriculture and the forest industry. The small family farm that dominated the Quebec rural scene is studied in M. Morisset, *L'Agriculture familiale au Québec* (M: L'Harmattan 1987). Changes in the rural economy, especially since the 1960s, are charted in a collection of articles by Gérald Fortin, *La fin d'un règne* (M: HHM 1971).

Pierre Trépanier, *Siméon Le Sage: un haut fonctionnaire québécois face aux défis de son temps (1867–1909)* (M: Bellarmin 1979) is the biography of Quebec's minister of public works for the first thirty years after Confederation. The author stresses his efforts to modernize the Quebec economy, in particular agriculture, and does not hide his sympathies for Le Sage's nationalist endeavours.

SOCIAL HISTORY

Sociologists cast their eyes on Quebec's social structure long before social historians scrutinized the development of social classes and the French-Canadian position in Canadian society. While Everett C. Hughes's *French Canada in Transition* (1943, Chicago: University of Chicago Press 1965) is still of interest, the changes brought about by the Quiet Revolution of the 1960s fostered new approaches to understanding Quebec society. The most important examples of these can be found in Rioux and Martin, eds., *French Canadian Society*, (cited above).

The upheavals of the 1960s, the politicization of sociologists, and the Marxist influence on the social sciences have resulted in important theoretical writings on social class in Quebec. These early essays are complied and annotated in Fernand Harvey and Gilles Houde, eds., *Les classes sociales au Canada et au Québec: bibliographie annotée* (Q: Institut supérieur des sciences humaines 1979). The concept of ethnic class underlines Jacques Dofny and Marcel Rioux, 'Social Classes in French Canada,' in Martin and Rioux, eds., *French-Canadian Society*. John Porter, *The Vertical Mosaic: An Analysis of Social Class and Power in Canada* (T: UTP 1965) is a landmark in the analysis of Canadian elites, and its discussion of socio-economic and ethnic stratification is directly relevant to Quebec society. Sociologist Hubert Guindon's pioneering articles on social class and modernization, first published in the 1960s and 1970s, have been brought together in *Quebec Society: Tradition, Modernity, and Nationhood*, (T: UTP 1988), edited by Roberta Hamilton and John L. McMullan. Roch Denis, *Luttes des classes et question nationale au Québec, 1948–1968* (M: Presses socialistes internationales 1979) brings together the questions of nationalism and labour political action. In Paul R. Bélanger et al., *Animation et culture en mouvement: fin ou début d'une époque?* (Sillery: PUQ 1987), we see current concerns for social movements, community organizations, and popular groups that have been springing up since the 1960s.

The dramatic drop in the birthrate in the last thirty years, as well as the shifts in the distribution of ethnic groups, have elicited the concerns of all sectors of society, not the least those of demographers, who have moved from gathering data on New France to drafting projections into the future. The first volume devoted to the topic, *La population du Québec: études rétrospectives* (M: BE 1973), edited by Hubert Charbonneau, offers examples of the early spadework on demography from New France to the twentieth century. Since then, worries about the future of Quebec's francophone population have led to distinctly natalist positions such as those of Jacques Henripin in *Naître ou ne pas être* (Q: IQRC 1989). A new specialization, demolinguistics, traces the evolution of language groups and linguistic transfers. Réjan Lachapelle and Jacques Henripin, *La situation démolinguistique au Canada: évolution passée et prospective* (M: Institut de Recherches politiques 1980), and Marc Termote and Danielle Gauvreau, *La situation démolinguistique du Québec* (Q: Conseil de la langue française 1988) analyse these phenomena, especially, since 1951.

LABOUR AND WORKING-CLASS HISTORY

Recent work in social history reflects Quebec society in its specific class, gender, and ethnic components. The evolution of labour history in Quebec and in Canada, and their different *problématiques*, are compared by Joanne Burgess, 'Exploring the Limited Identities of Canadian Labour: Recent Trends in English Canada and Quebec,' *IJCS* 1990. Here, the major books and articles published since the mid-seventies are placed in their historiographical and social context. To keep up with the latest trends, one should consult the *Bulletin du Regroupement des chercheurs-chercheures en Histoire des travailleurs et travailleuses du Québec*.

Labour history took off in the 1970s, but at first limited itself to trade union history. Then historians turned to labour political action and more recently to the working class. Anglophone readers wanting an overview of Quebec labour organizations would do well to read Bernard Dionne's short and clear synthesis, *Le syndicalisme au Québec* (M: BE 1991), and Louis Fournier et al., *The History of the Labour Movement in Quebec* (M: Black Rose 1987). The latter, a collective endeavour, was sponsored by the Confédération des Syndicats nationaux and the Centrale de l'enseignement du Québec and is aimed at an audience of trade unionists. Do not expect footnotes, but it is useful for its descriptions of strikes and labour legislation.

Much more comprehensive is Jacques Rouillard's *Histoire du syndicalisme au Québec: des origines à nos jours* (M: BE 1989). Based on exhaustive research, this straightforward account of the development of trade unions is the main reference text on labour organizations. Historians have long been intrigued by Catholic unionism, stressing its religious character and its submission to authority. Rouillard's *Histoire de la CSN, 1921–1981* (M: BE 1981) and his *Les Syndicats nationaux au Québec de 1900 à 1930*

(M: PUL 1979) challenge this simplistic view by showing a more complex picture of the preachings on class harmony and the reality of labour conflicts.

International unions have not only been more numerous but also more militant than the Catholic unions. While a definitive monograph on their activities is still not forthcoming, there are some articles on unions affiliated with the American Federation of Labor. To cite but a few: Robert Babcock, 'Samuel Gompers et les travailleurs québécois, 1900–1914,' in Fernand Harvey, ed., *Le mouvement ouvrier au Québec: aspects historiques*, (M: BE 1980); Bernard Dionne, 'Les Canadiens français et les syndicats internationaux: le cas de la direction du Conseil des Métiers et du Travail de Montréal (1938–1958),' *RHAF* 1980, and his *Cents ans de solidarité: Histoire du CTM, 1886–1986* (M: VLB 1987). In a rather admiring mode, journalist Louis Fournier, *Louis Laberge: le syndicalisme c'est ma vie* (M: Q/A 1992), provides an informative biography of the colourful leader of the Fédération des travailleurs du Québec.

Fernand Harvey ed., *Révolution industrielle et travailleurs: une enquête sur les rapports entre le capital et le travail au Québec à la fin du 19e siècle* (M: BE 1978), using the findings of the Royal Commission on the Relations of Capital and Labour, documents working conditions and labour relations in the 1880s. Fernand Harvey, ed., *Aspects historiques du mouvement ouvrier au Québec* (M: BE 1973) includes pieces on early labour political action.

Radical unionism and labour involvement in left politics have attracted a new generation of historians, no doubt influenced by the political turmoil and the growth of militancy in the 1970s. A substantial collection of essays edited by Robert Comeau and Bernard Dionne, *Le droit de se taire: histoire des communistes au Québec, de la Première Guerre mondiale à la Révolution tranquille* (M: VLB 1989), touches upon various aspects of the Communist Party of Canada's activities in politics, in the labour movement, and in the arts. It includes biographical articles on famous Communists such as Norman Bethune, Stanley Bréhaut Ryerson, Fred Rose, and Henri Gagnon. Robert Comeau and Bernard Dionne, *Les communistes au Québec, 1936–1956: sur le Parti communiste du Canada, Parti ouvrier-progressiste* (M: Presses de l'Unité 1981), translated as *Communism in Québec, 1936–1956; The Communist Party of Canada, Labour-Progressive Party* (M: Presses de l'Unité 1982), surveys twenty crucial years of Communist activities. Bernard Gauvin, *Les communistes et la question nationale, 1921–1938: sur le Parti communiste du Canada de 1921 à 1938* (M: Presses de l'Unité 1981), tackles an issue which proved a major stumbling block to the Communist Party in Quebec. Journalist Merrily Weisbord, relying on extensive interviews, sketches lively portraits of Communist militants from the 1930s to the 1960s in *The Strangest Dream: Canadian Communists, the Spy Trials, and the Cold War* (T: Lester & Orpen Dennys 1983). More recent studies of labour in politics include Roch Denis and Serge Denis, *Les syndicats face au pouvoir: Syndicalisme et politique au Québec de 1960 à 1992* (M: Vermillion 1992), a not too rigorous study dealing with the unions' attitude to nationalism and their relations with the main political parties. Covering the same period is Pierre Vennat's journalistic account, *Une révolution non-tranquille: le syndicalisme au Québec de 1960 à l'an 2000* (M: Méridien 1992).

Research on labour organization by trade is still incomplete. In editing *The Asbestos Strike* (T: James Lewis and Samuels 1974), Pierre Elliott Trudeau expounded his views on nationalism as the culprit for Quebec's backwardness. Gilbert Vanasse, *Histoire de la Fédération des travailleurs du papier et de la forêt (CSN)*, vol. 1, *1907–1958* (M: Editions Albert Saint-Martin 1986), examines the long record of exploitation and difficult labour relations in what was, since the nineteenth century, the first sector of Quebec's economy. One lumbermen's strike in 1933, involving the communist Workers' Unity League in north-west Quebec, has been the object of Béatrice Richard's published MA thesis, *'Péril rouge' au Témiscamingue: la grève des bûcherons de Rouyn-Noranda, 1933–1934* (M: RCHTQ 1993).

The longest tradition of labour organization belongs to what is commonly referred to as the 'aristocracy of labour,' the printing trades. In *Fédération professionnelle des journalistes du Québec* (M: Méridien 1989), François Demers, a journalist active in the Fédération nationale des communications, surveys the struggles of the printing trades in the nineteenth and twentieth centuries, and those involving journalists after their inclusion in the union in 1946. The newspapers' reaction to the serious union clashes with the government over the wage freeze in 1982–3 is analysed by semiotician Maryse Souchard, *Le discours de presse: L'image des syndicats au Québec (1982–1982)* (Q: Préambule 1989). This is unfortunately limited to the deconstruction of texts published in *Le Devoir* but still illustrates very eloquently the anti-labour bias in its reporting.

Organizations that defend class interests can also be found among farmers who, during the progressive wave following the Great War, formed the Union catholique des cultivateurs, later the Union des Producteurs agricoles. Jean-Pierre Kesteman et al., *Histoire du syndicalisme agricole au Québec, UCC-UPA, 1924–1984* (M: BE 1984) is an innovative monograph on a long-neglected topic.

While labour historians went on documenting the evolution of the labour movement, another group of social historians pursued their interest in the 'condition of the working class,' that is, the experience of workers' neighbourhoods, families, and institutions outside the workplace. They first concentrated on the Montreal proletariat, and Yvan Lamonde, Lucia Ferretti, and Daniel Leblanc, eds., *La culture ouvrière à Montréal (1880–1920): bilan historiographique* (Q: IQRC 1982) is an early assessment of this new labour history. For the period before the Great War, Jean de Bonville, *Jean-Baptiste Gagnepetit: les travailleurs montréalais à la fin du XIXe siècle* (M: Aurore 1975), gives a picture of male workers in Montreal before 1900, while Terry Copp, *The Anatomy of Poverty: The Condition of the Working Class in Montreal, 1897–1929* (T: M&S 1974) remains a classic study of working-class living conditions in nineteenth-century Montreal.

Since the 1970s, we have witnessed an increasing number of publications on the working-class family, and more specifically on working-class women and women workers. Family history owes much to Bettina Bradbury's two pathbreaking articles, 'Pigs, Cows, and Boarders: Non-Wage Forms of Survival among Montreal Families, 1861–1891,' *Labour* 1984, and 'Women and Wage Labour in a Period of Transition: Montreal, 1861–1881,' *HS/SH 1984*. These are brought together and expanded in *Working Families: Age, Gender, and Daily Survival in Industrializing Montreal* (T: M&S 1993). At the junction of labour and women's history, Denyse Baillargeon, *Ménagères au temps de la Crise* (M: Editions du Remue-Ménage 1991) uses the techniques of oral history to follow the experience of a sample of working-class housewives during the economic depression of the 1930s. The situation of women industrial workers is as yet documented in only a few articles. Textile workers are investigated by Gail Cuthbert-Brandt in '"Weaving it together": Life Cycle and the Industrial Experience of Female Cotton Workers in Québec, 1910–1959,' *Labour/ Le Travail* 1981, and her 'Transformation of Women's Work in the Quebec Cotton Industry, 1920–1950,' in Bryan Palmer, ed., *The Character of the Class Struggle: Essays in Canadian Working-Class History, 1850–1985* (T: M&S 1986), and in Jacques Rouillard's *Les travailleurs du coton au Québec, 1900–1915* (M: PUQ 1974), which tackles mainly labour organization and working conditions. Besides the textile industry, there are too few studies of women in the labour force outside Montréal. An exception of note is Odette Vincent Domey, *Filles et familles en milieu ouvrier: Hull, Québec à fin du XIXe siècle* (M: RCHTQ 1991).

WOMEN AND THE FAMILY

In the last decade, women's history has been the fastest developing field of Quebec history. Apart from the bibliography in Rouillard's *Guide d'histoire*, there is an interdisciplinary bibliography: Denise Lemieux and Lucie Mercier, *La recherche sur les femmes au Québec: bilan et bibliographie* (Q: IQRC 1982), and a historiographical essay on books published between 1985 and 1990 by Andrée Lévesque, 'Historiography: History of Women in Quebec since 1985,' *Quebec Studies* 1991. In a more polemical vein, one can consult Fernand Ouellet, 'La question sociale au Québec, 1880–1930: la condition féminine et le mouvement des femmes dans l'historiographie,' (HS/SH) 1988, and Micheline Dumont's reply to Ouellet, 'L'histoire des femmes,' (HS/SH) 1990.

The basic text remains *Quebec Women: A History* (T: Women's Press 1987) by the Clio Collective. Written when the history of women was in its early stages (the book was first published in French in 1982), it is sometimes uneven. Nevertheless, it was an ambitious pioneering project and deals in some detail with the areas of specialization of each of the four authors. In French, the Clio Collective has come with a new, revised, and up-to-date edition: *L'histoire des femmes au Québec depuis quatre siècles* (2nd ed., M: Le Jour 1992).

Education was one of the first fields mined by historians of women. Articles on the subject appear in Nadia Fahmy-Eid and Micheline Dumont, eds., *Maîtresses de maison, maîtresses d'école: femmes, famille, et éducation dans l'histoire du Québec* (M: BE 1983), and in the same authors' *Les Couventines: l'éducation des filles au Québec dans les congrégations religieuses enseignantes, 1840–1960* (M: BE 1986). The authors deal with socialization, curricula, private schools, and teachers' unions. In an innovative and thorough monograph, Nicole Thivierge, *Ecoles ménagères et instituts familiaux: un modèle féminin traditionnel* (Q: IQRC 1982) throws new light on the Quebec counterparts to the home science schools from 1882 to their demise with the educational reforms brought about the Quiet Revolution. It stresses the efforts to socialize young women, and the growing discrepancy between the ideals fostered by the schools and Quebec's increasingly urban and industrial reality. Life in a convent school is examined by Marie-Paule Malouin, *Ma soeur, à quelle école allez-vous?: deux écoles de filles à la fin de XIXe Siècle* (M: Fides 1985).

Given the prominent role of religious communities in educational institutions, it is no surprise that nuns have fascinated historians. Marta Danylewycz, *Taking the Veil: An Alternative to Marriage, Motherhood, and Spinsterhood in Quebec, 1840–1920* (T: M&S 1987), is an original study on a subject that has not stopped attracting scholars. The temptation is great for feminists to see a model in those women who escaped the bonds of marriage and submission to the patriarchal family. Nicole Laurin et al., *A la recherche d'un monde oublié: les communautés religieuses de femmes au Québec de 1900 à 1970* (M: Editions du Jour 1991) is the first volume of an in depth investigation of the labour accomplished by nuns, adopt a materialist feminist perspective to document the appropriation of the nuns' labour by a patriarchal society.

Young Quebec women outside the working class had few options if they wanted to enter the labour market. Apart from teaching, nursing was viewed as particularly well suited to feminine qualities of abnegation and sensitivity. A traditional account of the professionalization of a female occupation can be found in André Petitat, *Les Infirmières: de la vocation à la profession* (M: BE 1989). Previously mentioned works by Bettina Bradbury, Denyse Baillargeon, and Gail Cuthbert-Brandt consider the experience of working-class women. Marie Lavigne and Yoland Pinard, eds., *Travailleuses et féministes: Les femmes dans la société québécoise* (M: BE 1983) is a collection that adds to our knowledge of women's wage labour since the 1880s, labour and feminist militancy, and discourse on women. Françine Barry, *Le Travail de la femme au Québec: l'evolution de 1940 à 1970* (M: PUQ 1977) reviews thirty years of participation in paid labour. The twentieth century has witnessed the swelling of the tertiary sector as well as it feminization. Despite Montreal's role as the head office of numerous banks and insurance companies, publications on female office workers have so far been scarce, apart from the Ronald Rudin's work on banking, which touches on the sexual division of labour. Michèle Martin, *'Hello Central?' Gender, Technology, and Culture in the Formation of Telephone Systems* (M and K: MQUP 1991) challenges some received ideas about feminization in a poorly paid occupation enjoying a relatively good social status.

It has often been assumed that, because of the labour of the nuns in the social sector, Quebec women did not engage in volunteer work as much as women did in English Canada. Unpaid labour was never absent, especially for middle-class women, as seen in Aline Charles' *Travail d'ombre et de lumière: le bénévolat féminin à l'Hôpital Sainte-Justine, 1907–1960* (Q: IQRC 1990), an empirical study of volunteers in Montreal's hospital for children. Women's supportive role in the labour movement has been the subject of a published thesis by Sylvie Murray, *A la jonction du mouvement ouvrier et du mouvement des femmes; la Ligue auxiliaires de l'Association internationale des machinistes, 1903–1980* (M: RCHTQ 1990).

Women's first role was that of mothers; making an extensive use of autobiographies, memoirs, and diaries, Denise Lemieux and Lucie Mercier, *Les femmes au tournant du siècle: 1880–1940: âges de la vie, maternité, et quotidien*

(Q: IQRC 1989), with a rather broad definition of 'turn-of-the-century,' examine each stage of women's life cycle as defined by their reproductive function. Juxtaposing society's prescriptions and women's actual behaviour during the interwar period, Andrée Lévesque, *La Norme et les déviantes: des femmes au Québec pendant l'entre-deux-guerres* (M: Editions du Remue-Ménage 1989), translated by Yvonne Klein as *Making and Breaking the Rules* (T: M&S 1994), investigates groups that did not conform to the models: single mothers, prostitutes, and women who resorted to abortion. Aimed at a broad audience, yet based on solid documentation, Geneviève Auger and Raymonde Lamothe's *De la poêle à frire à la ligne de feu: la vie quotidienne des Québécoises pendant la guerre, 1939–1945* (M: BE 1981) presents a lively, well-illustrated chronicle of women's lives during World War II.

ETHNICITY

Françoise Noël, *Bibliographie des thèses et des mémoires sur les communautés culturelles et l'immigration au Québec* (M: PUM 1985) and Gary Caldwell, *Les études ethniques au Québec: bilan et perspectives* (Q: IQRC 1983) should guide the students of ethnic minorities in Quebec.

Anthropological reports on Native people are not lacking, but there are not many historical studies of Amerindians and the Inuit in the twentieth century. The excellent journal *Recherches amérindiennes* publishes the most recent research in the field. Important data, not just for Quebec but for Canada as a whole, have been gathered in Louise Normandeau and Victor Piché, *Les populations amérindiennes et inuit du Canada: Aperçu démographique* (M: PUM 1984). Hélène Bédard, *Les Montagnais et la réserve de Betsiamites: 1850–1900* (Q: IQRC 1988) paints a broad picture of a reservation on the north shore of the St Lawrence.

The Anglo-Canadian minority has long been associated with Montreal's commercial elites. Margaret W. Westley, *Remembrance of Grandeur: The Anglo-Protestant Elite of Montreal, 1900–1950* (M: Libre Expression 1990) reinforces this vision of an affluent enclave in Montreal's 'Golden Mile.' Ronald Rudin. *The Forgotten Quebecers: A History of English-Speaking Quebec, 1759–1980* (Q: IQRC 1985) casts a wide net over anglophone minorities of different social classes, both inside and outside Montreal. For some impressionistic as well as sociological contributions, Gary Caldwell and Eric Waddell, eds., *The English of Quebec: From Majority to Minority Status* (Q: IQRC 1982), gather a collection of articles, often strongly opinionated. The Scottish contribution to the development of Montreal is acknowledged in Lynda Price, *Introduction to the Social History of Scots in Quebec, 1780–1840* (O: National Museums of Canada 1981).

Bruno Ramirez, *Les premiers Italiens de Montréal: l'origine de la Petite Italie du Québec* (M: BE 1984) documents the first wave of Italian immigrants to Montreal at the turn of the century. Many of them assimilated to the francophone majority, and Ramirez's *On the Move: French-Canadian and Italian Migrants in the North Atlantic Economy, 1860–1914* (T: M&S 1991) tells the story of the relations between the two communities.

The Jews, one of the oldest ethnic groups in Quebec, have attracted the attention of social scientists concerned with ethnic relations and anti-semitism. Pierre Anctil, *Le rendez-vous manqué: les Juifs de Montréal face au Québec de l'entre-deux-guerres* (Q: IQRC 1988) focuses on Jews and the established francophone and anglophone communities, while his monograph *Le Devoir, les Juifs et l'immigration de Bourassa à Laurendeau* (Q: IQRC 1988) analyses the attitude of Henri Bourassa's daily newspaper to Jewish immigration. One can also find some useful information in some of the pieces in the collection edited by Pierre Anctil and Gary Coldwell, *Juifs et réalités juives au Québec* (Q: IQRC 1984). Jacques Langlais and David Rome's *Juifs et Québécois français: 200 ans d'histoire commune* (M: Fides 1986) is presented in a conciliatory spirit by a Jewish archivist and a Catholic cleric involved in multiculturalism. Apart from its treatment of anti-Semitism, it is particularly useful for its section on education.

Denise Helly, *Les Chinois à Montréal, 1871–1951* (Q: IQRC 1987) looks at the problems and the strategies of assimilition of a cohesive, long-established community, while Dorothy W. Williams, *Blacks in Montreal, 1628–1986: An Urban Demography* (Cowansville: Yvon Blais 1989) offers an overview of a community still awaiting a comprehensive history.

URBAN HISTORY

Much of the social and economic history written about Quebec has centred on Montreal. Robert Rumilly's événementiel narrative, *Histoire de Montréal,* 5 vols. (M: Fides 1970–75), is superseded by a more scholarly survey: *Histoire de Montréal depuis la Confédération* (M: BE 1992), by urban historian Paul-André Linteau. Terry Copp's monograph *The Anatomy of Poverty* pertains as much to urban history as to working-class history. Paul-André Linteau, *The Promoters' City: Building the Industrial Town of Maisonneuve, 1883–1918* (T: JL 1985) follows the evolution of an industrial suburb until its annexation to Montreal in 1918. This is considered in the framework of local businessmen's interests and dreams of grandeur for their city. The parish long played an important religious and social role for urban as well as rural families. One working-class parish of the Oblates of Mary Immaculate forms the subject of Lucia Ferretti, *Entre*

Voisins: la société paroissiale en milieu urbain, Saint-Pierre-Apôtre de Montréal, 1848–1930 (M: BE 1992).

Jean-Rémi Brault, ed., *Montréal au XIXe siècle: des gens, des idées, des arts, une ville* (M: Leméac 1990) is a collection of articles discussing topics ranging from popular culture to immigration, housing, and health. Marc H. Choko, *Crises du logement à Montréal (1860–1939)* (M: Editions Albert Saint-Martin 1980) offers a preliminary exploration of working-class housing, while in *Une Cité-jardin à Montréal: la Cité-jardin du Tricentenaire, 1940–1947* (M: Méridien 1988), he analyses an example of urban planning after the war. Wendell MacLeod, Libbie Park, and Stanley Bréhaut Ryerson, *Bethune: The Montreal Years* (T: JL 1978) re-creates the social climate of Montreal during the 1930s, when Bethune was a thoracic surgeon at the Royal Victoria Hospital and the Hôpital du Sacré-Coeur.

If the dominant discourse has been the object of numerous studies, deviance from the prescribed norm and the treatment of non-conformity also is starting to draw some interest. Criminologist Jean-Paul Brodeur, in *La Délinquance de l'ordre: Recherches sur les commissions d'enquête* (M: HMH 1984) sifts through the commissions of enquiry into the Montreal police force for an understanding of social control exercised by every level of authority. Jacques Laplante, *Prison et ordre social au Québec* (O: UOP 1989) also adopts a Foucaultian approach to prisons as agents of social control.

REGIONAL HISTORY

Starting in the 1930s, Raoul Blanchard, a French geographer, criss-crossed Quebec on foot, observing, taking notes, and proceeding to lay the foundations of physical and human geography in Quebec in his as yet unequaled *L'est du Canada-français: Province de Québec, Le centre du Canada français: Province de Québec,* and *L'ouest du Canada français* (M: Beauchemin 1935, 1947, and 1953–4).

In the last ten years, the Institut québécois de recherche sur la culture has sponsored a number of bibliographies as well as regional histories, some merely descriptive accounts, others more analytical. Among these, Jules Bélanger et al., *Histoire de la Gaspésie* (Q: BE/IQRC 1981), have produced an impressive synthesis at a time when research on that region was just beginning. Mainly a narrative of events, it remains very informative. Camil Girard and Normand Perron, eds., *Histoire du Saguenay-Lac-Saint-Jean* (Q: IQRC 1989), and Serge Laurin, ed., *Histoire des Laurentides* (Q: IQRC 1989) both contain interesting articles, whereas Chad Gaffield, ed., *Histoire de l'Outaouais* (Q: IQRC 1994) more consistently stems from the collaborative efforts of a team of scholars successfully contributing to our knowledge of western Quebec.

Most regions have their own journal. *Cap-aux-Diamants* sometimes breaks out of amateur and anecdotal stories of the past to publish solid research on the history of Quebec City. While many of the articles in regional journals would not meet the test of rigorous scholarship, one sometimes finds gems, if not mines, of information published by local historians. For this reason, one should be familiar with journals such as *La Revue d'histoire du Bas-Saint-Laurent, Gaspésie, Sagnenayensia*, and *Asticou* for the Outaouais region.

FRENCH OUTSIDE CANADA

It is estimated that between 1830 and 1920 a million people emigrated from Quebec to New England, some 410,000 in the first thirty years of this century. Yves Roby, *Les Franco-Américains de la Nouvelle-Angleterre, 1776–1930* (Q: Septentrion 1990) describes their emigration to the mill towns south of the border, their jobs in the textile mills, and then their preoccupation with survival and the institutions created to protect their religion and their values. The decision to emigrate, the adaptation to life in the United States, and for many the decision to return to Quebec are examined by Jacques Rouillard in *Ah les Etats! Les travailleurs canadiens-français dans l'industrie textile de la Nouvelle-Angleterre d'après le témoignage des derniers migrants* (M: BE 1985), which is largely based on interviews with fifty people who experienced life in the New England textile towns before 1930.

CULTURAL AND INTELLECTUAL HISTORY

Yvan Lamonde, 'L'histoire culturelle et intellectuelle du Québec: tendances et aspects méthodologiques,' *JCS* 1989, appraises trends in this field of history. The same author has gathered twelve articles on various aspects of socio-cultural history in *Territoires de la culture québécoise* (Q: PUL 1991).

Nationalism is surely the ideology that has most fascinated historians of Quebec. The ideas of Lionel Groulx, Quebec's nationalist historian, and of the intellectual group around him, have been studied by Susan Mann Trofimenkoff in *Action Française: French Canadian Nationalism in the Twenties* (T: UTP 1975). Taking the press as the main exponent of various ideologies, some very uneven essays, mainly concerned with marginal or minority ideologies, are gathered in Fermand Dumont, Jean-Paul Montminy, and Jean Hamelin, eds., *Idéologies au Canada-français*, 1850–1900 (Q: PUL 1971); Fernand Dumont, Jean Hamelin, Fernand Harvey, and Jean-Paul Montminy, eds., *Idéologies au Canada-français, 1900–1929* (Q: PUL 1973); and Fernand Dumont, Jean Hamelin, and Jean-Paul Montminy, eds., *Idéologies au Canada français, 1940–76*, 3 vols. (Q: PUL 1981).

By focusing on a short period of ideological conflict, social unrest, and governmental change, André-J. Bélanger, *L'apolitisme des idéologies québécoises: Le grand tournant de 1934–1936* (Q: PUL 1974) draws conclusions about the political impotence of ideologies. Political scientist Denis Monière's *Ideologies in Quebec: The Historical Development* (T: UTP 1981), at times based on obsolete empirical research, is a controversial attempt to follow the evolution of political ideas.

Liberalism, not nationalism, has been Quebec's dominant ideology since the nineteenth century. Fernande Roy, *Progrès, harmonie, liberté: le libéralisme des milieux d'affaires francophones de Montréal au tournant du siècle* (M: BE 1988) provides a solid analysis of the social ideas of the Quebec business community, stressing its similarity with the anglophone community. For a discussion of a minority ideology which has had an impact on intellectual Quebec thinking, see Lucille Beaudry et al., eds., *Un siècle de marxisme: avec deux textes inédits de Karl Polanyi* (Q: PUQ 1990).

Few individuals have reflected and interpreted their time with as much acumen and integrity as André Laurendeau. A journalist by profession, he was politically active in the 1940s, and also wrote plays and a novel before ending his career as co-chair of the Royal Commission of Bilingualism and Biculturalism. The 1989 UQAM annual Colloquium on political personalities was devoted to this multifaceted intellectual. The proceedings, edited by Robert Comeau and Lucille Beaudry, *André Laurendeau, un intellectuel d'ici* (Sillery: PUQ 1990), provide a wide range of articles and first-hand accounts for those interested in his career and his commitments.

Marcel Trudel, *Mémoires d'un autre siècle* (M: BE 1987) is an autobiographical account by one of Quebec's leading historians, about growing up and starting an academic career in a traditional Quebec. Here the reader can find substance for intellectual, social, and literary history. In *Souvenances: entretiens avec Simon Jutras*, 3 vols. (M: La Presse 1983–1989), Georges-Henri Lévesque, the father of social science in Quebec, gave lengthy interviews to journalist Simon Jutras, and provides insights into the reaction of an oppressive milieu to the efforts at modernization of the last fifty years.

Before engaging in research on religious history, students would do well to first consult Guy Laperrière, 'L'histoire religieuse du Québec, principaux courants, 1978–1988,' *RHAF* 1989, which reveals how far religious history has come, from hagiographies of clerical leaders to well-grounded examples of social history. Under the direction of Nive Voisine, a major project to write the history of the Catholic Church in Quebec had yielded a broad synthesis by Jean Hamelin and Nicole Gagnon, *Histoire du catholicisme québécois*, vol. 1, *Le XXe siècles*, and vol. 2, *De 1940 à nos jours* (M: BE 1984), an institutional history of the Catholic Church and its leaders in this century. Lucien Lemieux, *Histoire du catholicisme au Québec: les XVIIIe et XIXe siècles*, 2 vols. (M: BE 1989) covers the earlier period. A good collection on nineteenth-century religious issues has been assembled by Pierre Savard, ed., *Aspects du catholicisme canadien-français au XIXe siècle* (M: Fides 1980).

Ultramontanism, which rocked the political scene at the end of last century, has aroused the interest of specialists in religious, political, and intellectual history. Nadia Fahmy-Eid, *Le clergé et le pouvoir politique au Québec: une analyse de l'idéologie ultramontaine au milieu du XIXe siècle* (M: HMH 1978), and Nive Voisine and Jean Hamelin, eds., *Les Ultramontains canadiens-français* (M: BE 1985), complement each other. Touching on the same period, Pierre Savard, *Jules-Paul Tardivel, la France et les Etats-Unis, 1851–1905* (Q: PUL 1967) enlarges the scope of his biography to include, through the life of Tardivel, Quebec relations with France and the United States.

François Rousseau, in a study of Quebec's first hospital and the religious community that administered it, *La Croix et le Scalpel: Histoire des Augustines et de l'Hôtel-Dieu de Québec, 1639–1989*, vol. 1, *1639–1892* (Q: Septentrion 1989), illuminates the history of *mentalité* and of medicine as much as it does that of religion.

The Catholic Church's hegemony did not prevent the formation of small groups of dissidents. Denounced with a vehemence out of proportion to its real strength, freemasonry, as a free thinking and progressive movement, is put in perspective in Roger LeMoine, *Deux loges montréalaises du Grand-Orient de France* (O: UOP 1991).

Relations with Rome dominated not only clerical matters but also minority rights and French-English relations. Roberto Perin's success in exploring the Vatican archives had led to an important contribution to religious and diplomatic history, *Rome in Canada: The Vatican and Canadian Affairs in the Late Victorian Age* (T: UTP 1990). René Hardy, *Les Zouaves pontificaux: une stratégie du clergé québécois au XIXe siècle* (M: BE 1980) argues the strategic importance of the pontifical guards for Quebec ultramontanism between 1868 and 1870. Pertaining as much to the intellectual history as to that of religious practices, the special issue of *Culture du Canada français* (1991) published the proceedings of the colloqium *La morale prescrite et vécue au Canada-français de l'après-guerre, 1945–1960*, an uneven collection on a period whose significance is just being discovered.

One of the outstanding reforms of the 1960s was the transformation of the traditional educational system. Claude Galarneau in *Les collèges classiques au Canada français 1620–1970* (M: Fides 1978) outlines the broad features of the basic institutions of the much-maligned classical educational system. After an introductory chapter on education from New France to 1919, the bulk of the book concentrates on the period from 1920 to the dismantlement of classical colleges in 1970.

The history of science is only recently developed as a field in Quebec. Luc Chartrand, Raymond Duchesne, and Yves Gingras's *Histoire des Sciences au Québec* (M: BE 1987) provides an important survey of the development of scientific thought and achievements since New France. Using a thematic approach, the authors document the achievements of French Canadians and the evolution of French–Canadian scientific tradition. Robert Gagnon, *Histoire de l'Ecole Polytechnique de Montréal* (M: BE 1991) presents the history of the school of engineering in Montreal.

Jacques Bernier, *La Médecine au Québec: naissance et évolution d'une profession* (Q: PUL 1989) covers the years from the professionalization of medicine with the Medical Act of 1788, to 1909, and examines the evolution of medical science and techniques, and of medical legislation, placing the profession in its political, economic, and ideological context. A comprehensive history of the faculty of medicine of the Université de Montréal, since its foundation one hundred and fifty years ago, as the private and bilingual Ecole de médecine et de chirurgie de Montréal, is charted by Denis Goulet, *Histoire de la Faculté de Médecine de l'Université de Montréal, 1843–1993* (M: VLB 1993).

The social history of medicine opens a window on intellectual history, as demonstrated in a good selection of essays gathered by Marcel Fournier, Yves Gingras, and Othmar Keel, eds., *Sciences & médecine au Québec: perspectives sociohistoriques* (Q: IQRC 1987). One also finds articles on the social history of medicine in *Norman Bethune: His Times and His Legacy*, edited by David A.E. Shephard and Andrée Lévesque (O: Canadian Public Health Assocation 1982).

THE MEDIA, ART, AND LITERATURE

In the last decades, historians have limited themselves to studies of the printed media, as witnessed in the bibliography put together by Manon

Brunet et al., *Bibliographie des études québécoises sur l'imprimé, 1970–1987* (M: BNQ 1991). In ten volumes published in the last twenty years, André Beaulieu and Jean Hamelin et al., eds., *La Presse québécoise, des origines à nos jours*, vol. 10, *1964–1975* (Q: PUL 1990) follows the trends in the development of the printed media; the 1987 volume provides an index to the first seven volumes.

Jean de Bonville, *La presse québécoise de 1884 à 1914: genèse d'un média de masse* (Q: PUL 1988), based on 373 dailies and weeklies, shows the quantitative and qualitative growth and transformation of the press, which de Bonville approaches as a business, an integral part of the economy. Victor Teboul, *Le Jour: Emergence du libéralisme moderne au Québec* (M: HMH 1984) considers the ideas expressed in the 1930s liberal newspaper founded by Jean-Charles Harvey.

There are a number of bibliographical tools and biographical dictionaries, usually edited by specialists of literature rather than by historians. They are of use not only to intellectual historians but to all those interested in understanding the past, and one should not forget that until the beginning of the twentieth century a number of politicians were also well known as writers. Historians also collaborated on the four-volume *Histoire de la littérature française du Québec* (M: Beauchemin 1967–1969), edited by Pierre de Grandpré. Lucie Robert, *L'institution littéraire au Québec* (Q: PUL 1989), focuses on the production of literary works.

Most major literary figures have warranted a biography. Marcel-Aimé Gagnon, *Jean-Charles Harvey: Précurseur de la révolution tranquille* (M: Beauchemin 1970) is an uneven work, but it contributes to our understanding of the antecedents of the Quiet Revolution by placing it in the same liberal tradition as the liberal journalist and novelist. Of the most recent biographies, Sandra Djwa, *The Politics of the Imagination: A Life of F.R. Scott* (T: M&S 1987) is not the definitive work on Scott, and is more interested in him as a writer than as a constitutionalist, social-democrat, founding member of the CCF, and civil libertarian.

The tensions between advocates of modernism and its adversaries point to a much less homogeneous Quebec than was once believed. In Yvan Lamonde and Esther Trépanier, eds., *L'avènement de la modernité culturelle au Québec* (Q: IQRC 1986) some very fine articles on modernization help our understanding of the intellectual and artistic climate before 1945. Of particular interest in this collection is Esther Trépanier's 'L'émergence d'un discours de la modernité dans la critique d'art (Montréal 1918–1938).' The debate on modern art centred on Father M.-A. Couturier is the subject of Robert Schwartzwald's 'The "Civic presence" of Father Marie-Alain Couturier, O.P. in Québec,' *Quebec Studies* 1990. Students should also consult the numerous works by art historians on the history of Quebec painting and exhibition catalogues, which are sometimes a rich source of art and intellectual history.

The last twenty years have seen a growing interest in urban architecture. Montreal's ecclectic landscape is considered by Jean-Claude Marsan, *Montreal in Evolution: Historical Analysis of the Development of Montreal's Architecture and Urban Environment* (M and K: MQUP 1981). Madeleine Forget, *Les gratte-ciel de Montréal* (M: Méridien 1990), follows the erection of large commercial buildings from 1887 to 1930 by placing the metropolis in its North American context. Christina Cameron, *Charles Baillargé: Architect and Engineer* (M and K: MQUP 1989), is a well-crafted biography of an architect who left his mark on Quebec's landscape. Montreal's centre of ethnic diversity, the famous and infamous boulevard Saint-Laurent, has been studied as the stage of one hundred years of theatre in André-G. Bourassa and Jean-Marc Larue, *Les Nuits de la 'Main': Cent Ans de Spectacles sur le boulevard Saint-Laurent (1891–1991)* (M: VLB 1993). The history of Montreal as the jazz capital of Canada has been successfully charted by journalist John Gilmore, *Swinging in Paradise: the Story of Jazz in Montreal* (M: Véhicule 1988).

Québec stands at a historiographical crossroad, influenced both by Anglo-Saxon and French historiographical traditions, and this is reflected in current debates, research, and publications, where one can find both empirical enquiries into the making of the Quebec working class, and a more continental concern with intellectual history.

If we take a long look at the writing of history in Quebec, we see a change in focus from politicians and political history, to Quebec society in its specificity, to the blossoming of social history in all its diversity. Some trends emerge from this bibliography: the importance of social history, especially women's history and labour history, with the emphasis on institutions such as trade unions and professions, is well established, yet we are just starting to find scholarly research on popular culture and on the socially marginal groups. The multicultural debate gives rise to an interest in various ethnic groups and this reinforces the importance of urban history. Rural history has long been neglected, despite the traditional view of Quebec as a rural province. This will soon be remedied by the regional histories sponsored by the IQRC, which promise some important findings to be published in the next few years. There are gaps to be filled: economic history remains underdeveloped for the twentieth century, while political history is too easily left to political scientists. Ours is a discipline that borrows from other social sciences; witness the annual prizes given by the *Institut d'histoire de l'Amérique française* to geographers, sociologists, demographers, and anthropologists.

Judging from the orientation of many graduate students – tomorrow's historians – social history is likely to reign supreme for more years to come. The present *éclatement* of the discipline inspires the investigations of social groups too long neglected by historians fascinated by political movements. Yet, the seductiveness of new fields and original subjects may lead us to lose sight of the political implications of social relations. This in turn will no doubt be followed by a rediscovery of political history. As each generation makes and writes its own history, this one no doubt reflects our own fragmented times.

DAVID MILLS

Ontario

Ontario is the largest, most powerful, and wealthiest province in Canada; yet it has been called the 'unknown province.' Peter Oliver wrote in an earlier edition of this *Guide*: 'There has been surprisingly little effort by Canadian historians consciously to write the regional history of Ontario. As a result, while there has been much history written by Ontario historians and while there is much about Ontario in that work, there does not at the moment exist a historical literature devoted to Ontario in the sense that such may be said to exist for other Canadian regions.'[1] But Ontario does not readily lend itself to a regional approach; Carl Berger wryly observed that 'possessing no tradition of regional grievance, having confidently accepted its dominant role within Confederation, Ontario has simply been confused by historians with the country as a whole.'[2] Elwood Jones, for example, baldly asserted that 'There is a good reason to see Ontario as the most representative region of Canada ... In a real sense, all parts of Canada are a part of Ontario's experience, partly because of the migration of its people, its institutions and its values.'[3]

It is one thing to try to understand Ontario through an examination of the early development of Manitoba or the establishment of Vulcan, Alberta; it is quite another to understand Ontario on its own terms. It has neither a unifying provincial identity like Nova Scotia nor a unifying cultural identity like French-speaking Quebec. There is no unity apart from its political and territorial definition. Consequently, most general histories of Ontario have focused upon provincial politics as the overarching theme. Alexander Fraser's *A History of Ontario: Its Resources and Development*, 2 vols. (T: Canada History Company 1907) provides an uncritical political narrative in the few chapters that deal with the province after Confederation. The four-volume *Province of Ontario: A History, 1615–1927* by Fred Landon and J.E. Middleton (T: Dominion Publishing Company 1927) provides a more balanced discussion of social, economic, and political developments and examines particular regions in Ontario through census and assessment data, as well as material drawn from late nineteenth-century county atlases. Recent provincial histories do not offer much improvement. Joseph Schull's *Ontario since 1867* (T: M&S 1978) notes important social and economic changes in the province but focuses primarily on politics from the premier's office. It is not very useful for the period after the 1930s and assumes that the cultural life of Ontario is that of English Canada as a whole. *Ontario 1610–1985: A Political and Economic History* by Randall White (T: Dundurn 1985) outlines the regional, ethnic, and cultural diversity of Ontario as background to the development of the provincial economy and government. White argues that the state becomes the dynamic for change and the means to solve social problems. Robert Bothwell's *A Short History of Ontario* (E: Hurtig 1986) also deals with economic development and social change, but provincial politics and federal-provincial relations remain the central themes. Bothwell's cynical perspective on politics is refreshing; he condemns ideology and radicalism in favour of the pragmatic and marginally progressive but conservative leaders who were successful. Yet overall the book is disappointing. Although Bothwell searches for the 'common experience of the province,' his popular history remains Toronto-focused and ignores women, the working class, and ethnic groups.

Two important series should be noted. The Ontario series of the Champlain Society offers collections of primary sources. The Ontario Historical Studies Series, edited by Goldwin French, Jeanne Beck, and Peter Oliver, is intended to produce a comprehensive history of Ontario aimed at the intelligent reader. It was launched in 1971 with provincial government funding, its aim being to reveal Ontario's values and convictions and to strengthen the provincial identity. There are excellent volumes on the economy and the development of the educational system, but the real priority of the series seems to be political biography; the lives and times of the provincial premiers provide the main focus.

Although politics has largely shaped provincial histories, it must be recognized that Ontario is a province of sub-regions, characterized by social diversity and economic complexity. J.M.S. Careless's insight about Canada also holds true for Ontario; the province must be understood in terms of its 'limited identities.' See his 'Limited Identities in Canada,' *CHR* 1969. Its people, as S.F. Wise perceptively argued, have traditionally been identified by reference to the groups to which they belonged – groups defined by ethnicity, religion, class, gender, and region. See his

'Liberal Consensus or Ideological Battleground: Some Reflections on the Hartz Thesis,' CHA *HP* 1974. The result has been the development of what David Gagan has called 'a distinctive society,' in his article 'Writing the History of Ontario in the 1980s: Defining a Distinctive Society,' *Acadiensis* 1991.

The history of this pluralist society is more difficult to capture because it lacks a unifying theme. In the early twentieth century the *Canada and Its Provinces* series offered two volumes on Ontario which included essays on education, the municipal and judicial systems, and economic development; these works may still be usefully consulted. G.P. de T. Glazebrook, *Life in Ontario: A Social History* (T: UTP 1968) is old-fashioned social history, that is, history with the politics left out. Roger Hall and Gordon Dodds produced *A Picture History of Ontario* (E: Hurtig 1978), which provides an interesting visual account of the province and concludes that since 1960 there are no Ontarians, only people who live in Ontario. For Ontario's bicentennial, Hall and Dodds produced *Ontario: Two Hundred Years in Pictures* (T: Dundurn 1991). A less satisfactory effort along the same lines is Mary Beacock Fryer and Charles J. Humber, eds., *Loyal She Remains: A Pictorial History of Ontario* (T: United Empire Loyalists Association of Canada 1984). A big book, with lots of pictures, it contains a number of short essays by prominent historians on topics such as business and labour, Northern Ontario, and the Great Depression. It was intended for a popular audience, but the quality of the essays is uneven and consequently it offers a weak analytical overview of Ontario's history. A more successful attempt to discuss provincial development has been written by historical geographers, not historians. Louis Gentilcore, ed., *Ontario* (T: UTP 1972) surveys the environment, settlement, the economy, urbanization, and the political-territorial structure.

Much of the recent scholarly writing about Ontario, influenced as it is by the new social history, has addressed the theme of pluralism more explicitly. Many historians have turned away from politicians to examine previously ignored groups such as women, ethnic communities, and the working class, shifting their emphasis away from politics to look instead at economic development, social change, and ideas. The focus of study has become more narrow and specialized, drawing upon the methodologies of the social sciences in order to understand past behaviour through the application of concepts such as gender, ethnicity, and class. The field of Ontario history reveals a broad and varied body of literature and is found in both periodicals and collections of essays. *Ontario History*, the longest-established journal of provincial history, is produced quarterly by the

Ontario Historical Society. At one time most of the articles were about the pre-Confederation era, but for the last decade or so about half have focused on Ontario. There is also Hilary Bates and Robert Sherman, eds., *Index to the Publications of the Ontario Historical Society, 1899–1972* (T: Ontario Historical Society 1974). Several periodicals devoted to local history should be noted; these include *Wentworth Bygones*, *Historic Kingston*, *Western Ontario History Nuggets*, and *The Bruce County Historical Society Yearbook*. Other local historical societies have publications but there is no general guide to these.

Articles about Ontario appear occasionally in the *Canadian Historical Review*, the *Journal of Canadian Studies*, *Histoire sociale/Social History*, and the *Urban History Review*. Ironically, the best discussions of Ontario historiography have been in *Acadiensis: Journal of the History of the Atlantic Region*; see Richard Clippingdale, 'The Renaissance of Ontario History,' 1978; Elwood Jones, 'Diversity at the Centre: Ontario's Local and Political History,' 1982; and David Gagan, 'Writing the History of Ontario in the 1980s' (cited above).

There are several collections of essays available which provide an introduction to Ontario history and indicate contemporary trends in historical writing. The Ontario Historical Society has produced Edith Firth, ed., *Profiles of a Province: Studies in the History of Ontario* (T: Ontario Historical Society 1967); it is an uneven collection with sections on politics, the economy, and the Ontario outlook. Donald Swainson, ed., *Oliver Mowat's Ontario* (T: MAC 1972) is a better collection, with articles by Michael Bliss on business, H.V. Nelles on the resource economy, and Graeme Decarie on prohibition. F.H. Armstrong, H.A. Stevenson, and J.D. Wilson, eds., *Aspects of Nineteenth-Century Ontario: Essays Presented to James J. Talman* (T: UTP 1974) contains some interesting articles on education, newspapers, Northern Ontario, and the provincial mind. *Old Ontario: Essays in Honour of J.M.S. Careless*, a *festschrift* edited by David Keane and Colin Read (T: Dundurn 1990), includes articles by former students of one of the best historians of Ontario. Although most of the essays deal with the pre-Confederation period, there are important works by Neil Semple on the Protestant revival, Gerald Tulchinsky on Toronto's clothing industry, and Alison Prentice on teachers. The centennial of the establishment of the Ontario Historical Society was celebrated by the publication of *Patterns of the Past: Interpreting Ontario's History*, edited by Roger Hall, William Westfall, and Laurel Sefton MacDowell (T: Dundurn 1988). It clearly reveals the shift away from politics as a major theme of study; its articles focus on topics such as the economy, social reform, science and technology, labour, ethnic groups, and conservation. The same broad range of interests is shown in Michael Piva, ed., *A History of Ontario: Selected Readings* (T: CPP 1988). A number of important articles are available in this volume, including David Gagan on families, Greg Kealey on the Orange Order, Craig Heron on metal workers, Peter Oliver on bilingual schools, and Sylvia Bashevkin on women and politics. David Gagan and Rosemary Gagan, eds., *New Directions for the Study of Ontario's Past* (Hamilton: McMaster University 1988) presents papers delivered at a conference on Ontario's bicentennial; they outline the current state of Ontario historiography and suggest research initiatives. Most of the authors included in this collection have followed up their articles with monographs.

The most recent books do not define their topics of study in provincial terms; instead broad themes are examined with Ontario as their context. This should be regarded as a strength not a weakness. Perhaps the best way to understand Ontario is to explore the province through a number of inter-related areas of study. There are demographic works which examine the distribution of population by location, sex, age, ethnicity, and religion. Historians have provided micro-studies of particular communities and studies of the family or immigrant groups. They also explain how social relations can be defined by ethnicity or gender. The economy is an important focus for analysis. How has Ontario's economy functioned? How have natural and human resources been used? What were the occupations and standards of living of different groups? More important, how has the economy defined social relations through class formation? Do Ontarians continue to believe that economic development and material progress can overcome ethnic differences and class tensions? Ideas must be examined in their historical context because they reveal broader social attitudes and values. Religion, for example, cannot be understood simply in terms of theology; it was also a means of group identification and defined Ontario's Protestant culture well into the twentieth-century. Finally there are the studies of social and political change. Responses to the province's social and economic transformation found expression in movements for social reform as well as in the political arena.

BIBLIOGRAPHICAL WORKS

Before the topical literature is discussed, readers should be directed to the bibliographical tools available. The most comprehensive is Olga B. Bishop et al., eds., *Bibliography of Ontario History, 1867–1976: Cultural, Economic, Political, Social*, 2 vols. (T: UTP 1980). It is organized thematically and

includes books, articles, pamphlets, theses, government reports, and Royal
Commissions. Since 1980, the Ontario Historical Society has published
an 'Annual Bibliography of Ontario History.' The editors, Gaetan Gervais,
Gwenda Hallsworth, and Ashley Thomson, have also produced *The Bibli-
ography of Ontario History, 1976–1986* (T: Dundurn 1989). The *Canadian
Historical Review* contains a section on Ontario in its 'Recent Publications
Relating to Canada,' published in each issue but it is generally quite
short.

More topical bibliographies include Benjamin Fortin and Jean-Pierre
Gaboury, eds., *Bibliographie analytique de l'Ontario français* (O: Editions de
l'Université d'Ottawa 1975), along with the update prepared by Jean-Yves
Pelletier, *Bibliographie Sélective de l'Ontario Français* (O: Centre franco-
ontarien de ressources pédagogiques 1989). The Toronto area Archivists'
Group has prepared a series of guides to local archival resources: *Ontario's
Heritage: A Guide to Archival Resources* (Erin: Boston Mills Press 1978–).
There are also two useful guides to local histories in Ontario: William
F.E. Morley, comp., *Canadian Local Histories to 1950: A Bibliography*, vol. 3,
Ontario and the Canadian North (T: UTP 1978), and Barbara B. Aitken,
ed., *Local Histories of Ontario Municipalities, 1951–1977: A Bibliography*
(T: Ontario Library Association 1978). Finally, it is worthwhile examining
Peter Oliver's 'Ontario' in the earlier version of *A Reader's Guide to Cana-
dian History*, vol. 2, *Confederation to the Present*, edited by J.L. Granatstein
and Paul Stevens (T: UTP 1982); it is especially good on Ontario politics.

THE PEOPLE

Traditionally politics has dominated the historical writing about Ontario;
works about women, ethnic groups, and working people were few and
usually lumped together in the catch-all category of social history. But in
the past generation there has been greater interest in the history of ordinary people. Historians, influenced by the outlook of the social sciences
and interested in a more comprehensive analysis of society and social
relations, championed the study of women and the family, immigrants,
and industrial workers – concerns that often arose in part from their own
identities. Their attempts were facilitated by new sources of data and new
methods for analysing them. To uncover the lives of previously neglected
groups, new social historians moved away from government records, political correspondence, and newspapers and instead began to seek documents which yielded mass data, such as registers of births and deaths,
censuses, church lists, factory rolls, tax records, wills, or records from

courts, prisons, and hospitals. They looked at more popular sources like diaries, personal letters, and so forth. The result has been an explosion of historical writing which must now be discussed in terms of sub-disciplines like historical demography, women's history, family history, or ethnic studies. Local histories can also provide insights into the lives of the people of Ontario. The society then can be understood in terms of its component groups, their attitudes and values, and the social relations which developed.

DEMOGRAPHY

One place to start when looking at Ontario's demography is F.H. Leacy, ed., *Historical Statistics of Canada* (2nd ed., O: Statistics Canada 1983). It provides raw data on population – numbers, origins, household and family statistics, interprovincial migration, and international immigration figures. A statistical profile of Ontario from Confederation to 1976 is provided (this will be updated when the 1991 census becomes available), although provincial figures are presented in terms of national aggregates. A guide to provincial sources of statistical information is Dean Tudor, ed., *Sources of Statistical Data for Ontario* (O: Canadian Library Association 1972).

The *Historical Atlas of Canada*, vol. 3, *Addressing the Twentieth Century, 1891–1961*, edited by historical geographers Donald Kerr and Deryck W. Holdsworth (T: UTP 1990), is a superb source. Its maps integrate both statistical data and historical analysis to provide a striking visual picture of the changing Canadian population between 1901 and 1961. The national focus of this work should not limit its importance to students of Ontario. Population data for post-war Ontario can be found in W.G. Dean, ed., *Economic Atlas of Ontario* (T: UTP 1969). There are maps illustrating the distribution of population, and its changes over time, ethnicity, and so on; it is a valuable source for social historians and should not be ignored.

There are a number of important monographs which address the social reality of Old Ontario. David Gagan's comprehensive Peel County Project laid the foundation for several articles, including Gagan and Herbert Mays, 'Historical Demography and Canadian Social History: Families and Land in Peel County, Ontario,' *CHR* 1973; Gagan, 'Land, Population, and Social Change: The 'Critical Years' in Rural Canada West,' *CHR* 1978; Mays, '"A Place to Stand": Families, Land, and Permanence in Toronto Gore Township, 1820–1890,' *CHA* 1980; and finally Gagan's book, *Hopeful Travellers: Families, Land, and Social Change in Mid-Victorian Peel County, Canada West* (T: UTP 1981). This work seriously challenged the traditional view about the stability of Ontario rural communities in this period by using census material, wills, and other data to illustrate the massive mobility of the rural population and the means by which they dealt with social and economic dislocations. The work also produced an interesting debate in the *Canadian Historical Review* between Gagan and George Emery and José Igartua over methodology (1981).

The 1980s saw the publication of a number of other examples of historical demography which incorporated the concept of ethnicity into their analyses. From the time of the Loyalist migration in the 1780s through to the modern period, Ontario's population has been characterized by diversity. People traditionally have been identified by the ethnic group to which they belonged; this is especially true for the Irish. At the time of Confederation, the Irish formed the largest ethnic group in Ontario and yet for a long time their experience was ignored. This is no longer the case, for there is a growing and dynamic literature dealing with the Irish. In 1984, Donald H. Akenson published *The Irish in Ontario: A Study in Rural History* (M and K: MQUP 1984), which demolished the old stereotypes of this group. From a micro-study of Leeds and Lansdowne Townships in eastern Ontario, he concluded that Irish farmers successfully adapted to rural life. The churches, schools, and the Orange Order also facilitated this process. While Akenson's interpretation has been challenged, notably by Murray Nicolson in 'Peasants in an Urban Society: The Irish Catholics in Victorian Toronto,' in Robert Harney, ed., *Gathering Place: Peoples and Neighbourhoods of Toronto, 1834–1945* (T: MHSO 1985), it has influenced other works. Two of the most important also deal with the Irish in eastern Ontario: Bruce S. Elliott's *Irish Migrants in the Canadas: A New Approach* (M and K: MQUP 1988) follows Irish immigrants from Tipperary to March Township near Ottawa, and their continued movements, land-holding strategies, and economic lives, and Glenn Lockwood wrote *Montague: A Social History of an Irish Ontario Township, 1783–1980* (Smith Falls: Township of Montague 1980).

Cecil J. Houston and William J. Smyth have produced two studies of the Irish. In *The Sash Canada Wore: A Historical Geography of the Orange Order in Canada* (T: UTP 1980), they looked at the location and numbers of Orangemen and showed how the Order spread as settlement developed, but they ignore the larger social and political context, particularly the question of class in urban areas which Greg Kealey addressed in 'Orangemen and the Corporation: The Politics of Class during the Union of the Canadas,' in Victor L. Russell, ed., *Forging a Consensus: Historical Essays on Toronto* (T: UTP 1984). Houston and Smyth's most recent book,

Irish Emigration and Canadian Settlement: Patterns, Links, and Letters (T: UTP 1990), looks at the process of chain migration from Ireland to Ontario but also examines the cultural life of the Irish through their books and letters.

The Franco-Ontarian communities in eastern and northern Ontario have received a great deal of attention. The publications of La Societé Historique du Nouvel-Ontario are uneven in quality but deal with important topics like community life, education, religion, economic development, prominent individuals, and so on. The *Laurentian University Review* is also useful for studies of Franco-Ontarians.

An overview is provided in Robert Choquette, *L'Ontario français, historique*. (M: Editions études vivantes 1980). General essays on the subject include Leopold Lamontagne, 'Ontario: The Two Races,' in Mason Wade, ed., *Canadian Dualism: Studies of French-English Relations* (T: UTP 1960); T.H.B. Symons, 'Ontario's Quiet Revolution: A Study of Change in the Position of the Franco-Ontarian Community,' in R.M. Burns, ed., *One Country or Two?* (M and K: MQUP 1971); Archibald Clinton, 'La Pensée politique des Franco-Ontariens au XXe siècle' in *Revue du Nouvel Ontario* 1979; Pierre Savard, 'De la difficulté d'être Franco-Ontarien,' *Revue du Nouvel Ontario* 1978; and Antonio D'Iorio, 'Les idéologies de l'Ontario française: un choix de textes (1912–1980),' *Revue du Nouvel Ontario* 1981. Sheila McLeod Arnopoulos has compiled *Voices from French Ontario* (M and K: MQUP 1982), which provides portraits of individual Franco-Ontarians. There are also two important doctoral dissertations: D.G. Cartwright, 'French Canadian Colonization in Eastern Ontario to 1910,' PhD thesis, University of Western Ontario, 1973, and Gail Cuthbert Brandt's quantitative study, '"J'y suis, j'y reste": The French Canadians of Sudbury, 1883–1913,' PhD thesis, York University, 1976.

Robert Choquette has addressed the tensions between the Franco-Ontarians and the Irish in the Roman Catholic Church; his book *Language and Religion: A History of French-English Conflict in Ontario* (O: UOP 1975) looks at the period from 1900 to 1927; *L'Eglise catholique dans l'Ontario français du neuvième siècle* (O: UOP 1984) examines the earlier period. The importance of the clergy in maintaining cultural identity is stressed, but both works could be better focused. The major source of controversy for the Franco-Ontarian community has been the struggle for educational rights; useful sources include Franklin A. Walker, *Catholic Education and Politics in Ontario*, vol. 2, *A Documentary Study*, and vol. 3, *From the Hope Commission to the Promise of Completion (1964–1986)* (T: Nelson 1964; T: Catholic Education Foundation of Ontario 1986); Marilyn Barber, 'The

Ontario Bilingual Schools Issue: Sources of Conflict,' *CHR* 1966; Margaret Prang, 'Clerics, Politicians, and the Bilingual Schools Issue in Ontario, 1910–1917,' *CHR* 1960; Peter Oliver, 'The Resolution of the Ontario Bilingual Schools Crisis, 1919–1929,' *JCS* 1972; David Millett, 'The Social Context of Bilingualism in Eastern Ontario,' *American Review of Canadian Studies* 1983; and Andre Lalonde, *Le Règlement XVII et ses répercussions sur le Nouvel-Ontario* (Sudbury: Société historique du Nouvel-Ontario 1965). The best work has been done by Chad Gaffield in *Language, Schooling, and Cultural Conflict: The Origins of the French-Language Controversy in Ontario* (M and K: MQUP 1987). Gaffield uses historical demography to explain the origins of the language issue in two francophone townships in Prescott County in the Ottawa Valley. Francophones on the social and economic margins were frustrated in their attempts to control their own schools by a provincial government that sought to assimilate them and the result was a political eruption. Gaffield skilfully handles these issues and, in the process, sheds new light on the schools controversy.

IMMIGRANT GROUPS AND ETHNICITY

The pluralism of Ontario's society has been reinforced by immigration patterns, especially of non-British and non-French groups in the twentieth-century. There is no general history of immigration to Ontario, although *'Coming Canadians': An Introduction to a History of Canada's Peoples*, edited by Jean Burnet and Howard Palmer (T: M&S 1988), and Robert F. Harney and Harold Troper, *Immigrants: A Portrait of the Urban Experience, 1890–1930* (T: Van Nostrand Reinhold 1975) are useful starting points. One topic which has received some attention is the movement of poor British women and children to Canada; the important sources are Joy Parr's scholarly treatment, *Labouring Children: British Immigrant Apprentices to Canada, 1869–1924* (2nd ed., T: UTP 1994), and two popular works: Kenneth Bagnell, *The Little Immigrants: The Orphans who Came to Canada* (T: MAC 1980), and Phyllis Harrison, *The Home Children: Their Personal Stories* (W: Watson & Dwyer 1979). There are also several important articles: Marilyn Barber's 'The Women Ontario Welcomed: Immigrant Domestics for Ontario Homes, 1870–1930,' *OH* 1980, and her 'Sunny Ontario for British Girls, 1900–1930,' in Jean Burnet, ed., *'Looking into My Sister's Eyes': An Exploration in Women's History* (T: MHSO 1986); Barbara Roberts, '"A Work of Empire": Canadian Reformers and British Female Immigration,' in Linda Kealey, ed., *A Not Unreasonable Claim: Women and Reform in Canada, 1880s–1920s* (T: Women's Press 1979).

Useful background material on specific ethnic groups in Canada can be found in the *Generations* series published by McClelland & Stewart for the Department of the Secretary of State, and the Canadian Historical Association's *Canada's Ethnic Groups* booklet series. Ontario has a dynamic literature in the field of ethnic history as the result of the establishment of the Multicultural History Society in the 1970s. The Society collects and preserves archival materials, records oral history, organizes conferences and publishes papers, and produces its own journal, *Polyphony*, which has published special issues on both the Finns and the Poles in northern Ontario, Hungarians in Toronto, and Ontario's Ukrainians. Robert Harney, a former president of the Society and editor of *Polyphony*, made important contributions to ethnic history in Ontario through his studies of the Italians in Toronto before World War II. He looked at the slow transition from sojourning to settlement through the creation of Italian neighbourhoods where the culture could flourish, the nature of work, and the reactions of the Anglo-Protestant community in articles like 'Toronto's Little Italy, 1885–1945,' in Harney and J. Vincenza Scarpaci, eds., *Little Italies in North America* (T: MHSO 1981) and 'Boarding and Belonging: Thoughts on Sojourner Institutions,' *UHR* 1978.

Harney's work has stimulated interest in the Italian community and the result has been the production of a number of excellent monographs. John E. Zucchi's *Italians in Toronto: Development of a National Identity, 1875–1935* (M and K: MQUP 1988) examines the social and cultural forces affecting Italians who came to live in Toronto and shows how the changes they experienced gave them an Italian identity. In *The Italian Immigrant Experience* (Thunder Bay: Canadian Italian Historical Association 1988), John Potestio and Antonio Pucci focus on the working experience of Italians, especially in northern Ontario. *'Such Hardworking People': Italian Immigrants in Postwar Ontario* by Franca Iacovetta (M and K: MQUP 1992) discusses how a large population of southern Italian peasants came to Toronto after 1945 in spite of efforts to keep them out. Iacovetta examines the work of both men and women, and she argues that home ownership was central to cultural survival. Her work is shaped by a feminist perspective, which is also a strength in her articles, including 'New Canadians: Social Workers, Women, and the Reshaping of Immigrant Families,' in Iacovetta and Mariana Valverde, eds., *Gender Conflicts: New Essays in Women's History* (T: UTP 1992).

There is a large amount of material on other ethnic groups, much of which has been produced by those communities themselves to show the contribution of their group to Canada's development; it is often nonacademic in approach. However, there is also a growing scholarly literature. The ethnic pluralism of Toronto has been illustrated in Peter S. Li, 'The Stratification of Ethnic Immigrants: The Case of Toronto,' in *Canadian Review of Sociology and Anthropology* 1978 and, more important, Robert F. Harney, ed., *Gathering Place: Peoples and Neighbourhoods of Toronto, 1834–1945* (T: MHSO 1985), which reprinted articles from *Polyphony* on groups such as the Chinese, Greeks, Finns, and Jews. There is also Raymond Breton et al., *Ethnic Identity and Equality: Varieties of Experience in a Canadian City* (T: UTP 1990).

Stephen A. Speisman's *The Jews of Toronto: A History to 1937* (T: M&S 1979) examines the social, economic, and political activities of the Jewish community and emphasizes its religious and ethnic diversity. It tends to focus on the elites, ignoring the working class, and does not explore the relationship with the host society. Ruth A. Frager has addressed some of these issues in *Sweatshop Strife: Class, Ethnicity, and Gender in the Jewish Labour Movement of Toronto, 1900–1939* (T: UTP 1992). Anti-Semitism in Toronto is discussed in Cyril H. Levitt and William Shaffir, *The Riot at Christie Pits* (T: Lester & Orpen Dennys 1987). The Ukrainians have also been a focus of attention; Lubomyr Y. Luciuk and Iroida L. Wynnyckyj edited *Ukrainians in Ontario* (T: MHSO 1986), which explains how the Ukrainians who came to Ontario after World War II were different from the Prairie groups. There is also Luciuk and Stella Hryniuk, eds., *Canada's Ukrainians: Negotiating an Identity* (T: UTP 1991), and more important, Orest Martynowich, *Ukrainians in Canada: The Formative Period, 1891–1924* (E: CIUS 1991). Perhaps the most significant new work on Ukrainian Canadians is being done by Frances Swyripa on women; see her *Wedded to the Cause: Ukrainian-Canadian Women and Ethnic Identity, 1891–1991* (T: UTP 1993), and 'Outside the Bloc Settlement: Ukrainian Women in Ontario during the Formative Years of Community Consciousness,' in Burnet, ed., *'Looking into My Sister's Eyes.'* The other articles in Burnet's volume also show the interaction between ethnicity and gender; of particular note is Varpu Lindström-Best's '"I Won't Be a Slave": Finnish Domestics in Canada.' There are special issues of *Polyphony* on women and ethnicity (1986), *Canadian Ethnic Studies* on ethnicity and feminism (1981), and *Canadian Women's Studies* on women and multiculturalism and selected ethnic groups (1982, 1987–8). The interrelationships between gender, race, and class are explored in a collection of interviews edited by Dionne Brand, *No Burden to Carry: Narratives of Black Working Women in Ontario, 1920s to 1950s* (T: Women's Press 1991).

There is also a strong link between ethnicity and the development of a working-class identity as the following articles indicate: Jean Morrison, 'Ethnicity and Violence: The Lakehead Freight Handlers before World War I,' *Lakehead University Review* 1976; Alan Seager, 'Finnish-Canadians and the Ontario Miner's Movement,' and Ian Radforth, 'Finnish Lumber Workers in Ontario, 1919–1946,' both in *Polyphony* 1981; and in the same journal, Gilbert Stelter, 'The People of Sudbury: Ethnicity and Community in an Ontario Mining Region' 1983.

WOMEN'S HISTORY AND GENDER STUDIES

The study of women used to be on the periphery of historical writing; now some of the best work focuses on women. Historians of women's experience have made women in the past visible and revealed a distinctive world of women's relationships, work, and ideas. In doing so, they have drawn attention to the concept of gender as an analytical concept. Gender is a socially constructed category of behaviour which defines the relations between women and men; historically women have been subordinate to men and their maternal, domestic, and economic functions have been devalued. Moreover, it is argued that in patriarchal social systems women are denied autonomy.

Canadian Women: A History by Alison Prentice et al. (T: HBJ 1988) provides an overview of women's history. Veronica Strong-Boag and Anita Clair Fellman have edited *Rethinking Canada: The Promise of Women's History* (2nd ed., T: CCP 1991), which contains essays on women in Ontario, as does Kealey, ed., *A Not Unreasonable Claim*. Jean Burnet's collection, *'Looking into My Sister's Eyes'* has already been noted.

One of the most innovative approaches to the study of women is found in Veronica Strong-Boag's *The New Day Recalled: Lives of Girls and Women in English Canada, 1919–1939* (T: CCP 1988). It focuses on the life course, that is, the significant changes in women's lives – early socialization, paid labour, courtship and marriage, housework, motherhood, and aging. Although the book is mostly about urban middle-class women, it does offer an interesting method of examining women's experience.

There are a number of articles on female schooling in Ontario; these include works by M.V. Royce, 'Arguments over the Education of Girls,' *OH* 1975, 'Education for Girls in Schools in Ontario,' *Atlantis* 1977, and 'Methodism and the Education of Women in 19th Century Ontario,' *Atlantis* 1977; Chad Gaffield, 'Schooling, the Economy, and Rural Society in 19th century Ontario,' in Joy Parr, ed., *Childhood and Family in Canadian History* (T: M&S 1982), and his 'Children, Schooling, and Family

Reproduction in Nineteenth-Century Ontario,' *CHR* 1991. Ruby Heap and Alison Prentice, eds., *Gender and Education in Ontario: An Historical Reader* (T: Canadian Scholars Press 1991) is a collection of articles on female students and teachers in the nineteenth and early twentieth centuries. The unifying theme is that gender relations shape the female experience in the educational system.

Some interesting work has been done in the area of women's paid labour. Two early sources are Janice Acton et al., eds., *Women at Work: Ontario, 1850–1930* (T: Women's Educational Press 1974), and Wayne Roberts, *'Honest Womanhood': Feminism, Femininity, and Class Consciousness among Toronto Working Women, 1893–1914* (T: New Hogtown Press 1976). The contribution of women to Ontario's economic development is examined in Marjorie Griffin Cohen's excellent *Women's Work, Markets, and Economic Development in Nineteenth-Century Ontario* (T: UTP 1988). Beginning with an examination of women's economic role on the farm, this monograph argues that women's work was essential to the development of a capitalist economy. Women controlled the household economy, allowing men to produce staples for the market and to accumulate capital. Thus work was divided by sex and controlled by men. As household production shifted to the factory, women increasingly participated in the paid labour force. Industrialization did not begin the sexual division of labour; it simply reinforced existing patterns. *The Gender of Breadwinners: Women, Men, and Change in Two Industrial Towns, 1880–1950* (T: UTP 1990) by Joy Parr is outstanding. It is a thoroughly researched and complex study of the industrial structures in Paris and Hanover, Ontario, and the processes which shaped their work forces and influenced community relationships and social development. Paris was a 'women's town' where the women who worked in Penman's textile plant had more power and autonomy in their households and the community because they were breadwinners; women in Hanover were largely confined to domestic labour. Parr's work analyses gender and class relationships in a conscious and integrated manner. Graham S. Lowe's *Women in the Administrative Revolution: The Feminization of Clerical Work* (T: UTP 1987) is an excellent examination of the role of women in the growth and development of the modern office.

Other sources which look at women's paid labour and address the theme of gender and class include: Michèle Martin, *'Hello Central?': Gender, Technology, and Culture in the Formation of Telephone Systems* (M and K: MQUP 1991); Ruth Roach Pierson, *'They're Still Women after All': The Second World War and Canadian Womanhood* (T: M&S 1986); and Eileen

Sufrin, *The Eaton Drive: The Campaign to Organize Canada's Largest Department Store, 1948–1952* (T: Fitzhenry & Whiteside 1982). Ruth A. Frager also incorporates ethnicity into her study of Jewish immigrants involved in Toronto's needle trade, in her book *Sweatshop Strife* (cited above). While the theme of gender interests and identities is important, the book provides a solid and straight-forward examination of Toronto's Jewish labour movement. There are also a number of significant articles: John Bullen, 'Hidden Workers: Child Labour and the Family Economy in Late Nineteenth-Century Urban Ontario,' *Labour* 1986; Meg Luxton and June Corman, 'Getting to Work: The Challenge of the Women Back into Stelco Campaign,' *Labour* 1991; R. Marvin McInnis, 'Women, Work, and Childbearing: Ontario in the Second Half of the Nineteenth Century,' *HS/SH* 1991; Mark Rosenfeld, 'It was a Hard Life: Class and Gender in the Work and Family Rhythms of a Railway Town, 1920–1950,' CHA *HP* 1988; Joan Sangster, 'The 1907 Bell Telephone Strike: Organizing Women Workers,' *Labour* 1978; Shirley Tillotson, 'Human Rights as Prism: Women's Organizations, Unions, and Ontario's Female Employees Fair Remuneration Act, 1951,' *CHR* 1991; and Susan Mann Trofimenkoff, 'One Hundred and Two Muffled Voices: Canada's Industrial Women in the 1880's,' *Atlantis* 1977.

The theme of courtship and marriage has been addressed in W. Peter Ward's *Courtship, Love, and Marriage in Nineteenth-Century English Canada* (M and K: MQUP 1990). This book examines the attitudes and activities of men and women quite well and discusses the religious, legal, and demographic structures within which these relations developed. It has been called a traditional approach to family history, though, because it does not emphasize gender inequalities. There is also an article by Stephen D.E. Marshall, 'Courtship and Marriage in Nineteenth-Century Ontario,' in *Families* 1990, and two important works by James G. Snell, 'The White Life for Two: The Defence of Marriage and Sexual Morality in Canada, 1890–1914,' *HS/SH* 1983, and with Cynthia Comacchio Abeele, 'Regulating Nuptuality: Restricting Access to Marriage in Early Twentieth-Century English-Speaking Canada,' *CHR* 1988. Two monographs which focus on women and the law are Constance Backhouse, *Petticoats and Prejudice: Women and the Law in Nineteenth-Century Canada* (T: Women's Press 1991), and James G. Snell, *In the Shadow of the Law: Divorce in Canada, 1900–1939* (T: UTP 1991).

The topic of reproduction has also produced a lively historical literature. Angus McLaren and Arlene Tigar McLaren, *The Bedroom and the State: The Changing Practices and Politics of Contraception and Abortion in Canada, 1880–1980* (T: M&S 1986) provides an excellent starting point. A special issue of *Ontario History* (1983) contains five articles on motherhood issues and reproduction, and there are other useful articles: Suzann Buckley, 'Ladies or Midwives? Efforts to Reduce Infant and Maternal Mortality,' in L. Kealey, ed., *A Not Unreasonable Claim;* Cynthia Comacchio Abeele, '"The Mothers of the Land Must Suffer": Child and Maternal Welfare in Rural and Outpost Ontario,' *OH* 1988; and Eric G. Moore and Brian S. Osborne, 'Marital Fertility in Kingston, 1861–1871: A Study of Socioeconomic Differentials,' *HS/SH* 1987. Attitudes about motherhood and sexuality are addressed in Wendy Mitchinson's excellent book, *The Nature of Their Bodies: Women and Their Doctors in Victorian Canada* (T: UTP 1991); it examines doctors' perception of women, the changing nature of interventional medicines, and the social conventions that shaped medical attitudes. There is also, of course, Michael Bliss, 'Pure Books on Avoided Subjects: Pre-Freudian Sexual Ideas in Canada,' in Michiel Horn and Ronald Sabourin, eds., *Studies in Canadian Social History* (T: M&S 1974). An interesting perspective on gender and sport is found in Helen Lenskyj, *Out of Bounds: Women, Sport, and Sexuality* (T: The Women's Press 1986).

Finally, there are a number of biographical studies of Ontario women worth noting. Veronica Strong-Boag edited, *'A Woman with a Purpose': The Diaries of Elizabeth Smith, 1872–1884* (T: UTP 1980); it provides useful insights into the life of one of Ontario's first women doctors by discussing education, courtship, and medicine. Terry Crowley's *Agnes Macphail and the Politics of Equality* (T: JL 1990) looks at the life and career of Canada's first woman MP. It is far more analytical than Doris Pennington's *Agnes Macphail, Reformer: Canada's First Female M.P.* (T: Simon & Pierre 1989). Two other popular biographies are also weak: Mary Beacock Fryer, *Emily Stowe: Doctor and Suffragist* (T: Dundurn 1990), and Cheryl MacDonald, *Adelaide Hoodless: Domestic Crusader* (T: Dundurn 1986). Of more use is Terry Crowley, 'Madonnas before Magdalenes: Adelaide Hoodless and the Making of the Canadian Gibson Girl,' *CHR* 1986. An excellent analysis of Charlotte Whitton, one of Canada's earliest proponents of social welfare and the first woman mayor of Ottawa, is contained in P.T. Rooke and R.L. Schnell, *No Bleeding Heart: Charlotte Whitton, A Feminist on the Right* (V: UBCP 1987). Also of note is James Struthers, 'A Profession in Crisis: Charlotte Whitton and Social Work in the 1930s,' *CHR* 1981.

REGIONAL AND LOCAL STUDIES AND URBAN HISTORY

Regional and local identities are also important in defining Ontario's character. Some of the best historical writing has been done on northern

Ontario. Angus Gilbert has edited a special issue of the *Laurentian University Review* (1979), on 'Historical Essays on Northern Ontario,' and the March 1990 issue of *Ontario History* is devoted to the region. Morris Zaslow's *The Opening of the Canadian North, 1870–1914* (T: M&S 1971) provides a good introduction to settlement, the forest and mining industries, transportation, and the role of government. There is also Matt Bray and Ernie Epp, eds., *A Vast and Magnificent Land: An Illustrated History of Northern Ontario* (Thunder Bay: Lakehead University 1984).

Much of the existing literature deals with the economic exploitation of Northern Ontario. *The Canadian Frontiers of Settlement* series vol. 9 (T: MAC 1936) contains studies by Arthur R.M. Lower, *Settlement and the Forest Frontier in Eastern Canada* and by Harold A. Innis, *Settlement and the Mining Frontier*. Dianne Newell examines the resource-extractive industries of northern Ontario, emphasizing the economic and technological changes, in *Technology on the Frontier: Mining in Old Ontario* (V: UBCP 1986). Philip Smith, *Harvest from the Rock: A History of Mining in Ontario* (T: MAC 1986), and R. Matt Bray and Ashley Thomson, eds., *At the End of the Shift: Mines and Single-Industry Towns in Northern Ontario* (T: Dundurn 1992) are popular histories. H.V. Nelles, *The Politics of Development: Forests, Mines, and Hydro-Electric Power in Ontario, 1849–1941* (T: MAC 1974) is an excellent study of the natural resource industries, the entrepreneurs who developed them, and government policies. Albert Tucker, *Steam into the Wilderness: Ontario Northland Railway, 1902–1962* (T: Fitzhenry & Whiteside 1978) looks at the railway company and the political context of development. *Steel at the Sault: Francis H. Clergue, Sir James Dunn, and the Algoma Steel Corporation, 1901–1956* (T: UTP 1984) by Duncan McDowall is also not simply a company history; it explores the economic and political context for Algoma Steel with some facility and contributes to an understanding of northern Ontario. The social and economic relations defined by the resource industries of the region are analysed in three excellent works: Wallace Clement, *Hardrock Mining: Industrial Relations and Technological Changes at Inco* (T: M&S 1981), which focuses on the period since 1945; Ian Radforth, *Bushworkers and Bosses: Logging in Northern Ontario, 1900–1980* (T: UTP 1987), which discusses the pulpwood logging industry and company strategies but is primarily concerned with the workers' struggles against the impact of mechanization; and Laurel Sefton MacDowell's *'Remember Kirkland Lake': The History and Effects of the Kirkland Lake Gold Miners' Strike, 1941–1942* (T: UTP 1983), which looks at the devastation to workers' families and the community as a result of the strike.

One of the most important books on the region is Bruce W. Hodgins and Jamie Benidickson, *The Temagami Experience: Recreation, Resources, and Aboriginal Rights in the Northern Ontario Wilderness* (T: UTP 1989). It presents an environmentalist perspective in its analysis of the conflict between sustainable development, Native rights, and conservation as the logging and mining companies, the Teme-augama Anishnabai tribe, and vacationers competed for the Temagami Forest Reserve.

Other regions have also been well serviced, notably eastern Ontario. Chad Gaffield has written that there is a tendency to study the ideological and political dimensions of regionalism rather than the demographic and economic ones in 'The New Regional History: Rethinking the History of the Outaouais,' *JCS* 1991. His 'Boom or Bust: The Demography and Economy of the Lower Ottawa Valley in the Nineteenth Century,' *CHA* 1982, first outlined the approach that was to shape *Language, Schooling, and Cultural Conflict*. Other important sources have already been noted – Akenson's *The Irish in Ontario* and Elliot's *Irish Migrants in the Canadas*, for example. Royce MacGillivray and Ewan Ross produced a good local history, *A History of Glengarry* (Belleville: Mika Publishing 1979), and Ruth McKenzie wrote *Leeds and Grenville: Their First Two Hundred Years* (T: M&S 1967). The area around Bruce County has been discussed in Norman Robertson, *The History of the County of Bruce and of the Minor Municipalities Therein* (1906, Owen Sound: Richardson, Bond & Wright 1969); Norman McLeod *The History of the County of Bruce and of the Minor Municipalities Therein, 1907–1968* (Southhampton: Bruce County Historical Society 1969); W. Sherwood Fox, *The Bruce Beckons: The Story of Lake Huron's Great Peninsula* (T: UTP 1952); and W.R. Wightman, *Forever on the Fringe: Six Studies in the Development of the Manitoulin Island* (T: UTP 1982).

Most local histories are done by amateurs. Few are useful for the post-Confederation period because they focus on the pioneers and early settlement and often simply list schools, churches, prominent individuals and families, and local political developments; there are, for example, over two hundred Tweedsmuir histories prepared by Women's Institutes. One notable local history has been done by the professional historian Leo A. Johnson, *History of the County of Ontario 1615–1875* (Whitby: Corporation of the County of Ontario 1973); an interesting amateur study is *Greenbank: Country Matters in 19th Century Ontario* (Peterborough: Broadview Press 1988) by W.H. Graham which won a CHA regional history award for its discussion of the social and economic history of rural Ontario from 1835 to 1935 by focusing upon four farms.

There are also numerous studies of cities and towns in the province. Jacob Spelt's *Urban Development in South-Central Ontario* (1955, O: Carleton UP 1983) is a comparative overview of urban growth. Also useful are John U. Marshall, *The Location of Service Towns: An Approach to the Analysis of Central Place Systems* (T: UTP 1969) and John U. Marshall and W.R. Smith, 'The Dynamics of Growth in a Regional Urban System: Southern Ontario, 1851–1971,' *Canadian Geographer* 1978. The *Urban History Review* is the best source for periodical literature on urban development in Ontario.

As might be expected, there is a large literature on Toronto. The older sources link economic development and urban growth by emphasizing the metropolitan interpretation. These include: D.C. Masters, *The Rise of Toronto, 1850–1890* (T: UTP 1947), and Jacob Spelt, *Toronto* (T: Collier-Macmillan 1973). More recently, urban history has focused upon the internal history of the city and the social patterns of its inhabitants. G.P. de T. Glazebrook offers an old-fashioned narrative in *The Story of Toronto* (T: UTP 1971) and Peter G. Goheen's *Victorian Toronto, 1850 to 1900: Pattern and Process of Growth* (Chicago: University of Chicago 1970) is a quantitative analysis, heavy on methodology and light on interesting historical detail. The History of Canadian Cities Series has produced two volumes on Toronto. J.M.S. Careless's *Toronto to 1918: An Illustrated History* (T: JL 1984) emphasizes the economic relationship of the metropolis of Toronto to its hinterland; political, social, and cultural developments of the period are also covered. Few new themes are explored and the work is based on secondary sources. *Toronto since 1918: An Illustrated History* (T: JL 1985) by James Lemon, a historical geographer, looks at the evolution of Toronto from an Anglo-Protestant community to a pluralistic and multi-ethnic city by the 1980s, and explores the process of suburbanization quite well. It is not a comprehensive study; the treatment of municipal government and politics is weak. There are also some important collections of articles on Toronto: Russell has edited *Forging a Consensus* (cited above), which includes essays on municipal services, the creation of the board of control, public transportation, office development, and public utilities. Russell has also edited the two-volume *Mayors of Toronto*, vol. 1, *1834–1899*; and vol. 2, *1900–1984* (Erin: Boston Mills Press 1982, 1984) and Frederick H. Armstrong has collected his articles in *A City in the Making: Progress, People, and Perils in Victorian Toronto* (T: Dundurn 1988), although only a few of the essays deal with the post-Confederation period.

The impact of industrialization on Toronto's workers has been analysed in Gregory S. Kealey's excellent study, *Toronto Workers Respond to Industrial Capitalism, 1867–1892* (2nd ed., T: UTP 1991). He discusses institutions and strategies of skilled workers facing the social and economic changes accompanying industrial capitalism. Michael Piva has written *The Condition of the Working Class in Toronto, 1900–1921* (O: UOP 1979), and Frager's *Sweatshop Strife* has been noted previously.

Some of the most interesting work on Toronto has focused on the topic of municipal politics and urban reform. There are two important general sources: Paul Rutherford, ed., *Saving the Canadian City: The First Phase, 1880–1920* (T: UTP 1974), and John C. Weaver, ed., *Shaping the Canadian City: Essays on Urban Politics and Policy, 1890–1920* (T: Institute of Public Administration of Canada 1977). Christopher Armstrong and H.V. Nelles, *The Revenge of the Methodist Bicycle Company: Sunday Streetcars and Municipal Reform in Toronto, 1888–1897* (T: Peter Martin Associates 1977) is an amusing account of municipal reform. There is also John Weaver's 'Order and Efficiency: S. Morley Wickett and the Urban Progressive Movement in Toronto, 1900–1915,' *OH* 1977, and Michael J. Doucet, 'Mass Transit and the Failure of Private Ownership: The Case of Toronto in the Early Twentieth Century,' *UHR* 1978. The best works on recent municipal politics in Metropolitan Toronto are Albert Rose, *Governing Metropolitan Toronto: A Social and Political Analysis, 1953–1971* (Los Angeles: University of California Press 1972), and Timothy J. Colton's biography of the first chairman of the Metropolitan Toronto Council, *Big Daddy: Frederick G. Gardiner and the Building of Metropolitan Toronto* (T: UTP 1980). An official history, *Metro's Housing Company: The First 35 Years* by Michael McMahon (T: Metropolitan Housing Co. 1990), addresses the topic of housing for seniors.

While Toronto has a large quantity of historical writing, the best quality work has focused on Hamilton. John C. Weaver's *Hamilton: An Illustrated History* (T: JL 1982) is one of the best books in the Canadian Cities series. It discusses the spatial evolution of Hamilton and examines the economic transition from commerce to industry in the nineteenth century. Themes like social class and ethnicity are explored and the cultural development of the city is examined. There are also some important monographs which focus on Hamilton. The Hamilton project, headed by Michael B. Katz, exploited quantitative data in order to reconstruct the social patterns of the city; the transiency and inequality which characterized the local population is analysed with some facility in *The People of Hamilton, Canada West: Family and Class in a Mid-Nineteenth-Century City* (Cambridge: HUP 1975). Bryan D. Palmer's *A Culture in Conflict: Skilled Workers and Indus-*

trial Capitalism in Hamilton, Ontario, 1860–1914 (M and K: MQUP 1979) examines the breakdown of working-class culture among the skilled artisans of the city in the face of industrial-capitalist development. *Working in Steel: The Early Years in Canada, 1883–1935* by Craig Heron (T: M&S 1988) discusses the business of steel-making and the responses of workers. A study of major importance is Michael Doucet and John Weaver, *Housing the North American City* (M and K: MQUP 1991), which focuses on Hamilton. An impressive amount of data is assembled to explore land speculation and the development of suburbs, government policy, the demography of home owners and the psychology of home ownership, the quality of homes, and the relationship between landlords and tenants, among others. More important, this is not just a narrow, local study; the perspective is broader than Hamilton.

There are a number of popular histories of Ottawa but the city was not particularly well served until John H. Taylor's *Ottawa: An Illustrated History* (T: JL 1986). It addresses both the biculturalism of Ottawa and its evolution from a lumbering town to a government city. Peter Gillis has written 'Big Business and the Origins of the Conservative Reform Movement in Ottawa, 1890–1912,' *JCS* 1980. There are a couple of sources on Kingston: Gerald Tulchinsky, ed., *To Preserve and Defend: Essays on Kingston in the Nineteenth Century* (M and K: MQUP 1976), and Brian S. Osborne and Donald Swainson, *Kingston: Building on the Past* (Westport: Butternut Press 1988). Leo Johnson has written a *History of Guelph, 1827–1927* (Guelph: Guelph Historical Society 1977); and John English and Kenneth McLaughlin produced *Kitchener: An Illustrated History* (Wa: WLUP 1983).

THE ECONOMY AND CLASS FORMATION

Having discussed the historical writing about Ontario's people, how their social relations have been constructed and their identities defined, the next question to be asked is: what did they do? Thus the economy becomes the focus for discussion. A number of topics are addressed through an examination of the development of the provincial economy: the manner in which primary resources have been exploited, and the social consequences of exploitation; the impact of industrialization; the growth of the service sector; and, finally, how the economy has structured social classes in Ontario.

The provincial economy cannot be understood in isolation from both the international and national contexts; therefore Kenneth Norrie and

Doug Owram's *A History of the Canadian Economy* (T: HBJ 1991), is a good starting point. This interdisciplinary synthesis is a comprehensive study and emphasizes the staples framework as the organizing theme. Michael Bliss has produced the best study of national business development, notably the shift from a commercial to an industrial economy in the nineteenth century and the emergence of the service economy in the twentieth century, the activities of Canada's businessmen, and the problems associated with government intervention, in *Northern Enterprise: Five Centuries of Canadian Business* (T: M&S 1987). Ontario became the heartland of the national economy and *Heartland and Hinterland: A Geography of Canada*, edited by L.D. McCann (2nd ed., Scarborough: PH 1987) outlines the emergence of the industrial heartland, industrial and urban growth, and the heartland-hinterland relationship.

Statistical data on economic development can be found in F.H. Leacy, ed., *Historical Statistics of Canada* (2nd ed., O: Statistics Canada 1983); there is material on staple production, manufacturing, construction and housing, transportation and communications, as well as internal trade, although provincial figures are presented in national aggregates. The *Historical Atlas of Canada*, vol. 3, *Addressing the Twentieth Century, 1891–1961*, edited by Donald Kerr and Deryck W. Holdsworth (T: UTP 1990), provides the visual pictures of patterns of economic growth, primary production, manufacturing, trade, the development of power resources, the crisis of the Great Depression, the nature of the workforce, and the responses of labour to economic changes. Also of use is Dean, ed., *Economic Atlas of Ontario* (cited above), for the period from 1945 to the 1960s.

There are two essential overviews of Ontario's economic development from the 1860s to 1973, published as part of the Ontario Historical Studies Series. Ian M. Drummond's *Progress without Planning: The Economic History of Ontario from Confederation to the Second War* (T: UTP 1987) is a very good examination of natural resource exploitation, industrialization, transportation, and services, although these themes are not as integrated as they might be. Drummond argues that Ontario's economy was largely shaped by market forces rather than government planning and that local demands were more important than national markets in shaping the provincial economy and fuelling prosperity. The work is situated in the political-economy tradition, though, and does not offer a broader social and political context. K.J. Rea's *The Prosperous Years: The Economic History of Ontario, 1939–1975* (T: UTP 1985), on the other hand, emphasizes the important role that government spending played in stimulating the provincial economy after World War II. Rea discusses economic productivity, population growth, the shift to a service-oriented economy, and public planning, but concludes that increasing government intervention, especially at the federal level, led to a loss of provincial autonomy in the economic sector and then to diminishing faith in state management because there was no long-term strategy or consistent policy. The book explains what happened very well, but the broader analysis is weaker.

The Staples Industries

Ontario is a province rich in natural resources and therefore staple production laid the foundation for the development of the provincial economy. It attracted immigrants and capital, boosted living standards, stimulated urban and industrial development, and shaped political responses. Each sector of the staples economy has a strong body of literature.

The classic overview of agricultural development is Robert Leslie Jones, *History of Agriculture in Ontario, 1613–1880* (T: UTP 1946); not as good is a work which continues into the twentieth century, G. Elmore Reaman's *A History of Agriculture in Ontario*, 2 vols. (T: Saunders 1970). John McCallum, *Unequal Beginnings: Agriculture and Economic Development in Quebec and Ontario until 1870* (T: UTP 1980) is a comparative study which, while concentrating on the pre-Confederation period, argues that Ontario's competitive advantage lay in its superior agricultural resources and the farming that laid the foundation for the growth of towns, transportation systems, and industry. There is also J. de Visser, R. Sallows, and J. Carroll, *The Farm: A Celebration of Two Hundred Years of Farming in Ontario* (T: Methuen 1984).

Donald H. Akenson has edited the series *Canadian Papers in Rural History* (Gananoque: Langdale Press 1978–1992), which contains several important articles on agriculture in Old Ontario; in the most recent collection, R. Marvin McInnis has outlined 'Perspectives on Ontario Agriculture, 1815–1930,' and Robert E. Ankli has written about 'Ontario's Dairy Industry, 1880–1920.' Alan A. Brookes has edited a number of the *Proceedings* of the Agricultural History of Ontario Seminar held at the University of Guelph. There are several important articles about agriculture, including Robert E. Ankli and Wendy Millar, 'Ontario Agriculture in Transition: The Switch from Wheat to Cheese,' *Journal of Economic History* 1982; D.A. Lawr, 'The Development of Ontario Farming, 1870–1914: Patterns of Growth and Change,' *OH* 1972; William L. Marr, 'The Wheat Economy in Reverse: Ontario's Wheat Production, 1887–1917,' *CJE* 1981; and Joy Parr, 'Hired Men: Ontario Agricultural Wage Labour in Historical Perspective,' *Labour* 1985.

The crucial role of women on the farm is discussed in Rosemary Ball, 'A Perfect Farmer's Wife: Women in the 19th Century Rural Ontario,' *Canada: An Historical Magazine* 1975; a far more important work which incorporates gender into economic history is Marjorie Griffin Cohen's *Women's Work, Markets, and Economic Development* (cited above). Cohen emphasizes women's contribution to the productive economy of the farm and argues that women's work was essential to the development of a market economy. Also to be noted are A.A. Brookes and C.A. Wilson, 'Working away from the Farm: The Young Women of North Huron, 1910–1930,' *OH* 1985, and in the same volume, M. McKechnie, 'The United Farm Women of Ontario: Developing a Political Consciousness.'

Agriculture is not just an economic activity; it shaped the rural way of life with its physical isolation, extended family networks, simple social organization, and seasonal labour patterns. The result was the development of a set of values best outlined in the classic *Rural Life in Canada: Its Trends and Tasks* by John MacDougall (1913, T: UTP 1973). Responses to social and economic change are analysed in David Gagan, *Hopeful Travellers* (cited above). The political reactions of farmers are discussed in Louis Aubrey Wood, *A History of Farmers' Movements in Canada: The Origins and Development of Agrarian Protest, 1872–1924* (1924, T: UTP 1975); *Farmers Confront Industrialism: Some Historical Perspectives on Ontario Agrarian Movements* by Russell G. Hann (3rd ed., T: New Hogtown Press 1975); and articles by S.E.D. Shortt, 'Social Change and Political Crisis in Rural Ontario: The Patrons of Industry, 1889–1896,' in Swainson, ed., *Oliver Mowat's Ontario*; W.R. Young, 'Conscription, Rural Depopulation, and the Farmers of Ontario, 1917–1919,' *CHR* 1972; B.C. Tennyson's 'The Ontario General Election of 1919: The Beginnings of Agrarian Revolt,' *JCS* 1969; and Terry Crowley, 'The New Canada Movement: Agrarian Youth Protest in the 1930s,' *OH* 1988. An essential source for the rise and fall of the United Farmers of Ontario is Charles M. Johnston, *E.C. Drury: Agrarian Idealist* (T: UTP 1986), while *Agnes Macphail and the Politics of Equality* by Terry Crowley discusses Macphail's emergence as a farmers' candidate.

The forest industry has been examined in Arthur R.M. Lower, *Settlement and the Forest Frontier in Eastern Canada*, and John Guthrie, *The Newsprint Paper Industry: An Economic Analysis* (Cambridge: HUP 1941). A work focusing on conservation is Richard S. Lambert with Paul Pross, *Renewing Nature's Wealth: A Centennial History of the Public Management of Lands, Forests, and Wildlife in Ontario, 1763–1967* (T: Ontario Department of Lands and Forests 1967). Ian Radforth has written an excellent study of Ontario's pulpwood logging industry and the workers' responses to changes in the industry, *Bushworkers and Bosses* (cited above).

Studies of the mining economy begin with Harold A. Innis, *Settlement and the Mining Frontier*; E.S. Moore's two works, *The Mineral Resources of Canada* (T: RP 1933) and *The American Influence in Canadian Mining* (T: UTP 1941); and O.W. Main, *The Canadian Nickel Industry: A Study in Market Control and Public Policy* (T: UTP 1955). There are popular histories, such as *Metals and Men: The Story of Canadian Mining* (T: M&S 1957) and *Sudbury Basin: The Story of Nickel* (T: RP 1953), both by Donat M. LeBourdais, and Philip Smith's *Harvest from the Rock*. The most important source is now Dianne Newell, *Technology on the Frontier*, which discusses the exploitation of Ontario's resource hinterland for the American metal processing industry. It is especially strong on the economic and technological changes which affected mining.

An impressive monograph (cited above) on the natural resource industry in Ontario is H. Nelles, *The Politics of Development*; it offers an excellent appraisal of government developmental policies. *Power at Cost: Ontario Hydro and Rural Electrification, 1911–1958* by Keith R. Fleming (M and K: MQUP 1992) illustrates the response of the provincial government and Ontario Hydro to rural demands for electricity. In a detailed examination, Fleming argues that this was a response to both the ethic of public good and political pressure. Christopher Armstrong and H.V. Nelles have produced *Monopoly's Moment: The Organization and Regulation of Canadian Utilities, 1830–1930* (2nd ed., T: UTP 1988), which discusses the process of governmental control over utilities; there is a chapter on Ontario Hydro.

Industrial Development

There is no general synthesis on industrialization in Ontario. There has been some good specialized work by historical geographers, including James M. Gilmour, *Spatial Evolution of Manufacturing: Southern Ontario, 1851–1891* (T: UTP 1972). There is an interesting and informative debate on 'Ontario's Industrial Revolution,' *CHR* 1988. The importance of the protective tariff to Ontario's industrial growth cannot be understated and Ben Forster's *A Conjunction of Interests: Business, Politics, and Tariffs, 1825–1879* (T: UTP 1986) provides a comprehensive discussion of the events which led up to the adoption of the National Policy. The close ties between business and government are also illustrated in Elizabeth Bloomfield, 'Municipal Bonusing of Industry: The Legislative Framework in Ontario to 1930,' *UHR* 1981.

There are a few good studies of individual companies. William Kilbourn wrote *The Elements Combined: A History of the Steel Company of Canada*

(T: CI 1960) and E.P. Neufeld produced *A Global Corporation: A History of the International Development of Massey-Ferguson Limited* (T: UTP 1969). Peter Cook's *Massey at the Brink: The Story of Canada's Greatest Multinational and it Struggle to Survive* (T: Collins 1981) deals with the collapse of the company. One of Canada's finest business historians, Duncan McDowall, has published two excellent business histories: *Steel at the Sault* (cited above) and *The Light: Brazilian Traction, Light, and Power Co., Ltd. 1899-1945* (T: UTP 1988).

Class Formation

One of the important consequences of urban and industrial development in Ontario was increasing social stratification. Some attention has been paid to the business elite although the approach has focused more on the 'great man' than on class relationships; Peter C. Newman's popular books on *The Canadian Establishment*, vol. 1, vol. 2, *The Acquisitors*, and vol. 3, *The Establishment Man: A Portrait of Power* (T: M&S 1975, 1981, 1982) on Conrad Black, provide the best examples. The 'businessman as villain' approach is best illustrated by Wallace Clement's *The Canadian Corporate Elite: An Analysis of Economic Power* (T: M&S 1975).

The changing nature of the business class in the country is outlined in T.W. Acheson, 'Changing Social Origins of the Canadian Industrial Elite,' in Glenn Porter and Robert D. Cuff, eds., *Enterprise and National Development: Essays in Canadian Business and Economic History* (T: Hakkert 1973). The attitudes of businessmen about competition, the tariff, farmers, and unions are examined in *A Living Profit: Studies in the Social History of Canadian Business, 1883-1911* by Michael Bliss (T: M&S 1974). There are a number of good biographies of individual businessmen. Michael Bliss has written one of the best in *A Canadian Millionaire: The Life and Business Times of Sir Joseph Flavelle, Bart., 1858-1939* (2nd ed., T: UTP 1992); it offers a superb analysis of financial leadership, business organization, and management structures as well as offering insights into Methodism and philanthropy. Duncan McDowall's *Steel at the Sault* examines the entrepreneurial capitalism of Francis Clergue and Sir James Dunn; Joy L. Santink's *Timothy Eaton and the Rise of His Department Store* (T: UTP 1990) offers a chronological look at the growth of the business and emphasizes Eaton's personal role as the key to success.

Most work on the topic of class formation focuses not on businessmen but on working people. The dominant school, influenced by the work of E.P. Thompson and Herbert Gutman, emphasizes the development of class consciousness and attempts by the working class to protect its distinctive culture. Marxist ideology shapes this type of analysis and thus every strike becomes an example of class conflict. The best example of this approach is Bryan D. Palmer's synthesis *Working-Class Experience: Rethinking the History of Canadian Labour, 1800–1991* (T: M&S 1992), which is an essential starting-point for any examination of working people in Ontario; a narrower focus is offered in his article written with Craig Heron, 'Through the Prism of the Strike: Industrial Conflict in Southern Ontario, 1901–1914,' *CHR* 1977. A more international perspective, although with Canadian material, is Michael B. Katz, Michael J. Doucet and Mark J. Stern, *The Social Organization of Early Industrial Capitalism* (Cambridge HUP 1982). The journal *Labour/Le Travail* has a number of articles on Ontario subjects; the most comprehensive collection of essays in this field is *Canadian Working-Class History: Selected Readings*, edited by Laurel Sefton MacDowell and Ian Radforth (T: Canadian Scholars Press 1992).

An impressive body of monographic literature has been produced on the working class in Ontario by a new generation of labour historians. Bryan D. Palmer's *A Culture in Conflict* examines the development of a working-class culture among the skilled artisans in Hamilton, and the ways in which workers protested the emerging industrial-capitalist structures. Gregory S. Kealey's *Toronto Workers Respond to Industrial Capitalism* also stresses the dynamic of class when examining Toronto's industrial revolution. He analyses the impact of industrialization on Toronto's skilled workers and how the artisans sought to maintain control of production in the factories. He looks at both labour organizations and the political responses of workers as well, emphasizing the traditions upon which the artisans built. Kealey and Palmer together produced *Dreaming of What Might Be: The Knights of Labor in Ontario, 1880–1900* (NY: Cambridge UP 1982). This romantic study, emphasizing successes rather than failures, argues that the Knights built on the working-class culture to create an organization which united working people of diverse backgrounds, both men and women, along reformist and cooperative lines. The idealistic Knights of Labor were a transitional group, between the traditional artisan societies and industrial trade unions, which fought the emerging industrial-capitalist economy and ultimately lost.

Michael Piva has examined the material conditions of Toronto's working class and the problems it faced in *The Condition of the Working Class in Toronto, 1900–1921* (O: UOP 1979); he concludes that a conscious militant working class did not appear. There are a number of important studies of others groups of working people. Craig Heron's *Working in Steel: The Early Years in Canada* (T: M&S 1988) provides a useful discussion of the organization of the steel industry and an insightful discussion of life in the steel mills as well as the responses of workers to changes in the workplace. Wallace Clement's *Hardrock Mining* discusses working conditions and labour's responses to changes in the mining industry since World War II. Ian Radforth's *Bushworkers and Bosses* examines the pulpwood logging industry, conditions in the camps, and the organization and struggle of the unions dealing with the impact of mechanization on the workers. There are some useful articles in the periodical literature: Wayne Roberts has two published in *Labour*, 'Artisans, Aristocrats, and Handymen: Politics and Unionism among Toronto's Skilled Building Trades Workers, 1896–1914,' 1976 and 'Toronto Metal Workers and the Second Industrial Revolution,' 1980; also in that journal is Desmond Morton, 'Taking on the Grand Trunk: The Locomotive Engineers' Strike of 1876–7,' 1977.

There are some good monographs on union activity and strikes. A more traditional approach is presented in Robert H. Babcock, *Gompers in Canada: A Study in American Continentalism before the First World War* (T: UTP 1974); Sally F. Zerker has produced an institutional study, *The Rise and Fall of the Toronto Typographical Union, 1832–1972: A Case Study of Foreign Domination* (T: UTP 1982); and *The Eaton Drive: The Campaign to Organize Canada's Largest Department Store* (cited above) was written by one of the organizers, Eileen Sufrin. Two important works are James Naylor, *The New Democracy: Challenging the Social Order in Industrial Ontario, 1914–1925* (T: UTP 1991), which focuses upon post-war labour discontent, examines working-class views of the state, unions and women, and emphasizes the link between strikes and political activity; and Laurel Sefton MacDowell, *Remember Kirkland Lake*, which illustrates an interesting new direction for labour history by examining the impact of a strike on the union, its members and their families, and the community in general. The work is critical of the government, which played an active role in breaking the strike, and emphasizes the weakness of organized labour in its attempts to achieve its demands.

Books which successfully link gender and class are Marjorie Griffin Cohen's *Women's Work, Markets, and Economic Development*; Graham S. Lowe's *Women in the Administrative Revolution*; Joy Parr's outstanding work, *The Gender of Breadwinners*; *It's a Working Man's Town: Male Working-Class Culture in Northwestern Ontario* by Thomas W. Dunk (M and K: MQUP 1991); and Ruth A. Frager's *Sweatshop Strife*.

The relationship between the Ontario government and the working class is explored in Eric Tucker, *Administering Danger in the Workplace: The Law and Politics of Occupational Health and Safety Regulation in Ontario, 1850–1914* (T: UTP 1990), which argues that industrial safety legislation was largely an expression of the political desire to attract working-class support and a consequence of the expansion of the state's role. But as workers lost control of the workplace, the legislation offered little real protection because it was not enforced.

Analyses of class formation, especially for the late nineteenth and early twentieth centuries, still leave some questions unanswered: did the pace of urban and industrial development advance so quickly in this period that working people were unable to adapt? How important was the family in providing a stable and secure environment for the working class? When did class lines crystallize in Ontario? Was the society divided by class conflict or was it characterized by class consciousness among all groups, each with its own social ideal?

SOCIAL AND CULTURAL HISTORY

Ontario's cultural history remains an underdeveloped topic of study; there is, in fact, some debate about the nature of the provincial culture and the best means to understand its development. A.B. McKillop, for example, favours the intellectual history approach, although in 'Culture, Intellect, and Context: Recent Writing on the Cultural and Intellectual History of Ontario,' *JCS* 1989, he argues that ideas transcend provincial boundaries. Elwood Jones, on the other hand, believes that historians must explore more fully the links between social history and culture, and between politics and culture: see his article 'English-Canadian Culture in the Nineteenth Century: Love, History, and Politics,' *JCS* 1990–1. An examination of ideas in their historical context does reveal broader social attitudes and values, especially in areas like religion, because the religious dimension shaped Ontario's social, cultural, and intellectual history in the nineteenth century. Moreover, demands for reform, especially in the area of education, illustrate how Ontario society responded to the social and economic changes which were transforming it in this period.

Religion

In the previous edition of this *Guide*, Peter Oliver commented that: '... most work to date has been national in approach and institutional in character

... Generally, however, religious history remains the most neglected area of post-Confederation Ontario history.' This is no longer the case, as a number of dynamic works have appeared recently in this field.

With the development of a commercial economy in Old Ontario by the mid-nineteenth century, power was in the hands of the progressive classes, the entrepreneurs, and the professionals, and the new ethos became development, not just existence. As a result, the Protestant denominations had to face the challenge of maintaining their position as society's moral foundation. There was a shift from theology based on faith to a concern with family morals and social responsibility; the churches thus supported the creation of voluntary institutions to achieve reform. With this new emphasis on the whole community, old ethnic and denominational identities began to break down and a Protestant culture began to emerge in Ontario.

The best synthesis is John Webster Grant's *A Profusion of Spires: Religion in Nineteenth-Century Ontario* (T: UTP 1988), which was prepared for the Ontario Historical Studies Series. It discusses the religious evolution of the province and concludes that a general Protestant consensus shaped Ontario's culture. There was no crisis of confidence in the churches, but rather, through their missions and links to the social reform movements, the Protestant denominations believed that religion could respond to new challenges and transform the society. *Two Worlds: The Protestant Culture of Nineteenth-Century Ontario* (M and K: MQUP 1989) is a complex and provocative study by William Westfall. He examines the development of a Protestant consensus by 1870 which united the Anglican culture of order with the Methodist emphasis on experience. The linkage between rational development and morality shaped the social system and social consciousness, defining the family, the school, and the community. Ontario's Protestant culture reconciled the secular and the sacred, giving strength to the idea that this world could be reformed. By contrast, Neil Semple has stressed the Methodist influence rather than consensus in the shift from a theology based on faith to one based on family morality and social reform in his 'The Quest for Kingdom: Aspects of Protestant Revivalism in Nineteenth-Century Ontario,' in David Keane and Colin Read, eds., *Old Ontario: Essays in Honour of J.M.S. Careless* (T: Dundurn 1990).

The relationship between religion and secular society was first explored in Richard Allen's *The Social Passion: Religion and Social Reform in Canada, 1914–1928* (T: UTP 1973), which stressed the positive impact of religious ideas on reform thought. This relationship is also the main theme in Ramsay Cook's *The Regenerators: Social Criticism in Late Victorian English*

Canada (T: UTP 1985), but the conclusion is different. Cook argues that modern Protestant theology accommodated itself to the challenges posed by Darwinian science, criticism of the Bible, and free thought by focusing on social salvation. Moral reformers looked increasingly to the social sciences for secular explanations of social problems and abandoned religious views of human sin; religion, therefore, became less relevant in modern society. In *A Disciplined Intelligence: Critical Inquiry and Canadian Thought in the Victorian Era* (M and K: MQUP 1979), A.B. McKillop examined philosophical thought among the intellectual leaders in Canadian universities, where it was generally agreed that social morality could be understood from the nature of things and where traditional religion had given way to philosophic idealism. Carl Berger looked at the connection between the enthusiasm for science and religion in *Science, God, and Nature in Victorian Canada* (T: UTP 1983). David B. Marshall has also explored the ways in which religious leaders addressed the intellectual challenges which they faced in his *Secularizing the Faith: Canadian Protestant Clergy and the Crisis of Belief, 1850–1940* (T: UTP 1992), but he concludes that the churches became marginalized by the changes taking place and thus focused on missions and social reform. Also of note are Brian J. Fraser, *The Social Uplifters: Presbyterian Progressives and the Social Gospel in Canada, 1875–1915* (Wa: WLUP 1988), and Phyllis D. Airhart, *Serving the Present Age: Revivalism, Progressivism, and the Methodist Tradition in Canada* (M and K: MQUP 1992).

The religious reaction to the crisis of secularization is rejected by Marguerite Van Die in *An Evangelical Mind: Nathanael Burwash and the Methodist Tradition in Canada, 1839–1918* (M and K: MQUP 1989). Burwash, one of Canada's most influential educators and theologians, remained an evangelical, focusing upon individual redemption rather than social reform. He did not fear social and intellectual challenges because of his faith. In *The Evangelical Century: College and Creed in English Canada from the Great Revival to the Great Depression* (M and K: MQUP 1991), Michael Gauvreau stresses the flexibility of Protestant thought in the Victorian period; evangelicals were able to integrate elements of modern thought into their theology without challenging their faith. This complex work of revision makes an important contribution to our understanding of religious thought. Gauvreau also develops this argument in a thoughtful historiographical piece, 'Beyond the Half-Way House: Evangelicalism and the Shaping of English-Canadian Culture,' in *Acadiensis* 1991. The tensions which existed between church leaders and the general lay population are illustrated in N. Keith Clifford, *The Resistance to Church Union in Canada, 1904–1939*

(V: UBCP 1985). Even though the union was supported by most ministers and reformers, it was resisted in many towns and cities in Ontario.

One theme which has attracted an increasing amount of attention is the role of women in the church. According to the 'Cult of True Womanhood,' women were naturally pious and could work outside the home in the respectable helping roles within the church or as missionaries. C. Headon, 'Women and Organized Religion in Mid- and Late Nineteenth-Century Canada,' *Journal of the Canadian Church Historical Society* 1978; J.D. Thomas, 'Servants of the Church: Canadian Methodist Deaconess Work, 1890–1926,' *CHR* 1984; M.F. Whiteley, 'Doing Just About What They Please: Ladies' Aids in Ontario Methodism,' *OH* 1990; Wendy Mitchinson, 'Canadian Women and the Church Missionary Societies in the Nineteenth Century: A Step towards Independence,' *Atlantis* 1977; and Rosemary Gagan, 'More than a Lure to the Gilded Bower of Matrimony: The Education of Methodist Women Missionaries,' *Historical Studies in Education* 1989, and her book, *A Sensitive Independence: Canadian Methodist Women Missionaries in Canada and the Orient, 1881–1925* (M and K: MQUP 1992) all address these themes.

Women were especially attracted to the evangelical denominations, which in turn emphasized the social importance of the 'moral mother.' Women were to inculcate proper moral values in their families, as Neil Semple discusses in 'The Nurture and Admonition of the Lord: Nineteenth-Century Methodism's Response to Childhood.' *HS/SH* 1981, and they were also to extend their moral superiority into the larger society as part of the movement for social reform.

Social Reform and Social Welfare

The social reform movement addressed a number of problems, each of which has attracted a substantial body of literature. Richard Allen's *The Social Passion* provides a general overview for the study of social reform, although a more interesting approach is presented in *The Age of Light, Soap, and Water: Moral Reform in English Canada, 1885–1925* by Mariana Valverde (T: M&S 1991); it looks at the social purity movement through the theoretical framework provided by discourse on class, ethnicity, and gender.

The best starting point is Richard B. Splane's *Social Welfare in Ontario, 1791–1893: A Study of Public Welfare Administration* (T: UTP 1965), which provides an institutional approach to issues such as child welfare, care of the poor, public health, and crime and punishment. Any examination of child-centred reform must take into account Neil Sutherland's pioneering work, *Children in English-Canadian Society: Framing the Twentieth-Century Consensus* (T: UTP 1976), which looks at the changing views of children and explains the growing concern of middle-class Canadians with the social problems which affected children, notably public health and education. *Studies in Childhood History: A Canadian Perspective*, edited by Patricia T. Rooke and R.L. Schnell (C: Detselig 1982), contains some useful articles; they also produced 'The Rise and Decline of British North American Protestant Orphan's Homes as Women's Domain,' *Atlantis* 1982, and 'Childhood and Charity in 19th Century British North American,' *HS/SH* 1982. T.R. Morrison wrote '"Their Proper Sphere": Feminism, the Family, and Child-Centred Social Reform in Ontario, 1875–1900,' *OH* 1976, which argues that middle-class reformers were motivated by the desire for social control. *In the Children's Aid: J.J. Kelso and Child Welfare in Ontario* (T: UTP 1981) by Andrew Jones and Leonard Rutman focuses on an individual crusader for reform and his efforts directed at children and their environment. Kelso also became Superintendent of Ontario's Department of Neglected and Dependent Children and thus was able to influence the laws about child protection, juvenile delinquency, and institutional care. The work is based exclusively on Kelso's papers and should be supplemented with John Bullen, 'J.J. Kelso and the New Child Savers: The Genesis of the Children's Aid Movement in Ontario' *OH* 1990.

Useful articles on reform of the urban environment and public health include: S. Speisman, 'Munificent Parsons and Municipal Parsimony,' *OH* 1973; James Pitsula, 'The Treatment of Tramps in late Nineteenth-Century Toronto,' CHA *HP* 1980; Paul Bator, 'The Struggle to Raise the Lower Classes: Public Health and the Problems of Poverty in Canada,' *JCS* 1979, and 'The Health Reformers versus the Common Canadian: The Controversy over Compulsory Vaccination against Smallpox in Toronto and Ontario, 1900–1920,' *OH* 1983; and Heather MacDougall, 'The Genesis of Public Health Reform in Toronto, 1869–1890,' *UHR* 1982. MacDougall has also written *Activists and Advocates: Toronto's Health Department, 1883–1983* (T: Dundurn 1990), which illustrates the shift from reformers involved in the sanitation movement to professionals concerned with the scientific management of public health. Other important works also examine the development of professional health care. David Gagan's *'A Necessity Among Us': The Owen Sound General and Marine Hospital, 1891–1985* (T: UTP 1990) is an excellent study, not just of a hospital, but of the broader policies which transformed medical services in Ontario. *Moments of Unreason: The Practice of Canadian Psychiatry and the Homewood Retreat, 1883–1923* by Cheryl Krasnick Warsh (M and K: MQUP 1989) discusses the treatment of insanity, the professionalization of psychiatry, the world of the asylum, and the patients with much facility. She links her study to the intellectual and moral world of late nineteenth- and early twentieth-century Ontario. Harvey G. Simmons has written two works on government policy towards mental disability: *From Asylum to Welfare* (Downsview: National Institute on Mental Retardation 1982) and *Unbalanced: Mental Health Policy in Ontario, 1930–1989* (T: Wall & Thompson Publishing 1990).

Social reformers were also concerned with the problems associated with crime and punishment, and there is a growing body of literature which focuses on the law to offer insights into the attitudes and values of Ontarians. Volume 2 of *Essays in the History of Canadian Law*, edited by David H. Flaherty (T: UTP 1983), includes a number of articles of interest to historians of Ontario, ranging from examinations of the courts system to workers' compensation to the conflict between private rights and public purposes. R.C. Macleod, ed., *Lawful Authority: Readings on the History of Criminal Justice in Canada* (T: CCP 1988) contains articles on Toronto's police court, the Kingston penitentiary, and attempts to rehabilitate prisoners. Susan Houston's early work argued that reform was simply an expression of social control: 'The Victorian Origins of Juvenile Delinquency,' in M. Katz and P. Mattingly, eds., *Education and Social Change: Themes from Ontario's Past* (NY: New York UP 1975), and 'The "Waifs and Strays" of a Late Victorian City: Juvenile Delinquents in Toronto,' in Joy Parr, ed., *Childhood and Family in Canadian History* (T: M&S 1982). Harvey J. Graff wrote, 'Crime and Punishment in the Nineteenth Century: A New Look at Crime,' *Journal of Interdisciplinary History* 1977. Recently two monographs have appeared which deal with different aspects of legal history and touch upon developments in Ontario: Paul Romney, *Mr Attorney: The Attorney General for Ontario in Court, Cabinet, and Legislature, 1791–1899* (T: UTP 1986); and Dorothy E. Chunn, *From Punishment to Doing Good: Family Courts and Socialized Justice in Ontario, 1880–1940* (T: UTP 1992), which examines how changes in the application of the laws were related to views of the family, and how the emergence of 'socialized justice' was the result of pragmatic rather than idealistic motives. Michael Barnes, *Policing Ontario: The OPP Today* (Erin: Boston Mills 1991) is a popular history of the provincial police force.

The two great moral crusades of the period have attracted some attention. Prohibition has been addressed in Gerald A. Hallowell's political study, *Prohibition in Ontario, 1919–1923* (T: Ontario Historical Society

1972); Graeme Decarie's 'Something Old, Something New ... : Aspects of
Prohibitionism in Ontario in the 1890s,' in Donald Swainson, ed., *Oliver
Mowat's Ontario*; and Wendy Mitchinson's 'The WCTU: For God, Home,
and Native Land: A Study in Nineteenth-Century Feminism,' in Linda
Kealey, ed., *A Not Unreasonable Claim*. Several articles in Kealey's collec-
tion also focus on the topic of women's suffrage; other important sources
include Catherine L. Cleverdon, *The Woman Suffrage Movement in Canada*
(2nd ed., T: UTP 1974), which has a chapter on Ontario; Carol Lee
Bacchi, *Liberation Deferred? The Ideas of the English-Canadian Suffragists,
1877–1918* (T: UTP 1983); and the documents in Barbara Wilson, ed.,
Ontario and the First World War, 1914–1918: A Collection of Documents
(T: CS 1977).

After World War I the social reform movement, having attained its
two great goals, diminished in enthusiasm and professionals rather than
amateurs began to assume greater control over the direction of social
welfare. Dennis Guest, *The Emergence of Social Security in Canada* (2nd ed.,
V: UBCP 1985) provides a useful overview of this change. There is also
some important periodical literature, including K. McCuaig, 'From Social
Reform to Social Service: The Changing Role of Volunteers, the Anti-
tuberculosis Campaign, 1900–1930,' *CHR* 1980; James Pitsula, 'The
Emergence of Social Work in Toronto,' *JCS* 1979; and James Struthers,
'How Much is Enough? Creating a Social Minimum in Ontario, 1930–
1944,' *CHR* 1991. The works by Rooke and Schnell, and Struthers on
Charlotte Whitton, cited earlier, are also of some use. But the study of
social policy still remains a largely untouched field by Ontario historians.

Education

It was in the area of education that the social reformers achieved their
greatest success; by 1871 Ontario had a free, compulsory, non-denomina-
tional public school system and a separate Roman Catholic system. Contentious issues of the past had been resolved for the time being – schools
would retain their religious base to inculcate proper moral values, class
values would be instilled, and the state would control education to ensure
social stability and progress. The literature on the creation of the Ontario
school system in the pre-Confederation period will be assessed in the
other volume of the *Guide*, although Neil McDonald and Alf Chaiton,
eds., *Egerton Ryerson and His Times* (T: MAC 1978), should be noted.

The sources discussing the development of the Ontario school system
after Confederation include general works like C.E. Phillips, *The Develop-*

ment of Education in Canada (T: Gage 1957), and J. Donald Wilson, Robert M. Stamp, and Louis-Philippe Audet, eds., *Canadian Education: A History* (T: PH 1970); and institutional approaches, such as Robin S. Harris, *Quiet Evolution: A Study of the Educational System of Ontario* (T: UTP 1967); David M. Cameron, *Schools for Ontario: Policy-making, Administration, and Finance in the 1960s* (T: UTP 1972); and W.G. Fleming, *Ontario's Educative Society*, seven vols. (T: UTP 1971–2). The development of the separate school system is examined in two volumes by Franklin Walker, *Catholic Education and Politics in Ontario*. These works emphasize the evolution of public policy and political conflict.

With the emergence of the 'new educational history,' social science methodology was applied to the study of school systems. Educational reform was interpreted as an expression of social control by the middle class in the mid-nineteenth century; works such as Michael B. Katz and Paul Mattingly, eds., *Education and Social Change*; Alison Prentice, *The School Promoters: Education and Social Class in Mid-Nineteenth-Century Upper Canada* (T: M&S 1977); and Harvey J. Graff, *The Literacy Myth: Literacy and Social Structure in the Nineteenth-Century City* (NY: Academic Press 1979) are good examples of this approach. A far more sophisticated methodology has been outlined by Chad Gaffield in 'Children, Schooling, and Family Reproduction in Nineteenth-Century Ontario,' *CHR* 1991.

Two recent monographs produced for the Ontario Historical Studies Series have made valuable contributions to the history of education. Susan E. Houston and Alison Prentice wrote a superb synthesis in *Schooling and Scholars in Nineteenth-Century Ontario* (T: UTP 1988). No longer was educational reform viewed simply as a means of social control; it was seen to be the key to economic development in this period. The authors discuss the shift from a private and family-based system to a public system financed and controlled by the state. Moreover, they examine attitudes about families and theories of child-raising and explore, with a sharp feminist perspective, the theme of women in the schools, both as students and teachers. *The Schools of Ontario, 1876–1976* by Robert M. Stamp (T: UTP 1982) examines the development of the educational system in the larger economic, social, and political contexts. Stamp looks at the roles of administrators and teachers, the changing theories of education, curriculum, the students' experience, and public attitudes to schools. He emphasizes the growing centralization of the system under the Department of Education and the weakness of local forces. A third work is also very important: *Inventing Secondary Education: The Rise of the High School in Nineteenth-Century Ontario* by R.D. Gidney and W.P.J. Millar (M and K: MQUP 1990). Gidney and

Millar discuss the transformation of the old grammar schools into practical secondary schools with broad-based curricula and co-education as the result of pressures from the middle-class parents who supported the system. Also of note is Terry Crowley, 'Parents in a Hurry: The Early Home and School Movement in Ontario,' *HS/SH* 1986.

The theme of women and education has attracted much attention in the periodical literature and articles worth examining include: Alison Prentice, 'The Feminization of Teaching,' in Susan Mann Trofimenkoff and Alison Prentice, eds., *The Neglected Majority: Essays in Canadian Women's History* (T: M&S 1977); Marta Danylewicz, Beth Light, and Alison Prentice, 'The Evolution of the Sexual Division of Labour in Teaching: A Nineteenth-Century Ontario and Quebec Case Study,' *HS/SH* 1983; Danylewicz and Prentice, 'Teachers' Work: Changing Patterns and Perceptions in the Emerging School Systems of 19th and early 20th Century Central Canada,' *Labour* 1986; and John Abbott, 'Accomplishing "a Man's Task": Rural Women Teachers, Male Culture, and the School Inspectorate in Turn-of-the-Century Ontario,' *OH* 1986. Many of these articles are reprinted in Ruby Heap and Alison Prentice, eds., *Gender and Education in Ontario* (cited above).

The history of post-secondary education is dominated by institutional histories, some of which are very good. These include Charles M. Johnston's two-volume work on *McMaster University*, vol. 1, *The Toronto Years*, and vol. 2, *The Early Years in Hamilton, 1930–1957* (T: UTP 1976, 1981); Hilda Neatby's *Queen's University*, vol. 1, *And Not to Yield: 1841–1917* and vol. 2, *To Serve and Yet be Free: 1917–1961* by Frederick W. Gibson (M and K: MQUP 1978, 1983). An overview for the country is provided in Robin S. Harris, *A History of Higher Education in Canada, 1663–1960* (T: UTP 1976); A.B. McKillop's provincial overview, *Matters of Mind: The University in Ontario, 1791–1951*, is forthcoming (T: UTP 1994). *Scholars and Dollars: Politics, Economics, and the Universities of Ontario, 1945–1980* by Paul Axelrod (T: UTP 1982) is an excellent examination of the forces behind the expansion of the post-secondary school system after World War II. Axelrod argues that the corporate and government forces behind this expansion were motivated by the desire to produce skilled professionals for the expanding economy; universities were to serve the public interest. Cutbacks were imposed during the economic downturn of the 1970s because government had no long-term strategy for the universities, and the institutions themselves were slow to adapt to the new fiscal realities, thereby creating a crisis.

An interesting new theme is the focus on the university communities themselves, especially the students. Keith Walden, for example, wrote 'Respectable Hooligans: Male Toronto College Students Celebrate Hallowe'en, 1884–1910,' *CHR* 1987. Paul Axelrod is again in the forefront of this field with his *Making a Middle Class: Student Life in English Canada during the Thirties* (M and K: MQUP 1990), which examines the characteristics and significance of university life in the 1930s. He concludes that university students shared the aspirations of the middle class. Axelrod has also edited, with John G. Reid, *Youth, University, and Canadian Society: Essays in the Social History of Higher Education* (M and K: MQUP 1989), which contains a number of articles on Ontario, ranging from an examination of late nineteenth- and early twentieth-century student life to an account of the financial support available to postgraduates; from the student movement in the 1930s to the student critique of the arts curriculum in the 1960s. The book includes articles on women in universities, a topic also examined by Lynn Marks and Chad Gaffield, 'Women at Queen's University, 1895–1905: A "Little Sphere" All Their Own?,' *OH* 1986, and Mona Gleason, 'A Separate and "Different" Education: Women and Co-education at the University of Windsor's Assumption College, 1950–1957,' *OH* 1992.

POLITICS

Ontario, as a province, is a politically defined territory, and for many years the responses to social and economic changes were explained in terms of political development. Although the reality is more complex, there remains a strong tradition of writing about the government and politics of the province.

There are some useful bibliographical guides to government documents: Olga B. Bishop, ed., *Publications of the Government of Ontario, 1867–1900* (T: Ontario Ministry of Government Services 1976); and Hazel I. MacTaggart's two edited collections, *Publications of the Government of Ontario, 1901–1955: A Checklist* (T: QP 1964) and *Publications of the Government of Ontario, 1956–1971* (T: Ontario Ministry of Government Services 1975). Debra Forman has compiled constituency histories and the electoral careers of members, plus lists of ministries, in two volumes, *Legislators and Legislatures of Ontario: A Reference Guide*, vol. 2, *1867–1929*, and vol. 3, *1930–1984* (T: Ontario Legislative Library 1984). The *Canadian Annual Review of Politics and Public Affairs* (T: UTP 1960–) contains essays on Ontario.

Political scientists have contributed a number of useful general works;

one of the most important is Graham White, ed., *The Government and Politics of Ontario* (4th ed., Scarborough: Nelson 1990), which contains broad overviews of Ontario politics, and selections on government institutions, politics, and policy. The classic study of government administration before Confederation is J.E. Hodgetts, *Pioneer Public Service: An Administrative History of the United Canadas, 1841–1867* (T: UTP 1956); an interesting counterpoint, because of its foundations in the methodology of the new social history, is *Colonial Leviathan: State Formation in Mid-Nineteenth-Century Canada*, edited by Allan Greer and Ian Radforth (T: UTP 1992). The essays focus upon the intrusive expansion of state power. For the post-Confederation period, two works should be consulted: F.F. Schindeler, *Responsible Government in Ontario* (T: UTP 1969), which emphasizes the growing power of the executive over the legislature, and Graham White, *The Ontario Legislature: A Political Analysis* (T: UTP 1989), which stresses the importance of the legislative assembly as a forum for contending political ideologies and an institution to shape laws. Other works to be noted are François-Pierre Gingras, 'Ontario,' in David J. Bellamy, Jon H. Pammett, and Donald C. Rowat, eds., *The Provincial Political Systems: Comparative Essays* (T: Methuen 1976), and Graham White, 'Governing from Queen's Park: The Ontario Premiership,' in Leslie Pal and David Taras, eds., *Prime Ministers and Premiers: Political Leadership and Public Policy in Canada* (T: PH 1988).

As late as 1980, students were largely dependent on periodical literature and theses for material on Ontario politics; Peter Oliver's contribution to the earlier editions of the *Guide* makes this quite clear, and his article is still indispensable for these types of sources on provincial politics. Since that time, however, the Ontario Historical Studies Series has produced a number of biographies of provincial premiers, and these works will provide the foundation for future study.

The Confederation period is still adequately served by J.M.S. Careless, *Brown of the Globe*, vol. 2, *Statesman of Confederation, 1860–1880* (T: MAC 1963), and *The Pre-Confederation Premiers: Ontario Government Leaders, 1841–1867* (T: UTP 1980); Bruce W. Hodgins, *John Sandfield Macdonald, 1812–1872* (T: UTP 1971); and Dale C. Thomson, *Alexander Mackenzie: Clear Grit* (T: MAC 1960). Two useful articles are D.G. Kerr, 'The 1867 Elections in Ontario: The Rules of the Game,' *CHR* 1970, and J.D. Livermore, 'The Ontario Election of 1871: A Case Study of the Transfer of Power,' *OH* 1979.

From 1872 to 1896, the premier of Ontario was Sir Oliver Mowat, the subject of A. Margaret Evans's biography of the same name (T: UTP 1992). Mowat's government played an active role in both promoting economic development and expanding the state role in industrial relations, public health, education, agriculture, and resource development; the 'conservative liberalism' of his administration began a tradition that continued to be successful well into the twentieth century. This authoritative but traditional political narrative should be supplemented by other sources; Mowat's articulation of provincial rights and the 'compact theory' of Confederation, for example, is also examined in Ramsay Cook, *Provincial Autonomy, Minority Rights, and the Compact Theory, 1867–1921* (O: QP 1969). H.V. Nelles, *The Politics of Development* explores more fully the relationship between the provincial government and business interests seeking to exploit natural resources. His work illustrates the emergence of the idea of the public interest, especially in the hydroelectric power sector, and offers perceptive insights into the nature of Ontario's politics from the mid-nineteenth century. Also important is *The Politics of Federalism: Ontario's Relations with the Federal Government, 1867–1942* by Christopher Armstrong (T: UTP 1981), which argues that beginning with Mowat, Ontario premiers sought to defend and expand provincial interests to pursue economic development. The emergence of 'empire Ontario' led to conflict with the federal government over control of natural resources and spheres of power. The relationship between provincial and federal Liberals is explored in Carman Miller, 'Mowat, Laurier, and the Federal Liberal Party, 1887–1897,' in Swainson, ed. *Oliver Mowat's Ontario*, and in Brian P.N. Beaven, 'Partisanship, Patronage, and the Press in Ontario, 1880–1914: Myths and Realities,' *CHR* 1983. Also of note are Desmond Morton, 'The *Globe* and the Labour Question: Ontario Liberalism in the "Great Upheaval," May, 1886,' *OH* 1981; and Kenneth McLaughlin, 'Ontario's "Grand Old Man": Oliver Mowat's Last Hurrah,' *OH* 1992.

The dominance of Ontario's Protestant culture caused religious tensions in this period which had political consequences. Some of the pertinent literature is discussed in the sections of this article on religion and Franco-Ontarians, with Franklin Walker's traditional political approach, in *Catholic Education and Politics in Ontario*, vol. 2, and Chad Gaffield's excellent demographic study, *Language, Schooling, and Cultural Conflict*, being the most useful. There are also some articles on this theme: Peter Dembski, 'A Matter of Conscience: The Origins of W.R. Meredith's Conflict with Archbishop J.J. Lynch,' *OH* 1981; J.R. Miller, '"Equal Rights for All": The E.R.A. and the Ontario Election of 1890,' *OH* 1973, 'The Jesuit Estates Act Crisis,' *JCS* 1974, and 'Anti-Catholic Thought in Victorian Canada,' *CHR* 1985; and James T. Watt, 'Anti-Catholicism in Ontario Politics: 1894,' *OH* 1967.

The period after 1896 was marked by the transitional administration of

Sir George Ross, for whom there is not yet a biography, who came before the advent of the 'progressive Conservativism' which dominated Ontario politics for most of the twentieth century. Charles W. Humphries, *'Honest Enough to be Bold': The Life and Times of Sir James Pliny Whitney* (T: UTP 1985) provides background on the 1890s and early 1900s in this straight-forward political biography of the man who was Ontario's premier from 1905 to 1914. The work tends to focus on Whitney rather than his times; and there is little on the social and economic changes of the period, although the politics are fully discussed. The emphasis is upon the Whitney government's promotion of economic and technological progress through the creation of Ontario Hydro, railway construction, and improved industrial relations with the Workmens' Compensation Act. The creation of Ontario Hydro has been the subject of a number of works: W.R. Plewman, *Adam Beck and the Ontario Hydro* (T: RP 1947); an official history by Merrill Denison, *The People's Power: The History of Ontario Hydro* (T: M&S 1960); and Keith R. Fleming, *Power at Cost*. Once again, Nelles's *The Politics of Development* is indispensable. There is also a biography of Whitney's minister of lands, forests, and mines, *Silent Frank Cochrane: The North's First Great Politician* by Scott and Astrid Young (T: MAC 1973).

A number of political developments between World War I and the Great Depression have been examined in Peter Oliver's important collection, *Public and Private Persons: The Ontario Political Culture, 1914–1934* (T: CI 1975), including the collapse of Hearst's Conservatives, the resolution of the bilingual schools issue, moral reform in politics, the Conservative and Liberal parties in the 1920s, and political scandals. Barbara Wilson edited *Ontario and the First World War*, a compilation of documents illustrating the views of Ontario's elites on several issues; the introduction is good. Margaret Prang has written a major biography, *N.W. Rowell: Ontario Nationalist* (T: UTP 1975), which examines the career of the Methodist social reformer and corporation lawyer who was the leader of the opposition from 1911 to 1917.

The growth of rural unrest during the war which culminated in the election of the United Farmers of Ontario in 1919 has already been noted in the section on staple industries. Two UFO leaders wrote their memoirs: *Farmer Premier: Memoirs of Honourable E.C. Drury* (T: M&S 1966), and W.C. Good, *Farmer Citizen: My Fifty Years in the Canadian Farmers' Movement* (T: RP 1958). More important is Charles M. Johnston's biography, *E.C. Drury*, which focuses on Drury and his ideas to explore the tensions in Ontario society which led to the farmers' movement and pressures for moral reform. The UFO was torn apart by the division between the reformers who supported prohibition, educational changes, conservation, and social welfare and the political realists who wanted financial restraint. The party lost the next election to the Conservatives led by *G. Howard Ferguson: Ontario Tory*, whose biography was written by Peter Oliver (T: UTP 1977). This sound political study addresses issues like bilingual schools, prohibition, resource development, rural-urban tensions, and federal-provincial relations. Oliver uses Ferguson to explain the Orange and Tory Ontario political culture which rejected dualism and embraced imperialism in the 1920s.

The Great Depression produced political demagogues in a number of provinces and Ontario was no exception. Mitch Hepburn, an onion farmer from southwestern Ontario who was premier from 1934 to 1943, has attracted the attention of two historians. Neil McKenty's older work, *Mitch Hepburn* (T: M&S 1967), emphasizes the conservatism of Hepburn in his reactions to issues like hydroelectric power, separate schools, the liquor question, labour unrest in Oshawa, and federal-provincial relations. John T. Saywell's much longer book *'Just call me Mitch': The Life of Mitchell F. Hepburn* (T: UTP 1991) addresses the same issues and deals fully with Hepburn's close ties to the entrepreneurs who supported the Liberals and the 'exuberance' of his private life. Although it is an exhausting read, Saywell does an excellent job placing Hepburn in the context of the times.

The politics of postwar Ontario into the 1980s were dominated by the Progressive Conservatives and two more premiers have received biographical attention. Roger Graham's *Old Man Ontario: Leslie M. Frost* (T: UTP 1990) is the more successful effort. The book concentrates on Frost as an administrator during the boom of the 1950s; the activities of the provincial government expanded in this period to promote economic growth and provide services like health and education, although the perspective is somewhat different than that outlined in Paul Axelrod's *Scholars and Dollars*. In the end, though, Ontario was not able to counter the postwar centralization of the federal government. The Frost administration did not ignore the more practical benefits of government activity like road construction, and the book is especially effective when discussing party organization and machine politics. One of the products of that machine was Frost's successor, John Robarts, who has not been well served in A.K. McDougall's biography, *John P. Robarts: His Life and Government* (T: UTP 1986); this is a straightforward political account of his years as premier. Peter Oliver has written an impressive biography of an 'ethnic Tory,' *Unlikely Tory: The Life and Politics of Allan Grossman*

(T: Lester & Orpen Dennys 1985), which discusses political organiza-
tion, ethnic politics, and the process of government. There are no scholarly
studies of Ontario's premiers after Robarts as of yet, although there are
three journalistic accounts: Jonathan Manthorpe, *The Power and the Tories:
Ontario Politics, 1943 to the present* (T: MAC 1974), Clair Hoy, *Bill Davis:
A Biography* (T: Methuen 1985), and Georgette Gagnon and Dan Rath,
Not Without Cause: David Peterson's Fall from Grace (Scarborough:
HarperCollins 1991).

Until the provincial election which placed Bob Rae in the premier's
office, the CCF/NDP has always been more popular with the academic
community than the electorate. There is Gerald L. Caplan's *The Dilemma
of Canadian Socialism: The CCF in Ontario* (T: M&S 1973) and Leo Zakuta's
A Protest Movement Becalmed: A Study of Change in the CCF (T: UTP
1964). *Secular Socialists: The CCF/NDP in Ontario, A Biography* by J. Terence
Morley (M and K: MQUP 1984) examines the ability of the party to
adapt to changing social, economic, and political conditions – a process
labelled 'secularization.' The book is stronger on party leaders, political
organization, and ideology than on more general concepts like political
culture. Donald C. MacDonald, a former leader of the party, has written
The Happy Warrior: Political Memoirs (Markham: Fitzhenry & Whiteside
1988). There are also two articles of note: John Wilson and David
Hoffman, 'Ontario: A Three-Party System in Transition,' in Martin Robin,
ed., *Canadian Provincial Politics: The Party Systems of the Ten Provinces* (2nd
ed., T: PH 1978) and John Bullen, 'The Ontario Waffle and the Struggle
for an Independent Socialist Canada: Conflict within the NDP,' *CHR*
1983.

There is some interesting new work appearing on the theme of women
in Ontario politics. Sylvia B. Bashevkin's *Toeing the Lines: Women and
Party Politics in English Canada* (T: UTP 1985) emphasizes the NDP but
does contain material on all political parties and their activities in Ontario;
there is also her 'Women's Participation in the Ontario Political Parties,
1971–1981,' *JCS* 1982. Other articles to be noted are: John Manley,
'Women and the Left in the 1930s: The Case of the Toronto CCF
Women's Joint Committee,' *Atlantis* 1980; Dean Beeby, 'Women in the
Ontario CCF, 1940–1950,' *OH* 1982; and Pauline Rankin, 'The
Politicization of Ontario Farm Women,' in Linda Kealey and Joan
Sangster, eds., *Beyond the Vote: Canadian Women and Politics* (T: UTP 1989).

Finally, the topic of Ontario's political culture has been addressed,
although it has generated little of the debate that has attracted historians
of Upper Canada. S.F. Wise has argued in 'The Ontario Political Cul-

ture: A Study in Complexities,' in Graham White, ed., *The Government and Politics of Ontario*, that the Upper Canadian experience shaped Ontario's political culture because of the development of a consensus which believed in the superiority of British values and institutions, rejected American examples, and accepted the integrative role of the state in economic and social affairs. As a result, the Ontario government supported economic development projects – the 'politics of affluence' – and expansion to the West, as Doug Owram has so brilliantly shown in *Promise of Eden: The Canadian Expansionist Movement and the Idea of the West, 1856–1900* (2nd ed., T: UTP 1992). It also created a centralized school system to assimilate immigrants and inculcate proper moral and political values. This progressive conservative political culture gave rise to what might be called a sense of Ontario nationalism in the nineteenth and early twentieth centuries.

Gordon T. Stewart's *The Origins of Canadian Politics: A Comparative Approach* (V: UBCP 1986) reinforces this argument about the development of a complex political culture, different from those of Great Britain and the United States. By the 1860s, Canada entered a period of political stability in which a system of patronage, influence, and active government flourished, especially under John A. Macdonald at the federal level and Oliver Mowat in Ontario, and which shaped political responses until the early twentieth century. This view is developed more fully in S.J.R. Noel, *Patrons, Clients, Brokers: Ontario Society and Politics, 1791–1896* (T: UTP 1990). Noel argues that the political development of Old Ontario can be defined by studying the relationships between patrons and clients, relationships which were crafted into the political machine of the Liberal Party led by Mowat. A consensus had developed that the provincial government was to manage provincial economic development and that patronage was the best means to effect sound administration. In the words of Vaughn Lyon, it became a political culture of 'complacency'; Ontario would generally be governed by a conservative elite: *JCS* 1987. Also of note is John Wilson, 'The Red Tory Province: Reflections on the Character of the Ontario Political Culture,' in Donald C. MacDonald, ed., *The Government and Politics of Ontario* (2nd ed., T: Van Nostrand Reinhold 1980).

Ontario, in the words of S.F. Wise, is 'geographically vast, regionally and demographically diverse, historically complex, and yet seemingly lacking in distinctiveness or special character.' Some historians have tried to define this character; Royce MacGillivray, for example, sought to examine *The Mind of Ontario* (Belleville: Mika Publishing 1985) but could only conclude that Ontarians are moderate, enlightened – although prone to intellectual conformity – and compassionate; they prefer compromise to confrontation, are deferential to authority, and exhibit a smug sense of moral superiority. But identifying Ontario's distinct character remains elusive.

Arthur Lower once asked: 'Ontario – does it exist?' If historians look for a common experience, whether it is social, economic, or political, the answer remains no. Ontario must be understood in terms of its diversity – its pluralism – and recent historical writing, while making the past more accessible, has revealed the complexity of the provincial experience by focusing on identities and social relations defined by ethnicity, religion, class, gender, and region. Ontario can no longer be called the 'unknown province,' and the old complaint that there is not enough Ontario history has clearly been supplanted by the cry that there is now too much. But no one has yet attempted to draw the themes developed in the literature together in a comprehensive history. There are many historians who write about Ontario; what the province needs is a good Ontario historian.

JOHN HERD THOMPSON

The West and the North

The differences in the three versions of this *Reader's Guide* attest to the constant shifting of historians' paradigms. The original 1974 *Guide* combined British Columbia and the Prairie provinces as one chapter and ignored the North. The outpouring of regional history in the 1970s was reflected by separate chapters on British Columbia, the Prairie provinces, and the North in the 1982 *Guide*. In this edition of the *Reader's Guide*, one chapter must now serve all three regions. The task is difficult; it is not impossible only because several topics which would once have been included in individual regional chapters have chapters of their own: Native history, labour history, and women's history. There are historiographical reasons for unifying the Pacific West and the Prairie, but the North has been placed in this chapter more for editorial than historiographical reasons; W.L. Morton's comment that 'the North has yet to be incorporated into the historiography of Canada' remains valid. It could also be argued that the North is not one but several distinct regions. Our ideas of a monolithic 'North' were constructed by southerners, people outside the region, as D.A. West points out in 'Re-searching the North in Canada: An Introduction to Canadian Northern Discourse,' *JCS* 1991.

ATLASES, BIBLIOGRAPHIES, AND SCHOLARLY JOURNALS

Maps are indispensable sources for all historians, and especially important to those who would study the vastness of the West and the North. The best cartographic depictions of regional history are those in the magnificent *Historical Atlas of Canada* (T: UTP 1987, 1990, 1993). More than simple physical and political geography, the plates in Volume 3,

Addressing the Twentieth Century, 1891–1961, are superb visual images of the economic and social history of the Prairie provinces and of British Columbia, although the North is less adequately represented. Each plate has an accompanying list of sources and suggestions for further reading. Volume 2, *The Land Transformed, 1800–1891*, is of similar quality. Atlases of varying utility exist for individual provinces: John Warkentin and Richard I. Ruggles, *Manitoba Historical Atlas: A Selection of Facsimile, Maps, Plans, and Sketches from 1612 to 1969* (W: Historical and Scientific Society of Manitoba 1970), William C. Wonders et al., *Atlas of Alberta* (E and T: UAP/UTP 1969), and A.L. Farley, *Atlas of British Columbia: People, Environment, and Resource Use* (V: UBCP 1979).

Specialized regional bibliographies go into more detail than is possible in this single chapter. The most comprehensive listing of books, articles, and graduate theses is Alan F.J. Artibise, *Western Canada since 1870: A Select Bibliography and Guide* (V: UBCP 1978). Bruce Braden Peel's encyclopedic *A Bibliography of the Prairie Provinces to 1953 with Biographical Index* (2nd ed., T: UTP 1973) is an indispensable tool for students doing advanced research. The third edition, with some one thousand new entries should be available in late 1994. Peel lists literally everything ever written about the Prairies, and includes brief biographies of many authors, subject bibliographies, and an excellent index. There are also provincial bibliographies: Richard A. Enns, ed., *A Bibliography of Northern Manitoba* (W: UMP 1991); Gloria M. Strathern, comp., *Alberta, 1954–1979: A Provincial Bibliography* (E: University of Alberta 1982); Barbara J. Lowther with Muriel Laing, eds., *A Bibliography of British Columbia*, vol. 2, *Laying the Foundations, 1849–1899* (Vi: University of Victoria 1968); Margaret H. Edwards and John C.R. Lort, eds., *A Bibliography of British Columbia* , vol. 3, *Years of Growth, 1900–1950* (Vi: University of Victoria 1975); and Frances Woodward, *Theses on British Columbian History and Related Subjects in the Library of the University of British Columbia* (V: UBC Library 1971; supplement 1974). Linda L. Hale, *Vancouver Centennial Bibliography* (V: Vancouver Historical Society 1986) has over fifteen thousand items. On the North, the chapter by Morris Zaslow in the 1982 edition of this *Reader's Guide* has entries which are not included in this chapter. *The Arctic Bibliography*, sixteen volumes, published by the Arctic Institute of North America from 1953 to 1975, has unfortunately not been continued. Alan Cooke and Fabien Caron, comps., *Bibliographie de la peninsule du Québec-Labrador*, 2 vols. (Q: Centre d'Etudes Nordiques 1968) is now dated.

Historiographical essays are often more useful to students than simple bibliographies, because these essays not only list relevant works, but put them into an interpretive context. Excellent examples are Gerald Friesen's 'Historical Writing on the Prairie West,' in R. Douglas Francis and Howard Palmer, eds., *The Prairie West: Historical Readings* (2nd ed., E: Pica Pica Press 1992), and Allan Smith's 'The Writing of British Columbia History,' *BCS* 1980. T.D. Regehr's 'Historiography of the Canadian Plains after 1870,' in Richard Allen, ed., *A Region of the Mind: Interpreting the Western Canadian Plains* (R: CPRC 1973), is still worth looking at, as are W.L. Morton, 'The North in Canadian Historiography,' *TRSC* 1971, and T.H.B. Symons, 'The Arctic and Canadian Culture,' in Morris Zaslow, ed., *A Century of Canada's Arctic Islands, 1880-1980* (O: RSC 1981). *Acadiensis*, a journal of Atlantic history, sometimes publishes review articles on other regions, such as Patricia E. Roy '"The Company Province" and Its Centennials: A Review of Recent British Columbia Historiography,' 1974; David Breen, 'The Canadian Prairie West: A Review of Recent Studies,' 1982; and Gordon Hak, 'Workers, Schools, and Women: Some Recent Writings on the History of British Columbia,' 1990.

Much of the historical research on the West and the North appears as articles in journals devoted to provincial and regional history. The *Transactions of the Historical and Scientific Society of Manitoba* began publication in 1882 and continued, with interruptions, until 1979 when it became *Manitoba History*. *Saskatchewan History*, the most scholarly of the Prairie provincial journals, has appeared since 1948, and *Alberta History* (until 1985 *Alberta Historical Review*) since 1953. *BC Studies*, which succeeded the *British Columbia Historical Review* in 1968, is officially interdisciplinary but in practice devotes many of its pages to history. The same may be said of *Prairie Forum* (1976–), published by the Canadian Plains Research Center at the University of Regina. A new scholarly journal, *Alberta: Studies in the Arts and Sciences* (1989–92), died in its infancy. *The Beaver* (1920–), published by the Hudson's Bay Company, is the closest to being a comprehensive regional history journal. Its articles, written for general readers as well as scholars, cover the Prairies, British Columbia, and the North. *The Northern Review* (1987–) examines northern issues and themes, some of which are historical. *The Polar Record* is published three times a year by the Scott Polar Research Institute at Cambridge University. Articles on regional history also now appear frequently in national journals like the *Canadian Historical Review* and the *Journal of Canadian Studies*.

Because it is impossible to list any but the most significant journal articles (or those written by cronies of the author) in this chapter, students should search for references to their subjects in the tables of contents of relevant journals, in the indexes which the periodicals publish (usually shelved alongside the journal), or in the *Canadian Periodicals Index*. These journals are also important sources of references to new books and articles. Each publishes book reviews, and *Manitoba History* and *BC Studies* publish comprehensive bibliographies of their respective provinces. Finally, in the 'Recent Publications Relating to Canada' section of every issue of the *Canadian Historical Review* there are listings on 'The Prairie Provinces,' 'British Columbia,' and 'The North West Territories, the Yukon, and the Arctic.' These listings are particularly useful because they include graduate theses, but students should note that (as of this *Guide*) some titles of interest to regional historians of the North and West appear under other categories.

GENERAL HISTORIES AND COLLECTIONS
OF ARTICLES

Students are fortunate to have recent general histories of the Prairie West, BC, and the North with which to begin their reading in the regions' histories. Gerald Friesen's *The Canadian Prairies: A History* (T: UTP 1984) is a superbly crafted survey which encompasses social, economic, and political history. Unfortunately, Friesen was unable to include a bibliography, but his extensive endnotes in part make up for this. Jean Barman's *The West beyond the West: A History of British Columbia* (T: UTP 1991) falls short of Friesen's achievement, but it is the obvious point of departure for BC history. Barman has both endnotes and a sixteen-page list of references. No survey adequately synthesizes the histories of both the Pacific and Prairie Wests, despite J.F. Conway's attempt in *The West: The History of a Region in Confederation* (T: JL 1983). The North has been well served by Morris Zaslow's meticulous scholarship. In his two volumes of the *Canadian Centenary* series, *The Opening of the Canadian North, 1870–1914* and *The Northward Expansion of Canada, 1914–1967* (T: M&S 1971, 1988), Zaslow defines the North very broadly, so that both books also contain much that is of interest to historians of the Prairies and BC. Both volumes also have bibliographical essays. Kenneth S. Coates, *Canada's Colonies: A History of the Yukon and Northwest Territories* (T: JL 1985) is a comprehensive short survey tipped towards the Yukon, whose interpretative thesis is proclaimed in its title.

Provincial and territorial survey histories are the next step in general research. John H. Archer's *Saskatchewan: A History* (S: WPPB 1980), prepared to celebrate the seventy-fifth anniversary of Saskatchewan's provincehood, is thorough, well documented, and well written. James A. Jackson, *The Centennial History of Manitoba* (T: M&S 1970), is another fine commemorative history. James G. MacGregor's *A History of Alberta* (rev. ed., E: Hurtig 1981) is banal boosterism; much better is Howard and Tamara Palmer, *Alberta: A New History* (E: Hurtig 1990). George Woodcock's *British Columbia: A History of a Province* (V: Douglas & McIntyre 1990) has earned effusive praise from academic reviewers. Two older scholarly provincial histories remain worthwhile: W.L. Morton, *Manitoba: A History* (2nd ed., T: UTP 1967), and Margaret Ormsby, *British Columbia: A History* (rev. ed., T: MAC 1971). Kenneth S. Coates and William R. Morrison's *Land of the Midnight Sun: A History of the Yukon* (E: Hurtig 1988) provides a popular introduction to territorial history.

The growth of university history courses on the West has inspired collections of journal articles and book excerpts designed to be used as required reading for undergraduate discussion groups. These books usually include bibliographies. For this reason the most recent are the most useful: Patricia E. Roy, ed., *A History of British Columbia: Selected Readings* (T: CCP 1989), and Francis and Palmer, *The Prairie West* (cited above). Three useful older collections are also widely available in libraries: W. Peter Ward and Robert A.J. McDonald, eds., *British Columbia: Historical Readings* (V: Douglas & McIntyre 1981); Donald Swainson, ed., *Historical Essays on the Prairie Provinces* (T: M&S 1970); and Jean Friesen and H.K. Ralston, eds., *Historical Essays on British Columbia* (T: M&S 1976).

Between 1969 and 1984, the University of Calgary sponsored Western Canadian Studies conferences. The published collections of conference papers represent virtually every aspect of Western regional history, and are useful for exploring the historiographical evolution of the field. It is impossible to list titles of individual articles, but in most cases the titles of the volumes suggest their contents: David Gagan, ed., *Prairie Perspectives* (T: HRW 1970); A.W. Rasporich and Henry C. Klassen, eds., *Prairie Perspectives 2* (T: HRW 1973); Susan Mann Trofimenkoff, ed., *The Twenties in Western Canada* (O: National Museums of Canada 1972); David J. Bercuson, ed., *Western Perspectives 1* (T: HRW 1974); A.W. Rasporich, ed., *Western Canada: Past and Present* (C: University of Calgary/M&S West 1975); Howard Palmer, ed., *The Settlement of the West* (C: University of Calgary Comprint Publishing 1977); Henry C. Klassen, ed., *The Canadian West: Social Change and Economic Development* (C: University of Calgary Comprint Publishing 1977); R. Douglas Francis and Herman Ganzevoort, eds., *The Dirty Thirties in Prairie Canada* (V: Tantalus 1980); Howard

Palmer and Donald Smith, eds., *The New Provinces: Alberta and Saskatchewan, 1905–1980* (V: Tantalus 1980); David Jay Bercuson and Phillip A. Buckner, eds., *Eastern and Western Perspectives* (T: UTP 1981); A.W. Rasporich, ed., *The Making of the Modern West: Western Canada since 1945* (C: UCP 1984).

On the North, Morris Zaslow, ed., *A Century of Canada's Arctic Islands* (cited above), collects a series of interdisciplinary conference papers on issues as diverse as Inuit cultural change, exploration, and Arctic sovereignty. Another form of collection is the *festschrift*, essays published to honour a senior scholar. Three contain important work on the Prairies: John E. Foster, ed., *The Developing West: Essays in Canadian History in Honour of Lewis H. Thomas* (E: UAP 1983), Lewis H. Thomas, ed., *Essays on Western History in Honour of Lewis Gwynne Thomas* (E: UAP 1976), and Carl Berger and Ramsay Cook, eds., *The West and the Nation: Essays in Honour of W.L. Morton* (T: M&S 1976). John Norris and Margaret Prang's *Personality and History in British Columbia: Essays in Honour of Margaret Ormsby* (Vi: Morris Printing 1977) is a special edition of *BC Studies* 1976–7. Canada's most important Northern historian inspired K.S. Coates and W.R. Morrison, *For Purposes of Dominion: Essays in Honour of Morris Zaslow* (T: Captus Press 1989).

EXTENDING CANADIAN CONTROL WEST AND NORTH

The annexation of the Hudson's Bay Company's northwestern empire and British Columbia was an explicit goal of Canadian Confederation. W.L. Morton summarizes Canada's acquisition of the Prairies in *The West and Confederation, 1857–1871* (O: CHA 1958) and explores regional subordination to central Canada in 'Clio in Canada: The Interpretation of Canadian History,' *University of Toronto Quarterly* 1946. Doug Owram's brilliant *Promise of Eden: The Canadian Expansionist Movement and the Idea of the West, 1856–1900* (2nd ed., T: UTP 1992) explains how Canadians came to see the West as their patrimony awaiting exploitation. Why the West was won for Canada and not annexed to the United States is the subject of Alvin C. Gluek, *Minnesota and the Manifest Destiny of the Canadian Northwest: A Study in Canadian-American Relations* (T: UTP 1965), and of Donald F. Warner, *The Idea of Continental Union: Agitation for the Annexation of Canada to the United States, 1849–1893* (Lexington: University of Kentucky Press 1960). There is also an extensive discussion of the Red River community's resistance in 1869–70 to Canada's westward expansion in the literature on the Métis and on Louis Riel described below. Three edited collections of documents make possible student primary research on the resistance: W.L. Morton, ed., *Manitoba: The Birth of a Province* (Altona: Manitoba Record Society/D.W. Friesen 1965) and his *Alexander Begg's Red River Journal and Other Papers Relative to the Red River Resistance of 1869–1870* (T: CS 1956); and Hartwell Bowsfield, ed., *The James Wickes Taylor Correspondence, 1859–1870* (Altona: Manitoba Record Society/D.W. Friesen 1968), which reprints the correspondence of an American agent at Red River. In *A Snug Little Flock: The Social Origins of the Riel Resistance of 1869–70* (W: Watson and Dwyer 1991), Frits Pannekoek suggests that the real question should not be 'How Was the West Won for Confederation?,' but 'Why Did the Red River Community Change?' Pannekoek sees the failure of the resistance to Canadian expansion as the result of deep divisions among the groups within Red River, especially between the Catholic Métis and the Protestant mixed-bloods. And change it did, with astonishing rapidity. In 'John A. Macdonald, Confederation and the Canadian West,' in R.C. Brown, ed., *Minorities, Schools, and Politics* (T: UTP 1969), Donald Creighton paints Riel as a dictator who imposed an inappropriate bicultural constitution on Manitoba against its will and against the better judgment of Macdonald. Ralph Heintzman has challenged this in 'The Spirit of Confederation: Professor Creighton, Biculturalism, and the Use of History,' *CHR* 1971. The reasons the West became an extension of Ontario rather than Quebec are explored in Arthur Silver, 'French Canada and the Prairie West,' *CHR* 1968.

British Columbia's entry into Confederation has attracted less historical attention. W. George Shelton, ed., *British Columbia and Confederation* (Vi: University of Victoria 1967), an uneven collection of eight essays, remains the best single source. Margaret A. Ormsby's 'Frederick Seymour: The Forgotten Governor,' and Robert Louis Smith's 'The Hankin Appointment, 1868,' both in *BCS* 1974, discuss the contributions of two colonial officials. Gordon R. Elliott's 'Henry P. Pellew Crease: Confederation or No Confederation,' *BCS* 1971–2, describes the lukewarm support of BC's attorney general for union with Canada – an attitude probably typical of the colonial elite. James E. Hendrickson, ed., *Journals of the Legislative Council of British Columbia*, vol. 5 of the *Journals of the Colonial Legislatures of the Colonies of Vancouver Island and British Columbia, 1851–1871* (Vi: Provincial Archives of British Columbia 1980), contains the colony's debates on Confederation, and Dorothy Blakey Smith has edited *The Reminiscences of Doctor John Sebastian Helmcken* (V: UBCP 1975), one of the three delegates who negotiated the terms of entry which made the province 'the spoiled child of Confederation.'

Unlike those to the West, Canadian claims to the North were extended and defended sluggishly. The process of northern exploration is described in R. St J. Macdonald, ed., *The Arctic Frontier* (T: UTP 1966), Alan Cooke and Clive Holland, comps., *The Exploration of Northern Canada, 500 to 1920: A Chronology* (T: Arctic History Press 1978), and A. Taylor, *Geographical Exploration in the Queen Elizabeth Islands* (O: QP 1955). Daniel Francis, *Discovery of the North: The Exploration of Canada's Arctic* (E: Hurtig 1986), is a well-written popular synthesis, as is Pierre Berton, *The Arctic Grail: The Quest for the North West Passage and the North Pole, 1818–1909* (T: M&S 1988). Vilhjalmur Stefansson, Canada's most famous northern explorer, wrote four books about the process, and is himself the subject of two modern biographies. William R. Hunt's *Stef: A Biography of Vilhjalmur Stefansson, Canadian Arctic Explorer* (V: UBCP 1986) has been pronounced by a reviewer as 'resolutely in favour of Stefansson's interpretation of virtually everything'; Richard J. Diubaldo's *Stefansson and the Canadian Arctic* (M and K: MQUP 1978) will be more useful for most researchers. Northern sovereignty must be constantly asserted, as Franklyn Griffiths, ed., *Politics of the Northwest Passage* (M and K: MQUP 1987), and John Honderich, *Arctic Imperative: Is Canada Losing the North?* (T: UTP 1987), remind us.

Canada had to control indigenous Native peoples in order to extend its industrial and agricultural frontiers north-westward. Gary Kelly, 'Class, Race, and Cultural Revolution: Treaties and the Making of Western Canada,' *Alberta* 1989, places Canada's treaty-making in the context of 'a global process of which the making ... of western Canada was only one episode.' John Tobias, 'Canada's Subjugation of the Plains Cree, 1879–1885,' *CHR* 1983, and Frank Tough, 'Economic Aspects of Aboriginal Title in Northern Manitoba: Treaty 5 Adhesions and Métis Script,' *Manitoba History* 1988, offer detailed examinations of parts of this process. Hana Samek, *The Blackfoot Confederacy, 1880–1920: A Comparative Study of Canadian and US Indian Policy* (Albuquerque: University of New Mexico Press 1987) does the same for another. Samek's work is particularly interesting for its bi-national perspective; although she describes Canadian policies as more humane than those of the US, she notes that the end result for the Blackfoot was almost identical on both sides of the international boundary. Hugh A. Dempsey has written biographies of two plains chiefs who coped differently with the new order, *Crowfoot: Chief of the Blackfoot* (Norman: University of Oklahoma Press 1972), and *Big Bear: The End of Freedom* (V: Douglas & McIntyre 1984). Sarah Carter's *Lost Harvests: Prairie Indian Reserve Farmers and Government Policy* (M and K:

MQUP 1990) explains how pernicious government policies doomed to failure plains Indians' attempts to adapt to farming. Like Carter's book, Peter D. Elias, *The Dakota of the Canadian Northwest: Lessons for Survival* (W: UMP 1988), shows that Native peoples could be active agents in shaping their future rather than simply passive victims of Euro-Canadian policies. There are several useful essays in F. Laurie Barron and James B. Waldram, eds., *1885 and After: Native Society in Transition* (R: CPRC 1986).

Similar attempts to marginalize the Métis eventually provoked the 1885 North-West Rebellion. Two historiographical articles are useful road maps to the copious and complicated literature on the Métis and their controversial leader, Louis Riel: Doug Owram, 'The Myth of Louis Riel,' *CHR* 1982, and George F.G. Stanley's 'The Last Word on Louis Riel,' in Barron and Waldram, eds., *1885 and After*. There is a host of Riel biographies – and, accordingly, a host of different Louis Riels. Joseph Kinsey Howard's lyric *Strange Empire: Louis Riel and the Métis People* (2nd ed., T: James Lewis & Samuel 1974) was the first account in English to make Riel a tragic hero. George F.G. Stanley's *Louis Riel* (rev. ed., T: MHR 1985) portrays Riel as both tragic and mentally ill; it remains the best scholarly treatment. E.B. Osler's *The Man Who Had to Hang: Louis Riel* (T: Longmans Green 1961) and Hartwell Bowsfield's *Louis Riel: The Rebel and the Hero* (T: OUP 1971) are worthwhile shorter biographies. George F.G. Stanley, *The Birth of Western Canada: A History of the Riel Rebellions* (1936, 3rd ed., T: UTP 1992) is partially summarized in his short monograph *Louis Riel, Patriot or Rebel?* (2nd ed., O: CHA 1970). Bob Beal and Rod Macleod provide a superb synthesis of the crisis of 1885 in *Prairie Fire: The 1885 North-West Rebellion* (E: Hurtig 1984). The most important new entrant into the Riel industry is Thomas Flanagan, whose *Louis 'David' Riel: Prophet of the New World* (T: UTP 1979) and *Riel and the Rebellion: 1885 Reconsidered* (S: WPPB 1983) reject the thesis that Riel was insane and blame Riel for provoking the armed conflict in 1885. *The Collected Writings of Louis Riel/Les écrits complets de Louis Riel* (E: UAP 1985) have been printed in five volumes, but are very difficult for any but specialists to work with.

Accounts of the Métis and their resistance have been too Riel-centred in any event, argues J.R. Miller in 'From Louis Riel to the Métis,' *CHR* 1988. In *Gabriel Dumont: The Métis Chief and His Lost World* (E: Hurtig 1975), George Woodcock simply substitutes Dumont for Riel as the Métis 'great man.' There are detailed discussions of the Métis in Marcel Giraud, *Le Métis canadien* (1945, St Boniface: Editions du blé 1984), which was translated by George Woodcock as *The Métis in the Canadian West* (E: UAP

1986); and in A.H. de Tremaudan, *Histoire de la nation métisse dans l'ouest canadien* (1936, St Boniface: Editions du blé 1979), translated by Elizabeth Mauget as *Hold High Your Heads: The History of the Métis Nation in Western Canada* (W: Pemmican 1982). Don McLean's *1885, Métis Rebellion or Government Conspiracy?* (W: Pemmican 1985), and D.N. Sprague's *Canada and the Métis, 1869–1885* (Wa: WLUP 1988) vigorously condemn federal policies. Thomas Flanagan, *Métis Lands in Manitoba* (C: UCP 1991) defends the federal government and is hotly contested by Sprague in 'Métis Dispersal from Manitoba, 1870–1881,' *Prairie Forum* 1991. Gerhard Ens, 'Dispossession or Adaptation? Migration and Persistence of the Red River Métis, 1835–1890,' CHA *HP* 1988, argues that the Métis move west from Red River was as much economic adaptation as enforced dispersal. In *'The Free People – Otipemisiwak', Batoche, Saskatchewan, 1870–1930* (O: Parks Canada 1990), Diane Payment demonstrates forcefully that the Métis as a people did not disappear after their defeat at Batoche.

British Columbia's white settler governments got to shape their own Indian policies to a larger degree. In his prize-winning book *Contact and Conflict: Indian-European Relations in British Columbia, 1774–1890* (2nd ed., V: UBCP 1992), and in 'An Exercise in Futility: The Joint Commission on Indian Land in British Columbia, 1875–1880,' *CHAR* 1975, Robin Fisher argues that the Indian-white partnership which had characterized the fur trade era ended abruptly as Canadians sought natural resources other than fur. Robert E. Cail, *Land, Man, and the Law: The Disposal of Crown Lands in British Columbia, 1871–1913* (V: UBCP 1974) discusses the appropriation of Indian lands, as does Paul Tennant, *Aboriginal Peoples and Politics: The Indian Land Question in BC, 1849–1989* (V: UBCP 1990). In *Gunboat Frontier: British Maritime Authority and the Northwest Coast Indians, 1846–1890* (V: UBCP 1984), Barry M. Gough reminds us that military force was used to suppress the Pacific Coast tribes. In *Captured Heritage: The Scramble for Northwest Coast Artifacts* (V: Douglas & McIntyre 1985), Douglas Cole explains how stripping Native peoples of their cultural heritage could be part of the pattern of subordination, and in *An Iron Hand upon the People: The Law against the Potlach on the Northwest Coast* (V: Douglas & McIntyre 1990), Cole and Ira Chaikin recount the sixty-five-year attempt by government to suppress this Northwest Pacific Coast cultural institution. Different perspectives on the role of missionaries in persuading Indians to accommodate to change are provided by Jean Usher in *William Duncan of Metlakatla: A Victorian Missionary in British Columbia* (O: National Museums of Canada 1974) and by David Mulhall in *Will to Power: The Missionary Career of Father Morice* (V: UBCP 1986).

Although dispossessed, British Columbia's Indians did not silently vanish. Rolf Knight, *Indians at Work: An Informal History of Native Indian Labour in British Columbia, 1858–1930* (V: New Star 1978), and James K. Burrows, '"A Much-Needed Class of Labour": The Economy and Income of the Southern Interior Plateau Indians, 1897–1910,' *BCS* 1986, show that Indians adapted to the new economy of mining, forestry, and settlement as wage workers. Peter Carstens, *The Queen's People: A Study of Hegemony, Coercion, and Accommodation among the Okanagan of Canada* (T: UTP 1991) is a historical ethnography which follows a Native group of the BC southern interior from contact to the 1980s. E. Palmer Patterson, 'Andrew Paull and the Early History of British Columbia Indian Organization,' in Ian A.L. Getty and Donald B. Smith, eds., *One Century Later: Western Canadian Reserve Indians since Treaty 7* (V: UBCP 1978), and John Lutz, 'After the Fur Trade: The Aboriginal Labouring Class of British Columbia, 1849–1890,' CHA *HP* (1992) explore the roots of Indian resurgence against white domination. Daniel Raunet, *Without Surrender, Without Consent: A History of the Nishga Land Claims* (V: Douglas & McIntyre 1984), chronicles a century of effective resistance.

Native peoples farther north were spared the Euro-Canadian onslaught until demand for northern resources eventually exposed them to the same pressures. In *Best Left as Indians: Native-White Relations in the Yukon Territory, 1840–1973* (M and K: MQUP 1991), Kenneth S. Coates shows how different federal policy could be when there was no foreseeable need for a region's land and resources. The papers in the special edition of the *American Review of Canadian Studies* (1988) relate what happens once resources are sought after, as does James B. Waldram, *As Long as the Rivers Run: Hydroelectric Development and Native Communities in Western Canada* (W: UMP 1988).

For sixty years after Confederation, the western interior was in many respects a colony of the federal government. Alberta and Saskatchewan were part of the North-West Territories until 1905; along with Manitoba, their natural resources were controlled from Ottawa until 1930. The politics of this relationship are effectively summarized in Lewis H. Thomas, *The North-West Territories, 1870–1905* (O: CHA 1970), and described at length in his *The Struggle for Responsible Government in the North-West Territories, 1870–1897* (2nd ed., T: UTP 1978). In *Territorial Government in Canada: The Autonomy Question in the Old North-West Territories* (T: UTP 1946), C. Cecil Lingard emphasizes the acquisition of provincial status. Doug R. Owram, ed., *The Formation of Alberta: A Documentary History* (C: Alberta Records Publication Board 1979) contains primary document

on the development of provincial status. Because his department con-
trolled territorial and Indian affairs, the federal minister of the interior
was the most important individual in the colonial rule of the West and
North. Macdonald considered the portfolio so important that he held it
himself for six years, but Donald Creighton's *John A. Macdonald*, vol. 2,
The Old Chieftain (T: MAC 1955) mentions this role only to justify
Macdonald's every decision. David Hall's two-volume biography of *Clifford
Sifton*, vol. 1, *The Young Napoleon, 1861–1900*, and vol. 2, *A Lonely Eminence, 1901–1929* (V: UBCP 1981, 1985), who ran the department from
1896 to 1905, is infinitely better.

The most written-about institution of federal control was the North-
West Mounted Police. Two important articles provide a good introduction
to the force's origins and significance: S.W. Horrall, 'Sir John A.
Macdonald and the Mounted Police Force for the North-West Territories,'
CHR 1972 and Desmond Morton, 'Cavalry or Police: Keeping the Peace
on Two Adjacent Frontiers,' *JCS* 1977. Philip Goldring's 'The First
Contingent: The N-WMP, 1873–74' and 'Whisky, Horses, and Death:
The Cypress Hills Massacre and Its Sequel,' in *Occasional Papers in Arch-
aeology and History* (O: Canadian Historic Sites 1979) are fascinating accounts of two events from the force's formative period; they illustrate the
many important contributions made to regional historiography by public
historians. There are several studies of the force's first three decades: J.P.
Turner, *The North-West Mounted Police, 1873–1893*, 2 vols. (O: KP 1950)
is dry official chronology; Ronald Atkin, *Maintain the Right: The Early
History of the North West Mounted Police, 1873–1900* (L: MAC 1973), is a
better read, but unscholarly. R.C. Macleod, *The North-West Mounted Police
and Law Enforcement, 1873–1905* (T: UTP 1976) is the best scholarly
monograph, and there are excellent articles by Macleod, John Jennings,
and David Breen in Hugh A. Dempsey, ed., *Men in Scarlet* (C: Historical
Society of Alberta/M&S West 1974). Paul F. Sharp's *Whoop-up Country:
The Canadian-American West, 1865–1885* (Minneapolis: University of
Minnesota Press 1955) credits the police for the relative non-violence of
the Canadian frontier. Carl Betke's 'Pioneers and Police on the Canadian
Prairies, 1885–1914,' CHA *HP* 1980, explains the myriad other functions
the force performed in addition to law enforcement. The essays in Louis
A. Knafla, ed., *Law and Justice in a New Land: Essays in Western Canadian
Legal History* (T: Carswell 1986) are an earnest beginning in this as-yet-
undeveloped field.

The Mounties were also critical in the northward extension of Canada's
authority. Two full-scale histories of the RCMP also have significant

sections on both the West and the North, but neither book is very good. In *An Unauthorized History of the RCMP* (T: James Lewis and Samuel 1973), Lorne and Caroline Brown make the Mounties into hired thugs of Canadian capitalism, while Nora and William Kelly transform them into saints in scarlet in *The Royal Canadian Mounted Police: A Century of History, 1873–1973* (E: Hurtig 1973). There are so many memoirs of Northern policing that reviewers have joked that the Mounties 'got their book as well as their man'; these memoirs are described on pages 307–8 of the 1982 *Reader's Guide*. William R. Morrison's *Showing the Flag: The Mounted Police and Canadian Sovereignty in the North, 1894–1925* (V: UBCP 1985) explains its thesis in its title.

ECONOMIC CHANGE

Canada's north-western economic expansion took place within the 'National Policy' of tariff protection. Its effects on Western development are discussed in W.A. Mackintosh's *The Economic Background of Dominion-Provincial Relations* for the Rowell-Sirois Commission on Dominion-Provincial Relations (1939, T: M&S 1964). 'New' economic historians eschew narrative for quantitative analysis; the best examples of this are two articles by Kenneth Norrie, 'The National Policy and the Rate of Prairie Settlement: A Review,' *JCS* 1979, and 'The National Policy and Prairie Economic Discrimination, 1870–1930,' in Donald H. Akenson, ed., *Canadian Papers in Rural History* (Gananoque: Langdale Press 1978). Gerald Friesen's 'Imports and Exports in the Manitoba Economy, 1870–1890,' *Manitoba History* 1988, shows how the province was integrated into a national and global economy in this period.

Railways linked the West and the North to central Canada so that the National Policy's developmental designs could be fulfilled. The CPR was the first of these, and *A History of the Canadian Pacific Railway* (1923, T: UTP 1970) helped establish Harold A. Innis's reputation as a brilliant scholar and a dreadful writer. W. Kaye Lamb, *History of the Canadian Pacific Railway* (NY: MAC 1977) is a sympathetic and comprehensive popular account. Pierre Berton's two volumes, *The National Dream: The Great Railway, 1871–1881* and *The Last Spike: The Great Railway, 1881–1885* (T: M&S 1970, 1971), are dramatic narratives laced with an overdose of patriotic pride; readers seeking an antidote should consult Robert Chodos, *The CPR: A Century of Corporate Welfare* (T: James Lewis and Samuel, 1973). W.A. Waiser, 'A Willing Scapegoat: John Macoun and the Route of the CPR,' *Prairie Forum* 1985, assesses the reasons for the CPR's choice of the southern route across the Prairies. Hugh A. Dempsey, ed., *The CPR West: The Iron Road and the Making of a Nation* (V: Douglas & McIntyre 1984) has fifteen mostly good essays on the CPR and the Prairies and BC. John A. Eagle, *The Canadian Pacific Railway and the Development of Western Canada, 1896–1914* (M and K: MQUP 1989) is a detailed study of the company's activities during two formative decades.

There were other railways besides the Canadian Pacific, of course. T.D. Regehr has provided an excellent study of *The Canadian Northern Railway: Pioneer Road of the Northern Prairies, 1895–1918* (T: MAC 1976), although his uncritical admiration for its entrepreneurs approaches that of Pierre Berton. Ena Schnieder, *Ribbons of Steel: The Story of the Northern Alberta Railways* (C: Detselig 1989) is a rare history of a small provincial railway. Three railways that opened the North to development are the subjects of Albert Tucker, *Steam into Wilderness: Ontario Northland Railway, 1902–1962* (T: Fitzhenry & Whiteside 1978), on the Ontario Northland; Roy Minter, *The White Pass: Gateway to the Klondike* (T: M&S 1987), on the White Pass and Yukon; and Howard A. Fleming, *Canada's Arctic Outlet: A History of the Hudson Bay Railway* (Berkeley: University of California Press 1957), on the Hudson Bay Railway. The airplane replaced the railway farther north: see J.R.K. Main, *Voyageurs of the Air: A History of Civil Aviation in Canada: 1858–1967* (O: QP 1967), Frank H. Ellis, *Canada's Flying Heritage* (T: UTP 1954), and William Paul Ferguson, *The Snowbird Decades: Western Canada's Pioneer Aviation Companies* (V: BUT 1979). Gordon Bennett, *Yukon Transportation: A History* (O: Parks Canada 1978) surveys air, rail, and water transport. The papers collected in Kenneth S. Coates, ed., *The Alaska Highway* (V: UBCP 1985) assess the significance of the link from Edmonton to Fairbanks.

The most valuable resource of the Prairie West was land for agricultural settlement. Vernon C. Fowke, *The National Policy and the Wheat Economy* (T: UTP 1957) is the book to read first. Carl E. Solberg's *The Prairies and the Pampas: Agrarian Policy in Canada and Argentina, 1880–1930* (Stanford: Stanford UP 1987) is an interesting comparative overview based on secondary sources. Although fifty years old, several volumes of the *Canadian Frontiers of Settlement* series remain important sources for serious inquiry: William A. Mackintosh, *Prairie Settlement, the Geographical Setting* (T: MAC 1934), Arthur S. Morton, *A History of Prairie Settlement* (T: MAC 1938), and Chester Martin, *Dominion Lands Policy* (T: MAC 1938), the latter reissued in abridged form with an introduction by L.H. Thomas (T: M&S 1973). The resale of the tens of millions of acres given the CPR is the subject of J.B. Hedges, *The Federal Railway Land Subsidy Policy of Canada*

(Cambridge: HUP 1934), and of his *Building the Canadian West: The Land and Colonization Policies of the Canadian Pacific Railway* (NY: MAC 1939). Wheat was the Prairie West's staple crop, but studies of wheat marketing are too numerous to list them all here. Charles F. Wilson, *A Century of Canadian Grain: Government Policy to 1951* (S: WPPB 1978); Garry Fairbairn, *From Prairie Roots: The Remarkable Story of Saskatchewan Wheat Pool* (S: WPPB 1984); William E. Morriss, *Chosen Instrument: A History of the Canadian Wheat Board, The McIvor Years* (E: Reidmore Books 1987); and Allan G. Levine, *The Exchange: 100 Years of Trading Grain in Winnipeg* (W: Peguis 1987) will answer most questions and point out the other studies. George E. Britnell and V.C. Fowke's neglected *Canadian Agriculture in War and Peace, 1935–50* (Stanford: Stanford UP 1962) includes both Prairie and BC agriculture. Grant MacEwan's *Illustrated History of Western Canadian Agriculture* (S: WPPB 1980) is as shallow as his dozens of other popular Prairie histories. The sense of crisis which has surrounded Prairie agriculture since the 1960s is captured in Barry Wilson, *Beyond the Harvest: Canadian Grain at the Crossroads* (S: WPPB 1981), and in the essays in G.S. Basran and David A. Hay, eds., *The Political Economy of Agriculture in Western Canada* (T: Garamond Press 1988).

Emphasis on the grain trade and on government policy has meant that there are fewer scholarly studies of the actual farm families and the communities they built. Two recent outstanding contributions which come to very different conclusions are Paul Voisey, *Vulcan: The Making of a Prairie Community* (T: UTP 1988), and Lyle Dick, *Farmers 'Making Good': The Development of Abernethy District, Saskatchewan, 1880–1920* (O: Parks Canada 1989). Wendy Owen's edited collection, *The Wheat King: The Selected Letters and Papers of A.J. Cotton, 1888–1913* (W: Manitoba Record Society 1985), tells the story of an early agri-businessman. David C. Jones, *Empire of Dust: Settling and Abandoning the Prairie Dry Belt* (E: UAP 1987) describes the failure that met many other would-be kings. Heather Robertson's *Grass Roots* (T: James Lewis and Samuel 1973) does the same for a later period. The ten chapters of David C. Jones and Ian MacPherson, eds., *Building beyond the Homestead: Rural History on the Prairies* (C: UCP 1985) explore several important themes. There are dozens of homesteading memoirs of variable quality: Wilfrid Eggleston, *Homestead on the Range* (O: Borealis Press 1982) is one of the best. The utility (or lack thereof) of the hundreds of local histories is discussed in Paul Voisey, 'Rural Local History and the Prairie West,' *Prairie Forum* 1985. Works on Prairie communities by sociologists and anthropologists are also useful to historians: C.A. Dawson and Eva R. Young, *Pioneering in the Prairie Provinces:*

The Social Side of the Settlement Process (T: MAC 1940); Jean Burnet, *Next-Year Country: A Study of Rural Social Organization in Alberta* (T: UTP 1951); and John W. Bennett, *Northern Plainsmen: Adaptive Strategy and Agrarian Life* (Chicago: Aldine 1969). Donald H. Akenson's almost-annual collection of *Canadian Papers in Rural History* (Gananoque: Langdale Press 1978–93) is another source of articles on both the Prairie West and occasionally BC, which has been neglected by historians of agriculture. From these volumes, Ian MacPherson's 'Divisions in the Struggle for Orderly Marketing in British Columbia, 1900–1940,' 1990, deserves specific mention, as does Margaret Ormsby, 'Agricultural Development in British Columbia,' *Agricultural History* 1945; and Morag MacLachlan, 'The Success of the Fraser Valley Milk Producers' Association,' *BCS* 1974–5. David Dendy and Kathleen Kyle, *A Fruitful Century: The BC Fruit Growers' Association* (Kelowna: BC Fruit Growers 1990) is a history of the tree-fruit industry as well as the organization.

BC's ranching industry has a single good historian in G.E.G. Thomas, 'The British Columbia Ranching Frontiers, 1858–1896,' MA thesis, University of British Columbia 1976. In southern Alberta, argue David H. Breen in *The Canadian Prairie West and the Ranching Frontier, 1874–1924* (T: UTP 1983), and L.G. Thomas in *Ranchers' Legacy: Alberta Essays by Lewis G. Thomas*, edited by Patrick A. Dunae (E: UAP 1986), Canada's ranching frontier was institutionally and socially distinct from that of the United States. Instead, the range cattle industry incorporated the Prairie West into a Canadian metropolitan network and transplanted a British-Canadian society to southern Alberta. Simon M. Evans disagrees in 'American Diffusion or Victorian Transplant: The Origin of Ranching in Western Canada,' *Great Plains Quarterly* 1983, and in 'The End of the Open Range Era in Western Canada,' *Prairie Forum* 1983. Sheilagh Jameson provides a short overview in 'The Ranching Industry of Western Canada: Its Initial Epoch, 1873–1910,' *Prairie Forum* 1986.

British Columbia's most important resources were its forests and minerals, but neither industry as yet has a comprehensive history. Two articles in *BC Studies* examine provincial policy: Stephen Gray, 'The Government's Timber Business: Forest Policy and Administration in BC, 1912–1928,' 1989; and Jeremy Wilson, 'Forest Conservation in BC, 1935–85: Reflections on a Barren Political Debate,' 1987–8. Geoffrey W. Taylor, *Timber: A History of the Forest Industry in BC* (V: J.J. Douglas 1975) is uncritical but provides useful information, as do two corporate histories: Sue Baptie, *First Growth: The Story of British Columbia Forest Products Limited* (V: BC Forest Products 1975); and Donald MacKay, *Empire of Wood: The MacMillan Bloedel Story* (V: Douglas & McIntyre 1982). Patricia Marchak,

Green Gold: The Forest Industry in British Columbia (V: UBCP 1983) has several historical sections. Andrew Mason Prouty, *More Deadly than War!: Pacific Coast Logging, 1827–1981* (2nd ed., NY: Garland 1988) compares BC favourably with the United States with regard to workers safety. Three older studies are worth dusting off: W.A. Carrothers's chapter in A.R.M. Lower, ed., *The North American Assault on the Canadian Forest: A History of the Lumber Trade between Canada and the United States* (T: RP 1938); F.W. Howay, W.N. Sage, and H.F. Angus, *British Columbia and the United States: The North Pacific Slope from Fur Trade to Aviation* (RP 1942, NY: Russell and Russell 1970), which considers both forestry and mining in a binational context; and Harold A. Innis *Settlement and the Mining Frontier* and A.R.M. Lower, *Settlement and the Forest Frontier in Eastern Canada*, published together (T: MAC 1936). Mark Wyman explains hard-rock mining in 'Industrial Revolution in the West: Hard-Rock Miners and the New Technology,' *Western Historical Quarterly* 1974. Raymond W. Payne, 'Corporate Power, Interest Groups, and the Development of Mining Policy in British Columbia, 1972–77,' *BCS* 1982, is a lonely study of provincial policy towards this important industry. Gold in the Klondike attracted Euro-Canadians north in large numbers for the first time; see Pierre Berton, *Klondike: The Last Great Gold Rush* (rev. ed., T: M&S 1972).

Academic, public, and corporate historians have studied BC's salmon fishery. Keith Ralston, 'Patterns of Trade and Investment on the Pacific Coast, 1867–1892: The Case of the British Columbia Salmon Canning Industry,' *BCS* 1968–9, and David J. Reid, 'Company Mergers in the Fraser River Salmon Canning Industry, 1885–1902,' *CHR* 1975, discuss the corporate structure of the nineteenth-century industry. William A. Carrothers, *The British Columbia Fisheries* (T: UTP 1941) is a now-dated survey, and Cicely Lyons, *Salmon Our Heritage: The Story of a Province and an Industry* (V: BC Packers 1969) is an encyclopedic celebration. Duncan A. Stacey, *Sockeye & Tinplate: Technological Change in the Fraser River Canning Industry, 1871–1912* (Vi: BC Provincial Museum 1982) is a fascinating material history of canning. Dianne Newell, ed., *The Development of the Pacific Salmon-Canning Industry: A Grown Man's Game* (M and K: MQUP 1989) contains the letters and documents written between 1902 and 1928 from the papers of Henry Doyle, founder of the BC Packers Association. Although neither book is a formal history, Patricia Marchak et al., *Uncommon Property: The Fishing and Fish-Processing Industries in British Columbia* (T: Methuen 1987) and Geoff Meggs, *Salmon: The Decline of the British Columbia Fishery* (V: Douglas & McIntyre 1991) examine the industry's contemporary crisis.

The exploitation of ocean mammals – whales and seals – is a theme which unites the histories of BC and the North. Robert Lloyd Webb, *On the Northwest: Commercial Whaling in the Pacific Northwest, 1790–1967* (V: UBCP 1988) is a scholarly survey of the industry; W. Gillies Ross, *Whaling and Eskimos: Hudson Bay, 1860–1915* (O: National Museums of Canada 1975) looks at the eastern Arctic; Daniel Francis, *Arctic Chase: A History of Whaling in Canada's North* (St John's: Breakwater 1984) is a solid popular treatment. Dorothy Harley Eber, *When the Whalers Were Up North: Inuit Memories from the Eastern Arctic* (M and K: MQUP 1989) collects Inuit accounts; W. Gillies Ross's two edited collections, *An Arctic Whaling Diary: The Journal of Captain George Comer in Hudson Bay, 1903–1905* (T: UTP 1984) and *Arctic Whalers, Icy Seas: Narratives of the Davis Strait Whale Fishery* (T: Irwin 1985) are well-introduced and well-annotated documentary sources. Briton Cooper Busch, *The War against the Seals: A History of the North American Seal Fishery* (M and K: MQUP 1985) considers Northern and North Pacific sealing from the seals' perspective, while Peter Murray, *The Vagabond Fleet: A Chronicle of the North Pacific Sealing Schooner Trade* (Vi: Sono Nis Press 1988) is both a survey of the sea hunt and a nautical history. Although it diminished in importance to Europeans, the fur trade remained a significant primary industry, especially to northern Native peoples. Harold A. Innis explains the changes in the last section of *The Fur Trade in Canada: An Introduction to Canadian Economic History* (1930, 4th ed., T: UTP 1970), and Arthur J. Ray's *The Canadian Fur Trade in the Industrial Age* (T: UTP 1990) extends the history of this staple industry to 1945. Hugh Brody, *The Living Arctic: Hunters of the Canadian North* (V: Douglas & McIntyre 1987) is more fun to read. Shepard Krech III, ed., *The Subarctic Fur Trade: Native Economic and Social Adaptations* (V: UBCP 1984) is an interdisciplinary collection which has some discussion of the post-Confederation period, as does Peter J. Usher, *Fur Trade Posts of the Northwest Territories, 1870–1970* (O: Northern Scientific Research Group 1971). In *A Gentleman Adventurer: The Arctic Diaries of R.H.G. Bonnycastle* (T: Lester & Orpen Dennys 1984), Heather Robertson has edited the diaries of an HBC employee between 1928 and 1931.

The search for oil, gas, and minerals also unites Western and Northern history. In the North, oil development remains an incendiary political issue. Francois Bregha, *Bob Blair's Pipeline: The Business and Politics of Northern Energy Development Projects* (T: JL 1979) is critical; Donald Peacock, *People, Peregrines, and Arctic Pipelines: The Critical Battle to Build Canada's Northern Gas Pipelines* (V: J.J. Douglas 1977) is pro-development; Peter H. Pearse, ed., *The Mackenzie Pipeline: Arctic Gas and Canadian En-*

ergy Policy (T: M&S 1974) is an attempt at a dispassionate study. David Breen, ed., *William Stewart Herron: Father of the Petroleum Industry in Alberta* (C: Alberta Records Publication Board 1984) is a book of documents with an excellent introduction which can serve as a survey history of the early development of the Turner Valley fields, while Barry Glen Ferguson, *Athabasca Oil Sands: Northern Resource Exploration, 1875–1951* (R: CPRC 1985) sets oil sands' development in the broader context of the development of the petroleum industry. Larry Pratt, *The Tar Sands: Syncrude and the Politics of Oil* (E: Hurtig 1976) looks at the later period. J.D. House, *The Last of the Free Enterprisers: The Oilmen of Calgary* (T: MAC 1980) is a sympathetic sociological study of oil entrepreneurs.

The role of the entrepreneur in regional economic development is the subject of A.A. den Otter, *Civilizing the West: The Galts and the Development of Western Canada* (E: UAP 1982), and J.M.S. Careless, 'The Business Community in the Early Development of Victoria, BC,' in David S. Macmillan, ed., *Canadian Business History: Selected Studies, 1497–1971* (T: M&S 1972). D.G. Paterson attributes a major role to BC entrepreneurs in 'European Financial Capital and British Columbia: An Essay on the Role of the Regional Entrepreneur,' *BCS* 1974, but Patricia E. Roy proves the opposite in 'Direct Management from Abroad: The Formative Years of the British Columbia Electric Railway,' *Business History Review* 1973. In 'Managerial Crisis: The Emergence and Role of the West Coast Logging Engineer, 1900–1930,' *Canadian Papers in Business History*, vol. 1, (Vi: Public History Group 1989), ed., Peter A. Baskerville, Richard Rajala explains how a managerial elite used engineers as 'lesser managers' to control workers. Brett Fairbairn looks at a very different form of entrepreneurship prevalent in the West in *Building a Dream: The Co-operative Retailing System in Western Canada, 1928–1988* (S: WPPB 1989). The best efforts of regional entrepreneurs were never able to reduce the West's dependence on resource-extractive industries and build a diversified economy. Two articles about BC manufacturing explore this theme: John Lutz, 'Losing Steam: The Boiler and Engine Industry as an Index of British Columbia's Deindustrialization,' *CHA HP* 1988, and John Stewart, 'The Kamloops Canneries: The Rise and Fall of a Local Industry, 1913–1990,' *BCS* 1992. In their provocative *Prairie Capitalism: Power and Influence in the New West* (T: M&S 1979), John Richards and Larry Pratt discuss 'the re-emergence during the 1970s of provincial entrepreneurship' in Saskatchewan under the NDP and in Alberta through an alliance between the provincial Conservative government and 'an arriviste local bourgeoisie,' K.J. Rea recognizes in *The Political Economy of the Canadian*

North: An Interpretation of the Course of Development in the Northern Territories of Canada to the Early 1960s (T: UTP 1968) that the federal government has been the critical actor in Northern economic development.

The Prairies, BC, and the North have been 'urban frontiers' as well as rural ones; towns and cities were integral to regional development. Three articles provide excellent introductions to the broad themes of Western urbanization: Alan F.J. Artibise, 'The Urban West: The Evolution of Prairie Towns and Cities to 1930,' *Prairie Forum* 1979; Robert A.J. McDonald, 'Victoria, Vancouver, and the Economic Development of British Columbia, 1881–1914,' and Paul Phillips, 'The Prairie Urban System, 1911–1961: Specialization and Change.' The latter two articles are chapters in Artibise's edited collection *Town and City: Aspects of Western Canadian Urban Development* (R: CPRC 1981). The most ubiquitous form of urban history is the 'urban biography' of an individual city. Artibise's *Winnipeg: A Social History of Urban Growth, 1874–1914* (M and K: MQUP 1975) was one of the first and remains one of the best, although Reuben Bellan, *Winnipeg First Century: An Economic History* (W: Queenston House 1978) covers a longer period. Several of James H. Gray's books, most notably *The Winter Years: The Depression on the Prairies* (T: MAC 1966), *The Boy from Winnipeg* (T: MAC 1970), and *The Roar of the Twenties* (T: MAC 1975), are essentially social histories of Winnipeg. Artibise has also contributed *Winnipeg: An Illustrated History* (T: JL 1977) to the National Museums of Canada's *History of Canadian Cities* series, which includes J. William Brennan's *Regina: An Illustrated History* (T: JL 1989), Max Foran's *Calgary: An Illustrated History* (T: JL 1978), Patricia Roy's *Vancouver: An Illustrated History* (T: JL 1980), and P. Koroscil's *Whitehorse: An Illustrated History* (T: JL 1979). Don Kerr and Stan Hanson, *Saskatoon: The First Half-Century* (E: NeWest Press 1982); Peter A. Baskerville, *Beyond the Island: An Illustrated History of Victoria* (Burlington: Windsor Publications 1986); and Alex Johnston and A.A. den Otter, *Lethbridge: A Centennial History* (Lethbridge: Historical Society of Alberta/City of Lethbridge 1985) are intended for a popular readership but useful to researchers. In *Distant Neighbors: A Comparative History of Seattle and Vancouver* (Lincoln: University of Nebraska Press 1987), Norbert MacDonald describes the dissimilar evolution of two Pacific coast cities from their frontier foundations to the present – an approach other urban historians might consider. Vancouver is also well served by the ten essays in Robert A.J. McDonald and Jean Barman, eds., *Vancouver Past: Essays in Social History*, a special double edition of *BC Studies* (1986), also published as a book (V: UBCP 1986). Smaller urban centres have received less attention from professional historians, but every community of any size has a history compiled by an enthusiastic amateur. Single industry towns are a significant part of western and northern Canada's urban frontier, but they have found more sociologists than historians. Rex A. Lucas, *Minetown, Milltown, Railtown: Life in Communities of Single Industry* (T: UTP 1971) provides a general analysis, while Robert Robson, 'Manitoba's Resource Towns: The Twentieth Century Frontier,' *Manitoba History* 1988 puts several towns into historical perspective.

'LIMITED IDENTITIES': ETHNICITY

Region is only one of Canada's 'limited identities'; class, gender, and ethnicity are the others which historians have emphasized. Peopled by Native North Americans and immigrants from Europe and Asia, the West and the North historically have been ethnically diverse, but there is no good single study which considers ethnic history within the regional context. Thus a good place to begin is by reading Roberto Perin, 'Writing about Ethnicity,' in John Schultz, ed., *Writing about Canada: A Handbook for Modern Canadian History* (Scarborough: PH 1990). For an overview of the Prairie West, the starting point should be Gerald Friesen's 'Immigrant Communities, 1870–1940,' chapter 11 of *The Canadian Prairies*. For BC, John Norris, ed., *Strangers Entertained: A History of the Ethnic Groups of British Columbia* (V: BC Centennial '71 Committee 1971) is unfortunately typical of much ethnic history in that it is an uneven collection of twenty-six laudatory chapters, each written by a loyal member of the group. Howard and Tamara Palmer, eds., *Peoples of Alberta: Portraits of Cultural Diversity* (S: WPPB 1985) contains chapters on the histories of seventeen ethnic groups within that province.

On the shaping and implementation of immigration policy, the important studies are David Hall, *Sifton*; Pierre Berton, *The Promised Land: Settling the West, 1896–1914* (T: M&S 1984); Norman Macdonald, *Canada: Immigration and Colonization, 1841–1903* (T: MAC 1966); Harold Troper, *Only Farmers Need Apply: Official Canadian Government Encouragement of Immigration from the United States, 1896–1911* (T: Griffin House 1972); and especially Donald H. Avery, *'Dangerous Foreigners': European Immigrant Workers and Labour Radicalism in Canada, 1896–1932* (T: M&S 1979). Avery provides an excellent discussion of the response of Anglo-Canadians to immigrants, a subject further considered in Howard Palmer, *Patterns of Prejudice: A History of Nativism in Alberta* (T: M&S 1982), and in John Herd Thompson, *The Harvests of War: The Prairie West, 1914–1918* (T: M&S

1978). John Lehr, 'The Government and the Immigrant: Perspectives on Ukrainian Block Settlement in the Canadian West,' 1977, is but one of dozens of useful articles to be found in *Canadian Ethnic Studies* (University of Calgary 1969–). Anglo-Canadians in the Prairie provinces insisted upon unilingual schools to assimilate the children of European immigrants, and to do this stripped French Canadians of their constitutional rights. These bitter struggles are discussed in Lovell Clark, ed., *The Manitoba School Question: Majority Rule or Minority Rights?* (T: CC 1968); Paul Crunican, *Priests and Politicians: Manitoba Schools and the Election of 1896* (T: UTP 1974); Manoly R. Lupul, *The Roman Catholic Church and the North-West School Question: A Study in Church-State Relations in Western Canada, 1875–1905* (T: UTP 1974); and in the essays in Brown, ed., *Minorities, Schools, and Politics* (cited above). Mary Ashworth, *The Forces Which Shaped Them: A History of the Education of Minority Group Children in BC* (V: New Star 1979) looks at popular attitudes and public policy toward the education of Native Indians, Chinese, Japanese, Doukhobors, and East Indians.

There are many studies of specific ethnic groups in the West, some scholarly and others filiopietistic. The former group are listed here; their notes will lead readers to the latter. Jaroslav Petryshyn with Luba Dzubak, *Peasants in the Promised Land: Canada and the Ukrainians, 1891–1914* (T: JL 1985) is the first book to read on Ukrainians in Western Canada; and Manoly R. Lupul, *A Heritage in Transition: Essays in the History of Ukrainians in Canada* (T: M&S 1982) has five relevant articles and an historiographical essay. Frances Swyripa, *Wedded to the Cause: Ukrainian-Canadian Women and Ethnic Identity, 1891–1991* (T: UTP 1993), brilliantly explores the intersection of gender, ethnicity, and region. The Canadian government's flexible attitude to group settlement attracted religious groups to block settlements in the West, groups discussed in George Woodcock and Ivan Avakumovic, *The Doukhobors* (2nd ed., T: M&S 1977); Victor Peters, *All Things Common: The Hutterian Way of Life* (Minneapolis: University of Minnesota Press 1965); Royden K. Loewen, *Family, Church, and Market: A Mennonite Community in the Old and the New Worlds, 1850–1930* (T: UTP 1993); E.K. Francis, *In Search of Utopia: The Mennonites in Manitoba* (Altona: D.W. Friesen 1955); and Carl A. Dawson, *Group Settlement: Ethnic Communities in Western Canada* (T: MAC 1936). The only study of immigrants from the United States, Karel Bicha's *The American Farmer and the Canadian West, 1896–1914* (Lawrence: Coronado Press 1968), is limited in scope. Immigrants from Great Britain also used ethnic group strategies for economic advantage: see Jean Barman, *Growing Up British in British Columbia: Boys in Private School: 1900–1950* (V: UBCP

1984); Patrick A. Dunae, *Gentlemen Emigrants: From the British Public Schools to the Canadian Frontier* (V: Douglas & McIntyre 1981); and A. Ross McCormack, 'Networks among British Immigrants and Accommodation to Canadian Society: Winnipeg 1900–1914,' *HS/SH* 1984.

Migrants to BC from China, Japan, and Southeast Asia have been the most and best studied groups. W. Peter Ward, *White Canada Forever: Popular Attitudes and Pubic Policies toward Orientals in British Columbia* (2nd ed., M and K: MQUP 1990) and Patricia E. Roy, *A White Man's Province: British Columbia Politicians and Chinese and Japanese Immigrants, 1858–1914* (V: UBCP 1989) are both careful studies. There are very different perspectives on Vancouver's Chinese community in Paul Yee, *Saltwater City: An Illustrated History of the Chinese in Vancouver* (V: Douglas & McIntyre 1988), and in Kay J. Anderson, *Vancouver's Chinatown: Racial Discourse in Canada, 1875–1980* (M and K: MQUP 1991). Ken Adachi's *The Enemy that Never Was: A History of the Japanese Canadians* (T: M&S 1976) is really about the 1942 internment of Japanese-Canadians. Ann Gomer Sunahara vilifies the Canadian government for the interment in *The Politics of Racism: The Uprooting of Japanese Canadians during the Second World War* (T: JL 1981), while Patricia Roy et al. excuse the internment in their curiously titled *Mutual Hostages: Canadians and Japanese during the Second World War* (T: UTP 1990). In *The Voyage of the Komagata Maru: The Sikh Challenge to Canada's Colour Bar* (2nd ed., V: UBCP 1989), Hugh Johnston explains how Anglo-Canadian racism turned back the 'challenge.'

Individual Western immigrant communities are also considered in general studies of the larger ethnic group's presence in Canada. The fastest way to find the titles of these studies is in the bibliography compiled by Jean Burnet with Howard Palmer, for *'Coming Canadians': An Introduction to a History of Canada's Peoples* (T: M&S 1988). The twenty-one pamphlets in the Canadian Historical Association's *Canada's Ethnic Groups* series (O: CHA 1982–) are mercifully short and have excellent bibliographies.

'LIMITED IDENTITIES': CLASS

Class is another 'limited identity' which intersects regional identity, but although historians are actively recreating the world of workers in the West, there is no general history of the working class or of the labour movement in Western Canada. BC has had the most written about it. The basic survey, Paul Phillips's *No Power Greater: A Century of Labour in British Columbia* (V: BC Federation of Labour 1967), is dated. Carlos A. Schwantes, *Radical Heritage: Labor, Socialism, and Reform in Washington and British Columbia, 1885–1917* (V: Douglas & McIntyre 1979) is a comparative overview. When W. Peter Ward proposed in 'Class and Race in the Social Structure of British Columbia, 1870–1939' *BCS* 1980, that 'the major cleavages in British Columbia's social structure ... were those based on race,' he drew an angry rejoinder from Rennie Warburton, 'Race and Class in British Columbia: A Comment,' *BCS* 1981, to which Ward in turn replied in *BCS* 1981. Rennie Warburton and David Coburn, eds., *Workers, Capital, and the State in British Columbia* (V: UBCP 1988) contains twelve essays unified by unanimous rejection of Ward's argument. Two important BC unions are the subjects of Jerry Lembcke and William M. Tattam, *One Union in Wood: A Political History of the International Woodworkers of America* (V: Harbour Publishing 1984), and Elaine Bernard, *The Long Distance Feeling: A History of the Telecommunications Workers Union* (V: New Star 1982). There are also two studies of the IWW: Jack Scott, *Plunderbund and Proletariat: A History of the IWW in British Columbia* (V: New Star 1975), and Mark Leier, *Where the Fraser River Flows: The Industrial Workers of the World in British Columbia* (V: New Star 1990). Lynne Bowen's fine books on BC coal mining communities, *Boss Whistle: The Coal Miners of Vancouver Island Remember* and *Three Dollar Dreams* (Lantzville: Oolichan Books 1982, 1987), are sensitive histories based on oral sources. Howard White, *A Hard Man to Beat: The Story of Bill White, Labour Leader, Historian, Shipyard Worker, Raconteur: An Oral History* (V: Pulp Press 1983) contains factual errors but paints a vivid portrait.

For Manitoba, Doug Smith has provided an overview and a bibliography in *Let Us Rise! An Illustrated History of the Manitoba Labour Movement* (V: New Star 1985). The Winnipeg General Strike of 1919 has attracted many historians. Norman Penner's *Winnipeg 1919: The Strikers' Own History of the Winnipeg General Strike* (T: James Lewis and Samuel 1973) reprints primary testimony. D.C. Masters, *The Winnipeg General Strike* (T: UTP 1950), the first scholarly account, has been superseded by David Jay Bercuson, *Confrontation at Winnipeg: Labour, Industrial Relations, and the General Strike* (rev. ed., M and K: MQUP 1990), which was abbreviated as Kenneth McNaught and Bercuson, *The Winnipeg General Strike: 1919* (T: Longmans 1974). In his interpretive article 'Labour Radicalism and the Western Industrial Frontier, 1897–1919,' *CHR* 1978, Bercuson argued that 'class consciousness and radical working-class attitudes' were more prevalent in the West than in other regions because of the harsh conditions on the 'hinterland-extractive frontier.' Becuson developed this thesis in *Fools and Wise Men: The Rise and Fall of the One Big Union* (T: MHR 1978); in *Reformers, Rebels, and Revolutionaries: The Western Canadian*

Radical Movement, 1899–1919 (T: UTP 1977), A. Ross McCormack made a similar case. This idea that the West was a radical regional exception has been vigorously challenged, most notably by Gregory S. Kealey in '1919: The Canadian Labour Revolt,' *Labour* 1984, who denies any 'unique regional fermentation.' Two more recent articles provide further detail and discussion: James R. Conley, 'Frontier Labourers, Crafts in Crisis, and the Western Labour Revolt: The Case of Vancouver, 1900–1919,' *Labour* 1989, and Jeremy Mouat, 'The Genesis of Western Exceptionalism: British Columbia's Hard Rock Miners, 1895–1903,' *CHR* 1990.

Since 1976, *Labour/le travail* has poured out articles on Western workers until there are now too many to list here by title. Students should look through the index for the work of William M. Baker, W.J.C. Cherwinski, Alvin Finkel, Gordon Hak, Larry Hannant, Mark Leier, Jerry Lembcke, David Monod, Robert Robson, David Schulze, Stanley Scott, Allen Seager, Jeffrey Taylor, Michael R. Welton, and Glen Makahonuk. Makahonuk seems to be writing a working-class history of Saskatchewan a chapter at a time; in addition to 'Class Conflict in a Prairie City: The Saskatoon Working-Class Response to Prairie Capitalism,' *Labour* 1987, see his article in *Saskatchewan History* 1980, 1982, 1986, and in *Prairie Forum* 1984, 1985. *BC Studies* also publishes articles in labour history, among them John Norris, 'The Vancouver Island Coal Miners, 1912–1914: A Study of an Organizational Strike,' *BCS* 1980, and Gordon Hak, '"Line Up or Roll Up": The Lumber Workers Industrial Union in the Prince George District,' *BCS* 1990.

'LIMITED IDENTITIES': GENDER

There is not yet a monograph which surveys women's history in a Western or Northern regional context. The discussion of women's history in Barman's *The West beyond the West* is very good, but Friesen's *Canadian Prairies* has been criticized for lack of attention to women. Alison Prentice et al., *Canadian Women: A History* (T: HBJ 1988) covers the western provinces and Yukon well and has an excellent index and extensive endnotes. Useful bibliographies are Susan Jackel, 'Canadian Prairie Women's History: A Bibliographic Survey,' (T: Canadian Research Institute for the Advancement of Women 1987), and Mary Kinnear and Vera Fast, *Planting the Garden: An Annotated Archival Bibliography of the History of Women in Manitoba* (W: UMP 1987). Two collections of essays discuss a wide range of topics: Mary Kinnear, ed., *First Days, Fighting Days: Women in Manitoba History* (R: CPRC 1987), and Barbara Latham and

Cathy Kess, eds., *In Her Own Right: Selected Essays on Women's History in BC* (Vi: Camosun College 1980).

The history of the women who led suffrage struggles in the Prairie provinces and BC is told in chapters 3 and 4 of Catherine L. Cleverdon's *The Woman Suffrage Movement in Canada* (2nd ed., T: UTP 1974). Carol Lee Bacchi looks at regional and class divisions within the suffrage movement in her book *Liberation Deferred?: The Ideas of the English-Canadian Suffragists, 1877–1918* (T: UTP 1983) and in 'Divided Allegiances: The Response of Farm and Labour Women to Suffrage,' in Linda Kealey, ed., *A Not Unreasonable Claim: Women and Reform in Canada, 1880s–1920s* (T: Women's Press 1979). Prominent Western feminists are the subjects of Elsie Gregory MacGill, *My Mother the Judge: A Biography of Helen Gregory MacGill* (1955, T: Peter Martin Associates 1981), and Mary Kinnear, *Margaret McWilliams: An Interwar Feminist* (M and K: MQUP 1991). The most famous Western suffragist is captured in Veronica Strong-Boag's thoughtful chapter 'Nellie McClung: First-Wave Feminist,' in Strong-Boag and Anita Fellman, eds., *Rethinking Canada: The Promise of Women's History* (2nd ed., T: CCP 1991). Strong-Boag's seminal article 'Pulling in Double Harness or Hauling a Double Load: Women, Work, and Feminism on the Canadian Prairie,' *JCS* 1986, shows that feminism didn't expire with the achievement of suffrage.

Appropriately, the lives of Western women who were not prominent suffragists are now receiving more attention, in books like Barbara Latham and Roberta J. Pazdro, eds., *Not Just Pin Money: Selected Essays on the History of Women's Work in British Columbia* (Vi: Camosun College 1984). Carol Fairbanks and Sara Brooks Sundberg, *Farm Women on the Prairie Frontier: A Sourcebook for Canada and the United States* (Metuchen: Scarecrow Press 1983) and Fairbanks, *Prairie Women: Images in American and Canadian Fiction* (New Haven: Yale UP 1986) have a comparative focus. Five edited collections draw upon the writings of English gentlewomen in the West: Margaret A. Ormsby, ed., *A Pioneer Gentlewoman in British Columbia: The Recollections of Susan Allison* (V: UBCP 1976); W.L. Morton, ed., *God's Galloping Girl: The Peace River Diaries of Monica Storrs, 1929–1931* (V: UBCP 1979); Monica Hopkins, *Letters from a Lady Rancher* (C: Glenbow Museum 1981); Susan Jackel, ed., *A Flannel Shirt and Liberty: British Emigrant Gentlewomen in the Canadian West, 1880–1914* (V: UBCP 1982); and R. Cole Harris and Elizabeth Phillips, eds., *Letters from Windermere, 1912–1914* (V: UBCP 1984). Obtaining equal access to higher education, a much discussed theme in women's history, is the subject of Lee Stewart's *'It's Up to You': Women at UBC in the Early Years*

(V: UBCP 1990). Elaine Leslau Silverman looked beyond the middle class in her *The Last Best West: Women on the Alberta Frontier, 1880–1930* (M: Eden Press 1984), as does Star Rosenthal in 'Union Maids: Organized Women Workers in Vancouver, 1900–1915,' *BCS* 1979.

POLITICAL HISTORY

Given that historians pretend that 'the West' is a single region, it is surprising that there are only two studies which look at BC and Prairie politics from a common regional perspective, both of which look at radical parties: Walter D. Young, *Democracy and Discontent: Progressivism, Socialism, and Social Credit in the Canadian West* (2nd ed., T: MHR 1978), is a slight monograph intended as a text; and J. William Brennan, ed., *Building the Co-operative Commonwealth: Essays on the Democratic Socialist Tradition in Canada* (R: CPRC 1984), is a series of essays on the CCF in all four Western provinces. Several historians interpret the Prairie provinces as a regional entity. The central thesis of Roger Gibbin's *Prairie Politics and Society: Regionalism in Decline* (T: BUT 1980) is now tenuous, but the book remains an excellent survey of Prairie politics through the 1970s. The agrarian insurgencies of the 1920s are discussed in W.L. Morton, *The Progressive Party in Canada* (T: UTP 1950), in Paul F. Sharp, *The Agrarian Revolt in Western Canada: A Survey Showing American Parallels* (1948, NY: Octagon Books 1971), and in David Laycock's *Populism and Democratic Thought in the Canadian Prairies, 1910–1945* (T: UTP 1990), which also considers the CCF and Social Credit. Three trans-Prairie studies look at the regional alienation of the 1960s and 1970s: John J. Barr and Owen Anderson, eds., *The Unfinished Revolt: Some Views on Western Independence* (T: M&S 1971); Larry Pratt and Garth Stevenson, eds., *Western Separatism: The Myths, Realities, and Dangers* (E: Hurtig 1981); and David E. Smith's excellent *The Regional Decline of a National Party: Liberals on the Prairies* (T: UTP 1981). Other than these works, Western politics have been studied in their individual provincial contexts. The essays on each of the four provinces in two political science textbooks are a good place to begin: Rand Dyck, *Provincial Politics in Canada* (2nd ed., Scarborough: PH 1991), and Martin Robin, ed., *Canadian Provincial Politics: The Party Systems of the Ten Provinces* (2nd ed. Scarborough: PH 1978). Dyck's book has useful tables of provincial election results and lists of provincial ministries.

The best short analysis of Manitoba politics is Thomas Peterson's essay 'Manitoba: Ethnic and Class Politics' in Robin's *Canadian Provincial Poli-*

tics. M.S. Donnelly, *The Government of Manitoba* (T: UTP 1963) sprinkles political history through a study of provincial institutions. Gerald Friesen's 'Homeland to Hinterland: Political Transition in Manitoba, 1870–1879,' CHA *HP* 1979, is a thoughtful explanation of political change in the new province. Although the Liberal and Conservative parties await histories, the Manitoba CCF-NDP has been studied in Nelson Wiseman, *Social Democracy in Manitoba: A History of the CCF-NDP* (W: UMP 1983), and in James A. McAllister, *The Government of Edward Schreyer: Democratic Socialism in Manitoba* (M and K: MQUP 1984). Susan Mann Trofimenkoff, *Stanley Knowles: The Man from Winnipeg North Centre* (S: WPPB 1982) is an affectionate portrait of a distinguished Manitoba member of the CCF-NDP federal caucus. John Kendle, *John Bracken: A Political Biography* (T: UTP 1979) substitutes well for a history of the Liberal-Progressive government Bracken led from 1922 to 1942. Doug Smith, *Joe Zuken: Citizen and Socialist* (T: JL 1990) reminds us of the importance of Communists in Winnipeg politics. The essays in James Silver and Jeremy Hull, eds., *The Political Economy of Manitoba* (R: CPRC 1990) are also useful.

In *Saskatchewan Government: Politics and Pragmatism* (S: WPPB 1980), Evelyn Eager exaggerates the 'conservatism of the Saskatchewan electorate,' which is also the title of Eager's article in the excellent collection edited by Norman Ward and Duff Spafford, *Politics in Saskatchewan* (Don Mills: Longmans 1968). David E. Smith, *Prairie Liberalism: The Liberal Party in Saskatchewan, 1905–71* (T: UTP 1975) is a good general discussion of provincial politics. Norman Ward and David E. Smith look at a Liberal premier and regional cabinet representative in *James G. Gardiner: Relentless Liberal* (T: UTP 1990), while Dale Eisler's, *Rumours of Glory: Saskatchewan and the Thatcher Years* (E: Hurtig 1987) and Barry Wilson's, *Politics of Defeat: The Decline of the Liberal Party in Saskatchewan* (S: WPPB 1980) tell the unhappy (for the Liberals) recent history of the party that once dominated the province. S.M. Lipset's ancient *Agrarian Socialism: The Cooperative Commonwealth Federation in Saskatchewan; A Study in Political Sociology* (2nd ed., NY: Anchor 1968) remains required reading. Doris French Shackleton, *Tommy Douglas* (T: M&S 1975), and Lewis H. Thomas, ed., *The Making of a Socialist: The Recollections of T.C. Douglas* (E: UAP 1982), reject Lipset's argument that the CCF in power lost the radical direction of its early years. A second social democratic premier is the subject of Dennis Gruending, *Promises to Keep: A Political Biography of Allan Blakeney* (S: WPPB 1990). The struggle for Saskatchewan medicare is covered in Robin F. Badgley and Samuel Wolfe, *Doctor's Strike: Medical*

Care and Conflict in Saskatchewan (T: MAC 1967), in essays by Cynthia Krueger and Janet Walker Gouldner in the 1968 edition of Lipset's *Agrarian Socialism*, and in 'Medicare: Saskatchewan Moves the Nation,' chapter seven of J.L. Granatstein's *Canada 1957–1967: Years of Uncertainty and Innovation* (T: M&S 1986). Patrick Kyba, *Alvin: A Biography of the Honorable Alvin Hamilton, PC* (R: CPRC 1989) recounts the career of a federal Conservative minister of agriculture. On the Conservative provincial government of the 1980s, see Lesley Biggs and Mark Stobbe, eds., *Devine Rule in Saskatchewan: A Decade of Hope and Hardship* (S: Fifth House 1991). The Saskatchewan Archives Board has published two helpful guides: a *Directory of Saskatchewan Ministries, Members of the Legislative Assembly, and Elections, 1905–1953* (R: QP 1954) and a *Directory of Members of Parliament and Federal Elections for the North-West Territories and Saskatchewan, 1887–1966* (R: QP 1967).

L.G. Thomas, *The Liberal Party in Alberta: A History of Politics in the Province of Alberta, 1905–1921* (T: UTP 1959) leads off any reading list on Alberta political history. D.R. Babcock looks at the origins of provincial exceptionalism in 'Autonomy and Alienation in Alberta: Premier A.C. Rutherford,' *Prairie Forum* 1981. James H. Gray describes a frustrated Alberta Conservative in *R.B. Bennett: The Calgary years* (T: UTP 1991). There is as yet no history of the UFA government, 1921–1935, but Carl Betke's 'Farm Politics in an Urban Age: The Decline of the United Farmers of Alberta after 1921,' in Thomas, *Essays on Western History*, is helpful, as are two biographies: William Kirby Rolph, *Henry Wise Wood of Alberta* (T: UTP 1950), and Anthony Mardiros, *William Irvine: The Life of a Prairie Radical* (T: JL 1979). Social Credit, which held power in Edmonton from 1935 to 1971, has been the most written-about movement/party. Alvin Finkel's comprehensive *The Social Credit Phenomenon in Alberta* (T: UTP 1989) identifies the radical roots which began to wither during William Aberhart's second premiership and atrophied under Ernest Manning after 1943. David R. Elliott and Iris Miller, *Bible Bill: A Biography of William Aberhart* (E: Reidmore Books 1987) shows that the Social Credit party in Alberta had little connection with Aberhart's personal religious beliefs, and that he had little conception of where he was actually leading Albertans. Three older books from the *Social Credit in Alberta* series are also worthwhile: John A. Irving, *The Social Credit Movement in Alberta* (T: UTP 1959); C.B. Macpherson, *Democracy in Alberta: Social Credit and the Party System* (2nd ed., T: UTP 1962); and especially J.R. Mallory, *Social Credit and the Federal Power in Canada* (T: UTP 1954). There are also two documentary collections on Social Credit: Joseph A.

Boudreau, ed., *Alberta, Aberhart, and Social Credit* (T: HRW 1975); and Lewis H. Thomas, *William Aberhart and Social Credit in Alberta* (T: CC 1977), which emphasizes the too-easily-forgotten radical reform background of Social Credit. John J. Barr, *The Dynasty: The Rise and Fall of Social Credit in Alberta* (T: M&S 1974) explains the Conservative victory of 1971, and David G. Wood, *The Lougheed Legacy* (T: Key Porter 1985) looks at Alberta's first Tory premier. The essays in Carlo Caldarola, ed., *Society and Politics in Alberta: Research Papers* (T: Methuen 1979), and in Larry Pratt, ed., *Democracy and Socialism in Alberta: Essays in Honour of Grant Notley* (E: NeWest Press 1986) touch many aspects of provincial political history.

British Columbia is the subject of Martin Robin's two-volume political history *The Company Province*, vol. 1, *The Rush for Spoils, 1871–1933*, and vol. 2, *Pillars of Profit, 1934–1972* (T: M&S 1972, 1973), which Robin summarizes in the chapter on BC in his *Canadian Provincial Politics*. Alan Cairns and Daniel Wong offer a different interpretive overview in 'Socialism, Federalism, and the BC Party System 1933–1983,' in Hugh G. Thorburn, ed., *Party Politics in Canada*, (6th ed., Scarborough: PH 1991). The eight chapters in J. Terence Morley et al., eds., *Reins of Power: Governing British Columbia* (V: Douglas & McIntyre 1983) collectively constitute a general introduction to BC politics and institutions. Five venerable articles remain important for the study of the nineteenth century: Margaret A. Ormsby, 'Prime Minister Mackenzie, the Liberal Party, and the Bargain with British Columbia,' *CHR* 1945; W.N. Sage, 'Federal Parties and Provincial Groups in British Columbia, 1871–1903,' *BCHQ* 1948; Edith Dobie, 'Some Aspects of Party History in British Columbia, 1871–1903,' *Pacific Historical Review* 1932; J.T. Saywell, 'The McInnes Incident in British Columbia,' *BCHQ* 1950; and George F.G. Stanley, 'A "Constitutional Crisis" in British Columbia,' *CJEPS* 1955. Patricia Roy, 'Progress, Prosperity, and Politics: The Railway Policies of Richard McBride,' *BCS* 1980, is the best introduction to BC's first partisan premier. Two articles by Margaret Ormsby look at political failures: 'The United Farmers of British Columbia: An Abortive Third Party Movement,' *BCHQ* 1953; and 'T. Dufferin Pattullo and the Little New Deal,' *CHR* 1962. BC politics in the interwar years can be followed through three good biographies: Robin Fisher, *Duff Pattullo of British Columbia* (T: UTP 1991) depicts the Liberal premier as the reformist regional victim of conservative centralists in Ottawa; David Ricardo Williams, *Mayor Gerry: The Remarkable Gerald Gratton McGeer* (V: Douglas & McIntyre 1986) describes the BC MLA, MP, senator, and Vancouver mayor 'warts and all'; and Dorothy G. Steeves,

The Compassionate Rebel: Ernest E. Winch and the Growth of Socialism in Western Canada (2nd ed., V: J.J. Douglas 1977) is a sympathetic life and times of a major Socialist politician. In *The Anatomy of a Party: The National CCF, 1932–1961* (T: UTP 1969), Walter D. Young devotes many pages to the party in BC.

Social Credit, which has ruled the province almost continuously since 1952, still awaits a scholarly history, but the complexity of BC politics since the 1940s is explored in Donald E. Blake, et al., *Two Political Worlds: Parties and Voting in British Columbia* (V: UBCP 1985). Ronald B. Worley, *The Wonderful World of W.A.C. Bennett* (T: M&S 1971), and two books by David J. Mitchell, *W.A.C. Bennett and the Rise of British Columbia* (V: Douglas & McIntyre 1983) and *Succession: The Political Reshaping of British Columbia* (V: Douglas & McIntyre 1987) are uncritical accounts by party insiders. Dave Barrett's NDP government lasted only one term, a failure which Philip Resnick attributes to its lack of radical courage in 'Social Democracy in Power: The Case of British Columbia,' *BCS* 1977; and which Paul Tennant explains as the result of poor planning in 'The NDP Government of British Columbia: Unaided Politicians in an Unaided Cabinet,' *Canadian Public Policy* 1977. The resurgence of Social Credit under Bill Bennett is chronicled in Stan Persky's *Son of Socred: Has Bill Bennett's Government Got BC Moving Again?* and its sequel *Bennett II: The Decline and Stumbling of Social Credit Government in BC, 1979–1983* (V: New Star 1979, 1983). These books are better than the partisan diatribes implied by the titles, as are Warren Magnusson et al., eds., *The New Reality: The Politics of Restraint in British Columbia*, Stan Persky, *Fantasy Government: Bill Vander Zalm and the Future of Social Credit* (V: New Star 1984, 1989), and Gary Mason and Keith Baldrey, *Fantasyland: Inside the Reign of Bill Vander Zalm* (Scarborough: MHR 1989). Bryan D. Palmer dissects an unsuccessful popular insurgency against the SoCreds in *Solidarity: The Rise and Fall of an Opposition in BC* (V: New Star 1987).

Because the northern territories are still in many respects federal colonies, the politics of territory-Ottawa relations predominate as Northerners – like Westerners a century before – try to gain control of their destinies. Kenneth S. Coates, 'Controlling the Periphery: The Territorial Administration of the Yukon and Alaska, 1867–1959,' *Pacific Northwest Quarterly* 1987, provides an interpretive setting. Robert Page, *Northern Development: The Canadian Dilemma* (T: M&S 1986) is a good introduction to development issues – the most important political issues – in the post-1970 North. Other books which consider them include Edgar J. Dosman, *The National Interest: The Politics of Northern Development, 1968–*

75 (T: M&S 1975); L.-E. Hamelin's *Canadian Nordicity: It's Your North, Too* (M: Harvest House 1979); and Gurston Dacks, *A Choice of Futures: Politics in the Canadian North* (Agincourt: Methuen 1981). In *The Modern North: People, Politics, and the Rejection of Colonialism* (T: JL 1989), Kenneth S. Coates and Judith Powell carry this discussion from the 1975 Berger Mackenzie Valley Pipeline Inquiry to the end of the 1980s. R. Quinn Duffy, *The Road to Nunavut: The Progress of the Eastern Arctic Inuit since the Second World War* (M and K: MQUP 1988) is both a study of federal government colonial policy and an economic, social, and political history of what the Inuit call Nunavit – 'Our Land.' Other significant contributions are Shelagh D. Grant, *Sovereignty or Security? Government Policy in the Canadian North, 1936–1950* (V: UBCP 1988), and Mark O. Dickerson, *Whose North?: Political Change, Political Development, and Self-Government in the Northwest Territories* (V: UBCP/Arctic Institute of North America 1992).

INTELLECTUAL AND CULTURAL HISTORY

'Region is less important in Canadian intellectual history than in many other sub-disciplines,' argues Doug Owram in 'Intellectual History in the Land of Limited Identities,' *JCS* 1989. Two articles in the same issue illustrate Owram's contention: R. Douglas Francis, 'In Search of a Prairie Myth: A Survey of Intellectual and Cultural Historiography of Prairie Canada,' and Douglas Cole, 'The Intellectual and Imaginative Development of British Columbia.' Allan Pritchard examines 'Literature of British Columbia' in two articles in *Canadian Literature* (1982, 1984). Three studies of Prairie literature deserve mention: Dick Harrison, *Unnamed Country: The Struggle for a Canadian Prairie Fiction* (E: UAP 1977), Harrison, ed., *Crossing Frontiers: Papers in American and Canadian Western Literature* (E: UAP 1979), and Laurie Ricou, *Vertical Man/Horizontal World: Man and Landscape in Canadian Prairie Fiction* (V: UBCP 1973). Studies of Emily Carr dominate writing about BC painters; begin reading with Maria Tippett's *Emily Carr: A Biography* (T: OUP 1979). Ronald Rees, *Land of Earth and Sky: Landscape Painting of Western Canada* (S: WPPB 1984) discusses Prairie painters. Colin Browne, *Motion Picture Production in BC, 1898–1940: A Brief Historical Background and Catalogue* (Vi: BC Provincial Museum 1979) is an extraordinary catalogue.

Two edited collections introduce Western educational history: J. Donald Wilson and David C. Jones, eds., *Schooling and Society in Twentieth Century British Columbia* (C: Detselig 1980), and Nancy M. Sheehan, Wilson, and Jones, eds., *Schools in the West: Essays in Canadian Educational History* (C: Detselig 1986). Higher education in the West has the usual institutional biographies. Westerners at prayer are discussed in William E. Mann, *Sect, Cult, and Church in Alberta* (T: UTP 1955); Ben Smillie, *Beyond the Social Gospel: Church Protest on the Prairies* (S: Fifth House 1991); and Dennis L. Butcher et al., eds., *Prairie Spirit: Perspectives on the Heritage of the United Church in the West* (W: UMP 1985). Westerners at play are the subjects of Donald G. Wetherell and Irene Kmet, *Useful Pleasures: The Shaping of Leisure in Alberta, 1896–1945* (R: CPRC 1990); and of Morris Mott and John Allardyce, *Curling Capital: Winnipeg and the Roarin' Game, 1876–1988* (W: UMP 1989), which reaches much more than the usual level of sports history.

J.M.S. Careless has complained that there has been so much regional history written that he feels like 'a farmer in a flood: "Lord, I know I prayed for rain, but this is ridiculous."' (see his 'Limited Identities – Ten Years Later,' *Manitoba History* 1980). The bibliographical entries above represent but a fraction of the inundation of written history on Manitoba, Saskatchewan, Alberta, British Columbia, and the North since 1867. The water is now rising more slowly, in that region and regionalism as tools of historical analysis appear to be in decline. This will not, however, make the task of keeping current with historical literature on the West and the North any easier; instead, it will force students to search through other sub-fields of Canadian history to find studies with relevant regional settings.

Contributors

T.W. Acheson is Professor of History at the University of New Brunswick.

Robert Bothwell is Professor of History at Trinity College, University of Toronto.

John English is on leave from his position as Professor of History at the University of Waterloo. He is currently serving as the MP for the region.

Ben Forster is Professor of History at the University of Western Ontario.

Craig Heron is Professor of History at York University.

Andrée Lévesque is Professor of History at McGill University.

J.R. Miller is Professor of History at the University of Saskatchewan.

David Mills is Associate Professor of History at the University of Alberta.

Wendy Mitchinson is Professor of History at the University of Waterloo.

Doug Owram is Professor of History at the University of Alberta.

John Herd Thompson is Professor of History and Canadian Studies at Duke University.

Paul Voisey is Associate Professor of History at the University of Alberta.

Author Index

Abbott, John, 332
Abeel, Cynthia, 223, 310, 311
Abel, Kerry, 188
Abella, Irving, 35, 37, 75, 88, 98, 110, 119
Acheson, Dean, 78
Acheson, T.W., 5, 127, 229, 236, 250, 252, 254, 258, 266, 321
Acton, Janice, 102, 214, 309
Adachi, Ken, 39, 363
Adams, Ian, 91
Adams, Roy, 117
Adamson, Nancy, 211
Adshead, Gordon R., 125
Ahenakew, Freda, 225
Airhart, Phyllis B., 326
Aitken, Barbara, B., 301
Aitken, Hugh, 125, 129, 149, 154
Akenson, Donald, 212, 303, 313, 318, 353, 356
Albert, Jim, 39, 93
Albinson, John G., 97
Alexander, David, 133, 137, 251, 254
Allardyce, John, 373
Allen, Richard, 163, 167, 325, 327
Allen, R.S., 192
Altman, Morris, 128

Ames, Herbert, 240
Anctil, Pierre, 35, 287
Anderson, John C., 113
Anderson, Kay, 363
Anderson, Oscar E., 71
Anderson, Owen, 367
Andrew, Caroline, 241
Anglin, Douglas G., 70
Angus, H.F., 66, 357
Angus, Ian, 119
Ankli, Robert, 318
Annett, Douglas R., 57
Arat-Koc, Sedef, 90
Arbuckle, Franklin, 180
Archer, John H., 344
Archer, Keith, 120
Archibald, Edith, 262
Argue, Rober, 113
Armour, Leslie, 174
Armstrong, Christopher, 14, 97, 132, 142, 151, 154, 244, 253, 315, 320, 335
Armstrong, Elizabeth, 26, 273
Armstrong, Fredrick, 232, 299, 314
Armstrong, Robert, 126, 277
Arnopoulis, Sheila McLeod, 304
Arnup, Katherine, 223

Aronsen, Lawrence, 73
Arsenault, Georges, 263
Arthurs, H.W., 112
Artibise, Alan F.J., 91, 128, 229, 231, 232, 233, 235, 240, 241, 242, 243, 342, 360
Asch, Michael, 200
Ashworth, Mary, 362
Assu, Harold, 187
Aster, Sidney, 37
Atkin, Ronald, 352
Aubin, Paul, 269
Audet, Louis Phillipe, 172–3, 258, 331
Auger, Geneviève, 286
Augerot-Arend, Sylvie d', 209
Austin, Barbara, 144
Avakumovic, Ivan, 30, 119, 120, 168, 362
Avery, Donald, 24, 107, 361
Axelrod, Paul, 174, 175, 220, 259, 333, 337
Axline, Andrew W., 77
Axworthy, Tom, 47, 80

Babad, Michael, 155
Babcock, D.R., 369
Babcock, Robert H., 106, 252, 260, 281
Bacchi, Carol Lee, 160, 207, 330, 366
Bacher, John, 91
Backhouse, Constance, 211, 220, 310
Badgley, Robert F., 368
Baetz, Mark C., 146
Baeudry, Lucille, 290
Baglole, Harry, 13, 249
Bagnell, Kenneth, 305
Bailey, A.G., 249
Baillargeon, Denyse, 283
Baker, Melvin, 106, 257, 266
Baker, William, 13, 25, 116, 250

Baldry, Keith, 371
Ball, Norman, 141, 142, 237, 244
Ball, Rosemary, 319
Balawyder, Aloysius, 62
Baldwin, Douglas, 232, 253, 266
Bannerman, Jean, 206
Banting, Keith, 48
Baptie, Sue, 356
Barber, Joseph, 75
Barber, Marilyn, 26, 212, 304, 305
Barkley, Muray, 266
Barman, Jean, 95, 169, 186, 197, 225, 240, 344, 360, 362, 365
Barnes, Michael, 329
Barnett, Corelli, 55, 67
Barr, Elinor, 103
Barr, John J., 367, 370
Barron, F. Laurie, 192, 196, 349
Barros, James, 71
Barrett, L.G., 251, 265
Barrett, L. Jean, 101
Barrett, Jane R., 51
Barry, Francine, 100, 214, 285
Bartlett, Eleanor A., 91
Bashevkin, Sylvia, 300, 338
Baskerville, Peter, 126, 130, 145, 146, 147, 151, 233, 359, 360
Basran, G.S., 355
Bassler, Gerald, 257
Bates, Hilary, 299
Bator, Paul, 328
Battye, John, 104
Baulin, Jean, 83
Baum, Gregory, 257, 265
Beal, Bob, 18, 194, 349
Beamish, Paul W., 146
Bearden, Jim, 226
Beaucage, André, 113
Beaudry, Lucille, 290
Beaulieu, André, 293

Beaumont, Jane, 51
Beaven, Brian, 11, 335
Beck, J. Murray, 8, 13, 242, 247, 249, 255
Beck, Jeanne, 297
Bédard, Hélène, 286
Bedford, Judy, 215
Beeby, Dean, 338
Beeby, William, 76
Beeching, William, 119
Behiels, Michael, 10, 41, 50, 166, 269, 274, 275
Beigie, Carl, 81
Bélanger, André J., 290
Bélanger, Guy, 111
Bélanger, Jules, 288
Bélanger, Noel, 103
Bélanger, Paul R., 279
Bélanger, Réal, 20, 25, 272
Bélanger, Yves, 274, 278
Bellamy, David J., 334
Bellan, Rueben, 235, 360
Beloff, Max, 55, 64
Belshaw, John Douglas, 103
Benidickson, Jamie, 189, 313
Benjamin, Jacques, 82
Bennett, Gordon, 354
Bennett, John W., 356
Benoit, Cecilia, 217
Bérard, R.N., 257
Bercuson, David J., 10, 13, 28, 38, 49, 75, 87, 88, 105, 108, 116, 168, 263, 345, 346, 364
Berger, Carl, 21, 22, 26, 56, 158, 159, 164, 175, 208, 230, 326, 346
Berger, Thomas R., 199
Bergren, Myrtle Woodward, 110
Bernard, André, 271
Bernard Elaine, 114, 364
Bernard, Jean Paul, 16, 165, 166

Bernier, Gérald, 270
Bernier, Jacques, 161, 292
Berton, Pierre, 4, 16, 18, 24, 34, 134, 348, 353, 357, 361
Bertram, Gordon W., 141
Best, Patricia, 133
Betcherman, Lita-Rose, 35, 119
Betke, Carl, 241, 352, 369
Bettison, David G., 242
Bibby, Reginald, 162
Bicha, Karel, 362
Bickerton, James, 46, 254
Biggs, Leslie, 369
Biddiscombe, Perry, 263
Bilson, Geoffery, 161
Binhammer, H.H., 131
Binnie-Clark, Georgina, 211
Bird, Florence, 211
Bischoff, Peter, 104
Bishop, Charles A., 189
Bishop, Olga, 300, 333
Bissell, Claude, 64, 173
Bitterman, Rusty, 100
Black, Conrad, 41, 273
Black, Errol, 94
Black, Tom, 94
Blackburn, Robert H., 173
Blake, Donald, 371
Blanchard, Paula, 216
Blanchard, Raoul, 288
Blanchette, Arthur, 53
Bland, Salem, 163
Bland, Susan, 207
Bliss, Michael, 17, 24, 62, 124, 125, 126, 129, 143, 151, 152, 160, 161, 223, 299, 311, 317, 321
Bloomfield, Elizabeth, 235, 240, 244, 320
Bloomfield, Gerald T., 143, 215
Bochachevsky-Choniak, Martha, 226

Bogaard, Paul, 266
Boily, Robert, 270
Boivin, H.B., 269
Boismenu, Gérard, 273
Bolger, Francis, 13, 248
Bonenfant, Jean-Charles, 14
Borden, Henry, 25
Borins, Sandford F., 47, 153
Bosnitch, Milan, 122
Bothwell, Robert, 7, 33, 34, 37, 41, 45, 47, 57, 64, 66, 67, 68, 69, 70, 74, 80, 126, 139, 152, 174, 297
Bouchard, Gerard, 96
Boudreau, Emile, 112
Boudreau, Joseph A., 369–70
Bourassa, André-G., 294
Bourassa, Jean, 114
Bourne, Kenneth, 56
Bourne, Paula, 214
Boutillier, James A., 59, 70
Bowen, Lynne, 114, 364
Bowen, Roger W., 72
Bowles, Roy T., 233
Bowsfield, Hartwell, 347, 349
Boyle, George, 265
Bradbury, Bettina, 87, 89, 93, 102, 103, 104, 211, 213, 215, 283
Bradwin, Edmund, 105
Brand, Dionne, 226, 307
Brandt, Gail Cuthbert, 109, 213, 215, 219, 283, 304
Brault, Jean-Rémi, 288
Bray, Matt, 26, 312
Brecher, Irving, 131, 150
Brecher, Michael, 76
Breen, David H., 140, 141, 343, 352, 356, 359
Bregha, Francois, 358
Brennan, J. William, 24, 120, 232, 360, 366

Breton, Raymond, 307
Brimelow, Peter, 48
Briskin, Linda, 100, 107, 211
Britnell, George E., 140, 355
Broadfoot, Barry, 39
Broadhead, Lee-Anne, 51
Brodie Janine, 8, 46, 120
Brodeur, Jean-Paul, 288
Brody, Hugh, 169, 181, 187, 358
Brookes, A.A., 266, 319
Brookes, Alan, 101, 318
Brooks, I.R., 179
Brooks, W.H., 162
Brown, Caroline, 353
Brown, Ian, 145, 147
Brown, John J., 141
Brown, Lorne, 110, 353
Brown, Robert Craig, 5, 6, 18, 25, 26, 27, 55, 58, 59, 61, 126, 149, 256, 346, 362
Brown, S.H., 193
Browne, Colin, 372
Brouwer, Ruth Compton, 164, 224
Bruce, Harry, 147
Brunet, Manon, 292–3
Bryce, Robert, 35, 150
Brym, R.J., 101, 265
Buchlock, H.D., 94
Buck, Tim, 62, 121
Buckley, Helen, 198
Buckley, Kenneth A.H., 131
Buckley, Suzanne, 311
Buckner, Philip, 11, 165, 248, 263, 346
Bullen, Jane, 89
Bullen, John, 99, 103, 213, 310, 328, 338
Bumsted, J.M., 158, 248
Burgess, Joanne, 87, 103, 269, 280
Burghardt, Andrew F., 235

Burnet, Jean, 95, 205, 305, 307, 356, 363
Burns, R.M., 46, 304
Burrows, James K., 351
Busch, Briton Cooper, 261, 358
Butcher, Dennis L., 373
Butler, Linda, 226
Byers, R.B., 47

Cadigan, Sean, 109
Cahill, Jack, 48
Cail, Robert E., 198, 350
Cairns, Alan, 10, 370
Caldarola, Carl, 370
Caldwell, Gary, 286
Calhoun, Sue, 260–1
Calliste, Agnus, 108
Callwood, June, 4
Cameron, Christina, 294
Cameron, David, 331
Cameron, Duncan, 150, 155
Cameron, Silver Donald, 101
Camp, Dalton, 41, 256
Campbell, Colin, 16
Campbell, Douglas, 221, 264
Campbell, G.G., 261
Campbell, Marie, 107
Campbell, Robert, 147
Cantelon, Hart, 97
Caplan, Gerald L., 338
Caragata, Raymond, 99
Cardin, Jean-Francois, 275
Cardinal, Harold, 200
Careless, Anthony, 255
Careless, J.M.S., 3, 12, 58, 170, 232, 233, 234, 247, 297, 314, 334, 359, 373
Carington, Philip, 163
Carroll, J., 318
Cartwright, D.G., 304

Caron, Fabien, 342
Carroll, John E., 84
Carroll, William K., 148
Carrothers, William A., 137, 357
Carstens, Peter, 351
Carter, Gwendolen, 67
Carter, Sarah, 197, 198, 348
Carty, R. Kenneth, 8
Casgrain, Thérèse, 209
Castle, Geoffery, 84
Cathcart, Ruth, 144
Cardin, Jean-François, 112
Carrigan, D. Owen, 8
Chadwick, St. John, 256
Chafe, W.J., 122
Chaikin, Ira, 196, 350
Chaiton, Alf, 330
Chambers, Allan, 152
Chan, Anthony, B., 89
Chapman, J.K., 265
Chapman, Terry, 222
Chaput-Rolland, Solange, 276
Charbonneau, Hubert, 222, 279
Charland, Jean-Pierre, 115, 142, 277
Charles, Aline, 285
Chartrand, Luc, 292
Cherwinski, W.J.C., 88, 101, 260
Chisholm, Jessi, 106
Chodos, Robert, 353
Choquette, Robert, 26, 304
Chown, Alice A., 210
Christaller, Walter, 234
Christian, William, 16
Christian, William A., 70, 175, 176
Chrétien, Jean, 48
Chunn, Dorothy, 98, 329
Clairmont, Donald, 264
Clark, Lovell, 19, 362
Clark, S.D., 91, 240
Clarkson, Stephen, 46, 80, 83

Clement, Wallace, 101, 115, 138, 148, 312, 321, 323

Cleverdon, Catherine, 27, 207, 261, 330, 366

Clifford, N. Keith, 163, 326

Clinton, Archibald, 304

Clippingdale, Richard, 20, 299

Coates, Kenneth S., 182, 184, 188, 344, 345, 346, 351, 354, 371, 372

Coates, Robert, 43

Coburn, David, 88, 364

Cohen, Albert D., 144

Cohen, Andrew, 49

Cohen, Marjorie Griffin, 100, 102, 109, 141, 212, 309, 319, 323

Cohen, Yolande, 212

Coldwell, Gary, 287

Cole, Douglas, 178, 187, 196, 350, 372

Coleman, William, 41, 149, 275

Collins, Edward, 80

Colton, Timothy J., 242, 315

Comeau, Robert, 119, 270, 274, 276, 290

Conley, James, 87, 365

Connelly, M. Patricia, 102

Conrad, Margaret, 43, 203, 206, 250, 254, 256, 262, 267

Conway, J.F., 344

Cook, George L., 95

Cook, G. Ramsay, 6, 10, 12, 13, 19, 27, 28, 55, 126, 164, 165, 170, 178, 205, 208, 275, 325, 335, 346

Cook, Peter, 155, 321

Cooke, Alan, 342, 348

Cooke, Owen, 52

Cooper, Andrew, 31

Cooper, Barry, 10

Cooper, Ian, 238

Cooper, John I., 232

Copp, Terry, 88, 91, 110, 111, 241, 283, 287

Corcoran, James, 22

Corcoran, Terence, 133

Corman, June, 310

Cornell, Paul, 14

Corry, J.A., 152

Coté, Luc, 114

Coulon, Jocelyn, 84

Coulter, Rebecca, 214

Couture, Claude, 273

Couturier, J.P., 263, 264

Cox, Mar, 117

Craig, Andy A., 135

Craig, Beatrice, 100

Crane, David, 125

Craven, Paul, 23, 98, 115, 116, 125, 171

Crawley, Ron, 266

Creese, Gillian, 107, 108, 205

Creighton, D.G., 3, 6, 7, 12, 15, 40, 58, 68, 170, 175, 249, 346, 352

Creighton, Philip, 146

Crête, Jean, 271

Crispo, John H.G., 112

Cross, Michael, 88, 92

Crowe, Keith, J., 188

Crowley, T.A., 29, 120, 208, 210, 311, 319, 332

Cruikshank, Douglas, 99

Cruikshank, Ken, 151, 253

Crunican, Paul, 19, 362

Cruise, David, 132, 149

Cuff, Robert, 24, 27, 40, 62, 74, 130, 150, 266, 321

Cumming, Peter, 200

Currie, Arthur W., 133

Curtis, Clifford, 131

Dacks, Gurston, 372

Dafoe, J.W., 21, 23
Dahlie, Jorgen, 95
Dahms, F.A., 234
Daigle, Jean, 248, 263
Dales, John H., 17, 140, 149, 277
Dancocks, Daniel G., 27
Daniel, Richard C., 198
Danylewycz, Marta, 114, 164, 225, 284, 332
Danysk, Cecilia, 101
Darroch, Gordon, 90, 91
Davey, Keith, 45, 48
Davidson, J.D., 261
Davidson, Joe, 122
Davies, Gwendolyn, 267
Davies, S., 135
Davis, C.M., 264
Davis, Donald F., 135, 233
Davis N. Brian, 96
Dawson, C.A., 240, 355, 362
Dawson, R. MacGregor, 23, 63
Day, Douglas, 101
Dean, Malcolm, 98
Dean, W.G., 302
Dear, M.J., 232
Decarie, Graeme, 299, 330
Dechêne, Louis, 269
de Kiewiet, C.W., 56
de Bonville, Jean, 90, 176, 283, 293
Delainey, William, 232
Del Balso, Michael, 95
Degenais, Michele, 107
de Grandpré, Pierre, 293
DeLottinville, Peter, 96, 104, 244, 260
Dembski, Peter, 335
de Menthon, Pierre, 82
Demers, François, 282
DeMont, John, 147, 254
Dempsey, Hugh, 184–5, 192, 348, 354
den Otter, Andrew, 18, 134, 359, 360

Dendy, David, 356
Denham, Robert, 176
Denis, Roche, 279, 282
Denis, Serge, 282
Denison, Merrill, 131, 140, 143, 336
Derdak, Thomas, 125
Désilets, Andrée, 12, 16, 272
Dessaulles, Henriette, 222
Deverell, John, 122
deVisser, J., 318
Dewdney, Selwyn, 180
Dick, Lyle, 355
Dick, Trevor J.O., 124
Dickason, Olive P., 181
Dickerson, Mark, 372
Dickinson, Harley, 88
Dickinson, James, 94
Dickinson, John, 269
Dickinson, T. Kelley, 125
Diefenbaker, John, 43, 77
Dilks, David, 64
Dion, Léon, 274
Dionne, Bernard, 119, 280, 281
Dirks, Gerald, E., 73
Diubaldo, Richard J., 348
Djwa, Sandra, 36, 172, 293
D'lorio, Antonio, 304
Dobell, Peter, 47, 80
Dodd, Dianne, 224
Dodds, Gordon, 298
Dodds, W.D., 154
Doern, Bruce, 47, 83, 84, 151
Dofny, Jacques, 279
Doherty, Bill, 106
Domey, Odette Vincent, 283
Donaghy, Greg, 75
Donald, W.J.A., 143
Donnely, M.S., 368
Donneur, André, 52
Donovan, Kenneth, 95, 260

Doran, Charles F., 84
Dosman, Edgar J., 371
Doucet, Michael, 91, 237, 315, 316
Douglas, W.A.B., 36, 70
Dow, Bradley, 110
Doyle, A.T., 255
Drache, Daniel, 113, 155
Drake-Terry, Joanne, 198
Driben, Paul, 190
Driezeger, N.F., 62, 69, 152
Drouilly, Pierre, 271
Drover, Glenn, 94
Drummond, Ian, 35, 65, 66, 68, 91,
    126, 127, 129, 132, 174, 317
Dubinksy, Karen, 222
Duchesne, Raymond, 292
Duff, Wilson, 186
Duffey, R. Quinn, 188, 372
Dumas, Evelyn, 110
Dumont, Fernand, 33, 165, 290
Dumont, Micheline, 99, 217, 220, 284
Dunae, Patrick, 169, 356, 363
Dunk, Thomas, 97, 323
Dunn, Charles W., 264
Dupont, Antonin, 272
Durocher, René, 14, 33, 127, 227,
    269, 276
Du Vernet, Sylvia, 190
Dyck, Noel, 196, 197
Dyck, Rand, 367
Dyckes, James, 135
Dzubian, W., 70

Eager, Evelyn, 368
Eagle, John A., 134, 354
Earle, Michael, 89, 110, 260, 265
Easterbrook, W.T., 125, 126, 129
Eastman, Mack, 67
Eayrs, James, 9, 35, 40, 65, 67, 73
Eber, Dorothy Harley, 188–9

Edwards, Margaret H., 342
Edwards, Peter, 122
Eggleston, Wilfrid, 355
Ehrhardt, Roger, B., 79
Eisler, Dale, 368
Elias, Peter, 184, 349
Elkin, Frederick, 146
Elliot, David, 34, 167, 369
Elliot, Gordon R., 347
Elliott, Bruce, S., 303
Ellis, Frank H., 354
Ellis, Lewis E., 25, 57, 150
Emery, George, 303
Ennals, P., 267
Engerman, Stanley L., 128
English, John, 7, 25, 27, 28, 40, 45, 59,
    64, 66, 67, 68, 69, 74, 78, 85, 126,
    170, 171, 232, 316
Enns, Richard A., 342
Ens, Gerhard, 195, 350
Epp, Ernie, 312
Esberey, Joy, 28, 171
Evans, Gary, 177
Evans, Lewis T., 127
Evans, Margaret, 14, 334
Evans, Paul, 84
Evans, Simon, 356
Everest, Allan S., 66

Fahmy-Eid, Nadia, 17, 99, 217, 218,
    220, 284
Falardeau, Jean-Charles, 277
Fairbairn, Brett, 359
Fairbairn, Garry, 355
Farley, A.L., 342
Farr, David, 56
Fast, Vera, 365
Faucher, Albert, 126
Fecteau, Jean-Marie, 92
Fellman, Anita Clair, 205, 262

Felt, L., 252
Felt, P., 252
Ferguson, Barry G., 139, 174, 359
Ferguson, William Paul, 354
Fergusson, C.B., 23, 255, 256
Fergusson, Norman H., 114
Ferland, Jacques, 103, 107, 142, 218
Ferland, Philippe, 272
Fernando, Tissa, 95
Ferns, H.B., 23, 71
Ferretti, Lucia, 95, 96, 283
Fetherling, Doug, 132
Fiddler, Thomas, 189
Fingard, Judith, 91, 92, 102, 220, 221, 241, 248, 250, 262, 264, 265,
Finkel, Alvin, 33, 34, 116, 151, 167, 369
Finkelman, Jacob, 113
Finlay, J.L., 5
Finlayson, Ann, 131
Firestone, O.J., 128
Firth, Edith, 299
Fischer, David Hackett, 4
Fischer, Lewis R., 133, 236, 251, 252
Fisher, Robin, 34, 182, 186, 350, 370
Flaherty, David H., 98, 115, 209, 211, 329
Flanagan, Thomas, 18, 168, 171, 191, 194, 195, 349, 350
Flem-Ath, Rand, 52
Fleming, Berkeley, 254
Fleming, Donald, 43, 77
Fleming, Howard, 354
Fleming, Keith R., 140, 320, 336
Fleming, R.B., 23
Fleming, W.G., 331
Flenley, Robert, 16
Foggo, Cheryl, 226
Foran, Max, 232
Forbes, Ernest, 14, 29, 39, 97, 165,
207, 209, 247, 248, 253, 254, 257, 261, 264
Forbes, H.D., 170
Ford, Anne Rochon, 220
Ford, Clelland S., 187
Forestell, Nancy, 109, 261
Forget, Madeleine, 294
Forrest, Anne, 125
Forrester, Maureen, 216
Forsey, Eugene, 98, 139, 172, 259, 260
Forster, Ben, 17, 144, 150, 320
Forster, Donald, 29, 36, 68
Fortin, Benjamin, 301
Fortin, Gérard, 122, 278
Foster, John E., 346
Foster, Peter, 140, 147, 152
Fournier, Louis, 275, 280, 281
Fournier, Marcel, 119, 292
Fournier, Pierre, 278
Fowke, Edith, 97
Fowke, Vernon, 140, 354, 355
Fox, W. Sherwood, 313
Frager, Ruth A., 107, 119, 218, 226, 307, 323
Francis, Daniel, 189, 190, 348, 358
Francis, Douglas, 5, 166, 168, 172, 343, 345, 372
Francis, E.K., 168, 362
Frank, David, 95, 97, 108, 118, 139, 165, 253, 260, 265
Frankfurter, Glen, 4
Franklin, Ursula, 202
Fransen, David, 35
Fraser, Alexander, 296
Fraser, Brian J., 326
Fraser, Dawn, 96
Fraser, Graham, 49, 274
Fraser, Matthew, 148
Fraser, W.B., 192
Fredericks, H.A., 152

Freeman, Barbara M., 216
Freeman, Bill, 111
French, Goldwin, 297
French, Richard D., 152
Friesen, Gerald, 28, 128, 183, 343,
    344, 353, 365, 368
Friesen, Jean, 345
Frizell, Alan, 49
Frolic, Michael B., 84
Frost, J., 253
Frost, J.D., 132
Frost, Stanley B., 173
Fry, Michael, 62
Fryer, Mary Beacock, 298
Fudge, Judy, 116
Fullerton, Douglas, 35
Fumoleau, R., 188, 191

Gaboury, Jean-Pierre, 301
Gad, Gunter, 239
Gaffield, Chad, 26, 89, 240, 288, 305,
    308, 313, 331, 333, 335
Gagan, David, 90, 221, 298, 299, 300,
    319, 328, 345
Gagan, Rosemary, 90, 224, 300, 327
Gagnon, Georgette, 338
Gagnon, Mona-Josée, 207
Gagnon, Nicole, 291
Gagnon, Robert, 292
Gagnon, Jean-Pierre, 273
Gagnon, Jean-Louis, 276
Gagnon, Marcel, Aimé, 293
Gagnon, Robert, 173
Gagnon, Serge, 158, 162
Gagnon, Nicholas, 162
Galambos, Louis, 124
Galarneau, Claude, 292
Gallman, Robert E., 128
Galt, A.T., 60
Gamberg, H., 265

Gannage, Charlene, 115
Ganzevort, Herman, 345
Garneau, Claude, 173
Gauthier, Armand, 173
Gauvin, Michel, 243
Gauvreau, Danielle, 280
Gauvreau, Michael, 162, 164, 174,
    258, 326
Gee, Ellen, 222
Gelber, Nancy, 60
Gelman, Susan, 114, 216
Gentilcore, Louis, 298
George, Roy E., 254–5
Gerin-Lajoie, Jean, 111
Germain, Annick, 243
Gertler, Meric S., 113
Gervais, Gaetan, 301
Getty, I.A.L., 182, 351
Ghent, Jocelyn, 44, 77
Gibbins, Roger, 183, 367
Gibson, Frederick, 13, 173, 332
Gibson, J. Douglas, 73
Gidney, R.D., 172, 331
Gilbert, Angus, 312
Gillespie, Bill, 99, 261, 266
Gillett, Margaret, 220
Gillis, Peter, 316
Gilmore, John, 97, 294
Gilmour, James M., 127, 235, 320
Gilson, C.H.J., 112
Gingras, François-Pierre, 334
Gingras, Yves, 174, 292
Girard, Camil, 288
Girard, Philip, 221, 262
Giraud, Marcel, 193, 349
Glassford, Larry, 32
Glazebrook, G.P. de T., 54, 62, 133,
    169, 298, 314
Gleason, Mona, 333
Gluek, Alvin C., 15, 58, 346

Goddard, John, 199
Godfrey, Dave, 78
Godfrey, W., 248
Godin, Pierre, 82, 274
Goheen, Peter G., 234, 237, 314
Goldberg, Michael, 241
Goldenberg, Shirely B., 113
Goldenberg, Susan, 148
Goldring, Philip, 188, 352
Golz, Eileen, 91
Good, W.C., 336
Goodspeed, Donald J., 54, 60
Goodwin, C.D.W., 130
Gordon, Manuel, 125
Gordon, Walter, 41, 45, 79
Gorham, Deborah, 209, 210
Gossage, Patrick, 48
Gosztonyi, Marianne, 216
Goudie, Elizabeth, 213
Gough, Barry, 350
Goulet, Denis, 292
Gould, Allen, 149
Gouldner, Janet Walker, 369
Gow, James Iain, 271
Gowans, Alan, 237
Gowing, Margaret, 71
Graff, Harvey, 329, 331
Graham, John F., 254
Graham, Roger, 19, 31, 62, 96, 337
Graham, W.H., 313
Granatstein, J.L.G., 7, 26, 28, 30, 36,
    37, 38, 39, 40, 44, 47, 55, 57, 61, 62,
    65, 67, 69, 70, 72, 74, 77, 79, 80,
    150, 152, 159, 177, 273, 301, 369
Grant, Gail Cuthbert, 203
Grant George M., 159
Grant, George, P., 44, 170, 175
Grant, Ian, 19
Grant, John Webster, 162, 163, 325
Grant, Madelaine, 51

Grant, Shelagh, 372
Graham, Ron, 48
Gray, Colin S., 81
Gray, Earle, 139
Gray, James H., 32, 96, 98, 215, 360,
    369
Gray, Stephen, 356
Green, Jim, 111
Greenhous, Brereton, 36–7, 70
Greening, William E., 114
Greenlee, James G., 173
Greer, Allan, 100, 334
Gregg, Allan, 49
Gregson, Harry, 233
Grescoe, Paul, 149
Gresko, Jacqueline, 197
Griffiths, Alison, 132
Griffiths, Franklyn, 348
Griffiths, Naomi, 165, 266
Groulx, Lionel, 14
Gruending, Dennis, 368
Gruneau, Richard S., 97
Guest, Dennis, 93, 330
Guildford, Janet, 258
Guillaume, Pierre, 83
Guillaume, Sylvie, 83
Guindon, Herbert, 279
Gunderson, Morley, 113
Gundy, H. Pearson, 136
Guppy, Neil, 138
Guthrie, John, 319
Gwyn, Richard J., 45, 46, 80, 83, 256
Gwyn, Sandra, 20

Hacker, Carlotta, 216, 217
Hadley, Michael L., 59, 61
Haiven, Larry, 116
Hak, Gordon, 109, 343
Hale, Linda L., 342
Hall, David, 12, 23, 24, 58, 352, 361

Hall, Roger, 97, 144, 154, 298, 299
Hallett, Mary, 225
Halloran, Mary, 72
Hallowell, Gerald S., 97, 329
Hallsworth, Gwenda, 301
Hamel, Therese, 214
Hamelin, Jean, 104, 126, 162, 165, 276, 290, 291, 293
Hamelin, L.-E., 372
Hamelin, Marcel, 270
Hamilton, Sylvia, 226
Hancock, W.K., 65
Hann, Russell, G., 319
Hansen, Eric, 139
Hansen, Marcus Lee, 58
Hanson, A.J., 251
Hanson, Stan, 360
Hardy, René, 291
Harkness, Ross, 136
Harney, Robert F., 89, 95, 107, 241, 305, 306, 307
Harper, J. Russell, 177
Harrington, D.F., 73
Harris R. Cole, 366
Harris, Richard, 91, 237
Harris, Robin S., 174, 331, 332
Harris, Stephen, 65
Harrison, Dick, 168, 372
Harrison, Phyllis, 305
Hart, Michael, 84
Hartz, Louis, 169
Harvey, Fernand, 99, 102, 103, 104, 279, 281
Harvey, Kathryn, 90, 222
Harvey, Jean-Charles, 293
Hatfield, Michael, 250
Hathorn, Ramond, 168
Hawkins, John, 33
Hawthorn, H.B., 187, 200

Hay, David, A., 355
Hay, Keith A.J., 128–9
Haycock, Ronald G., 27, 61, 85
Hayden, Michael, 174
Headon, C., 327
Heap, Ruby, 216, 309, 332
Heaps, Leo, 121
Hébert, Y., 197
Hedges, J.B., 354
Henney, Arnold, 75
Heggie, Grace F., 52
Heick, W.H., 96
Heintzman, Ralph, 12, 346
Helley, Denise, 287
Hellyer, Paul, 45, 79
Henderson, Sir Nicholas, 72
Hendrickson, James E., 347
Henripin, Jacques, 222, 280
Hero, Alfred O., 81, 83, 275
Heron, Craig, 88, 94, 98, 105, 106, 115, 118, 130, 142, 260, 300, 316, 322, 323
Hewlett, Richard G., 71
Hickey, Daniel, 262, 266
Higgins, Benjamin, 236
Hill, Frank E., 154
Hill, Mary O., 30, 60, 150
HIll, Roderick, 83
Hiller, Harry H., 174
Hiller, James K., 13, 248, 249, 252, 257
Hilliker, John, 30, 60, 64
Hillmer, Norman, 31, 33, 35, 37, 63, 64, 66, 67, 85
Hitsman, J.M., 26, 39, 56, 61, 273
Hives, Christopher L., 132
Hoar, Victor, 67, 119
Hobbs, Margaret, 219
Hodge, Gerald, 238
Hodgetts, J.E., 30, 334

Hodgins, Bruce, 14, 189, 250, 313, 334
Hody, H.D., 263
Hoerder, Dirk, 108
Hoffman, David, 338
Holdsworth, Deryck W., 91, 239, 267, 302, 317
Holland, Clive, 348
Holland, Patrick, 168
Holland, R.F., 64
Hollands, Robert, 97
Homel, Gene Howard, 97, 98, 118
Holmes, John W., 38, 73, 79, 83
Honderich, John, 348
Hooker, Harvison, 70
Hopkin, Deian R., 89
Hopkins, J. Castell, 54
Hopkins, Monica, 366
Horn, Michiel, 33, 36, 115, 171, 311
Horne, Allistair, 77
Horowitz, Gad, 120, 169
Horrall, S.W., 98, 116, 352
Horwood, Harold, 256
Houde, Gilles, 279
House, J.D., 359
Houston, Cecil J., 303
Houston, Susan, 172, 220, 329, 331
Howard, Irene, 110, 210
Howard, Joseph Kinsey, 349
Howard, Victor, 110
Howay, F.W., 357
Howell, Colin, 13, 96, 249, 259
Hoy, Clair, 338
Hryniuk, Stella, 307
Hughes, Everett C., 101, 279
Hulchanski, J. David, 238
Hull, Jeremy, 195, 368
Humber, Charles J., 298
Humphries, Charles, 336
Hunt, B.B., 85
Hunt, Russell, 147

Hunt, William R., 348
Hunter, Peter, 121
Hurl, Lorna, 103
Hurtig, Mel, 50
Hutchison, Bruce, 41, 63
Huxley, Christopher, 117
Hyatt, A.J.M., 27
Hyde, Francis, 133

Iacovetta, Franca, 90, 93, 96, 205, 222, 226, 306
Igartua, José, 109, 154, 303
Iinio, Masako, 39, 69
Inglis, Gordon, 101, 261
Inglis, Joy, 187
Innis, Harold, 18, 98, 123, 124, 134, 136, 138, 277, 353, 312, 319, 357, 358
Innis, Mary Quayle, 126, 206
Inwood, Kris, 127, 129, 142, 253
Irving, John, 34, 369
Isbester, Fraser, 112
Ismael, Jacqueline S., 94
Ismael, Tareq Y., 78

Jackel, Susan, 211, 212, 365
Jackson, James A., 345
James, R. Warren, 69
Jameson, Sheilagh, 356
Jamieson, Don, 48, 80
Jamieson, Stuart Marshall, 99, 116
Jasen, Patricia, 175
Jean, Dominique, 93, 214
Jenkins, Brian, 56
Jenkins, Glen P., 79
Jenness, Diamond, 180, 181
Jennings, John, 352
Jenson, Jane, 8, 120
Jockel, Joseph T., 74
Joe, Rita, 191

Johns, Walter, 174
Johnson, A.A., 257
Johnson, Barbara, 80
Johnson, F. Henry, 172
Johnson, Leo, 313
Johnson, Walter, 112
Johnston, Alex, 360
Johnston, Catherine, 252
Johnston, Charles M., 173, 319, 332, 336
Johnston, Donald, 48
Johnston, Hugh, 24
Johnston, Jean, 206
Johnston, Wendy, 92
Jones, Andrew, 93, 328
Jones, David C., 101, 355, 372
Jones, Elwood, 299
Jones, Robert L., 141, 318
Jull, Peter, 188

Kallmann, Helmut, 177
Kaplan, Harold, 243
Kaplan, William, 75, 76, 111
Kapstein, Ethan B., 81
Karr, Clarence, 158
Kasurak, Peter, 66
Katz, Michael, B., 90, 221, 229, 315, 329, 331
Kealey, Greg, 16, 87, 88, 89, 90, 92, 99, 100, 102, 104, 106, 107, 108, 116, 260, 300, 303, 315, 322, 365
Kealey, Linda, 29, 107, 120, 208, 210, 305, 338, 366
Keane, David, 299, 325
Keating, Tom, 84
Keefer, Janice Kulyk, 165, 267
Keel, Othmar, 292
Keenleyside, Hugh, 38, 65, 172
Kehoe, Alice B., 180
Kelly, Gary, 348

Kelly, Norah, 353
Kelly, Robert, 16
Kelly, William, 353
Kendle, John, 33, 57, 368
Kennedy, Douglas, R., 104
Kent, Tom, 44, 48
Kerr, D.G., 302, 317, 334
Kerr, Don, 232, 360
Kerr, Donald P., 232
Kess, Cathy, 107, 205, 366
Kesteman, Jean-Pierre, 282
Kettler, David, 112
Kiefer, Nancy, 220
Kilbourn, William, 37, 41, 68, 75, 140, 142, 152, 320
Kimber, Stephen, 137
Kinnear, Mary, 205, 210, 212, 365, 366
Kirton, John, 66, 77, 78, 84
Kitagawa, Muriel, 226
Kitchen, Martin, 73
Klassen, Henry, 147, 233, 345
Klinck, C.F., 96
Kmet, Irene, 95, 373
Knafla, L.A., 116, 221, 352
Knight, David B., 235
Knight Phyllis, 122
Knight, Rolf, 94, 100, 121, 187, 225, 351
Knowles, Valerie, 29, 210
Koizumi, Maya, 121
Kolasky, John, 118
Koroscil, P., 360
Kostash, Myrna, 175
Kottman, Richard N., 150
Krawchuk, Peter, 118
Krech, Shepard III, 358
Kresl, Peter, 66
Krotz, Larry, 200
Krueger, Cynthia, 369
Kwavnick, David, 111

Kyba, Patrick, 369
Kyle, Kathleen, 356

Lacasse, Roger, 148
Lacelle, Claudette, 102, 214
Lachappelle, Eéjan, 280
Lacouture, Jacques, 82
Lacroix, Robert, 112
Lafleur, Gisette, 262
Laforce, Hélène, 217
Lai, David Chuenyan, 241
Laidlaw Toni, 206
Laine, Edward, 119
Laing, Muriel, 342
Lalonde, André, 305
Lalonde, Marc, 47, 81
LaMarsh, Judy, 45, 210
Lamb, W. Kaye, 18, 134, 353
Lambert, Richard S., 319
Lamonde, Yvan, 95, 158, 166, 176,
    289, 293
Lamontague, M., 126
Lamontagne, Leopold, 304
Lamothe, Raymonde, 286
Lamson, C., 251
Landon, Fred, 296
Landry, Irene, 263
Lang, Nichole, 263
Langdon, Elizabeth, 221
Langdon, Stephen, 104
Langlais, Jacques, 287
Lapèrriere, Guy, 291
Laplante, Jacques, 288
Lapointe-Roy, Huguette, 92
Lariviere, Claude, 121
Larue, Jean-Marc, 294
La Terreur, Marc, 271
Latham, Barbara K., 107, 203, 205,
    214, 365, 366
Latremouille, Joann, 91

Laurendeau, André, 273
Laureyssens, J., 154
Laurin, Nicole, 284
Laurin, Serge, 288
Laurendeau, André, 39
Lauzon, Gilles, 91
Lavigne, Marie, 100, 107, 109, 205,
    214, 285
Laviolette, F.E., 196
Laviolette, Gontran, 184
Lawr, D.A., 318
Laxer, Robert, 112
Laycock, David, 29, 167, 367
Leblanc, Daniel, 95, 283
Leblanc, Phyllis, 263
LeBourdais, Donat, 138, 320
Leacock, Stephen, 160
Leacy, F.H., 302
Lean, Cheryl, 178
Lecker, Robert, 80
Leeson, Howard, 48
Leger, Jean-Marc, 82
Léger, Raymond, 252
Leggett, Robert F., 134
LeGresley, Omer, 263
Lehr, John, 362
Leier, Mark, 105, 364
Lembcke, Jerry, 110, 364
Lemelin, Maurice, 112
Lemieux, Denise, 206, 284, 285
Lemieux, Lucien, 291
Lemieux, Vincent, 271
Lemon, James, 232, 314
Lenskyj, Helen, 222, 311
Léonard, Jean-François, 274
Lepan, Douglas, 69
Leslie, John, 183
Levant, Victor, 78
Lévesque, Andrée, 36, 97, 119, 215,
    223, 274, 284, 286, 292

Lévesque, Georges-Henri, 290
Lévesque, Michel 270, 274
Levine, Allan G., 243, 355
Levine, G., 91
Levitt, Cyril, 175, 307
Levitt, Joseph, 22, 166, 272
Levitt, Kari, 79, 153
Levy, George, 257
Lewis, Jefferson, 161
Leyton-Brown, David, 82
Li, Peter S., 307
Light, Beth, 114, 203, 205, 332
Lindstrom-Best, Varpu, 95, 119, 120, 225, 307
Lingard, C.C., 351
Linteau, Paul-André, 14, 17, 127, 227, 230, 232, 236, 239, 240, 269, 276, 287
Lipset, S.M., 36, 368
Lipsey, Richard, 50
Lipsig-Mumme, Carla, 113
Lipton, Charles, 98
Lisée, Jean-François, 83, 275
Lithwick, N.H., 255
Litt, Paul, 171
Little, Arthur J., 146
Livermore, J.D., 334
Logan, H.A., 98, 116
Longley, R.S., 251
Loo, Tina, 196
Lorimer, James, 94, 237, 239
Lort, John C., 342
Louis, William Roger, 75
Loveridge, Donald, 61
Lowe, Graham S., 105, 146, 215, 309, 323
Lower, A.R.M., 3, 138, 312, 319, 357
Lowther, Barbara, 342
Lucas, Rex, 94, 240, 361
Luciuk, Lubomyr, 307

Lumsden, Ian, 17, 79
Lupul, Manoly, 24, 362
Lussier, Antoine S., 182, 193
Lutz, John, 100, 138, 351, 359
Luxton, Meg, 89, 213, 310
Lyon, Peter, 32, 63
Lyon, Peyton, 78, 81
Lyons, Cicely, 357

Macdonald, David, 101
MacDonald, Donald C., 338
MacDonald, Martha, 102
MacDonald, Norbert, 233, 360
Macdonald, R. St. J., 348
MacDonald, Sheryl, 223
MacDougall, Heather, 244, 328
MacDougall, John, 319
MacDowell, G.F., 112
MacDowell, Laurel Sefton, 111, 116, 144, 299, 312, 323
MacEachren, George, 121
MacEwan, Grant, 185, 355
MacEwan, Paul, 99
MacGill, Elsie, 207, 366
Macgillivray, Don, 116, 253, 259
MacGillivray, Royce, 313, 339
MacGregor, James G., 233, 345
MacKay, Donald, 114, 138, 356
Mackintosh, W.A., 123, 353, 354
MacKenzie, A.A., 264
MacKenzie, David, 71, 133, 135, 256
MacKenzie, Lewis, 85
MacKinnon, Frank, 255
MacKinnon, Wayne, 255
MacLachlan, Morag, 356
MacLean, M.M., 114
MacLean, Raymond, 264
MacLeod, Donald, 258
MacLeod, Malcolm, 173, 257, 259

Macleod, Roderick C., 19, 194, 329, 349, 352
Macleod, Wendell, 288
MacMillan, David S., 129, 359
MacMillan, Margaret, 72
MacNaughton, Katherine, F.C., 250, 258
Macpherson, C.B. 34, 167, 369
Macpherson, Ian, 101, 141, 265, 355, 356
Macpherson, Kathryn, 211
Magnuson, Bruce, 122
Magnuson, Roger, 172
Magnusson, Warren, 242, 371
Maguire, Ron, 183
Mahler, Gregory, 52
Mailhot, Raymond, 263
Maillet, Chantal, 209
Main, J.R.K., 354
Main, Oscar W., 138, 320
Makahonuk, Glen, 105, 365
Mallen, Pierre-Louis, 82
Mallory, J.R., 369
Malouin, Marie-Paul, 284
Mandelbaum, David G., 184
Manley, John, 111, 338
Mann, William E., 94, 168, 373
Mansergh, Nicholas, 55
Manthorpe, Jonathan, 338
March, William, 256
Marchak, Patricia, 101, 115, 138, 356
Marchand, Philip, 176
Marchildon, Gregory, 132, 154
Marder, Arthur, 59
Mardiros, Anthony, 121, 369
Marks, Lynn, 96, 333
Maroney, Heather Jon, 112
Marquis, Greg, 244, 265
Marr, William, 124, 318
Marrus, Michael, 143

Marsan, Jean-Claude 237, 294
Marsh, James, 233
Marsh, John S., 239
Marsh, Leonard, 92
Marshall, David, 162, 163, 164, 326
Marshall, Herbert, 66, 153
Marshall, John U., 314
Marshall, Stephen D.E., 310
Martel, Gilles, 194
Martin Chester, 141, 354
Martin, Ged., 11
Martin, Lawrence, 65, 84
Martin, Michèle, 102, 115, 215, 285, 309
Martin, Patrick, 49
Martin, Paul, 38, 45, 65, 78, 80
Martin, Sandra, 131
Martin, Yves, 277
Martynowych, Orest T., 118, 307
Maslove, Allen, 116
Mason, Gary, 371
Massey, Vincent, 38, 64
Massicote, Louis, 271
Masters, D.C., 108, 314, 364
Mathias, Peter, 152
Mathias, Philip, 46, 255
Matters, Diane, 92, 219
Mathews, Ralph, 257
Matthews, Robert O., 84
Matthews-Klein, Yvonne, 207
Mattingly, P., 329, 331
Maynard, K.S., 262
Mays, Herbert, 302
Mayse, Susan, 121
Mazur, Carol, 203
McAllister, James A., 368
McCall, Christina, 46, 80
McCalla, Douglas, 123, 127, 129, 144
McCallum, John, 141, 318

McCallum, Margaret, 107, 109, 117, 146, 147, 219, 262
McCanless, Richard, 110
McCann, L.D., 100, 233, 235, 236, 247, 252, 258, 317
McCaskill, D., 197
McCirick, Donna, 94
McClung, Nellie, 207
McComber, Joseph-Edmond, 278
McCormack, A. Ross, 28, 95, 105, 118, 167, 231, 363, 365
McCuaig, K., 330
McCullagh, A.B., 137, 144
McDiarmid, O.J., 57, 150
McDonald, Ian D.H., 101, 261
McDonald, Neil, 330
McDonald, Robert, A.J., 18, 95, 105, 239, 240, 345, 360
McDougall, A.K., 337
McDougall, John N., 139
McDowall, Duncan, 76, 131, 142, 155, 312, 321
McEwen, Tom, 121
McGahan, Elizabeth, 265
McGee, H.F., 190
McGill, D., 136
McGinnis, Janice Dickin, 161
McGowan, Mark G., 162
McIlveen, John, 155
McInnis, R.M., 310, 318
McIntire, C.T., 224
McIntosh, Rober, 103, 260
McKay, Ian, 3, 87, 103, 104, 106, 113, 165, 253, 259, 260, 267
McKay, R.A., 53, 68
McKenna, Brian, 243
McKenna, Olga, 190
McKenty, Neil, 337
McKenzie, Ruth, 313

McKillop, A.B., 158, 164, 167, 173, 324, 326, 332
McKim, William A., 258
McKinsey, Laurn, 79
McLaren, Angus, 223, 224, 310
McLaren, Arlene Tigar, 223, 224, 310
McLaren, John P.S., 97
McLaren, Roy, 48
McLaughlin, Kenneth, 19, 232, 316, 335
McLean, Bruce, 112
McLean, Don, 350
McLin, Jon B., 77
McMahon, Michael, 315
McMillan, Alan D., 180
McMullen, John, 138
McNaught, Kenneth, 30, 87
McPhail, Margaret, 211
McQueen, Rod, 132
McRae, Kenneth, 169
McRoberts, Kenneth, 41, 274
McWhinney, Edward, 45
Meggs, Geoffery, 357
Meisel, John, 41, 44, 49
Mellen, Peter, 178
Mellett, Edward B., 146
Menzies, Heather, 115
Mercer, John, 241
Merchant, Livingston, 45, 78
Mercier, Lucie, 206, 284, 285
Merk, Frederick, 58
Metcalfe, Alan, 97
Metson, William, 178
Michell, Humfrey, 131
Michie, R.C., 132
Mickenberg, Neil H., 200
Middleton, J.E., 297
Millar, David, 88
Millar, W.P.J., 172, 331

Millar, Wendy, 318
Millard, J. Rodney, 142, 160
Miller, Carman, 23, 56, 335
Miller, David Hunter, 62
Miller, Iris, 34, 167, 369
Miller, J.D.B., 77
Miller, J.R., 19, 22, 159, 181, 182, 184, 191, 196, 349
Miller, Richard, 112
Millet, David, 305
Milligan, Frank, 172
Milloy, John S., 184
Mills, Allen, 30, 120, 167, 171
Milne, David, 48
Milner, Marc, 65, 70
Milroy, Beth Moor, 241
Minter, Roy, 354
Minville, Esdras, 118
Miron, John, 92, 238
Mitchell, David, 371
Mitchell, Harvey, 249
Mitchinson, Wendy, 161, 205, 208, 223, 224, 261, 311, 327, 330
Moir, John, 63, 163, 164, 224
Monad, David, 145
Monière, Denis, 165, 290
Montero, Gloria, 98
Montminy, Jean-Paul, 165, 290
Moody, Barry, 259
Moore, Eric, G., 311
Moore, E.S., 320
Morantz, Toby, 189
Moreira, James, 96, 264
Morici, Peter, 84
Morin, Claude, 45, 82
Morisset, M., 278
Morley, J. Terence, 120, 338, 370
Morley, William F.E., 301
Morris, Alexander, 191

Morris, Cerise, 210
Morris, James, 55
Morris, Peter, 177
Morrison, James. H., 96, 264
Morrison, Jean, 107, 308
Morrison, R. Bruce, 180
Morrison, T.R., 328
Morrison, W.R., 188, 345, 346, 353
Morriss, William E., 355
Morse, B.W., 200
Morton, Desmond, 5, 27, 29, 36, 54, 56, 59, 61, 87, 88, 93, 115, 120, 243, 323, 335, 352
Morton, Suzanne, 90, 108, 260, 266
Morton, W.L., 3, 6, 11, 15, 167, 170, 174, 211, 343, 345, 346, 347, 366, 367
Moscovitch, Allan, 39, 93, 94
Motiuk, Laurence, 51
Mott, Morris, 373
Mouat, Jeremy, 103, 105, 365
Mowat, Farley, 181
Moyles, R.G., 24
Muirhead, B.W., 74
Muise, D.A., 13, 103, 191, 248, 249, 262, 266
Mulcahey, Jerry, 125
Mulhall, David, 197, 350
Mulroney, Catherine, 155
Munn, Edwidge, 122
Munro, Jack, 122
Munro, John, 24, 59
Munro, Kenneth, 272
Munton, Don, 72, 78, 84
Murray, Hilda, 102, 213
Murray, Peter, 358
Murray, Sylvie, 285
Murrow, Casey, 22
Muszynski, Alicja, 100, 101, 102

Myers, Gustavus, 148

Nader, George, 230
Nash, Knowlton, 44, 76
Naylor, James, 87, 108, 323
Naylor, R.T., 7, 148
Neary, Peter, 13, 71, 248, 249, 256, 257
Neatby, H. Blair, 17, 22, 28, 34, 63, 175, 272
Neatby, Hilda, 173, 332
Neice, David, 221
Neill, Robin, 129, 130, 176
Neis, Barbarba, 101
Nelles, H.V., 97, 140, 142, 151, 154, 244, 253, 299, 312, 315, 320, 335
Nesbitt, Joy, 217
Neufeld, Edward P., 131, 155, 321
Newell, Dianne, 137, 312, 320, 357
Newhook, F.J., 249
Newman, Peter, 42, 78, 137, 143, 147, 321
Newsome, Eric, 103
Newton, Janice, 120
Newton, Lord, 56
Nicholson, G.W.L., 60, 70, 217
Nicholson, Murray, 303
Nicks, Trudy, 195
Niosi, Jorge, 8, 148, 155
Nish, Ian H., 63
Noble, Joey, 92
Nock, David, A., 197
Noel, Françoise, 286
Noel, S.J.R., 256, 339
Nolan, Brian, 36
Nolan, Michael, 136, 147
Noon, Alan, 94
Normandeau, Louise, 286
Norrie, Kenneth, 126, 141, 316, 353
Norris, John, 105, 346, 361, 365

Nossal, Kim, 9, 79
Nye, Joseph, 83

O'Brien, P., 259
O'Donovan, Joan E., 176
Offen, Karen, 203
O'Flaherty, Patrick, 165
Ogle, Edmund, 136
Oglesby, J.C.M., 76
O'Hara, Jane, 122
Oliver, Peter, 297, 300, 301, 305, 336, 337
Olsen, Greg, 113
O'Malley, Martin, 199
Ommer, Rosemary, 101, 102, 133, 137, 251
O'Neill, Paul, 231, 265
O'Neill, Pierre, 82
Ormsby, Margaret, 15, 212, 345, 347, 356, 366, 370
Ornstein, Michael, 90
Orvik, Nils, 81
Osborne, B.S., 91, 311
Osler, E.B., 349
Ostry, Bernard, 16, 23, 104
Ouellet, Fernand, 87, 236, 269, 284
Ovendale, Ritchie, 67
Overton, James, 92
Owen, Roger, 76
Owen, Wendy, 355
Owram, Doug, 15, 24, 30, 34, 64, 126, 152, 158, 159, 168, 171, 194, 317, 339, 346, 349, 351, 372

Page, Donald, 51, 66
Page, Robert, J.D., 22, 82, 199, 371
Pal, Leslie A., 93, 334
Palmer, Bryan D., 16, 87, 88, 97, 99, 104, 106, 113, 158, 215, 283, 315, 322, 371

Palmer, Howard, 24, 168, 235, 305, 343, 345, 361
Palmer, Tamara, 345, 361
Pammette, Jon H., 334
Panitch, Leo, 7, 116, 170
Pannekoek, Frits, 15, 194, 347
Panting, Gerald, 102, 133, 250, 251, 252
Paquet, Gilles, 276
Pariseau, J.B., 116
Park, Libby, 288
Parkinson, J.F., 69
Parr, Joy, 89, 93, 100, 101, 103, 109, 144, 202, 205, 213, 215, 222, 305, 308, 309, 318, 329
Paterson, Donald G., 124, 154, 359
Paterson, Thomas G., 77
Patrias, Camela, 109
Patterson, E. Palmer III, 181, 351
Patterson, Graeme, 176
Payment, Dianne, 195, 350
Payne, Raymond, 357
Pazdro, Roberta J., 203, 214, 366
Peacock, Donald, 358
Pearse, Peter H., 358
Pearson, Lester, 38, 64
Peden, Murray, 70
Pedersen, Diana, 203, 208, 220
Peel, Bruce, 342
Peers, Frank, 177
Pelletier, Gérald, 276
Pelletier, Réjean 271
Pelletier-Baillargeon, Hélène, 209
Penlington, Norman, 22, 24, 59
Penner, Norman, 30, 108, 119, 171, 364
Penniman, Howard, 49
Pennington, Doris, 311
Penny, S.M., 259
Pentland, H. Clare, 88, 105

Penton, James M., 163
Pepper, Sheila, 203
Perin, Roberto, 19, 361
Perkins, Bradford, 59
Perlin, George, 44, 49
Perreault, Ernest G., 138
Perron, Normand, 288
Persky, Stan, 371
Pestieau, Caroline, 144
Peterson, Jacqueline, 193
Peterson, James O., 141–2
Peterson, Larry, 108
Peterson, Thomas, 367
Petitat, André, 285
Petryshyn, J., 116, 362
Pettipas, Katherine, 197
Phillips, C.E., 330
Phillips, Elizabeth, 366
Phillips, Jim, 221, 262, 266,
Phillips, Paul, 99, 360, 363
Phillips, Myfanwy, 94
Piché, Lucie, 100, 218
Piché, Victor, 286
Pickersgill, J.W., 29, 36, 37, 41, 44, 68
Pierson, Ruth Roach, 38, 93, 109, 152, 202, 203, 204, 205, 209, 219, 220, 309
Pinard, Maurice, 121
Pinard, Yolande, 100, 107, 205, 214, 285
Pindera, Loreen, 190, 196
Pinnock, Clark, 164
Pitsula, James, 92, 330,
Piva, Michael, 91, 117, 121, 241, 300, 315, 322,
Plaice, Evelyn, 191
Plewman, W.R., 336
Plumptre, A.F.W., 69, 74, 131
Poelzer, Irene, 217
Pomfret, Richard, 126

Ponack, Allen, 113
Pontaut, Alain, 271
Ponting, J. Rick, 183
Pope, Joseph, 12, 60
Pope, Maurice, 71
Porritt, Edward, 17, 149
Porter, Bernard, 55
Porter, Glenn, 130, 321
Porter, John, 148, 279
Porter, Marilyn B., 102
Porter, Michael, 155
Posius, Gerald, 267
Potestio, John, 306
Poulin, Pierre, 278
Powe, B.W., 80
Powell, Judith, 372
Power, Charles G., 37
Prang, Margaret, 26, 61, 305, 336, 346
Pratt, Cranford, 84
Pratt, Larry, 84, 139, 359, 367, 370
Pred, Allan R., 234
Prentice, Alison, 27, 114, 172, 204,
    205, 216, 220, 299, 309, 331, 332
Prentice, Susan, 90
Presnell, L.S., 69
Preston, Richard, 22, 56
Price, B.J., 266
Price, Jane B., 221
Price, Lynda, 286
Price, Richard, 192
Prince, Robert, 74
Pross, Paul, 319
Prouty, Andrew Mason, 357
Provencher, Jean, 274
Pryke, Kenneth, 13, 249
Pucci, Antonio, 306
Purcell, Susan, 243
Purich, Donald, 193, 198, 200

Quigley, Neil C., 127, 132

Quinn, Herbert, 33, 273
Quintal, Claire, 266

Raddall, Thomas, 231, 265
Radforth, Ian, 115, 138, 308, 312, 319,
    323, 334
Radwansky, George, 46, 80
Rajala, Richard, 105, 359
Ralston, H.K., 345, 357
Ramirez, Bruno, 87, 95, 101, 287
Rankin, Pauline, 338
Rasmussen, Linda, 211
Rasporich, A.W., 168, 197, 233, 345,
    346
Rath, Dan, 338
Raunet, Daniel, 351
Rawlyk, George, 14, 162, 164, 247,
    249, 258
Ray, Arthur, J., 100, 137, 187, 358
Rayner-Canham, Geoffery W., 216
Rayner-Canham, Marlene, 216
Rea, J.E., 167
Rea, Kenneth J., 127, 128, 317, 359
Read, Colin, 299, 325
Reader, William J., 154
Reaman, G. Elmore, 318
Reasons, Charles E., 115
Redekop, Clarence G., 79
Rees, Ronald, 168, 178
Reilly, Nolan, 260
Reves, W.G., 257
Reford, Robert W., 75
Regehr, T.D., 23, 31, 134, 140, 343,
    353
Reid, David G., 357
Reid, Dennis, 177
Reid, Escott, 38, 65, 72, 73, 76, 172
Reid, John G., 173, 174, 175, 220,
    248, 258, 259, 261
Reid, Laura, 133

Reid, Richard, 144
Reigenstreif, Peter, 44
Reilly, Nolan, 108, 118, 265
Reisman, S.S., 150
Rendell, Jane, 203
Render, Shirley, 216
Repka, Kathleen, 119
Repka, William, 119
Resnick, Philip, 41, 371
Reynolds, Cecilia, 114
Reynolds, Lloyd G., 151
Ricard, F., 127, 269
Rich, George, 129
Richard, Béatrice, 282
Richards, John, 139, 359
Richardson, Boyce, 122, 199
Richardson, Douglas, 173
Ricou, Laurie, 372
Riddell, Walter, 67
Rioux, Marcel 277, 279
Ritchie, Charles, 64, 78
Ritchie, Thomas, 237
Roback, Leo, 112
Robert, Jean-Claude, 14, 127, 227,
    240, 269, 275
Roberts, Barbara, 35, 116, 210, 305
Roberts, Hayden, 96
Roberts, Leslie, 72
Roberts, Wayne, 99, 106, 111, 208,
    309, 323
Robertson, Heather, 20, 43, 355, 358
Robertson, I.R., 248
Robertson, Norman, 313
Robertson, Terence, 75
Robin, Martin, 28, 118, 367, 370
Robinson, Basil, 43
Robson, Robert, 110, 361
Roby, Yves, 126, 276, 278, 289
Rodney, William, 119
Rogers, E.B., 68

Rohmer, Richard, 143, 147
Rolland, C.G., 161
Rolph, William K., 369
Romanow, Roy, 48
Rome, David, 287
Romney, Paul, 329
Ronning, Chester, 76
Rooke, Patricia T., 93, 210, 311, 328
Roper, Henry, 265
Rose, Albert, 92, 243, 244, 315
Rose, Clifford, 264
Rosenberg, Harriet, 90
Rosenfeld, Mark, 90, 310
Rosenthal, Star, 367
Ross, Alexander, 132, 149
Ross, David P., 91
Ross, Douglas, 78
Ross, Evelyn, 239
Ross, Ewan, 313
Ross, Rupert, 189
Ross, Victor, 131
Ross, W.G., 188, 358
Rothchild, John, 155
Rothney, G.O., 258
Rouillard, Jacques, 99, 106, 268, 280,
    283, 289
Roussel, Stephane, 52
Rowat, Donald C., 334
Rowe, Frederick W., 248, 258
Roy, Fernand, 290
Roy, Jean-Louis, 271
Roy, Michel, 263
Roy, Patricia, 24, 39, 69, 105, 169,
    233, 343, 345, 359, 360, 363, 370
Roy, Reginald, 43, 77
Royce, Marion, 218, 308
Rubio, Mary, 206
Rudin, Ronald, 131, 236, 269, 278,
    285, 286
Ruggles, Richard, 342

Rugman, Alan M., 155
Rumilly, Robert, 19, 22, 25, 263, 270, 272, 287
Russell, Peter, 159
Russell, Robert, 89, 94, 117, 219
Russell, Victor, 232, 303, 314
Rutherford, Paul, 11, 136, 176, 177, 243, 315
Rutman, Leonard, 93, 328
Ryan, Shannon, 137, 251
Ryan, Toby Gordon, 96
Ryan, W.F., 277
Ryerson, Stanley B., 288

Saarienen, Oiva W., 238
Sabourin, Ronald, 115, 311
Sacouman, R. James, 101, 265
Safarian, A.E., 34, 79, 129, 154
Sage, W.N., 357, 370
Sager, Eric. W., 102, 133, 236, 250, 251, 252
Saint-Germain, Maurice, 277
Salisbury, Richard F., 199
Sallows, R., 318
Salutin, Rick, 122
Salverson, Laura Goodman, 225
Samek, Hana, 184, 348
Sancton, Andrew, 242
Sandberg, L. Anders, 252
Sanger, Clyde, 79, 80
Sangster, Joan, 29, 107, 120, 210, 218, 310, 338
Santink, Joy L., 145, 321
Sargeant, William A.S., 232
Sarra-Bournet, Michel, 273
Sarty, Roger, 59, 61
Saunders, E.M., 12
Saunders, Stanley A., 127, 138, 251, 252
Sautter, Udo, 117

Savard, Pierre, 162, 166, 269, 275, 304
Savoie, A.J., 258, 263
Sawatsky, John, 49
Sayers, R.S., 68
Saywell, J.T., 17, 19, 21, 33, 43, 54, 56, 337, 370
Scarpaci, J. Vincenza, 306
Schindeler, F.F., 334
Schlegel, John P., 83
Schmalz, Peter S., 189
Schnell, R.L., 93, 210, 311, 328
Schnieder, Ena, 353
Schrodt, Barbara, 97
Schull, Joseph, 15, 21, 132, 272, 297
Schultz, John, 69, 129, 158
Schulz, Particia, 109
Schwantes, Carlos, A., 105, 363
Schwartzwald, Robert, 293
Scott, Bruce, 109
Scott, Jack, 122, 364
Scrafton, Derek, 135
Seager, Allen, 64, 107, 110, 118, 126, 253, 260, 308
Sealey, D.B., 193
Séguin, Maurice, 276
Séguin, Norman, 100, 141, 278
Semple, Neil, 299, 325, 327
Senese, P.M., 166
Sewell, John, 239
Shackleton, Doris French, 368
Shadbolt, Doris, 178, 216
Shaffir, William, 307
Sharp, Mitchell, 81
Sharp, Paul, 352, 367
Sharpe, C.A., 257
Sharpe, David, 175
Sheddon, Leslie, 94
Sheehan, Nancy, 95, 197, 372
Sheils, Jean Evans, 121
Shelton, George, 15, 347

Shephard, David A.E., 292
Sheppard, Robert, 47, 200
Sherman, Robert, 299
Shippee, L.B., 57, 150
Shkilnyk, Anastasia M., 189
Shore, Marlene, 174
Shortt, Adam, 123, 131
Shortt, S.E.D., 161, 164, 319
Shortell, Ann, 133
Shugarman, David, 9, 10
Siegfried, André, 21
Silman, Janet, 225
Silver, A.I., 14, 15, 19, 159, 270, 346
Silver, James, 195, 368
Silverman, Elaine Leslau, 203, 211, 367
Simeon, Richard, 10, 47, 48
Simley, John, 125
Simmons, Christina, 92, 261
Simmons, Harvey G., 329
Simmons, James W., 234
Simpson, Jeffery, 48
Simpson, Michael, 238
Sinclair, Bruce, 141
Sinclair, Peter R., 137
Sioui, Georges E., 201
Skelton, O.D., 12, 21, 63, 123
Skilling, Gordon, 60
Slobodin, Richard, 188
Sluman, Norma, 185
Smaller, John, 111
Smiley, Donald, 9, 10
Smillie, Benjamin, 168, 373
Smith, Allan, 159, 160, 343
Smith, David, 34, 367, 368
Smith, Denis, 45, 73
Smith, Derek G., 200
Smith, Donald B., 24, 166, 185, 346, 351
Smith, Dorothy Blakey, 347

Smith, Doug, 99, 364, 368
Smith, Goldwin, 17, 19, 159
Smith, Michael, 259, 262
Smith, Miriam, 113
Smith, Norman, 72
Smith, Peter J., 128, 237
Smith, Philip, 133, 135, 138, 139, 140, 257, 312
Smith, W. Randy, 235, 314
Smitheram, V., 248
Smyth, Donna, 206
Smyth, William J., 303
Snell, James, 160, 221, 262, 310
Snider, Norman, 49
Snow, Duart, 111
Socknat, Thomas, 27, 164, 209
Solberg, Carl E., 354
Solski, Michael, 111
Sorenson, David S., 72
Souchard, Maryse, 282
Southard, Frank A., 66, 153
Soward, F.H., 68
Spafford, Duff, 368
Spelt, Jacob, 232, 235, 314
Spencer, Robert, 84
Spicer, Keith, 79
Speisman, Stephen, 92, 307, 328
Spigelman, M.S., 263
Spira, Thomas, 232, 266
Splane, Richard, 92, 327
Spradley, James, 187
Spragge, Shirley, 91
Sprague, D.N., 18, 193, 195, 350
Spry, Irene, 194
St-Onge, Nicole, 195
Stacey, C.P., 22, 24, 28, 31, 37, 54, 56, 63, 69
Stacey, Duncan, 357
Stairs, Denis, 57, 74
Stamo, Robert M., 172

Stamp, R.M., 258, 331
Stanbury, W.T., 149, 151
Stanley, Della, 255, 263
Stanley, G.F.G., 15, 18, 54, 191, 194, 250, 263, 349, 370
Steed, Judy, 49
Steedman, Mercedes, 107
Steeves, Dorothy, G., 121, 370
Stefanson, Vilhjalmur, 348
Stein, Michael B., 275
Stelter, Gilbert, 91, 230, 231, 234, 241, 242, 243, 308
Stengos, Thomasis, 129
Stevens, George R., 23, 134, 253
Stevens, James R., 189
Stevens, Paul, 21, 24, 25, 56
Stevenson, Garth, 47, 367
Stevenson, H.A., 299
Stewart, Gordon, 11, 66, 339
Stewart, John, 359
Stewart, Larry, 53, 81
Stewart, Lee, 220, 366
Stitch, K.P., 225
Stobbe, Mark, 369
Stoddart, Jennifer, 107, 109, 209
Stone, Leroy O., 230
Stonechild A. Blair, 192
Storey, Robert, 109, 111, 115, 130, 260
Storrie, K., 212
Story, Donald, 66
Strange, Carolyn, 97, 221
Stratford, Philip, 166
Strathcona, Lord, 60
Strathearn, Gloria, 342
Street, Margaret, 217
Strong, Cyril, 122
Strong-Boag, Veronica, 29, 93, 109, 174, 203, 204, 205, 208, 209, 217, 218, 242, 262, 308, 311, 366

Struthers, James, 93, 117, 311, 330
Stuart, Marian, 218
Stuart, Reginald C., 58
Stubbs, John O., 29, 67
Stursberg, Peter, 42, 77, 78
Sufrin, Eileen, 111, 309–10, 323
Sunhara, Gomer, 363
Surtees, Robert J., 179
Sussman, Jennifer, 134
Sutherland, Duff, 261
Sutherland, Neil, 89, 93, 327
Swainson, Donald, 12, 14, 159, 299, 316, 319, 330, 335, 345
Swainson, Neil, 46, 77
Swanick, E.L., 248
Swankey, Ben, 121
Swanson, Roger Frank, 53
Swartz, Donald, 116
Sweeney, Alistair, 12, 272
Swerdlow, Max, 122
Swettenham, John, 27, 38, 60, 62
Swimmer, Gene, 113, 116
Swyripa, Frances, 226, 307, 362
Symons, T.H.B., 304, 343
Synge, Jane, 89

Takamura, Hiroko, 39, 69
Tan, Jin, 108
Tansill, C.C., 57, 150
Taras, David, 334
Tattam, William M., 110, 364
Taylor, A., 348
Taylor, Charles, 78, 170
Taylor, Don, 110
Taylor, Geoffery W., 135, 138, 356
Taylor, Georgina, 212
Taylor, Graham, 126, 129, 136, 154
Taylor, John H., 232, 242, 316
Taylor, John Leonard, 183, 191
Taylor, Kenneth, 66, 131, 153

Taylor, Malcolm G., 39
Taylor, S., 139
Teboul, Victor, 293
Tennant, Paul, 186, 198, 350, 371
Tennyson, B.C., 319
Tennyson, Brian D., 249, 259
Termot, Marc, 280
Thacker, Robert, 168
Theobold, Majorie R., 114
Thibault, Claude, 269
Thivierge, Nicole, 284
Thomas, G.E.G., 356
Thomas, J.D., 327
Thomas, John, 224
Thomas, Lewis G., 241, 356, 369
Thomas, Lewis H., 167, 346, 351, 368, 370
Thompson, John Herd, 6, 27, 64, 126, 101, 128, 253, 361
Thompson, Mark, 113
Thomson, Anthony, 112
Thomson, Ashley, 301, 312
Thomson, Dale C., 16, 37, 45, 75, 82, 274, 275, 334
Thorardson, Bruce, 45, 80
Thorburn, Hugh G., 13, 255, 370
Thornton, A.P., 55
Thornton, Patricia, 266
Tillman, Seth, 62
Tillotson, Shirley, 107, 117, 219, 310
Tippett, Maria, 158, 178, 216, 372
Titley, Brian, 183, 191, 196, 197
Tobias, John L., 182, 184, 191, 348
Tomlin, Brian W., 81, 84
Toner, Glen, 47, 83
Toner, Peter, 250
Tough, Frank, 348
Traves, Tom, 125, 129, 151
Tremaudan, A.H. de., 350
Tremblay, Arthur, 271

Tremblay, H., 112
Trépanier, Esthier, 166, 293
Trépanier, Pierre, 278
Trigg, Arthur, 131
Trigs, S., 154
Trofimenkoff, Susan Mann, 14, 25, 26, 33, 102, 166, 205, 206, 226, 270, 273, 289, 310, 332, 368
Troper, Harold, 35, 241, 305, 361
Trott, Elizabeth, 174
Trudeau, Pierre, 46, 47, 111, 170, 282
Trudeau, Robert S., 190
Trudel, Marcel, 290
Tuck, J.H., 106
Tucker, Albert, 134, 312, 353
Tucker, Eric, 115, 117, 324
Tucker, Gilbert, 59, 61
Tudor, Dean, 302
Tulchinsky, Gerald, 232, 299, 316
Tulloch, Elspeth, 261
Tunbridge, John E., 239
Tupper, Sir Charles, 60
Turner, J.P., 352

Uisikin, Roz, 119
Ullman, Walter, 14
Underhill Frank H., 11, 16, 20, 56, 170
Upton, L.F.S., 264
Urquhart, M.C., 128, 130
Ursell, Jane, 94
Usher, Jean. See also Friesen, Jean, 197, 350
Usher, Peter, 188, 358
Uukw, Delgam, 198

Vaillancourt, Yves, 271
Valentine, Victor V., 181
Vallee, Frank G., 181
Vallières, Marc, 277

Valpey, Michael, 47, 200
Valverde, Mariana, 93, 96, 160, 205, 208, 327
Vanasse, Gilbert, 114, 282
Vance, Catharine, 121
Van Die, Marguerite, 163
Van Dusen, Thomas, 43
Van Kirk, Sylvia, 193, 202, 212, 225
van Nus, Walter, 238
Van Praagh, David, 78
van Steenburgh, Susan, 135
Vardalas, John, 142
Vastel, Michel, 46, 83
Veatch, Richard, 66
Vennat, Pierre, 282
Vernux, J.C., 263
Verzuh, Ron, 96, 104
Viennot, R., 262
Vietor, Richard H.K., 81
Vigod, Bernard, 33, 272
Villeneuve, Larry, 190
Viner, Jacob, 129
Vipond, Mary, 177
Voisey, Paul, 141, 240, 355

Wa, Gisday, 198
Waddell, Eric, 286
Wadden, Marie, 199
Wade, Mason, 247, 270, 304
Wagner, Jonathan, 35
Waiser, W.A., 160, 353
Waite, P.B., 6, 11, 12, 13, 32, 55, 159, 174, 256
Walden, Keith, 144, 168, 333
Waldram, J.B., 192, 199, 349, 351
Walker, Franklin, 304, 331, 335
Wall, Geoffery, 239
Wallace, Carl, 249, 256
Wallace, W. Stewart, 61, 256
Warburton, Rennie, 88, 115, 364

Ward, Norman, 34, 63, 368
Ward, Patricia, 223
Ward, Peter, 8, 20, 108, 159, 169, 222, 223, 310, 345, 363, 364
Warkentin, John, 342
Warner, Donald, 58, 346
Warrian, Peter, 88, 106, 107
Warsh, Cheryl Krasnick, 329
Waterston, Elizabeth, 206
Watkins, Ernest, 32
Watkins, Melville, 78, 129, 153, 175, 199
Watson, Louise, 121
Watt, Donald Cameron, 67
Watt, F.W., 96
Watt, James T., 335
Watts, Ronald, 9
Wayman, Tom, 96
Wayne, Randi, 209–10
Weale, David, 13
Wearing, Joseph, 44
Weart, Spencer, R., 71
Weaver, John C., 91, 98, 232, 237, 239, 243, 244, 315, 316
Weaver, John Kent, 83
Weaver, Sally, 183
Webb, J.H., 256
Webb, Robert Lloyd, 358
Webber, Jeremy, 116
Weinberg, Albert, 57
Weir, Gail, 114
Welton, Michael, R., 96
Winrich, Peter, 87
Wenzel, George, 189
Weisbord, Merrily, 72, 120, 281
Well, Donald M., 117
West, D.A., 341
Westfall, William, 144, 162, 299, 325
Westley, W., 286
Wetherall, Donald, 95, 373

Whalen, Hugh J., 242
Whalley, 83
Whebell, C.F.J., 235
Whelan, Eugene, 48
Whitaker, Reg, 8, 9, 37, 40, 73, 116, 170, 171
White, Bob, 122
White, Clinton O., 140
White, Graham, 334, 339
White, Howard, 122, 364
White, Jerry, 113
White, Randall, 150, 297
Whiteley, M.F., 327
Whiteside, J.F., 132
Whyte, John, 48
Wightman, W.R., 313
Wigley, Philip, 31, 62
Wilbur, Richard, 33
Wilgus, William J., 134
Wilkie, Robert, 94
Wilkins, Mira, 154
Williams, Dorothy, 287
Williamson, Janice, 210
Willms, A.M., 26
Wilmot, Chester, 70
Willes, John A., 117
Williams, David Ricardo, 370
Willison, John, 20
Willoughby, William R., 65, 77
Wilson, Alan, 145
Wilson, Barbara, 330, 336
Wilson, Barry, 355, 368
Wilson, C.A., 141, 319
Wilson, C. Roderick, 180
Wilson, Catherine A., 101
Wilson, Charles F., 69, 140, 355
Wilson, Garrett, 43
Wilson, Harold, 59
Wilson, J.D., 172, 197, 258, 299
Wilson, J. Donald, 331, 372

Wilson, Jeremy, 356
Wilson, John, 338, 339
Wilson, Kevin, 43
Wilson, R.S., 250
Wilson, Susannah, 207
Wilton, Carol, 146
Winham, Gilbert R., 57
Winks, Robin, 264
Wise, S.F., 58, 60, 96, 297, 338
Wiseman, Nelson, 120, 368
Wolfe, Samuel, 368
Wolpart, H.C., 225
Wonder, Edward, 82
Wonders, William, 342
Wong, Daniel, 370
Wood, David G., 370
Wood, H.F., 74
Wood, Louis Aubrey, 319
Woodcock, George, 168, 194, 345, 349, 362
Woodham, David C., 181
Woods, Shirley E., 143
Woodsworth, Charles, 67
Woodsworth, J.S., 163, 240
Woodward, Frances, 342
Worley, Ronald B., 371
Wright, Glenn, 27
Wright, Mary Ellen, 224
Wright, Richard, 96
Wykie, P.J., 254
Wyman, Mark, 357
Wynn, Graeme, 94
Wynnyckyj, Iroida, 307

Yantz, Lynda, 100, 107
Yee, Paul, 363
York, Geoffery, 190, 196, 200
Young, Astrid, 336
Young, Brian, 12, 269, 272, 278
Young, Eva R., 355

Young, John H., 57
Young, R.A., 254
Young, Robert, 39
Young, Roger, 79
Young, Scott, 336
Young, Walter, 36, 120, 167, 367, 371
Young, William, 27, 38, 49, 319

Zacher, Mark W., 80
Zakuta, Leo, 338

Zaslow, Morris, 128, 160, 187, 312, 342, 344
Zeller, Susanne, 160
Zeman, Jerold K., 164
Zerker, Sally F., 114, 323
Zimmerly, David, 213
Zimmerman, David, 70
Zucchi, John, 241, 306
Zur-Mehlen, Max Von, 146

Subject Index

Editor's note: The *Guide* itself is arranged on a subject basis. This index is not intended to supplant that arrangement and readers should be careful to consult the table of contents.

Aberhart, William, 167
Acadia University, 259
Acadians, 248, 258, 262–3
Action française, 166, 289
Africa, Canadian relations with, 83
Africville, 264
agriculture, 27, 100, 140–1, 354; agricultural labour, 101, 318; in Ontario, 318–19; in Quebec, 278; in the West, 354–5; and women, 211–12, 319, 366
Aitken, Max, 132
Alaska boundary dispute, 23–4, 59
Alaska Highway, 354
Alberta, 46, 95, 99, 139–40, 342, 367, 373; alcohol, 96, 97, 264; Conservative party in, 370; creation of the province, 351–3; Indians in, 184–5; Liberal party in, 369; municipal government in, 242; University of, 174
Algoma Steel Corporation, 312
Anglican church, 163
Anglin, Timothy Warren, 13, 250

Annand, W., 255
Antigonish movement, 265
anti-Semitism, 35–6, 306
architecture, 237, 238, 267, 294
Arctic, 82, 188–9, 343, 346, 347; whaling and sealing in, 358. *See also* Yukon, Northwest territories
armed forces, 23, 54, 56, 60–1, 70; Newfoundland and, 257; unification of, 79; in World War I, 26–7. *See also* under individual services
art and artists, 169, 177–8, 216
aviation, 47, 135–6, 216, 354
Asia, Canadian relations with, 78
atomic energy, 70–1
Australia, comparative history, 89, 250
automobile industry, 135, 143; unions and, 111

Bank of Canada, 35
banking, 127–8, 131–2, 133, 253, 278
Banks, Hal, 75, 111, 122
Banting, Frederick, 161
Baptist church, 164, 257, 258

Beaver Indians, 187
Belaney, Archie. *See* Grey Owl
Bennett, R.B., 32–3, 116
Benyon, Frances Marion, 208
Bethune, Norman, 292
Big Bear, 185, 192, 348
bilingualism, 83
birth control, 223–4, 310
Black, Conrad, 147, 323
Blackfoot, 184
blacks in Canada, 226, 264, 307
Blake, Edward, 14–15, 16
Blakeney, Allan, 368
Bloc Populaire, 274–5
Blood Indians, 185
Board of Railway Commissioners, 253
Boer War, 22, 59
Bombardier, Joseph-Armand, 148
Borden, Robert Laird, 60, 61
Bourassa, Henri, 272
Bracken, John, 33, 368
Brascan, 155
Brazil, 76, 155
brewing industry, 143
British Columbia, 99, 100, 108, 112,
    113, 169, 187–8, 342, 344, 347, 356;
    education in 172, 174; fishery of,
    101, 137–8, 357–8; forest industry
    in, 356–7; mining in, 357; native
    peoples in, 186–7, 350; politics in,
    370–1
British Empire-Commonwealth, 31,
    32–3, 55–7, 59, 62, 64, 68, 76;
    Anglo-Japanese alliance, 62–3;
    colonial-imperial conferences, 57;
    Commonwealth secretariat, 79;
    trade and investment, 35, 57, 65–6,
    69, 154
Bronfman family, 143
Brown, George, 12, 58

Bruce County, 313
Bucke, Richard M., 161
Buller, Annie, 121
Burwash, Nathaniel, 163, 326

Caisses populaires, 278
Calgary, 233, 240
Campeau, Robert, 155
Canada Council, 177
Canadian Congress of Labour, 110
Canadian Labour Congress, 112
Canadian-American relations; 25, 35,
    40, 41, 43–4, 46, 47, 49, 56–8, 59,
    62, 65, 68, 74–5, 81–2, 149, 159;
    and the Cold War, 73–5;
    Diefenbaker and Kennedy, 43–4;
    during World War II, 40, 70;
    international unionism, 106, 112,
    281; ownership of Canadian
    industry, 66, 78–9, 153–4; and
    Quebec, 275; representation in
    Washington, 64; trade with, 19, 35,
    40, 49, 57, 66, 69, 83, 150, 155;
    Vietnam War, 78
Canadian-Israeli relations, 75
Canadian National Railway, 134
Canadian Northern Railway, 23
Canadian Pacific Railway, 18, 134, 353
Canadian-Russian relations, 62, 76–7
Canadian-Soviet relations. *See*
    Canadian-Russian relations
Cape Breton, 95, 99, 103, 108, 116,
    138, 259, 266
Carr, Emily, 178, 216, 372
Cartier, George-Etienne, 12, 272
CCF (Co-operative Commonwealth
    Federation), 36, 75, 120, 167, 212,
    371; in Ontario, 120, 338; in
    Quebec, 274; in Manitoba, 120, 368;
    in Saskatchewan, 120, 368

censorship, 98
Chapleau, Sir Adolphe, 17, 272
Chaput-Rolland, Solange, 276
Charlottetown, 232, 266
childhood, 89–92
child labour, 103, 213–4, 260
child welfare, 328
China, Canadian relations with, 76, 84
Chinese in Canada, 24, 89, 108, 169, 363
Chown, Alice A., 210
Christie, Loring, 57, 61
Churchill Falls, 257
CIO (Congress of Industrial Organizations), 37, 75, 110
City Beautiful movement, 238
civil service, 30, 34, 59–60, 64, 106, 112, 152, 171, 334; and Indian policy, 183, 348–9; and unions, 112, 113
Clark, Joe, 48
Claxton, Brooke, 38
Clergue, Francis, 321
clerical work, 105
clothing and textiles, 107, 144, 283
coal mining, 103, 105, 107–8, 110, 138, 259–60
Cold War, 40, 72–3; and impact upon unions, 111, 116
Coleman, Kathleen, Blake,   216
Colonial Office, 56
Columbia River treaty, 46, 77
Communism, 71, 110, 116, 122, 274. See also Cold War.
Communist Party of Canada, 30, 75, 110, 119–20, 281–2
Confederation, 11–12, 159; and Atlantic Canada, 249; and British Columbia, 347
conscription, 26, 39, 61, 273, 319

Conservative party, 16, 37, 44, 49, 59, 121, 170; in Alberta, 370; in Manitoba, 3, 68; in Ontario, 24–5; in Saskatchewan, 368
conservative tradition in Canada, 170
constitutional issues 45, 47–8; Natives and, 200. See also federal-provincial relations
craft unions, 106, 113–14, 260, 323
Cree: Plains, 184; of James Bay, 199
Crowfoot, 185, 348
Currie, Sir Arthur, 27

Dafoe, John W., 28
Dalhousie University, 220, 259
Davis, Bill, 338
defence policy 22, 35, 37, 54, 56, 59, 60–1, 65, 69–70, 74, 77, 81, 84–5. See also armed forces
De Gaulle, Charles, 82
Dené, 188
Diefenbaker, John, 42–4, 76–7
divorce, 221
domestic servants, 90, 102, 214–5
Dorion Commission, 209
Douglas, T.C., 167, 368
Doukhobors, 362
Drapeau, Jean, 243
Drury, E.C., 336
Dumont, Gabriel, 194, 349
Duncan, William of Metlakatla, 197, 350
Dunn, Sir James, 321
Duplessis, 33, 273, 274

Eaton's department store, 111, 145, 321
economic theory, 334–5
Edmonton, 233, 241
education, 95, 172–3, 216–7, 250,

261–2; and Natives, 179, 196–7, 225; and women, 219–221, 284, 308–9, 332; in Atlantic Canada, 258–9; in Ontario, 330–1, 335; in Quebec, 271, 284. *See also* teachers

elections, 8; 1896, 19; 1911, 25; 1988, 49; in Ontario, 334; in Quebec, 271

electricity, 140, 142, 254, 277, 320

Energy and Chemical Workers Union, 111

energy policy, 81–2

engineering in Canada, 142, 160

environmental issues, 84

ethnicity, 35, 37, 39, 95, 107, 119, 165; and women, 225–6; and the West, 362–3. *See also* under specific ethnic groups

Evans, Arthur H., 121

External Affairs, Department of, 30, 38, 60, 81

Falconer, Sir Robert, 173

family allowances, 93

federal-provincial relations, 9–10, 13, 14, 35, 45, 47–8, 49–50, 123, 254, 335

Ferguson, G. Howard, 337

Fielding, W.S., 23, 255

Finance, Department of, 150

Finnish Canadians, 95, 226, 308

fire prevention, 244

fisheries, 100, 101, 109, 123, 137, 213, 357–8

Fishermen's Protective Union, 261

Flavelle, Sir Joseph, 62, 143, 160, 321

Fleming, Donald, 77

FLQ (Front de libération du Québec), 275

Forsey, Eugene, 172

Foster, George, 61, 256

Franco-Ontarians, 304

francophonie, 82–3

free trade, 35, 49, 57

French-Canadian relations, 275

Frost, Leslie M., 337

Frye, Northrop, 176

FTQ (Fédération provinciale du travail du Québec), 112

fur trade, 100, 136–7, 187, 358; and women, 212

Galt, A.T., 12, 60, 359

Gardiner, Frederick G., 242

Gardner, Jimmy, 34, 37

Gaspé, 288

Gault, Bella Hall, 121

Geological Survey of Canada, 160

Gladstone, James, 185

Good, W.C., 336

Gordon, Walter, 41, 44, 45

Gouin, Paul, 272

Gouzenko, Igor, 72

grain trade, 123–4, 144

Grand Trunk Railway, 106

Grant, George P., 176

Great Depression, 32–3, 34, 129, 132, 345

Grey Owl, 185–6

Grossman, Allan, 337–8

Groulx, Abbé Lionel, 166; attitude toward women, 206–7

Group of Seven, 178

Guelph, 316

Gulf War, 84–5

Gutteridge, Helena, 210

Halifax, 91, 93, 231, 241, 265; labour in, 260–1

Hamilton, Alvin, 43

Hamilton (Ontario), 90, 98, 104, 106, 221, 229, 315–6
Hartz, Louis, 169–70
Harvey, Jean-Charles, 293
Heaps, A.A., 121
Helmcken, J.S., 347
Hepburn, Mitch, 33, 337
Hind, Cora E., 216
homes. *See also* Housing
Hoodless, Adelaide, 208
housing, 91–2, 237–8, 244
Howe, C.D., 37, 41, 68–9, 152
Howe, Joseph, 249
Hughes, Sam, 27, 61

immigration, 24, 35, 58, 93, 107, 241, 305, 361–3. *See also* specific ethnic groups
imperialism; in Canada, 19, 21–2, 24; British, 55–6. *See also* British Empire-Commonwealth
Inco Limited, 115, 312
India, 76
Industrial relations, 112, 113, 116–7. *See also* strikes
industrial unions, 109–110
Industrial Workers of the World, 105, 364
industrialization, 91, 102
Innis, Harold, 175–6
Innuit, 180–1, 199, 372
Intercolonial Railway, 253
international trade, 129. *See also* British Empire; Canadian-American relations
International Union of Mine, Mill, and Smelter Workers, 111
International Woodworkers of America, 110
Irish in Canada, 264, 303, 313

Irvine, William, 121
Irving, K.C., 147, 254
Italian Canadians, 89, 90, 101, 107, 226, 306

Japan, 62–3, 69
Japanese Canadians, 39, 69, 121, 226, 363
Jehovah's Witnesses, 273
Jewish Canadians, 35, 107, 119, 226, 287, 307
Johnson, Daniel, 274
juvenile delinquency, 329

Kennedy, J.F., 43, 44, 76–7
King, William Lyon Mackenzie, 6, 23, 28–9, 36–7, 63, 170, 171
King–Byng affair, 31
Kingston, 232, 316
Kitchener (Ontario), 232, 235, 316
Knights of Labor, 96, 104, 322
Korean War, 74
Krieghoff, C., 177–8
Kurelek, William, 178
Kwakiutl Indians, 187

Labrador, 109, 191; women in, 213
LaMarsh, Judy, 210
land claims, Native, 198–9
Landry, Pierre-Armand, 263
Langevin, Hector, 12, 272
Lansdowne, Lord, 56
Lapalme, Georges-Emile, 274
Lapointe, Ernest, 63
Laurendeau, André, 39, 290
Laurentians, 288
Laurier, Wilfrid, 17, 20–1, 58, 59, 272
law, 98, 266, 329; women and the law, 220–1, 310. *See also* policing
Law of the Sea, 80

League for Social Reconstruction, 171
League of Nations, 66–7
Leeds and Grenville counties, 313
leisure, 95
Lesage, Jean, 45, 274
Lethbridge, 360
Lévesque, René, 274
Lévesques, Georges-Henri, 290
Liberal party (federal), 16–17, 22, 36–7, 40, 41, 44, 335, in Alberta, 369; in Ontario, 24, 335; in Quebec, 270, 272; on the Boer War, 22
life insurance, 132
literature, history of, 96, 372; in Quebec, 293; in western Canada, 168
logging, 105
Longfellow, 266
lumber industry. *See* wood products

Macdonald, Angus L., 33
MacDonald, Cheryl, 311
Macdonald, Sir John A., 11–12, 15, 17, 58
Macdonald, John Sandfield, 14, 334
MacEachren, George, 121
MacGill, Helen, 207, 366
Machar, Agnes, 208
Mackenzie, Alexander, 16, 334
Mackenzie, Larry, 174
Mackenzie, William, 23
Macmillan-Bloedel, 138
Macoun, John, 160, 353
McClung, Nellie L., 207, 225
McGeer, Gerald Gratton, 370
McGill University, 173, 220
McLuhan, Marshall, 176
McMaster University, 164, 332
McNaughton, General A.G.L. 38
McPhail, Agnes, 29, 210, 311

McWilliams, Margaret, 210
Manitoba, 99, 120, 342, 345, 350, 361; politics in, 368; schools question in, 362; University of, 174
Maritime Rights Movement, 254, 267
marriage, 221–2
Marsh, Leonard, 39
Martin, Paul, 38
Massey, Vincent, 64. *See also* Royal Commission on the Arts, Letters and Sciences
Massey-Ferguson Limited, 155, 321
maternal feminism, 208
medicare, 368–9
medicine in Canada, 160–1, 217, 259, 292; women and, 223, 311
Meech Lake Accord, 10, 49–50
Meighen, Arthur, 31
Memorial University, 173
Mennonites, 168, 362
Methodism, 162, 163, 258, 326–7
Métis, 18–19, 188, 192–5, 349–50
Micmacs, 190
mining, 103, 105, 110, 111, 138, 151, 312, 320
Minto, fourth earl of, 21, 56
Mohawks, 190, 196
Moncton, 263, 266
Monk, Frederick, 25
Montgomery, Lucy Maud, 206
Montreal, 97, 102, 103, 213, 232, 236, 240, 241, 287, 294; minorities in, 286–7; municipal government in, 243
morality, history of, 97–8
Mount Allison University, 173, 258
movies, 98, 177
Mowat, Oliver, 14, 334
Mulroney, Brian, 49, 84
music, 97, 177

National Council of Women, 208

National Film Board, 177, 207

National Policy, 17, 127, 149, 326; and the Maritimes, 252–3; and West, the, 353

NATO (North Atlantic Treaty Organization), 72, 81, 84

Natives, 100, 313, 348–9, 350. *See also* chapter on Native history

New Brunswick, 39, 106, 110, 252, 266; and Confederation, 249; municipal government in, 242; schools question, 250, 263

naval debate 59

Nazis in Canada, 35

New Democratic Party (NDP), 371. *See also* CCF

Newfoundland, 13, 45, 71, 92, 99, 109, 165, 248, 249, 256; fishing industry in, 137, 251

newspapers, 96, 136, 176, 256, 293

Norman, Herbert, 71–2

North-West Mounted Police. *See* Royal Canadian Mounted Police

North-West Rebellion. *See* Rebellion of 1885

North-West Territories (to 1905), 24, 351; schools question in, 362

Northwest Territories (after 1905), 128, 372. *See also* Arctic

Notman, William, 154

Nova Scotia, 13, 33, 46, 139, 165, 253, 254, 255, 265; and Confederation, 249; labour in, 259–60; municipal government in, 242; women in, 206, 221, 262

Nowlan, George, 43, 254

nuclear power, 152, 216

nuns, 284

nursing, 217–8

occupational health and safety, 117

October Crisis (1970), 113

oil and natural gas, 139–40, 358–9

Ojibwa, 189

One Big Union, 28, 108, 168

Ontario, 14–15, 127, 151, 255; auto industry, 111; CCF in, 120; Conservative party in, 24–5; economy of, 317–8; Liberal party in, 24; mining in, 138, 151; natives in, 189–90; population of, 302; schools question, 304, 305; urban development in, 235, 314

Ontario, county of, 313

Ontario Hydro, 336

Orange Order, 303

Ottawa, 232, 316

Otter, W.D., 59

Outaouais, 289

Pacific Scandal, 16, 18

pacifism, 164; universities and, 173, 175, 209–10

Paper Makers Union, 114

Pattullo, Duff, 34, 370

Pearkes, George, 43

Pearson, Lester, 38, 40, 42–5, 64, 77–8, 171

Peel County, 302–3

Peggy's Cove, 267

Penfield, Wilder, 161

Peterson, David, 338

philosophy, 164, 174

physics, 174

policing, 98, 244, 265, 352. *See also* Royal Canadian Mounted Police

Pope, J.C., 255

Pope, Joseph, 60

Pope, Maurice, 71

populism, 29, 367

potlach, 196
Poundmaker, 185
poverty, 91, 92, 240, 261, 264
Power, C.G., 37, 63
prairie settlement, 141
Presbyterian church, 164, 224
Prince Edward Island, 13, 248, 255
Prince George, 110
Progressive Conservatives. See
    Conservative party
Progressive party, 28, 367
prohibition, 97, 257, 264, 329–30.
    See also alcohol
prostitution, 97–8, 215
public health, 244, 328
Public Works, Department of, 30
pulp and paper, 142, 277. See also
    wood products industry

Quebec, 41, 45–6, 93, 99, 110, 112,
    121; birthrate in, 279–80; business
    in, 148; class in, 279; Confederation,
    14; economic history of, 126–7,
    276–9; education in, 172, 217, 220;
    and foreign policy, 82, 275; ideology
    in 165–6; and Laurier, 22–3;
    nationalism and, 275; natives in,
    190; syndicalism in, 282; urban
    development in, 236; women in
    206–7, 209, 212–13, 220, 283–6;
    and World War I, 26–7
Quebec City, 236
Queen's University, 173, 174, 332
Quiet Revolution, 41, 45, 166, 273,
    274

radio, 136, 177
railways, 134–5, 146, 312; in the
    Maritimes, 253; in Quebec, 278; in
    the West, 353–4; unions and, 106,

114. See also under individual
    railways
ranching, 141, 356; and women, 212,
    241
Reagan, Ronald, 83
Rebellion of 1885, 192, 194, 349
reciprocity, 25, 150; (1911), 57
Reconstruction, 38, 109
Red River, 15, 194; resistance, 1870,
    193, 347
Regina, 232, 360
Reichmann family, 147
religion, 96, 162–3, 224, 291, 325;
    utopianism in, 167, 373; native
    missions, 188. See also under
    individual denominations
retail trade, 111, 145
Riddell incident, 67
Riel, Louis, 18, 168, 194, 347, 349
Robarts, John P., 337
Robertson, Norman, 38, 65
Robichaud, Louis, 255
Roman Catholics, 19, 162, 166, 257,
    263, 265, 304–5; anti-Catholicism,
    159, 335; in Quebec, 272, 277, 284,
    291
Ross, Sir George, 336
Rouges, les, 16–17
Rowell, Newton, 61
Rowley, Kent, 122
Royal Canadian Air Force, 60–1, 70
Royal Canadian Mounted Police, 98,
    116, 168, 352–3
Royal Canadian Navy, 59, 61, 70
Royal Commission on Bilingualism
    and Biculturalism, 276
Royal Commission on Canada's
    Economic Prospects, 41
Royal Commission on Dominion-
    Provincial Relations, 35

Royal Commission on the Arts, Letters and Sciences, 171–2
Royal Commission on the Status of Women, 210–11
Russia. *See* Canadian–Russian relations

Saguenay, 288
Saint John, 106, 229, 236, 260, 265
St John's, 106, 231, 266
St Laurent, Louis, 37–8, 75–6
St Lawrence Seaway, 133–4
Saint-Martin, Albert, 121
Salvation Army, 96
Saskatchewan, 36, 212, 217, 344, 356; education in, 217; Métis in, 195; politics in, 368
Saskatoon, 106, 232, 365
science, 160–1, 266, 292, 326
Scots in Canada, 165, 264
Scott, Duncan Campbell, 183
Scott, F.R., 36, 172, 293
Sévigny, Albert, 25
sexual morality/regulation, 97, 160, 162, 223
Seymour, Frederick, 347
Sharp, Mitchell, 81
shipping, 133–4, 250–1; seafaring, 102, 115, 250
Sifton, Clifford, 23, 58–9, 352
Sikhs, 24
Sioux, 184
Sitting Bull, 185
Skelton, O.D., 32, 63–4
Smallwood, Joey, 256–7
Smith, Elizabeth, 217, 311
Social Credit party: in Alberta, 167, 367, 369–70; in British Columbia, 371; in Quebec, 275
social gospel, 163–4, 257, 325–6
social security/welfare, 39, 92–4, 117, 152, 327–8, 330. *See also* occupational health and safety
social work, 93, 306
socialism, 36, 105, 118, 170–1, 265, 363–4; and women, 120
South Africa, 79. *See also* Boer War
South America, 76, 155
Soviet Union. *See* Canadian-Russian relations
Spanish civil war, 67, 119
sports, 96–7, 222–3, 262, 373
Stanley Park, 239
steel industry, 142–3, 253; workers in, 105, 115, 260
Stefansson, V., 348
Stelco, 310, 320
stock exchanges, 132
Stoney Indians, 185
Stowe, Emily, 311
strikes, 99, 104, 106, 108, 111, 112, 282
suburbs, 94, 239
Sudbury, 304, 308, 320
Suez crisis, 75–6
suffrage. *See* women's suffrage

tariffs, 17–18, 149–50. *See also* Canadian-American relations and National Policy
Taschereau, L-A., 33, 272
Tax Rental Agreements, 46
Taylor, E.P., 143
teachers, 114–15, 216, 284
telephones, 136, 215, 218, 285, 309; unions and, 102, 107, 115
television, 136, 177
textiles. *See* clothing and textiles
Third World, relations with, 76
Thompson, Sir John, 13
Thomson family, 148

Tilley, Samuel Leonard, 256
Tootoosis, John, 185
Toronto, 90–1, 94, 97, 104, 114, 232, 237, 314–5; labour in, 303, 322–3; municipal government in, 242–3
Toronto Typographical Union, 114, 323
Towers, Graham, 35
town planning, 238–9
Trade and Commerce, Department of, 59–60, 150
trade unions, 75, 98–9, 106, 109, 112, 281; labour law and, 115–16; in Quebec, 280–1; women and, 218, 310; TransCanada PipeLines, 41, 75. See also under specific unions
Trudeau, Pierre Elliott, 46–8, 80, 170–1
Tupper, Sir Charles, 12–13
Turner, John, 48–9

Ukrainian Canadians, 118–19, 226, 307, 362
ultramontanism, 17, 291
Underhill, F. H., 172
unemployment/unemployment policy, 93, 109, 110, 117, 214, 219, 311
Union Nationale, 33, 273
Union of Mine, Mill and Smelter Workers, 111
United Church of Canada, 163
United Farmers of Alberta, 369
United Farmers of Ontario, 336
United Nations, 73
United States, 4, 57–8. See also Canadian-American Relations
University of Alberta, 174
University of British Columbia, 174, 220, 367

University of Manitoba, 174
University of Saskatchewan, 174
University of Toronto, 173–4, 220
University of Windsor, 333
urban reform, 243, 315
utilities, 151

Vancouver, 94, 95, 107, 114, 233, 240, 342, 360
Victoria, 233, 359
Vietnam War, 78
Vulcan, Alberta, 355

Wartime Information Board, 38
westward expansion, 15, 159, 346–7; and Natives, 348
wheat, 123–4, 140–1; in Ontario, 318; in the West, 354–6
Wetmore, A.R., 255
Whelan, Eugene, 48
White, Bill, 122
Whitney, Sir James Pliny, 336
Whitton, Charlotte, 93, 210, 311
Willison, Sir John, 21
Wilson, Cairine, 210
Wilson, E.F., 197
Winch, Ernest E., 121, 371
Winnipeg, 95, 128, 232, 235, 360; General Strike of 1919, 107, 108, 364
Women, image of, 207; and politics, 120, 160, 338; and religion, 164, 224; wage earners, 99–100, 102, 106–7, 109, 117, 141, 214–16, 261, 309. See also the chapter on Women's History, 89–90, 308–10.
women's suffrage movement, 207, 330, 366; in Quebec, 209

wood products industry, 100, 114, 138, 151, 251–2, 312, 356
Woodsworth, J.S., 30, 120
workmen's compensation. *See* occupational health and safety
World War I, 25–6, 60–2; and Ontario, 336; and the West, 128
World War II, 36–7, 38, 40, 62, 67–9; and conscription, 39; and Peace Conference, 62; and the Maritimes,

254; and women, 38–9, 204, 286, 309

Yarmouth, 252
Yukon, 128, 344, 345, 371; natives in, 188
YWCA, 220

Zuken, Joe, 368